AI Forensics

AI Forensics provides a comprehensive framework for investigating artificial intelligence systems when they fail, cause harm, or become subjects of legal or regulatory scrutiny. As artificial intelligence (AI) systems power critical decisions in healthcare, finance, autonomous vehicles, and public safety, traditional digital forensics techniques prove inadequate for understanding their complex, opaque, and dynamic behaviors.

You'll master systematic approaches for evidence collection across distributed cloud environments, training data analysis for bias detection and intellectual property violations, model parameter examination to identify tampering or discrimination, and output analysis to validate system performance and detect adversarial attacks. The book provides detailed investigation templates, Python code examples, and statistical validation techniques that can be immediately applied to active cases. Each chapter builds upon previous techniques, creating an integrated investigation framework that scales from small regional deployments to enterprise systems spanning multiple jurisdictions. Through real-world case studies spanning healthcare bias investigations, financial fraud detection failures, and autonomous system malfunctions, you'll learn to answer critical questions: Was the AI system modified after deployment? Does training data contain unauthorized content? Are there signs of model tampering? Does system behavior match specifications?

This practical guide equips forensic investigators, legal professionals, and AI practitioners with specialized methodologies tailored to AI's unique characteristics. It provides both technical depth for expert practitioners and accessible explanations for legal professionals who must understand and present AI evidence in court proceedings.

Joseph C. Sremack is a computer scientist and forensic examiner with over 20 years of experience in data, software, and systems analysis, having worked on more than 500 investigations across numerous industries, regulatory bodies, and courts in over 50 countries. He is a recognized expert in both traditional digital forensics and emerging AI forensics methodologies, bridging the gap between established investigative practices and cutting-edge artificial intelligence systems.

AI Forensics

Investigation and Analysis of Artificial Intelligence Systems

Joseph C. Sremack

CRC Press
Taylor & Francis Group
Boca Raton London New York

CRC Press is an imprint of the
Taylor & Francis Group, an **informa** business
A CHAPMAN & HALL BOOK

Designed cover image: Web Large Image (Public)

First edition published 2026
by CRC Press
2385 NW Executive Center Drive, Suite 320, Boca Raton FL 33431

and by CRC Press
4 Park Square, Milton Park, Abingdon, Oxon, OX14 4RN

CRC Press is an imprint of Taylor & Francis Group, LLC

ISBN: 978-1-041-06304-9 (hbk)
ISBN: 978-1-041-06303-2 (pbk)
ISBN: 978-1-003-63478-2 (ebk)

DOI: 10.1201/9781003634782

Typeset in Times
by Apex CoVantage, LLC

Contents

Preface

ABOUT THIS BOOK

This book is a guide for forensic analysis of artificial intelligence systems. AI systems are increasingly found in our work, our personal lives, and our way of life. As the ubiquity of AI grows, so too does the need for systematically investigating its behaviors, failures, and impacts. This book explains how different types of AI systems are designed and operate, how to perform forensic analysis on these systems, and the need to tailor the forensic approach based on the type of issue being investigated.

There are many books on that range from explainers on effectively using LLMs with prompt engineering, technical guides for designing AI system's architecture, and automation tutorials for security to futurist explorations of what AI means for humankind's future—and everything else about working *on* or *with* AI. This book is not that. This book is a guide for understanding how AI systems *were* designed, what they contain, and what they *did*. This book teaches you how to investigate AI systems to better understand how they were designed and how they operate.

My motivation for writing this book consists of several factors that led me to compiling this information and putting it in the public domain. First, AI systems are rapidly expanding and taking over elements of how we live and work, and they are changing our understanding of *knowledge* and *information*. Knowledge and information are foundational to digital forensics. If the subject of a forensic investigation, an AI system, does not follow the traditional norms of knowledge and information, then we need to have a methodology and set of techniques that allow us to understand AI systems.

Second, AI systems are not the monolithic "AI" that seems to prevail in media and sales marketing. These systems are varied in how they are designed, trained, used, deployed, and maintained. The functions they serve are different, so I want to do my part in explaining how these functional differences necessitate different forensic approaches.

Finally, forensic literature and research has not kept pace with AI development. Many books, papers, and talks on digital forensics provide detailed technical explanations on how to perform digital forensic analysis, whereas with AI, those same types of papers and talks seem to lack technical depth and do not offer a framework or approach on analyzing AI systems. Several practitioners and researchers have published information about the subject, but most of the knowledge is shared in smaller circles. I hope this book helps fill that void and that this information helps encourage the growth of knowledge sharing in this domain.

WHAT THIS BOOK COVERS

The book provides a comprehensive introduction to AI forensics, starting with fundamental concepts and progressing to advanced investigation techniques. We begin by establishing the core principles of AI forensics and how they differ from traditional digital forensics. The text then explores the various components of AI systems that may require investigation, from training data to model architectures and deployment infrastructure.

Subsequent chapters detail specific investigation procedures, including evidence collection, training data analysis, model examination, and output validation. Throughout the book, we emphasize practical applications and real-world considerations, supplementing theoretical frameworks with case studies and hands-on examples.

This book will equip you to answer fundamental questions that arise during AI system investigations, such as:

1. Was the AI system modified after its initial deployment?
2. Did the training data contain unauthorized or problematic content?
3. Are there signs of tampering with the model weights or architecture?
4. Does the system behavior match its documented specifications?
5. Were proper access controls maintained throughout the system lifecycle?
6. Can we verify the provenance of all training data sources?
7. Are there undisclosed biases in the system outputs?
8. Did the system maintain appropriate logging and monitoring?
9. Were model updates and modifications properly documented?
10. Can we establish a complete chain of custody for the AI system components?

These questions represent just a sample of the investigative scenarios covered in the book. Each chapter provides detailed methodologies and practical techniques for addressing these and similar forensic challenges.

This book gives you a broad perspective of the different categories of AI and which forensic methodologies and techniques can be used for the different categories. Right now, LLMs are all the rage. We are also on the cusp of advanced reasoning models supplanting LLMs in general AI discussions, and who knows when and where the next major breakthrough and focus will happen. This book does cover LLMs, including their foundation models, but the world of AI is so much bigger. Complex AI systems typically make use of different types of AI in their design, development, and maintenance. Understanding the different types of AI will better equip you to perform AI forensics, regardless of what the technology looks like in the coming years.

AI systems are evolving at a breathtaking pace. New model architectures, training methodologies, and deployment patterns emerge almost monthly, creating a moving target for forensic investigators. This book acknowledges this challenge by focusing on forensic principles rather than current implementations. Step-by-step instructions will become obsolete with the next technological shift, so this book emphasizes fundamental investigative principles that will remain relevant regardless of how AI systems evolve. These principles include evidence preservation, chain of custody, artifact analysis, and system behavior characterization—concepts that transcend specific technologies or implementations.

The methodologies presented are designed with adaptability in mind. Each framework can be extended and modified to accommodate new AI paradigms as they emerge. For instance, the model investigation techniques presented for today's neural networks establish patterns that can be applied to whatever replaces them tomorrow. The data provenance tracking approaches work regardless of whether the system uses traditional supervised learning or more advanced techniques that have not yet been developed.

Beyond specific techniques, this book aims to enhance your investigative approach. By understanding not just how to analyze today's AI systems but why certain approaches work, you will develop the critical thinking skills needed to adapt to future developments. I believe that this approach-building method proves far more valuable than prescriptive procedures that might not apply to tomorrow's technologies.

WHAT THIS BOOK IS NOT

This book is not a comprehensive tutorial on all types of AI forensics. While this book covers the fundamental principles and most common forensic scenarios, the field of AI is wide—and growing. Instead of attempting to address every possible AI forensics scenario, the book focuses on explaining the core methodologies and analysis frameworks that can be adapted to various situations.

Readers will learn transferable investigation skills that can be applied to both current and future AI systems.

This book is not a step-by-step guide for AI forensics. The beauty of AI forensics is that AI systems are so varied. Most AI systems are unique and require scoping and examination to determine how to perform the forensic analysis. This differs from common types of digital forensics, such as that of mobile devices or email data, where the structures of the data are quite standardized. A step-by-step guide AI forensics guide would not work, unless it were for one specific AI model that followed a very defined implementation. That is not what you will encounter in the field, so this guide provides frameworks and techniques that can be adapted to any AI system.

This book is not an introduction to AI. This book assumes that the reader has some familiarity with AI model development, data analysis, and programming concepts. I do provide high-level explanations about the concepts, and I do my best to provide tips and recommendations about learning more about these. The subjects of AI and data analysis are too deep and broad to do a deep-drive discussion while still covering AI forensics. The good news is that AI forensics does not require that you have a PhD-level mastery of the intricacies for AI model development and management, just as mobile device forensics examiners are not required to have such a deep understanding of mobile device hardware engineering, operating systems, and application development that they could develop their own mobile device.

The subject of AI forensics does not include the evaluation of known AI algorithms. The focus is on investigating the implementation, deployment, and use of AI systems rather than analyzing the mathematical foundations or theoretical properties of specific algorithms. While understanding how an algorithm works can inform an investigation, forensic analysis primarily focuses on how the algorithm was implemented, used in training, and operated in practice. A forensic investigator will do better by understanding the algorithms—just like they better perform forensics on a laptop with an understanding of operating system kernel design and operations—but such knowledge does not preclude them from conducting an effective investigation.

Finally, this book is not a legal guide. The subject of AI is a developing area in legal and regulatory fields, with those developments rapidly increasing to keep pace with technological advancements. The legal standards for the admissibility of AI-based evidence are being tested in new, novel cases, and those are quickly across global legal and regulatory bodies, including at both the state and federal levels in the United States. While this book provides guidance on how to collect and examine AI-based evidence, the use and applications of the forensic analysis depend on situation-specific legal analysis.

INTENDED AUDIENCE

This book is written for anyone who is interested in AI and forensic methods. This audience includes forensic examiners, information security professionals, attorneys, regulators, compliance professionals, academic researchers, and anyone else interested in the subject. AI systems and their impact apply to many different people. The subject applies to technology, legal, compliance, and beyond. While the book is primarily aimed at forensics and information security professionals whose work involves AI forensics, the audience is anyone who has an interest in the subject. The subject applies to legal professionals who want to better understand the concepts for litigation and regulatory compliance. In addition, AI developers will benefit from this book. Forensic methods are extremely useful for AI developers for their evaluation, testing, and reverse engineering of issues with their own AI systems.

The following people will benefit from this book:

- Digital forensics professionals
- Information security professionals
- AI/ML engineers and data scientists

- Legal and compliance professionals
- Risk management professionals
- Academic researchers

INTERDISCIPLINARY NATURE OF AI FORENSICS

AI forensics stands at the intersection of multiple disciplines, requiring practitioners to develop knowledge across several domains to perform effectively. This book acknowledges this interdisciplinary reality and strives to bridge these diverse knowledge areas.

The field draws heavily from computer science and software engineering, providing the foundation for understanding system architecture, code execution, and data structures. Data science and statistical analysis form another crucial pillar, as investigators must often evaluate training methodologies, test for statistical anomalies, and understand the mathematical principles underlying model behavior.

Legal and regulatory knowledge provides essential context for investigations, informing evidence collection methods, documentation standards, and compliance requirements. Without this legal foundation, even the most technically sound investigation may fail to meet admissibility standards or address regulatory concerns.

Domain expertise in the specific application area of the AI system being investigated—whether healthcare, finance, autonomous systems, or another field—proves invaluable for understanding expected behaviors, industry standards, and contextual significance of findings. This expertise helps investigators distinguish between normal operations and concerning anomalies.

Additionally, understanding human factors and psychology becomes increasingly important when investigating systems that interact with users, as these factors often influence system design, training data collection, and performance evaluation.

This book does not attempt to make you an expert in all these disciplines—that would be impossible. Instead, it acknowledges these interdisciplinary connections and provides enough context to help you recognize when you might need to collaborate with specialists from these fields. Throughout the text, you'll find callouts highlighting these interdisciplinary touchpoints and suggestions for effective collaboration with experts from related domains.

The most successful AI forensic investigators are those who can navigate these disciplinary boundaries, speaking the language of each field well enough to integrate diverse perspectives into a cohesive investigation framework. This book aims to lay the groundwork for this interdisciplinary approach.

HOW TO USE THIS BOOK

This book is organized to support multiple approaches to learning AI forensics, allowing you to engage with the material in whatever way best suits your needs. For those new to the field of digital forensics or AI, reading the book sequentially from start to finish is the best way to progressively develop your understanding of the subject. This approach incrementally builds your knowledge and capabilities, starting with fundamental concepts and moving toward more advanced investigation techniques. Each chapter builds upon the previous ones, helping you develop a comprehensive understanding of AI forensics principles and practices.

For practitioners who need information about specific aspects of AI forensics, this book also serves as a practical reference guide. Each chapter is self-contained enough to be useful on its own, with detailed information that can be quickly accessed during active investigations. You will find specific technical procedures, checklists, and template documents that can be immediately applied to your work, making it easy to find the exact information you need when you need it.

Throughout the book, you will encounter case studies drawn from real-world incidents and investigations. These examples demonstrate how theoretical concepts and procedures are applied in practice, illustrating both successful approaches and common pitfalls. The case studies are designed to help you understand not just what to do, but why certain approaches work better than others in specific situations.

Additionally, you will find references for further reading that point you toward more detailed information on specific topics. Whether you are reading cover-to-cover, using the book as a reference, or focusing on case studies, these resources help ensure you can effectively apply what you have learned to real-world investigations.

PREREQUISITES

While this book does not require extensive prior knowledge of AI systems or forensics, readers will benefit from having some foundational technical background. A basic understanding of digital systems, general investigation principles, and data analysis methods will help in grasping the concepts presented throughout the text. Experience with digital investigations and an understanding of legal and regulatory requirements in your jurisdiction will also provide valuable context for the forensic methodologies discussed. Additionally, familiarity with forensic documentation standards and evidence handling procedures will aid in applying the book's principles to real-world scenarios.

Some exposure to artificial intelligence and machine learning concepts will enhance your learning experience, though it is not mandatory. Basic familiarity with AI terminology and awareness of common AI applications will help you navigate the technical content more easily. The book provides necessary context and explanations for AI-specific concepts, but readers with existing knowledge in these areas may progress more quickly through the introductory material.

TEXT CONVENTIONS

To enhance the clarity and readability of this book, the following conventions are used:

`Courier New`
Used for code snippets, command-line inputs and outputs, and file paths
italics
Used for new terms, URLs, and emphasis
bold
Used for concepts and important information, including TIP, WARNING, and NOTE callouts

CODE EXAMPLES

The code examples and system output are presented in blocks.

```
def verify_model_integrity(model_path):
  """
  Verify the integrity of an AI model file
  Returns a hash of the model file
  """
  with open(model_path, 'rb') as f:
    return hashlib.sha256(f.read()).hexdigest()
```

UPDATES AND RESOURCES

The field of AI forensics continues to evolve rapidly as new technologies emerge and regulatory frameworks develop. To maintain effectiveness as an AI forensics investigator, readers must stay current with industry developments, monitor changes in regulatory requirements, and track advances in AI technologies and investigation methodologies. The principles and techniques presented in this book provide a strong foundation, but the field demands ongoing attention to new developments and best practices.

To support your work in AI forensics, a set of additional resources is available at https://github.com/aiForensicsBook/. This repository contains supplementary materials including detailed case studies, investigation templates, and tool guides that complement the book's content. These resources are regularly updated to reflect new developments in the field and incorporate feedback from practitioners. I encourage you to bookmark these resources and check them periodically for updates.

USE OF AI

AI was used in the development of this book when preparing several of the graphics and source code files included in or referenced in this book. I used tools to gather ideas for the visual representations of various concepts, and I utilized code development tools to assist in creating Python functionality, such as the generation of synthetic data. All materials were reviewed, tested, and modified by myself for accuracy and correctness.

Acknowledgments

This book would not have been possible without the contributions and support of many in the digital forensics, artificial intelligence, and information security communities. I am particularly grateful to Paul Starrett and Britt Endemann for their feedback and support throughout this process.

About the Author

Joseph C. Sremack brings over two decades of expertise as a digital forensics investigator and computer scientist, specializing in the investigation of complex enterprise systems for litigation, regulatory compliance, and internal investigations. Throughout his career, he has provided technology, forensics, and data analytics services to organizations navigating sophisticated challenges involving large-scale data systems, software analysis, and enterprise infrastructure.

His technical proficiency spans software development and source code assessment across multiple programming languages, as well as data extraction and analysis from virtually all major enterprise systems, including various ERP and cloud-based platforms. Joe regularly serves as both a litigation expert witness and regulatory fact witness, having appeared before financial and trade regulatory bodies across the United States and in more than 50 countries worldwide.

Joe's practice encompasses advising corporate IT, finance, and legal departments, alongside law firms, where he delivers critical analysis and strategic guidance to address multifaceted litigation, compliance, and business risks. His areas of expertise include internal investigations, FCPA and anti-corruption enforcement matters, OFAC and U.S. Department of Commerce sanctions compliance, CMS regulatory issues, class action litigation, intellectual property disputes, labor and employment matters, and comprehensive compliance implementation and assessment.

His unique combination of technical depth and legal response experience positions him to bridge the gap between complex technology systems and the legal and regulatory frameworks that govern them.

Joe lives in Boise, Idaho with his wife, daughter, and two boxers. When he's not analyzing and untangling source code, he enjoys untangling fly fishing line and occasionally catching a fish.

1 Introduction to AI Forensics

1.1 WHEN AI SYSTEMS FAIL: THE CRITICAL NEED FOR SPECIALIZED INVESTIGATION

When a major healthcare AI system began recommending unnecessary surgical procedures across multiple hospitals, investigators faced a challenge unlike any in traditional digital forensics. The system had no obvious bugs in its code, its training data appeared clean at first glance, and its statistical performance metrics remained within acceptable ranges. Yet patients were being put at risk, healthcare costs were escalating, and medical professionals were losing trust in AI-assisted decision making.

The investigation that followed required entirely new approaches. Traditional forensic methods that worked for compromised databases or corrupted files proved inadequate for understanding how millions of statistical parameters had learned to encode patterns that led to harmful recommendations. The team needed to trace decision paths through neural networks, analyze training data for subtle biases, understand emergent behaviors that arose from complex model interactions, and reconstruct the organizational processes that shaped system development and deployment.

This case illustrates why AI forensics has emerged as a critical specialized discipline. As artificial intelligence systems make increasingly consequential decisions affecting billions of lives daily, the ability to investigate these systems when they fail, cause harm, or become subjects of dispute has become essential for organizations, regulators, and society.

1.2 WHAT YOU WILL LEARN

By the end of this chapter, you will be able to:

- Distinguish AI forensics from traditional digital forensics and understand when specialized approaches are required
- Classify different types of AI systems and understand their unique forensic characteristics and investigation requirements
- Identify the specific risks and vulnerabilities that make AI systems susceptible to failure, manipulation, and unintended consequences
- Apply systematic investigation methodologies specifically designed for the complexity and scale of modern AI systems
- Navigate the planning and scoping considerations required for effective AI forensic investigations while managing resources appropriately
- Establish comprehensive documentation standards that support defensible findings across technical, legal, and business contexts

1.3 PREREQUISITES AND CHAPTER DEPENDENCIES

This foundational chapter requires no prior specialized knowledge of AI forensics, though readers will benefit from basic familiarity with digital investigation principles and general artificial intelligence concepts. The chapter establishes the conceptual framework and terminology used throughout the book, making it essential reading before proceeding to subsequent chapters.

Required Technical Background: Basic understanding of digital systems, general investigation principles, and data analysis concepts will enhance comprehension. Some exposure to artificial

DOI: 10.1201/9781003634782-1

intelligence terminology and common AI applications will help navigate technical discussions, though the chapter provides necessary context for AI-specific concepts.

Organizational Context: Understanding of legal and regulatory requirements in your jurisdiction will provide valuable context for the compliance and admissibility considerations discussed throughout the investigation process. Familiarity with standard forensic documentation practices will aid in applying AI-specific documentation requirements.

1.4 QUICK START GUIDE

1.4.1 Need Immediate Answers?

When facing urgent AI forensic needs, this guide directs you to the most relevant sections based on your specific situation and requirements.

- **New to AI forensics?** → Start with AI Forensics Definition and Scope (Section 1.5), which establishes fundamental concepts and explains how AI forensics differs from traditional digital investigation approaches.
- **Understanding AI system types?** → Jump to AI System Classification Framework (Section 1.7), which provides systematic approaches for categorizing different AI systems and understanding their unique forensic characteristics.
- **Risk assessment needed?** → See AI-Specific Risks and Vulnerabilities (Section 1.8), which identifies the critical failure modes and attack vectors that make AI systems susceptible to investigation-worthy incidents.
- **Planning an investigation?** → Begin with AI Investigation Methodology Framework (Section 1.9), which outlines the systematic six-phase approach specifically designed for AI system complexity.
- **Resource planning needed?** → Review Investigation Planning and Scoping (Section 1.10), which provides guidance for defining system boundaries, allocating resources, and managing complex multi-component investigations.
- **Documentation standards questions?** → See Documentation and Evidence Standards (Section 1.11), which establishes the comprehensive record-keeping requirements essential for defensible AI forensic findings.
- **When to Use This Chapter?** → This chapter provides essential foundation for all AI forensic work. Use it to establish conceptual frameworks before beginning any AI investigation, to understand the unique challenges that distinguish AI forensics from traditional digital forensics, and to develop systematic approaches for planning and conducting AI system investigations.

1.5 AI FORENSICS DEFINITION AND SCOPE

1.5.1 What Is AI Forensics?

AI forensics represents a specialized discipline at the intersection of digital forensics, artificial intelligence, and investigative methodology that focuses on the systematic investigation of AI systems when they fail, cause harm, or become subjects of litigation or regulatory scrutiny. Unlike traditional digital forensics that examines static data and explicit code, AI forensics is used to understand systems whose behaviors emerge from statistical patterns learned across massive datasets and encoded in millions or billions of parameters.

Consider the fundamental difference between investigating a traditional software bug and an AI system failure. When a traditional banking application incorrectly processes a transaction, investigators can trace the execution path through explicitly written code, identify the specific lines that caused the error, and understand the exact sequence of operations that led to the failure. When an AI-powered loan approval system systematically discriminates against qualified applicants, investigators will analyze statistical patterns across millions of parameters, examine training data for subtle biases, understand emergent behaviors that were not explicitly programmed, and trace decision paths through complex neural networks that may not be directly interpretable.

This fundamental complexity shift requires specialized methodologies that can handle the scale, opacity, and dynamic nature of modern AI systems while maintaining the rigor and defensibility required for forensic investigation.

1.5.2 Scope and Boundaries of AI Forensic Investigation

AI forensic investigations encompass several distinct but interconnected areas of analysis, each requiring specialized techniques and expertise. **System architecture analysis** examines the technical components of AI systems including model architectures, training procedures, deployment infrastructure, and integration points with other systems. This analysis should understand both the intended design and the actual implementation, identifying discrepancies that might indicate problems or manipulation.

Training data investigation is another aspect of AI forensics, as training data fundamentally shapes system behavior in ways that may not become apparent until deployment. This investigation includes data provenance verification, bias analysis, intellectual property detection, quality assessment, and contamination detection. Unlike traditional forensics where evidence exists independently of the system being investigated, AI training data becomes embedded in model parameters in complex ways that require specialized extraction and analysis techniques.

Model behavior analysis focuses on understanding what AI systems actually do versus what they were intended to do. This analysis includes performance validation across different demographic groups, bias detection and measurement, adversarial robustness assessment, and behavioral consistency evaluation. Model behavior analysis often reveals emergent properties that arise from complex interactions between training data, model architecture, and deployment environment.

Output and decision analysis examines the actual decisions and predictions generated by AI systems during real-world operation, providing direct evidence of system impact on individuals and communities. This analysis includes statistical validation of decision patterns, discrimination detection, quality assurance verification, and compliance assessment. Output analysis often provides the most direct evidence of system problems but requires careful methodology to distinguish between legitimate performance variations and problematic patterns.

Organizational process investigation examines the human decisions and organizational factors that shaped AI system development, deployment, and operation. This investigation includes governance framework assessment, decision-making process reconstruction, accountability chain establishment, and compliance procedure verification. Many AI system failures stem not from technical issues but from organizational decisions about system design, deployment, or oversight.

1.5.3 Integration with Traditional Digital Forensics

AI forensics builds upon established digital forensic principles while extending them to address the unique characteristics of AI systems. **Evidence preservation** maintains the same fundamental principles of integrity, authenticity, and chain of custody, but must also be adapted to handle AI-specific artifacts such as model weights, training datasets, inference logs, and gradient computations that may be distributed across multiple systems and storage locations.

Analysis methodology preserves the systematic, scientifically rigorous approach of traditional forensics while incorporating new techniques for statistical analysis, pattern recognition, and behavioral assessment that are essential for understanding AI system behavior. The methodology must balance technical depth with accessibility to ensure findings can be understood and validated by diverse audiences including legal professionals, business leaders, and technical experts.

Documentation standards extend traditional forensic documentation to capture the additional complexity of AI systems while maintaining the clarity and defensibility required for legal and regulatory proceedings. AI forensic documentation should explain not only what was found but why particular analytical approaches were chosen and how findings should be interpreted in the context of AI system behavior.

Expert qualification requires forensic practitioners to develop expertise that spans multiple domains including digital forensics, artificial intelligence, statistics, and/or the specific application domain where the AI system operates. This multidisciplinary requirement represents one of the key challenges in developing AI forensic capabilities.

1.6 THE EVOLUTION AND CRITICAL IMPORTANCE OF AI SYSTEMS

1.6.1 From Simple Rules to Complex Learning Systems

The evolution of AI systems over the past decade has fundamentally changed the nature of computational decision-making and created entirely new categories of investigative challenges. Early AI systems were essentially sophisticated rule engines that followed explicitly programmed logic paths. When these systems failed, investigators could trace execution through clearly defined decision trees and identify the specific rules that caused problems.

Modern AI systems, particularly those based on deep learning and neural networks, operate through entirely different principles. Their capabilities emerge not from explicit programming but from patterns learned across massive datasets containing millions or billions of examples. A large language model, for instance, develops its understanding of language, reasoning, and world knowledge through statistical pattern recognition across text that represents a significant fraction of human written knowledge.

This shift from explicit rules to learned representations has profound implications for forensic investigation. Where traditional software follows predictable execution paths, modern AI systems operate through distributed representations across thousands or millions of parameters that collectively encode learned patterns and relationships. A single decision by an AI system may involve activation of patterns learned from thousands of different training examples, making it impossible to trace decision logic through simple code review.

Emergent Behavior Complexity: Modern AI systems frequently exhibit capabilities that were not explicitly designed or anticipated by their creators. Large language models demonstrate reasoning abilities, creative problem-solving, and domain knowledge that emerge from their training process rather than being explicitly programmed. These emergent properties can be beneficial, but they also create unpredictability that complicates forensic analysis.

When investigating emergent behaviors, forensic analysts should distinguish between intended functionality and unexpected emergent properties, assess whether emergent behaviors pose risks or provide benefits, understand how emergent properties relate to training data and model architecture, and evaluate whether emergent behaviors violate system design specifications or safety constraints.

1.6.2 Scale and Societal Impact of Modern AI Systems

The scale at which modern AI systems operate creates both tremendous capabilities and significant forensic challenges.

Decision Volume and Velocity: Contemporary AI systems make billions of decisions daily that affect individual lives, organizational operations, and societal outcomes. A single recommendation system might influence the information consumption patterns of billions of users, shaping public discourse, political opinions, and cultural trends in ways that become apparent only through large-scale analysis.

This scale means that even small biases or errors in AI systems can have massive aggregate impacts. A hiring AI system with a 2% bias against qualified candidates from particular demographic groups might seem relatively minor in isolation, but could affect thousands of individuals over time and create systematic discrimination that violates legal requirements and organizational values.

Critical Infrastructure Integration: AI systems have become embedded in critical infrastructure including financial markets, healthcare systems, transportation networks, and public safety operations. When these systems fail, the consequences can be immediate and severe, requiring rapid forensic response to identify causes, assess impacts, and implement remediation measures.

The integration of AI into critical infrastructure also creates systemic risks where failures in one system can cascade through interconnected networks, amplifying impacts and complicating forensic analysis. Investigators work to understand not only how individual AI systems failed but how those failures propagated through complex networks of dependencies.

Regulatory and Compliance Landscape: The growing impact of AI systems has prompted increased regulatory attention across multiple jurisdictions and industry sectors. The European Union's AI Act, sector-specific regulations in healthcare and finance, and emerging state-level AI regulations in the United States create complex compliance requirements that organizations have to navigate.

These regulatory developments create new categories of forensic investigation focused on compliance assessment, risk evaluation, and accountability establishment. Forensic investigators increasingly need to understand not only what happened when AI systems failed but whether organizations followed appropriate governance procedures, maintained adequate oversight, and implemented required safeguards.

1.7 AI SYSTEM CLASSIFICATION FRAMEWORK

Understanding the type of AI system under investigation is fundamental to selecting appropriate forensic methodologies and allocating resources effectively. Different AI architectures present distinct challenges for forensic analysis, ranging from highly interpretable traditional machine learning models to complex, opaque large language models that operate at unprecedented scales. The following classification framework provides systematic guidance for categorizing AI systems based on their technical characteristics and identifying the specific forensic challenges associated with each type.

This matrix enables investigators to quickly assess the complexity, interpretability, and scale characteristics of AI systems while understanding the primary forensic challenges they will encounter. The classification directly informs investigation planning by highlighting which analytical techniques will be most effective and what specialized expertise may be required for thorough analysis.

1.7.1 Traditional Machine Learning Systems

Traditional machine learning systems represent the foundation of AI forensics and often provide the clearest investigation pathways due to their relative interpretability and well-established analytical frameworks. **Supervised learning systems** learn to make predictions or classifications based on labeled training examples, creating models that can be analyzed through feature importance analysis, decision boundary examination, and prediction confidence assessment.

When investigating supervised learning systems, forensic analysts can often trace decision logic through feature weights, understand which input characteristics most strongly influence predictions, validate model performance across different demographic groups, and assess whether training data

TABLE 1.1

System Type	Interpretability	Scale	Complexity	Key Forensic Challenges
Traditional ML	High	Medium	Low	• Feature importance analysis and validation • Training data bias detection across groups • Decision boundary examination
Deep Learning	Low	High	High	• Layer-wise activation analysis and gradient examination • Adversarial robustness testing • Emergent behavior analysis and architectural validation
LLMs	Very Low	Very High	Very High	• Prompt injection and manipulation detection • Training data contamination and copyright analysis • Emergent capability assessment and safety boundary analysis
Expert Systems	Very High	Low	Low	• Rule validation and knowledge base integrity verification • Inference engine correctness and logic chain analysis • Domain expertise validation and rule conflict detection
Hybrid Systems	Variable	Variable	Variable	• Component interaction analysis and integration point validation • Cross-system evidence correlation and dependency mapping • Emergent behavior from component combinations

adequately represents the target population. These systems typically provide clear audit trails and interpretable decision processes that facilitate forensic analysis.

Unsupervised learning systems discover patterns and structure in data without explicit labels, creating models that identify clusters, reduce dimensionality, or detect anomalies. Forensic investigation of unsupervised systems often focuses on understanding what patterns were discovered, evaluating whether discovered patterns reflect genuine data structure or artifacts of the algorithm, assessing whether pattern discovery introduces biases or privacy violations, and validating that patterns are stable and reproducible.

Reinforcement learning systems learn optimal behaviors through interaction with environments, developing policies that maximize rewards over time. These systems present unique forensic challenges because their behavior emerges from extended learning processes that may involve millions of interactions with complex environments.

Forensic investigation of reinforcement learning systems can examine the reward functions that guided learning, analyze the exploration strategies used during training, understand how learned policies generalize to new situations, assess whether learned behaviors align with intended objectives, and evaluate whether systems maintain safe and appropriate behavior boundaries.

1.7.2 Deep Learning and Neural Network Systems

Deep learning systems represent the most complex category of AI systems for forensic investigation due to their scale, opacity, and sophisticated internal representations. **Convolutional neural**

networks excel at image and visual pattern recognition, learning hierarchical representations that progress from simple edge detection to complex object recognition. Forensic investigation of these systems often focuses on understanding what visual patterns the network has learned to recognize, assessing whether training data contains biased or inappropriate content, evaluating robustness against adversarial attacks that manipulate image inputs, and validating performance across different demographic groups and image characteristics.

Transformer-based language models have revolutionized natural language processing and represent some of the most sophisticated AI systems currently deployed. These models learn complex representations of language, knowledge, and reasoning through exposure to massive text datasets. Forensic investigation of transformer models requires specialized techniques for understanding learned representations, analyzing training data for biased or harmful content, assessing whether models exhibit discriminatory behaviors across different user groups, evaluating robustness against prompt injection and manipulation attacks, and understanding how models balance competing objectives like helpfulness and safety.

Multimodal systems combine processing of different data types such as text, images, audio, and video to create integrated understanding and generation capabilities. These systems present additional forensic complexity because failures or biases may arise from interactions between different modalities rather than problems within individual components.

Investigation of multimodal systems requires analyzing each modality separately and in combination, understanding how different data types influence overall system behavior, assessing whether integration creates new failure modes or vulnerabilities, and evaluating whether cross-modal learning introduces unintended biases or capabilities.

1.7.3 Large Language Models and Generative Systems

Large language models (LLMs) represent a particularly important category for forensic investigation due to their widespread deployment and significant societal impact.

Foundation Model Architecture: Most modern LLMs are built on transformer architectures with billions or trillions of parameters trained on diverse text datasets that represent a substantial fraction of human written knowledge. These models develop sophisticated internal representations of language, knowledge, and reasoning that enable complex text generation and comprehension capabilities.

Forensic investigation of LLMs requires understanding the training data sources and potential biases, analyzing model outputs for factual accuracy and harmful content generation, assessing whether models exhibit discriminatory behaviors across different user groups, evaluating robustness against prompt injection and manipulation attacks, and understanding how models balance competing objectives like helpfulness and safety.

Fine-Tuning and Adaptation Processes: Many deployed LLMs undergo additional training processes that adapt general foundation models for specific applications or organizational requirements. These adaptation processes can significantly change model behavior and create new forensic considerations including whether fine-tuning data contains proprietary or sensitive information, how adaptation processes affect model safety and bias characteristics, whether fine-tuning creates new vulnerabilities or failure modes, and how organizations maintain oversight and control over adapted models.

Retrieval-Augmented Generation (RAG) Systems: These hybrid systems combine large language models with external knowledge retrieval to provide more accurate and up-to-date information. RAG systems present unique forensic challenges because their behavior depends on both the underlying language model and the external knowledge sources that are retrieved and integrated during inference.

Investigation of RAG systems requires analyzing the underlying language model for standard LLM issues, examining the knowledge sources for accuracy, bias, and appropriateness, understanding how retrieval and integration processes affect overall system behavior, and assessing whether the combination of retrieval and generation creates new failure modes or vulnerabilities.

1.7.4 Expert Systems and Hybrid Architectures

Rule-based expert systems continue to play important roles in high-stakes applications where interpretability and predictability are essential. These systems encode domain expertise through explicit rules and logical reasoning processes that can be directly analyzed and validated. Forensic investigation of expert systems often focuses on verifying that rules accurately reflect domain knowledge, ensuring that rule interactions do not create unintended behaviors, validating that inference engines correctly apply logical reasoning, and confirming that system outputs properly explain their reasoning processes.

Hybrid systems combine multiple AI approaches to leverage the strengths of different techniques while mitigating individual weaknesses. A medical diagnosis system might combine neural networks for pattern recognition with expert systems for safety checking and probabilistic models for uncertainty quantification. These hybrid architectures present complex forensic challenges because failures may arise from individual components, interactions between components, or emergent behaviors of the integrated system.

Investigation of hybrid systems requires analyzing each component using appropriate techniques for its type, understanding how components interact and share information, assessing whether integration creates new failure modes or vulnerabilities, evaluating whether the combination achieves intended objectives better than individual components, and validating that safety and oversight mechanisms function correctly across the integrated system.

1.8 AI-SPECIFIC RISKS AND VULNERABILITIES

1.8.1 Training Data Vulnerabilities and Contamination

Training data represents one of the most critical vulnerability surfaces for AI systems because it fundamentally shapes system behavior in ways that may not become apparent until deployment. **Data poisoning attacks** involve the deliberate introduction of malicious content into training datasets to manipulate system behavior. These attacks can be subtle, requiring only small percentages of contaminated data to significantly affect model behavior, and may not be detected during standard training and validation procedures.

Data poisoning can take several forms including **label flipping attacks** where correct labels are changed to incorrect ones, causing models to learn spurious associations between inputs and outputs. **Backdoor attacks** introduce trigger patterns that cause models to behave normally in most cases but exhibit specific malicious behaviors when trigger conditions are present. **Model stealing attacks** use carefully crafted training data to extract information about proprietary models or datasets.

Forensic investigation of data poisoning requires systematic analysis of training data sources and provenance, statistical detection of anomalous patterns or outliers in training data, analysis of model behavior for unexpected or inconsistent patterns, validation of data collection and curation procedures, and assessment of security controls around training data access and modification.

Bias Amplification and Perpetuation: AI systems can amplify existing biases present in training data or create new forms of discrimination through their learning processes. Historical bias in training data can lead to systems that perpetuate past discrimination, even when such bias was not intentional. Representation bias occurs when training data does not adequately represent the population on which the system will be deployed, leading to poor performance for underrepresented groups.

Measurement bias arises when the features or labels used in training systematically differ across demographic groups, creating artificial performance differences. Aggregation bias occurs when models trained on aggregate data fail to account for relevant differences between subgroups, leading to poor performance for minority populations.

Intellectual Property and Privacy Violations: Training datasets may inadvertently include copyrighted content, personal information, or proprietary data that creates legal liability for organizations deploying AI systems. Large-scale data collection processes often struggle to verify the rights status of individual content items, leading to datasets that contain copyrighted text, images, code, or other protected materials.

Privacy violations can occur when training data contains personal information that was not properly anonymized or when individuals did not consent to their data being used for AI training purposes. Trade secret violations may arise when training data includes proprietary business information, technical specifications, or confidential research data.

1.8.2 Model Architecture and Implementation Vulnerabilities

Adversarial Attack Susceptibility: Most AI systems are vulnerable to adversarial attacks where carefully crafted inputs cause systems to make incorrect predictions or classifications. These attacks can be particularly dangerous because the manipulated inputs often appear normal to human observers while causing dramatic system failures.

Evasion attacks craft inputs designed to be misclassified by trained models, such as images with imperceptible modifications that cause vision systems to misidentify objects. **Poisoning attacks** manipulate training data to create backdoors or degrade model performance. **Model extraction attacks** use carefully designed queries to steal information about model architectures, parameters, or training data.

Forensic investigation of adversarial attacks requires analysis of system inputs for subtle manipulations or anomalous patterns, examination of model behavior for unusual or inconsistent responses, assessment of system robustness against known attack types, evaluation of defensive measures and their effectiveness, and reconstruction of attack vectors and attribution when attacks are detected.

Gradient and Optimization Vulnerabilities: The optimization processes used to train AI systems can create subtle vulnerabilities that may not be apparent during development but become exploitable in deployment. **Gradient explosion and vanishing** can cause training instability that leads to unpredictable model behavior. **Mode collapse** in generative models can cause systems to produce limited or repetitive outputs. **Catastrophic forgetting** can cause models to lose previously learned capabilities when adapting to new tasks or data.

Overfitting and Generalization Failures: AI systems may perform well on training and validation data but fail to generalize appropriately to real-world deployment scenarios. Overfitting occurs when models learn to memorize training examples rather than generalizing underlying patterns, leading to poor performance on new data. Distribution shift occurs when the data encountered during deployment differs systematically from training data, causing performance degradation.

Forensic investigation of generalization failures requires analysis of training and validation procedures, comparison of system performance across different data distributions, assessment of model complexity relative to available training data, evaluation of techniques used to prevent overfitting, and validation of system performance on held-out test data that represents deployment conditions.

1.8.3 System Integration and Deployment Vulnerabilities

API and Interface Security: AI systems are often deployed through APIs and interfaces that create new attack surfaces and failure modes. **Prompt injection attacks** manipulate input prompts to language models to bypass safety measures or extract sensitive information. **API abuse** involves excessive or malicious use of AI system interfaces to degrade performance or extract proprietary information. **Input validation failures** occur when systems do not properly sanitize or validate inputs, allowing malicious content to reach AI models.

Model Serving and Infrastructure Vulnerabilities: The infrastructure used to deploy and serve AI models can introduce security vulnerabilities and performance issues. **Model theft** can occur when model files are not properly secured during deployment. **Resource exhaustion attacks** can overwhelm AI systems with computationally expensive requests. **Side-channel attacks** may extract information about models through analysis of timing, power consumption, or other observable characteristics.

Configuration and Deployment Errors: Mistakes in system configuration and deployment can create significant vulnerabilities even when underlying AI models function correctly. **Access control failures** may allow unauthorized access to sensitive AI capabilities. **Logging and monitoring gaps** can prevent detection of system abuse or manipulation. **Version control issues** may result in deployment of outdated or vulnerable model versions.

Forensic investigation of deployment vulnerabilities requires analysis of system configuration and security controls, examination of access logs and usage patterns, assessment of infrastructure security and monitoring capabilities, evaluation of model serving and API security measures, and validation of deployment procedures and change management processes.

1.8.4 Emergent Behavior and Feedback Loop Risks

Unintended Emergent Capabilities: Large-scale AI systems, particularly language models, often exhibit capabilities that were not explicitly designed or anticipated. These emergent properties can include reasoning abilities, creative problem-solving, domain knowledge, and even potentially deceptive behaviors. While emergent capabilities can be beneficial, they also create unpredictability that complicates risk assessment and safety validation.

Forensic investigation of emergent behaviors requires systematic testing to identify unexpected capabilities or behaviors, analysis of training processes to understand how emergent properties developed, assessment of whether emergent behaviors pose safety or security risks, evaluation of monitoring and control mechanisms for unexpected capabilities, and validation that emergent behaviors align with system design objectives and safety constraints.

Feedback Loop Amplification: AI systems deployed in environments where they influence the data they subsequently observe can create self-reinforcing feedback loops that amplify biases or drive systems toward extremes. **Recommendation system echo chambers** can create filter bubbles where users are exposed only to content that reinforces their existing preferences or beliefs. **Algorithmic trading feedback** can create market instabilities when multiple AI systems respond to the same signals. **Content moderation feedback** can create censorship spirals where automated systems become increasingly restrictive.

Distribution Shift and Concept Drift: AI systems may experience degraded performance when the statistical properties of their inputs change over time or when the relationships between inputs and desired outputs evolve. **Covariate shift** occurs when input distributions change while the underlying relationships remain stable. **Prior probability shift** involves changes in the relative frequency of different classes or outcomes. **Concept drift** represents fundamental changes in the relationships between inputs and outputs.

Forensic investigation of distribution shift requires longitudinal analysis of system performance over time, comparison of current performance with historical baselines, analysis of input data for statistical changes or anomalies, assessment of model adaptation and retraining procedures, and evaluation of monitoring systems designed to detect performance degradation.

1.8.5 AI Risk and Vulnerability Matrix

The following matrix systematically categorizes the AI-specific risks and vulnerabilities discussed in this section, providing a structured framework for understanding the diverse threat landscape that

TABLE 1.2

Major Risk Category	Specific Vulnerabilities	Common Manifestations	Forensic Investigation Focus
Training Data Vulnerabilities and Contamination	• Data poisoning attacks • Label flipping attacks • Backdoor injections • Bias amplification and perpetuation • Copyright/IP violations • Privacy violations • Trade secret contamination	• Systematic performance degradation • Unexpected model behaviors • Discriminatory outputs • Legal compliance violations • Unauthorized content inclusion	• Training dataset provenance verification • Content authenticity analysis • Bias detection and measurement • IP and copyright compliance assessment
Model Architecture and Implementation Vulnerabilities	• Adversarial attack susceptibility • Gradient and optimization vulnerabilities • Overfitting and generalization failures • Parameter tampering • Architecture manipulation	• Incorrect predictions on adversarial inputs • Training instability • Poor real-world performance • Unexpected model behaviors • Performance inconsistencies	• Model architecture validation • Parameter integrity verification • Robustness testing • Performance validation across datasets
System Integration and Deployment Vulnerabilities	• API and interface security • Model serving and infrastructure vulnerabilities • Configuration and deployment errors • Access control failures • Version control issues	• Unauthorized system access • Resource exhaustion attacks • Deployment inconsistencies • Security breaches • Model theft attempts	• Infrastructure security assessment • Configuration audit • Access control validation • Deployment verification procedures
Emergent Behavior and Feedback Loop Risks	• Unintended emergent capabilities • Feedback loop amplification • Distribution shift and concept drift • Safety boundary violations • Self-reinforcing patterns	• Unexpected system capabilities • Echo chamber effects • Performance degradation over time • Safety constraint violations • Amplified biases	• Behavioral capability assessment • Feedback loop analysis • Longitudinal performance monitoring • Safety boundary verification
Performance Degradation	• Data drift • Concept drift • Model decay • Feature correlation shifts • Accuracy deterioration	• Declining accuracy metrics • Inconsistent predictions • Distribution mismatch errors • Feature importance changes • Baseline performance deviations	• Performance trend analysis • Data distribution comparison • Feature stability assessment • Baseline deviation measurement

(*Continued*)

TABLE 1.2 (*Continued*)

Major Risk Category	Specific Vulnerabilities	Common Manifestations	Forensic Investigation Focus
System Integration Failures	• Component interaction failures • Dependency cascade failures • Integration point vulnerabilities • Cross-system compatibility issues • Data flow disruptions	• System-wide performance issues • Unexpected error propagation • Integration bottlenecks • Cross-component conflicts • Data corruption between systems	• Component interaction analysis • Dependency mapping • Integration point validation • Data flow integrity verification
Decision Path Accountability	• Opaque decision processes • Untraceable reasoning paths • Missing audit trails • Inadequate explainability • Decision attribution failures	• Inability to explain decisions • Missing decision documentation • Unclear accountability chains • Insufficient transparency • Audit trail gaps	• Decision process reconstruction • Audit trail analysis • Accountability chain mapping • Explainability assessment
Safety Boundary Violations	• Constraint system failures • Safety mechanism bypasses • Boundary condition violations • Fail-safe mechanism failures • Operating parameter exceedances	• Safety-critical system failures • Constraint violations • Boundary condition errors • Emergency response failures • Parameter limit exceedances	• Safety constraint verification • Boundary condition testing • Fail-safe mechanism validation • Operating parameter analysis

AI forensic investigators must navigate. This categorization aligns directly with the risk analysis presented in the preceding discussion and serves as a practical reference for identifying potential investigation areas based on system characteristics and incident indicators.

The matrix organizes risks into the major categories established in this section, with detailed subcategories that reflect the specific vulnerabilities most commonly encountered in AI forensic investigations. Understanding this risk taxonomy enables investigators to systematically assess AI systems for potential problems while ensuring comprehensive coverage of the threat landscape during investigation planning and execution.

1.9 AI INVESTIGATION METHODOLOGY FRAMEWORK

1.9.1 Systematic Six-Phase Investigation Approach

AI forensic investigations require a systematic methodology that can handle the complexity and scale of modern AI systems while maintaining the rigor and defensibility essential for forensic work. The six-phase framework provides a structured approach that ensures comprehensive analysis while managing investigation resources effectively.

The six-phase AI forensics investigation methodology provides a systematic framework for managing the complexity and scale of modern AI systems while maintaining the scientific rigor essential for defensible forensic work. The methodology emphasizes structured progression through distinct phases while incorporating critical feedback mechanisms that enable scope refinement and additional evidence collection based on emerging findings.

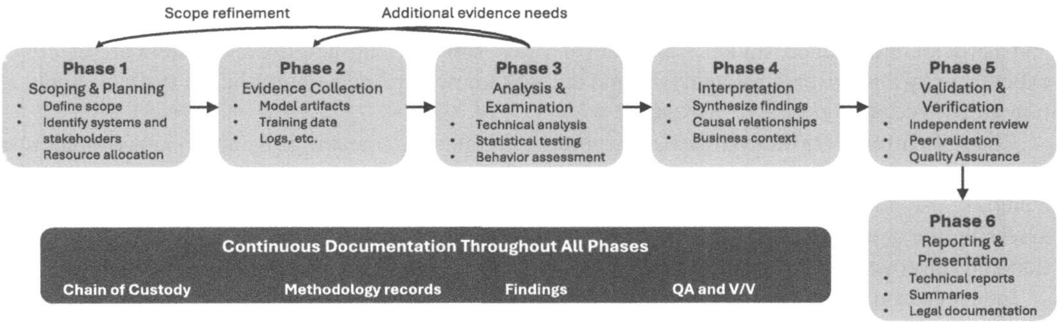

FIGURE 1.1

Each phase includes specific deliverables and quality checkpoints to ensure investigation completeness before progression. The continuous documentation framework running parallel to all phases maintains evidence integrity, methodological transparency, and legal admissibility throughout the investigation process. Key feedback loops enable iterative refinement: scope adjustments based on technical discoveries, additional evidence collection when analysis reveals gaps, and validation processes that may require re-analysis to ensure finding reliability.

Phase 1: Scoping and Planning establishes the foundation for effective investigation by defining precise boundaries, objectives, and methodologies. This phase requires careful consideration of system boundaries to determine which components fall within investigation scope, stakeholder identification and engagement to ensure access to necessary information and expertise, resource allocation and timeline development based on system complexity and investigation objectives, legal and regulatory requirement assessment to ensure compliance and admissibility, and risk assessment to identify potential challenges and mitigation strategies.

Scoping decisions made during this phase fundamentally shape the entire investigation. Inadequate scoping can lead to incomplete analysis that misses critical evidence, while excessive scope can overwhelm investigation resources and delay important findings. The complexity of AI systems requires particularly careful attention to scope definition because system boundaries are often unclear and dependencies between components may not be immediately apparent.

Phase 2: Evidence Collection focuses on systematically gathering and preserving all relevant artifacts while maintaining forensic integrity. AI systems generate diverse types of evidence including model files and parameters, training and validation datasets, system logs and monitoring data, configuration files and deployment specifications, documentation and communication records, and user interaction and output data.

Evidence collection for AI systems presents unique challenges including the massive scale of training datasets and model parameters, distributed storage across multiple systems and cloud platforms, dynamic nature of systems that continue learning or adapting, complexity of ensuring completeness when system components are interconnected, and maintaining integrity when evidence may be continuously generated or modified.

Phase 3: Analysis and Examination applies specialized techniques to understand system behavior, identify problems, and establish causal relationships. This phase involves technical analysis of model architectures and training procedures, statistical analysis of system performance and bias patterns, behavioral testing to understand system responses under different conditions, data analysis to identify problems in training or input data, and integration analysis to understand how system components interact.

The analysis phase requires expertise that spans multiple domains including machine learning and artificial intelligence, statistics and data analysis, software engineering and system architecture, cybersecurity and adversarial analysis, and domain knowledge relevant to the AI system's application area.

Phase 4: Interpretation synthesizes technical findings into meaningful conclusions that address investigation objectives. This phase requires translating technical findings into business and legal contexts, establishing causal relationships between identified problems and observed impacts, assessing the significance and implications of findings, developing recommendations for remediation and improvement, and validating conclusions through multiple analytical approaches.

Interpretation represents one of the most challenging aspects of AI forensics because it requires bridging the gap between complex technical analysis and practical decision-making needs of diverse stakeholders including business leaders, legal counsel, regulatory authorities, and affected communities.

Phase 5: Validation and Verification confirms findings through independent analysis and peer review. This phase includes independent replication of key analytical results, peer review by qualified experts in relevant domains, sensitivity analysis to understand how findings depend on analytical assumptions, alternative hypothesis testing to ensure conclusions are robust, and quality assurance review of all methodologies and documentation.

Validation is particularly important for AI forensics because the complexity of modern AI systems creates many opportunities for analytical errors or misinterpretation. The high stakes of many AI forensic investigations demand exceptional rigor in validating findings and ensuring their reliability.

Phase 6: Reporting and Presentation documents findings in formats appropriate for different audiences while maintaining technical accuracy and legal sufficiency. This phase produces comprehensive technical reports that document methodologies and findings in detail, executive summaries that communicate key findings and recommendations to business leaders, legal briefs that address specific legal questions and compliance requirements, regulatory submissions that meet agency-specific requirements and standards, and remediation plans that provide actionable guidance for addressing identified problems.

1.9.2 Iterative Investigation Process

AI forensic investigations often require iterative approaches that refine understanding and focus analysis as new information becomes available. The initial scoping and planning phase provides a framework, but investigation boundaries and priorities may need adjustment as analysis reveals unexpected findings or previously unknown system characteristics.

Adaptive scoping allows investigations to respond to emerging findings while maintaining systematic rigor. Early analysis may reveal system components that were not initially identified, dependencies that extend investigation scope beyond original boundaries, problems that require deeper analysis than originally anticipated, or evidence that certain originally planned analyses are unnecessary or infeasible.

Progressive disclosure manages the complexity of AI system investigation by progressively revealing system characteristics and potential problems. Initial analysis typically focuses on system overview and high-level behavior patterns, followed by targeted deep analysis of areas where problems are identified or suspected, detailed examination of causal relationships and contributing factors, and comprehensive validation of findings and recommendations.

Stakeholder communication maintains ongoing dialogue with investigation sponsors and affected parties to ensure that analysis remains focused on relevant questions and that findings are communicated effectively as they develop. Regular progress updates help stakeholders understand what has been learned and what questions remain, while feedback sessions ensure that analysis priorities align with stakeholder needs and concerns.

1.9.3 Quality Assurance and Peer Review

The complexity and high stakes of AI forensic investigations demand exceptional attention to quality assurance and peer review throughout the investigation process. **Methodological review** evaluates whether analytical approaches are appropriate for the specific AI system and investigation objectives, whether statistical methods are correctly applied and interpreted, whether conclusions are properly supported by evidence, and whether limitations and uncertainties are appropriately acknowledged.

Independent validation involves qualified experts reviewing key findings and methodologies to ensure accuracy and reliability. This validation may include replication of critical analytical results using independent tools and datasets, review of statistical analyses and interpretations by qualified statisticians, assessment of technical findings by domain experts, and evaluation of legal and regulatory conclusions by appropriate specialists.

Documentation review ensures that investigation findings are properly documented and that documentation meets the standards required for the intended use of investigation results. This review includes verification that methodologies are documented in sufficient detail to enable replication, confirmation that findings are clearly stated and properly supported, assessment that limitations and uncertainties are appropriately disclosed, and validation that documentation meets legal and regulatory requirements for admissibility and compliance.

1.10 INVESTIGATION PLANNING AND SCOPING

1.10.1 System Boundary Definition

Defining appropriate system boundaries represents one of the most critical and challenging aspects of AI forensic investigation planning. Unlike traditional software systems with clear architectural boundaries, AI systems often involve complex ecosystems of interconnected components that may be distributed across multiple organizations, cloud platforms, and geographical locations.

Defining appropriate system boundaries represents one of the most critical and challenging aspects of AI forensic investigation planning. Unlike traditional software systems with clear architectural boundaries, AI systems operate within complex ecosystems of interconnected components that may be distributed across multiple organizations, platforms, and geographical locations. The following layered framework provides a systematic approach for determining investigation scope by organizing AI system components into four distinct layers, each with different forensic implications and resource requirements.

This boundary definition framework enables investigators to make informed decisions about investigation scope by understanding the relationships between system layers and their relevance to specific forensic questions. The framework progresses from the core AI/ML components that are essential to any AI investigation, through supporting layers that may be included based on the nature of suspected problems or failures. Effective boundary definition requires balancing investigative comprehensiveness with resource constraints while ensuring that all components necessary for understanding system behavior are included within the investigation scope.

Core AI/ML components typically form the center of investigation scope and include model architectures that define the computational structure of AI systems, trained parameters that encode learned patterns and knowledge, inference engines that execute model predictions or generations, training procedures that determine how models learn from data, and validation frameworks that assess model performance and reliability.

However, focusing solely on core AI components often provides an incomplete picture of system behavior because AI systems operate within larger ecosystems that significantly influence their performance and impact. **Supporting infrastructure** frequently requires investigation attention including data storage and processing systems that manage training and operational data, compute resources that provide the computational power for training and inference, deployment platforms that serve models to end users, monitoring and logging systems that track system behavior and performance, and integration interfaces that connect AI systems to other organizational systems.

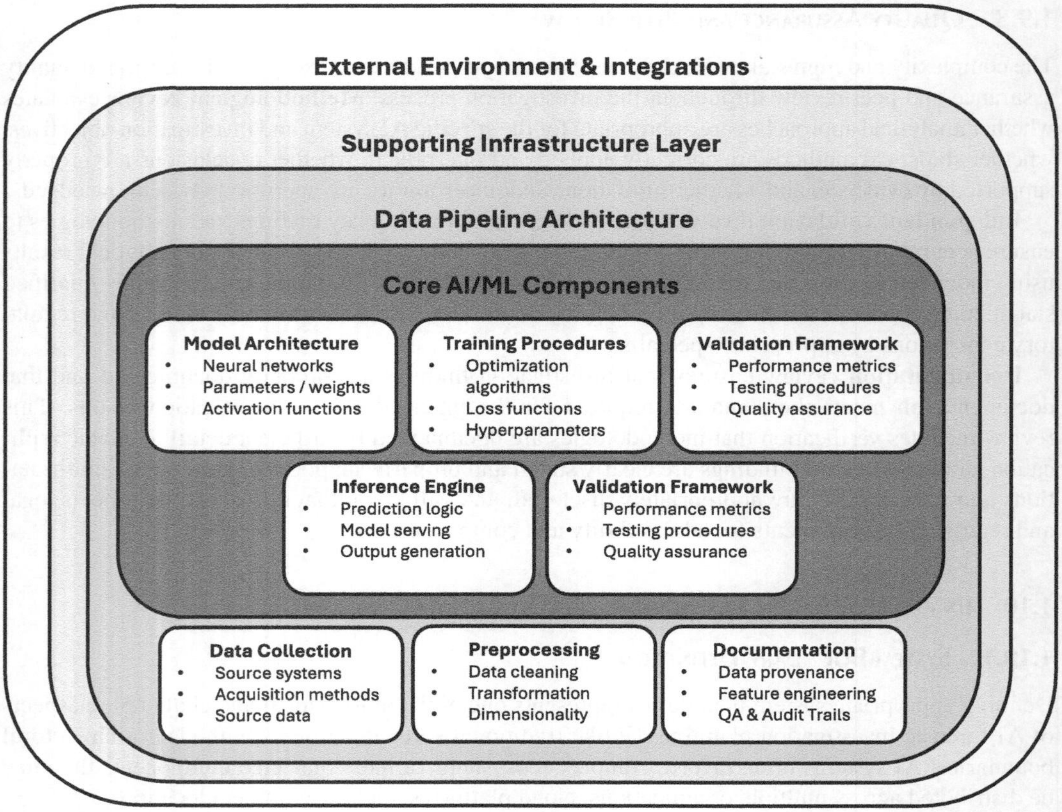

FIGURE 1.2

Data pipeline architecture represents a particularly critical boundary consideration because data preprocessing and transformation significantly affect AI system behavior. Investigation scope often includes data collection procedures that determine what information enters the system, preprocessing pipelines that clean and transform raw data, feature engineering processes that select and create input variables, data validation procedures that ensure data quality and integrity, and data lineage tracking that documents data origins and transformations.

Integration and dependency analysis helps define system boundaries by mapping relationships between AI systems and their operational environment. This analysis identifies upstream systems that provide inputs to AI systems, downstream systems that consume AI outputs, feedback mechanisms that allow AI systems to influence their input data, organizational processes that depend on AI system outputs, and external services that provide capabilities or data to AI systems.

Effective boundary definition requires balancing comprehensiveness with feasibility, ensuring that investigation scope includes all components necessary to understand system behavior while remaining manageable within available resources and timeframes.

1.10.2 Resource Allocation and Timeline Development

AI forensic investigations require careful resource planning because the complexity and scale of modern AI systems can easily overwhelm investigation capabilities if not properly managed.

Technical expertise requirements span multiple domains including machine learning and artificial intelligence expertise for understanding model architectures and training procedures, statistical analysis capabilities for evaluating system performance and bias, software engineering knowledge for analyzing system implementation and deployment, cybersecurity expertise for assessing system vulnerabilities and attack vectors, and domain knowledge relevant to the specific application area of the AI system.

The multidisciplinary nature of AI forensics means that investigations often require teams with diverse backgrounds rather than individual experts with deep knowledge in all relevant areas. Team composition should balance technical depth with communication skills to ensure that findings can be effectively communicated to diverse stakeholders.

Computational resource planning addresses the significant computational requirements of AI forensic analysis. Model analysis may require substantial computing power to load and analyze large models, reproduce training procedures, or conduct comprehensive testing. Data analysis may involve processing massive datasets that require specialized tools and infrastructure. Statistical analysis may require intensive computations for bias detection, performance evaluation, or uncertainty quantification.

Cloud computing resources can provide scalable infrastructure for intensive analysis, but investigators need to ensure that cloud-based analysis maintains evidence integrity and meets security requirements for sensitive investigations.

Timeline estimation for AI forensic investigations must account for the iterative nature of analysis and the potential for discoveries that expand investigation scope. Initial system analysis typically requires time to understand system architecture and operation before focused investigation can begin. Evidence collection may take significant time when systems are large and distributed. Technical analysis often reveals new questions that require additional investigation. Validation and peer review require time for independent experts to review findings.

Investigators should plan for iterative analysis cycles that progressively refine understanding and focus investigation efforts while maintaining flexibility to address unexpected findings or complications.

1.10.3 Stakeholder Engagement and Communication

Effective AI forensic investigations require ongoing engagement with diverse stakeholders who bring different perspectives, expertise, and requirements to the investigation process. **Technical stakeholders** include development teams who created AI systems and can provide insider knowledge about design decisions and implementation details, data science teams who understand model training and validation procedures, infrastructure teams who manage deployment and operations, and security teams who understand system vulnerabilities and protective measures.

Engaging technical stakeholders requires balancing their detailed system knowledge against potential conflicts of interest if the investigation concerns system problems or failures. Investigators should structure stakeholder engagement to gather essential information while maintaining investigation independence and objectivity.

Business stakeholders include product managers who understand business requirements and success metrics, compliance officers who understand regulatory requirements and organizational policies, risk management teams who assess potential organizational impacts, and legal counsel who advise on litigation and regulatory matters.

Business stakeholder engagement ensures that investigation priorities align with organizational needs and that findings are presented in formats suitable for business decision-making.

External stakeholders may include regulatory authorities who have jurisdiction over AI system deployment, affected communities who may have been harmed by system failures, customer organizations who depend on AI system outputs, and advocacy groups who represent interests of affected populations.

External stakeholder engagement requires careful consideration of confidentiality and disclosure requirements while ensuring that investigation scope and priorities adequately address legitimate concerns and interests.

Communication planning establishes regular communication channels and formats that keep stakeholders informed of investigation progress while managing expectations about timelines and potential findings. Progress reports should provide clear updates on what has been learned without premature conclusions about final findings. Technical briefings can provide detailed information to stakeholders with appropriate expertise. Executive summaries can communicate key findings and implications to senior leadership.

Effective communication planning anticipates potential controversial findings and prepares stakeholders for difficult conversations about system problems or organizational responsibilities.

1.10.4 Risk Assessment and Mitigation Planning

AI forensic investigations often involve significant risks that require careful assessment and mitigation planning. **Evidence preservation risks** arise from the dynamic nature of AI systems that may continue operating and generating data during investigation periods. Investigators must balance the need to preserve evidence integrity against operational requirements to maintain system functionality. Risk mitigation may involve creating forensic copies of critical evidence before beginning analysis, implementing monitoring to detect evidence modification during investigation, establishing procedures for handling evidence that continues to be generated, and coordinating with system operators to minimize evidence contamination.

Confidentiality and privacy risks emerge from the sensitive nature of AI training data and the potential for investigations to reveal proprietary information or personal data. Training datasets may contain copyrighted content, trade secrets, or personal information that requires special handling procedures. Investigation findings may reveal competitive advantages or organizational vulnerabilities that require confidential treatment.

Risk mitigation requires implementing appropriate security controls for investigation evidence and findings, establishing clear confidentiality agreements with all investigation participants, developing procedures for handling proprietary or personal information, and planning for potential disclosure requirements in legal or regulatory proceedings.

Technical complexity risks stem from the possibility that investigation analysis may be incomplete or incorrect due to the complexity of modern AI systems. Complex systems may exhibit behaviors that are difficult to understand or reproduce. Novel AI architectures may require analytical approaches that have not been fully validated. Investigation findings may be misinterpreted by stakeholders who lack technical expertise.

Risk mitigation involves implementing comprehensive peer review and validation procedures, engaging qualified experts for complex technical analysis, maintaining clear documentation of analytical assumptions and limitations, and providing appropriate caveats and uncertainty estimates with investigation findings.

Organizational impact risks consider potential negative consequences of investigation findings for organizations, employees, or stakeholders. Investigation findings may reveal system problems that require expensive remediation, organizational practices that violate legal or regulatory requirements, or individual actions that warrant disciplinary measures.

Risk mitigation requires early communication with organizational leadership about potential findings and implications, development of remediation plans that address identified problems constructively, coordination with legal counsel to ensure appropriate handling of potentially damaging findings, and establishment of fair procedures for addressing individual accountability questions.

1.10.5 Technology and Tool Requirements

Effective AI forensic investigations require specialized technological capabilities that extend beyond traditional digital forensic tools. The complexity and scale of modern AI systems demand computational resources, programming expertise, and analytical frameworks specifically designed to handle the unique characteristics of machine learning artifacts. Understanding these technical requirements is essential for proper investigation planning and ensures that forensic teams have the capabilities necessary to conduct thorough, defensible analysis.

The technology stack for AI forensics centers on flexible, programmable analysis environments that can adapt to the diverse architectures and data formats encountered in AI systems. Unlike traditional forensics where standardized tools can handle most evidence types, AI forensics requires investigators to develop custom analytical approaches for each unique system configuration while maintaining the rigor and documentation standards essential for forensic work.

1.10.5.1 Programming Languages and Analysis Environments

Python serves as the primary programming language for AI forensic analysis due to its extensive ecosystem of machine learning and data analysis libraries. The language provides investigators with direct access to the same tools used for AI development, enabling analysis of model architectures, training procedures, and system behaviors using familiar frameworks. Python's interpreted nature and interactive capabilities make it particularly suitable for exploratory analysis and iterative investigation approaches that characterize AI forensic work.

R provides complementary statistical analysis capabilities that prove essential for bias detection, performance evaluation, and significance testing. The language excels at statistical modeling and hypothesis testing procedures that are central to demonstrating discriminatory patterns or performance anomalies in AI systems. R's extensive statistical libraries and visualization capabilities make it particularly valuable for generating the rigorous statistical evidence required for legal and regulatory proceedings.

SQL and database technologies become necessary when investigating training data sources, data lineage, and the complex data pipelines that feed AI systems. Many AI forensic investigations require analysis of the databases and data warehouses that store training data, user interactions, and system logs. Understanding database technologies and query optimization becomes essential when working with the massive datasets typical of AI systems.

Jupyter notebooks and interactive environments provide the foundation for conducting reproducible forensic analysis while maintaining comprehensive documentation of investigative procedures. These environments enable investigators to combine code, visualizations, and explanatory text in formats that support both analysis and communication of findings to diverse stakeholders. The notebook format proves particularly valuable for creating audit trails that demonstrate analytical rigor and enable independent validation of findings.

1.10.5.2 Core Python Libraries for AI Forensics

Data analysis and manipulation requires robust tools for handling the massive datasets and complex data structures common in AI systems. Pandas provides the foundation for data manipulation, cleaning, and analysis, with capabilities for handling diverse data formats and performing complex transformations. NumPy supports numerical computing and array operations essential for analyzing model parameters and training data. SciPy extends these capabilities with advanced statistical functions and optimization algorithms needed for sophisticated analytical procedures.

Machine learning and model analysis demands tools that can examine trained models, reproduce training procedures, and validate system behaviors. Scikit-learn provides accessible implementations of traditional machine learning algorithms and evaluation metrics that enable investigators to benchmark AI system performance and detect anomalies. TensorFlow and PyTorch support analysis of deep learning systems, providing access to model architectures, parameter inspection, and gradient analysis capabilities essential for understanding complex neural networks.

Statistical analysis and hypothesis testing requires specialized libraries for the rigorous statistical analysis essential to AI forensic work. Statsmodels provides comprehensive statistical modeling capabilities including regression analysis, time series analysis, and hypothesis testing procedures. SciPy.stats offers additional statistical functions and probability distributions needed for significance testing and confidence interval estimation. These tools enable investigators to provide the statistical rigor required for legal and regulatory contexts.

Data visualization and communication capabilities enable investigators to create compelling presentations of complex technical findings for diverse audiences. Matplotlib provides foundational plotting capabilities with fine-grained control over visualization appearance. Seaborn offers statistical visualization tools particularly suited for exploring relationships in complex datasets. Plotly enables interactive visualizations that can help stakeholders understand technical findings and explore data relationships dynamically.

1.10.5.3 Specialized AI Forensic Analysis Tools

Model architecture analysis requires tools capable of examining the structure and parameters of trained AI models across different frameworks and architectures. Netron provides visualization capabilities for neural network architectures, enabling investigators to understand model complexity and identify potential manipulation. TensorBoard offers detailed analysis of training procedures and model performance over time. Custom tools may be required for analyzing proprietary model formats or unusual architectures encountered in investigations.

Training data analysis demands capabilities for processing and analyzing the massive, diverse datasets used to train AI systems. Dask enables parallel processing of datasets that exceed memory limitations, while Apache Spark provides distributed computing capabilities for analyzing datasets at enterprise scale. Great Expectations offers data validation and profiling capabilities that can detect anomalies or contamination in training datasets.

Bias detection and fairness analysis requires specialized tools designed specifically for identifying discriminatory patterns in AI system outputs. Fairlearn provides bias detection and mitigation tools specifically designed for machine learning systems. AI Fairness 360 offers comprehensive bias detection across multiple fairness metrics and demographic groups. What-If Tool enables interactive exploration of model behavior across different demographic groups and input conditions.

Security and adversarial analysis tools help investigators detect manipulation attempts and assess system robustness. Foolbox provides implementations of adversarial attack techniques that can be used to test system robustness. CleverHans offers additional adversarial analysis capabilities and defense mechanisms. Art (Adversarial Robustness Toolbox) provides comprehensive tools for testing AI system security and detecting potential vulnerabilities.

1.10.5.4 Infrastructure and Environment Considerations

Computational resources for AI forensic analysis often require substantial processing power, particularly when analyzing large models or extensive training datasets. GPU Computing becomes essential for analyzing deep learning models, with investigation teams requiring access to modern graphics processing units capable of handling model inference and analysis tasks. Memory Requirements can be substantial when loading large models or processing extensive datasets, often requiring systems with 32GB or more of RAM for effective analysis.

Storage infrastructure considers the massive scale of AI evidence while maintaining forensic integrity. Training datasets may require terabytes of storage, while model artifacts and analysis results can quickly accumulate to substantial sizes. Network-Attached Storage or cloud storage solutions may be necessary but must be configured to maintain evidence integrity and chain of custody requirements.

Forensic environment isolation ensures that analysis activities do not contaminate evidence or compromise investigation integrity. Containerization using Docker or similar technologies can provide isolated analysis environments that can be precisely documented and reproduced. Virtual machines offer another approach for creating isolated analysis environments while maintaining clear separation between evidence and analysis tools.

Cloud vs. on-premise considerations involve complex trade-offs between computational capabilities, security requirements, and cost considerations. Cloud platforms offer scalable computational resources and managed services that can accelerate analysis, but may introduce data sovereignty and security concerns that conflict with forensic requirements. On-premise infrastructure provides greater control over security and evidence handling but may lack the computational scale necessary for analyzing large AI systems.

Version control and reproducibility requires systematic approaches for managing analysis code, documentation, and intermediate results throughout the investigation process. Git provides version control for analysis scripts and documentation, while MLflow or similar tools can track analysis experiments and results. Docker containers can package complete analysis environments to ensure reproducibility of forensic procedures.

1.10.5.5 Tool Selection and Evaluation Criteria

Forensic suitability should guide tool selection decisions, with preference for open-source tools that enable independent validation of analytical procedures. Tools should provide comprehensive logging and audit capabilities that support forensic documentation requirements. Reproducibility becomes essential, requiring tools that can produce consistent results across different computing environments and enable independent verification of findings.

Scalability considerations account for the potential size and complexity of AI systems under investigation. Tools should be capable of handling enterprise-scale datasets and model architectures while maintaining reasonable performance. Extensibility enables investigators to adapt tools for novel AI architectures or unusual investigation requirements that may not be supported by standard tools.

Legal and compliance requirements may impose constraints on tool selection, particularly regarding data handling, encryption, and audit trail capabilities. Tools used in forensic contexts should support the documentation and chain of custody requirements necessary for legal admissibility. Licensing considerations become important when analysis tools may be subject to legal scrutiny or when findings may be used in litigation contexts.

Community and support factors influence the long-term viability of forensic tools and the availability of expertise for complex investigations. Tools with active development communities and extensive documentation reduce the risk of encountering unsupported analysis scenarios. Training and expertise requirements should be considered when selecting tools, as the specialized nature of AI forensics may limit the availability of qualified personnel.

This technology foundation enables the systematic, rigorous analysis approaches detailed in subsequent chapters while ensuring that forensic investigations can adapt to the rapidly evolving landscape of AI technologies and deployment architectures.

1.11 DOCUMENTATION AND EVIDENCE STANDARDS

1.11.1 Comprehensive Documentation Framework

AI forensic investigations generate complex evidence that requires systematic documentation to ensure admissibility, enable peer review, and support effective decision-making. **Technical documentation standards** capture both the methodologies used and the rationale for analytical choices while remaining accessible to diverse audiences including legal professionals, business leaders, and technical experts who were not involved in the investigation.

Methodology documentation provides detailed descriptions of all analytical approaches, statistical techniques, software tools, and procedural decisions used during investigation. This documentation should be sufficiently detailed to enable independent replication while explaining why particular approaches were chosen over alternatives. For AI forensics, methodology documentation also addresses the selection of statistical techniques appropriate for AI system analysis, software tools and configurations used for model analysis, data processing procedures and quality assurance measures, validation approaches used to confirm findings, and peer review processes used to ensure analytical reliability.

Evidence documentation creates comprehensive records of all evidence collected and analyzed during investigation, including detailed inventories of model files, datasets, logs, and other artifacts, chain of custody records that track evidence handling from collection through analysis, integrity verification procedures that confirm evidence authenticity, analysis results and intermediate findings, and quality assurance records that document validation procedures.

Decision documentation records the reasoning behind key investigation decisions including scope definition rationale and boundary-setting criteria, stakeholder engagement strategies and communication plans, resource allocation decisions and timeline development, analytical priorities and sequencing decisions, and limitation acknowledgments and risk assessments.

This decision documentation helps readers understand not only what was found but why particular analytical approaches were taken and how investigation limitations might affect the reliability of findings.

1.11.2 Legal Admissibility and Chain of Custody

AI evidence presents unique challenges for maintaining legal admissibility standards because of the dynamic nature of AI systems and the complexity of ensuring evidence completeness and integrity. **Chain of custody procedures** have to be adapted to handle AI-specific evidence types while maintaining the fundamental principles of evidence authentication, integrity preservation, and accountability tracking.

Model evidence management requires procedures for identifying and collecting model files that may be distributed across multiple storage systems, preserving model metadata including version information and training timestamps, documenting model architecture and configuration details, maintaining integrity verification for potentially large model files, and tracking access to and modifications of model evidence throughout investigation.

Training data chain of custody presents particular challenges because training datasets may be extremely large, continuously updated, or distributed across multiple systems. Effective procedures address identification of relevant training data subsets for analysis, preservation of data in original format while creating working copies for analysis, documentation of data lineage and transformation procedures, verification of data integrity and completeness, and tracking of data access and processing throughout investigation.

Log and monitoring data management handles evidence that may be continuously generated during investigation periods. Procedures should establish cutoff times for log collection to ensure evidence completeness, implement monitoring to detect log modification or deletion during investigation, create forensic copies of critical logs before beginning analysis, document log format and content interpretation procedures, and maintain chain of custody for potentially massive log datasets.

Digital signature and verification procedures ensure that evidence authenticity can be verified throughout investigation and legal proceedings. These procedures may involve cryptographic signing of evidence collections at time of acquisition, regular integrity verification throughout investigation process, documentation of all personnel who access evidence, and procedures for detecting and documenting any evidence modifications.

1.11.3 Multi-Audience Documentation Strategy

AI forensic investigations communicate findings to diverse audiences with different expertise levels, information needs, and decision-making responsibilities. **Technical documentation** provides comprehensive detail for expert audiences including complete methodology descriptions with tool specifications and configuration parameters, detailed statistical analyses with confidence intervals and significance testing, comprehensive evidence listings with integrity verification results, validation procedures with peer review documentation, and limitation acknowledgments with uncertainty quantification.

Technical documentation serves as the authoritative record of investigation procedures and findings while providing the detailed information necessary for expert review and independent validation.

Executive documentation translates technical findings into business-focused presentations that enable organizational decision-making. Executive documentation should lead with clear statements of key findings and their business implications, provide concise technical summaries that explain reliability without overwhelming detail, emphasize actionable recommendations with clear implementation guidance, include resource requirements and timeline estimates for recommended actions, and conclude with success metrics that enable progress monitoring.

Legal documentation addresses specific requirements for litigation and regulatory proceedings while explaining technical concepts in ways that legal professionals can understand and present effectively. Legal documentation establishes expert qualifications and methodology reliability, provide clear explanations of technical findings and their implications, address potential challenges to analytical approaches or conclusions, maintain appropriate limitations and uncertainty acknowledgments, and organize findings to support specific legal arguments or compliance requirements.

Regulatory documentation meets specific requirements of relevant regulatory agencies while demonstrating organizational commitment to compliance and improvement. Regulatory documentation should map findings to specific regulatory requirements and standards, provide evidence of good faith investigation and remediation efforts, include comprehensive remediation plans with accountability assignments, establish ongoing monitoring and reporting procedures, and document compliance with applicable investigation and reporting requirements.

1.11.4 Quality Assurance and Validation Documentation

The complexity and potential impact of AI forensic investigations demand exceptional attention to quality assurance and validation throughout the investigation process. **Peer review documentation** provides records of independent expert review including identification of qualified reviewers and their relevant expertise, detailed review procedures and validation criteria, reviewer findings and recommendations for improvement, resolution of reviewer concerns and recommended modifications, and final reviewer approval or qualification of investigation findings.

Peer review documentation demonstrates that appropriate scientific safeguards were followed while providing evidence that findings have been subjected to independent expert scrutiny.

Validation procedure documentation records all steps taken to confirm investigation reliability including replication testing using independent tools and datasets, sensitivity analysis to assess how findings depend on analytical assumptions, alternative hypothesis testing to ensure conclusions are robust against competing explanations, cross-validation using different analytical approaches where feasible, and uncertainty quantification to provide appropriate confidence estimates.

Quality control documentation establishes systematic procedures for ensuring investigation accuracy and completeness including verification checklists for evidence collection and analysis procedures, supervisory review requirements and approval processes, error detection and correction procedures, version control for investigation documents and findings, and audit trails for all investigation activities and decisions.

Limitation and uncertainty documentation provides honest and complete acknowledgment of investigation constraints including scope limitations and their potential impact on findings, data availability constraints and their effect on analysis completeness, methodological limitations and their implications for finding reliability, time and resource constraints that may have affected investigation thoroughness, and uncertainty estimates that help readers understand finding reliability.

Comprehensive limitation documentation strengthens rather than weakens investigation credibility by demonstrating scientific integrity and helping readers appropriately interpret and apply investigation findings.

1.12 TRADITIONAL DIGITAL FORENSICS VS. AI FORENSICS

1.12.1 Fundamental Similarities and Shared Principles

AI forensics builds upon the established foundation of traditional digital forensics while extending core principles to address the unique characteristics of AI systems. **Evidence integrity** remains fundamental to both disciplines, requiring systematic procedures for evidence identification, collection, preservation, and analysis that maintain authenticity and enable independent verification. Both traditional and AI forensics establish clear chain of custody procedures, implement appropriate security controls, document all evidence handling procedures, and provide mechanisms for detecting evidence tampering or modification.

Scientific methodology provides the analytical foundation for both disciplines, emphasizing systematic investigation procedures, empirical analysis based on observable evidence, peer review and validation of findings, and clear documentation that enables independent replication. Both disciplines require rigorous statistical analysis where appropriate, careful consideration of alternative explanations, honest acknowledgment of limitations and uncertainties, and presentation of findings that separate observations from interpretations.

1.12.2 Critical Differences and Unique Challenges

Despite shared foundations, AI forensics presents fundamentally different challenges that require specialized approaches and expertise. **System complexity and scale** represents the most obvious difference, with AI systems often involving millions or billions of parameters, massive training datasets, and complex distributed architectures that dwarf traditional software systems in scope and sophistication.

Traditional digital forensics typically deals with systems where behavior can be understood through code review and execution tracing. AI systems, by contrast, operate through learned statistical patterns that may not be directly interpretable and whose behaviors emerge from complex interactions between training data, model architecture, and deployment environment.

Dynamic and adaptive behavior distinguishes AI systems from traditional software that follows predetermined execution paths. AI systems may continue learning or adapting during deployment, exhibit different behaviors based on accumulated experience, respond to inputs in ways that depend on prior interactions, and demonstrate emergent capabilities that were not explicitly programmed.

This dynamic nature complicates forensic analysis because system behavior at the time of investigation may differ from behavior during the incident being investigated. Traditional forensic techniques for reconstructing system state at particular times become much more complex when applied to systems that continuously evolve.

Interpretability and explainability challenges represent perhaps the most fundamental difference between traditional and AI forensics. Traditional software can typically be understood through code analysis that reveals explicit logic and decision processes. Modern AI systems, particularly deep learning models, operate through distributed representations that may not admit straightforward interpretation.

TABLE 1.3

Aspect	Traditional Digital Forensics	AI Forensics
Evidence Type	Files, logs, network traffic, database records, memory dumps	Models, training data, inference outputs, gradient computations, hyperparameters
Analysis Approach	Code review, execution tracing, file system analysis	Statistical analysis, behavioral testing, pattern recognition
System Behavior	Deterministic, rule-based, predictable execution paths	Statistical, emergent, adaptive, context-dependent
Typical Scale	Gigabytes to terabytes (10^3 to 10^{12} bytes)	Terabytes to petabytes (10^{12} to 10^{15} bytes)
Interpretability	High—Direct code analysis reveals logic and decisions	Low to none—Black box models, distributed representations
Evidence Preservation	Static snapshots, point-in-time captures	Dynamic, continuously evolving, distributed across systems
Expert Skills Required	Digital forensics, cybersecurity, software engineering	ML/AI, statistics, domain expertise, cybersecurity, data science
Typical Timeline	Days to weeks (rapid analysis possible)	Weeks to months (complex iterative analysis)
Reproducibility	High—Deterministic results from same evidence	Medium to low—Stochastic elements, version dependencies
Legal Precedent	Well-established standards and court acceptance	Emerging field with evolving standards and precedents

When a traditional software system makes an incorrect decision, investigators can often trace the execution path to identify the specific code responsible for the error. When an AI system makes a problematic decision, the causal factors may be distributed across millions of parameters in ways that cannot be easily traced or understood.

Evidence volume and computational requirements create practical challenges that exceed those typically encountered in traditional digital forensics. Training datasets may contain billions of examples requiring specialized tools and substantial computational resources for analysis. Model parameters may number in the trillions, requiring high-performance computing infrastructure for comprehensive analysis. Inference logs may capture billions of decisions requiring sophisticated analytical approaches to identify patterns or problems.

The evolution from traditional digital forensics to AI forensics represents a fundamental shift in investigative methodology driven by the unique characteristics of artificial intelligence systems. While both disciplines share core principles of evidence integrity and systematic analysis, AI forensics operates in an environment of unprecedented complexity that requires specialized approaches across multiple dimensions.

The following comparison matrix illustrates these critical differences and demonstrates why AI systems demand forensic methodologies that extend far beyond conventional digital investigation techniques. Understanding these distinctions is essential for properly scoping AI forensic investigations and ensuring that analytical approaches match the unique challenges presented by modern AI systems.

1.12.3 Methodological Adaptations and Extensions

AI forensics requires significant methodological adaptations that extend traditional forensic approaches while maintaining core principles of scientific rigor and legal admissibility. **Statistical analysis integration** becomes central to AI forensics in ways that are typically optional for traditional digital forensics. Understanding AI system behavior requires sophisticated statistical techniques for bias detection, performance evaluation, uncertainty quantification, and pattern recognition that go beyond the basic statistical analysis sometimes used in traditional forensics.

AI forensic investigators should be proficient in machine learning evaluation metrics, statistical hypothesis testing, confidence interval estimation, effect size calculation, and causal inference techniques that are not typically required for traditional digital forensics.

Behavioral testing and analysis represents a new category of forensic technique specific to AI systems. While traditional forensics focuses on analyzing static evidence, AI forensics often involves active testing to understand system behavior under different conditions. This testing may involve systematically varying inputs to understand system responses, evaluating performance across different demographic groups, assessing robustness against adversarial attacks, testing system behavior under edge cases or unusual conditions, and comparing system behavior to documented specifications or expectations.

Multi-modal evidence integration becomes necessary because AI systems often involve multiple types of evidence that must be analyzed together to understand system behavior. Traditional forensics typically focuses on single evidence types like file systems, network logs, or database records. AI forensics often integrates analysis of training data, model parameters, system outputs, infrastructure logs, organizational documentation, and stakeholder communications to develop comprehensive understanding of system behavior and organizational context.

Adversarial analysis requires AI forensic investigators to understand and detect sophisticated attacks that have no equivalent in traditional digital forensics. Data poisoning attacks, adversarial examples, model extraction attacks, and prompt injection represent entirely new categories of investigation that require specialized knowledge and analytical techniques.

1.13 FUTURE DIRECTIONS AND EMERGING CHALLENGES

1.13.1 Technological Evolution and Investigation Implications

The rapid pace of AI technological development creates ongoing challenges for forensic methodologies that must evolve to keep pace with new system architectures, training techniques, and deployment approaches. **Foundation model evolution** represents one of the most significant trends affecting AI forensics, with increasingly large and capable models that demonstrate emergent capabilities, require massive computational resources for analysis, operate through complex training procedures that may be difficult to reconstruct or validate, and exhibit behaviors that emerge from scale rather than explicit programming.

Future foundation models may operate at scales that exceed current analytical capabilities, requiring new tools and methodologies for forensic investigation. The emergence of multimodal models that integrate text, images, audio, and video creates additional complexity for understanding system behavior and potential failure modes.

Automated AI development through automated machine learning (AutoML) and neural architecture search creates systems whose design and training procedures may not be fully documented or understood by human developers. Forensic investigation of automatically designed systems may require new approaches for understanding system architecture, reconstructing training procedures, and assessing whether automated design processes introduced problems or vulnerabilities.

Federated learning and distributed training create AI systems that are trained across multiple organizations or devices without centralizing training data. These architectures present new challenges for forensic investigation including distributed evidence collection across multiple organizations, analysis of systems whose training data cannot be directly examined, assessment of security and privacy properties in federated settings, and understanding how distributed training affects system behavior and potential biases.

Continuous learning and adaptation enable AI systems to update their behavior based on ongoing experience rather than static training procedures. These systems require new forensic approaches for understanding how system behavior evolves over time, reconstructing system state at particular historical points, assessing whether adaptation introduces new problems or vulnerabilities, and maintaining appropriate oversight and control over continuously evolving systems.

1.13.2 Regulatory and Legal Development

The legal and regulatory landscape surrounding AI continues to evolve rapidly, creating new requirements and opportunities for AI forensic investigation. **Comprehensive AI legislation** in major jurisdictions will likely create standardized requirements for AI system documentation, testing, monitoring, and incident reporting that will shape forensic investigation practices. These regulations may establish mandatory forensic capabilities for organizations deploying high-risk AI systems, standardized reporting requirements for AI-related incidents, liability frameworks that require forensic analysis to establish responsibility, and professional standards for AI forensic practitioners.

Algorithmic accountability laws may require organizations to provide explanations for AI system decisions, demonstrate compliance with anti-discrimination requirements, implement ongoing monitoring for bias and harmful outputs, and provide mechanisms for individuals to challenge algorithmic decisions. These requirements will create new categories of forensic investigation focused on transparency, fairness, and accountability.

International harmonization efforts seek to create compatible regulatory frameworks across jurisdictions while respecting different legal traditions and policy priorities. Harmonization may facilitate cross-border forensic investigations while creating standardized approaches for evidence sharing, expert qualification, and investigation procedures.

Litigation evolution will likely see increasing numbers of legal cases involving AI systems, creating precedents for expert testimony, evidence admissibility, liability determination, and damage assessment. These cases will help establish professional standards for AI forensic practice while identifying areas where additional research and development are needed.

1.14 HOW THIS BOOK IS STRUCTURED

1.14.1 Foundation

This chapter has established the conceptual and methodological foundation essential for effective AI forensic investigation. We have explored how AI forensics emerges as a critical specialized discipline that builds upon traditional digital forensics while addressing the unique challenges of modern AI systems. The systematic classification of AI system types provides the framework for understanding when and how different investigative approaches should be applied, while the comprehensive analysis of AI-specific risks and vulnerabilities identifies the key failure modes and attack vectors that make AI systems subjects of forensic investigation.

The six-phase investigation methodology provides a systematic approach for managing the complexity and scale of AI forensic investigations while maintaining the scientific rigor and legal admissibility essential for effective forensic work. The planning and scoping guidance provides practical approaches for defining investigation boundaries and allocating resources effectively.

The documentation and evidence standards create the foundation for defensible findings that can withstand scrutiny across technical, legal, and business contexts. The comparison between traditional and AI forensics highlights both the continuity and the significant adaptations required for effective AI investigation, while the future directions discussion identifies emerging challenges and opportunities that will shape the continued evolution of this field.

1.14.2 Integration with Technical Analysis Chapters

The foundation established in this chapter directly supports the detailed technical methodologies presented in subsequent chapters.

Chapter 2: AI System Components builds upon the system classification framework introduced here to provide detailed technical understanding of different AI architectures and their forensic characteristics. The component analysis techniques presented in Chapter 2 will enable investigators to systematically understand AI system architecture and identify the specific analytical approaches appropriate for different system types.

Chapter 3: Knowledge Gathering and Scoping operationalizes the planning and scoping principles established in this chapter by providing detailed procedures for stakeholder engagement, documentation discovery, and investigation scope refinement. The systematic approach to human intelligence gathering presented in Chapter 3 complements the technical analysis capabilities by ensuring that investigators understand the organizational and operational context essential for interpreting technical findings.

Chapter 4: Evidence Collection translates the evidence preservation principles established here into specific procedures for collecting and preserving AI-specific artifacts while maintaining forensic integrity. The comprehensive evidence collection framework ensures that subsequent analysis has access to all relevant information while meeting legal admissibility requirements.

Chapter 5: Training Data Analysis addresses one of the most critical aspects of AI forensic investigation by providing detailed methodologies for analyzing the datasets that fundamentally shape AI system behavior. The training data analysis techniques enable investigators to identify bias, contamination, intellectual property violations, and other problems that may not be apparent from examining trained models alone.

Chapter 6: Model Investigation provides specialized techniques for analyzing AI model architecture, parameters, and behavior to understand how systems operate and identify potential problems or manipulation. The model analysis methodologies complement training data analysis by examining how training procedures and data characteristics are encoded in model parameters and behavior.

1.14.3 Integration with Output and Documentation Analysis

Chapter 7: Output Analysis focuses on examining the actual decisions and predictions generated by AI systems during real-world operation, providing direct evidence of system impact on individuals and communities. The output analysis techniques enable investigators to detect discrimination, assess system performance, and evaluate compliance with organizational and legal requirements.

The integration between output analysis and the foundational concepts established in this chapter becomes particularly important for understanding how training data characteristics, model architecture decisions, and organizational processes manifest in real-world system behavior. Output analysis provides the empirical evidence needed to validate hypotheses developed through training data and model analysis.

Chapter 8: Documentation Analysis addresses the critical organizational and human factors that shape AI system development, deployment, and operation. The documentation analysis techniques complement technical analysis by revealing the decision-making processes, governance frameworks, and accountability structures that determine how AI systems are created and managed.

The synthesis of technical findings with organizational documentation provides the comprehensive understanding needed to assess not only what happened when AI systems failed but why those failures occurred and what organizational factors contributed to problems.

Chapter 9: Reporting and Presentation translates the comprehensive analysis enabled by all previous chapters into effective communication formats for diverse stakeholders. The reporting methodologies ensure that complex technical findings are presented in ways that enable effective decision-making by business leaders, legal counsel, regulatory authorities, and affected communities.

1.14.4 Comprehensive Investigation Framework

Together, these chapters provide a complete framework for conducting thorough, defensible investigations of AI systems that can address the full range of technical, organizational, and legal questions that arise when AI systems fail, cause harm, or become subjects of dispute. The systematic progression from foundational concepts through technical analysis to documentation and reporting ensures that investigators can handle the complexity of modern AI systems while maintaining the rigor and defensibility essential for forensic work.

As artificial intelligence continues to transform critical aspects of our economy and society, the ability to effectively investigate these systems when problems arise becomes increasingly important for maintaining public trust, ensuring legal compliance, and enabling continued innovation. The methodologies presented in this book provide the foundation for developing these critical capabilities while adapting to the rapidly evolving landscape of AI technology and regulation.

The investment you make in understanding these foundational concepts will enable effective application of the specialized techniques presented in subsequent chapters while providing the conceptual framework needed to adapt these approaches to new AI technologies and investigation scenarios as they emerge. With this foundation established, we can proceed to the detailed technical analysis that forms the core of effective AI forensic investigation.

2 Overview of AI Systems for Forensic Investigators

2.1 THE INVESTIGATION QUESTION THAT CHANGES EVERYTHING

When a major bank's loan approval AI started systematically rejecting qualified minority applicants, investigators faced a critical first question: What type of AI system are we dealing with? The answer completely determined their investigation strategy.

If it was a traditional machine learning system, they could examine explicit features and decision trees to trace bias directly. If it was a deep neural network, they would need sophisticated probing techniques to uncover hidden bias patterns. If it was a rule-based expert system, they would audit decision logic and knowledge bases. If it was a hybrid ensemble, they would need to investigate multiple interacting components.

The investigators discovered it was a deep learning system trained on decades of historical lending data. This single insight shaped their entire approach: they focused on training data bias analysis rather than rule auditing, used neural network probing techniques rather than decision tree analysis, and prepared for opacity challenges rather than transparent rule examination.

That identification decision—determining what type of AI system you are investigating—may be the most important choice you make in any AI forensic investigation.

2.2 WHAT YOU WILL LEARN

By the end of this chapter, you will be able to:

- **Rapidly classify any AI system** using a forensic-focused decision framework
- **Understand system components and architecture** including data flows, computational infrastructure, and storage patterns
- **Identify key evidence sources** specific to different AI system types and their operational components
- **Navigate modern LLM and RAG systems** including their unique forensic challenges and evidence artifacts
- **Map system infrastructure** from data ingestion through model inference to understand where evidence resides
- **Choose the right investigation strategy** based on system architecture, components, and operational characteristics
- **Collect relevant technical evidence** from servers, databases, APIs, and distributed computing environments
- **Analyze hybrid architectures** and understand how multiple AI components interact and affect forensic investigation
- **Understand filtering layers** and other processing components that affect AI system outputs

DOI: 10.1201/9781003634782-2

2.3 QUICK START GUIDE

2.3.1 Need to Identify Your AI System Type Immediately?

- **Unknown system type?** → Start with Classification Framework for Investigators (Section 2.4)
- **Traditional ML (trees, regression)?** → Jump to Traditional Machine Learning Systems (Section 2.5.1)
- **Neural networks or "deep learning"?** → See Deep Learning Systems (Section 2.5.2)
- **Large language model or chatbot?** → Focus on Large Language Model Systems (Section 2.5.3)
- **RAG system or knowledge retrieval?** → See Retrieval-Augmented Generation Architecture (Section 2.5.4)
- **Rule-based or expert system?** → Begin with Expert Systems and Rule-Based AI (Section 2.5.5)
- **Multiple AI components?** → Start with Hybrid and Ensemble Systems (Section 2.5.6)
- **Need component breakdown?** → See System Architecture and Technical Infrastructure (Section 2.6)
- **Infrastructure questions?** → Jump to Operational Infrastructure and Evidence Collection (Section 2.7)

2.4 CLASSIFICATION FRAMEWORK FOR INVESTIGATORS

Understanding what type of AI system you are investigating is not just academic curiosity—it fundamentally determines which investigation techniques will work, what evidence you can collect, and where bias or manipulation might hide. The differences between AI system types are so fundamental that using the wrong investigation approach can render an entire forensic investigation useless.

TABLE 2.1
Investigation Planning Quick Reference

System Type	Key Components	Primary Evidence	Infrastructure Focus
Traditional ML	Features, models, pipelines	Training data, model files	Application servers, databases
Deep Learning	Layers, parameters, checkpoints	Training logs, model weights	GPU clusters, distributed storage
LLMs	Tokenizers, embeddings, attention	Prompt logs, fine-tuning data	Inference servers, model caches
RAG Systems	Retrievers, knowledge bases, embeddings	Vector stores, retrieval logs	Search infrastructure, embedding servers
Expert Systems	Rules, facts, inference engines	Knowledge bases, rule logs	Application servers, rule databases
Multimodal AI	Vision, language, audio components	Cross-modal training data	Specialized hardware, integration servers
Reinforcement Learning	Agents, environments, policies	Reward logs, action histories	Simulation environments, policy servers
Federated Learning	Distributed models, aggregation	Local training logs, communication records	Edge devices, coordination servers

Consider the difference between investigating a traditional machine learning system versus a large language model. In a traditional ML system, you can directly examine decision trees, trace feature weights, and understand exactly why each decision was made. The evidence is explicit, interpretable, and often stored in human-readable formats. In contrast, investigating an LLM requires understanding distributed representations across billions of parameters, analyzing statistical patterns in prompt-response pairs, and using sophisticated probing techniques to uncover bias hidden in learned associations.

2.4.1 System Behavior Categories

Before diving into specific AI types, investigators should understand fundamental behavioral categories that affect investigation approach. These categories represent different ways AI systems adapt and change over time, creating different evidence patterns and preservation requirements.

Static systems maintain consistent behavior throughout their operational lifetime, providing stable and predictable investigation targets. These systems do not modify their behavior based on new data or changing conditions, making them the most straightforward for forensic analysis. Static systems include most traditional machine learning models deployed without continuous learning capabilities.

Static systems generate consistent evidence patterns that remain stable throughout investigation. Their behavior can be completely characterized through point-in-time analysis, making them ideal for controlled testing and verification. The evidence from static systems is highly reproducible, as the same inputs will always produce the same outputs.

Evidence Strategy: Point-in-time model snapshots, training data analysis, static configuration examination, deployment artifact collection, performance benchmark validation

Investigation Focus: Training bias analysis, model parameter examination, deployment configuration verification, input-output relationship mapping, decision boundary analysis

Adaptive systems continuously modify their behavior based on new data or changing conditions, creating complex evidence challenges as their behavior may have changed since an incident occurred. These systems learn from ongoing interactions, environmental changes, or updated training data. Adaptive systems include online learning models, recommendation systems that update user profiles, and fraud detection systems that adapt to new attack patterns.

These systems present complex forensic challenges because their behavior may have changed since an incident occurred, requiring sophisticated temporal analysis to reconstruct historical behavior. Adaptive systems generate continuous evidence throughout their operational lifetime. They create logs of learning episodes, adaptation triggers, and behavioral changes that must be preserved and analyzed to understand system evolution.

Evidence Strategy: Continuous monitoring throughout system lifetime, adaptation tracking with detailed logging, temporal behavior analysis, version control throughout deployment, trigger event preservation

Temporal Scope: Requires evidence collection throughout the entire system operational period, with particular focus on adaptation events and behavioral changes

Investigation Challenges: System behavior may have changed since incident, requires temporal reconstruction of historical behavior, more complex evidence preservation requirements, ongoing monitoring needs

Dynamic systems modify their behavior based on context, user characteristics, or environmental conditions without necessarily learning from new data. These systems use rule-based adaptation, contextual switching, or user personalization to vary their behavior. Dynamic systems create forensic complexity because their behavior depends on context that may not be fully captured in logs.

Dynamic systems generate evidence about contextual triggers and behavioral variations that require careful analysis to understand bias patterns. The same input may produce different outputs depending on user characteristics, time of day, system load, or other contextual factors that may not be obvious from simple input/output analysis.

Evidence Strategy: Context tracking with comprehensive logging, user interaction pattern analysis, environmental condition monitoring, dynamic configuration change tracking, contextual bias analysis

Investigation Focus: Context-dependent behavior patterns, user-specific adaptations, environmental influences on decisions, dynamic configuration effects, contextual bias emergence

2.4.2 Understanding the Fundamental Differences

The differences between AI system types are not just technical details—they represent fundamentally different approaches to creating intelligent behavior, each with unique forensic implications, evidence patterns, and investigation requirements.

2.4.2.1 The Learning Spectrum: From Explicit to Implicit Knowledge

At one end of the spectrum, expert systems store knowledge explicitly as human-readable rules and facts. Investigating these systems involves examining rule bases, tracing logical inference paths, and verifying knowledge sources. The investigation process resembles auditing a complex set of business rules rather than analyzing learned patterns.

At the other end, deep neural networks store knowledge implicitly through millions or billions of numerical parameters that do not correspond to interpretable concepts. Investigating these systems requires statistical analysis, pattern recognition techniques, and sophisticated probing methods to understand what has been learned and how it affects behavior.

This spectrum fundamentally affects investigation methodology. Explicit knowledge systems allow direct examination of decision logic, while implicit knowledge systems require indirect inference about learned patterns. The choice of investigation techniques must match the knowledge representation used by the target system.

2.4.2.2 The Interpretability Divide: Transparent versus Opaque Systems

The interpretability of decision processes fundamentally affects which forensic techniques will be effective. This question determines whether you can directly examine decision logic or instead rely on indirect analysis methods.

Interpretable systems provide transparent decision pathways where every step from input to output can be examined and understood. These systems use algorithms like decision trees, linear models, or explicit rules that create clear audit trails. Interpretability is the forensic investigator's best friend—it enables direct bias detection, individual case analysis, and clear explanation of system behavior.

Interpretable systems generate evidence that directly corresponds to their decision-making process. You can examine feature weights in linear models to understand which inputs most influence decisions. You can trace decision tree paths to see exactly which conditions led to specific outcomes. You can audit rule firing sequences in expert systems to verify logical consistency.

Forensic Advantages: Direct analysis of decision pathways, individual case investigation capabilities, transparent bias detection methods, clear explanation of system behavior, straightforward tampering detection

Investigation Approach: Importance analysis, decision pathway tracing, rule consistency checking, direct bias measurement, logical verification

Evidence Types: Decision trees (visual representations of decision logic), feature weights (numerical importance scores), rule firing logs (sequences of applied rules), explanation outputs (system-generated justifications), individual case traces (step-by-step decision records)

Black-box systems make decisions through opaque processes that resist direct interpretation. These systems, primarily deep neural networks, encode their decision-making in millions or billions of parameters that do not correspond to interpretable concepts. Black-box systems present significant forensic challenges because their decision processes cannot be directly examined.

Understanding black-box systems requires thinking statistically rather than logically. Instead of examining decision rules, you must probe system behavior across large numbers of test cases to infer bias patterns. Instead of tracing individual decisions, you must analyze aggregate behavior to understand system tendencies. This indirect approach requires more sophisticated analysis techniques and larger evidence datasets.

Forensic Challenges: Indirect analysis requirements, statistical inference needs, large-scale testing requirements, sophisticated tooling needs, interpretation uncertainty

Investigation Approach: Behavioral probing, statistical pattern analysis, adversarial testing, representation analysis, counterfactual examination

Evidence Types: Input-output behavior patterns, statistical bias measurements, adversarial test results, activation pattern analysis, counterfactual analysis results

2.4.3 Forensic Decision Framework

The forensic decision framework provides a systematic method for classifying any AI system you encounter based on observable characteristics and investigation requirements. This framework emphasizes forensic considerations rather than academic classifications, focusing on factors that directly affect evidence collection and analysis strategies.

Figure 2.1 provides a systematic approach to AI system classification specifically designed for forensic investigators. This decision framework emphasizes characteristics that directly affect investigation strategy, evidence collection, and analysis techniques.

The framework guides investigators through four critical classification questions that determine investigation approach. The first level examines input types to understand what data the system processes and where evidence might reside. The second level focuses on output generation methods, which affects how bias manifests and how system behavior can be analyzed. The third level assesses decision transparency, fundamentally determining whether direct examination or indirect behavioral analysis is required. The fourth level evaluates learning and adaptation characteristics, which affects temporal evidence requirements and the stability of system behavior.

Each decision point leads to specific investigation strategies and evidence priorities. For example, systems processing natural language require different analysis techniques than those processing structured data, and systems with transparent decision processes enable direct bias detection while opaque systems require statistical behavioral analysis. This framework ensures that investigators select appropriate techniques from the start rather than discovering mismatched approaches after significant investigation effort.

The framework's strength lies in its practical focus on forensic characteristics rather than technical implementation details. Two systems using similar algorithms but with different transparency levels require fundamentally different investigation approaches, while systems using different algorithms but similar transparency levels can often be investigated using similar techniques. This decision framework helps investigators quickly identify the most critical system characteristics for their investigation planning.

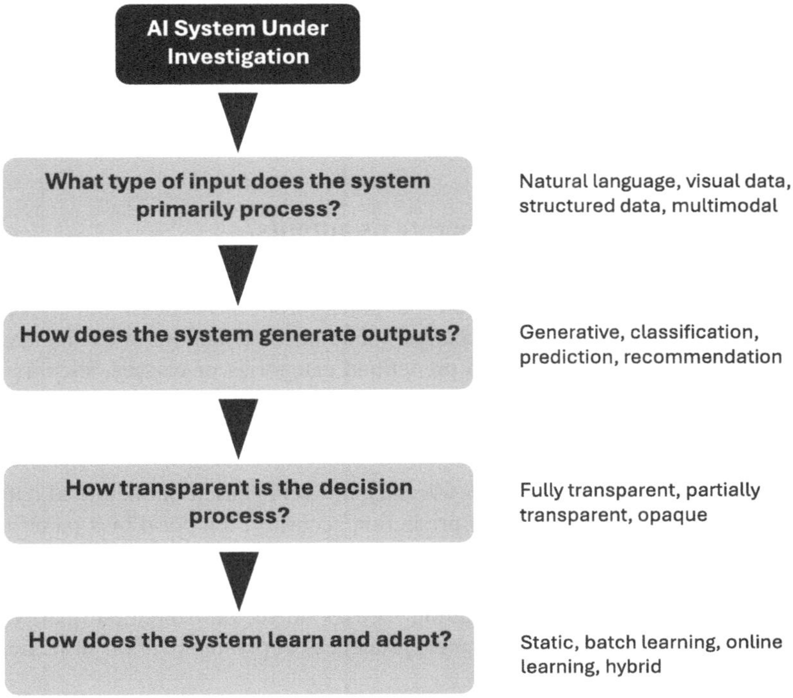

FIGURE 2.1

2.4.3.1 Primary Classification Questions

The framework begins with fundamental questions about system capabilities and behavior that determine the broad category of investigation approach required.

Question 1: What type of input does the system primarily process?

Natural language systems process text or speech as their primary input, including chatbots, translation systems, sentiment analysis tools, and content moderation systems. These systems require investigation techniques focused on linguistic patterns, semantic understanding, and text-based bias detection. Evidence collection emphasizes prompt logs, conversation histories, and text processing pipelines.

Visual systems process images, videos, or other visual data as their primary input, including facial recognition systems, medical imaging analysis, autonomous vehicle perception, and content classification systems. These systems require investigation techniques focused on visual pattern recognition, image bias analysis, and computer vision testing. Evidence collection emphasizes training image datasets, visual processing logs, and image feature analysis.

Structured data systems process tabular data, databases, or other structured information as their primary input, including credit scoring systems, fraud detection, recommendation engines, and business intelligence tools. These systems require investigation techniques focused on feature analysis, statistical relationships, and structured data bias detection.

Evidence collection emphasizes training datasets, feature engineering logs, and statistical model parameters.

Multimodal systems process multiple types of input simultaneously, combining text, images, audio, or other data types. These systems require hybrid investigation approaches that address each modality while also examining cross-modal interactions and integration effects.

Question 2: How does the system generate its outputs?

Generative systems create new content, text, images, or other outputs that did not exist in their training data. Investigation focuses on the quality, appropriateness, and bias patterns in generated content, requiring careful analysis of output distributions and content evaluation.

Classification systems assign inputs to predefined categories or classes, such as approved/denied decisions, risk scores, or content categories. Investigation focuses on decision boundaries, classification accuracy across different groups, and the appropriateness of category assignments.

Prediction systems forecast future values, trends, or events based on historical data and current inputs. Investigation focuses on prediction accuracy, temporal bias patterns, and the appropriateness of prediction horizons and confidence intervals.

Recommendation systems suggest items, content, or actions to users based on preferences, behavior, or characteristics. Investigation focuses on recommendation quality, diversity, fairness across user groups, and the appropriateness of personalization strategies.

Question 3: How transparent is the system's decision process?

Fully transparent systems provide complete visibility into their decision-making process, typically through explicit rules, decision trees, or linear models. Investigation can directly examine decision logic and trace individual cases through the system.

Partially transparent systems provide some insight into their decision process through feature importance scores, attention weights, or explanation systems, but the full decision process cannot be directly observed. Investigation combines direct analysis of available information with indirect probing techniques.

Opaque systems provide no direct insight into their decision process, requiring purely indirect analysis techniques such as behavioral testing, statistical analysis, and pattern inference. Investigation focuses on input-output relationships and behavioral patterns rather than internal decision logic.

Question 4: How does the system learn and adapt?

Static systems do not change their behavior after initial training and deployment, providing stable investigation targets with consistent behavior patterns. Investigation can focus on point-in-time analysis without concern for temporal changes.

Batch learning systems update their behavior periodically through retraining on new data, creating discrete investigation periods with different system behaviors. Investigation must consider which version of the system was active during incidents of interest.

Online learning systems continuously adapt their behavior based on new data or interactions, creating complex temporal investigation challenges where behavior may have changed since incidents occurred. Investigation requires temporal analysis and behavior reconstruction techniques.

Hybrid learning systems combine multiple learning approaches, such as pretrained models with online adaptation or ensemble systems with different update schedules. Investigation must understand each learning component and their interactions.

2.4.3.2 Secondary Classification Questions

After answering primary questions, secondary questions refine the classification and determine specific investigation approaches.

For Natural Language Systems:

- Does it generate human-like text responses? → Generative Language Analysis
- Does it classify or analyze existing text? → Text Classification Analysis
- Does it translate between languages? → Translation System Analysis
- Does it understand speech or convert speech to text? → Speech Processing Analysis

For Visual Systems:

- Does it generate images or videos? → Generative Visual Analysis
- Does it recognize or classify visual content? → Computer Vision Analysis
- Does it track objects or detect motion? → Video Analysis Techniques
- Does it combine visual and textual understanding? → Multimodal Analysis

For Structured Data Systems:

- Can individual decision pathways be examined? → Interpretable ML Analysis
- Does it use ensemble methods or multiple models? → Ensemble Analysis
- Does it process time-series or temporal data? → Temporal Analysis
- Does it make real-time or batch predictions? → Deployment Analysis

2.4.3.3 Integration and Architecture Questions

Question 5: Does the system combine multiple AI approaches?

Single-component systems use one primary AI technique, allowing focused investigation using techniques appropriate for that specific approach. Evidence collection and analysis can concentrate on the characteristics of the single AI method used.

Multi-component systems combine different AI approaches, requiring investigation of each component plus analysis of integration patterns and interaction effects. Evidence collection must address all component types plus integration evidence.

Pipeline systems process data through sequential AI components, where the output of one component becomes the input to the next. Investigation must trace data flow through the entire pipeline and understand how errors or biases propagate between components.

Ensemble systems combine outputs from multiple AI components through voting, averaging, or other combination methods. Investigation should analyze each component plus the combination methodology and its effects on overall system behavior.

Question 6: What filtering and processing layers affect the output?

Content filtering systems apply post-processing rules to modify or block AI outputs based on content policies, safety requirements, or business rules. Investigation of these will examine both the core AI system and the filtering layers that may significantly alter final outputs delivered to users.

Safety and alignment layers include constitutional AI, reinforcement learning from human feedback (RLHF), and other techniques designed to ensure AI outputs align with human values and safety requirements. These layers may suppress certain types of outputs or modify AI behavior in ways that affect forensic analysis.

Business logic integration layers apply organizational rules, compliance requirements, or process automation that transforms AI outputs into business decisions. Investigation will help to understand how AI recommendations are integrated into broader business processes.

User interface and presentation layers determine how AI outputs are presented to end users, potentially affecting interpretation and decision-making even when the underlying AI outputs are unbiased. Investigation will consider the complete user experience, not just raw AI outputs.

2.4.3.4 Evidence Collection Planning

Once investigators have classified an AI system using the forensic decision framework, the next critical step involves planning evidence collection strategies that match the system's characteristics and investigation objectives.

Figure 2.2 presents an evidence collection priority matrix that enables efficient investigation planning by showing which evidence types are most critical for different AI system categories. This matrix represents the distillation of forensic experience across numerous AI investigations, providing investigators with data-driven guidance for resource allocation and collection sequencing.

The matrix uses a three-tier priority system where high-priority evidence is essential for successful investigation, medium-priority evidence provides important supporting information, and low-priority evidence may be useful but is not critical for most investigation objectives. These priorities reflect both the investigative value of different evidence types and the practical constraints investigators face in terms of time, resources, and access limitations.

The priority assignments reflect fundamental differences in how different AI system types generate, store, and process information. Traditional machine learning systems prioritize training data and model parameters because these directly determine system behavior and can be directly examined. Deep learning systems emphasize training logs and configuration files because their distributed knowledge representation requires understanding the training process. LLM systems prioritize prompt logs and API interactions because these systems are often accessed indirectly and behavioral analysis is more feasible than direct parameter examination.

Hybrid systems show consistently high priorities across multiple evidence categories because they require coordinated analysis of multiple component types. This reflects the increased complexity and resource requirements for investigating systems that combine multiple AI approaches. Investigators should use this matrix not as rigid requirements but as starting points for developing investigation strategies that balance thoroughness with practical constraints and specific investigation objectives.

AI System Type	Training Data	Model Parameters	Training Logs	Inference Logs	System Logs	Configuration Files	API Logs	Knowledge Bade	Rule Base	Prompt Logs	Safety Filters
Traditional ML	H	H	M	M	L	M	L	L	L	L	L
Deep Learning	H	H	H	M	M	H	L	L	L	L	L
LLM Systems	M	M	M	H	M	H	H	L	L	H	H
RAG Systems	M	M	L	H	M	H	H	H	L	H	M
Expert Systems	L	L	L	H	M	M	M	M	H	L	L
Hybrid Systems	H	H	H	H	H	H	M	M	M	M	H
Multimodal AI	H	H	H	M	M	H	M	L	L	M	M
Reinforcement Learning	M	H	H	H	M	M	L	L	L	L	L

FIGURE 2.2

2.5 AI SYSTEM TYPES AND FORENSIC CHARACTERISTICS

2.5.1 Traditional Machine Learning Systems

Traditional machine learning systems form the foundation of many deployed AI applications, representing the most mature and well-understood category of AI from a forensic investigation perspective. These systems use well-established algorithms like decision trees, linear regression, logistic regression, support vector machines, and random forests to process structured data and make predictions or classifications.

The architecture of traditional ML systems follows a relatively straightforward pipeline: data flows from storage systems through feature engineering components to trained models, then to inference engines that serve predictions. This linear architecture creates clear evidence trails and makes these systems particularly amenable to forensic analysis. Unlike more complex AI architectures, traditional ML systems maintain explicit relationships between inputs and outputs that can be directly examined and understood.

From an investigative standpoint, traditional ML systems offer significant advantages because their decision-making processes are generally interpretable. When a loan application is rejected by a logistic regression model, investigators can examine the exact coefficients applied to each feature and understand precisely why that decision was made. This transparency makes traditional ML systems ideal starting points for investigators new to AI forensics, as the investigation techniques closely parallel those used in traditional business process auditing.

However, this apparent simplicity can be deceptive. While the models themselves may be interpretable, the feature engineering processes that prepare data for these models can introduce significant bias or hide important relationships. The human decisions embedded in feature selection, data preprocessing, and model configuration often prove more consequential than the algorithmic choices, requiring investigators to pay careful attention to the entire system ecosystem rather than just the model itself.

Figure 2.3 illustrates the linear architecture of traditional ML systems that creates clear evidence trails and enables systematic forensic investigation. The diagram shows how data flows through distinct, interpretable stages from storage through feature engineering to model training and inference. This linear pipeline architecture is fundamental to understanding why traditional ML systems are more amenable to forensic analysis than other AI system types.

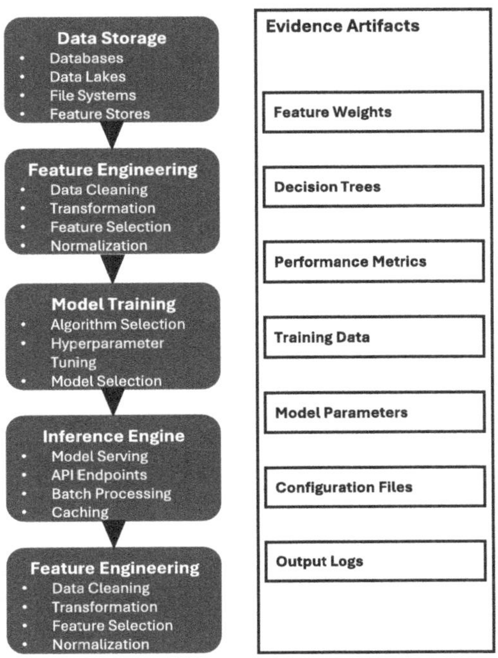

FIGURE 2.3

Each component in the pipeline generates specific types of evidence that can be directly examined and understood. The data storage layer provides access to training datasets and feature definitions. The feature engineering component reveals the human decisions about data transformation and selection that often determine system behavior more than the model itself. The model training stage produces interpretable parameters like feature weights and decision trees that can be directly analyzed for bias or accuracy. The inference engine provides clear logs of how individual predictions are made.

The clear separation between components means that investigators can isolate problems to specific stages of the pipeline. If bias is discovered in system outputs, investigators can trace backward through the inference engine to the model parameters, then to the training process, and finally to the feature engineering and data storage to identify the root cause. This traceability makes traditional ML systems ideal for establishing accountability and understanding exactly how discriminatory decisions are made.

2.5.1.1 System Components and Architecture

Core Components:

- **Feature Engineering Pipeline:** Data preprocessing, transformation, and selection systems
- **Model Training Infrastructure:** Training algorithms, hyperparameter optimization, cross-validation
- **Model Storage:** Serialized models, version control, model registries
- **Inference Engine:** Prediction serving, batch processing, real-time scoring
- **Monitoring Systems:** Performance tracking, drift detection, error logging

Training Infrastructure:

- **Data Pipeline:** ETL processes, data validation, feature store integration
- **Experiment Tracking:** Model versioning, hyperparameter logs, performance metrics
- **Validation Framework:** Cross-validation, holdout testing, statistical significance testing
- **Model Selection:** Algorithm comparison, ensemble construction, final model selection

Deployment Infrastructure:

- **Serving Platform:** REST APIs, batch processing jobs, embedded scoring
- **Caching Layer:** Feature caching, prediction caching, model caching
- **Load Balancing:** Request distribution, failover mechanisms, scaling policies
- **Integration Points:** Database connections, external API calls, downstream systems

2.5.1.2 Forensic Investigation Focus

Traditional ML Evidence:

- **Training Data:** Complete datasets with feature definitions and transformations
- **Feature Engineering:** Preprocessing steps, transformation logic, feature selection criteria
- **Model Parameters:** Learned weights, tree structures, support vectors, ensemble components
- **Training Logs:** Algorithm convergence, validation scores, hyperparameter search results
- **Deployment Configuration:** Serving infrastructure, integration settings, monitoring thresholds

Interpretability Advantages:

- **Direct Parameter Examination:** Feature weights can be directly inspected and interpreted
- **Decision Path Tracing:** Individual predictions can be traced through decision trees
- **Feature Importance Analysis:** Statistical measures show which features most influence decisions
- **Linear Relationship Analysis:** Coefficients in linear models provide clear influence direction
- **Rule Extraction:** Decision trees can be converted to human-readable rules

Investigation Strategies:

- **Feature Bias Analysis:** Examining training data and feature engineering for demographic bias
- **Model Fairness Testing:** Statistical parity, equalized odds, demographic parity analysis
- **Decision Boundary Analysis:** Understanding how the model separates different classes
- **Sensitivity Analysis:** Testing how changes in individual features affect predictions
- **Outlier Detection:** Identifying unusual cases that may indicate problems or tampering

2.5.2 Deep Learning Systems

Deep learning systems represent a paradigm shift from traditional ML, using artificial neural networks with multiple layers to automatically learn complex patterns from high-dimensional data. These systems excel at processing images, text, speech, and other unstructured data types that traditional ML struggles with, but they introduce significant challenges for forensic investigation due to their opacity and computational complexity.

The architecture of deep learning systems is fundamentally different from traditional ML. Instead of explicit feature engineering, these systems learn hierarchical representations automatically through layers of interconnected neurons. Data flows through embedding layers that convert raw inputs into numerical representations, then through multiple hidden layers that progressively extract higher-level features, finally reaching output layers that make predictions. This layered architecture means that the system's "knowledge" is distributed across millions or billions of parameters rather than concentrated in interpretable rules or weights.

Understanding deep learning systems requires investigators to think in terms of learned representations rather than explicit logic. A facial recognition system, for example, might learn to detect edges in early layers, facial features in middle layers, and complete face representations in later layers. However, these representations are not explicitly programmed but emerge from the training process, making them difficult to interpret and analyze directly.

Figure 2.4 demonstrates the fundamental architectural differences that make deep learning systems challenging for forensic investigation, contrasting sharply with the linear pipelines of traditional ML systems. The layered neural network structure shows how information flows through multiple transformation stages, with each layer learning increasingly abstract representations that cannot be directly interpreted or traced back to specific input features.

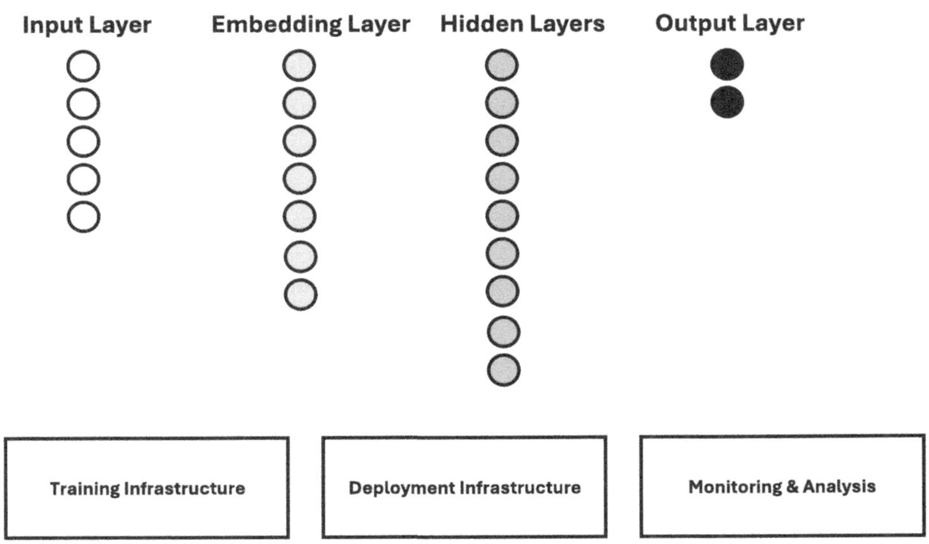

FIGURE 2.4

The diagram illustrates the critical forensic challenge of distributed knowledge representation. Unlike traditional ML systems where decision logic is concentrated in interpretable parameters, deep learning systems distribute their "understanding" across millions of parameters in the hidden layers. Each node in these layers captures statistical patterns that contribute to the final decision, but individual nodes or weights rarely correspond to human-interpretable concepts that investigators can directly examine.

The supporting infrastructure components shown below the network highlight the scale and complexity that investigators navigate. Training infrastructure involves distributed computation across multiple GPUs with complex synchronization requirements, generating massive logs that require specialized analysis tools. Deployment infrastructure handles the computational demands of large models while maintaining performance, creating additional layers of abstraction between investigators and the core AI behavior.

The forensic implications become clear when comparing this architecture to traditional ML systems: investigators cannot simply examine feature weights or trace decision trees to understand bias or errors. Instead, they rely on behavioral analysis, statistical testing, and sophisticated probing techniques to infer what the distributed network has learned. The scale indicators shown in the figure that represent millions of parameters requiring billions of operations underscore why deep learning investigations require fundamentally different approaches, specialized tools, and significantly more computational resources than traditional ML forensics.

The forensic investigation of deep learning systems accounts for this distributed knowledge representation. Evidence collection focuses on training processes, parameter evolution, and behavioral analysis rather than direct examination of decision logic. Investigators need to understand how the training infrastructure distributed computation across multiple GPUs, how data was preprocessed and augmented, and how the model's behavior changed throughout the training process. The scale and complexity of these systems require specialized tools and techniques, but they also generate comprehensive logs and artifacts that can provide detailed insights into system behavior when properly analyzed.

2.5.2.1 System Components and Architecture

Core Model Components:

- **Neural Network Architecture:** Layer definitions, activation functions, skip connections
- **Parameter Storage:** Weights, biases, normalization parameters, optimizer states
- **Loss Functions:** Training objectives, regularization terms, custom loss definitions
- **Optimization Components:** Gradient computation, parameter updates, learning rate schedules
- **Activation Analysis:** Layer outputs, attention patterns, intermediate representations

Training Infrastructure:

- **Distributed Training:** Multi-GPU coordination, gradient synchronization, communication protocols
- **Data Loading:** Batch processing, data augmentation, parallel data pipelines
- **Checkpointing:** Model state preservation, training resumption, best model selection
- **Monitoring Systems:** Loss tracking, gradient analysis, resource utilization, convergence detection
- **Experiment Management:** Hyperparameter tracking, configuration management, result comparison

Deployment Infrastructure:

- **Inference Optimization:** Model quantization, pruning, distillation, hardware acceleration
- **Serving Platforms:** GPU clusters, edge deployment, cloud inference, model serving frameworks

- **Batch Processing:** Large-scale inference, distributed processing, result aggregation
- **Real-time Serving:** Low-latency inference, load balancing, auto-scaling, caching strategies

2.5.2.2 Forensic Investigation Focus

Deep Learning Evidence:

- **Model Architecture:** Network topology, layer configurations, parameter counts, computational graphs
- **Training Process:** Loss curves, gradient statistics, learning rate schedules, data augmentation policies
- **Parameter Analysis:** Weight distributions, activation patterns, learned representations, feature maps
- **Training Data:** Dataset composition, preprocessing steps, augmentation techniques, data validation
- **Optimization History:** Training logs, checkpoint analysis, convergence behavior, hyperparameter evolution

Investigation Challenges:

- **Parameter Opacity:** Millions of parameters do not correspond to interpretable concepts
- **Distributed Representations:** Information is spread across many parameters rather than localized
- **Nonlinear Interactions:** Complex relationships between inputs and outputs resist direct analysis
- **Scale Complexity:** Large models require specialized tools and computational resources for analysis
- **Version Complexity:** Multiple checkpoints and model versions require careful temporal analysis

Investigation Strategies:

- **Behavioral Testing:** Systematic input-output analysis to infer learned patterns
- **Representation Analysis:** Examining intermediate layer outputs to understand learned features
- **Adversarial Testing:** Using carefully crafted inputs to probe model vulnerabilities and biases
- **Attribution Methods:** Gradient-based and perturbation-based techniques to understand input influence
- **Probing Experiments:** Training diagnostic models to test what information is captured in representations

2.5.3 Large Language Model Systems

Large language models represent the current frontier of AI systems, using transformer architectures with billions of parameters to process and generate human-like text. These systems create unique forensic challenges due to their scale, complexity, and novel capabilities.

2.5.3.1 System Components and Architecture

Core Model Components:

- **Tokenizer:** Converts text to numerical tokens and back to text
- **Embedding Layers:** Convert tokens to high-dimensional vectors with positional information

- **Transformer Blocks:** Self-attention and feed-forward layers (dozens to hundreds of blocks)
- **Language Modeling Head:** Converts final hidden states to probability distributions over vocabulary
- **Position Encodings:** Mechanisms for understanding sequence order and relationships

Training Infrastructure:

- **Pre-Training Data:** Massive text corpora (CommonCrawl, books, web pages, academic papers)
- **Distributed Training:** Multi-GPU, multi-node systems with specialized communication protocols
- **Gradient Accumulation:** Techniques for handling large batch sizes across distributed systems
- **Mixed Precision Training:** FP16/BF16 optimization for memory efficiency and training speed
- **Checkpointing Systems:** Fault-tolerant training with periodic state saves and recovery mechanisms

Deployment Components:

- **Inference Engines:** Optimized serving systems (vLLM, TensorRT-LLM, Triton Inference Server)
- **Prompt Templates:** System instructions, formatting rules, and conversation management
- **Safety Filters:** Content moderation, harmful output detection, and response filtering
- **Response Caching:** Systems for storing and reusing common responses to improve efficiency
- **Load Balancing:** Distribution of requests across multiple model instances and hardware

Fine-tuning Infrastructure:

- **Instruction Tuning:** Training on instruction-following datasets to improve task performance
- **Reinforcement Learning from Human Feedback (RLHF):** Training to align outputs with human preferences
- **Parameter-Efficient Fine-Tuning:** LoRA, adapters, and other techniques for efficient customization
- **Safety Training:** Constitutional AI, red teaming, and other safety-focused training procedures
- **Domain Adaptation:** Specialized training for specific domains or use cases

2.5.3.2 Forensic Investigation Focus

LLM-Specific Evidence:

- **Prompt Engineering:** System instructions, prompt templates, conversation management logic
- **Interaction Logs:** Complete prompt and response histories with timestamps and user identification
- **Safety Systems:** Content filter configurations, activation logs, bypass attempts, escalation procedures
- **Fine-Tuning Data:** Task-specific training datasets, human feedback data, preference rankings
- **Performance Monitoring:** Response quality metrics, safety violations, user satisfaction scores

Unique Investigation Challenges:

- **Scale Complexity:** Billions of parameters require specialized analysis tools and techniques
- **API-Only Access:** Many LLMs are only accessible through APIs, limiting direct model analysis
- **Dynamic Behavior:** Outputs may vary for identical inputs due to sampling and generation strategies
- **Context Dependencies:** Long conversation histories and complex prompt interactions affect behavior
- **Safety Layer Interactions:** Multiple filtering and safety systems may modify or suppress outputs

Investigation Strategies:

- **Prompt Pattern Analysis:** Systematic testing of different prompt types and conversation patterns
- **Bias Probing:** Targeted prompts designed to reveal demographic, cultural, or ideological biases
- **Safety Testing:** Red team exercises to identify harmful output generation or filter bypasses
- **Consistency Analysis:** Testing response consistency across similar prompts and conversation contexts
- **Knowledge Boundary Testing:** Understanding what information the model has learned and its limitations

Evidence collection addresses multiple phases of the LLM lifecycle, from pre-training through deployment and ongoing operation.

Development Phase Evidence: Pre-training datasets (when accessible), model architecture specifications, training hyperparameters and optimization settings, computational resource allocation records, checkpoint and version control systems

Fine-Tuning Phase Evidence: Task-specific training datasets, fine-tuning procedures and parameters, RLHF training data and human feedback records, performance evaluation results, safety testing and red team results

Deployment Phase Evidence: Prompt templates and system instructions, safety filter configurations and activation logs, API access controls and authentication records, load balancing and scaling configurations, monitoring and alerting system settings

Operational Phase Evidence: Complete prompt and response logs, user interaction patterns and session data, safety filter activation and bypass attempts, performance metrics and error rates, model update and versioning records

2.5.4 Retrieval-Augmented Generation Systems

Retrieval-augmented generation (RAG) systems represent a sophisticated hybrid architecture that combines the language generation capabilities of LLMs with the ability to access and reason over external knowledge bases. These systems address one of the fundamental limitations of standalone LLMs—their reliance on information learned during training—by dynamically retrieving relevant information from external sources to inform their responses.

The architecture of RAG systems involves a complex orchestration of multiple specialized components working in concert. When a user submits a query, the system first processes that query through an embedding model to create a vector representation. This vector is then used to search through a pre-indexed knowledge base, where documents have been broken into chunks and converted into similar vector representations. The retrieval system identifies the most relevant document chunks, which are then combined with the original query and fed to a language generation model that synthesizes a response drawing from both its training knowledge and the retrieved information.

This multi-component architecture creates unique forensic challenges because problems can arise at any stage of the pipeline and propagate through subsequent components. A bias in the knowledge base composition will affect what information is available for retrieval. Biases in the retrieval algorithms will determine which information is actually selected for different types of queries. The language generation component may introduce additional biases when synthesizing retrieved information into responses. Understanding how these different bias sources interact requires investigators to analyze each component independently while also examining their integration points.

Figure 2.5 illustrates the complex multi-component orchestration that defines RAG systems and creates unique forensic investigation challenges not present in single-component AI architectures. The sequential flow diagram shows how user queries trigger a sophisticated pipeline involving multiple specialized systems that work in coordination to produce final responses, with each component representing a potential source of bias, error, or manipulation.

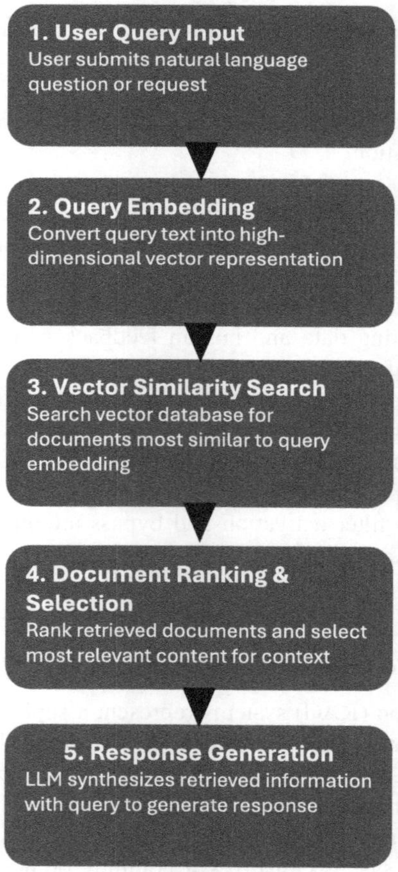

FIGURE 2.5

The five-step process reveals the critical forensic insight that RAG systems can fail or exhibit bias at multiple distinct points in the pipeline. A user query must first be successfully converted to vector embeddings, then matched against a knowledge base through similarity search, ranked and selected through potentially biased algorithms, and finally synthesized by a language model that may introduce additional distortions. Each step can introduce or amplify bias independently, meaning investigators should analyze not just individual components but also their cumulative effects.

The diagram emphasizes the unique evidence trail that RAG systems create through their citation and retrieval mechanisms. Unlike other AI systems that produce outputs without clear source attribution, RAG systems generate verifiable links between inputs, retrieved knowledge, and outputs. This creates both opportunities and challenges for forensic investigation: while the citation trail provides accountability mechanisms absent in other AI types, it also requires investigators to validate the accuracy of these citations and understand how retrieval bias affects what information is selected and presented.

The forensic complexity shown in this architecture requires investigators to coordinate analysis across multiple domains simultaneously. Investigators examine knowledge base composition for bias, analyze retrieval algorithms for systematic preferences, validate citation accuracy against source documents, and assess how the generation component synthesizes retrieved information. This multi-domain requirement makes RAG investigations more resource-intensive than single-component systems but potentially more tractable than opaque neural networks due to the explicit knowledge retrieval process.

The evidence landscape for RAG systems spans multiple domains: knowledge management systems track document ingestion and processing, vector databases store searchable embeddings, retrieval logs record what information was accessed for each query, and generation logs capture how that information was synthesized into responses. Perhaps most critically, RAG systems generate citation and attribution information that can be verified against source documents, providing a level of accountability and traceability that is often missing from other AI system types. This makes RAG systems somewhat more amenable to forensic investigation than pure LLMs, but the multi-component nature requires investigators to coordinate analysis across different system types and evidence sources.

2.5.4.1 System Components and Architecture

Core RAG Components:

- **Document Corpus:** Large collection of text documents serving as the external knowledge base
- **Embedding Model:** Neural network that converts text to vector representations for similarity search
- **Vector Database:** Specialized storage for high-dimensional embeddings (Pinecone, Weaviate, Chroma)
- **Retrieval System:** Search mechanism that finds relevant documents for user queries
- **Generation Model:** LLM that synthesizes retrieved information into coherent responses
- **Fusion Module:** Component that combines retrieval results with generation capabilities

Knowledge Processing Pipeline:

- **Document Ingestion:** Systems for loading and parsing diverse document types and formats
- **Text Chunking:** Algorithms for splitting documents into manageable pieces for embedding
- **Embedding Generation:** Batch processing to create vector representations of text chunks
- **Index Construction:** Building searchable vector indexes with metadata and optimization
- **Metadata Management:** Tracking document sources, dates, authors, and other attributes

Retrieval Infrastructure:

- **Query Processing:** Converting user questions into effective search queries and embeddings
- **Similarity Search:** Vector similarity computation and ranking of relevant content
- **Reranking Systems:** Secondary ranking based on relevance, recency, or other criteria
- **Context Window Management:** Fitting retrieved content into LLM input limits and constraints
- **Citation Tracking:** Maintaining links between generated content and original sources

2.5.4.2 Forensic Investigation Focus

RAG-Specific Evidence:

- **Knowledge Base Content:** Complete document corpus with source attribution and metadata
- **Embedding Vectors:** High-dimensional representations of all indexed content for analysis
- **Retrieval Logs:** Records of what documents were retrieved for each query with rankings
- **Ranking Algorithms:** Logic determining which documents are most relevant for different queries
- **Citation Accuracy:** Verification that generated responses accurately cite and represent sources
- **Update Logs:** Records of knowledge base modifications, additions, and version management

Bias and Quality Issues:

- **Knowledge Base Bias:** Systematic bias in the underlying document collection and sources
- **Retrieval Bias:** Search algorithms favoring certain types of content or sources over others
- **Temporal Bias:** Knowledge base freshness and currency issues affecting response accuracy
- **Source Quality:** Reliability and accuracy of information sources in the knowledge base
- **Citation Hallucination:** Generated responses claiming false source support or attribution

Investigation Strategies:

- **Knowledge Base Auditing:** Systematic analysis of document collection for bias and quality issues
- **Retrieval Pattern Analysis:** Understanding what content is retrieved for different query types
- **Citation Verification:** Cross-checking generated citations against actual source content
- **Source Diversity Analysis:** Ensuring balanced representation across different perspectives and sources
- **Temporal Analysis:** Tracking how knowledge base updates affect system behavior over time

2.5.4.3 Server Infrastructure and Evidence Collection

RAG systems create complex evidence trails across multiple components that require systematic collection and analysis approaches. The distributed architecture requires understanding both individual component evidence and integration patterns.

Knowledge Management Infrastructure: Document storage and versioning systems, text processing and chunking pipelines, embedding generation and update procedures, vector database indexing and backup systems, metadata management and source attribution systems

Retrieval Infrastructure: Query processing and transformation systems, similarity search and ranking algorithms, reranking and filtering mechanisms, context assembly and prompt generation systems, response caching and optimization systems

Integration Infrastructure: API gateways and request routing systems, load balancing across retrieval and generation components, monitoring and performance tracking systems, error-handling and fallback mechanisms, security and access control systems

2.5.5 Expert Systems and Rule-Based AI

Expert systems represent the most transparent and auditable category of AI systems, encoding human expertise through explicit rules and logical inference mechanisms. These systems store knowledge in human-readable formats and make decisions through clearly traceable logical processes, making them particularly amenable to forensic investigation. Unlike machine learning systems that learn patterns from data, expert systems embody explicit human knowledge that has been carefully encoded into rule bases and inference engines.

The architecture of expert systems follows classical artificial intelligence principles, with clear separation between knowledge representation and reasoning mechanisms. The knowledge base contains facts, rules, and domain expertise encoded in structured formats like IF-THEN rules or logical statements. The inference engine applies these rules systematically to derive conclusions, maintaining detailed logs of which rules were applied in which order. This separation means that investigators can independently examine the knowledge content and the reasoning process, providing multiple avenues for analysis and validation.

From a forensic perspective, expert systems offer unique advantages because their decision-making processes are completely transparent and reproducible. Every conclusion can be traced back through the exact sequence of logical steps that led to it. Every rule can be examined for accuracy, bias, or appropriateness. The knowledge sources can be validated against domain expertise and organizational policies. This transparency makes expert systems ideal for high-stakes applications where accountability and explainability are paramount, but it also means that any flaws in the encoded knowledge or reasoning logic will be clearly visible upon examination.

However, the apparent simplicity of expert systems can mask significant complexity in knowledge acquisition and validation. The process of extracting expert knowledge and encoding it into rules is inherently subjective and may introduce biases or omit important considerations. The logical inference mechanisms, while transparent, may not accurately reflect how human experts actually make decisions in practice. Investigators should examine not just the technical implementation of expert systems, but also the knowledge engineering process that created them and the ongoing maintenance procedures that keep them current and accurate.

2.5.5.1 System Components and Architecture

Core Components:

- **Knowledge Base:** Structured collection of facts, rules, and domain expertise
- **Inference Engine:** System that applies logical reasoning to derive conclusions from knowledge
- **Working Memory:** Temporary storage for facts and intermediate conclusions during reasoning
- **User Interface:** System for querying the expert system and receiving explanations
- **Explanation System:** Component that provides justification for conclusions and recommendations

Knowledge Representation:

- **Rule Base:** IF-THEN rules encoding expert decision-making logic and procedures
- **Fact Base:** Declarative knowledge about the domain, entities, and relationships
- **Ontologies:** Formal representations of domain concepts and their relationships
- **Decision Trees:** Structured representations of decision-making processes and outcomes
- **Semantic Networks:** Graph-based representations of knowledge and relationships

Inference Mechanisms:

- **Forward Chaining:** Reasoning from facts to conclusions using available rules
- **Backward Chaining:** Reasoning from goals to required facts and evidence
- **Conflict Resolution:** Strategies for choosing among multiple applicable rules
- **Uncertainty Handling:** Methods for dealing with incomplete or uncertain information
- **Explanation Generation:** Systems for providing reasoning traces and justifications

2.5.5.2 Forensic Investigation Focus

Expert System Evidence:

- **Rule Base Examination:** Direct analysis of decision rules and logical structures
- **Knowledge Source Verification:** Tracing rules back to expert knowledge and validation
- **Inference Logs:** Complete traces of reasoning processes and rule applications
- **Consistency Checking:** Verification that rules do not contradict each other
- **Completeness Analysis:** Assessment of whether rule coverage is adequate for the domain

Transparency Advantages:

- **Complete Auditability:** Every decision can be traced through explicit logical steps
- **Rule-Level Analysis:** Individual rules can be examined for bias, accuracy, and appropriateness
- **Expert Validation:** Domain experts can directly review and validate encoded knowledge
- **Explanation Quality:** Systems can provide complete justification for their recommendations
- **Modification Tracking:** Changes to rules and knowledge can be precisely documented

Investigation Strategies:

- **Rule Consistency Auditing:** Checking for logical contradictions and inconsistencies in the rule base
- **Knowledge Source Validation:** Verifying that encoded rules accurately represent expert knowledge
- **Coverage Analysis:** Ensuring that rules adequately cover the expected range of cases
- **Bias Detection:** Examining rules for systematic bias against particular groups or situations
- **Performance Validation:** Testing system recommendations against expert judgment and outcomes

Infrastructure Components:

- **Knowledge Management Systems:** Rule base storage and versioning systems for tracking changes
- **Inference Infrastructure:** Rule engine implementations and configurations for processing logic
- **Maintenance Infrastructure:** Knowledge base backup and recovery, testing frameworks, expert interfaces

2.5.6 Hybrid and Ensemble Systems

Modern AI deployments increasingly combine multiple approaches to leverage the strengths of different AI techniques while mitigating individual weaknesses. These hybrid and ensemble systems represent the growing sophistication of production AI architectures, but they also create the most complex forensic investigation challenges because problems can arise from individual components, component interactions, or emergent behaviors that only appear when multiple systems work together.

The architecture of hybrid systems varies dramatically depending on how different AI components are integrated. Pipeline systems process data sequentially through different AI components, where the output of one system becomes the input to the next. Ensemble systems run multiple AI models in parallel and combine their outputs through voting, averaging, or more sophisticated fusion techniques. Hierarchical systems use different AI approaches for different levels of decision-making, such as using simple rules for initial filtering and complex neural networks for detailed analysis. Each integration pattern creates different evidence trails and requires different investigation approaches.

Understanding hybrid systems requires investigators to think systemically about how different AI components interact and influence each other. A recommendation system might combine collaborative filtering algorithms to identify user preferences, content-based filtering to analyze item characteristics, and deep learning models to capture complex interaction patterns. The final recommendations emerge from the interaction of all these components, meaning that bias or errors in any individual component can affect the overall system behavior in ways that may not be immediately obvious from examining components in isolation.

The forensic investigation of hybrid systems requires addressing multiple levels of complexity simultaneously. At the component level, each AI system is investigated using techniques appropriate for its type—traditional ML components require feature analysis, neural networks require behavioral testing, and rule-based components require logical auditing. At the integration level, investigators should understand how data flows between components, how decisions are combined or prioritized, and how conflicts between different components are resolved. At the system level, investigators should identify emergent behaviors that arise from component interactions and may not be present in any individual component.

This multi-level analysis is further complicated by the filtering and processing layers that are increasingly common in production AI systems. Content filtering systems may modify or suppress outputs based on safety policies. Business logic integration may apply organizational rules that transform AI recommendations into final decisions. User interface systems may present AI outputs in ways that affect human interpretation and decision-making. Each of these layers can introduce additional sources of bias or error that should be considered alongside the core AI components.

2.5.6.1 System Architecture Types

Ensemble Models:

- **Voting Ensembles:** Multiple models make independent predictions combined through voting mechanisms
- **Bagging Systems:** Multiple models trained on different data subsets with aggregated predictions
- **Boosting Systems:** Sequential models that learn from previous model errors and weaknesses
- **Stacking Systems:** Meta-models that learn how to optimally combine predictions from base models

Hybrid Architectures:

- **Pipeline Systems:** Sequential processing through different AI components with data flow dependencies
- **Parallel Systems:** Multiple AI systems processing same input independently with result combination
- **Hierarchical Systems:** Different AI approaches for different decision levels or complexity tiers
- **Contextual Systems:** AI approach selection based on input characteristics, user context, or environmental conditions

Integration Patterns:

- **Loose Coupling:** Independent systems with simple output combination and minimal interaction
- **Tight Integration:** Shared components and data between different AI approaches with complex dependencies
- **Feedback Loops:** Output from one system influences another system's processing and decision-making
- **Dynamic Switching:** Runtime selection of AI approach based on conditions, performance, or context

2.5.6.2 Filtering and Processing Layers

Modern AI systems incorporate multiple layers of processing that can significantly affect outputs and investigation requirements. Understanding these layers is crucial for comprehensive forensic analysis.

Figure 2.6 reveals the critical but often overlooked reality that modern AI systems involve multiple processing layers that can significantly modify outputs between the core AI computation and final user delivery. This layered architecture demonstrates why investigators cannot simply analyze core AI models in isolation—they should understand how safety filters, business logic, and presentation systems can introduce bias, suppress information, or alter decision-making in ways that may be invisible from examining only the underlying AI components.

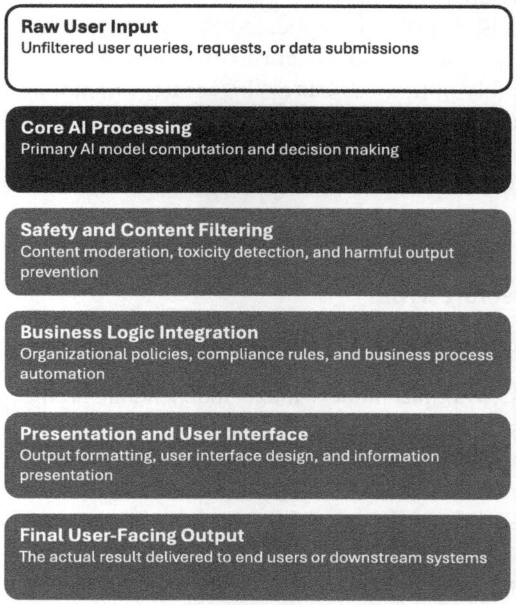

FIGURE 2.6

The vertical flow diagram illustrates how each processing layer represents a potential intervention point where bias can be introduced, amplified, or theoretically mitigated. Raw user inputs pass through increasingly sophisticated filtering and transformation systems, with each layer applying different criteria, policies, and business rules that may have disparate impacts across different user groups or use cases. A core AI system that produces unbiased outputs can still result in discriminatory outcomes if subsequent layers apply biased filtering criteria or present information in ways that affect human interpretation.

The forensic implications of this architecture are significant. Investigators should analyze not just the technical AI components but also the complete sociotechnical system that shapes how AI outputs become real-world decisions. Safety filters may suppress legitimate information for certain user groups, business logic may apply organizational policies that create disparate impacts, and user interface design may present identical AI outputs in ways that lead to different human decisions depending on user characteristics.

This layered approach to AI systems means that accountability and responsibility are distributed across multiple teams, technologies, and organizational functions. Investigators should coordinate analysis across technical AI teams, safety and policy teams, business process owners, and user experience designers to understand how problems emerge from the interaction of multiple systems rather than from any single component failure.

2.5.6.3 Content Filtering and Safety Layers

Safety Filtering Systems:

- **Content Moderation:** Automated detection and filtering of harmful, inappropriate, or policy-violating content
- **Toxicity Detection:** Systems that identify and suppress toxic, abusive, or harassment-related outputs
- **Bias Mitigation:** Post-processing systems designed to reduce discriminatory outputs across demographic groups
- **Factual Verification:** Systems that attempt to verify the accuracy of generated factual claims
- **Legal Compliance:** Filtering based on jurisdiction-specific legal requirements and regulations

Constitutional AI and Alignment Layers:

- **Value Alignment:** Systems trained to ensure AI outputs align with specified human values and principles
- **Harmlessness Training:** RLHF and other techniques to reduce harmful output generation
- **Helpfulness Optimization:** Training to maximize useful and constructive responses while minimizing harmful ones
- **Truthfulness Enhancement:** Systems designed to improve factual accuracy and reduce hallucination
- **Respectfulness Training:** Ensuring outputs maintain appropriate tone and respect for all users

2.5.6.4 Business Logic and Integration Layers

Organizational Policy Enforcement:

- **Business Rule Application:** Post-processing that applies organization-specific policies and constraints
- **Compliance Integration:** Systems that ensure AI outputs meet regulatory and legal requirements

- **Process Automation:** Integration with broader business processes that may modify or contextualize AI outputs
- **Approval Workflows:** Human-in-the-loop systems that review AI outputs before final deployment
- **Audit Trail Generation:** Logging and documentation systems that track decision-making processes

Output Transformation Layers:

- **Format Conversion:** Systems that transform AI outputs into required formats for downstream consumption
- **Aggregation Logic:** Components that combine multiple AI outputs or integrate with other data sources
- **Threshold Application:** Business rules that convert continuous AI outputs into discrete business decisions
- **Personalization Layers:** Systems that customize AI outputs based on user characteristics or preferences
- **Presentation Formatting:** User interface components that affect how AI outputs are displayed and interpreted

2.5.6.5 Forensic Investigation Complexity

Multi-Component Evidence:

- **Component-Level Analysis:** Each AI component requires investigation using appropriate techniques for its type
- **Integration Evidence:** Logs and configurations showing how components interact and share information
- **Meta-Level Decisions:** Evidence about which components are used when and why for different situations
- **Emergent Behavior:** System-level behavior that emerges from component interactions rather than individual components
- **Failure Propagation:** How problems in one component affect overall system behavior and other components

Interaction Analysis:

- **Data Flow Tracking:** Following data through multiple processing stages and transformation points
- **Decision Fusion:** Understanding how multiple predictions are combined into final system outputs
- **Conflict Resolution:** How the system handles disagreement between components or contradictory outputs
- **Performance Attribution:** Determining which components contribute to overall system performance and failures
- **Bias Amplification:** How biases from individual components combine or interact to create system-level bias patterns

2.5.6.6 Investigation Strategy Framework

Hybrid System Investigation Approach:

1. **Component Identification:**
    - Map all AI components and their types with detailed architectural documentation
    - Identify integration points and data flows between components
    - Document decision fusion mechanisms and conflict resolution strategies
2. **Individual Component Analysis:**
    - Apply appropriate investigation techniques for each component type
    - Collect component-specific evidence using relevant forensic methods
    - Analyze component-level bias and performance characteristics
3. **Integration Analysis:**
    - Examine component interaction logs and communication patterns
    - Test integration point behavior under various conditions
    - Analyze decision fusion for bias amplification or mitigation effects
4. **System-Level Analysis:**
    - Test overall system behavior and performance characteristics
    - Compare system performance to individual component performance
    - Identify emergent behaviors not present in individual components
5. **Correlation Analysis:**
    - Map relationships between component evidence and system-level outcomes
    - Identify system-level patterns that emerge from component interactions
    - Trace end-to-end decision pathways through the complete system

2.6 SYSTEM ARCHITECTURE AND TECHNICAL INFRASTRUCTURE

Understanding the technical infrastructure that supports AI systems is essential for forensic investigation because it determines where evidence resides, how it can be accessed, and what preservation challenges investigators will face. Modern AI systems operate within complex distributed architectures that span multiple storage systems, computational resources, and operational platforms, each creating different types of evidence and requiring different collection strategies.

The infrastructure supporting AI systems has evolved from simple single-server deployments to sophisticated distributed architectures capable of handling massive datasets and computational workloads. This evolution creates both opportunities and challenges for forensic investigators: while modern systems generate more comprehensive logs and artifacts, they also distribute evidence across multiple platforms, storage systems, and geographical locations that may require coordinated collection efforts.

2.6.1 Data Storage and Management Through the Investigation Lens

Data storage and management systems form the foundation of every AI system, determining how training data, model artifacts, and operational logs are organized, preserved, and accessed. The choice of storage architecture affects not just system performance, but also what evidence can be collected, how it can be verified, and what temporal analysis is possible during forensic investigations.

2.6.1.1 Centralized Storage Architectures in Practice

Centralized storage systems concentrate data management in unified platforms that provide consistent access controls, backup procedures, and data governance policies. These systems offer significant advantages for forensic investigation because they centralize evidence collection and provide unified audit trails.

Data lakes represent large-scale storage systems that accommodate diverse data types in their native formats, creating comprehensive repositories of raw information that investigators can analyze systematically. When forensic investigators encounter data lakes, they gain access to comprehensive metadata about data lineage and transformation processes that reveals how information flows through the AI system. The evidence generated includes raw data files with complete provenance information, detailed processing logs that document every transformation, comprehensive access patterns showing who accessed what data when, and transformation histories that enable investigators to understand exactly how raw data became training data.

Data warehouses provide structured storage systems optimized for analytical queries and reporting, offering investigators access to processed datasets with detailed schemas and transformation logs. The forensic value emerges through detailed schemas that document how data is organized and what transformations have been applied, transformation logs that provide complete audit trails of data processing, query histories that reveal how data has been accessed and analyzed, and data quality reports that document known issues or limitations affecting the data.

Feature stores serve as specialized systems for managing machine learning features with versioning and lineage capabilities that prove invaluable for forensic analysis. These systems document feature engineering decisions and temporal evolution, providing investigators with feature definitions that explain exactly what information the AI system uses for decision-making, transformation code that can be analyzed for bias or errors, version histories that enable temporal analysis of how features have changed, and usage statistics that reveal which features are most important for system decisions.

Model registries function as centralized repositories for managing model artifacts and deployment information, creating complete audit trails of model lifecycle and approval workflows. Investigators benefit from access to model versions with complete deployment histories, performance metrics that document how well models perform across different populations, deployment configurations that reveal how models are actually used in production, and approval records that show what review processes were followed before deployment.

Artifact repositories provide version-controlled storage for training scripts and experimental results, documenting complete development history and decision-making processes. The forensic evidence includes code changes with complete revision histories, configuration files that document how systems were set up, experiment logs that show what approaches were tried and why they were rejected, and dependency tracking that reveals what external components influence system behavior.

2.6.1.2 Distributed Storage Complexities and Evidence Challenges

Distributed storage systems spread data across multiple nodes and locations to achieve scalability and fault tolerance that exceed centralized system capabilities. While these systems enable large-scale AI operations, they create additional complexity for forensic investigators who coordinate evidence collection across multiple locations and understand distributed consistency models.

Distributed file systems like Hadoop Distributed File System (HDFS) partition large datasets across clusters, creating forensic challenges related to data distribution across multiple nodes and complex replication patterns. Investigators can collect distributed metadata that documents how data is partitioned, replication logs that show how data is duplicated for fault tolerance, node health records that reveal system reliability, and data placement decisions that may affect system performance and behavior.

NoSQL databases designed for scale and flexibility present forensic challenges including flexible schemas that change over time, eventual consistency that means data may be temporarily inconsistent, and distributed transactions that span multiple systems. The evidence types include document versions that show how data structures evolve, consistency logs that document when data becomes synchronized, distributed query patterns that reveal how the system accesses information, and schema evolution records that show how data organization changes over time.

Object storage systems optimized for large-scale cloud-based data access provide comprehensive access logs and global distribution tracking that prove valuable for forensic analysis. Investigators can access detailed access patterns showing who accessed what data when and from where, geographic distribution information that reveals where data is stored and processed, version histories that document changes to stored objects, and permission changes that show how access controls have evolved.

Content delivery networks create distributed caching systems that affect AI output delivery, introducing forensic considerations around geographic caching decisions and content availability variations. The evidence includes cache hit-and-miss patterns that reveal performance optimizations, geographic performance data that shows how users in different locations experience the system, and content modification logs that document changes to cached information.

Edge storage systems provide local storage at edge computing locations for reduced latency, creating forensic challenges around distributed evidence locations and varying jurisdiction requirements. Investigators can collect local processing logs that document edge-specific behavior, data residency records that show where sensitive information is stored, and edge-specific user interactions that may differ from centralized processing.

2.6.1.3 Specialized Storage Systems and AI-Specific Evidence

Specialized storage systems address specific AI requirements that general-purpose storage cannot efficiently handle. These systems often contain the most AI-specific evidence but require specialized knowledge to analyze effectively.

Vector databases optimize high-dimensional storage for similarity search and retrieval, providing forensic significance through revealing how AI systems understand relationships between data points. The evidence includes similarity scores that show how the system compares different inputs, indexing structures that reveal how information is organized for retrieval, embedding vectors that represent how the system understands different concepts, and search patterns that document what information the system retrieves for different queries.

Time series databases specialize in temporal data storage with efficient querying capabilities, enabling forensic applications including temporal bias analysis, seasonal effects assessment, and long-term trend impact evaluation. Investigators can access temporal aggregations that show how data changes over time, trend calculations that reveal long-term patterns, seasonal patterns that may affect system behavior differently at different times, and anomaly detection results that highlight unusual events.

Graph databases optimize storage for complex relationship data and network analysis, providing forensic value through understanding how AI systems navigate information networks. The evidence types include relationship metadata that documents connections between entities, traversal patterns that show how the system explores relationships, network analysis results that reveal important connections, and connection weights that indicate the strength of different relationships.

Streaming platforms manage real-time data processing for continuous data flows, enabling forensic applications for analyzing AI adaptation to changing conditions over time. Investigators can examine stream processing logs that document real-time decision-making, real-time decision patterns that reveal how systems respond to live data, and data velocity metrics that show how quickly information flows through the system.

Cache systems provide high-speed storage for frequently accessed data and computed results, creating forensic considerations around performance optimizations that might influence decision-making. The evidence includes cache hit patterns that reveal what information is accessed most frequently, eviction policies that show how the system manages limited cache space, and performance impact measurements that document how caching affects system behavior.

2.6.2 Computational Infrastructure and Evidence Generation

The computational infrastructure supporting AI systems determines system capabilities, performance characteristics, and the types of evidence generated during training and inference operations. Understanding these computational architectures is essential because different infrastructure choices create different logging patterns, artifact types, and evidence preservation challenges.

2.6.2.1 Training Infrastructure and Evidence Generation Patterns

Training infrastructure represents the computational backbone that enables AI systems to learn from data. The scale and complexity of modern AI training creates extensive evidence trails that can provide detailed insights into system development and behavior.

GPU clusters serve as specialized hardware for parallel matrix operations and neural network training, generating comprehensive evidence through resource allocation logs that document how computational resources are distributed across training tasks. Investigators can analyze utilization patterns that reveal whether adequate resources were allocated for thorough training, training performance metrics that show how efficiently the system learned, and hardware-specific behavior patterns that may affect model development. The forensic applications include verifying training completion by examining resource usage patterns and identifying hardware-related biases that might emerge from uneven resource allocation.

CPU farms provide general-purpose computing for traditional machine learning algorithms and data processing, creating different evidence patterns through system logs that document general computational activities, job scheduling records that show how tasks are prioritized and executed, and resource utilization statistics that reveal computational bottlenecks. The forensic applications focus on feature engineering analysis to understand how input data is transformed and data preprocessing verification to ensure data handling meets expectations.

Tensor processing units (TPUs) represent Google's optimized hardware for specific AI workloads, generating TPU-specific performance logs that document specialized processing characteristics, optimization metrics that show how well the system utilizes specialized hardware, and hardware utilization patterns unique to tensor processing architectures. These systems prove particularly valuable for Google Cloud Platform investigations and hardware-specific behavior analysis that may not be apparent with other computational approaches.

Cloud platforms provide scalable computing resources from major cloud providers, creating evidence through resource allocation records that document how computational capacity is distributed, billing information that reveals usage patterns and cost optimization decisions, and service interaction logs that show how different cloud services work together. The forensic applications include multi-tenant environment analysis to understand how shared resources might affect system behavior and cost-based behavior verification to determine whether financial constraints influenced system development.

Edge computing delivers local processing capabilities for reduced latency and improved privacy, generating local processing logs that document edge-specific behavior, geographic performance data that shows how location affects system performance, and network interaction records that reveal communication patterns between edge and central systems. The forensic applications include location-specific behavior analysis to understand geographic variations and privacy compliance verification to ensure data handling meets regulatory requirements.

2.6.2.2 Infrastructure Orchestration and Coordination Evidence

Modern AI systems rely on sophisticated orchestration systems that manage distributed workloads and coordinate complex processing pipelines. These systems generate detailed evidence about how computational resources are allocated and how different system components interact.

Container orchestration systems like Kubernetes manage distributed workloads across multiple machines, providing complete container lifecycle documentation that shows how different system components are deployed and managed. The evidence value includes resource allocation decisions that reveal how computational capacity is distributed, deployment patterns that show how system architecture evolves over time, and configuration drift detection that identifies when systems diverge from intended configurations. Investigation applications focus on understanding deployment patterns that may affect system behavior and identifying configuration drift that could introduce unexpected behaviors or vulnerabilities.

Workflow management systems coordinate complex AI pipeline operations through platforms like Airflow and Kubeflow, generating detailed execution logs that document every step of data processing and model training. The evidence value includes dependency tracking that shows how different components depend on each other, error-handling records that document how systems respond to failures, and pipeline performance metrics that reveal bottlenecks or inefficiencies. Investigation applications include tracing data flow problems to understand how information moves through the system and identifying pipeline bottlenecks that may affect system performance or reliability.

Resource scheduling systems allocate computing resources based on priority and availability, creating evidence through scheduling decisions that show how computational tasks are prioritized, resource competition logs that document conflicts between different workloads, and priority enforcement records that reveal how the system manages competing demands. The investigation applications focus on understanding resource constraints that might affect AI behavior and identifying situations where resource limitations could create systematic biases or performance problems.

Auto-scaling systems provide dynamic resource allocation based on workload demands, generating scaling decision logs that document when and why additional resources are allocated, performance threshold triggers that show what conditions cause scaling events, and resource allocation changes that reveal how system capacity adapts to demand. The investigation applications include analyzing consistency under variable computational resources to understand whether system behavior changes when resource availability fluctuates.

Fault tolerance mechanisms handle hardware failures and ensure training continuity, creating evidence through failure detection logs that document system problems, recovery procedures that show how systems respond to failures, and checkpoint restoration records that reveal how training processes resume after interruptions. The investigation applications focus on verifying training integrity after infrastructure problems to ensure that system failures do not compromise model development.

2.6.2.3 Inference Infrastructure and Production Evidence Patterns

Inference infrastructure handles the deployment and serving of trained AI models for production use, generating different types of evidence than training infrastructure and requiring different investigative approaches focused on real-world system behavior and user interactions.

Model serving platforms specialize in deploying and serving trained models for production use, generating inference request logs that document every interaction with the system, response time metrics that show how quickly the system responds to different types of requests, and model version tracking that enables investigators to understand exactly which model version was used for specific decisions. The forensic applications include production bias analysis to identify discriminatory patterns in real-world usage, performance verification to ensure systems meet promised capabilities, and version consistency analysis to verify that the deployed system matches documented specifications.

API gateways manage access to AI services and enforce security policies, creating evidence through access control logs that document who can use the system and how, rate limiting records that show how the system manages usage limits, and authentication audit trails that provide accountability for system access. The forensic applications include usage pattern analysis to understand how different users interact with the system, security compliance verification to ensure access controls work as intended, and access accountability to determine who was responsible for specific system interactions.

Load balancers distribute traffic across multiple system instances to ensure scalability and availability, generating traffic distribution logs that show how requests are routed across different system components, instance health monitoring data that documents system reliability, and failover records that show how the system responds to component failures. The forensic applications include consistency verification across model instances to ensure all system components behave identically and traffic bias analysis to determine whether routing decisions might create systematic advantages or disadvantages for different users.

Caching layers store frequently requested predictions or intermediate results to improve system performance, creating evidence through cache performance logs that document hit and miss rates, hit and miss patterns that reveal what information is accessed most frequently, and eviction policy records that show how the system manages limited cache space. The forensic applications focus on understanding performance optimization impacts on AI behavior, particularly whether caching decisions might create different experiences for different users or whether cache policies could introduce systematic biases.

Monitoring systems provide real-time tracking of system performance, accuracy, and resource utilization, generating comprehensive performance metrics that document how well the system works over time, accuracy measurements that show whether system performance meets expectations, and resource utilization trends that reveal how system demands change over time. The forensic applications include anomaly detection to identify unusual system behavior, performance degradation analysis to understand how system capabilities change over time, and behavior baseline establishment to determine normal operating parameters.

2.6.2.4 Performance Optimization Technologies and Their Forensic Implications

Modern inference systems employ various optimization techniques that can affect system behavior in ways that have forensic significance.

Model quantization techniques reduce model size and improve inference speed but may introduce forensic considerations around potential accuracy impacts from model compression. The evidence types include quantization parameters that document how models are compressed, accuracy comparison metrics that show how compression affects performance, and performance improvements that reveal the benefits and costs of optimization. Investigators should understand whether optimization techniques introduce systematic changes in how the system treats different types of inputs.

Pruning systems remove unnecessary model parameters while attempting to preserve performance, creating forensic considerations around understanding which model components were removed and why. The evidence includes pruning criteria that document decision-making about what to remove, removed parameter logs that show exactly what was eliminated, and performance impact assessments that measure how pruning affects system behavior.

Hardware acceleration through specialized inference chips and optimized software stacks creates forensic considerations around hardware-specific behavior that might affect investigation outcomes. The evidence types include hardware utilization logs that document how specialized processors are used, acceleration performance metrics that show optimization benefits, and optimization settings that reveal how hardware capabilities are configured.

Batch processing systems efficiently handle multiple requests together, creating forensic applications around understanding how batching affects individual request processing. The evidence includes batch composition logs that show how requests are grouped together, processing order records that document how requests are prioritized within batches, and timing correlations that reveal how batch processing affects response times for individual users.

Stream processing systems provide real-time inference for continuous data streams, enabling forensic applications for analyzing real-time decision patterns and temporal consistency. The evidence includes stream processing logs that document real-time system behavior, real-time performance metrics that show how the system handles continuous data, and data flow records that reveal how information moves through streaming systems.

2.7 OPERATIONAL INFRASTRUCTURE AND EVIDENCE COLLECTION

The operational infrastructure surrounding AI systems creates the foundation for comprehensive forensic investigation through systematic monitoring, logging, and evidence preservation. Understanding how these systems generate, capture, and preserve evidence enables investigators to reconstruct system behavior, identify problematic patterns, and establish accountability for AI system decisions.

2.7.1 Monitoring and Logging Systems as Evidence Generators

Effective forensic investigation depends on comprehensive monitoring and logging systems that capture the full spectrum of AI system behavior from training through production deployment. These systems operate continuously, generating the evidence trails that investigators rely on to understand system performance, identify bias patterns, and reconstruct decision-making processes.

2.7.1.1 Performance Monitoring Through the Evidence Collection Process

Performance monitoring systems generate quantitative evidence about AI system capabilities and behavior patterns that prove essential for forensic analysis. The monitoring process begins with resource utilization tracking that captures CPU, memory, disk, and network usage patterns during both training and inference operations. This comprehensive resource monitoring provides investigators with detailed evidence about whether adequate computational resources were allocated for thorough model development, whether resource constraints during production might affect system performance differently for different users, and whether unusual resource usage patterns might indicate tampering or system compromise.

Throughput metrics extend performance monitoring to capture system capacity under varying load conditions through requests per second measurements that document how many interactions the system can handle, batch processing rates that show how efficiently the system handles grouped operations, and system capacity measurements that reveal maximum operational limits. These metrics enable investigators to assess whether performance claims match operational reality, identify periods when resource constraints might have affected system behavior, and understand whether throughput limitations might create systematic disadvantages for certain user groups.

Latency measurements provide direct evidence of user experience through response times that document how quickly the system responds to different types of requests, processing delays that reveal internal system bottlenecks, and user experience metrics that show how performance affects actual usage patterns. This latency evidence proves particularly valuable for bias investigations because systematic differences in response times between user groups may indicate discriminatory treatment or resource allocation problems.

Error rate monitoring captures system failures, prediction errors, and anomaly detection results that reveal system reliability and potential bias patterns. Error tracking provides investigators with comprehensive documentation of system failures including their frequency, patterns, and impacts on different user populations. This evidence proves essential for understanding whether system failures affect different groups disproportionately and whether error-handling procedures introduce additional bias into system behavior.

Availability metrics document uptime, service availability, and disaster recovery capabilities that affect user access to AI systems. Availability evidence enables investigators to assess whether system downtime affects different user groups differently and whether recovery procedures maintain system fairness and accuracy during restoration processes.

2.7.1.2 AI-Specific Monitoring for Forensic Investigation

Beyond general system performance, AI systems require specialized monitoring that captures behavior patterns unique to machine learning applications. Model performance monitoring tracks accuracy, precision, recall, and other performance metrics over time, providing investigators with evidence about whether system capabilities deteriorate and whether performance changes affect different user groups differently. This monitoring proves essential for identifying concept drift, data drift, and other temporal changes that may introduce bias or reduce system effectiveness.

Data drift detection systems monitor changes in input data distribution that may affect model performance, generating evidence about whether the data the system encounters in production matches the data used for training. Data drift evidence enables investigators to understand whether systematic changes in user populations or usage patterns might cause AI systems to perform differently over time, potentially creating discriminatory outcomes as the system encounters data that differs from its training experience.

Concept drift monitoring tracks changes in the relationship between inputs and outputs over time, providing evidence about whether the fundamental assumptions underlying system training remain valid in production. Concept drift evidence proves crucial for understanding whether AI systems maintain their intended behavior as real-world conditions change and whether these changes might affect different user groups differently.

Bias monitoring provides ongoing assessment of fairness and bias patterns across different user groups through systematic tracking of performance differences, outcome disparities, and demographic impact patterns. This specialized monitoring generates evidence that directly supports discrimination investigations and regulatory compliance assessments by documenting whether AI systems treat different groups fairly over time.

Safety monitoring focuses on detection of harmful outputs, policy violations, and security incidents that may not be captured by general performance metrics. Safety monitoring evidence includes detection of inappropriate content generation, identification of policy violations, and documentation of security incidents that might compromise system integrity or user privacy.

2.7.1.3 Comprehensive Logging Strategy for Forensic Readiness

Effective forensic investigation often involves comprehensive logging strategies that capture all relevant system behavior while preserving evidence integrity and maintaining operational efficiency. The logging architecture balances the need for complete documentation with practical constraints around storage capacity, processing overhead, and privacy protection.

Application logs form the core of forensic evidence through request and response logs that provide complete records of inputs, outputs, and system interactions for every user session. These logs capture sufficient detail to enable reconstruction of individual decisions while protecting sensitive user information and maintaining system performance. The logging strategy should include unique session identifiers that enable tracking of user interactions across multiple system components, timestamps with sufficient precision to enable temporal correlation analysis, input data with appropriate privacy protections to enable bias analysis, output decisions with confidence scores or other metadata that reveals system certainty, and system context information that documents the system state during each interaction.

Error logs provide detailed information about system failures, exceptions, and recovery actions that may reveal bias patterns or system vulnerabilities. Comprehensive error logging includes error classifications that enable systematic analysis of failure patterns, stack traces or other technical details that support root cause analysis, recovery actions that document how the system responds to problems, and impact assessments that show how errors affect user experience.

Performance logs capture timing information, resource usage, and optimization metrics that enable investigators to understand system efficiency and identify potential bias sources related to performance variations. Performance logging should include request processing times broken down by system component, resource utilization patterns that reveal computational bottlenecks, optimization decisions that might affect different users differently, and caching behavior that could create different experiences for different users.

Security logs document authentication events, authorization decisions, and security policy enforcement that provide accountability and access control evidence. Security logging must capture user authentication success and failure patterns, authorization decisions that show who can access what system capabilities, security policy violations that might indicate attempts to compromise system integrity, and access patterns that enable detection of unusual or potentially malicious usage.

Configuration logs track changes to system settings, model parameters, and deployment configurations that affect system behavior over time. Configuration logging provides investigators with complete audit trails of system modifications including what changes were made, who made them, when they occurred, and what authorization processes were followed.

2.7.1.4 Infrastructure Logging for Distributed System Evidence

Modern AI systems operate within complex distributed infrastructures that require coordinated logging strategies to capture evidence across multiple system components, geographic locations, and organizational boundaries.

System logs capture operating system events, hardware status, and resource allocation decisions that provide the foundation for understanding how AI systems interact with underlying infrastructure. System logging documents hardware failures that might affect AI system behavior, operating system events that provide context for application behavior, resource allocation decisions that might create performance differences, and network events that affect system communication and data access.

Network logs track traffic patterns, communication protocols, and security events that reveal how different system components interact and how user requests flow through distributed architectures. Network logging enables investigators to understand data flow patterns, identify communication bottlenecks, detect security incidents, and reconstruct the path of information through complex systems.

Database logs record data access patterns, query performance, and transaction records that provide evidence about how AI systems interact with underlying data storage. Database logging captures data access patterns that might reveal bias in information retrieval, query performance variations that could affect different users differently, transaction records that enable reconstruction of data modifications, and schema changes that might affect system behavior over time.

Container logs document application container lifecycle events, resource consumption, and orchestration decisions that affect how AI applications are deployed and managed. Container logging provides evidence about deployment configurations, resource allocation decisions, scaling events that might affect system performance, and container communication patterns that reveal system architecture.

Cloud platform logs capture service usage, billing information, and platform-specific events that provide evidence about how AI systems utilize cloud infrastructure. Cloud logging enables investigators to understand resource utilization patterns, cost optimization decisions that might affect system behavior, service integration patterns that could introduce bias or vulnerabilities, and geographic distribution decisions that might affect different user populations differently.

2.7.2 Model-Related Evidence and Artifact Preservation

The preservation and management of model-related evidence requires specialized approaches that maintain the integrity of complex digital artifacts while enabling comprehensive forensic analysis. Model artifacts exist in various formats and locations, requiring systematic collection and preservation strategies that account for their technical complexity and legal significance.

2.7.2.1 Model Artifacts and Their Forensic Significance

Parameter files represent the core learned knowledge of AI systems through binary files containing learned weights in various formats including PyTorch (.pt), Keras (.h5), and SafeTensors (.safetensors) formats. These files encode the complete decision-making capability of AI systems, making them critical evidence for understanding system behavior and identifying bias patterns. Forensic preservation of parameter files requires maintaining bit-exact copies with cryptographic verification, preserving metadata about model architecture and training procedures, documenting the relationship between different model versions, and ensuring compatibility with analysis tools that can interpret different file formats.

Architecture definitions provide the structural blueprint of AI systems through code or configuration files that define model structure and components. These definitions reveal how information flows through the system, what types of processing occur at each stage, and what design decisions were made during system development. Architecture evidence includes neural network layer definitions that show how information is processed, connection patterns that reveal information flow, activation function choices that affect system behavior, and optimization objectives that influenced model training.

Hyperparameter configurations document the training settings and optimization choices that shaped model development. These configurations provide evidence about whether appropriate training procedures were followed, whether training settings might introduce bias, and whether the training process was likely to produce reliable models. Hyperparameter evidence includes learning rates that affect training speed and quality, batch sizes that influence training stability, regularization parameters that prevent overfitting, and optimization algorithm choices that affect model convergence.

Training scripts and experimental configurations provide complete documentation of the model development process through code that implements training procedures, configuration files that specify training parameters, and experimental logs that document what approaches were attempted. This evidence enables investigators to understand exactly how models were developed, what alternatives were considered, and whether appropriate validation procedures were followed.

Checkpoint files preserve intermediate model states during training, enabling investigators to understand how models evolved and whether training procedures followed expected patterns. Checkpoint evidence includes intermediate model weights that show training progress, optimizer states that reveal training dynamics, validation scores that document performance evolution, and training metadata that provides context about training conditions.

2.7.2.2 Evidence Chain Preservation for Model Artifacts

Maintaining the integrity of model artifacts requires sophisticated chain of custody procedures that account for the technical complexity of AI systems while meeting legal standards for evidence preservation. The preservation process needs to ensure that model artifacts remain unchanged, that their relationships to other system components are maintained, and that sufficient metadata is captured to enable comprehensive analysis.

Cryptographic verification forms the foundation of model artifact preservation through hash values that detect any changes to model files, digital signatures that verify authenticity, and checksums that enable integrity verification. The verification process accounts for the binary nature of model files, the potential for format conversion during analysis, and the need to maintain verification across different storage systems and analysis platforms.

Version control integration ensures that model artifacts are preserved with complete historical context through repository systems that track model evolution, branching structures that show experimental directions, and merge histories that document how different development efforts were integrated. Version control evidence enables investigators to understand when changes were made, who was responsible for different modifications, and what validation processes were followed for different model versions.

Metadata preservation captures essential information about model context including training data descriptions, performance benchmarks, validation procedures, and deployment configurations. Metadata should be preserved in structured formats that enable systematic analysis while maintaining the relationships between different types of information.

Access control documentation tracks who has accessed model artifacts and what actions they have performed, providing accountability and detecting potential tampering. Access logs should include user identification, timestamp information, action descriptions, and authorization validation to enable comprehensive audit trails.

2.7.2.3 Training Data Provenance and Lineage Evidence

Understanding the complete lineage of training data proves essential for forensic investigation because data quality and representativeness issues often underlie AI system failures. Data provenance evidence allows you to trace information flow from original sources through all transformation processes to final model inputs.

Data source documentation provides evidence about where training data originated, including external data sources with licensing terms and usage restrictions, internal data sources with access controls and privacy considerations, real-time data feeds with update frequencies and quality monitoring, and synthetic data with generation procedures and validation methods. Source documentation enables investigators to understand whether data collection procedures might introduce bias and whether data usage complies with legal and ethical requirements.

Transformation pipeline evidence documents how raw data becomes training data through preprocessing procedures, feature engineering logic, data cleaning operations, and quality validation steps. Pipeline evidence reveals potential sources of bias introduction and enables investigators to understand whether data processing procedures treat different groups fairly.

Validation dataset evidence documents how model performance was assessed including test data selection procedures, validation methodology descriptions, cross-validation strategies, and performance measurement approaches. Validation evidence enables investigators to assess whether performance testing was adequate and whether validation procedures might mask bias or other performance problems.

Data quality metrics provide evidence about the completeness, accuracy, and representativeness of training data through missing data patterns, outlier detection results, bias assessment reports, and coverage analysis across different demographic groups. Quality metrics enable investigators to understand whether training data was adequate for the intended application and whether data limitations might affect system performance for different user populations.

2.7.3 Security and Access Control Evidence

Security and access control systems generate critical evidence for forensic investigations by documenting who has access to AI systems, how that access is used, and whether security controls function as intended. This evidence proves essential for establishing accountability, detecting unauthorized access, and understanding whether security vulnerabilities might affect system behavior.

2.7.3.1 Authentication and Authorization Evidence Trails

Authentication systems provide the foundation for accountability by documenting who accesses AI systems and when those access events occur. Authentication evidence includes login attempts with success and failure patterns that may reveal unauthorized access attempts, multi-factor authentication usage that provides stronger identity verification, session management that tracks user activity over time, and password policy compliance that affects security posture.

Authorization systems control what authenticated users can do within AI systems, generating evidence about permission structures, access decisions, and policy enforcement. Authorization evidence includes role-based access controls that show what capabilities different users possess, permission changes that document how access evolves over time, policy violations that may indicate security incidents, and privilege escalation events that require special attention during investigations.

API access controls manage programmatic access to AI systems through service accounts, rate limiting, and usage monitoring. API evidence includes service account usage patterns that reveal automated system interactions, rate limiting enforcement that shows how usage controls function, API key management that affects access accountability, and endpoint access patterns that reveal how different system components interact.

Single sign-on (SSO) integration affects how users authenticate across multiple systems, creating evidence about user identity federation, cross-system access patterns, and authentication policy consistency. SSO evidence enables investigators to understand user access patterns across complex system ecosystems while maintaining accountability across organizational boundaries.

2.7.3.2 Audit Trail Generation and Preservation

Comprehensive audit trails provide detailed documentation of user actions, system changes, and administrative activities that affect AI system behavior. Audit trail generation should balance the need for complete documentation with practical constraints around storage capacity and system performance.

User activity logging captures individual user interactions with AI systems through request logs that document what users ask the system to do, response logs that show how the system responds to user requests, session tracking that enables reconstruction of user interaction patterns, and behavioral analytics that identify unusual usage patterns requiring investigation.

Administrative action logging documents system changes and configuration modifications through privilege usage that shows when administrative capabilities are exercised, configuration changes that affect system behavior, user management actions that modify access controls, and system maintenance activities that might affect system performance or security.

Data access logging tracks how users and systems interact with underlying data through database query logs that show what information is accessed, file access logs that document data retrieval patterns, data modification logs that track changes to training or reference data, and data export logs that show when sensitive information leaves the system.

System modification logging captures changes to AI system components through model deployment logs that document when new models are put into production, parameter changes that affect system behavior, infrastructure modifications that might affect system performance, and security configuration changes that affect access controls or monitoring capabilities.

2.7.3.3 Security Incident Detection and Response Evidence

Security monitoring systems generate evidence about potential threats, attacks, and compromises that might affect AI system integrity. This evidence proves essential for understanding whether security incidents might have affected investigation results or whether AI systems might have been deliberately manipulated.

Anomaly detection systems identify unusual patterns in user behavior, system access, or AI system outputs that might indicate security incidents. Anomaly evidence includes behavioral baselines that define normal activity patterns, deviation alerts that identify unusual activity, investigation results that document how anomalies are resolved, and false positive tracking that shows monitoring system accuracy.

Intrusion detection systems monitor network traffic and system access for signs of unauthorized activity. Intrusion detection evidence includes network traffic analysis that reveals communication patterns, access attempt monitoring that identifies potential unauthorized access, malware detection that protects system integrity, and vulnerability assessments that identify potential security weaknesses.

Incident response procedures generate evidence about how organizations detect, investigate, and resolve security incidents affecting AI systems. Incident response evidence includes incident classification that shows how different types of problems are categorized, response timelines that document how quickly incidents are addressed, containment actions that show how threats are mitigated, and recovery procedures that restore normal operations.

Security assessment results provide evidence about overall system security posture through penetration testing that identifies vulnerabilities, compliance audits that verify security control effectiveness, risk assessments that evaluate potential threats, and remediation tracking that shows how security issues are addressed.

This comprehensive operational infrastructure provides the foundation for effective forensic investigation by ensuring that all relevant evidence is captured, preserved, and made available for analysis. The systematic approach to monitoring, logging, and security enables investigators to reconstruct system behavior, identify problematic patterns, and establish accountability for AI system decisions while maintaining the evidence integrity necessary for legal and regulatory proceedings.

2.8 CONCLUSION

This comprehensive overview of AI systems provides the technical foundation necessary for effective forensic investigation. Understanding the architecture, components, and operational characteristics of different AI system types enables investigators to:

- **Rapidly classify** unfamiliar AI systems using the forensic decision framework
- **Identify relevant evidence sources** based on system architecture and components
- **Plan appropriate collection strategies** matching technical infrastructure to investigation needs
- **Navigate modern complexities** including LLMs, RAG systems, and hybrid architectures
- **Understand operational context** including data flows, computational requirements, and security considerations

The figures and technical details provided serve as practical references during active investigations. When encountering an unfamiliar AI system, return to the classification framework and component analysis guides to quickly orient your investigation approach.

In Chapter 3, we will build on this technical foundation to address the human element of AI forensic investigation: gathering knowledge from stakeholders, understanding organizational context, and scoping investigations effectively. The system types and technical components identified in this chapter will inform stakeholder identification and knowledge-gathering strategies.

The investment you make in understanding AI system architecture and components will pay dividends throughout your investigation. Technical complexity should not intimidate—with the right framework and systematic approach, even the most sophisticated AI systems can be effectively investigated and understood.

3 Knowledge Gathering and Scoping

3.1 FROM INITIAL ISSUE TO INVESTIGATION FRAMEWORK: BUILDING UNDERSTANDING THROUGH HUMAN INTELLIGENCE

When a healthcare AI system began recommending unnecessary procedures, investigators did not start by analyzing algorithms or examining training data—they began by talking to people. Radiologists revealed that the system's confidence scores did not match their clinical experience. Data scientists disclosed preprocessing decisions made months earlier under tight deadlines. Hospital administrators explained workflow pressures that affected how recommendations were being interpreted and applied. Only after gathering this human intelligence could investigators determine what technical evidence to collect and how to analyze it meaningfully.

When a financial services AI started producing inconsistent loan decisions, the path to understanding did not begin with model analysis. It started with underwriters explaining how they expected the system to work, data engineers describing what preprocessing steps were actually implemented, and compliance officers revealing concerns raised in previous internal audits. The gap between intention, implementation, and application only became clear through systematic knowledge gathering from individuals across the organization.

3.2 WHAT YOU WILL LEARN

By the end of this chapter, you will be able to:

- Conduct structured interviews that reveal critical system context, undocumented practices, and tacit knowledge
- Systematically discover and prioritize documentation across formal repositories and informal sources
- Transform initial incident notifications into comprehensive investigation frameworks through iterative scope refinement
- Navigate the complex socio-technical relationships that characterize modern AI systems
- Build and maintain key personnel contacts that provide ongoing investigation support throughout technical analysis
- Synthesize human intelligence from multiple sources into actionable technical investigation plans

3.3 QUICK START GUIDE

- **Investigation planning confusion?** → Start with AI-Specific Objectives for Knowledge Gathering and Scoping (Section 3.6)
- **Missing documentation?** → Go to AI Bill of Materials and Critical Documentation Framework (Section 3.7)
- **Unknown system complexity and scope?** → See AI System Classification and Comprehensive Scoping Framework (Section 3.8)

DOI: 10.1201/9781003634782-3

- **Interview confusion?** → Start with Personnel Engagement and Interview Strategies (Section 3.9)
- **Complex system dependencies?** → Iterative Investigation Framework and Knowledge Integration (Section 3.10)
- **Investigation integrity concerns?** → Review Quality Assurance and Validation (Section 3.12)

3.4 IMPORTANT DISCLAIMER

Knowledge gathering in AI investigations is inherently contextual and requires careful adaptation to specific organizational cultures, system architectures, and investigation contexts. The interview techniques, documentation strategies, and synthesis approaches presented here provide frameworks that must be tailored to particular situations. No two AI systems, organizations, or incidents are identical. Always consider legal privilege implications, confidentiality requirements, and regulatory constraints when gathering information, and consult qualified counsel when litigation is anticipated or ongoing.

3.5 THE EVOLUTION OF INVESTIGATION SCOPE

AI forensic investigations rarely follow the scope originally envisioned at the outset. What begins as a straightforward model performance issue often reveals complex organizational, technical, and regulatory challenges requiring comprehensive multi-phase investigation. Understanding and managing this scope evolution process is crucial for effective investigation planning and resource allocation.

Figure 3.1 illustrates how investigation scope typically evolves through systematic knowledge-gathering activities. Each phase builds on previous understanding while revealing new areas requiring investigation attention and deeper analysis.

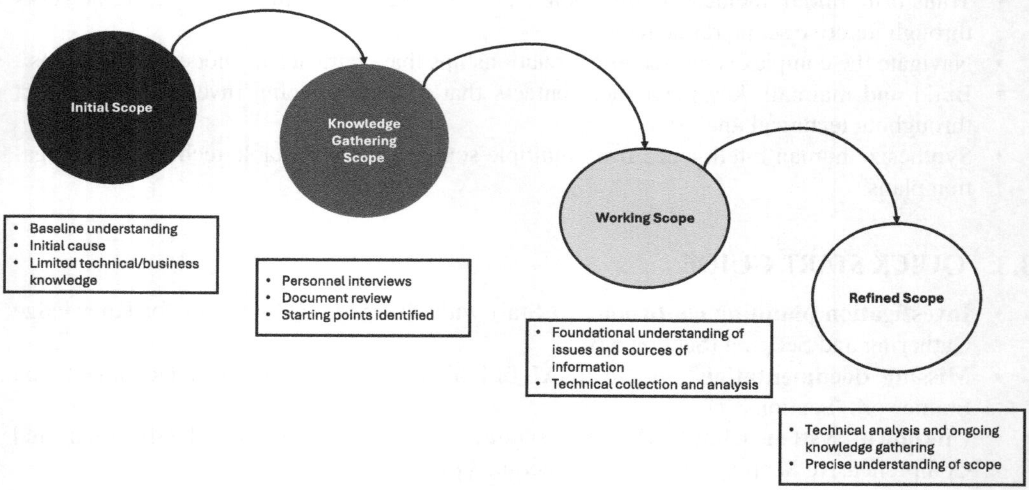

FIGURE 3.1

Initial Scope represents the starting point based on incident reports, complaints, or regulatory notices. At this stage, investigators typically operate under assumptions about narrow technical issues affecting limited systems over relatively short timeframes. The knowledge base consists primarily of baseline understanding derived from incident reports, initial cause hypotheses, and limited technical or business context about the affected systems.

Knowledge-Gathering Scope emerges after structured interviews and systematic document discovery activities. This phase typically reveals previously unknown system dependencies, longer historical timelines than initially assumed, and additional interview groups whose perspectives prove essential for understanding system behavior. The expanded knowledge base now includes interview insights, discovered documentation, and identified starting points for deeper technical investigation.

Working Scope develops as investigators gain foundational understanding of both technical issues and business context through ongoing analysis and validation activities. This phase establishes practical boundaries for evidence collection and technical investigation while acknowledging resource constraints, legal limitations, and investigation timeline requirements that affect what can realistically be accomplished.

Refined Scope represents the comprehensive investigation framework that guides technical evidence collection, analysis priorities, and reporting requirements. This final scope incorporates insights from ongoing knowledge-gathering activities and maintains precise understanding of investigation boundaries, success criteria, stakeholder expectations, and legal or regulatory requirements necessary for effective investigation execution.

This iterative scope evolution reflects the fundamental reality that AI systems are complex socio-technical constructs embedding human decisions, organizational processes, and technical implementations in ways that only become apparent through systematic knowledge gathering. The scope refinement process ensures investigations address the actual issues affecting organizations and stakeholders rather than the simplified problems initially reported while maintaining focus on achievable objectives within available resources and constraints.

3.6 AI-SPECIFIC OBJECTIVES FOR KNOWLEDGE GATHERING AND SCOPING

3.6.1 Foundational Objectives in Forensic Investigations

Traditional forensic investigations operate on well-established principles that guide the collection and analysis of evidence. These foundational objectives provide the framework for all forensic activities, ensuring that investigations maintain legal admissibility, technical rigor, and methodological consistency. In conventional digital forensics, these objectives typically focus on establishing factual timelines, identifying responsible parties, preserving evidence integrity, and documenting findings in a manner suitable for legal proceedings.

The primary objective of establishing factual foundation requires investigators to determine what events occurred, when they happened, who was involved, and what systems or processes were affected. This objective drives systematic evidence collection and analysis designed to create an accurate and complete record of relevant events. In traditional forensics, this often involves analyzing system logs, file timestamps, network traffic, and user activity records to construct chronological sequences of events.

3.6.2 AI-Specific Adaptations and Challenges

AI systems present unique challenges that require adaptation of traditional forensic objectives. Unlike conventional software systems where behavior can often be understood through code analysis, AI systems exhibit emergent behaviors that result from complex interactions between training data, model architecture, and deployment environment. These emergent behaviors cannot be predicted or understood through examination of individual components alone.

The socio-technical nature of AI systems means that human decisions about data collection, model design, validation procedures, and deployment configurations profoundly influence system behavior. Understanding these human elements requires specialized knowledge-gathering approaches that can elicit tacit knowledge, undocumented practices, and organizational context that may not be captured in traditional technical evidence.

3.6.2.1 AI-Specific Investigation Complexities

- **Emergent Behavior Understanding**: AI systems develop behaviors through statistical learning rather than explicit programming, making causation analysis more complex
- **Multi-Disciplinary Teams**: AI development involves diverse expertise areas requiring specialized stakeholder engagement strategies
- **Temporal Complexity**: AI systems evolve continuously through training updates, data refresh cycles, and deployment modifications
- **Scale and Volume**: Modern AI systems process massive datasets and generate extensive operational logs requiring strategic sampling approaches
- **Interpretability Challenges**: Many AI architectures operate as "black boxes" where decision-making processes are not readily interpretable

3.6.3 Investigation-Specific Objective Translation

Each AI forensic investigation must translate these general objectives into specific, measurable goals that guide knowledge-gathering activities and resource allocation decisions. This translation process requires careful consideration of the context, system characteristics, organizational factors, and legal or regulatory requirements that shape the investigation scope.

Hypothesis-driven scoping ensures that knowledge-gathering activities focus on validating or refuting specific theories about potential causes, failure modes, or responsible parties. Rather than conducting unfocused interviews or document collection, investigators develop preliminary hypotheses based on incident characteristics and available information, then design knowledge-gathering activities to test these hypotheses systematically.

Risk-proportionate depth ensures that investigation intensity corresponds to potential impact and risk levels. High-stakes systems that affect safety, civil rights, or significant financial interests warrant

TABLE 3.1
Objective Translation Framework

General Objective	AI-Specific Translation	Knowledge-Gathering Focus	Key Personnel
Establish Facts	Document AI system behavior patterns, training procedures, and deployment configurations	Interview technical teams about system design and operation	Data scientists, ML engineers, operations teams
Determine Causation	Trace relationships between data quality, model decisions, and system outputs	Map data flows and model decision processes	Data engineers, model validators, domain experts
Assess Impact	Evaluate fairness impacts, business consequences, and regulatory violations	Understand affected user populations and business processes	Product managers, compliance officers, user research teams
Preserve Evidence	Secure model artifacts, training data, and operational logs with version control	Identify all system components and their storage locations	DevOps engineers, data platform teams, security teams
Optimize Resources	Focus on high-impact components while managing data volume and complexity	Prioritize system components based on risk and investigative value	Technical leadership, project managers

comprehensive stakeholder interviews and documentation review. Lower-impact systems might require more focused investigation approaches that balance thoroughness with resource constraints.

Stakeholder complexity requires investigators to develop comprehensive engagement strategies that address the interdisciplinary nature of AI development teams. Unlike traditional software development, AI projects typically involve business stakeholders who define success criteria, data scientists who design models and experiments, engineers who implement deployment infrastructure, operational teams who monitor system performance, and compliance professionals who ensure regulatory adherence.

3.7 AI BILL OF MATERIALS AND CRITICAL DOCUMENTATION FRAMEWORK

3.7.1 The AI Bill of Materials Concept

One of the most critical early requests in any AI forensic investigation should be the AI bill of materials (BOM)—a comprehensive inventory that documents all components, dependencies, data sources, and processes that comprise the AI system under investigation. The AI BOM concept, emerging from software supply chain security practices, provides investigators with a systematic map of system complexity that guides subsequent evidence collection and stakeholder engagement activities.

The AI BOM serves multiple forensic purposes that distinguish it from traditional software BOMs. It establishes system boundaries by clearly defining what components are included in the AI system and what external dependencies exist. It identifies data lineage by documenting all data sources, preprocessing pipelines, and transformation processes that affect model behavior. It maps technical dependencies by cataloging all software libraries, frameworks, platforms, and services that support system operation. It documents human responsibilities by identifying who is accountable for different system components and processes.

Unlike traditional software systems where components might be relatively static, AI systems involve dynamic elements that change over time through training updates, data refreshes, and model versioning. The AI BOM must capture these temporal dimensions while providing investigators with current system state and historical evolution understanding. This temporal complexity makes the AI BOM particularly valuable for forensic investigations because it helps investigators understand when changes occurred and who was responsible for different modifications.

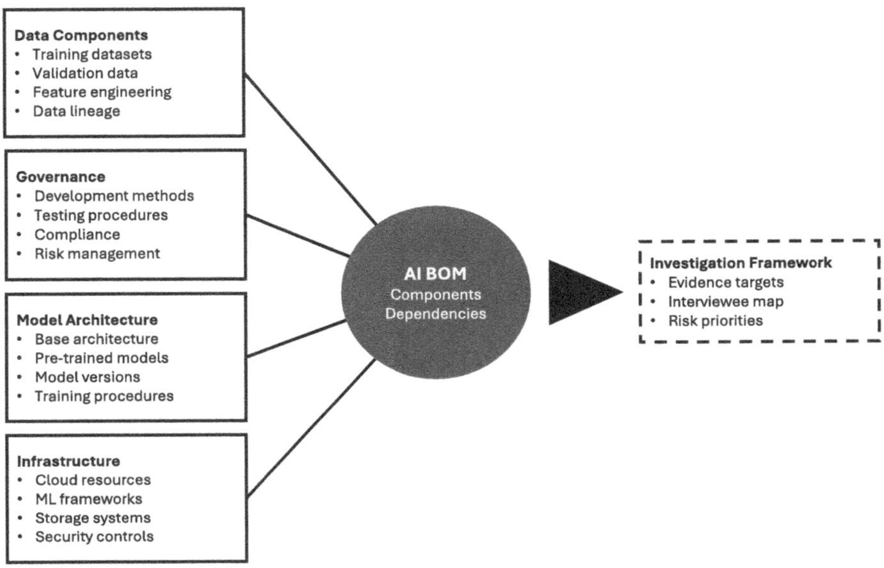

FIGURE 3.2

The AI BOM also addresses the multi-disciplinary nature of AI systems by documenting not just technical components but also organizational processes, governance frameworks, and business logic that influence system behavior. Traditional BOMs focus primarily on technical dependencies, but AI systems embed human decisions about data collection, model design, validation procedures, and deployment configurations that can profoundly affect system behavior.

WHAT IF THE ORGANIZATION DOES NOT HAVE AN AI BOM?

Many organizations, especially those with less mature AI governance practices, may not maintain formal AI bills of materials or may not be familiar with the concept. In these cases, request the following documentation as AI BOM components: system architecture diagrams and technical documentation, data source inventories and data flow diagrams, model development documentation including training procedures and validation reports, deployment and infrastructure documentation covering platforms and dependencies, and governance documentation such as AI policies, ethics reviews, and compliance assessments. Frame these requests as standard information needed for any AI system investigation rather than specialized forensic requirements to encourage cooperation and reduce defensive responses.

3.7.2 Core AI BOM Components

3.7.2.1 Data Components and Lineage

The data portion of the AI BOM represents one of the most critical elements for forensic investigations because data quality and representativeness issues often underlie AI system failures. This section should document all training datasets including source, collection methodology, size, quality metrics, and known limitations. Validation and test datasets must be cataloged with information about how they were selected, what they represent, and how they differ from training data. Feature engineering processes should be documented including transformation logic, feature selection criteria, and any domain-specific preprocessing steps.

Data lineage documentation within the BOM should trace information flow from original sources through all transformation processes to final model inputs. This includes external data sources such as public datasets, purchased data, or partner contributions, along with their licensing terms and usage restrictions. Internal data sources from organizational systems, user interactions, or business processes should be documented with access controls and privacy considerations. Real-time data feeds that provide ongoing input to deployed models should be cataloged with their update frequencies, quality monitoring, and failure handling procedures.

3.7.2.2 Model Components and Architecture

The model section of the AI BOM documents all algorithmic components that comprise the AI system. This includes base model architectures such as neural network designs, decision tree structures, or ensemble configurations. Pre-trained models and transfer learning components should be cataloged with their sources, training data, known biases, and licensing terms. Custom model components developed specifically for the system should be documented with design rationale, development history, and validation results.

Model versioning information becomes particularly important for forensic investigations because it enables investigators to understand when changes were made and how they might have affected system behavior. The BOM should document all model versions deployed in production, training procedures used for each version, performance metrics and validation results for different versions, and rollback procedures and model governance processes.

3.7.2.3 Infrastructure and Platform Dependencies

The infrastructure section documents all technical platforms, services, and tools that support AI system development and operation. Cloud computing resources should be cataloged including compute instances, storage systems, networking configurations, and security controls. Software dependencies should be documented with specific version numbers because different versions can exhibit different behaviors that might affect investigation findings.

Development and deployment tools form another critical component of the infrastructure documentation. Machine learning frameworks, data processing libraries, monitoring and observability tools, and CI/CD pipelines all influence how the AI system operates and what evidence might be available for forensic analysis. Understanding these dependencies helps investigators identify potential evidence sources and assess the reliability of different information types.

3.7.2.4 Governance and Process Documentation

The governance section of the AI BOM documents all organizational processes, policies, and controls that govern AI system development and operation. This includes development methodologies used for AI projects, testing and validation procedures, deployment and change management processes, and incident response and monitoring procedures.

Compliance and risk management documentation becomes particularly important for forensic investigations that involve regulatory violations or ethical concerns. This section should document all applicable regulatory requirements, risk assessment procedures, ethics review processes, and audit and compliance monitoring activities that influence system design and operation.

3.7.3 Documentation Discovery Process

Effective documentation discovery in AI investigations requires systematic approaches that accommodate both formal documentation repositories and informal knowledge sources. Unlike traditional software development where critical information might be concentrated in source code repositories, AI systems often involve documentation scattered across multiple platforms, formats, and organizational silos.

3.7.3.1 Formal Documentation Sources

Begin documentation discovery with systematic review of formal repositories including source code management systems that contain model implementations, training scripts, and configuration files. Project management systems often contain planning documents, requirement specifications, and progress tracking information that provides valuable context about system development. Corporate wikis and knowledge management systems may contain architectural decisions, best practices, and troubleshooting guides that reveal important operational information.

3.7.3.2 Informal Documentation Sources

AI development often involves extensive experimentation and iteration that may not be captured in formal documentation systems. Email communications between team members frequently contain important discussions about design decisions, performance issues, and operational challenges. Chat platforms used for team coordination may contain real-time discussions about problems, solutions, and decision-making processes. Personal notebooks and experiment tracking systems used by data scientists and researchers often contain critical information about model development and validation procedures.

Document quality assessment becomes critical for determining how much weight to give different sources during analysis and synthesis activities. Factors affecting quality include accuracy, completeness, currency, objectivity, and accessibility. High-quality documents that are accurate, complete, current, objective, and accessible can serve as primary evidence sources. Lower-quality documents may provide useful context or raise questions for further investigation but should not be relied upon as authoritative sources.

3.8 AI SYSTEM CLASSIFICATION AND COMPREHENSIVE SCOPING FRAMEWORK

3.8.1 AI System Classification and Investigation Planning

Understanding the type and complexity of the AI system under investigation is the foundation for effective scope definition, resource allocation, and methodological selection. This systematic classification process enables investigators to tailor their approach to the specific technical, organizational, and regulatory challenges presented by different AI system architectures.

3.8.1.1 The AI System Classification Process

Effective classification requires a multi-dimensional assessment that considers technical architecture, deployment context, business criticality, and regulatory environment. This assessment drives all subsequent investigation planning decisions and determines the depth and breadth of knowledge-gathering activities required.

TABLE 3.2
Enhanced AI System Classification Matrix

System Type	Technical Complexity	Key Risk Areas	Critical Personnel	Investigation Focus	Specialized Expertise Required
Traditional ML (linear/tree-based)	Low-medium	Feature bias, data quality	Data scientists, business analysts	Feature engineering bias, statistical validation	Statisticians, domain experts
Deep Learning (neural networks)	High	Black-box decisions, training data bias	ML engineers, research teams	Model interpretability, architecture analysis	DL researchers, interpretability experts
Foundation Models (LLMs/vision)	Very high	Emergent behaviors, alignment issues	AI safety teams, ethics boards	Prompt engineering, safety alignment	AI safety researchers, ethicists
Reinforcement Learning	Very high	Reward hacking, unintended optimization	RL engineers, simulation teams	Reward function analysis, environment design	RL researchers, game theorists
Computer Vision	Medium-high	Demographic bias, adversarial attacks	Vision engineers, annotation teams	Dataset representativeness, edge case handling	Computer vision experts, human factors
NLP Systems	Medium-high	Language bias, cultural assumptions	Linguists, cultural consultants	Corpus bias, cross-cultural validation	Computational linguists, anthropologists
Ensemble/Hybrid	High	Component interactions, cascading failures	Systems architects, integration teams	Inter-component analysis, failure propagation	Systems engineers, reliability experts
Federated Learning	Very high	Privacy leakage, heterogeneous bias	Privacy engineers, distributed systems teams	Cross-client bias, privacy preservation	Privacy researchers, distributed computing experts

3.8.1.2 Step 1: Technical Architecture Assessment

Begin with systematic evaluation of the AI system's technical characteristics using the classification matrix below. This assessment determines the specialized expertise needed and the complexity of technical investigation required.

3.8.1.3 Step 2: Deployment Context Analysis

Assess the operational environment and business context to understand investigation scope and stakeholder complexity:

- **Deployment Scale**: Single-tenant, multi-tenant, global distribution
- **User Impact**: Internal tools, customer-facing, safety-critical
- **Data Sensitivity**: Public data, personal data, protected health information
- **Regulatory Environment**: Healthcare, financial services, hiring, criminal justice
- **Organizational Maturity**: Research prototype, production pilot, enterprise-scale

3.8.1.4 Step 3: Investigation Scope Determination

Use the classification results to determine appropriate investigation scope using this decision framework.

3.8.2 Scope Definition and Risk Assessment Methodologies

Once the AI system is classified, investigators should define precise investigation boundaries and assess risks that could affect investigation success. This process balances thoroughness with resource constraints while ensuring that critical issues are not overlooked.

3.8.2.1 Scope Definition Framework

3.8.2.1.1 Primary Scope Boundaries

Define the core investigation area by establishing clear boundaries:

- **System Components**: Which AI models, data pipelines, and infrastructure components are included
- **Temporal Boundaries**: What time period is relevant (training data collection, model development, deployment period)
- **Stakeholder Groups**: Which organizational roles and external parties must be engaged
- **Business Processes**: Which organizational workflows and decision-making processes are affected
- **Geographic Scope**: Which jurisdictions, data centers, or user populations are relevant

TABLE 3.3
Scope Determination Decision Matrix

Risk Level	System Complexity	Regulatory Stakes	Investigation Scope	Team Composition
Low	Simple traditional ML	Minimal regulation	Focused technical review	2–3 investigators, domain expert
Medium	Complex ML or simple DL	Industry standards	Standard investigation	4–6 investigators, technical specialists
High	Complex DL or novel systems	Regulated industry	Comprehensive investigation	6–10 investigators, interdisciplinary team
Critical	Foundation models or safety-critical	High-stakes regulation	Full forensic investigation	10+ investigators, external experts

3.8.2.1.2 Secondary Scope Considerations

Identify areas that may require investigation based on initial findings:

- **Upstream Dependencies**: Third-party data sources, pre-trained models, external APIs
- **Downstream Impacts**: Connected systems, dependent business processes, affected user groups
- **Historical Context**: Previous versions, deprecated components, legacy decision-making
- **Regulatory Context**: Applicable laws, industry standards, compliance frameworks

3.8.2.2 Risk Assessment Methodology

3.8.2.2.1 Technical Risk Assessment

Evaluate risks specific to the AI system type and complexity:

- **Interpretability Challenges**: How difficult will it be to understand system behavior?
- **Data Access Constraints**: What limitations exist for accessing training data or system components?
- **System Evolution**: How rapidly is the system changing during investigation?
- **Technical Expertise Gaps**: What specialized knowledge is required but potentially unavailable?

3.8.2.2.2 Organizational Risk Assessment

Assess risks related to organizational context and stakeholder cooperation:

- **Stakeholder Availability**: Are key personnel available and cooperative?
- **Documentation Quality**: How complete and reliable is existing documentation?
- **Political Sensitivity**: Are there organizational conflicts or defensive responses?
- **Resource Constraints**: What limitations exist on time, budget, or access?

3.8.2.2.3 Legal and Regulatory Risk Assessment

Evaluate legal and compliance risks that could affect investigation:

- **Privilege Concerns**: What information might be protected by attorney-client privilege?
- **Privacy Regulations**: What data protection laws constrain investigation activities?
- **Regulatory Deadlines**: Are there compliance deadlines that affect investigation timeline?
- **Litigation Risk**: How likely is litigation and what evidence standards apply?

TABLE 3.4
Risk Mitigation Planning Matrix

Risk Category	High Risk Indicators	Mitigation Strategies	Contingency Plans
Technical Complexity	Novel architectures, limited documentation	Early expert consultation, extended timeline	External specialist engagement
Stakeholder Resistance	Defensive responses, limited cooperation	Legal authority, executive sponsorship	Subpoena processes, alternative sources
Data Access	Privacy constraints, technical barriers	Legal review, technical workarounds	Sampling strategies, synthetic analysis
Timeline Pressure	Regulatory deadlines, business urgency	Parallel workstreams, priority focusing	Phased delivery, scope reduction

System classification guides stakeholder engagement, as different AI architectures require specialized knowledge from different expert communities.

3.9 PERSONNEL ENGAGEMENT AND INTERVIEW STRATEGIES

3.9.1 Personnel Identification and Mapping

Effective AI forensic investigations require systematic identification and engagement of personnel across multiple organizational functions and technical disciplines. Unlike traditional software development where stakeholder groups might be relatively contained, AI projects typically involve complex matrices of roles spanning business, technical, operational, and compliance functions. Understanding these stakeholder relationships and their respective knowledge domains enables investigators to design comprehensive engagement strategies that capture all relevant perspectives.

The stakeholder identification process begins with understanding the organizational structure and development processes associated with the AI system under investigation. Modern AI development follows diverse patterns including centralized teams within dedicated AI organizations, distributed teams embedded within business units, hybrid approaches that combine internal and external resources, and complex partnerships with vendors, consultants, or research institutions. Each organizational pattern creates different stakeholder groups with varying levels of system knowledge and investigation relevance.

Business personnel typically include product managers who define system requirements and success criteria, business analysts who understand operational context and user needs, executive sponsors who provide strategic direction and resource allocation, and domain experts who provide specialized knowledge about the problem area being addressed. These personnel possess critical knowledge about system objectives, business constraints, success metrics, and operational context that may not be captured in technical documentation.

Technical personnel encompass several specialized roles that emerged with AI development practices. Data scientists focus on model design, experimentation, and validation but may have limited knowledge about production deployment or operational monitoring. Machine learning engineers specialize in model implementation, optimization, and deployment infrastructure but may lack deep understanding of business requirements or data provenance. Data engineers design and maintain data pipelines, preprocessing systems, and storage infrastructure but may not understand model architecture or business logic. Software engineers implement application interfaces, integration logic, and supporting systems but may have limited knowledge about machine learning components.

Operational personnel include site reliability engineers who monitor system performance and availability, DevOps engineers who manage deployment and infrastructure, security professionals who address privacy and security requirements, and customer support teams who interact with users affected by system decisions. These personnel possess critical knowledge about real-world system behavior, operational challenges, and user feedback that may not be reflected in development documentation.

Compliance and oversight personnel include privacy officers who ensure data protection compliance, legal counsel who address regulatory requirements, audit professionals who conduct compliance assessments, and ethics review boards who evaluate fairness and bias issues. These personnel understand regulatory constraints, organizational policies, and oversight procedures that influence system design and operation.

Stakeholder mapping requires understanding not just individual roles but also relationships between different groups, communication patterns, and decision-making authorities. AI projects typically involve complex dependencies where business requirements influence data collection strategies, technical constraints affect business objectives, operational limitations impact deployment decisions, and compliance requirements constrain design choices. Understanding these relationships helps investigators identify potential sources of conflict or misalignment that might contribute to system issues.

3.9.2 Interview Design and Protocol Development

Successful interviews in AI forensic investigations require careful preparation and protocol development that addresses the specialized knowledge domains, technical complexity, and interdisciplinary nature of AI systems. Unlike traditional forensic interviews that might focus primarily on actions and observations, AI forensic interviews should elicit understanding about complex technical processes, business reasoning, and organizational dynamics that influence system behavior.

Interview protocol development begins with understanding the specific knowledge domain and organizational role of each interviewee category. Each category requires protocols that focus on requirements definition, success criteria, resource allocation, and operational context. Questions should explore how system objectives were defined, what constraints influenced design decisions, how success was measured, and what business processes were affected by system deployment. Technical interviewees require protocols that address implementation details, design decisions, testing procedures, and operational challenges. Questions should explore architectural choices, data processing decisions, model selection rationale, and validation procedures.

The technical complexity of AI systems requires interview protocols that can accommodate different levels of technical expertise while ensuring comprehensive coverage of relevant topics. Some interviewees may possess deep technical knowledge about specific components but limited understanding of broader system architecture. Others may understand high-level system behavior but lack detailed implementation knowledge. Effective protocols should be adaptable to different knowledge levels while ensuring that critical information is not overlooked due to communication barriers.

Pre-interview preparation becomes particularly important in AI investigations because technical complexity can make it difficult to formulate meaningful questions without substantial background knowledge. Investigators should review available documentation, understand system architecture, and identify specific technical processes or decisions that require clarification. This preparation enables more focused questioning and helps investigators recognize when interviewee responses reveal important information that might not be immediately obvious.

Interview structure should balance systematic coverage of relevant topics with flexibility to pursue unexpected information or insights. A typical AI forensic interview might begin with background questions about the interviewee's role and involvement with the system, proceed to systematic exploration of their knowledge domain, focus on specific technical or business decisions relevant to the investigation, and conclude with questions about documentation sources and additional interviewees who should be consulted.

Documentation and validation procedures ensure that interview information is accurately captured and verified. Audio or video recording provides complete preservation of interviewee responses but requires appropriate consent and security measures. Written summaries should be provided to interviewees for review and correction, ensuring that technical details are accurately captured and that any misunderstandings are identified and resolved.

3.9.3 Sample Interview Question Matrices by Interviewee Type

Effective AI forensic interviews require tailored questioning strategies that address the specific knowledge domains and responsibilities of different interviewee categories. The following matrices provide structured approaches for different interviewee types while maintaining flexibility for investigation-specific adaptations.

3.9.3.1 Universal Interview Questions (All Interviewees)

Before proceeding to role-specific questions, establish foundational information with every interviewee using this standard framework:

TABLE 3.5

Question Category	Sample Questions	Investigation Purpose
Background and Role	"What is your current job title and how long have you held this position? What are your primary responsibilities related to this AI system?"	Establish credibility, scope of knowledge, and potential biases
System Understanding	"In your own words, describe what this AI system does and how it fits into business operations. What aspects of the system do you interact with most?"	Assess understanding level and identify knowledge gaps
Historical Context	"How long have you been involved with this system? Were you part of its development, deployment, or ongoing operations?"	Determine temporal scope of knowledge and relevant experience
Documentation Access	"What documents, reports, emails, or other materials do you have that would help us understand this system and how it was developed or operates?"	Identify additional evidence sources and validate completeness of discovery
Network Mapping	"Who else in the organization has significant knowledge about this system? Are there external parties (vendors, consultants, contractors) we should speak with?"	Expand interviewee network and identify missing perspectives
Open-Ended Discovery	"Is there anything important about this system that I have not asked about? What concerns or observations do you have that might be relevant to our investigation?"	Capture tacit knowledge and unexpected insights

TABLE 3.6
Technical Interview Matrix

Question Category	Data Scientists	ML Engineers	Data Engineers
System Understanding	"Walk me through your model design process"	"Describe the deployment architecture you implemented"	"Explain the data pipeline you built"
Decision Rationale	"Why did you choose this algorithm approach?"	"What led to these infrastructure decisions?"	"How did you decide on this data processing strategy?"
Problem Areas	"What validation challenges did you encounter?"	"What deployment issues have you observed?"	"What data quality problems have you seen?"
Documentation Sources	"Where do you document your experiments?"	"How do you track deployment configurations?"	"Where are your data lineage documents?"
Collaboration	"Who reviews your model designs?"	"Which teams depend on your deployments?"	"Who consumes your data outputs?"

TABLE 3.7
Business Interview Matrix

Question Category	Product Managers	Domain Experts	Executive Sponsors
System Objectives	"What business problem was this AI system designed to solve?"	"How does this system fit into existing domain practices?"	"What strategic goals drove this AI investment?"
Success Criteria	"How do you measure whether the system is working correctly?"	"What domain-specific outcomes indicate success?"	"What ROI or KPIs demonstrate value?"
User Impact	"How do users interact with system outputs?"	"How has this changed professional workflows?"	"What stakeholder feedback have you received?"
Constraints	"What business constraints affected system design?"	"What domain limitations needed accommodation?"	"What resource or timeline pressures existed?"
Change Management	"How was the system rolled out to users?"	"What training or adaptation was required?"	"How were organizational changes managed?"

Interviews invariably reveal new documentation sources and technical evidence that can be systematically collected and analyzed.

3.10 ITERATIVE INVESTIGATION FRAMEWORK AND KNOWLEDGE INTEGRATION

3.10.1 The Iterative Knowledge-Gathering Cycle

AI forensic investigations require a fundamentally iterative approach that cycles between different knowledge-gathering activities as understanding deepens and new questions emerge. Unlike traditional forensic investigations that might follow linear evidence collection procedures, AI investigations must accommodate the complex interdependencies between technical systems, organizational processes, and human decision-making.

Knowledge gathering in AI forensic investigations follows a systematic iterative cycle that integrates technical analysis, stakeholder engagement, and cross-validation activities. This high-level framework guides the detailed investigation procedures while accommodating the complex interdependencies between technical systems, organizational processes, and human decision-making.

Phase 1: Technical Analysis establishes the technical foundation through systematic examination of available artifacts, documentation, and system components. **Phase 2: Stakeholder-Guided Discovery** leverages human intelligence to uncover informal knowledge, organizational context, and undocumented practices. **Phase 3: Iterative Analysis** synthesizes findings through cross-referencing and validation, identifying gaps that drive subsequent investigation cycles.

This three-phase conceptual framework is implemented through the detailed four-phase operational cycle described below, which provides specific procedures for managing the iterative knowledge-gathering process.

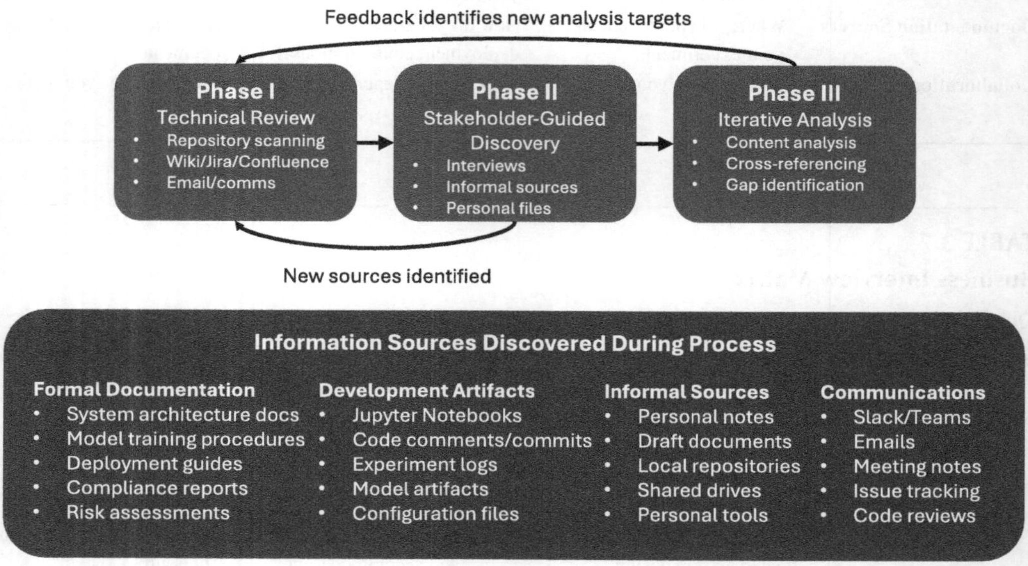

FIGURE 3.3

3.10.1.1 The Knowledge-Gathering Cycle

Each iteration of the knowledge-gathering cycle consists of four interconnected phases that build upon each other:

Phase 1: Information Collection

- Interviews and documentation discovery
- Technical artifact collection and initial analysis
- Preliminary hypothesis formation based on available evidence

Phase 2: Analysis and Synthesis

- Cross-validation of information from multiple sources
- Identification of inconsistencies and knowledge gaps
- Refinement of working hypotheses based on evidence

Phase 3: Scope Adjustment

- Expansion or refinement of investigation boundaries
- Identification of additional interviewees or evidence sources
- Resource reallocation based on emerging priorities

Phase 4: Planning and Coordination

- Design of next iteration activities
- Coordination between technical and human intelligence streams
- Communication of findings to investigation team

3.10.1.2 Iteration Triggers and Decision Points

Specific events or discoveries should trigger new investigation cycles:

- **Technical findings that contradict interview accounts**
- **Interviews that reveal unknown system components**
- **Documentation discovery that identifies new risk areas**
- **Regulatory requirements that expand investigation scope**

3.10.2 Cross-Stream Integration and Validation

The iterative approach requires systematic integration of findings from different knowledge-gathering streams to build comprehensive understanding while maintaining investigative rigor.

3.10.2.1 Multi-Source Validation Framework

3.10.2.1.1 Primary Evidence Sources

- **Technical Evidence**: System logs, configuration files, model artifacts, training data
- **Human Intelligence**: Interviews, institutional knowledge, tacit understanding
- **Documentary Evidence**: Formal documentation, email communications, meeting records

3.10.2.2 Cross-Validation Procedures

For each investigation finding, apply multiple validation approaches:

1. **Technical Validation**: Can the finding be verified through objective technical evidence?
2. **Source Triangulation**: Do multiple independent sources support the finding?

3. **Logical Consistency**: Is the finding consistent with other verified information?
4. **Expert Review**: Do subject matter experts find the finding credible?

3.10.2.3 Integration Checkpoints

Establish regular integration points throughout the investigation:

- **Weekly Synthesis Meetings**: Review findings across all investigation streams
- **Milestone Validation**: Comprehensive cross-validation at investigation milestones
- **Hypothesis Testing**: Systematic testing of working theories against accumulated evidence
- **Gap Assessment**: Identification of remaining uncertainties and information needs

3.10.3 Dynamic Scope Management and Quality Assurance

As investigations progress through multiple cycles, scope management becomes critical for maintaining focus while accommodating necessary scope expansions based on new discoveries.

3.10.3.1 Scope Evolution Management

Controlled Scope Expansion

- Document the rationale for all scope changes
- Assess resource implications of scope modifications
- Obtain stakeholder approval for significant expansions
- Maintain clear boundaries between core and extended scope

Quality Gates and Review Points

- Establish quality criteria for each investigation phase
- Implement peer review processes for critical findings
- Maintain chain of custody for all evidence sources
- Document limitations and uncertainties transparently

3.10.3.2 Investigation Conclusion Criteria

Define clear criteria for investigation completion:

- **Coverage Completeness**: All identified risk areas have been adequately assessed
- **Source Reliability**: Key findings are supported by multiple reliable sources
- **Scope Achievement**: Investigation objectives have been met within defined boundaries
- **Quality Standards**: All findings meet established quality and reliability standards

The iterative process continues until comprehensive understanding emerges, supported by quality assurance throughout, then transitions to guide technical evidence collection priorities.

3.11 INTEGRATION WITH TECHNICAL COLLECTION

3.11.1 Knowledge-Driven Technical Investigation

The knowledge-gathering phase establishes the foundation for technical evidence collection by identifying critical system components, potential failure modes, relevant time periods, and specific hypotheses that require technical validation. Unlike traditional forensic investigations where technical collection might proceed according to standard procedures, AI investigations require carefully targeted approaches that focus resources on the most relevant evidence sources while accommodating the complexity and scale of modern AI systems.

The integration process begins with translating knowledge-gathering findings into specific technical investigation requirements. Interviews and documentation analysis provide understanding of system architecture, data flows, deployment procedures, and potential problem areas that should be prioritized during technical collection. This understanding enables investigators to focus on specific system components, time periods, or data sources that are most likely to contain relevant evidence while avoiding unnecessary collection of low-value information.

Technical investigation planning must accommodate the distributed nature of AI systems, which typically span multiple platforms, environments, and organizational boundaries. Knowledge gathering reveals which systems contain relevant evidence, who has access and administrative privileges, what technical constraints might affect collection procedures, and what coordination is required between different technical teams or external providers.

The planning process should also address temporal considerations that are particularly important in AI investigations. Systems evolve continuously through training updates, configuration changes, and deployment modifications. Knowledge gathering helps identify critical time periods when problems may have been introduced, what changes were made during relevant timeframes, and what evidence sources might contain information about these changes.

Priority setting requires balancing the investigative value of different evidence sources against collection complexity, resource requirements, and access constraints. High-priority evidence includes information that directly addresses core investigation hypotheses, provides objective validation for interviewee claims, or reveals previously unknown aspects of system behavior. Medium-priority evidence provides supporting context or enables validation of secondary findings. Low-priority evidence offers general background information but does not significantly affect investigation conclusions.

3.11.2 Collaborative Investigation Processes

Effective integration between knowledge gathering and technical collection requires ongoing collaboration between team members with different expertise and responsibilities. This collaboration ensures that technical analysis is properly informed by human knowledge while human insights are validated through objective technical evidence.

Communication protocols establish regular interaction between knowledge-gathering and technical teams to share findings, identify new investigation priorities, and coordinate follow-up activities. These protocols should specify meeting schedules, information sharing procedures, escalation processes for urgent findings, and documentation requirements that ensure all team members have access to relevant information.

The collaborative process should address the different timelines and work patterns associated with knowledge-gathering and technical collection activities. Interviews typically require scheduling around availability and may be subject to travel or coordination delays. Technical collection may require system access during specific maintenance windows or may be constrained by processing time requirements for large datasets. Effective collaboration requires flexibility and advance planning to accommodate these different constraints.

Cross-validation procedures ensure that findings from different investigation streams are systematically compared and validated. Technical evidence should be used to verify claims made in interviews while human interpretation should provide context for technical findings. Discrepancies between sources should prompt follow-up investigation rather than being dismissed or ignored.

3.11.3 Iterative Knowledge Development

Rather than treating knowledge gathering as a preliminary phase that concludes before technical investigation begins, AI forensic investigations require continuous knowledge development throughout the entire investigative process. Technical findings frequently reveal new questions that require interviewee consultation, while ongoing engagement may identify additional evidence sources that require technical analysis.

This iterative approach recognizes that AI systems are sufficiently complex that complete understanding cannot be achieved through any single investigative approach. Initial knowledge gathering provides foundation understanding that enables effective technical investigation, but technical findings invariably reveal aspects of system behavior or configuration that were not apparent from documentation or interview accounts.

The iterative process requires systematic procedures for incorporating new information, updating investigation priorities, and coordinating between different investigation streams. New technical findings should prompt targeted follow-up interviews or documentation analysis rather than comprehensive re-investigation of all previously covered topics. Similarly, new information from interviewee engagement should guide additional technical analysis rather than requiring complete re-collection of technical evidence.

Documentation procedures should accommodate this iterative approach by maintaining current records of investigation findings, outstanding questions, and planned follow-up activities. Investigation teams should establish procedures for updating investigation plans, modifying resource allocation, and communicating changes to all relevant team members.

Knowledge-gathering conclusions guide technical evidence collection priorities and analytical approaches outlined in Chapter 4, while quality assurance ensures investigation integrity throughout.

3.12 QUALITY ASSURANCE AND VALIDATION

3.12.1 Information Reliability Assessment

The diverse sources and complex interdependencies involved in AI forensic investigations create substantial challenges for assessing information reliability and ensuring that investigation findings are based on accurate, complete, and appropriately validated evidence. Unlike traditional forensic investigations where evidence might be primarily technical and subject to objective verification, AI investigations must integrate individuals' subjective explanations, potentially biased documentation, and technical evidence that may require specialized expertise to interpret correctly.

Information reliability assessment begins with understanding the characteristics and limitations of different source types. Interviews provide valuable context and insights but are subject to memory limitations, cognitive biases, organizational pressures, and individual perspectives that may not reflect broader organizational understanding. Documentation sources vary significantly in accuracy, completeness, and currency depending on their purpose, authorship, and maintenance procedures. Technical evidence offers objective information about system behavior but may require interpretation to understand its significance or implications.

Source credibility evaluation requires systematic assessment of each information source's reliability characteristics. Interviewee credibility and reliability depend on their direct involvement with relevant systems, technical expertise in relevant domains, organizational position and access to information, potential conflicts of interest or biases, and consistency with other sources. Documentation credibility depends on authorship authority and expertise, creation and maintenance processes, version control and change tracking, official approval or review processes, and cross-referencing with other sources.

3.12.2 Validation Procedures and Cross-Checking

Systematic validation procedures ensure that investigation findings are appropriately supported by reliable evidence and that alternative explanations have been considered. These procedures address both the accuracy of individual information sources and the validity of synthesis and analysis processes that combine information from multiple sources.

Interview validation begins with accurate capture of interview responses, detailed note-taking, and systematic transcription procedures. For key information, the interviewee should be asked to confirm details and the interviewer should document that confirmation. Follow-up questions should be used to clarify ambiguous responses or explore apparent inconsistencies with other information sources.

Documentation validation involves verifying the authenticity, accuracy, and completeness of discovered documents while understanding their organizational context and limitations. Version control information, authorship records, and review histories provide insights into document reliability and currency. Cross-referencing with other documentation sources helps identify potential gaps or inconsistencies that require follow-up investigation.

Technical evidence validation requires appropriate expertise to ensure that system logs, configuration files, model artifacts, and other technical evidence are correctly interpreted and analyzed. This validation may require consultation with technical specialists who can provide independent assessment of technical findings and their implications for investigation conclusions.

Synthesis validation involves systematic review of analysis procedures and conclusions to ensure that findings are logically supported by available evidence and that alternative explanations have been appropriately considered. This review should address both the technical accuracy of analysis procedures and the logical validity of conclusions drawn from available evidence.

3.12.3 Completeness Assessment and Gap Management

Systematic assessment of investigation completeness ensures that all relevant information sources have been identified and appropriately addressed while acknowledging areas where additional information might be valuable but is not available or accessible within investigation constraints.

Completeness assessment requires systematic review of investigation coverage across all relevant dimensions including interview groups, documentation sources, system components, time periods, and business processes. This assessment should identify areas where investigation coverage is comprehensive, adequate, or potentially incomplete based on available evidence and investigation objectives.

Gap identification requires systematic review of investigation findings to identify areas where information is incomplete, uncertain, or contradictory. Common gaps in AI investigations include missing documentation about critical decisions, inconsistent accounts of technical procedures, limited understanding of system behavior under specific conditions, or inadequate information about organizational context and decision-making processes.

Some gaps reflect inherent limitations in available evidence such as missing log files, deleted documentation, or departed personnel who possessed unique knowledge. Other gaps result from investigation design limitations such as insufficient interview coverage, inadequate technical analysis, or limited access to relevant systems or information. Understanding the nature of different gaps helps investigators determine appropriate resolution strategies and assess the impact of remaining uncertainties on investigation conclusions.

Gap resolution strategies should balance the value of additional information against investigation resource constraints and timeline requirements. High-priority gaps that affect core investigation findings warrant significant effort to resolve through additional interviews, expanded technical analysis, or enhanced documentation discovery. Lower-priority gaps that provide contextual information but do not affect main conclusions might be noted as limitations without requiring extensive additional investigation.

The gap management process should maintain clear documentation of identified limitations, resolution efforts, and remaining uncertainties that affect investigation conclusions. This documentation supports the credibility of investigation findings while providing transparency about areas where additional information might change conclusions if it became available.

3.13 CONCLUSION

Knowledge gathering and scoping represent the critical foundation that enables effective AI forensic investigations, bridging the gap between understanding AI systems conceptually and investigating them with the technical rigor necessary for forensic applications. The frameworks, methodologies, and procedures outlined in this chapter provide investigators with systematic approaches for eliciting human knowledge, discovering critical documentation, and synthesizing complex information from multiple sources into actionable intelligence that guides technical investigation priorities.

The unique characteristics of AI systems—their socio-technical nature, evolutionary development patterns, and complex interdependencies—make knowledge gathering particularly critical for investigation success. Unlike traditional software systems where functionality can often be understood through code analysis alone, AI systems embed human decisions about problem framing, solution approaches, success criteria, and operational constraints that profoundly influence system behavior. Understanding these human elements requires specialized approaches that accommodate technical complexity while maintaining forensic rigor.

The iterative, multi-source approach emphasized throughout this chapter reflects the reality that AI forensic investigations cannot rely on any single information source to provide complete understanding. Interviews reveal critical context and tacit knowledge but require validation through documentation and technical evidence. Documentation provides intentional knowledge capture but may be incomplete, outdated, or aspirational rather than descriptive. Technical evidence offers objective information about system behavior but requires human interpretation to understand its significance and implications.

The integration of knowledge gathering with technical collection ensures that human intelligence and technical evidence work together throughout the investigation process rather than being treated as separate, sequential activities. This integration enables more efficient resource allocation, better hypothesis development, and more reliable conclusions that are grounded in both objective evidence and appropriate contextual understanding.

The quality assurance and validation procedures presented in this chapter help ensure that knowledge-gathering activities meet the standards necessary for forensic applications while acknowledging the inherent challenges of working with complex socio-technical systems. These procedures provide systematic approaches for assessing information reliability, validating findings across multiple sources, and managing gaps or limitations that inevitably arise in complex investigations.

As AI systems become more prevalent and sophisticated, the importance of effective knowledge gathering in forensic investigations will only increase. The frameworks provided in this chapter offer scalable approaches that can be adapted to different system types, organizational contexts, and investigation scenarios while maintaining the core principles necessary for forensic validity. Whether conducting internal investigations for system improvement, regulatory compliance assessments, or litigation support, these methodologies provide the foundation for thorough, reliable, and actionable investigation outcomes.

The transition to Chapter 4's technical evidence collection builds upon the foundation established here, ensuring that technical investigation activities are properly prioritized, efficiently conducted, and appropriately interpreted within their broader organizational and business contexts. The investment in comprehensive knowledge gathering pays dividends throughout the investigation process, often revealing critical evidence that might otherwise be overlooked and providing the contextual understanding necessary to transform technical findings into meaningful insights about system behavior, organizational practices, and potential remediation strategies.

4 Evidence Collection

4.1 BEYOND FILES AND FOLDERS: CAPTURING AI SYSTEM EVIDENCE

When investigators arrived at a major tech company to examine their facial recognition system's discriminatory behavior, they didn't find a single server to image or a database to preserve. Instead, they discovered training data scattered across three cloud platforms, model weights distributed among container registries, inference logs streaming to six different monitoring systems, and configuration files embedded in deployment pipelines that spanned multiple Kubernetes clusters. The evidence existed everywhere and nowhere simultaneously. They were present in fragments across a complex ecosystem but requiring systematic collection to become forensically meaningful.

When a healthcare AI began recommending dangerous drug combinations, investigators couldn't simply preserve a hard drive and call it complete. The evidence trail included training datasets with patient records across multiple hospitals, model checkpoints stored in cloud object storage, inference logs scattered across edge devices, configuration management systems tracking deployment changes, and performance monitoring data showing gradual degradation over months. Only through systematic evidence collection that preserved both individual artifacts and their interdependencies could investigators reconstruct how the system's behavior had evolved from safe recommendations to potentially lethal ones.

4.2 WHAT YOU WILL LEARN

By the end of this chapter, you will be able to:

- Systematically identify and catalog AI evidence across distributed cloud and on-premises infrastructure
- Implement forensically sound collection procedures that maintain legal admissibility while accommodating AI system complexity
- Preserve ephemeral training processes, model artifacts, and dynamic system configurations before they disappear
- Establish and maintain chain of custody for evidence that spans multiple jurisdictions, platforms, and organizational boundaries
- Document complex interdependencies between training data, model weights, configuration files, and system outputs
- Navigate the unique challenges of collecting evidence from live AI systems without disrupting critical operations

4.3 QUICK START GUIDE

- **Don't know where to start?** → Begin with Evidence Collection Process Overview (Section 4.5)
- **Production system is live and cannot shut down?** → Go to Live System Evidence Capture (Section 4.6.3)
- **Chain of custody concerns?** → Start with Legal Documentation Requirements (Section 4.6.4)
  Cloud platform evidence? → Jump to Platform-Specific (Section 4.12)

DOI: 10.1201/9781003634782-4

- **Petabyte-scale datasets?** → Review Sample-Based Collection Strategies (Section 4.12.5.1.1)
- **Container deployments?** → Start with Container Evidence Collection (Section 4.12.3)
- **Streaming systems?** → See Real-Time System Collection (Section 4.12.4)
- **Container or Kubernetes deployment?** → Begin with Container and Orchestration Evidence Collection (Section 4.12.3)

4.4 IMPORTANT DISCLAIMER

Evidence collection in AI investigations requires careful adaptation to specific technical architectures, organizational contexts, and legal jurisdictions. The procedures and frameworks presented in this chapter must be tailored to your investigation's unique requirements while maintaining forensic integrity standards.

4.5 EVIDENCE COLLECTION PROCESS OVERVIEW

AI evidence collection forms the foundation of AI forensic investigations, yet it presents unique challenges that distinguish it fundamentally from traditional digital forensics. Where conventional investigations might focus on preserving hard drives or network logs, AI forensics requires investigators to capture ephemeral training processes, distributed model artifacts, dynamic inference patterns, and complex interdependencies that span multiple cloud platforms and organizational boundaries. The evidence that determines AI system behavior exists not just in files and databases, but in the relationships between datasets, the evolution of model parameters over time, and the operational contexts that shape system deployment. This chapter provides comprehensive frameworks and practical methodologies for systematically collecting, preserving, and documenting AI evidence while maintaining the forensic integrity necessary for legal proceedings and technical analysis.

This section provides a comprehensive framework for understanding the AI evidence collection process before diving into the detailed methodologies that follow. The evidence collection phase forms the foundation of any successful AI forensic investigation, requiring systematic approaches that balance technical rigor with legal admissibility requirements.

4.5.1 Process Architecture and Flow

The evidence collection process follows a structured five-phase approach designed to ensure comprehensive coverage while maintaining forensic integrity. Each phase builds upon the previous one, creating a robust framework that supports both immediate investigation needs and future analysis requirements.

The systematic approach illustrated above demonstrates how evidence collection progresses from initial system identification through final verification, with quality assurance procedures applied throughout the collection, documentation, and verification phases. Each phase addresses specific technical and legal requirements while building toward comprehensive analysis capabilities.

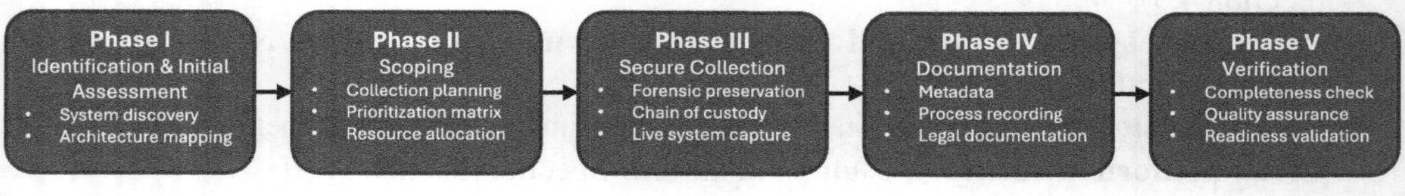

FIGURE 4.1

4.5.2 Core Principles and Methodology

The evidence collection framework operates on several fundamental principles that distinguish AI forensic investigations from traditional digital forensics:

Artifact interdependency recognition acknowledges that AI systems generate complex webs of related evidence where training data, model configurations, system logs, and outputs must be understood as interconnected components rather than isolated artifacts. This interdependency means that incomplete collection in any category can compromise the entire investigation's validity.

The AI Evidence Interdependency Framework illustrates the critical relationships between different categories of forensic evidence in AI systems. Unlike traditional digital forensics where evidence artifacts can often be analyzed independently, AI forensic investigations require an understanding of these interconnected evidence relationships to draw valid conclusions.

The framework shows three types of evidence relationships that guide collection strategy decisions:

Core Evidence Dependencies (solid arrows) represent critical relationships where model artifacts depend fundamentally on training data, configuration files, system logs, and output data. These dependencies mean that forensic analysis of AI behavior requires coordinated collection across all primary evidence categories. Missing any core evidence type severely limits the investigation's ability to understand system behavior or validate findings.

Supporting Context (dashed arrows) shows how version control and documentation provide temporal context and procedural understanding that enhances analysis of core evidence. While not always essential for basic analysis, this contextual evidence often proves crucial for understanding system evolution and identifying potential bias introduction points.

Cross-Category Links (dotted arrows) demonstrate how evidence types influence each other beyond their direct relationship to model artifacts. For example, training data characteristics influence configuration decisions, which in turn affect system log patterns and output data distributions.

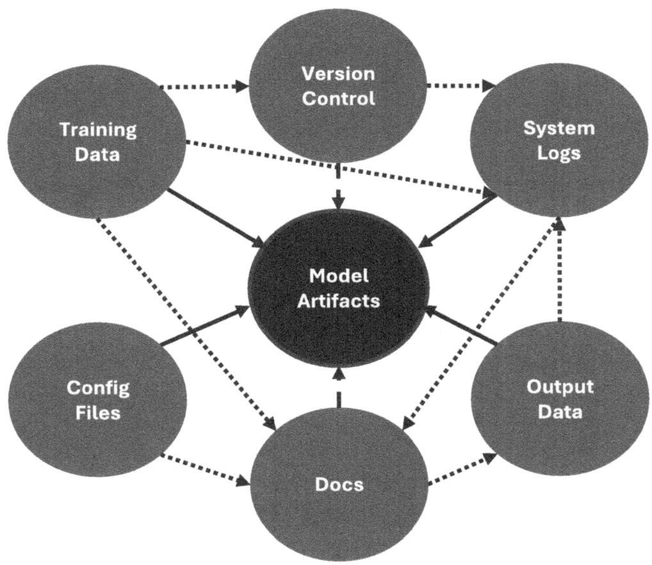

FIGURE 4.2

The framework supports different investigation approaches based on the specific questions being addressed. Targeted investigations may focus on a subset of evidence categories when addressing specific, well-defined issues—for example, a bias investigation might prioritize training data and output data with supporting configuration files, while a performance regression analysis might emphasize system logs and model artifacts. However, even targeted investigations should consider dependency relationships, as analyzing output bias without understanding training data characteristics often proves insufficient.

Comprehensive investigations require collection across all evidence categories when addressing complex systemic issues, regulatory compliance assessments, or investigations where the root cause is unknown. These investigations benefit from the complete evidence ecosystem to identify unexpected relationships and validate findings through multiple evidence sources.

The minimum viable collection scope is determined by the dependency relationships shown in the framework. Investigators cannot arbitrarily exclude evidence categories without considering how those exclusions might compromise their ability to answer investigation questions. The framework helps identify the minimum set of evidence categories needed to support specific analytical objectives while maintaining investigation integrity.

This interdependency framework directly impacts collection strategy decisions by showing investigators what evidence relationships must be preserved regardless of investigation scope. While not every investigation requires complete evidence collection, all investigations should consider the fundamental dependencies between evidence types to ensure analytical validity and legal defensibility.

Temporal integrity preservation ensures that evidence maintains accurate timestamps and sequencing across all collection activities. AI systems often operate continuously with frequent updates, making temporal accuracy crucial for understanding system behavior patterns and establishing causality between events.

Multi-platform coordination addresses the reality that modern AI systems span multiple cloud providers, on-premises infrastructure, and hybrid environments. Investigators should account for different storage formats, access methods, and preservation requirements across diverse technical platforms during the evidence collection phase in order to form a complete picture.

Legal admissibility standards require that all collection activities meet established forensic standards while accommodating the unique challenges of AI evidence. This includes maintaining chain of custody for dynamic data, establishing authenticity for automatically generated artifacts, and ensuring reproducibility of collection procedures.

4.6 PHASE-BY-PHASE COLLECTION METHODOLOGY

4.6.1 Phase I: Identification and Initial Assessment—AI System Discovery

The identification and initial assessment phase establishes the foundational understanding of the AI system under investigation. This phase focuses on system discovery and architectural mapping rather than detailed evidence collection planning, which occurs in the subsequent scoping phase.

AI architecture discovery begins by mapping the complete AI system ecosystem, which often spans multiple environments and platforms. Unlike traditional applications, AI systems typically involve separate development environments for experimentation, training infrastructure for model creation, staging environments for validation, and production systems for deployment. Each environment may contain unique evidence crucial to understanding system behavior.

The discovery process is where investigators identify all computational resources involved in the AI lifecycle including cloud-based training clusters that may have been spun up temporarily, distributed training systems across multiple geographic regions, model serving infrastructure that may auto-scale based on demand, and edge deployment systems that may operate independently. This discovery requires examining cloud billing records, AI TRiSM systems, infrastructure monitoring logs, and deployment automation scripts to ensure no computational resources are overlooked.

Data flow mapping traces how data moves through the AI system from initial collection through final output generation. AI systems often involve complex data pipelines with multiple transformation stages, making it crucial to understand data lineage completely. This mapping identifies data ingestion points where raw data enters the system, preprocessing pipelines that transform data for training, feature engineering systems that create model inputs, training data storage and versioning systems, and inference data flows in production systems.

Stakeholder and access identification documents all individuals and systems that interact with the AI system throughout its lifecycle. AI systems typically involve diverse stakeholders including data scientists who develop models, ML engineers who deploy systems, data engineers who manage pipelines, business users who consume outputs, and external vendors who provide data or services. Each stakeholder may have accessed different components and possessed different levels of system understanding crucial to the investigation.

4.6.2 Phase II: Scoping—Strategic Collection Planning

The scoping phase transforms the system understanding gained during identification into a strategic collection plan. This phase determines what evidence to collect based on investigation objectives, practical constraints, and system characteristics. Every investigation presents unique requirements, making scoping decisions highly context-dependent and requiring careful consideration of multiple factors.

Investigation goal alignment serves as the primary driver for scoping decisions. Different investigation types require different evidence priorities and collection depths. Bias discrimination investigations require comprehensive training data analysis, detailed output pattern examination, and extensive documentation of decision-making processes. Performance failure investigations focus on system logs, model degradation patterns, and infrastructure monitoring data. Intellectual property investigations emphasize training data provenance, model architecture documentation, and development history records.

Practical limitation assessment evaluates constraints that affect collection feasibility and strategy. Resource limitations include available investigation time, technical expertise, and financial budgets that constrain collection scope. Legal constraints encompass privacy regulations, data sovereignty requirements, and litigation hold obligations that affect what evidence can be collected and how it must be handled. Technical constraints involve system access restrictions, data format incompatibilities, and infrastructure limitations that may prevent comprehensive collection.

System design and volume considerations account for the technical characteristics that influence collection complexity and resource requirements. System scale affects collection strategies, with small experimental systems allowing comprehensive collection while enterprise-scale systems require sampling and prioritization strategies. System complexity influences collection depth, with simple single-model systems enabling complete artifact collection while complex multi-model systems requiring selective focus on critical components.

4.6.2.1 Evidence Collection Prioritization Matrix

The following matrix provides guidance for determining artifact collection priorities based on investigation characteristics and system constraints. This framework supports decision-making but should be adapted to specific investigation requirements and practical constraints.

Collection depth determination involves deciding the level of detail required for each artifact category based on investigation needs and resource constraints. Comprehensive collection captures complete artifact histories with full metadata and documentation, suitable for complex investigations with significant legal implications. Targeted collection focuses on specific time periods, system components, or artifact types relevant to particular investigation questions. Sample-based collection implements statistical sampling strategies for high-volume artifacts when comprehensive collection is impractical.

TABLE 4.1

Artifact Category	High-Priority Scenarios	Medium-Priority Scenarios	Collection Rationale	Resource Impact
Training Data	Bias/discrimination investigations, IP disputes, model performance failures	Regulatory compliance audits, security breaches not affecting training	Essential for understanding model behavior foundations and detecting systemic biases	Very high—Often largest volume artifacts
Model Artifacts	All investigations involving model behavior, IP disputes, regulatory compliance	Investigations focused solely on data processing or deployment issues	Core evidence for model analysis, required for behavioral reproduction	High—Multiple versions and formats
System Logs	Performance failures, security incidents, operational disputes	Bias investigations where system operation is well-documented	Critical for understanding operational context and identifying failure patterns	Medium to high—Continuous generation
Output Patterns	Bias investigations, performance disputes, regulatory compliance	IP investigations focused on training data or model architecture	Necessary for demonstrating actual system behavior and impact	Medium—Sampling strategies applicable
Configuration Files	All investigations requiring system reproduction, performance analysis	Investigations with well-documented system configurations	Essential for understanding system setup and reproducing analysis environments	Low to medium—Small volume, high importance
Communication Records	Investigations involving intent or knowledge, regulatory compliance	Technical performance investigations with clear system evidence	Provides context for technical decisions and awareness of issues	Medium—Requires legal review
Development History	IP investigations, compliance audits, investigations involving multiple system versions	Investigations focused on specific operational periods	Enables understanding of system evolution and decision rationale	Medium—Version control integration
External Dependencies	Investigations involving third-party data or services, security incidents	Internal system investigations with minimal external integration	Critical when external factors may influence system behavior	Variable—Depends on integration complexity

Temporal scope planning establishes the time periods for evidence collection based on investigation requirements and system characteristics. Incident-focused scoping collects evidence from specific time periods surrounding known issues or events. Trend analysis scoping captures evidence across extended periods to identify patterns and changes in system behavior. Lifecycle scoping attempts to collect evidence from the complete system development and operational lifecycle.

4.6.2.2 Evidence Collection Priority Timeline

The volatility and time-sensitivity of different AI evidence types require a prioritized collection approach that addresses the most ephemeral evidence first while ensuring comprehensive coverage of all critical artifacts. The following timeline framework provides guidance for sequencing collection activities based on evidence stability and investigation urgency.

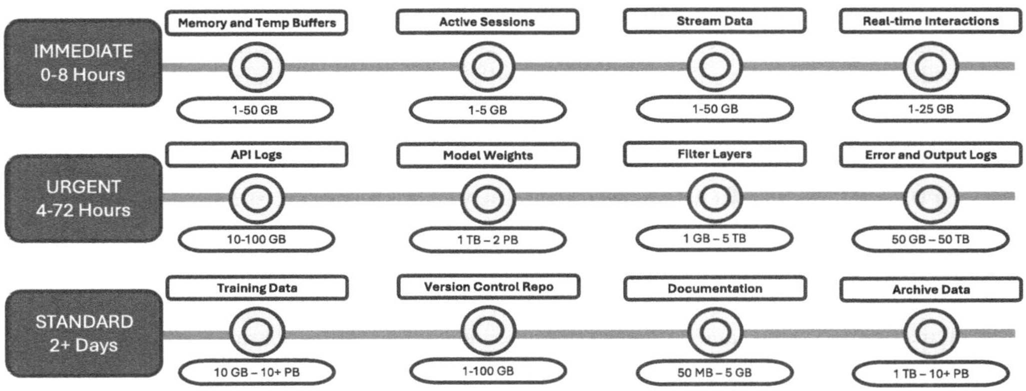

FIGURE 4.3

This prioritization framework addresses the unique challenges of AI evidence collection where different artifact types have dramatically different lifespans and collection requirements. Understanding these temporal constraints is essential for developing effective collection strategies that preserve critical evidence before it becomes unavailable.

Immediate Priority (0–8 Hours) addresses the most volatile evidence that may be lost within hours of system operation or investigation initiation. Memory and temporary buffers contain run-time state information that disappears when systems restart or processes terminate. Active sessions maintain user interaction state and model inference contexts that provide crucial evidence about system behavior at specific moments. Stream data includes real-time processing queues and message buffers that are continuously overwritten during normal operation. Configuration files in memory may contain temporary settings or runtime modifications that differ from stored configurations.

The immediate priority category requires rapid response capabilities and often necessitates live system collection techniques that minimize operational disruption while preserving ephemeral evidence. Collection teams must be prepared to act quickly when these evidence types are identified, as delays of even a few hours can result in permanent evidence loss.

Urgent Priority (4–72 Hours) encompasses evidence that remains stable for short periods but faces regular rotation, archival, or overwriting. API logs capture detailed interaction patterns but are typically rotated on daily or weekly cycles to manage storage costs. Model weights and parameters may be updated frequently in development environments or through automated retraining processes. Filter layers and preprocessing components can change rapidly during model optimization or deployment updates. Error and output logs provide detailed operational evidence but are often subject to retention policies that limit their availability.

The urgent priority category allows for more systematic collection planning while maintaining the need for prompt action. Investigation teams can coordinate with system administrators to temporarily extend log retention periods or pause automated cleanup processes to preserve evidence during collection activities.

Standard Priority (2+ Days) includes evidence that remains stable for extended periods and faces minimal risk of loss during typical investigation timeframes. Training data represents the foundation of model behavior and typically remains unchanged unless explicitly updated for retraining. Version control repositories maintain complete development history and are specifically designed for long-term preservation. Documentation including model cards, data sheets, and technical specifications changes infrequently and is usually backed up across multiple systems. Archive data encompasses historical datasets, deprecated models, and long-term storage that is designed for persistence.

The standard priority category enables comprehensive planning and resource allocation while accommodating investigation scheduling constraints and organizational coordination requirements. These evidence types can be collected systematically without time pressure, allowing for thorough validation and quality assurance procedures.

4.6.3 Phase III: Secure Collection—Forensically Sound Acquisition

The secure collection phase implements forensically sound acquisition procedures specifically adapted for AI system artifacts. This phase ensures that evidence maintains legal admissibility while accounting for the unique characteristics of AI evidence including dynamic data sources, distributed storage systems, and complex interdependencies. Quality assurance procedures begin at this phase and continue through documentation and verification.

Forensic imaging for AI systems extends traditional disk imaging concepts to accommodate the diverse storage formats used in AI environments. Unlike traditional systems where evidence exists primarily on local storage devices, AI evidence may span object storage systems, distributed databases, container registries, and streaming data platforms. Collection procedures create forensically sound copies of data across these diverse systems while maintaining timestamp accuracy and relationship integrity.

Live system evidence capture addresses the reality that many AI systems cannot be shut down for traditional forensic imaging without destroying crucial evidence. Training processes may run for days or weeks, generating continuous streams of performance metrics, gradient updates, and intermediate model states. The procedures in the evidence collection process should involve techniques for capturing evidence from live systems without disrupting ongoing operations or compromising evidence integrity.

Chain of custody for dynamic data establishes procedures for maintaining legal custody of evidence that changes continuously during normal system operation. AI systems generate new training examples, model updates, and prediction logs constantly, requiring chain of custody procedures that can accommodate this dynamic nature while maintaining the documentation necessary for legal admissibility.

4.6.4 Phase IV: Documentation—Comprehensive Metadata Capture

The documentation phase creates comprehensive metadata records that support both technical analysis and legal proceedings. AI evidence requires more extensive documentation than traditional digital evidence due to the complex relationships between different artifacts and the specialized knowledge required to interpret findings. Quality assurance procedures ensure documentation completeness and accuracy.

Technical documentation standards ensure that collected evidence includes sufficient information for independent analysis and reproduction of results. This documentation includes complete environment specifications with software versions and configurations, data lineage records tracing all transformations applied to datasets, training procedure documentation with hyperparameters and optimization settings, model selection, and performance baseline records that establish expected system behavior patterns.

Legal documentation requirements address the specific challenges of presenting AI evidence in legal proceedings. Expert qualification documentation establishes the credentials and experience necessary for testimony about AI systems. Methodology validation demonstrates that collection procedures follow accepted forensic standards adapted for AI evidence. Limitation acknowledgment provides honest assessment of uncertainties and constraints that may affect analysis conclusions.

4.6.5 Phase V: Verification—Integrity and Completeness Validation

The verification phase validates that collected evidence is complete, accurate, and ready for analysis. This phase implements comprehensive quality checks that ensure evidence integrity while confirming that all necessary artifacts have been preserved with appropriate metadata and documentation. This final phase completes the quality assurance framework applied throughout the collection process.

Integrity verification procedures employ multiple validation techniques to ensure evidence authenticity. Cryptographic hash verification confirms that artifacts have not been modified during collection or storage. Digital signature validation ensures that automated systems correctly captured evidence without corruption. Cross-reference verification confirms that relationships between different evidence types remain intact and that no dependencies have been broken during collection.

Completeness assessment protocols systematically verify that all identified evidence sources have been successfully collected according to the scoping plan. Dependency mapping validation ensures that relationships between training data, models, and system outputs can be traced completely. Gap analysis identifies any missing components that could compromise investigation conclusions. Statistical sampling validation confirms that collected evidence provides representative coverage of system behavior across different operational conditions.

4.7 AI-Specific Collection Challenges and Approaches

AI evidence collection presents unique challenges that differentiate it significantly from traditional digital forensics methodologies. The distributed architecture of AI systems, combined with the dynamic characteristics of machine learning infrastructure and the intricate relationships between different evidence categories, creates collection scenarios that require specialized approaches and careful consideration of technical constraints.

Ephemeral infrastructure management becomes critical when dealing with AI systems that rely heavily on temporary computational resources designed for automatic destruction after task completion. Many modern AI training workflows operate on auto-scaling clusters that terminate immediately following job completion, potentially eliminating crucial evidence about training processes, resource allocation patterns, and system performance characteristics. Effective collection procedures typically implement real-time evidence preservation mechanisms during active training phases. Additionally, automated collection systems often prove valuable when configured to activate upon temporary resource creation, ensuring that evidence capture begins before the ephemeral infrastructure enters its destruction cycle. Organizations frequently find that proactive monitoring of resource lifecycle events provides the timing necessary for successful evidence preservation in these dynamic environments.

Version control complexity in AI environments encompasses far more than traditional software code versioning systems. Modern AI development involves managing dataset versions across multiple iterations, preserving model checkpoints at various training stages, maintaining experimental configurations with different hyperparameter combinations, and tracking deployment variants across different operational environments. A single AI system commonly generates hundreds of experimental versions, each containing distinct training data subsets, architectural modifications, or configuration parameters that may significantly impact system behavior. Evidence collection frameworks generally need to preserve the complex relationships between these versions while maintaining the technical capability to reproduce specific system states during subsequent analysis phases. This requirement often involves capturing not only the artifacts themselves but also the dependency trees, build environments, and temporal sequences that enable accurate reconstruction of historical system states.

Data sensitivity and privacy protection requires evidence collection procedures to navigate complex regulatory landscapes while preserving information integrity necessary for thorough investigation. Training datasets frequently contain personally identifiable information, proprietary business intelligence, or content subject to industry-specific regulations that impose strict handling requirements. These constraints often prevent direct copying or unrestricted analysis without appropriate legal frameworks and technical safeguards. Collection procedures typically implement sophisticated data handling protocols that maintain forensic integrity while ensuring compliance with applicable privacy regulations. Many organizations develop specialized anonymization techniques, secure analysis environments, and controlled access procedures that enable investigation progress without compromising data protection obligations or regulatory compliance requirements.

Scale and performance considerations reflect the substantial computational and storage demands characteristic of modern AI systems. Contemporary training datasets routinely contain billions of individual examples spanning multiple data modalities, while model artifacts frequently require terabytes of storage capacity to preserve complete parameter sets and associated metadata. System logs in production AI environments often generate gigabytes of diagnostic information daily, creating substantial challenges for collection, storage, and subsequent analysis activities. Collection procedures typically require careful design to handle these scale requirements efficiently while maintaining the thoroughness necessary for comprehensive forensic analysis. This often involves implementing distributed collection strategies, developing efficient compression and storage techniques, and creating scalable analysis frameworks that can process large evidence volumes without compromising investigation quality or timeline requirements.

4.8 INTEGRATION WITH ANALYSIS PHASES

The evidence collection framework is specifically designed to support the analysis methodologies covered in subsequent chapters. Each collection activity generates documentation and metadata that enables specific analysis techniques:

Training data analysis integration ensures that collected datasets include the lineage documentation, sampling records, and quality assessments necessary for comprehensive bias detection and data quality analysis described in Chapter 5.

Model investigation preparation structures model artifact collection to support the architectural analysis and behavioral investigation techniques covered in Chapter 6, including version control integration and training environment preservation.

Output analysis readiness organizes system output collection to enable the statistical validation and pattern detection methodologies detailed in Chapter 7, including temporal organization and contextual metadata preservation.

Documentation analysis support structures audit trail and documentation collection to facilitate the compliance verification and audit trail examination techniques presented in Chapter 8.

4.9 SCALABILITY AND RESOURCE CONSIDERATIONS

The evidence collection framework accommodates investigations of varying scales and complexity while maintaining consistent quality standards:

Small-scale investigations involving single models or limited datasets can implement simplified versions of the collection procedures while maintaining core integrity and documentation requirements.

Enterprise-scale investigations spanning multiple AI systems across complex infrastructure require advanced automation, parallel collection strategies, and sophisticated coordination mechanisms to manage the volume and complexity of evidence.

Cross-organizational investigations involving multiple entities or cloud providers require careful coordination of access permissions, data sovereignty considerations, and standardized collection procedures to ensure consistent evidence quality across different technical environments.

The framework's modular design allows investigators to scale collection efforts appropriately while maintaining the systematic approach necessary for reliable analysis and legal admissibility.

4.10 COLLECTION TOOLS AND METHODOLOGY SELECTION

Traditional forensic tools like EnCase, FTK, and X-Ways have limited but important applications in AI forensics, primarily serving scenarios involving physical infrastructure rather than cloud-native deployments. These commercial tools excel at creating bit-for-bit disk images of on-premises AI servers, analyzing data scientist workstations for model development artifacts, and recovering deleted training datasets or model files from traditional file systems. However, their effectiveness is severely constrained by modern AI system architectures that predominantly rely on cloud platforms, distributed databases, API-based services, and containerized deployments that these tools cannot directly access or analyze.

The majority of AI evidence collection requires cloud-native tools and APIs that can interact directly with managed services while maintaining forensic integrity. AWS CLI, gcloud, and Azure CLI serve as the primary collection tools for most AI investigations, providing comprehensive access to machine learning platforms, object storage, audit logs, and operational telemetry with built-in integrity verification and chain of custody capabilities. Open-source alternatives like custom Python frameworks using boto3, pandas, and specialized libraries offer flexibility for unique requirements, while AI-specific tools like MLflow and DVC can provide model versioning and experiment tracking when properly configured for forensic evidence preservation.

CRITICAL: OPEN-SOURCE TOOL SELECTION FOR FORENSIC INTEGRITY

When selecting open-source tools for AI evidence collection, forensic integrity depends on careful tool evaluation. Poor tool choices can compromise evidence admissibility and investigation credibility. Before implementing any open-source solution, assess these critical factors:

MAINTENANCE AND DEVELOPMENT ACTIVITY

- Are there recent commits, bug fixes, and feature updates?
- Are critical security vulnerabilities being patched promptly?

DOCUMENTATION QUALITY

- Is installation and configuration clearly documented?
- Are there comprehensive API references and usage examples?

DEVELOPMENT TEAM CREDIBILITY

- Who are the primary maintainers and contributors?
- Do contributors have relevant expertise in forensics or security?

COMMUNITY SUPPORT

- Are there active forums, GitHub discussions, or Stack Overflow tags?
- Is there evidence of ongoing user adoption and support?

LEGAL AND COMPLIANCE CONSIDERATIONS

- Are there established procedures for expert testimony about the tool?
- Do licensing terms allow forensic and potential court use?

Selecting poorly maintained or undocumented tools can result in evidence collection failures, integrity challenges, and testimony difficulties that undermine entire investigations.

Successful AI evidence collection typically requires a hybrid approach combining multiple tool categories based on specific evidence types and system architectures. Cloud-native tools handle the bulk of evidence from managed AI services, traditional forensic tools address physical infrastructure and workstation analysis, and custom scripts bridge gaps for proprietary formats or specialized integrations. Tool selection must consider forensic integrity requirements (hash verification, chain of custody, non-destructive collection), platform compatibility (API support, authentication, rate limiting), scale considerations (data volume, parallel processing, network optimization), and legal admissibility standards (tool validation, documentation requirements, expert testimony support). This multi-tool strategy ensures comprehensive evidence collection while maintaining the forensic rigor necessary for technical analysis and legal proceedings.

4.11 RISK MANAGEMENT AND CONTINGENCY PLANNING

Evidence collection activities require the investigator to account for various risks that could compromise investigation integrity or legal admissibility. These include:

Technical risks include system failures during collection, data corruption, network interruptions, and access permission changes. Contingency planning includes backup collection methods, redundant storage systems, and automated integrity monitoring.

Legal risks encompass challenges to evidence admissibility, chain of custody breaches, and procedural compliance failures. Risk mitigation includes expert consultation, methodology validation, and comprehensive documentation standards.

Operational risks involve investigation timeline pressures, resource constraints, and coordination challenges across multiple stakeholders. Operational planning includes priority-based collection sequencing, resource allocation strategies, and stakeholder communication protocols.

This comprehensive process overview provides the foundation for understanding how the detailed methodologies presented in the following sections work together to create robust, legally admissible evidence collections that support thorough AI forensic analysis.

4.12 TECHNICAL COLLECTION IMPLEMENTATION: PLATFORM-SPECIFIC APPROACHES

Implementing AI evidence collection requires platform-specific expertise and specialized tools designed for the unique characteristics of machine learning systems. Each major deployment architecture presents distinct challenges and opportunities for evidence preservation, requiring investigators to master diverse technical approaches while maintaining forensic integrity throughout the collection process.

4.12.1 Cloud Platform Collection Strategies

Modern AI systems predominantly deploy on cloud platforms that provide both comprehensive logging capabilities and complex distributed architectures requiring specialized collection approaches. Each major platform offers different tools, access methods, and storage paradigms that shape collection strategies.

4.12.1.1 Amazon Web Services Evidence Collection Framework

Amazon Web Services (AWS) provides extensive logging and artifact storage capabilities that support comprehensive AI evidence collection, but the distributed nature of AWS services requires systematic approaches to identify and preserve all relevant evidence.

Core AWS AI services and evidence sources include AWS SageMaker for centralized machine learning model development and deployment with artifacts stored in predictable S3 bucket structures. Training jobs create detailed CloudWatch logs documenting training progress, resource utilization, and any errors or warnings. Model artifacts are automatically stored in S3 with comprehensive metadata including training parameters, model performance metrics, and dependency information.

Comprehensive AWS evidence collection approach begins with systematic CloudTrail audit log analysis to identify all AI-related activities including SageMaker job submissions, S3 bucket access patterns, IAM permission changes, and resource configuration modifications. This audit trail provides the foundation for understanding system scope and identifying evidence locations.

4.12.1.1.1 AWS Evidence Collection Framework

The systematic collection of AI evidence from Amazon Web Services requires a methodical approach that leverages AWS-native tools while maintaining forensic integrity throughout the process. This framework provides comprehensive procedures for identifying, cataloging, and preserving all AI-related artifacts across the AWS ecosystem.

4.12.1.1.2 Phase 1: System Discovery and Inventory

The initial discovery phase establishes the complete scope of AI resources within the AWS environment. This systematic enumeration ensures no critical evidence is overlooked during collection.

The training job inventory process begins by querying all SageMaker training activities to establish a comprehensive baseline of model development efforts. This inventory captures both active and completed training sessions, providing the foundation for understanding system scope and resource utilization patterns. The experiment tracking system provides additional context about model development workflows, grouping related training runs and revealing organizational structure that helps investigators understand relationships between different model versions and development approaches.

```
bash
aws sagemaker list-training-jobs --output json > training-jobs-
inventory.json
aws sagemaker list-experiments --output json > experiments-
inventory.json
```

4.12.1.1.3 Phase 2: Detailed Metadata Collection

Once the system inventory is complete, detailed metadata collection begins for each identified training job. This phase captures comprehensive configuration and execution details necessary for forensic analysis.

The metadata collection process retrieves complete training job specifications including hyperparameters, resource configurations, data source locations, and execution timelines. This information provides crucial context for understanding how models were developed and what factors may have influenced their behavior. The iteration through each training job ensures comprehensive metadata capture while maintaining organized file structures that support subsequent analysis activities.

```
bash
for job_name in $(jq -r
'.TrainingJobSummaries[].TrainingJobName' training-jobs-
inventory.json); do
    aws sagemaker describe-training-job --training-job-name
"$job_name" > "job-details-${job_name}.json"
done
```

4.12.1.1.4 Phase 3: Model Artifact Preservation with Integrity Verification

Model artifact collection focuses on preserving trained models along with all associated files necessary for model reproduction and analysis. This phase requires careful attention to file integrity and complete dependency capture.

The S3 synchronization process selectively collects model artifacts while excluding unnecessary files, focusing on compressed model packages that contain the essential components for forensic analysis. The integrity verification step generates cryptographic hashes for all collected files, creating tamper-evident records that ensure evidence authenticity throughout the investigation process.

```
bash
aws s3 sync s3://ml-models-bucket/ ./evidence/s3-artifacts/ --
exclude "*" --include "*.tar.gz"
find ./evidence/s3-artifacts/ -type f -exec sha256sum {} \; >
s3-artifacts-integrity.sha256
```

4.12.1.1.5 Phase 4: Comprehensive Log Collection and Export

Operational evidence collection captures runtime behavior and performance characteristics through comprehensive log aggregation and monitoring data preservation.

CloudWatch log collection begins with systematic enumeration of all SageMaker-related log groups, enabling comprehensive operational evidence gathering. The export task creation process establishes time-bounded log exports that capture relevant operational periods while managing data volume. The 30-day lookback period provides sufficient operational context while maintaining manageable collection scope for most investigations.

```
bash
aws logs describe-log-groups --log-group-name-prefix
"/aws/sagemaker" --output json > sagemaker-log-groups.json

for log_group in $(jq -r '.logGroups[].logGroupName' sagemaker-
log-groups.json); do
    aws logs create-export-task --log-group-name "$log_group" --
from $(date -d '30 days ago' +%s)000 --to $(date +%s)000 --
destination "ai-evidence-exports" --destination-prefix
"logs/$(basename $log_group)"
done
```

4.12.1.1.6 Phase 5: IAM and Access Control Evidence

Security and access control evidence collection documents the permissions and policies that govern AI system access, providing crucial context for understanding system security posture and potential access control issues.

The IAM role collection process identifies all SageMaker-related service roles and their associated permissions, capturing the security context within which AI systems operate. The policy collection focuses on custom policies that may affect ML resource access, providing evidence of organizational security decisions that could impact system behavior or investigation scope.

```
bash
aws iam list-roles --output json | jq '.Roles[] |
select(.RoleName | contains("SageMaker"))' >
sagemaker-roles.json
aws iam list-policies --scope Local --output json | jq
'.Policies[] | select(.PolicyName | contains("ML") or
.PolicyName | contains("SageMaker"))' > ml-policies.json
```

4.12.1.1.7 *Extended Infrastructure Evidence Collection*

Beyond core ML artifacts, comprehensive evidence collection includes VPC configurations and networking policies that affect system isolation and security, CloudWatch metrics and alarms that monitor system performance, and EC2 instance logs for compute resources supporting AI workloads. This extended collection ensures complete system context while maintaining focus on forensically relevant evidence.

4.12.1.1.8 *Data Pipeline and Integration Evidence*

The broader ecosystem evidence includes AWS Glue job logs and data catalog information for understanding data transformation processes, Amazon Kinesis stream configurations and processing logs for real-time data handling, Lambda function code and execution logs for serverless data processing, and RDS or DynamoDB configurations for data storage and retrieval patterns.

4.12.1.1.9 *Quality Assurance and Integrity Verification*

Throughout each collection phase, integrity verification procedures ensure that collected evidence maintains forensic standards. Hash generation, file verification, and chain of custody documentation provide the foundation for legally admissible evidence. The systematic approach ensures comprehensive coverage while maintaining the forensic rigor necessary for technical analysis and legal proceedings.

4.12.1.2 Google Cloud Platform Collection Methodology

Google Cloud Platform (GCP) organizes AI services around Vertex AI with integrated audit logging and artifact storage, but the platform's emphasis on managed services creates different evidence distribution patterns than AWS.

GCP Vertex AI Evidence Sources provide comprehensive model lifecycle management with detailed audit trails including Cloud Audit Logs capturing all administrative activities and data access, Vertex AI model registry containing versioned model artifacts with lineage tracking, BigQuery datasets often used for training data storage and analysis, and Cloud Storage buckets containing preprocessed datasets and experiment results.

4.12.1.2.1 *Google Cloud Platform Collection Methodology*

GCP organizes AI services around Vertex AI with integrated audit logging and artifact storage, but the platform's emphasis on managed services creates different evidence distribution patterns than AWS. The comprehensive collection approach typically needs to account for GCP's service-oriented architecture where evidence is commonly distributed across multiple specialized services.

4.12.1.2.2 *GCP Vertex AI Evidence Sources*

The platform provides comprehensive model lifecycle management with detailed audit trails including Cloud Audit Logs capturing all administrative activities and data access, Vertex AI model registry containing versioned model artifacts with lineage tracking, BigQuery datasets often used for training data storage and analysis, and Cloud Storage buckets containing preprocessed datasets and experiment results.

4.12.1.2.3 *Phase 1: Cloud Audit Log Collection for AI Activities*

The initial evidence collection phase focuses on capturing comprehensive audit trails that document all AI-related activities across the GCP platform. This systematic log collection establishes the foundation for understanding system usage patterns and identifying all relevant evidence sources.

Cloud Audit Logs provide detailed records of all administrative activities and API calls related to AI services. The Vertex AI platform audit logs capture model training activities, deployment events, and configuration changes, while BigQuery audit logs document data access patterns and query activities that may have influenced model training or evaluation processes.

```
gcloud logging read
'protoPayload.serviceName="aiplatform.googleapis.com"' --
limit=50000 --format=json > vertex-ai-audit-logs.json
gcloud logging read
'protoPayload.serviceName="bigquery.googleapis.com"' --
limit=50000 --format=json > bigquery-audit-logs.json
```

4.12.1.2.4 Phase 2: Vertex AI Model Registry Information Collection

The model registry collection phase systematically gathers comprehensive information about all AI models managed within the Vertex AI platform. This collection captures both high-level model inventory and detailed configuration metadata necessary for forensic analysis.

The model listing process enumerates all registered models within the specified region, providing the foundation for detailed metadata collection. The iterative metadata collection process ensures comprehensive documentation of each model's configuration, training parameters, and deployment history while maintaining organized file structures for subsequent analysis.

```
gcloud ai models list --region=us-central1 --format=json >
vertex-models-inventory.json

while IFS= read -r model_resource; do
    model_id=$(echo "$model_resource" | jq -r '.name')
    gcloud ai models describe "$model_id" --region=us-central1 -
-format=json > "model-details-$(basename "$model_id").json"
done < <(jq -c '.[]' vertex-models-inventory.json)
```

4.12.1.2.5 Phase 3: Training Pipeline Metadata Preservation

Training pipeline evidence collection captures the comprehensive development workflows that created the AI models under investigation. This phase documents both automated training pipelines and custom training jobs, providing crucial context for understanding model development processes.

The training pipeline inventory includes both managed training pipelines that use Vertex AI's automated workflow capabilities and custom training jobs that implement specialized training procedures. This comprehensive collection ensures that all aspects of model development are preserved for forensic analysis, including resource allocation decisions, training parameter configurations, and execution timelines.

```
gcloud ai training-pipelines list --region=us-central1 --
format=json > training-pipelines-inventory.json
gcloud ai custom-jobs list --region=us-central1 --format=json >
custom-jobs-inventory.json
```

4.12.1.2.6 Phase 4: BigQuery Dataset Export and Metadata Collection

BigQuery evidence collection focuses on preserving training data and analytical datasets that support AI model development and evaluation. This systematic approach ensures comprehensive data preservation while maintaining the metadata necessary for understanding data lineage and quality.

The dataset enumeration process identifies all BigQuery datasets within the project, providing the foundation for selective data collection based on investigation requirements. The metadata collection process captures detailed schema information, access patterns, and data lineage that may be crucial for bias investigations or data quality assessments. The conditional processing ensures robust handling of datasets while avoiding errors from missing or inaccessible resources.

```
bq ls --format=json > bigquery-datasets.json

while IFS= read -r dataset_info; do
    dataset_id=$(echo "$dataset_info" | jq -r
'.datasetReference.datasetId')
    if [ "$dataset_id" != "null" ]; then
       bq show --format=json "$dataset_id" > "dataset-metadata-
${dataset_id}.json"
       bq ls --format=json "$dataset_id" > "dataset-tables-
${dataset_id}.json"

    fi
done < <(jq -c '.[]' bigquery-datasets.json)
```

4.12.1.2.7 Phase 5: Cloud Storage Artifact Collection with Structure Preservation

Cloud Storage artifact collection preserves model artifacts, training data, and experimental results stored in Google Cloud Storage buckets. This comprehensive preservation maintains the original directory structure and file relationships that may be crucial for model reproduction and analysis.

The recursive listing process creates a complete inventory of all storage artifacts, enabling investigators to understand the scope and organization of stored evidence. The parallel copy operation efficiently transfers large volumes of data while preserving file timestamps, permissions, and directory structures that may contain important forensic evidence.

```
gsutil ls -r gs://ml-artifacts-bucket/** > cloud-storage-
inventory.txt
gsutil -m cp -r gs://ml-artifacts-bucket ./evidence/gcp-storage/
```

4.12.1.2.8 GCP-Specific Collection Considerations

The platform's service integration requires additional evidence collection to capture the complete AI system ecosystem. Cloud Build logs document automated model deployment pipelines, providing evidence of continuous integration and deployment processes that may affect model behavior. Cloud Functions execution logs capture serverless data processing activities, while Dataflow job monitoring preserves evidence of large-scale data transformation processes.

Cloud SQL audit logs document structured data access patterns that often prove relevant for understanding training data sources and data quality issues. The integration between these services generally means that comprehensive AI forensic investigations benefit from considering evidence from across the entire GCP ecosystem, rather than focusing solely on the core Vertex AI platform.

4.12.1.2.9 Advanced Collection Techniques for GCP

The managed service architecture requires specialized approaches for comprehensive evidence collection. Container Registry evidence preserves custom training environments and model serving containers, while Cloud Run logs document serverless model deployment activities. Kubernetes Engine clusters may host distributed training jobs that require coordination between multiple collection points.

The platform's emphasis on automation means that infrastructure-as-code definitions stored in Cloud Source Repositories may contain crucial evidence about system configuration and deployment decisions. Cloud Asset Inventory provides comprehensive resource enumeration that can guide evidence collection scope and priority decisions.

4.12.1.2.10 Quality Assurance and Integrity Verification

Throughout each collection phase, integrity verification procedures ensure that collected evidence maintains forensic standards. The JSON output formats provide structured data that can be systematically validated, while Cloud Storage transfer mechanisms include built-in integrity checking that verifies data consistency during collection operations.

The systematic approach leverages GCP's native tools and APIs to ensure comprehensive coverage while maintaining the forensic rigor necessary for technical analysis and legal proceedings. Each phase builds upon previous discoveries while maintaining detailed documentation of collection procedures and evidence relationships specific to the GCP platform architecture.

4.12.1.3 Microsoft Azure Collection Framework

Azure Machine Learning provides centralized model management with extensive metadata tracking, but the platform's enterprise focus creates additional compliance and governance considerations.

Azure ML workspace evidence organizes AI development around workspaces that contain comprehensive development and deployment history including experiment runs with detailed parameter and metric tracking, dataset registrations with version control and lineage information, model registrations with deployment history and performance monitoring, and compute target configurations showing resource allocation and scaling policies.

4.12.1.3.1 Microsoft Azure Collection Framework

Azure Machine Learning provides centralized model management with extensive metadata tracking, but the platform's enterprise focus creates additional compliance and governance considerations. The comprehensive collection approach typically needs to account for Azure's workspace-centric architecture and enterprise integration capabilities.

4.12.1.3.2 Azure ML Workspace Evidence

The platform organizes AI development around workspaces that contain comprehensive development and deployment history including experiment runs with detailed parameter and metric tracking, dataset registrations with version control and lineage information, model registrations with deployment history and performance monitoring, and compute target configurations showing resource allocation and scaling policies.

4.12.1.3.3 Phase 1: Azure ML Workspace Information Export

The initial collection phase systematically enumerates all Azure Machine Learning workspaces within the subscription, establishing the foundation for comprehensive evidence collection across the enterprise environment.

The workspace listing process identifies all Azure ML workspaces accessible within the current subscription context, providing the complete scope of AI development environments that require investigation. The systematic processing approach ensures comprehensive metadata collection for each workspace while maintaining robust error handling for environments with access restrictions or configuration issues.

```
az ml workspace list --output json > azure-ml-workspaces.json

# Process each workspace using proper JSON parsing
while IFS= read -r workspace_info; do
   workspace_name=$(echo "$workspace_info" | jq -r '.name')
   resource_group=$(echo "$workspace_info" | jq -r
'.resource_group // .resourceGroup')

   if [ "$workspace_name" != "null" ] && [ "$resource_group" !=
"null" ]; then
       az ml experiment list --workspace-name "$workspace_name"
--resource-group "$resource_group" --output json > "experiments-
${workspace_name}.json" 2>/dev/null || true
      az ml model list --workspace-name "$workspace_name" --
resource-group "$resource_group" --output json > "models-
${workspace_name}.json" 2>/dev/null || true
```

```
        az ml dataset list --workspace-name "$workspace_name" --
resource-group "$resource_group" --output json > "datasets-
${workspace_name}.json" 2>/dev/null || true
    fi
done < <(jq -c '.[]' azure-ml-workspaces.json)
```

4.12.1.3.4 Phase 2: Azure Activity Log Collection with Proper Date Formatting

Activity log collection captures comprehensive audit trails of all Azure operations related to AI and machine learning services. This phase documents administrative activities, resource management operations, and access patterns across the Azure environment.

The date formatting process ensures proper temporal scope for log collection, typically covering the investigation period with sufficient context for trend analysis. The activity log collection captures all subscription-level activities including resource provisioning, configuration changes, access events, and operational activities that may be relevant to the AI system investigation.

```
start_date=$(date -d '30 days ago' '+%Y-%m-%dT%H:%M:%SZ')
az monitor activity-log list --start-time "$start_date" --output
json > azure-activity-logs.json
```

4.12.1.3.5 Phase 3: Azure Policy Compliance Data Export

Policy compliance evidence collection documents governance and security controls applied to AI resources, providing crucial context for understanding organizational security posture and regulatory compliance efforts.

The policy state collection captures current compliance status for all resources, identifying any violations or non-compliant configurations that may affect AI system security or operation. The policy assignment collection documents which governance policies are applied to AI resources, providing evidence of organizational security and compliance intentions.

```
az policy state list --output json > azure-policy-compliance.json
az policy assignment list --output json > azure-policy-assignments.json
```

4.12.1.3.6 Phase 4: Azure DevOps Integration Evidence Collection

DevOps integration evidence captures software development lifecycle information including source code repositories, build pipelines, and deployment automation that may be crucial for understanding AI system development processes.

The conditional extension checking ensures robust operation in environments where Azure DevOps integration may not be configured, preventing collection failures while maintaining comprehensive coverage where integration exists. The project and repository collection captures development workflow evidence including source code management, build processes, and deployment automation that may contain crucial forensic evidence.

```
if az extension list --query "[?name=='azure-devops'].name" -o
tsv | grep -q azure-devops; then
    az devops project list --output json > devops-projects.json
2>/dev/null || echo "[]" > devops-projects.json
    az repos list --output json > devops-repositories.json
2>/dev/null || echo "[]" > devops-repositories.json
fi
```

4.12.1.3.7 Phase 5: Azure Monitor Metrics and Logs Preservation

Monitor metrics collection captures operational telemetry and performance data for Azure ML workspaces, providing evidence of system behavior, resource utilization, and operational patterns.

The subscription ID retrieval and resource ID construction enable systematic metrics collection for each identified workspace. The iterative processing ensures comprehensive metrics collection while maintaining robust error handling for workspaces that may have restricted access or configuration issues. The conditional processing and error suppression ensure collection continues even when individual workspaces encounter access or configuration problems.

```
subscription_id=$(az account show --query id -o tsv)

while IFS= read -r workspace_info; do
    workspace_name=$(echo "$workspace_info" | jq -r '.name')
    resource_group=$(echo "$workspace_info" | jq -r
'.resource_group // .resourceGroup')

    if [ "$workspace_name" != "null" ] && [ "$resource_group" !=
"null" ]; then
resource_id="/subscriptions/$subscription_id/resourceGroups/$resource_
group/providers/Microsoft.MachineLearningServices/workspaces/$workspace_
name"

        az monitor metrics list --resource "$resource_id" --
output json > "azure-ml-metrics-${workspace_name}.json"
2>/dev/null || true
    fi
done < <(jq -c '.[]' azure-ml-workspaces.json)
```

4.12.1.3.8 Azure Integration and Enterprise Evidence

The comprehensive enterprise evidence collection extends beyond core ML artifacts to include Azure Active Directory logs for authentication and authorization, providing crucial context for understanding access patterns and security events. Azure Policy compliance reports document governance and security controls applied to AI resources, while Azure Monitor metrics and logs provide operational telemetry for system behavior analysis.

Azure DevOps repositories capture software development lifecycle information including source code management, build pipelines, and deployment automation that may contain evidence of development practices, security controls, and operational procedures affecting AI system behavior.

4.12.1.3.9 Enterprise-Specific Collection Considerations

Azure's enterprise focus requires additional attention to compliance and governance evidence. Azure Security Center recommendations and alerts document security posture and threat detection activities. Azure Advisor recommendations provide evidence of performance optimization and best practice adherence. Azure Cost Management data documents resource utilization and cost allocation that may be relevant for understanding system scale and operational priorities.

The integration with Microsoft 365 and Azure Active Directory creates additional evidence sources including SharePoint document libraries containing AI development documentation, Teams conversations about AI projects, and Outlook communications regarding AI system decisions and approvals.

4.12.1.3.10 Advanced Collection Techniques for Azure

The enterprise architecture requires specialized approaches for comprehensive evidence collection. Azure Resource Manager templates and deployment history document infrastructure configuration decisions. Azure Logic Apps and Power Automate workflows may contain AI system integration logic. Azure Cognitive Services usage logs document AI service consumption patterns.

Azure Sentinel security information and event management (SIEM) data may contain security events and threat detection information relevant to AI system security incidents. Azure Application Insights provides detailed application performance monitoring and distributed tracing that can reveal AI system operational behavior.

4.12.1.3.11 *Quality Assurance and Integrity Verification*

Throughout each collection phase, integrity verification procedures ensure that collected evidence maintains forensic standards. The JSON output formats provide structured data that can be systematically validated, while Azure's built-in audit capabilities provide additional verification of collection completeness and accuracy.

The systematic approach leverages Azure's native CLI tools and APIs to ensure comprehensive coverage while maintaining the forensic rigor necessary for technical analysis and legal proceedings. The enterprise-focused design ensures that governance, compliance, and security evidence is preserved alongside technical artifacts, providing the complete context necessary for thorough AI forensic investigations.

4.12.2 Multi-Cloud and Hybrid Collection Coordination

Many enterprise AI systems span multiple cloud platforms requiring coordinated collection approaches that maintain referential integrity across different environments.

Cross-platform evidence correlation requires establishing consistent timestamp synchronization across different cloud providers, implementing unified naming conventions for evidence artifacts, maintaining comprehensive cross-reference databases linking related artifacts, and creating shared chain of custody documentation for distributed evidence.

Hybrid cloud and on-premises integration combines cloud resources with on-premises infrastructure requiring coordination between cloud-native collection tools and traditional digital forensics approaches, integration of cloud audit logs with on-premises system logs, and management of data transfer between different legal and technical jurisdictions.

4.12.3 Container and Orchestration Evidence Collection

Containerized AI deployments create layered evidence structures requiring specialized collection techniques that preserve both application artifacts and infrastructure context while maintaining the relationships between different abstraction layers.

4.12.3.1 Docker Container Evidence Preservation

Containers package complete execution environments including operating systems, runtime libraries, application code, model artifacts, and configuration files. This packaging creates comprehensive evidence units but requires specialized extraction and analysis techniques.

4.12.3.1.1 *Container Image Analysis and Preservation*

Containerized AI deployments create layered evidence structures requiring specialized collection techniques that preserve both application artifacts and infrastructure context while maintaining the relationships between different abstraction layers. Container image analysis involves documenting multiple layers that record the construction process including base operating system selection and configuration, software package installation and updates, application code and model artifact installation, and configuration file creation and modification.

Each layer represents a discrete change to the container environment and may contain evidence of security vulnerabilities, dependency conflicts, or configuration errors. This comprehensive preservation approach ensures that all aspects of the containerized AI system are available for forensic analysis while maintaining the integrity necessary for legal proceedings.

4.12.3.1.2 *Phase 1: Container Identification and Cataloging*

The initial discovery phase systematically identifies all AI-related containers within the environment, establishing the complete scope of containerized evidence that requires preservation.

The container catalog process uses Docker's filtering capabilities to identify containers specifically labeled as AI systems, ensuring comprehensive coverage while focusing collection efforts on relevant targets. The formatted output provides structured inventory information including container IDs, image references, container names, and current operational status, creating the foundation for detailed evidence collection.

```
docker ps -a --filter "label=ai-system" --format "table
{{.ID}}\t{{.Image}}\t{{.Names}}\t{{.Status}}" > docker-ai-
containers.txt
```

4.12.3.1.3 Phase 2: Complete Container Image Export for Analysis

Container image export creates comprehensive forensic copies of entire container images, preserving all layers, metadata, and configuration information necessary for detailed analysis.

The image export process uses Docker's native save functionality to create complete archives of container images, including all layers, metadata, and configuration information. The compression with gzip reduces storage requirements while maintaining complete fidelity of the original image. This approach ensures that the complete container environment can be reconstructed for analysis, including the specific versions of all software components and their configurations.

```
docker save ai-model-serving:v2.1 | gzip > evidence/ai-model-
serving-v2.1.tar.gz
```

4.12.3.1.4 Phase 3: Container Filesystem Extraction for Detailed Analysis

Filesystem extraction provides access to the complete container filesystem for detailed forensic examination of installed software, configuration files, model artifacts, and temporary data.

The container identification process selects a representative running container for filesystem analysis, ensuring that runtime state and temporary files are preserved alongside static configuration. The conditional processing ensures robust operation when containers may not be running, preventing collection failures while maintaining comprehensive coverage where active containers exist.

The filesystem extraction creates a complete TAR archive of the container's filesystem, preserving file permissions, timestamps, and directory structures. The subsequent extraction into an analysis directory enables detailed examination using standard forensic tools while maintaining the original archive for integrity verification.

```
container_id=$(docker ps -q --filter "label=ai-system" | head -1)

if [ ! -z "$container_id" ]; then
    docker export "$container_id" > evidence/container-
filesystem.tar
    mkdir -p evidence/filesystem-analysis
    tar -xf evidence/container-filesystem.tar -C
evidence/filesystem-analysis/
fi
```

4.12.3.1.5 Phase 4: Container Configuration and Runtime Information Collection

Configuration and runtime data collection captures the complete operational context of containerized AI systems, including environment variables, network configurations, resource allocations, and execution logs.

The iterative collection process ensures comprehensive coverage of all AI-related containers, both running and stopped, capturing configuration details that may differ between container instances. The container inspection process generates detailed JSON output documenting all container configuration parameters including environment variables, volume mounts, network settings, resource limits, and security contexts.

The log collection captures runtime operational evidence including application output, error messages, and system events that occurred during container execution. The output redirection ensures that both standard output and error streams are preserved, maintaining complete operational context for forensic analysis.

```
for container_id in $(docker ps -aq --filter "label=ai-system"); do
    docker inspect "$container_id" > "evidence/container-
configuration-${container_id}.json"
    docker logs "$container_id" > "evidence/container-runtime-
${container_id}.log" 2>&1
done
```

4.12.3.1.6 Phase 5: Container Registry Metadata Preservation

Registry metadata collection documents the complete build history and layer composition of container images, providing crucial evidence about how containers were constructed and what changes were made during the build process.

The container history command captures the complete build history including all layer creation commands, timestamps, and size information. The no-truncation flag ensures that complete command information is preserved, including full command lines and parameters that may contain important forensic evidence about build processes, installed software, and configuration decisions.

```
docker history ai-model-serving:v2.1 --no-trunc >
evidence/container-build-history.txt
```

4.12.3.1.7 Container Runtime Evidence Analysis

Beyond static image analysis, container runtime evidence includes operational data generated during container execution. This evidence encompasses process lists and resource utilization patterns that document how containers actually behaved during operation, network connections and communication logs that reveal data flow and external dependencies, file system changes and temporary file creation that may contain model artifacts or operational data, and environment variables and runtime configuration that may differ from static configuration.

4.12.3.1.8 Advanced Container Analysis Techniques

Container forensic analysis requires specialized techniques for examining layered filesystems and understanding container orchestration contexts. Layer-by-layer analysis reveals the construction process and can identify when specific software components, model artifacts, or configuration changes were introduced. Union filesystem analysis examines how different layers combine to create the final runtime environment, potentially revealing conflicting configurations or security vulnerabilities.

Multi-stage build analysis examines complex container builds that may use intermediate containers for compilation or data processing, ensuring that all relevant build artifacts are preserved. Build context analysis examines the source code and configuration files used during container construction, providing evidence of development practices and security controls.

4.12.3.1.9 Container Orchestration Integration

Containerized AI systems often operate within orchestration platforms like Kubernetes or Docker Swarm, requiring additional evidence collection to capture deployment configurations, service definitions, and operational policies. Pod specifications and deployment manifests document intended configuration and resource allocation. Service discovery and networking configurations reveal how containers communicate and access external resources.

Persistent volume claims and storage configurations document how containerized AI systems access training data and store model artifacts. Security policies and access controls document authorization mechanisms and potential attack vectors that may be relevant for security investigations.

4.12.3.1.10 Quality Assurance and Integrity Verification

Throughout each collection phase, integrity verification procedures ensure that collected container evidence maintains forensic standards. Image digest verification confirms that exported images match their original registry versions. Filesystem hash verification ensures that extracted filesystems maintain integrity throughout the analysis process.

Container signature verification, when available, provides cryptographic proof of image authenticity and publisher identity. Layer hash verification ensures that individual container layers maintain integrity and can detect tampering or corruption during the collection process.

The systematic approach leverages Docker's native tools and standard forensic practices to ensure comprehensive container evidence collection while maintaining the forensic rigor necessary for technical analysis and legal proceedings. The multi-phase approach ensures that both static configuration and runtime behavior evidence are preserved, providing the complete context necessary for thorough containerized AI system investigations.

4.12.3.2 Kubernetes Orchestration Evidence

Kubernetes clusters orchestrate complex AI systems across multiple containers and compute nodes, generating comprehensive audit trails about system behavior, resource allocation, and administrative actions.

4.12.3.2.1 Kubernetes Cluster State Evidence

Kubernetes clusters orchestrate complex AI systems across multiple containers and compute nodes, generating comprehensive audit trails about system behavior, resource allocation, and administrative actions. The cluster state evidence encompasses the complete cluster configuration including node specifications and resource allocation, namespace organization and access controls, persistent volume claims and storage provisioning, and network policies and service mesh configuration.

The comprehensive evidence collection approach will need to account for Kubernetes' distributed architecture where AI workloads span multiple pods, nodes, and namespaces, requiring systematic collection of both static configuration and dynamic operational state. This automated collection framework ensures continuous evidence preservation while maintaining system operational integrity.

4.12.3.2.2 Automated Kubernetes Evidence Collection Framework

The systematic evidence collection leverages Kubernetes' native tooling through an automated CronJob configuration that provides continuous, scheduled evidence collection without manual intervention. This approach ensures comprehensive coverage of AI workload evidence while maintaining consistent collection intervals that support temporal analysis and trend detection.

The CronJob configuration establishes a systematic collection schedule that captures AI workload state and configuration at regular intervals, providing the temporal granularity necessary for understanding system evolution and identifying behavioral changes over time. The automated approach eliminates manual collection errors while ensuring comprehensive coverage of all relevant Kubernetes resources.

```
# Kubernetes Evidence Collection Configuration
apiVersion: batch/v1
kind: CronJob
metadata:
  name: ai-evidence-collector
spec:
  schedule: "0 */6 * * *" # Collect every 6 hours
  jobTemplate:
    spec:
     template:
       spec:
         containers:
        - name: evidence-collector
           image: kubectl:latest
           command:
          - /bin/bash
          - -c
          - |
            # Collect AI workload state and configuration
             kubectl get pods -l app=ai-model -o yaml >
/evidence/ai-pods-$(date +%Y%m%d-%H%M%S).yaml
             kubectl get deployments -l app=ai-model -o yaml >
/evidence/ai-deployments-$(date +%Y%m%d-%H%M%S).yaml
             kubectl get services -l app=ai-model -o yaml >
/evidence/ai-services-$(date +%Y%m%d-%H%M%S).yaml
             kubectl get configmaps -l app=ai-model -o yaml >
/evidence/ai-configmaps-$(date +%Y%m%d-%H%M%S).yaml

            # Collect recent events and logs
             kubectl get events --sort-by='.lastTimestamp' --
field-selector involvedObject.name | grep ai-model >
/evidence/ai-events-$(date +%Y%m%d-%H%M%S).log

            # Collect pod logs for AI workloads
             kubectl get pods -l app=ai-model --no-headers -o
custom-columns=":metadata.name" | while read pod_name; do
               kubectl logs "$pod_name" > "/evidence/ai-pod-
logs-${pod_name}-$(date +%Y%m%d-%H%M%S).log" 2>/dev/null || true
             done

            # Generate integrity verification
            find /evidence -name "*$(date +%Y%m%d)*" -type f -
exec sha256sum {} \; > /evidence/integrity-$(date +%Y%m%d-
%H%M%S).sha256
           volumeMounts:
           - name: evidence-storage
             mountPath: /evidence
         volumes:
        - name: evidence-storage
          persistentVolumeClaim:
            claimName: forensic-evidence-pvc
         restartPolicy: OnFailure
```

4.12.3.2.3 Phase 1: AI Workload State and Configuration Collection

The workload state collection phase systematically gathers complete configuration and status information for all AI-related Kubernetes resources, providing comprehensive documentation of system deployment and current operational state.

The pod collection process captures complete pod specifications including container configurations, resource allocations, environment variables, volume mounts, and current operational status. The YAML output format preserves complete configuration detail including metadata, specifications, and status information necessary for forensic analysis.

The deployment collection documents how AI workloads are deployed and managed, including replica counts, rolling update strategies, resource requirements, and deployment history. This information provides crucial context for understanding system scaling behavior and deployment practices.

Service and ConfigMap collection captures networking configuration and application configuration data that may contain sensitive information or reveal system dependencies crucial for forensic analysis.

4.12.3.2.4 Phase 2: Event Collection and Temporal Analysis

Event collection provides temporal context for understanding system behavior changes, resource allocation issues, and administrative actions that may have affected AI workload operation.

The event sorting and filtering approach ensures that relevant events are captured with proper temporal ordering, enabling investigators to reconstruct sequences of system changes and identify correlations between administrative actions and system behavior changes. The field selector filtering focuses collection on AI-related events while maintaining comprehensive coverage of relevant system activities.

4.12.3.2.5 Phase 3: Pod Log Collection for Operational Evidence

Pod log collection captures the runtime operational evidence generated by AI workloads, including application output, error messages, and debugging information that may reveal system behavior patterns or operational issues.

The iterative log collection process ensures comprehensive coverage of all AI workload pods while maintaining organized file structures that support subsequent analysis. The custom column selection optimizes kubectl output for automated processing while the conditional error handling ensures collection continues even when individual pods may be inaccessible or terminated.

The timestamped log organization enables temporal correlation between different pods and system events, supporting comprehensive operational analysis and timeline reconstruction.

4.12.3.2.6 Phase 4: Integrity Verification and Evidence Authentication

The integrity verification process generates cryptographic hashes for all collected evidence, creating tamper-evident records that ensure evidence authenticity throughout the investigation process.

The automated hash generation process creates SHA-256 checksums for all evidence files collected during each collection cycle, enabling investigators to verify evidence integrity and detect any unauthorized modifications. The timestamped integrity files provide chronological verification records that support chain of custody requirements.

4.12.3.2.7 Kubernetes Workload Evidence Analysis

Beyond the automated collection framework, Kubernetes workload evidence includes comprehensive operational data that requires specialized analysis techniques. AI workloads generate extensive evidence including pod lifecycle events and status changes that document container creation, scheduling, execution, and termination processes.

Service discovery and networking configuration evidence reveals how AI workloads communicate with external services, access training data, and expose inference APIs. This networking evidence can reveal system dependencies, data flow patterns, and potential security vulnerabilities relevant to forensic investigations.

Persistent volume claims and storage access patterns document how AI workloads access training data, store model artifacts, and maintain operational state. Storage evidence can reveal data access patterns, model versioning practices, and potential data exfiltration activities.

Resource quotas and limit enforcement evidence documents how Kubernetes manages resource allocation for AI workloads, potentially revealing resource contention issues, capacity planning decisions, and operational constraints that may affect system behavior.

4.12.3.2.8 *Advanced Kubernetes Evidence Sources*

Enterprise Kubernetes deployments often include additional evidence sources that require specialized collection approaches. Role-based access control (RBAC) configurations document authorization policies and access controls applied to AI resources, providing crucial context for security investigations.

Network policies and service mesh configurations control traffic flow between AI workloads and external services, generating evidence about data access patterns and communication security. Admission controllers and policy engines may generate audit logs documenting policy enforcement decisions and configuration validation activities.

Custom resource definitions (CRDs) and operators may manage AI-specific resources like training jobs, model serving deployments, or data processing pipelines, requiring specialized collection procedures for non-standard Kubernetes resources.

4.12.3.2.9 *Quality Assurance and Forensic Integrity*

The automated evidence collection framework incorporates multiple quality assurance measures to ensure forensic integrity. The persistent volume storage ensures evidence preservation across collection cycles while maintaining organized directory structures that support systematic analysis.

The CronJob scheduling provides consistent collection intervals that enable temporal analysis while the container-based collection environment ensures reproducible collection procedures. The automated integrity verification creates cryptographic proof of evidence authenticity that supports legal admissibility requirements.

The systematic approach leverages Kubernetes' native tools and established DevOps practices to ensure comprehensive evidence collection while maintaining the forensic rigor necessary for technical analysis and legal proceedings. The automated framework reduces manual collection errors while ensuring comprehensive coverage of complex, distributed AI workload evidence.

4.12.4 Real-Time and Streaming System Collection

AI systems operating in real-time environments require specialized collection techniques that capture evidence without disrupting critical operations while preserving the temporal characteristics of streaming data and real-time decision-making.

4.12.4.1 Streaming Data Platform Evidence

4.12.4.1.1 *Streaming Data Platform Evidence Collection*

Real-time AI systems process continuous data streams through platforms like Apache Kafka, Amazon Kinesis, or Google Cloud Pub/Sub that maintain ordered logs of all processed messages. These streaming platforms create unique evidence preservation challenges due to their distributed architecture, continuous data flow, and temporal ordering requirements that are critical for forensic analysis.

Message stream preservation involves capturing comprehensive data flow information that encompasses multiple evidence categories. Message content preservation includes complete payload data along with precise timestamps and ordering metadata that establish sequence relationships. Partition assignment documentation tracks how data distribution occurs across the cluster, while consumer group coordination records provide insight into processing patterns and resource allocation. Performance metrics collection focuses on throughput measurements and processing latency data that reveal system behavior under different operational conditions. Error tracking encompasses failure rates and retry pattern documentation that may indicate system stress or configuration issues. Kafka's distributed log architecture typically requires collection procedures to span multiple brokers, topics, and consumer groups while preserving the temporal relationships essential for accurate forensic reconstruction and analysis.

4.12.4.1.2 Phase 1: Topic Configuration and Metadata Export

The initial discovery phase systematically identifies all Kafka topics within the environment and captures their complete configuration metadata, establishing the foundation for understanding message flow architecture and data organization patterns.

The topic inventory process enumerates all available topics within the Kafka cluster, providing the complete scope of data streams that may contain AI-related evidence. The iterative metadata collection ensures comprehensive documentation of topic configurations including partition counts, replication factors, retention policies, and security configurations that may affect evidence availability and integrity.

The conditional processing with empty string checks ensures robust operation in environments where topic lists may contain blank lines or formatting artifacts, preventing collection failures while maintaining comprehensive coverage of all valid topics.

```
# Kafka-based AI system evidence preservation
# 1. Export topic configurations and metadata
kafka-topics.sh --bootstrap-server localhost:9092 --list >
kafka-topics-inventory.txt
while IFS= read -r topic; do
    if [ ! -z "$topic" ]; then
        kafka-topics.sh --bootstrap-server localhost:9092 --
describe --topic "$topic" > "topic-config-${topic}.txt"
    fi
done < kafka-topics-inventory.txt
```

4.12.4.1.3 Phase 2: Consumer Group Information Capture

Consumer group evidence collection documents how AI applications consume message streams, providing crucial context for understanding data processing patterns, offset management, and potential data loss or duplication issues.

The consumer group inventory captures all active and inactive consumer groups within the cluster, revealing which applications are processing Kafka messages and how they coordinate distributed consumption. The detailed group descriptions document offset positions, lag metrics, and partition assignments that may reveal processing anomalies or performance issues relevant to AI system behavior.

The systematic iteration through all consumer groups ensures comprehensive coverage of consumption patterns while maintaining organized documentation that supports subsequent analysis of data flow and processing behavior.

```
# 2. Capture consumer group information
kafka-consumer-groups.sh --bootstrap-server localhost:9092 --list > con-
sumer-groups-inventory.txt

while IFS= read -r group; do
   if [ ! -z "$group" ]; then
       kafka-consumer-groups.sh --bootstrap-server
localhost:9092 --describe --group "$group" > "consumer-group-
${group}.txt"
   fi
done < consumer-groups-inventory.txt
```

4.12.4.1.4 Phase 3: Message Content Sampling with Ordering Preservation

Message content sampling captures representative examples of data flowing through AI prediction streams while preserving the temporal ordering and message structure essential for forensic analysis.

The console consumer configuration reads messages from the beginning of the topic to capture historical data patterns, with controlled message limits and timeout settings to prevent excessive resource consumption while ensuring adequate sample coverage. The JSON output format assumption indicates this stream likely contains structured AI prediction data that requires preservation for bias analysis or accuracy evaluation.

The ordering preservation approach maintains message sequence integrity that may be crucial for understanding AI system behavior patterns, temporal correlations, and data dependencies that could affect investigation conclusions.

```
# 3. Sample message content with preservation of ordering
kafka-console-consumer.sh --bootstrap-server localhost:9092 --
topic ai-predictions --from-beginning --max-messages 10000 --
timeout-ms 30000 > ai-predictions-sample.json
```

4.12.4.1.5 Phase 4: Broker Log and Storage Metrics Collection

Broker infrastructure evidence captures operational telemetry and storage information that provides context for understanding system performance, capacity constraints, and potential data retention issues.

The conditional log collection approach handles environments where Kafka logs may be stored in different locations or may not be accessible due to permissions restrictions. The graceful error handling ensures collection continues even when log access is restricted while providing clear documentation of access limitations that may affect evidence completeness.

The storage information collection captures detailed metrics about disk usage, log segment organization, and retention policy enforcement that may reveal data availability constraints or storage-related issues affecting evidence preservation.

```
# 4. Collect broker logs and metrics
if [ -d "/var/log/kafka" ]; then
   cp /var/log/kafka/*.log ./evidence/kafka-logs/ 2>/dev/null
|| echo "Kafka logs not accessible or do not exist"
fi

kafka-log-dirs.sh --bootstrap-server localhost:9092 --describe --
json > kafka-storage-info.json
```

4.12.4.1.6 Advanced Kafka Evidence Analysis

Beyond the basic collection framework, Kafka-based AI systems generate extensive operational evidence that requires specialized analysis techniques. Message throughput and latency patterns can reveal system performance characteristics and potential bottlenecks that may affect AI model training or inference quality.

Partition assignment and rebalancing events document how data distribution changes over time, potentially revealing system stability issues or configuration problems that could affect data processing consistency. Consumer lag metrics provide evidence of processing delays that may indicate system overload or resource constraints affecting AI system performance.

Message serialization and schema evolution evidence captures how data formats change over time, potentially revealing compatibility issues or data quality problems that could affect AI model accuracy. Offset management and commit patterns document data processing guarantees and potential data loss scenarios.

4.12.4.1.7 Stream Processing Integration Evidence

Many Kafka-based AI systems integrate with stream processing frameworks like Apache Flink, Kafka Streams, or Apache Storm that generate additional evidence sources. Stream processing topology configurations document data transformation logic and processing guarantees that may affect AI model input data quality.

State store evidence captures intermediate processing state that may contain model parameters, feature engineering transformations, or aggregated metrics relevant to AI system behavior. Checkpoint and recovery logs document fault tolerance mechanisms and potential data consistency issues.

Windowing and aggregation configurations reveal how temporal data is processed for AI model training or inference, potentially affecting system behavior during different time periods or under varying load conditions.

4.12.4.1.8 Real-Time Model Serving Evidence

Kafka-based AI systems often implement real-time model serving where inference requests and responses flow through Kafka topics. Request and response message correlation provides evidence of model behavior patterns, response times, and prediction accuracy that may be crucial for bias investigations.

Model versioning and deployment evidence captures how AI models are updated in real-time systems, potentially revealing version compatibility issues or deployment problems that could affect system behavior. A/B testing configurations document how different model versions are compared, providing evidence of experimental design and statistical validity.

4.12.4.1.9 Quality Assurance and Stream Integrity

Kafka's distributed architecture requires specialized integrity verification approaches that account for message ordering, partition distribution, and replication factors. Message offset verification ensures that sampled data represents the actual message sequences processed by AI systems.

Checksum verification for message content provides cryptographic proof of data integrity, while broker-level integrity checks ensure that storage systems maintain data consistency across replications. Consumer group offset verification documents processing progress and can identify potential data skipping or duplication issues.

The systematic approach leverages Kafka's native tooling and established streaming data practices to ensure comprehensive evidence collection while maintaining the forensic rigor necessary for technical analysis and legal proceedings. The multi-phase collection framework ensures that both configuration metadata and operational data are preserved, providing the complete context necessary for thorough streaming AI system investigations.

4.12.4.1.10 Temporal Analysis and Forensic Considerations

Time-based log retention in Kafka environments presents distinctive forensic challenges, as historical data faces automatic deletion according to configured retention policies. Evidence collection frameworks typically need to consider these temporal limitations while preserving sufficient historical coverage to support trend analysis and pattern recognition activities.

Message timestamp preservation enables temporal correlation analysis that may reveal seasonal patterns, system behavior changes, or external influence events that affected AI system performance. The combination of message content, timing information, and operational metrics provides comprehensive evidence for understanding system behavior evolution over time.

4.12.5 Advanced Collection Scenarios: Large-Scale Enterprise Systems

Enterprise-scale AI deployments present unique challenges requiring sophisticated coordination and resource management strategies.

4.12.5.1 High-Volume Training Data Collection

Large language models and computer vision systems may require training datasets measured in petabytes, creating unprecedented challenges for evidence preservation.

Distributed Dataset Management involves implementing parallel collection strategies across multiple storage systems, coordinating checksums and integrity verification at scale, managing bandwidth limitations and transfer costs, and implementing incremental collection for continuously updated datasets.

4.12.5.1.1 Sample-Based Collection Strategies

Large language models and computer vision systems may require training datasets measured in petabytes, creating unprecedented challenges for evidence preservation. When comprehensive collection becomes impractical due to resource constraints, sample-based collection strategies provide statistically valid approaches that maintain representativeness while managing computational and storage limitations.

Sample-Based Collection Strategies often become essential when comprehensive collection proves impractical due to scale or resource constraints. These approaches require careful implementation of statistical sampling methodologies that preserve dataset representativeness while enabling meaningful analysis. Bias evaluation helps identify potential artifacts introduced by sampling decisions, while cross-validation techniques using multiple sampling approaches provide confidence in collection adequacy. Sensitivity analysis typically assesses how sampling choices influence analytical conclusions and investigation outcomes.

Systematic sampling implementations need to navigate competing requirements that include adequate representation across all dataset segments and sufficient sample sizes for robust statistical analysis. Resource management considerations often influence sampling decisions, while investigators typically seek to preserve extrapolation capabilities that allow findings to be applied to complete datasets with appropriate confidence levels.

4.12.5.1.2 Statistical Foundation and Sample Size Calculation

The core sampling framework establishes mathematically sound approaches for determining appropriate sample sizes based on population characteristics and required statistical confidence levels. The sample size calculation incorporates standard statistical formulas while accounting for finite population corrections when necessary.

```
# Statistical approaches for managing petabyte-scale evidence
import random
import hashlib
import pandas as pd
from typing import Dict, List, Tuple

class ForensicDatasetSampler:
   def __init__(self, population_size: int, confidence_level:
float = 0.95, margin_error: float = 0.05):
       self.population_size = population_size
       self.confidence_level = confidence_level
       self.margin_error = margin_error

   def calculate_sample_size(self) -> int:
      """Calculate statistically valid sample size for population"""
       z_score = 1.96 if self.confidence_level == 0.95 else 2.576
       p = 0.5 # Conservative estimate for maximum variability

       numerator = (z_score ** 2) * p * (1 - p)
       denominator = (self.margin_error ** 2)
       sample_size = numerator / denominator
```

```
        # Finite population correction
        if self.population_size < 100000:
            sample_size = sample_size / (1 + ((sample_size - 1)
/ self.population_size))
        return int(sample_size)
```

4.12.5.1.3 Stratified Sampling for Bias Detection

Stratified sampling becomes essential when investigating potential discrimination, as bias often affects specific demographic groups that may represent small portions of the overall dataset. Without stratified sampling, these groups may be underrepresented in analysis samples, making bias detection impossible or unreliable.

The stratified approach ensures that all demographic groups have sufficient representation for meaningful statistical analysis, which is crucial for detecting discrimination patterns that might affect small subpopulations. The methodology maintains demographic proportions while ensuring adequate statistical power for each stratum.

```
    def stratified_sample(self, dataset_metadata: Dict[str, List],
strata_column: str) -> List[str]:
        """Generate stratified sample maintaining demographic
proportions"""
        strata_counts =
pd.Series(dataset_metadata[strata_column]).value_counts()
        total_sample_size = self.calculate_sample_size()
        sampled_items = []

        for stratum, count in strata_counts.items():
            stratum_proportion = count / self.population_size
            stratum_sample_size = int(total_sample_size *
stratum_proportion)

            stratum_items = [item for item, value in
zip(dataset_metadata['item_ids'],
                                 dataset_metadata[strata_column]) if
value == stratum]
            sampled_items.extend(random.sample(stratum_items,
                                     min(stratum_sample_size,
len(stratum_items))))
        return sampled_items
```

4.12.5.1.4 Temporal Sampling for Time-Series Analysis

Temporal sampling ensures representative coverage across different time periods, capturing seasonal variations, system evolution, and temporal dependencies that may affect AI system behavior. The temporal approach divides the time range into equal periods and samples proportionally from each period.

```
    def temporal_sample(self, timestamps: List[str],
time_periods: int = 12) -> List[str]:
        """Generate temporally representative sample across time periods"""
        sorted_timestamps = sorted(timestamps)
        period_size = len(sorted_timestamps) // time_periods
        sampled_timestamps = []

        for i in range(time_periods):
            period_start = i * period_size
            period_end = (i + 1) * period_size if i <
time_periods - 1 else len(sorted_timestamps)
            period_items = sorted_timestamps[period_start:period_end]
```

```
            if period_items:
                samples_per_period = max(1,
self.calculate_sample_size() // time_periods)

sampled_timestamps.extend(random.sample(period_items,
                                       min(samples_per_period,
len(period_items))))

return sampled_timestamps
```

4.12.5.1.5 Enhanced Bias Detection Sampling

For investigations specifically focused on bias detection, enhanced sampling approaches ensure adequate representation for protected groups while maintaining overall statistical validity. This specialized sampling approach creates intersectional groups from protected attributes and ensures minimum sample sizes for statistical validity.

```
def stratified_bias_detection_sample(dataset,
protected_attributes, sample_ratio=0.01, min_group_size=100):
    """Create stratified sample ensuring adequate representation
for bias detection"""
    samples = []

    # Create intersectional groups from protected attributes
    dataset['stratification_group'] =
dataset[protected_attributes].apply(
        lambda row: '_'.join(row.astype(str)), axis=1)

for group_value in dataset['stratification_group'].unique():

        group_data = dataset[dataset['stratification_group'] ==
group_value]

       # Ensure minimum sample size for statistical validity
        n_samples = max(min_group_size, int(len(group_data) *
sample_ratio))
        n_samples = min(n_samples, len(group_data)) # Don't
exceed available data

        if len(group_data) >= min_group_size:
            group_sample = group_data.sample(n=n_samples,
random_state=42)
            samples.append(group_sample)

   final_sample = pd.concat(samples, ignore_index=True)

    # Document sampling methodology for legal defensibility
    sampling_documentation = {
      'methodology': 'stratified_sampling',
      'stratification_criteria': protected_attributes,
      'min_group_size': min_group_size,
      'target_sample_ratio': sample_ratio,
      'groups_included': len(samples),
      'total_sample_size': len(final_sample),
      'original_dataset_size': len(dataset)
    }

    return final_sample, sampling_documentation
```

4.12.5.1.6 Quality Assurance for Sample Validity

Sample validation requires systematic verification that samples accurately represent the characteristics of the complete dataset. This validation process documents sample representativeness and identifies any systematic biases introduced by the sampling process itself.

Sample validation typically involves comparing key statistical properties between the sample and the complete dataset, testing for significant differences in demographic distributions, and documenting any limitations or constraints that affect the interpretation of sample-based findings.

4.12.5.1.7 Statistical Validation for Sampled Evidence

The validation framework addresses cases where comprehensive collection is impractical by implementing sample representativeness validation ensuring samples accurately reflect full datasets, demographic distribution comparisons between samples and full populations, temporal pattern validation ensuring samples capture relevant time periods, and feature distribution analysis confirming adequate representation of important variables.

4.12.5.1.8 Advanced Sampling Considerations

Beyond basic statistical sampling, specialized considerations apply to AI forensic investigations. Risk-based sampling focuses on high-priority evidence most likely to contain problematic patterns, while decision-type sampling targets specific categories of AI outputs for focused analysis.

Geographic targeting enables collection from specific locations or jurisdictions where regulatory requirements differ or complaints have been concentrated. Attribute-based collection ensures adequate representation of protected groups through demographic stratification or oversampling of underrepresented populations.

4.12.5.1.9 Legal and Forensic Compliance

The sampling framework ensures forensically sound approaches to managing large-scale evidence collection while maintaining statistical validity and legal admissibility standards. Comprehensive documentation of sampling methodology, statistical assumptions, and validation procedures provides the foundation for expert testimony and regulatory compliance.

Statistical power analysis determines minimum sample sizes needed to detect meaningful differences with specified confidence levels, while legal sufficiency standards guide sample size requirements for different types of legal proceedings and regulatory assessments.

4.12.5.2 Geographic Distribution and Jurisdictional Complexity

Modern AI training often spans multiple cloud regions and countries, creating evidence scattered across dozens of data centers and legal jurisdictions.

Multi-jurisdictional coordination requires navigating different privacy laws across jurisdictions, coordinating with cloud providers operating under various legal frameworks, managing data transfer restrictions and sovereignty requirements, and synchronizing collection activities across time zones and operational schedules.

Legal compliance framework addresses the complexity through jurisdiction-specific data handling protocols, privacy regulation compliance procedures, cross-border data transfer documentation, and regulatory notification requirements.

4.13 DOCUMENTATION AND LEGAL CONSIDERATIONS: BUILDING DEFENSIBLE EVIDENCE

Comprehensive documentation ensures that AI evidence collection meets legal admissibility standards while providing clear guidance for technical analysis. The complexity of AI systems requires enhanced documentation that addresses distributed collection, technical interdependencies, specialized preservation procedures, and the unique challenges of presenting technical evidence to legal audiences.

4.13.1 Comprehensive Documentation Requirements for AI Evidence

AI forensic investigations require extensive documentation that captures not only the technical artifacts but also the context, methodology, and chain of custody necessary for legal admissibility and technical reproducibility. This documentation serves multiple audiences while maintaining forensic integrity throughout the collection process.

4.13.1.1 Documentation Categories and Standards

Technical methodology documentation provides the detailed procedural record necessary for independent validation and reproduction of collection activities. This category forms the scientific foundation of the investigation by documenting exactly how evidence was collected, what tools were used, and what procedures were followed. The documentation should be sufficiently detailed that another qualified investigator could reproduce the collection process and achieve consistent results. This includes complete tool specifications with version numbers and configuration parameters, step-by-step collection procedures with timing and dependencies, environmental specifications documenting the collection context, quality assurance procedures with validation checkpoints, and limitation statements acknowledging constraints or uncertainties.

The importance of technical methodology documentation extends beyond mere record-keeping. In legal proceedings, opposing counsel will challenge collection procedures, and courts require evidence that proper forensic standards were followed. Technical documentation provides the foundation for expert testimony about methodology reliability and helps establish the scientific validity of the evidence collection process.

Chain of custody documentation maintains the legal foundation for evidence admissibility through comprehensive tracking of evidence handling from initial collection through final analysis. This documentation type addresses one of the most fundamental requirements in forensic investigations: proving that evidence has not been tampered with or altered since collection. The chain of custody must account for every person who accessed the evidence, every transfer or movement of evidence, and every procedure applied to the evidence.

For AI systems, chain of custody documentation becomes particularly complex due to the distributed nature of evidence sources and the dynamic character of many AI artifacts. Evidence may span multiple cloud platforms, involve automatically generated logs, and include artifacts that change continuously during normal operation. The documentation must address these unique challenges while maintaining the strict accountability required for legal admissibility. This includes collector identification and qualification records, collection timestamps with timezone specification, transfer logs documenting evidence movement, access controls and security measures, and integrity verification records with cryptographic validation.

System context documentation captures the operational environment and business context necessary for understanding evidence significance and interpreting technical findings. AI systems do not operate in isolation; they exist within complex business processes, regulatory frameworks, and technical ecosystems that influence their behavior and impact. Context documentation ensures that technical evidence can be properly interpreted by understanding the business purpose, operational constraints, and environmental factors that shaped system behavior.

This documentation category becomes critical when technical findings must be translated into business or legal conclusions. Understanding that a model was deployed during a period of high system load, regulatory change, or organizational restructuring may be essential for properly interpreting performance metrics or behavioral patterns found in the evidence. System context documentation includes system architecture documentation with component relationships, operational procedures and policies affecting system behavior, stakeholder interviews and knowledge capture, business process documentation explaining system integration, and regulatory compliance requirements affecting system design.

Analysis preparation documentation ensures that collected evidence can support comprehensive forensic analysis by providing the metadata, relationships, and structural information necessary for effective examination. This documentation type anticipates the needs of subsequent analysis phases and ensures that evidence is organized and described in ways that enable efficient and thorough investigation.

Analysis preparation documentation becomes particularly important in AI investigations due to the complex interdependencies between different evidence types. Training data influences model behavior, which affects system outputs, which may trigger operational responses that generate additional evidence. Understanding these relationships is essential for conducting meaningful analysis and drawing valid conclusions. This includes data lineage documentation tracing artifact origins, dependency mapping showing relationships between evidence types, sampling methodology documentation for partial collections, cross-reference indexes linking related artifacts, and metadata schemas defining evidence structure and content.

4.13.1.2 AI Model Collection Documentation Template

The following comprehensive template provides a standardized approach for documenting the collection of complete AI model evidence. This template ensures consistency across investigations while capturing all information necessary for forensic analysis and legal proceedings. The template addresses the unique challenges of AI evidence collection while maintaining compatibility with established forensic documentation standards.

4.13.1.2.1 AI Model Evidence Collection Report

Part A: Case Information

Case ID: [Unique case identifier]
Investigation Date: [YYYY-MM-DD]
Lead Investigator: [Name and credentials]
Collection Team: [Team member names and roles]
Legal Authority: [Court order, consent agreement, etc.]
Jurisdiction: [Legal jurisdiction and applicable laws]

Part B: Executive Summary

Model System: [High-level description of AI system]
Collection Scope: [Summary of evidence collected]
Key Findings: [Critical discoveries during collection]
Resource Requirements: [Time, storage, and personnel utilized]
Next Steps: [Recommended analysis procedures]

4.13.1.2.2 Part I: Model Identification and Scope

This section establishes the fundamental characteristics of the AI system under investigation, providing the essential context necessary for understanding the scope and significance of collected evidence. The identification process should capture both technical specifications and business context to ensure that subsequent analysis addresses the correct system and considers appropriate operational factors.

I.A System Identification

Model Name/Identifier: [Official system designation]
Model Version: [Current version and build information]
Deployment Environment: [Production, staging, development]
System Owner: [Responsible organization/department]
Business Purpose: [Intended system functionality and objectives]

I.B Technical Architecture

Model Type: [Neural network, ensemble, traditional ML]
Framework/Platform: [TensorFlow, PyTorch, cloud platform]
Model Size: [Parameters, file size, memory requirements]
Input/Output Specifications: [Data formats and interfaces]
Dependencies: [Libraries, services, external systems]

I.C Operational Context

Deployment Date: [When system was deployed]
Usage Volume: [Request volume, user base size]
Performance Metrics: [Accuracy, latency, throughput]
Integration Points: [Systems that feed data or consume outputs]
Business Impact: [Revenue impact, user experience effects]

4.13.1.2.3 Part II: Collection Methodology

This section documents the systematic approach used to identify, prioritize, and collect evidence while maintaining forensic integrity and legal admissibility standards.

II.A Collection Strategy

Approach: [Comprehensive/Targeted/Sampled collection rationale]
Prioritization: [Evidence priority matrix and decision criteria]
Timeline: [Collection schedule and milestones]
Resource Allocation: [Team assignments and tool selection]
Risk Mitigation: [Identified risks and mitigation strategies]

II.B Technical Procedures

Tools Used:

- [Tool name] v[version]—[Purpose and configuration]
- [Tool name] v[version]—[Purpose and configuration]
- [Continue for all tools]

Collection Commands:

bash

```
# [Include all commands used with full parameters]
# [Timestamp each major collection activity]
# [Document any errors or warnings encountered]
```

Quality Assurance Checks:

- Hash verification completed for all artifacts
- Chain of custody documentation complete
- Cross-reference validation successful
- Completeness assessment performed
- Legal compliance verified

II.C Environmental Documentation

Collection Environment:

- Operating System: [OS and version]
- Tool Versions: [Complete version inventory]
- Network Configuration: [Relevant network details]
- Security Context: [Permissions and access controls]
- Time Synchronization: [NTP configuration and validation]

Target System Environment:

- Cloud Provider: [Platform and region details]
- Service Versions: [ML platform and service versions]
- Access Methods: [APIs, CLIs, web interfaces used]
- Authentication: [Service accounts and credentials used]
- Rate Limiting: [API limits and throttling encountered]

4.13.1.2.4 Part III: Evidence Inventory

This section provides a comprehensive catalog of all collected evidence, organized by type and accompanied by metadata necessary for subsequent analysis. The inventory must capture sufficient detail to enable independent verification of evidence completeness and to support analysis planning.

4.13.1.2.5 III.A Training Data Evidence

This subsection documents all datasets used to train the AI model, including provenance information and quality assessments that may affect model behavior analysis.

TABLE 4.2
Primary Datasets

Dataset Name	Size	Format	Location	Hash (SHA-256)	Collection Status
[Dataset 1]	[Size]	[Format]	[Storage location]	[Hash value]	[Complete/Partial/Failed]
[Dataset 2]	[Size]	[Format]	[Storage location]	[Hash value]	[Complete/Partial/Failed]

Data Lineage Information:

- Original Source: [Data origin and provenance]
- Preprocessing Steps: [Transformations applied]
- Sampling Strategy: [If applicable]
- Quality Assessments: [Data quality reports]
- Version History: [Dataset versioning information]

Data Sensitivity Assessment:

- PII Content: [Personal information analysis]
- Proprietary Information: [Business sensitive content]
- Regulatory Constraints: [GDPR, CCPA, sector-specific regulations]
- Handling Requirements: [Special processing needs]

4.13.1.2.6 III.B Model Artifacts

This subsection documents the core technical components that implement the AI functionality, including all files necessary for model reproduction and analysis.

TABLE 4.3
Model Files

File Name	Type	Size	Hash (SHA-256)	Description
[model.pkl]	[Weights]	[Size]	[Hash]	[Primary model file]
[config.json]	[Config]	[Size]	[Hash]	[Model configuration]

Version Control Information:

- Repository URL: [Source control location]
- Commit Hash: [Specific version identifier]
- Branch/Tag: [Development branch information]
- Commit History: [Relevant development timeline]

4.13.1.2.7 III.C System Logs and Operational Data

TABLE 4.4
Log Categories

Log Type	Date Range	Size	Hash (SHA-256)	Coverage
[Application Logs]	[Start—End]	[Size]	[Hash]	[Complete/Partial]
[Access Logs]	[Start—End]	[Size]	[Hash]	[Complete/Partial]

4.13.1.2.8 III.D Configuration and Documentation

TABLE 4.5
Technical Documentation

Document Type	Title	Date	Author	Location	Hash (SHA-256)
Model Card	[title]	[date]	[author]	[path]	[hash]
Data Sheet	[title]	[date]	[author]	[path]	[hash]
API Documentation	[title]	[date]	[author]	[path]	[hash]
Deployment Guide	[title]	[date]	[author]	[path]	[hash]

Communication Records:

- Email Correspondence: [Relevant email threads and decisions]
- Meeting Records: [Design reviews, planning sessions, retrospectives]
- Issue Tracking: [Bug reports, feature requests, technical debt]
- Code Reviews: [Peer review comments and approval records]
- Incident Reports: [Operational issues and resolution procedures]

Business Documentation:

- Requirements Specifications: [Business requirements and acceptance criteria]
- Test Plans: [Testing strategies and validation procedures]
- Risk Assessments: [Security, privacy, and operational risk analysis]
- Compliance Reports: [Regulatory compliance and audit results]

4.13.1.2.9 Part IV: Chain of Custody

This section provides the legal foundation for evidence admissibility by documenting every aspect of evidence handling from collection through preservation. Chain of custody documentation must meet strict legal standards while accommodating the unique characteristics of AI evidence.

4.13.1.2.10 IV.A Collection Team

This subsection establishes the qualifications and responsibilities of all individuals involved in evidence collection, providing the foundation for expert testimony and methodology validation.

Lead Investigator:

- Name: [Full name]
- Credentials: [Relevant certifications and experience]
- Role: [Specific responsibilities in collection]
- Contact: [Contact information]

TABLE 4.6
Team Members

Name	Role	Credentials	Responsibilities	Contact
[Name]	[Role]	[Credentials]	[Responsibilities]	[Contact]
[Name]	[Role]	[Credentials]	[Responsibilities]	[Contact]

4.13.1.2.11 IV.B Collection Timeline

This subsection provides a chronological record of all collection activities, enabling verification of procedure adherence and identification of any deviations from planned methodology.

TABLE 4.7
Major Milestones

Date/Time	Activity	Team Member	Location	Notes
[Timestamp]	[Activity]	[Person]	[Location]	[Notes]
[Timestamp]	[Activity]	[Person]	[Location]	[Notes]

Critical Decisions:

- Scope Modifications: [Any changes to collection scope and rationale]
- Technical Challenges: [Obstacles encountered and resolution approaches]
- Access Issues: [Permission or technical access problems]
- Resource Constraints: [Limitations affecting collection completeness]

4.13.1.2.12 IV.C Evidence Handling

This subsection documents the security measures and procedures used to protect evidence integrity throughout the collection and preservation process.

Storage and Security:

- Primary Storage: [Storage system and location]
- Backup Storage: [Redundant storage configuration]

- Access Controls: [Who has access and authentication methods]
- Encryption: [Encryption methods for data at rest and in transit]
- Physical Security: [Physical storage security measures]

TABLE 4.8
Transfer Log

Date/Time	From	To	Items	Method	Verification
[Timestamp]	[Source]	[Destination]	[Items]	[Method]	[Verification]
[Timestamp]	[Source]	[Destination]	[Items]	[Method]	[Verification]

4.13.1.2.13 IV.D Integrity Verification

This subsection provides mathematical proof of evidence authenticity through cryptographic validation and systematic verification procedures.

Hash Verification Results:

- [Filename]: [SHA-256 hash]—[Timestamp]
- [Filename]: [SHA-256 hash]—[Timestamp]
- [Filename]: [SHA-256 hash]—[Status: VERIFIED/FAILED]
- [Filename]: [SHA-256 hash]—[Status: VERIFIED/FAILED]

4.13.1.2.14 Part V: Technical Analysis Preparation

This section organizes collected evidence to support efficient and comprehensive forensic analysis by documenting relationships between evidence types and preparing analysis roadmaps.

V.A Evidence Relationships

- **Dependency Mapping:** [Document relationships between different evidence types]
- **Cross-References:** [Index of related artifacts across categories]
- **Analysis Priorities:** [Recommended sequence for technical analysis]
- **Risk Areas:** [Potential issues identified during collection]

V.B Analysis Recommendations

- **Immediate Actions:** [Time-sensitive analysis steps]
- **Standard Procedures:** [Routine analysis recommendations]
- **Specialized Testing:** [Advanced analysis techniques recommended]
- **External Expertise:** [Areas requiring additional specialist knowledge]
- **Template Usage Notes:**

This template should be adapted based on specific case requirements, legal jurisdictions, and organizational standards while maintaining the core elements necessary for forensic integrity and legal admissibility. The structured format ensures consistency across investigations while providing flexibility for case-specific needs.

4.13.2 Quality Assurance and Validation Framework

The evidence collection process incorporates comprehensive quality assurance measures designed to ensure that collected evidence meets both technical analysis requirements and legal admissibility standards.

4.13.2.1 Integrity Verification Procedures

Evidence integrity forms the foundation of legal admissibility and requires multiple validation techniques throughout the collection process.

Cryptographic hash verification employs multiple hash algorithms to detect any modifications to collected evidence including SHA-256 hashing for all collected files, MD5 checksums for rapid integrity verification, blockchain-based timestamping for tamper-evident records, and regular re-verification throughout the storage period.

Digital chain of custody systems automate custody documentation while maintaining legal requirements including automated custody record generation with detailed timestamps and user identification, multi-platform custody coordination maintaining referential integrity across cloud providers, unified access logging and audit trail maintenance, and consistent documentation standards across diverse technical environments.

4.13.2.2 Completeness Assessment Protocols

Completeness validation ensures that all necessary evidence has been collected and that interdependencies between different evidence types are properly maintained.

Dependency mapping validation confirms that relationships between different evidence types remain intact including training data to model lineage verification, configuration dependency validation ensuring system reproducibility, cross-reference integrity checking for related artifacts across platforms, and temporal consistency validation ensuring proper sequencing of events.

Statistical validation for sampled evidence addresses cases where comprehensive collection is impractical including sample representativeness validation ensuring samples accurately reflect full datasets, demographic distribution comparisons between samples and full populations, temporal pattern validation ensuring samples capture relevant time periods, and feature distribution analysis confirming adequate representation of important variables.

This comprehensive documentation and quality assurance framework ensures that AI evidence collection produces legally admissible, technically sound evidence that supports robust forensic analysis while meeting the highest standards of professional practice and legal compliance.

4.14 CASE STUDY: EVIDENCE COLLECTION FOR A SMALL E-COMMERCE RECOMMENDATION SYSTEM

To demonstrate the practical application of the evidence collection framework and documentation template presented in this chapter, this section examines the complete evidence collection process for a real-world AI system. This case study illustrates how the theoretical principles and technical procedures translate into actual investigative practice while highlighting the adaptations necessary for smaller-scale systems.

4.14.1 System Background and Investigation Context

The SportZone Recommendation Engine represents a typical small-scale AI deployment found in many regional businesses. SportZone is a regional sporting goods retailer operating primarily in California, Nevada, and Arizona, serving approximately 50,000 registered customers through their e-commerce platform. The company implemented an AI-powered product recommendation system in January 2024 to improve customer engagement and increase sales conversion rates.

The recommendation system employs collaborative filtering algorithms enhanced with content-based features to suggest products to customers based on their browsing and purchase history. Built using scikit-learn and deployed on AWS infrastructure, the system processes customer interactions in real-time to generate personalized product recommendations displayed on the company website and in email marketing campaigns.

4.14.2 Investigation Trigger and Objectives

The investigation was initiated following a customer complaint alleging that the recommendation system exhibited demographic bias in product suggestions. Specifically, the complainant alleged that the system consistently recommended lower-priced items to customers from certain demographic groups while suggesting premium products to others with similar browsing patterns. The complaint triggered an internal compliance review to assess whether the recommendation system inadvertently incorporated demographic bias that could violate fair lending and anti-discrimination regulations.

The investigation objectives focused on three primary areas: determining whether the recommendation system exhibited systematic bias across demographic groups, evaluating the training data and model architecture for potential sources of discriminatory patterns, and assessing the company's compliance with applicable fair commerce regulations. Given the relatively small scale of the system and the cooperative nature of the investigation, the company authorized comprehensive evidence collection to support a thorough bias analysis.

4.14.3 Collection Strategy and Approach

The evidence collection strategy for the SportZone system balanced comprehensiveness with efficiency, taking advantage of the system's manageable scale to collect complete evidence rather than relying on sampling approaches required for larger systems. The investigation team consisted of two specialists: Dr. Sarah Mitchell, a certified forensic investigator with extensive experience in AI system analysis, and Tom Rodriguez, an AWS solutions architect with specialized knowledge of cloud-based machine learning deployments.

The team decided on comprehensive collection based on several factors. The system's relatively small data footprint (estimated at 500GB total) made complete collection feasible within resource constraints. The six-month operational history provided a manageable temporal scope that captured sufficient data for trend analysis without overwhelming storage requirements. The single-platform AWS deployment simplified collection procedures and reduced coordination complexity compared to multi-cloud investigations.

The collection approach prioritized model artifacts and training data as high-priority evidence essential for bias analysis while treating operational logs as medium priority for understanding system behavior patterns. The team planned a three-day collection window during off-peak business hours to minimize operational impact while ensuring thorough evidence preservation.

This flowchart representation visualizes the SportZone evidence collection as a systematic process, showing how training data flows through architecture artifacts to the core model and outputs, with clear visual indicators for collected versus excluded evidence types. The format effectively demonstrates the comprehensive collection strategy chosen for SportZone due to its manageable 500GB scope and single AWS platform deployment, making it ideal for process documentation and stakeholder communication during the three-day collection window. This visualization supports the case study's emphasis on systematic evidence preservation while clearly distinguishing between critical bias detection evidence (all collected) and peripheral components excluded from the investigation scope.

4.14.4 Technical Implementation and Challenges

The technical collection process leveraged AWS-native tools and standard forensic procedures adapted for cloud-based AI systems. The team used AWS CLI v2.7.1 for S3 and CloudWatch data collection, PostgreSQL pg_dump v14.2 for database export, and custom Python scripts for log processing and analysis preparation.

The collection began with model artifacts stored in S3, using the AWS sync command to preserve the complete model repository including trained model files, training scripts, configuration files, and experiment tracking data. The team implemented integrity verification using SHA-256 hashing for all collected files, generating checksums immediately upon collection and storing them in tamper-evident logs.

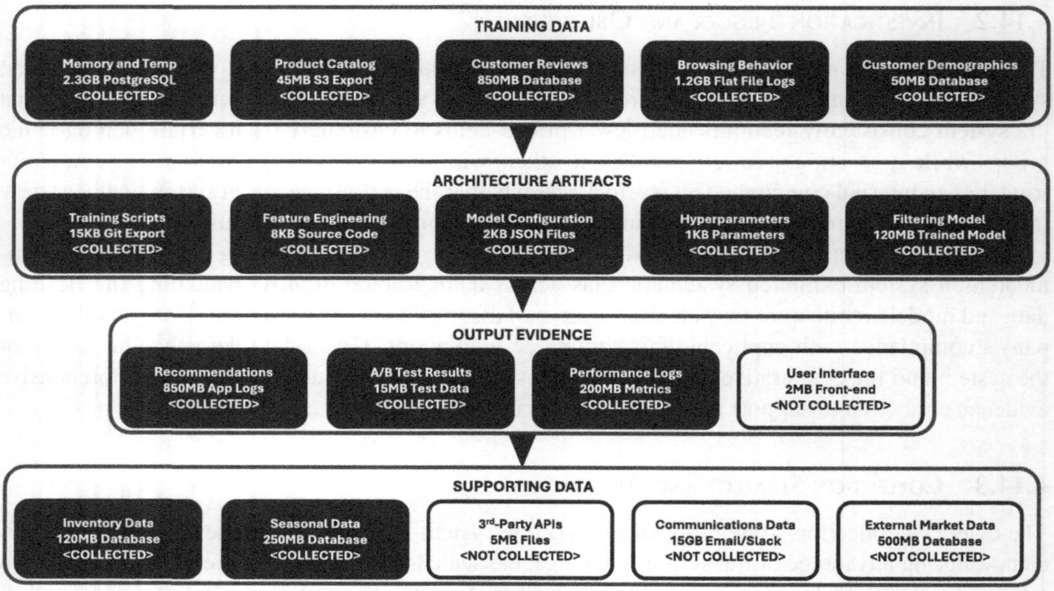

FIGURE 4.4

Database collection presented the primary technical challenge due to the size of customer interaction data and privacy considerations. The team used a read-only database user with restricted access to minimize system impact while ensuring complete data capture. The PostgreSQL export included customer interaction histories, product catalog data, and system configuration tables necessary for model analysis.

CloudWatch log collection required careful filtering to capture relevant application events while managing the volume of operational data. The team implemented time-based filtering to focus on the six-month investigation period and used log group filters to separate application logs, access logs, and system monitoring data into distinct evidence categories.

4.14.5 Evidence Inventory and Organization

The completed evidence collection produced a comprehensive inventory organized according to the documentation template structure. Training data evidence included the primary customer interactions database (2.3GB) containing purchase histories, browsing patterns, and demographic information where available, along with the product catalog (45MB) defining item characteristics and pricing information used by the recommendation algorithms.

Model artifacts comprised the core recommendation engine including the trained scikit-learn model file (120MB), training scripts (15KB), and configuration files (2KB) defining hyperparameters and model architecture. The team also collected version control information linking the deployed model to specific commits in the company's Git repository, providing complete traceability for model development decisions.

Operational evidence included application logs (850MB) documenting recommendation requests and responses, access logs (1.2GB) showing user interaction patterns, and system performance metrics demonstrating throughput, latency, and error rates. The team organized this evidence to support temporal analysis and pattern detection during subsequent bias analysis.

Configuration and infrastructure evidence documented the complete AWS deployment including EC2 instance configurations, RDS database settings, load balancer configuration, and networking policies. This evidence enables reproduction of the analysis environment and provides context for understanding system behavior patterns.

4.14.6 Quality Assurance and Validation Results

The quality assurance process implemented multiple validation layers to ensure evidence integrity and completeness. Hash verification confirmed the authenticity of all collected files, with no discrepancies detected between initial collection hashes and subsequent verification checks. Chain of custody documentation tracked every access and transfer of evidence, maintaining the legal foundation necessary for potential proceedings.

Completeness assessment verified that all identified evidence sources were successfully collected according to the investigation plan. The team confirmed that model artifacts could be loaded and analyzed using standard scikit-learn tools, that database exports could be successfully restored for analysis, and that log files parsed correctly without errors or corruption.

Technical validation included testing the collected model against known test cases to verify functional accuracy and confirming that training data maintained proper relationships and referential integrity. The team also validated that configuration files contained complete information necessary for reproducing the analysis environment.

4.14.7 Documentation and Legal Considerations

The investigation team produced comprehensive documentation following the template structure presented in this chapter, adapting the framework to the specific characteristics of the SportZone system. The documentation captured the complete collection methodology, evidence inventory, chain of custody records, and analysis preparation information necessary for independent validation.

Legal considerations focused on privacy compliance and evidence admissibility standards. The team ensured that customer data handling complied with California Consumer Privacy Act (CCPA) requirements, implementing appropriate access controls and data minimization practices. Documentation addressed the voluntary nature of the investigation while maintaining forensic standards necessary for potential legal proceedings.

The team acknowledged specific limitations including the six-month temporal scope that may not capture long-term bias patterns, the read-only access restriction that prevented certain system behavior tests, and the limited demographic data available in customer records that could constrain bias analysis depth.

4.14.8 Analysis Preparation and Next Steps

The evidence collection established a solid foundation for comprehensive bias analysis of the SportZone recommendation system. The collected evidence supports multiple analysis approaches including demographic parity testing to identify differential recommendation patterns, individual fairness analysis to examine similar customer treatment, and temporal analysis to detect bias emergence or evolution over time.

Analysis preparation included mapping evidence relationships to support systematic examination, identifying the customer interaction data as the primary driver for model training, the trained model as the mechanism for generating recommendations, and the operational logs as evidence of actual system behavior in production.

The team developed an analysis plan prioritizing demographic bias analysis as the primary investigation objective, model performance validation to establish baseline behavior expectations, and temporal pattern analysis to identify any systematic changes in recommendation patterns over the six-month operational period.

Resource requirements for analysis include moderate computational resources for model analysis and statistical testing, specialized bias analysis tools for demographic fairness assessment, and statistical software for pattern detection and significance testing. The team estimated a two-week analysis timeline with results suitable for both technical validation and regulatory compliance reporting.

4.14.9 Lessons Learned and Best Practices

The SportZone case study demonstrates several important principles for small-scale AI evidence collection. The comprehensive collection approach proved feasible and valuable for systems of this scale, providing complete evidence that supports thorough analysis without the sampling uncertainties associated with larger systems. The single-platform deployment simplified collection procedures but still required careful coordination and technical expertise to ensure forensic integrity.

Documentation proved essential for maintaining investigation credibility and supporting subsequent analysis activities. The structured template approach ensured consistent coverage of all critical elements while adapting appropriately to the system's scale and complexity. Chain of custody procedures required particular attention due to the distributed nature of cloud-based evidence sources.

The investigation highlighted the importance of early coordination with system administrators and stakeholders to minimize operational impact while ensuring evidence completeness. The cooperative investigation approach enabled comprehensive access while maintaining business continuity, demonstrating the value of proactive compliance programs for managing AI-related risks.

This case study illustrates how the evidence collection framework presented in this chapter scales effectively to smaller AI systems while maintaining the rigor necessary for forensic analysis and legal proceedings. The SportZone investigation provides a practical example of applying theoretical principles to real-world AI forensic challenges, demonstrating both the opportunities and constraints involved in contemporary AI evidence collection.

4.15 CONCLUSION

This chapter has presented a comprehensive framework for AI evidence collection that addresses the unique challenges posed by modern machine learning systems while maintaining the rigor necessary for forensic analysis and legal proceedings. The five-phase methodology provides a systematic approach that scales from small regional deployments to enterprise-scale systems, ensuring that investigators can adapt their procedures to match investigation requirements and resource constraints. Through detailed technical implementation guidance, comprehensive documentation templates, and practical case study illustration, this framework establishes the foundation for reliable, legally admissible AI evidence collection that supports the advanced analysis techniques presented in subsequent chapters of this book.

5 Training Data Analysis

5.1 GETTING TO THE ROOT: WHEN AI GOES WRONG, LOOK AT THE DATA

When a major online retailer discovered their AI recruiting tool was systematically downgrading resumes from women, the problem was not in the algorithm—it was in the decade of male-dominated hiring data the system learned from. When a large financial institution's loan approval AI started rejecting qualified minority applicants, investigators found the issue embedded in historical lending records that reflected decades of discriminatory practices.

These cases illustrate a fundamental truth about AI systems: training data drives behavior more than any other factor. When systems discriminate, fail, or exhibit unexpected behavior, the root cause usually traces to the data they learned from. Unlike debugging traditional software, AI forensics requires understanding how millions of examples shaped learned behaviors through statistical patterns rather than explicit programming.

5.2 WHAT YOU WILL LEARN

By the end of this chapter, you will be able to:

- Rapidly assess training datasets for bias, quality issues, and compliance violations
- Detect systematic discrimination using defensible statistical methods
- Identify data poisoning, synthetic content, and intellectual property violations
- Trace how data problems translate into deployed system failures
- Document findings that support legal proceedings and regulatory compliance

5.3 QUICK START GUIDE

5.3.1 Need Immediate Answers?

- **Investigation planning confusion?** → Start with The Data Investigation Challenge (Section 5.4) to understand the unique aspects of training data forensics and establish proper investigation scope.
- **Need systematic approach?** → Jump to Investigation Framework and Methodology (Section 5.6) for the structured five-phase approach to training data analysis and resource planning.
- **Bias detection required?** → Begin with demographic parity analysis and statistical bias detection techniques found throughout the chapter's bias analysis sections.
- **Data quality concerns?** → Focus on systematic completeness analysis and quality assessment methodologies for identifying missing data patterns and integrity issues.
- **IP violations suspected?** → See Intellectual Property Investigation (Section 5.10) for comprehensive copyright detection, fair use analysis, and legal risk assessment frameworks.
- **Large-scale dataset challenges?** → Review Decision Matrices for Training Data Analysis (Section 5.12) for technique selection, resource planning, and scalability considerations.
- **Integration with other forensic phases?** → Go to Conclusion and Integration (Section 5.15) for guidance on correlating training data findings with model investigation and output analysis results.

DOI: 10.1201/9781003634782-5

Note:

Training data investigations are inherently variable. No two AI systems, datasets, or organizational contexts are identical. The statistical methods and sampling approaches presented here require appropriate expertise for proper implementation and interpretation, many of which require tailored programming and testing. This chapter provides frameworks and techniques that must be adapted to specific investigation contexts. Always consult qualified statisticians for complex analyses and legal counsel for compliance interpretations.

5.4 THE DATA INVESTIGATION CHALLENGE

Training data analysis is an important aspect of AI forensic investigation because of the direct causal relationship between data characteristics and system behavior. Every decision an AI system makes reflects patterns it learned from training examples, making data analysis essential for understanding system failures, discrimination, and unexpected behaviors.

5.4.1 Why Training Data Matters

AI systems fundamentally differ from traditional software in how they acquire their capabilities. Instead of following explicitly programmed rules, they develop behaviors by finding statistical patterns in training data. This creates a direct causal chain where data characteristics directly influence system behavior in ways that may not be apparent until problems emerge.

The relationship between training data and AI behavior manifests in several ways. Representation patterns in training data directly affect which populations receive accurate service from deployed systems. Quality issues in training data create reliability problems that may only surface under specific operating conditions. Historical biases embedded in training labels perpetuate past discrimination in systematic ways that can be more consistent and pervasive than human decision-making.

Understanding these relationships requires investigators to think beyond traditional software debugging approaches. While conventional software failures can often be traced to specific code defects, AI system problems emerge from statistical patterns distributed across potentially millions of training examples. This distributed nature means that problems may not be apparent from examining any individual training example but become clear only through systematic statistical analysis.

5.4.2 The Human Element in Training Data

Training data doesn't exist in isolation—it reflects human decisions, social structures, and historical patterns that shape its content and characteristics. Understanding these human elements proves crucial for interpreting analysis results and developing effective remediation strategies.

Collection decisions made by data scientists and engineers fundamentally shape dataset characteristics. Choices about which sources to include, how to sample from available data, what quality standards to apply, and how to balance different considerations all influence the final dataset composition. These decisions often reflect the backgrounds, perspectives, and constraints of the people making them, potentially introducing systematic biases that aren't immediately apparent.

Annotation processes involve human judgments that become embedded in training data labels. Medical image annotation requires expert medical knowledge, legal document classification involves interpretation of complex regulations, and content moderation labeling reflects cultural and social norms. The humans performing these annotations bring their own expertise, biases, and limitations to the process, influencing how AI systems learn to interpret similar information.

The challenge for forensic investigators lies in uncovering these human elements through systematic analysis of data patterns. Unlike traditional digital forensics where human actions leave direct traces in logs and files, the human influence on training data manifests through statistical patterns that require specialized analysis techniques to detect and interpret.

5.5 ESSENTIAL TOOLS FOR TRAINING DATA FORENSICS

Understanding the magnitude and complexity of training data challenges makes clear why specialized tools and technologies are essential for effective forensic analysis. The scale and diversity of modern training datasets exceed the capacity of manual analysis, requiring systematic approaches supported by robust technical infrastructure.

5.5.1 Core Software Platforms

Effective training data forensics relies on software platforms specifically designed to handle the statistical analysis and large-scale data processing that these investigations require. The choice of platform significantly affects investigation efficiency and the sophistication of analysis that can be performed.

Python serves as the primary platform for most training data forensic analysis due to its extensive ecosystem of data science and machine learning libraries. Key Python libraries for forensic analysis include:

- **Pandas** for data manipulation and analysis, enabling efficient processing of large tabular datasets
- **NumPy** for numerical computing and statistical calculations that form the foundation of bias detection
- **Scikit-learn** for machine learning algorithms and statistical testing procedures used in fairness analysis
- **SciPy** for advanced statistical analysis and hypothesis testing required for legal defensibility
- **Matplotlib/Seaborn** for data visualization and exploratory analysis that reveals patterns in complex datasets
- **Jupyter Notebooks** for interactive analysis and documentation that maintains investigation transparency

R provides an alternative platform particularly strong in statistical analysis, with specialized packages for bias detection, fairness analysis, and advanced statistical modeling. R excels in generating publication-quality statistical reports and offers sophisticated packages for temporal analysis and change point detection that can identify when bias patterns emerged in training data.

Specialized AI forensics tools are emerging to address the unique challenges of training data analysis. These include commercial platforms for bias detection, open-source fairness toolkits, and cloud-based services for large-scale data analysis. Many organizations also develop custom tools tailored to their specific AI systems and compliance requirements.

5.5.2 Large-Scale Data Processing Tools

The massive scale of modern training datasets requires specialized tools that can efficiently process and analyze data volumes that exceed single-machine capacity. These tools enable investigators to perform comprehensive analysis without being limited by computational constraints.

Distributed computing frameworks like Apache Spark and Dask enable processing of datasets that exceed single-machine memory limitations. These frameworks distribute computation across multiple machines while providing familiar programming interfaces that don't require extensive distributed systems expertise.

Cloud-based analysis platforms offer scalable computing resources that can be provisioned on-demand for large investigations. These platforms often integrate with storage systems and provide specialized tools for AI analysis, enabling investigators to scale their computational resources to match investigation requirements.

5.6 INVESTIGATION FRAMEWORK AND METHODOLOGY

Effective training data forensics requires a systematic approach that ensures comprehensive analysis while managing the complexity and scale inherent in modern AI training datasets. This framework provides structure for investigations while maintaining the flexibility needed to address diverse scenarios and requirements.

5.6.1 Investigation Planning and Scoping

Successful training data investigations begin with careful planning that establishes clear objectives, defines appropriate scope, and allocates resources effectively. The systematic workflow shown in Figure 5.1 provides a structured five-phase approach that progresses from initial planning through comprehensive documentation, ensuring both forensic integrity and legal defensibility.

5.6.1.1 Planning Phase Foundation

The workflow begins with **Planning** to establish investigation objectives including scope and legal requirements, secure data access through appropriate sources and sampling protocols, and allocate necessary resources including team composition, analytical tools, and timeline constraints. Defining investigation objectives requires understanding what questions the investigation must answer and what evidence standards apply. Legal investigations may require different levels of

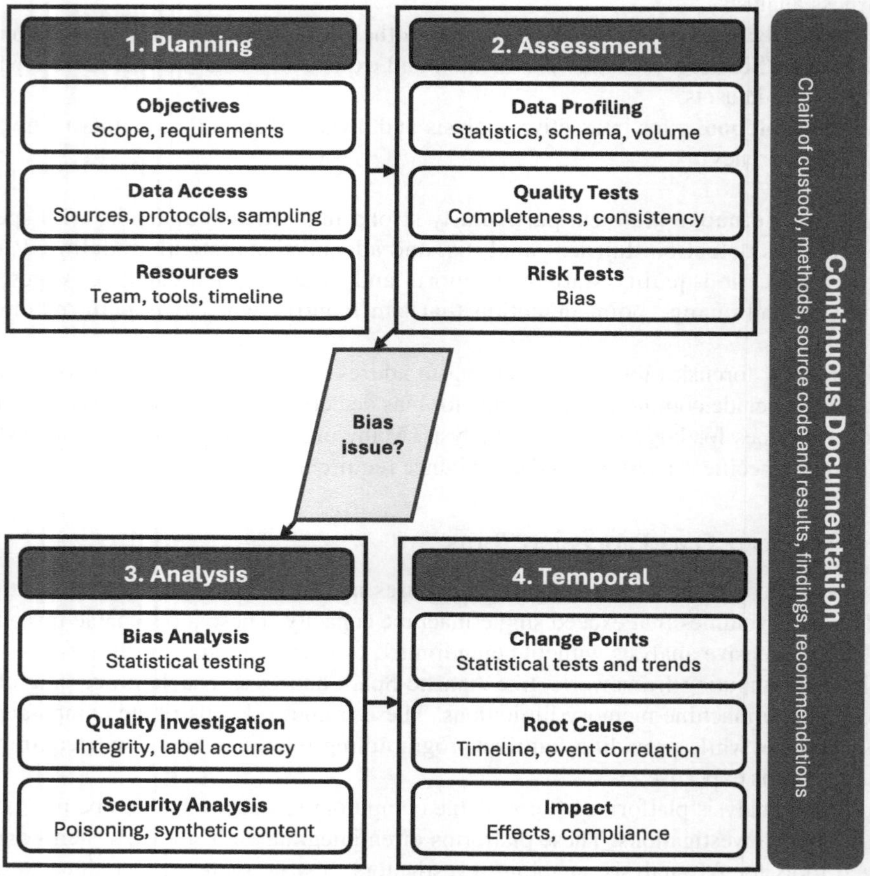

FIGURE 5.1

statistical certainty than internal compliance reviews, while regulatory investigations may focus on specific protected characteristics and security investigations emphasize data integrity and tampering detection.

Resource allocation should account for the computational requirements of large-scale data analysis, the expertise needed for different analytical approaches, and the time required for thorough statistical validation. Training data investigations often require coordination between technical analysts, statistical experts, legal counsel, and domain specialists. Complex bias detection may require consulting statisticians, while intellectual property analysis may need specialists in copyright law and content recognition technology.

5.6.1.2 Systematic Assessment and Analysis

Following planning, **Assessment** conducts initial data profiling to understand statistics, schema, and volume characteristics, quality testing to identify completeness and consistency issues, and risk testing to flag potential bias concerns. A critical decision point determines whether observed patterns constitute genuine issues warranting comprehensive analysis or can be resolved through simpler remediation approaches.

When detailed investigation is warranted, **Analysis** systematically examines bias patterns through statistical testing, quality issues including integrity and label accuracy problems, and security concerns such as poisoning attempts or synthetic content injection. **Temporal** analysis then establishes when problems emerged through change point detection, identifies root causes by correlating timeline events with organizational decisions, and assesses downstream effects on compliance and performance.

5.6.1.3 Legal and Compliance Integration

Legal and compliance considerations shape every aspect of this workflow, from data handling procedures to statistical methodology selection. Privacy regulations may limit access to certain types of data or require special handling procedures, while industry-specific regulations may mandate particular analytical approaches or documentation standards. The continuous **Documentation** process ensures comprehensive evidence preservation through detailed methodological records and findings that meet legal admissibility standards.

Understanding legal requirements early in the planning process prevents costly rework and ensures that investigation findings will be admissible and useful for their intended purposes. The decision-driven approach ensures efficient resource allocation by focusing detailed analysis only on cases where initial screening identifies genuine concerns requiring investigation.

5.6.2 Multi-Method Validation Approaches

Reliable training data forensics requires validation of findings through multiple independent analytical approaches. Single-method analysis may miss important patterns or produce false positives that comprehensive multi-method validation can identify and correct.

5.6.2.1 Statistical Sampling for Analytical Validation

Modern training datasets routinely exceed traditional forensic investigation capacities, often containing tens of millions of records that cannot be analyzed comprehensively within practical time and resource constraints. Effective sampling strategies balance statistical rigor with computational feasibility, ensuring that investigation findings maintain legal defensibility while managing the scale challenges inherent in contemporary AI systems.

The choice of sampling methodology directly impacts the validity and reliability of bias detection, quality assessment, and compliance analysis. **Simple random sampling** provides unbiased selection with equal probability for each record, making it ideal for homogeneous datasets where overall quality assessment is the primary objective. However, this approach may inadequately represent minority groups essential for bias detection.

Stratified sampling addresses representation concerns by dividing the population into demographic or categorical strata and sampling from each group independently. This approach ensures adequate representation of protected groups for bias analysis, though it requires prior knowledge of relevant stratification variables and may increase complexity when multiple intersecting characteristics must be considered.

Systematic sampling selects every kth record after a random starting point, providing efficient coverage for temporal analysis and large-scale quality assessment. This method works particularly well with chronologically ordered data where detecting temporal patterns is important but may introduce bias if the dataset contains hidden periodicities that align with the sampling interval.

Cluster sampling examines entire natural groupings rather than individual records, proving valuable when data sources, geographic regions, or other clustering structures are relevant to the investigation. This approach is particularly useful for intellectual property investigations where content may originate from common sources that should be analyzed together.

Sample size determination must account for multiple testing corrections, desired statistical power, and the specific analytical objectives of each investigation phase. The framework provides practical guidelines for minimum and recommended sample sizes across different analysis types while maintaining the statistical confidence levels required for legal proceedings and regulatory compliance.

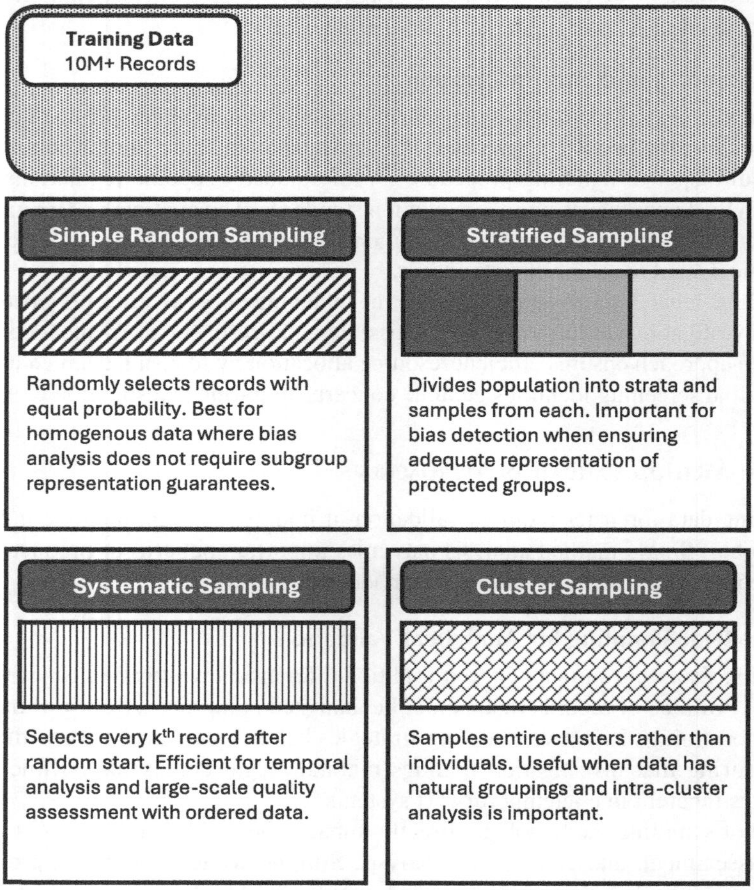

FIGURE 5.2

5.6.2.2 Cross-Validation and Statistical Validation

Cross-validation of findings across different analytical methods provides confidence that identified patterns represent genuine characteristics of the training data rather than artifacts of particular analytical approaches. Different statistical methods may have different sensitivities to various types of bias or quality issues.

Statistical significance testing ensures that identified patterns represent meaningful characteristics rather than random variation. Legal proceedings require evidence that meets established statistical standards, typically requiring confidence levels of 95% or higher for findings to be considered reliable.

Expert review integration points incorporate domain expertise and specialized knowledge that automated analysis cannot provide. Subject matter experts can validate whether identified patterns align with known characteristics of particular data sources, industries, or application domains.

The integration of multiple validation approaches creates a comprehensive picture of training data characteristics that can withstand scrutiny from opposing experts, regulatory agencies, and judicial review.

5.7 BIAS DETECTION AND DISCRIMINATION ANALYSIS

Several types of bias can emerge in training data, each requiring different detection approaches and having different implications for AI system behavior.

Sampling bias occurs when training data doesn't accurately represent the population the AI system will serve. This can happen when certain demographic groups are underrepresented or when data collection methods systematically exclude particular populations.

Label bias emerges when the training labels themselves reflect discriminatory human decisions or biased historical practices. For example, historical hiring decisions used as training labels may perpetuate past discrimination patterns.

Confirmation bias affects data collection and annotation when humans unconsciously seek evidence that confirms their existing beliefs, leading to datasets that reinforce rather than challenge problematic assumptions.

Aggregation bias occurs when data from different subgroups is combined without accounting for relevant differences between those groups. This can mask important subgroup-specific patterns or create models that work well for majority groups but poorly for minorities.

5.7.1 Understanding Bias Manifestations

Training data bias manifests in multiple forms, each requiring different detection approaches and presenting distinct challenges for forensic investigation. Understanding these different manifestations enables comprehensive bias assessment that addresses all potential sources of discrimination while providing legally defensible evidence of systematic unfair treatment.

5.7.2 Comprehensive Bias Detection Framework

Bias detection requires systematic application of appropriate statistical tests that can identify discrimination while controlling for legitimate factors. The choice of statistical test depends on the type of data being analyzed and the specific bias hypothesis being tested.

The foundation of bias detection begins with rapid screening to identify which protected attributes require detailed analysis. This screening process helps investigators prioritize their efforts while ensuring that no significant bias patterns are overlooked.

Bias detection requires systematic application of appropriate statistical tests that can identify discrimination while controlling for legitimate factors. Different types of bias manifest through distinct patterns and require tailored detection approaches to ensure comprehensive coverage while

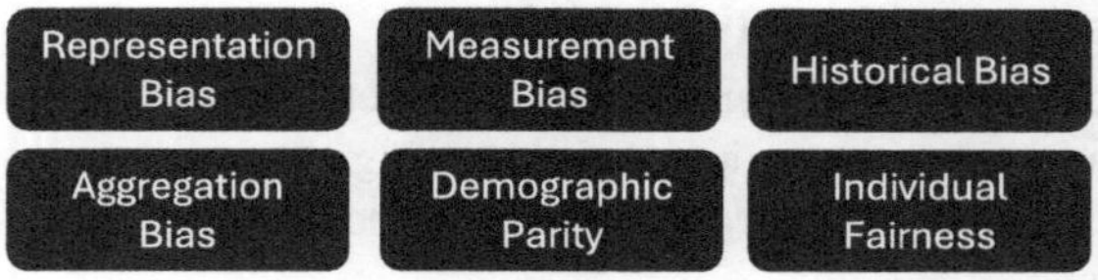

FIGURE 5.3

maintaining statistical rigor. The bias detection analysis matrix provides a structured framework for selecting appropriate methodologies based on the type of bias under investigation.

The matrix distinguishes between primary detection methods (the most effective initial approaches), secondary methods (supplementary techniques that provide additional insights), and validation approaches (methods for confirming and quantifying detected issues). This tiered approach ensures that investigations begin with the most reliable detection techniques while providing multiple validation pathways to confirm findings and support legal defensibility.

TABLE 5.1

Bias Type	Primary Detection Methods	Secondary Methods	Validation Approaches
Representation Bias	Statistical testing, demographic analysis, population comparisons	Temporal analysis, geographic distribution	Expert review, cross-validation, external benchmarks
Measurement Bias	Distribution analysis, consistency testing, quality metrics	Metadata examination, collection method review	Statistical significance testing, reproducibility testing
Historical Bias	Temporal analysis, pattern recognition, outcome trend analysis	Expert review, domain knowledge, policy change correlation	Counterfactual analysis, causal inference
Aggregation Bias	Subgroup analysis, stratified testing, interaction detection	Simpson's paradox testing, disaggregated metrics	Multi-level validation, domain expert review

Each bias type requires different detection strategies, and comprehensive investigations typically employ multiple methods from each category. Primary methods provide the foundation for bias detection, secondary methods offer corroborating evidence and alternative perspectives, while validation approaches ensure that identified patterns represent genuine bias rather than statistical artifacts or measurement errors.

5.7.2.1 Initial Bias Screening Process

The first step in bias detection involves a rapid screening analysis that examines outcome rates across different demographic groups. This screening helps investigators identify which protected attributes warrant detailed investigation and guides resource allocation for comprehensive analysis.

The initial bias screening function performs rapid statistical analysis to identify potential discrimination patterns across protected attributes. This screening process examines outcome rates for different demographic groups and flags attributes that show statistically significant disparities or practically meaningful differences that warrant detailed investigation.

```
def initial_bias_screening(dataset, protected_attributes,
outcome_variable):
    """
    Rapid bias screening to identify potential discrimination patterns
    """
```

```
    from scipy.stats import chi2_contingency
    import pandas as pd

    screening_results = {}

    for attribute in protected_attributes:
        if attribute not in dataset.columns:
            continue

      # Calculate basic outcome rates by group
      contingency = pd.crosstab(dataset[attribute],
dataset[outcome_variable])

       outcome_rates = contingency.div(contingency.sum(axis=1), axis=0)

       # Quick significance test
       chi2, p_value, dof, expected =
chi2_contingency(contingency)

       screening_results[attribute] = {
           'max_disparity': outcome_rates.iloc[:, 1].max() -
outcome_rates.iloc[:, 1].min(),
           'statistically_significant': p_value < 0.05,
           'requires_detailed_analysis': p_value < 0.05 or
               (outcome_rates.iloc[:, 1].max() -
outcome_rates.iloc[:, 1].min()) > 0.1
        }

    return screening_results
```

Sample Output and Interpretation:

```
{
    'race': {
        'max_disparity': 0.23,
        'statistically_significant': True,
        'requires_detailed_analysis': True
    },
    'gender': {
        'max_disparity': 0.08,
        'statistically_significant': False,
        'requires_detailed_analysis': False
    },
    'age_group': {
        'max_disparity': 0.15,
        'statistically_significant': True,
        'requires_detailed_analysis': True
    }
}
```

Interpretation: This output shows that race and age_group require detailed investigation, while gender does not. The race disparity of 23 percentage points is both statistically and practically significant, indicating potential discrimination. Age_group shows a 15-point disparity that warrants investigation. Gender shows only an 8-point difference that isn't statistically significant, suggesting no bias concern.

5.7.3 Demographic Parity Analysis

Demographic parity requires that positive outcomes occur at similar rates across different demographic groups. This represents one of the most straightforward fairness metrics and often serves as an initial screening tool for bias detection.

When conducting demographic parity analysis for legal proceedings, comprehensive statistical evidence that can withstand scrutiny becomes essential. The analysis needs to demonstrate not only that disparities exist, but that they are statistically significant and practically meaningful.

5.7.3.1 Statistical Foundation for Legal Evidence

The comprehensive demographic parity analysis provides robust statistical evidence suitable for legal proceedings. This analysis examines outcome rates across demographic groups and applies multiple statistical tests to establish both the existence and magnitude of any disparities. The function calculates approval rates, performs chi-square independence testing, measures effect sizes, and conducts pairwise comparisons between groups.

```
def comprehensive_demographic_parity_analysis(dataset,
protected_attribute, outcome_variable):
    """
    Comprehensive demographic parity analysis for legal proceedings
    """
    import pandas as pd
    from scipy.stats import chi2_contingency, fisher_exact
    import numpy as np

    # Create contingency table
    contingency = pd.crosstab(dataset[protected_attribute],
dataset[outcome_variable])

    # Calculate approval rates by group
    approval_rates = contingency.iloc[:, 1] / contingency.sum(axis=1)

    # Statistical significance testing
    chi2, p_value, dof, expected = chi2_contingency(contingency)

    # Effect size (Cramér's V)
    n = contingency.sum().sum()
    cramers_v = np.sqrt(chi2 / (n * (min(contingency.shape) - 1)))

    # Pairwise comparisons with Fisher's exact test
    group_names = approval_rates.index
    pairwise_results = {}

    for i, group1 in enumerate(group_names):
        for group2 in group_names[i+1:]:
            # Create 2x2 table for Fisher's exact test
            table_2x2 = contingency.loc[[group1, group2], :]
            odds_ratio, fisher_p = fisher_exact(table_2x2)

            pairwise_results[f"{group1}_vs_{group2}"] = {
                'odds_ratio': odds_ratio,
                'fisher_p_value': fisher_p,
                'rate_difference': approval_rates[group1] -
approval_rates[group2]
            }
```

```
    return {
        'approval_rates': approval_rates,
        'chi2_statistic': chi2,
        'p_value': p_value,
        'cramers_v': cramers_v,
        'pairwise_comparisons': pairwise_results,
        'legally_significant': p_value < 0.05 and cramers_v > 0.1
    }
```

Sample Output and Interpretation:

```
{
    'approval_rates': {
        'White': 0.72,
        'Black': 0.45,
        'Hispanic': 0.53,
        'Asian': 0.68
    },
    'chi2_statistic': 127.45,
    'p_value': 2.3e-28,
    'cramers_v': 0.18,
    'pairwise_comparisons': {
        'White_vs_Black': {
            'odds_ratio': 3.12,
            'fisher_p_value': 1.2e-15,
            'rate_difference': 0.27
        },
        'White_vs_Hispanic': {
            'odds_ratio': 2.31,
            'fisher_p_value': 3.4e-08,
            'rate_difference': 0.19
        }
    },
    'legally_significant': True
}
```

Interpretation: This output provides compelling evidence of racial discrimination. White applicants have a 72% approval rate compared to 45% for Black applicants—a 27 percentage point disparity. The extremely low p-value (2.3e-28) confirms statistical significance, while Cramér's V of 0.18 indicates a medium-to-large effect size. The odds ratio of 3.12 means White applicants are over 3 times more likely to be approved than Black applicants. This evidence would be legally defensible in discrimination proceedings.

5.7.4 Individual Fairness Assessment

Beyond group fairness, individual fairness requires that similar individuals receive similar treatment regardless of their demographic characteristics. This analysis provides compelling evidence of discrimination by identifying specific cases where comparable individuals were treated differently.

Individual fairness analysis typically employs nearest neighbor approaches to identify individuals with similar qualifications using appropriate distance metrics, then examines whether people with similar characteristics but different protected attributes receive consistent treatment.

5.7.4.1 Similarity-Based Fairness Analysis

The individual fairness analysis identifies cases where individuals with similar qualifications received different treatment based on protected characteristics. This analysis uses machine learning techniques to find nearest neighbors based on relevant qualifications, then examines whether outcomes differ systematically based on demographic group membership. The function standardizes features, computes similarity using euclidean distance, and flags cases where similar individuals from different groups experienced significantly different treatment.

```
def individual_fairness_analysis(dataset, protected_attribute,
features, outcome_variable, k=5):
    """
    Individual fairness analysis using nearest neighbor comparisons
    """
    from sklearn.neighbors import NearestNeighbors
    from sklearn.preprocessing import StandardScaler
    import pandas as pd
    import numpy as np

    # Prepare features for similarity calculation (exclude protected
attribute)
    feature_cols = [col for col in features if col !=
protected_attribute]
    X = dataset[feature_cols].copy()

    # Handle missing values and scale features
    X = X.fillna(X.median())
    scaler = StandardScaler()
    X_scaled = scaler.fit_transform(X)

    # Find nearest neighbors
    nbrs = NearestNeighbors(n_neighbors=k+1, metric='euclidean')
    nbrs.fit(X_scaled)
    distances, indices = nbrs.kneighbors(X_scaled)

    fairness_violations = []

    # Check each individual for fairness violations
    for i, row in dataset.iterrows():
        # Get nearest neighbors (excluding self)
        neighbor_indices = indices[i][1:] # Skip self (first element)
        neighbors = dataset.iloc[neighbor_indices]

        # Check if any neighbors have different protected
attribute and different outcome
        same_group_neighbors =
neighbors[neighbors[protected_attribute] ==
row[protected_attribute]]
        different_group_neighbors =
neighbors[neighbors[protected_attribute] !=
row[protected_attribute]]

        if len(different_group_neighbors) > 0:
            # Calculate outcome consistency
            same_group_outcome_rate =
same_group_neighbors[outcome_variable].mean() if
len(same_group_neighbors) > 0 else row[outcome_variable]
            different_group_outcome_rate =
different_group_neighbors[outcome_variable].mean()
```

```
            # Flag significant disparities
            if abs(same_group_outcome_rate -
different_group_outcome_rate) > 0.2: # 20% threshold
                fairness_violations.append({
                    'individual_id': i,
                    'protected_group': row[protected_attribute],
                    'outcome': row[outcome_variable],
                    'same_group_rate': same_group_outcome_rate,
                    'different_group_rate':
different_group_outcome_rate,
                    'disparity': abs(same_group_outcome_rate -
different_group_outcome_rate),
                    'neighbor_distances':
distances[i][1:].tolist()
                })

    return {
        'total_violations': len(fairness_violations),
        'violation_rate': len(fairness_violations) / len(dataset),
        'violations': fairness_violations[:50], # Return top 50
for review
        'average_disparity': np.mean([v['disparity'] for v in
fairness_violations]) if fairness_violations else 0
    }
```

Sample Output and Interpretation:

```
{
    'total_violations': 127,
    'violation_rate': 0.063,
    'violations': [
        {
            'individual_id': 1247,
            'protected_group': 'Black',
            'outcome': 0,
            'same_group_rate': 0.43,
            'different_group_rate': 0.71,
            'disparity': 0.28,
            'neighbor_distances': [0.12, 0.15, 0.18, 0.22, 0.25]
        },
        {
            'individual_id': 3891,
            'protected_group': 'Hispanic',
            'outcome': 0,
            'same_group_rate': 0.48,
            'different_group_rate': 0.75,
            'disparity': 0.27,
            'neighbor_distances': [0.09, 0.14, 0.19, 0.21, 0.26]
        }
    ],
    'average_disparity': 0.24
}
```

Interpretation: This analysis found 127 individual fairness violations affecting 6.3% of applicants. Individual 1247 (Black) was denied despite having very similar qualifications to approved White applicants (distance of 0.12–0.25). The 28 percentage point disparity shows that similar White applicants were approved at 71% vs. 43% for similar Black applicants. These specific cases provide concrete examples of discriminatory treatment that can be compelling in legal proceedings, moving beyond statistical aggregates to individual stories of unfair treatment.

5.8 QUALITY ASSESSMENT AND DATA INTEGRITY

Poor data quality in training datasets creates unreliable AI systems that may fail unexpectedly or exhibit biased behavior. Systematic quality assessment identifies completeness issues, labeling errors, and consistency problems that affect model reliability and legal defensibility.

5.8.1 Completeness and Consistency Analysis

Data completeness analysis examines whether training datasets contain adequate information across all relevant dimensions and demographic groups. Missing data patterns can create systematic bias if certain groups are systematically underrepresented or if important information is consistently absent for particular populations.

5.8.1.1 Systematic Missing Data Pattern Analysis

The completeness analysis examines whether missing data patterns correlate with protected characteristics, which could create systematic bias in AI training. This analysis determines whether data gaps disproportionately affect certain demographic groups, potentially leading to models that perform poorly for underrepresented populations. The function creates contingency tables cross-tabulating missing data patterns with protected attributes and applies chi-square tests to identify statistically significant associations.

```
def systematic_completeness_analysis(dataset,
protected_attributes, critical_features):
    """
    Analyze data completeness patterns that might create bias
    """
    import pandas as pd
    import numpy as np
    from scipy.stats import chi2_contingency

    completeness_analysis = {}

    for feature in critical_features:
        if feature not in dataset.columns:
            continue

        # Calculate missingness by protected groups
        missing_by_group = {}

        for protected_attr in protected_attributes:
            if protected_attr not in dataset.columns:
                continue

            # Create missingness indicator
            is_missing = dataset[feature].isna()

            # Cross-tabulate missingness with protected attribute
            contingency = pd.crosstab(dataset[protected_attr],
is_missing)
```

```
            # Statistical test for association
            if contingency.shape == (2, 2) and
contingency.min().min() >= 5:
                chi2, p_value, dof, expected =
chi2_contingency(contingency)

                missing_by_group[protected_attr] = {
                    'contingency_table': contingency,
                    'chi2_statistic': chi2,
                    'p_value': p_value,
                    'significant_association': p_value < 0.05
                }

        completeness_analysis[feature] = missing_by_group

    return completeness_analysis
```

Sample Output and Interpretation:

```
{
    'credit_score': {
        'race': {
            'contingency_table':
                       False  True
            race
            Asian       850    45
            Black       420    180
            Hispanic    380    120
            White      1200     75,
            'chi2_statistic': 89.34,
            'p_value': 4.2e-19,
            'significant_association': True
        },
        'gender': {
            'contingency_table':
                        False  True
            gender
            Female     1425    205
            Male       1425    215,
            'chi2_statistic': 0.24,
            'p_value': 0.62,
            'significant_association': False
        }
    }
}
```

Interpretation: This output reveals problematic missing data patterns. Credit scores are missing significantly more often for Black applicants (30% missing rate: 180/600) and Hispanic applicants (24% missing: 120/500) compared to White applicants (6% missing: 75/1275). The chi-square statistic of 89.34 with p-value 4.2e-19 confirms this isn't random. This systematic missing data pattern could cause the AI model to perform poorly for minority groups, as it has less complete information to learn from. Gender shows no significant pattern (p=0.62), indicating missing data is random across genders.

5.8.2 Integrity Verification Methods

Forensic documentation should include complete descriptions of all tools and techniques used, validation evidence for analytical methodologies, records of all personnel who accessed evidence, detailed timelines of all investigation activities, and clear explanations of limitations and uncertainties in findings.

Secure storage and access controls protect evidence integrity throughout lengthy investigations and legal proceedings. These controls must prevent unauthorized access while maintaining detailed audit logs of all legitimate access for chain of custody purposes.

Secure storage systems typically employ encryption for data protection, role-based access controls to limit evidence access, comprehensive audit logging of all access attempts, automated backup procedures for evidence preservation, and integration with legal e-discovery platforms for litigation support.

5.9 SYNTHETIC CONTENT AND DATA POISONING DETECTION

5.9.1 Synthetic Data Identification

Modern AI training datasets increasingly contain synthetic or artificially generated content. While legitimate synthetic data can augment training sets, identifying synthetic content becomes crucial for understanding data provenance and potential quality issues.

Detection methodologies include statistical analysis of data distributions for anomalous patterns, metadata examination for generation artifacts, consistency analysis across related data points, and temporal pattern analysis for batch generation indicators.

Synthetic content often exhibits subtle statistical signatures that distinguish it from naturally occurring data. These signatures may include unusual uniformity in certain features, statistical correlations that don't occur in natural data, or metadata patterns that reveal automated generation processes.

5.9.2 Data Poisoning Detection and Analysis

Data poisoning is a serious threat to AI system integrity, where malicious actors intentionally corrupt training data to influence model behavior. Unlike natural bias or quality issues, data poisoning is deliberately crafted to be subtle while achieving specific malicious objectives.

5.9.2.1 Understanding Data Poisoning Attacks

Data poisoning attacks can be categorized into several types, each with distinct characteristics and detection challenges. Label poisoning involves corrupting the labels associated with training examples while leaving the input data unchanged. This attack is often easier to execute but may be more detectable through label consistency analysis.

Feature poisoning modifies the input features themselves, potentially creating backdoor triggers or shifting decision boundaries in ways that favor specific outcomes. Clean-label poisoning represents the most sophisticated approach, where attackers craft examples that appear correctly labeled but actually push the model toward malicious behavior.

5.9.2.2 Detection Framework for Data Poisoning

The statistical anomaly detection framework examines training datasets for patterns that might indicate malicious manipulation. This analysis looks for unusual distributions, temporal patterns, and feature combinations that deviate from expected norms. The function applies multiple detection methods including distribution shift analysis, outlier concentration measurement, and temporal anomaly identification to flag potentially poisoned examples.

```
def detect_statistical_anomalies(dataset, protected_attributes):
    """
    Identify potential data poisoning through statistical anomaly
    detection
```

```
    """
    anomaly_indicators = {}

    # Distribution shift detection
    for feature in dataset.columns:
        if feature in protected_attributes:
            continue

        # Detect sudden distribution changes using statistical tests
        distribution_shifts = detect_distribution_shifts(dataset
        [feature])
        anomaly_indicators[feature] = {
            'distribution_shifts': distribution_shifts,
            'outlier_concentration': calculate_outlier_patterns(dataset
            [feature]),
            'temporal_anomalies': identify_temporal_anomalies(dataset
            [feature])
        }

return anomaly_indicators
```

Sample Output and Interpretation:

```
{
    'income': {
        'distribution_shifts': [
            {
                'position': 5000,
                'ks_statistic': 0.23,
                'p_value': 0.003,
                'significant_shift': True
            },
            {
                'position': 15000,
                'ks_statistic': 0.08,
                'p_value': 0.45,
                'significant_shift': False
            }
        ],
        'outlier_concentration': 0.15,
        'temporal_anomalies': ['2023-03-15', '2023-07-22']
    },
    'education_score': {
        'distribution_shifts': [
            {
                'position': 5000,
                'ks_statistic': 0.31,
                'p_value': 1.2e-06,
                'significant_shift': True
            }
        ],
        'outlier_concentration': 0.22,
        'temporal_anomalies': ['2023-03-15']
    }
}
```

Interpretation: This output indicates potential data poisoning around position 5000 in the dataset. Both income and education_score show significant distribution shifts at the same position (KS statistics of 0.23 and 0.31 with very low *p*-values), suggesting batch injection of anomalous examples. The temporal anomalies align on 2023–03–15, providing a specific date when suspicious data may have been added. High outlier concentrations (15% and 22%) further support the poisoning hypothesis. This pattern suggests coordinated manipulation rather than natural data variation.

Label consistency verification through systematic examination of label patterns can reveal inconsistencies that suggest poisoning attempts. This includes cross-validation of similar examples with different labels, temporal analysis of labeling patterns to identify sudden changes, expert review of high-confidence mismatches between features and labels, and statistical testing for unusual label distributions within demographic groups.

Temporal pattern analysis often reveals data poisoning signatures when malicious examples are added in batches:

5.9.2.3 Temporal Poisoning Pattern Detection

The temporal poisoning detection function analyzes how data characteristics change over time to identify periods when suspicious examples may have been injected into the dataset. This analysis examines data volume changes, feature distribution shifts, and quality degradation patterns that might indicate coordinated poisoning attempts.

The analysis process begins by dividing the dataset into time windows and examining changes between consecutive periods. Weekly analysis typically provides good balance between temporal resolution and statistical power for detecting batch injection patterns.

```
def temporal_poisoning_detection(dataset, time_column):
    """
    Detect potential batch injection of poisoned examples
    """
    import pandas as pd
    import numpy as np
    from datetime import datetime, timedelta

    # Convert temporal columns to datetime for analysis
    dataset[time_column] = pd.to_datetime(dataset[time_column])

    # Create time windows for analysis (weekly provides good balance)
    dataset['time_window'] = dataset[time_column].dt.to_period('W')
    time_windows = sorted(dataset['time_window'].unique())

    temporal_anomalies = {}

    # Analyze data characteristics over time windows
    for i in range(len(time_windows) - 1):
        current_window = time_windows[i]
        next_window = time_windows[i + 1]

        current_data = dataset[dataset['time_window'] == current_window]
        next_data = dataset[dataset['time_window'] == next_window]
        if len(current_data) < 50 or len(next_data) < 50: # Skip windows
        with insufficient data
            continue
        temporal_anomalies[str(current_window)] = {
            'sample_size': len(current_data),
            'next_sample_size': len(next_data),
            'volume_change_ratio': len(next_data) / len(current_data),
            'feature_distribution_changes': analyze_feature_shifts
```

```
                (current_data, next_data),
                'label_pattern_anomalies': detect_label_anomalies(current_
                data, next_data),
                'quality_degradation': assess_quality_changes(current_data,
                next_data)
            }

    return temporal_anomalies
```

5.9.2.4 Feature Distribution Shift Analysis

The feature shift analysis examines whether data distributions changed significantly between time periods, which could indicate injection of anomalous examples. This analysis uses statistical tests to identify sudden changes in feature characteristics that deviate from natural variation patterns.

```
def analyze_feature_shifts(data1, data2):
    """Analyze shifts in feature distributions between time windows"""
    from scipy.stats import ks_2samp

    shifts = {}
    numeric_columns = data1.select_dtypes(include=[np.number]).columns

    for col in numeric_columns:
        if col in data2.columns:
            ks_stat, p_value = ks_2samp(data1[col].dropna(), data2[col].
            dropna())

            shifts[col] = {
                'ks_statistic': ks_stat,
                'p_value': p_value,
                'significant_shift': p_value < 0.01,
                'mean_change': data2[col].mean() - data1[col].mean()
            }

return shifts
```

Sample Output and Interpretation:

```
{
    '2023-03-06/2023-03-12': {
        'sample_size': 245,
        'next_sample_size': 891,
        'volume_change_ratio': 3.64,
        'feature_distribution_changes': {
            'income': {
                'ks_statistic': 0.34,
                'p_value': 2.1e-08,
                'significant_shift': True,
                'mean_change': -15000
            },
            'credit_score': {
                'ks_statistic': 0.41,
                'p_value': 3.2e-12,
                'significant_shift': True,
                'mean_change': -85
            }
        },
```

```
        'label_pattern_anomalies': 0.23,
        'quality_degradation': 0.31
    }
}
```

Interpretation: This output reveals suspicious activity during the week of March 6–12, 2023. The data volume suddenly increased 364% (from 245 to 891 examples), which is highly unusual. Both income and credit scores shifted significantly (KS statistics >0.3, *p*-values <1e-07), with mean income dropping by $15,000 and credit scores falling by 85 points. The 23% label pattern anomaly rate and 31% quality degradation suggest these weren't legitimate data additions. This pattern strongly indicates batch injection of low-quality, potentially poisoned examples designed to manipulate model behavior against applicants with lower income/credit scores.

5.9.2.5 Investigation Methodology

The investigation process follows a systematic three-phase approach. Phase 1 involves initial screening through automated anomaly detection across all data dimensions, statistical testing for distribution shifts and outliers, temporal analysis to identify suspicious data addition patterns, and cross-reference with external threat intelligence about known attacks.

Phase 2 includes targeted analysis with deep examination of flagged examples and their characteristics, expert review of suspicious patterns identified in screening, cross-validation with similar datasets to establish baseline expectations, and correlation analysis between anomalies and model performance issues.

Phase 3 encompasses impact assessment through model behavior analysis to determine effects of suspected poisoning, counterfactual analysis to estimate impact if suspicious data were removed, risk assessment for deployed systems that may have been affected, and timeline reconstruction to understand when and how poisoning occurred.

5.9.2.6 Legal and Compliance Considerations

Data poisoning investigations require careful documentation to support potential legal proceedings. Evidence preservation of all suspicious examples and analysis results, chain of custody documentation for forensic integrity, expert testimony preparation with statistical evidence packages, and impact quantification for damages assessment and liability determination all become essential components of the investigation.

5.10 INTELLECTUAL PROPERTY INVESTIGATION

Modern AI training datasets may contain copyrighted material, trade secrets, or other intellectual property, creating legal liability. Systematic IP detection helps organizations identify violations and develop appropriate remediation strategies.

5.10.1 The Comprehensive IP Challenge in AI Training Data

Modern AI training datasets often contain millions of examples sourced from diverse origins, creating a complex landscape of intellectual property risks that organizations must systematically assess and manage. The scale and automated nature of data collection make inadvertent IP violations nearly inevitable without proper screening procedures.

Understanding the types of intellectual property that commonly appear in training data helps guide detection strategies and risk assessment. Copyright material represents the most prevalent IP risk, encompassing text content from books, articles, blogs, and publications; images, photographs, and artistic works; music, audio recordings, and sound effects; video content and multimedia presentations; and software code and documentation.

Trade secrets may be embedded in training data through proprietary business processes and methodologies, confidential research and development information, internal communications and strategic documents, customer lists and business intelligence, and proprietary algorithms and technical specifications.

5.10.2 IP Detection Methodologies

Different types of content require different detection approaches, each with distinct advantages and limitations. Understanding these trade-offs enables informed decisions about which methods to employ for specific content types and risk levels.

Exact hash matching provides the highest confidence detection for identical copies by comparing cryptographic fingerprints against databases of known copyrighted content. Perfect matches indicate definitive copyright violations that require immediate legal review. However, this approach misses modified or reformatted content and requires comprehensive reference databases.

Fuzzy hashing offers more flexibility by detecting modified versions of copyrighted content through perceptual similarity algorithms. This approach can identify cropped, resized, or lightly edited content but may produce false positives and requires careful threshold tuning.

Semantic similarity analysis uses natural language processing and computer vision techniques to identify content that might be derived from copyrighted sources without being identical copies. This approach is essential for text content analysis and detecting disguised copying attempts.

Perceptual hashing offers robustness against image modifications and catches cropped or resized content but may miss heavily edited material. This method works well for image and video content screening where exact duplicates are unlikely.

5.10.3 Systematic IP Investigation Framework

Comprehensive IP investigation requires a systematic approach that efficiently processes large datasets while maintaining accuracy and legal defensibility. The framework progresses through multiple phases, each building on previous analysis while increasing sophistication and accuracy.

5.10.3.1 Phase 1: Inventory and Classification

The investigation begins with systematic inventory of all content types requiring IP analysis. This inventory process creates a complete catalog of dataset contents, classifying each item by type and IP risk level to guide subsequent analysis priorities.

5.10.3.2 Comprehensive Content Inventory System

The IP inventory function systematically catalogs all content in the training dataset, classifying items by type and assessing initial risk levels to guide investigation priorities. This analysis examines file types, sizes, and characteristics to identify high-risk content that requires comprehensive screening versus lower-risk content that can be processed with automated methods.

The inventory process begins by establishing a structured classification system for different content types. This classification enables the investigation to apply appropriate detection methods for each content category while managing computational resources efficiently.

```
def comprehensive_ip_inventory(dataset_path, content_types):
    """
    Systematic inventory of all content types requiring IP analysis
    """
    import os
    import mimetypes
    from collections import defaultdict
```

```
    inventory = {
        'text_content': [],
        'image_files': [],
        'audio_files': [],
        'video_files': [],
        'code_files': [],
        'document_files': [],
        'unknown_types': []
    }

    risk_assessment = defaultdict(list)

    for root, dirs, files in os.walk(dataset_path):
        for file in files:
            file_path = os.path.join(root, file)
            mime_type, _ = mimetypes.guess_type(file_path)

            content_category = classify_content_type(file_path,
mime_type)
            inventory[content_category].append({
                'path': file_path,
                'size': os.path.getsize(file_path),
                'mime_type': mime_type,
                'risk_level': assess_initial_risk_level(file_path,
mime_type)
            })
    return inventory
```

5.10.3.3 Risk Assessment Classification

Once files are cataloged, the system assigns initial risk levels based on content characteristics and file types. This risk assessment helps prioritize investigation efforts by identifying content most likely to contain intellectual property violations.

```
def assess_initial_risk_level(file_path, mime_type):
    """
    Assign initial IP risk levels based on content characteristics
    """
    high_risk_extensions = ['.pdf', '.doc', '.docx', '.mp3', '.mp4',
'.jpg', '.png']
    medium_risk_extensions = ['.txt', '.csv', '.json']

    file_ext = os.path.splitext(file_path)[1].lower()

    if file_ext in high_risk_extensions:
        return 'HIGH'
    elif file_ext in medium_risk_extensions:
        return 'MEDIUM'
    else:
        return 'LOW'
```

Sample Output and Interpretation:

```
{
    'text_content': [
        {'path': '/data/text/doc1.txt', 'size': 15420, 'mime_type':
'text/plain', 'risk_level': 'MEDIUM'},
```

```
        {'path': '/data/text/doc2.txt', 'size': 8931, 'mime_type': 'text/
plain', 'risk_level': 'MEDIUM'}
    ],
    'image_files': [
        {'path': '/data/images/img1.jpg', 'size': 234567, 'mime_type':
'image/jpeg', 'risk_level': 'HIGH'},
        {'path': '/data/images/img2.png', 'size': 198234, 'mime_type':
'image/png', 'risk_level': 'HIGH'}
    ],
    'document_files': [
        {'path': '/data/docs/report.pdf', 'size': 1245678, 'mime_type':
'application/pdf', 'risk_level': 'HIGH'}
    ]
}
```

Interpretation: This inventory shows the dataset contains two text files (medium risk), two image files (high risk), and one PDF document (high risk). The high-risk files require comprehensive IP screening with multiple detection methods, while medium-risk text files can be processed with automated similarity detection. The classification guides resource allocation, ensuring thorough analysis of high-risk content while efficiently processing lower-risk items.

5.10.3.4 Phase 2: Multi-Method Detection Pipeline

The detection pipeline applies multiple analysis methods based on content type and risk level, using the most appropriate techniques for each content category while managing computational resources efficiently.

5.10.3.5 Multi-Method Detection Framework

The IP detection pipeline applies different detection methods based on content type and risk assessment. High-risk content receives comprehensive screening with multiple techniques including exact hash matching, fuzzy hashing, semantic analysis, and metadata examination. Lower-risk content is processed with efficient automated methods that still provide adequate coverage for potential violations.

The detection process is organized into tiers based on risk level. This tiered approach ensures thorough analysis of high-priority content while managing computational resources efficiently across the entire dataset.

```
def multi_method_ip_detection(inventory, reference_databases):
    """
    Apply multiple detection methods based on content type and risk level
    """
    detection_results = {}

    # High-risk content gets comprehensive screening with multiple
methods
    for item in inventory['high_risk_items']:
        detection_results[item['path']] = {
            'exact_hash': exact_hash_detection(item),
            'fuzzy_hash': fuzzy_hash_detection(item),
            'semantic_analysis': semantic_similarity_detection
(item, reference_databases),
            'watermark_check': watermark_detection(item),
            'metadata_analysis': extract_ip_metadata(item)
        }
```

```
    # Medium-risk content gets targeted screening with efficient methods
    for item in inventory['medium_risk_items']:
        detection_results[item['path']] = {
            'exact_hash': exact_hash_detection(item),
            'basic_similarity': basic_similarity_detection(item,
reference_databases)
        }
    return detection_results
```

5.10.3.6 Exact Hash Detection Implementation

The exact hash detection method provides the highest confidence identification of identical copyrighted content. This method compares cryptographic fingerprints against databases of known copyrighted material to identify perfect matches that represent definitive copyright violations.

```
def exact_hash_detection(content_item):
    """
    Exact hash matching against known copyrighted content databases
    """
    import hashlib

    try:
        with open(content_item['path'], 'rb') as f:
            content_hash = hashlib.sha256(f.read()).hexdigest()

        violation_found = check_copyright_database(content_hash)

        return {
            'hash': content_hash,
            'violation_detected': violation_found,
            'confidence': 1.0 if violation_found else 0.0,
            'method': 'exact_hash'
            }

    except Exception as e:
        return {
            'error': str(e),
            'method': 'exact_hash'
        }
```

Sample Output and Interpretation:

```
{
    '/data/images/img1.jpg': {
        'exact_hash': {
            'hash': 'a1b2c3d4e5f6 . . .',
            'violation_detected': True,
            'confidence': 1.0,
            'method': 'exact_hash'
        },
        'fuzzy_hash': {
            'similarity_score': 0.92,
            'potential_violation': True,
            'confidence': 0.85,
            'method': 'fuzzy_hash'
        },
```

```
        'metadata_analysis': {
            'copyright_notice': 'Getty Images',
            'rights_holder': 'Professional Photographer Inc',
            'violation_likely': True
        }
    },
    '/data/text/doc1.txt': {
        'exact_hash': {
            'violation_detected': False,
            'confidence': 0.0
        },
        'basic_similarity': {
            'max_similarity': 0.73,
            'potential_violation': True,
            'confidence': 0.6
        }
    }
}
```

Interpretation: The image file shows strong evidence of copyright violation with exact hash match (100% confidence) and high fuzzy hash similarity (85% confidence). The metadata reveals Getty Images copyright and professional photographer rights holder, confirming violation. The text file shows no exact match but 73% similarity to known content, suggesting potential paraphrasing that requires legal review. This tiered approach efficiently identifies definitive violations while flagging potential issues for human review.

5.10.3.7 Phase 3: Fair Use Analysis and Risk Assessment

The fair use analysis applies established legal frameworks to evaluate detected potential violations, helping organizations understand their legal exposure and develop appropriate responses.

5.10.3.8 Comprehensive Fair Use Legal Framework

The fair use analysis evaluates potential copyright violations using the established four-factor legal framework: purpose and character of use, nature of copyrighted work, amount and substantiality used, and effect on market. This analysis provides legal risk assessment to guide organizational decision-making about content removal, licensing, or fair use defense strategies.

The analysis begins by systematically evaluating each detected violation against all four factors of the fair use doctrine. This comprehensive approach ensures that legal decisions are based on thorough analysis rather than assumptions about copyright protection.

```
def comprehensive_fair_use_analysis(detected_violations,
business_context):
    """
    Apply four-factor fair use analysis to detected violations
    """
    fair_use_assessments = {}

    for violation_id, violation_data in detected_violations.items():
        if violation_data.get('violation_detected'):

            # Factor 1: Purpose and character of use
            purpose_score = assess_purpose_and_character(violation_data,
business_context)
```

```
            # Factor 2: Nature of copyrighted work
            nature_score = assess_nature_of_work(violation_data)

            # Factor 3: Amount and substantiality
            amount_score = assess_amount_and_substantiality
(violation_data)

            # Factor 4: Effect on market
            market_effect_score = assess_market_effect(violation_data,
business_context)

            # Calculate weighted overall assessment
            weighted_score = (
                purpose_score * 0.3 +
                nature_score * 0.2 +
                amount_score * 0.25 +
                market_effect_score * 0.25
            )

            fair_use_assessments[violation_id] = {
                'factor_1_purpose': purpose_score,
                'factor_2_nature': nature_score,
                'factor_3_amount': amount_score,
                'factor_4_market': market_effect_score,
                'overall_assessment': {
                    'weighted_score': weighted_score,
                    'fair_use_likely': weighted_score > 0.6,
                    'requires_legal_review': weighted_score
< 0.4 or weighted_score > 0.8,
                    'risk_level': categorize_fair_use_risk
(weighted_score)
                }
            }
    return fair_use_assessments
```

5.10.3.9 Purpose and Character Assessment

The first factor of fair use analysis examines the purpose and character of the use, with particular attention to whether the use is commercial or educational and whether it is transformative. Educational and research uses generally receive stronger fair use protection, while commercial uses face greater scrutiny.

```
def assess_purpose_and_character(violation_data, business_context):
    """Assess Factor 1: Purpose and character of use"""
    purpose_indicators = {
        'commercial_use': business_context.get('commercial_purpose',
True),
        'transformative_use': violation_data.get('transformative_
elements', False),
        'educational_purpose': business_context.get('educational_
context', False),
        'research_purpose': business_context.get('research_context',
False)
    }
```

```
    score = 0.5 # Neutral starting point

    if purpose_indicators['educational_purpose'] or purpose_
indicators['research_purpose']:
        score += 0.3
    if purpose_indicators['transformative_use']:
        score += 0.2
    if purpose_indicators['commercial_use']:
        score -= 0.2
    return max(0.0, min(1.0, score)) # Clamp to [0, 1]
```

Sample Output and Interpretation:

```
{
    '/data/images/img1.jpg': {
        'factor_1_purpose': 0.3, # Commercial use, not transformative
        'factor_2_nature': 0.4, # Creative work (photograph)
        'factor_3_amount': 0.2, # Used entire work
        'factor_4_market': 0.1, # Directly competes with original
        'overall_assessment': {
            'weighted_score': 0.25,
            'fair_use_likely': False,
            'requires_legal_review': True,
            'risk_level': 'HIGH'
        }
    },
    '/data/text/research_excerpt.txt': {
        'factor_1_purpose': 0.8, # Educational/research use
        'factor_2_nature': 0.6, # Factual content
        'factor_3_amount': 0.7, # Small excerpt used
        'factor_4_market': 0.8, # No market harm
        'overall_assessment': {
            'weighted_score': 0.72,
            'fair_use_likely': True,
            'requires_legal_review': False,
            'risk_level': 'LOW'
        }
    }
}
```

Interpretation: The image shows weak fair use protection (0.25 score) due to commercial use of the entire creative work that competes with the original, indicating high legal risk requiring immediate action. The research text excerpt shows strong fair use protection (0.72 score) due to educational purpose, factual content, limited use, and no market harm, suggesting low legal risk. This analysis enables risk-based decision making about which content requires immediate removal versus which might be defensible under fair use doctrine.

5.10.3.10 Phase 4: Legal Risk Assessment and Prioritization

The final phase prioritizes identified violations by legal risk and business impact, helping legal teams focus resources on the highest-risk situations while managing review workload efficiently.

5.10.3.11 Legal Risk Prioritization Framework

The risk prioritization function combines detection confidence, fair use analysis, business context, and copyright holder characteristics to create actionable risk rankings. This framework helps legal teams focus on the most serious violations while managing review resources efficiently.

The prioritization process considers multiple factors beyond simple detection confidence. Copyright holder enforcement history, business exposure levels, and content prominence all influence the overall risk assessment to provide realistic guidance for legal decision-making.

```
def ip_risk_prioritization(detection_results, fair_use_analyses, busi-
ness_context):
    """
    Prioritize IP violations by legal risk and business impact
    """
    risk_matrix = []

    for violation_id, detection in detection_results.items():
        fair_use = fair_use_analyses.get(violation_id, {})

        risk_score = calculate_composite_risk_score(
            detection_confidence=detection.get('confidence', 0),
            fair_use_strength=fair_use.get('overall_assessment',
{}).get('weighted_score', 0),
            content_prominence=assess_content_prominence(detection),
            copyright_holder_profile=assess_copyright_holder_
risk(detection),
            business_exposure=assess_business_exposure(detection, busi-
ness_context)
        )
        risk_matrix.append({
'violation_id': violation_id,
            'risk_score': risk_score,
            'risk_category': categorize_risk_level(risk_score),
            'immediate_action_required': risk_score > 0.8,
            'legal_review_priority': determine_review_priority
(risk_score),
            'recommended_timeline': determine_action_timeline(risk_score)
        })
    risk_matrix.sort(key=lambda x: x['risk_score'], reverse=True)

    return risk_matrix
```

5.10.3.12 Risk Score Calculation

The composite risk score integrates multiple factors to provide a comprehensive assessment of legal exposure. This calculation balances detection confidence with fair use strength while considering practical factors like copyright holder aggressiveness and potential business impact.

```
def calculate_composite_risk_score(detection_confidence,
fair_use_strength,
                                content_prominence, copyright_holder_
profile, business_exposure):
    """
    Calculate comprehensive risk score from multiple factors
    """
    # Base risk from detection confidence
    base_risk = detection_confidence

    # Adjust for fair use protection (inverse relationship)
    fair_use_adjustment = 1.0 - fair_use_strength
```

```
    # Weight and combine all factors
    composite_score = (
        base_risk * 0.4 +
        fair_use_adjustment * 0.3 +
        copyright_holder_profile * 0.15 +
        content_prominence * 0.1 +
        business_exposure * 0.05
    )
    return min(1.0, max(0.0, composite_score))
```

Sample Output and Interpretation:

```
[
    {
        'violation_id': '/data/images/getty_photo.jpg',
        'risk_score': 0.95,
        'risk_category': 'CRITICAL',
        'immediate_action_required': True,
        'legal_review_priority': 'URGENT',
        'recommended_timeline': '24_hours'
    },
    {
        'violation_id': '/data/text/news_article.txt',
        'risk_score': 0.72,
        'risk_category': 'HIGH',
        'immediate_action_required': False,
        'legal_review_priority': 'HIGH',
        'recommended_timeline': '1_week'
    },
    {
        'violation_id': '/data/research/academic_excerpt.txt',
        'risk_score': 0.23,
        'risk_category': 'LOW',
        'immediate_action_required': False,
        'legal_review_priority': 'LOW',
        'recommended_timeline': '30_days'
    }
]
```

Interpretation: The Getty Images photo requires immediate action within 24 hours due to high detection confidence, weak fair use protection, and aggressive copyright holder enforcement history. The news article needs review within one week as a high-priority item with moderate legal risk. The academic excerpt can be addressed within 30 days as a low-priority item with strong fair use protection. This prioritization enables efficient resource allocation while ensuring the most serious violations receive immediate attention.

5.10.4 Implementation Framework

The IP investigation process follows a structured sequence that ensures comprehensive coverage while managing complexity and resource requirements effectively.

Phase 1: Pre-Investigation Setup establishes the legal framework with counsel review of fair use policies, configures detection tools and reference databases, sets up secure analysis environments with appropriate access controls, defines sampling strategies for large datasets, and creates documentation templates for evidence preservation.

Phase 2: Automated Detection Phase runs inventory analysis to catalog all content types, executes the detection pipeline using appropriate methods for each content type, generates preliminary violation reports with confidence scores, flags high-confidence violations for immediate legal review, and documents all detection methodology for chain of custody requirements.

Phase 3: Fair Use Analysis applies four-factor analysis to detected violations, researches copyright holder profiles and enforcement history, assesses business context and usage circumstances, calculates risk scores and prioritization matrices, and prepares legal review packages with supporting evidence.

Phase 4: Legal Review and Action Planning involves legal counsel review of high-risk violations, develops mitigation strategies including removal, licensing, or fair use defense, creates compliance documentation for regulatory requirements, implements remediation actions based on legal advice, and establishes ongoing monitoring for future IP compliance.

Phase 5: Documentation and Reporting compiles comprehensive investigation reports with executive summaries, documents remediation actions taken and their legal justification, creates compliance evidence packages for regulatory requirements, establishes monitoring procedures for ongoing IP compliance, and updates data collection policies to prevent future violations.

5.10.5 Legal Documentation Requirements

IP investigations have to meet stringent documentation standards to support legal proceedings and regulatory compliance. Evidence preservation standards require chain of custody documentation for all analyzed content, methodology documentation with statistical validation, tool calibration records and accuracy testing results, expert qualification documentation for analysis personnel, and timestamp verification for all detection activities.

Reporting standards for legal proceedings include executive summaries with key findings and risk assessments, detailed methodology sections explaining detection approaches, statistical analysis with confidence intervals and error rates, fair use analysis following established legal frameworks, and remediation recommendations with implementation guidelines.

This comprehensive IP investigation framework provides organizations with systematic tools and methodologies for identifying intellectual property issues in training data while building legally defensible evidence and implementing effective remediation strategies.

5.11 TEMPORAL PATTERN ANALYSIS

Understanding how training data characteristics evolved over time provides crucial insights for forensic investigations. Temporal analysis helps establish causality, identify when problems emerged, and understand how external factors influenced dataset composition. Temporal analysis often proves crucial for establishing timelines in legal proceedings and understanding root causes of system failures.

5.11.1 Statistical Change Point Detection

Rather than relying solely on subjective observations about when changes occurred, statistical change point detection provides objective methods for identifying significant shifts in data characteristics over time.

5.11.1.1 Comprehensive Temporal Evolution Analysis

The temporal analysis function examines how data characteristics and bias patterns evolved over time, providing objective evidence of when significant changes occurred. This analysis divides datasets into time windows and tracks bias metrics, data quality measures, and external events to establish causal relationships and support legal timelines.

The temporal analysis process begins by establishing appropriate time windows that balance statistical power with temporal resolution. Quarterly windows typically provide sufficient sample sizes while capturing meaningful changes in organizational practices or external conditions.

```
def comprehensive_temporal_analysis(dataset, temporal_columns, protected_
attributes):
    """
    Analyze how data characteristics evolved over time using statistical
methods
    """
    import pandas as pd
    import numpy as np
    from datetime import datetime, timedelta

    # Convert temporal columns to datetime for analysis
    for col in temporal_columns:
        if col in dataset.columns:
            dataset[col] = pd.to_datetime(dataset[col])

            # Create time windows for analysis (quarterly provides good
balance)

    start_date = dataset[temporal_columns[0]].min()
    end_date = dataset[temporal_columns[0]].max()
    time_windows = pd.date_range(start=start_date, end=end_date,
freq='Q')

    temporal_bias_evolution = {}

    # Analyze bias patterns across time windows
    for i in range(len(time_windows) - 1):
        window_start = time_windows[i]
        window_end = time_windows[i + 1]

        window_data = dataset[
            (dataset[temporal_columns[0]] >= window_start) &
            (dataset[temporal_columns[0]] < window_end)
        ]

        if len(window_data) < 100: # Skip windows with insufficient data
            continue

        window_bias = analyze_bias_in_time_window(window_data, protected_
attributes)

        temporal_bias_evolution[window_start.strftime('%Y-Q%q')] = {
            'sample_size': len(window_data),
            'bias_metrics': window_bias,
            'data_quality': assess_data_quality_window(window_data),
            'external_events': identify_external_events(window_start,
window_end)
        }

    return temporal_bias_evolution
```

5.11.1.2 Time Window Bias Analysis

Once the dataset is divided into time windows, each window undergoes detailed bias analysis to track how discrimination patterns evolved over time. This analysis examines both demographic representation and outcome disparities within each time period.

```
def analyze_bias_in_time_window(window_data, protected_attributes):
    """Analyze bias patterns within a specific time window"""
    bias_metrics = {}

    for attr in protected_attributes:
        if attr in window_data.columns:
            # Calculate demographic representation

            representation = window_data[attr].
value_counts(normalize=True)

            # Calculate outcome rates by group (if outcome column exists)
            if 'outcome' in window_data.columns:
                outcome_rates = window_data.groupby(attr)['outcome'].
mean()
                bias_metrics[attr] = {
                    'representation': representation.to_dict(),
                    'outcome_rates': outcome_rates.to_dict(),
                    'max_disparity': outcome_rates.max() -
outcome_rates.min()
                }
            else:
                bias_metrics[attr] = {
                    'representation': representation.to_dict()
                }

    return bias_metrics
```

Sample Output and Interpretation:

```
{
    '2022-Q1': {
        'sample_size': 2547,
        'bias_metrics': {
            'race': {
                'representation': {'White': 0.68, 'Black': 0.15,
'Hispanic': 0.12, 'Asian': 0.05},
                'outcome_rates': {'White': 0.71, 'Black': 0.43,
'Hispanic': 0.48, 'Asian': 0.69},
                'max_disparity': 0.28
            }
        },
        'data_quality': 0.94,
        'external_events': ['policy_change_2022_01_15']
    },
    '2022-Q2': {
        'sample_size': 2891,
        'bias_metrics': {
            'race': {
                'representation': {'White': 0.65, 'Black': 0.18,
'Hispanic': 0.13, 'Asian': 0.04},
                'outcome_rates': {'White': 0.69, 'Black': 0.41,
'Hispanic': 0.46, 'Asian': 0.67},
```

```
                'max_disparity': 0.28
            }
        },
        'data_quality': 0.92,
        'external_events': []
    }
}
```

Interpretation: This output tracks bias evolution over time, showing persistent discrimination patterns. In Q1 2022, White applicants had 71% approval vs. 43% for Black applicants (28-point disparity). Despite a policy change on January 15, 2022, the disparity remained unchanged in Q2 (28 points: 69% vs. 41%). The slight increase in Black representation (15% to 18%) didn't improve outcomes. This temporal analysis provides evidence that the organization's policy changes were ineffective at reducing racial bias, potentially supporting claims of deliberate indifference to discriminatory outcomes. The consistent disparities across quarters strengthen legal arguments about systematic discrimination.

Quarterly analysis provides a good balance between temporal resolution and statistical power, ensuring adequate sample sizes in each time window while capturing meaningful changes over time.

5.12 DECISION MATRICES FOR TRAINING DATA ANALYSIS

The investigation techniques presented in this chapter can be overwhelming in their scope and complexity. To help forensic investigators navigate this complexity systematically, this section provides decision matrices that map investigation scenarios to appropriate analytical approaches.

The matrices serve multiple purposes: they accelerate decision-making during time-sensitive investigations, ensure comprehensive coverage of relevant analysis techniques, provide standardized approaches that support consistency across investigations, and enable efficient resource allocation based on investigation characteristics and constraints. Each matrix is designed to be both prescriptive enough to guide decision-making and flexible enough to accommodate the unique circumstances that characterize every AI forensic investigation.

5.12.1 Technique-to-Issue Mapping Matrix

This matrix provides a comprehensive cross-reference between specific analysis techniques and the types of training data issues they can effectively detect. The matrix uses a three-tier effectiveness rating system where checkmarks indicate high effectiveness (the technique is well-suited and

TABLE 5.2

Analysis Technique	Bias Detection	Quality Issues	IP Violations	Data Poisoning	Synthetic Content
Statistical Significance Testing	✓ High	✓ Medium	✗ Low	✓ Medium	✓ Low
Demographic Parity Analysis	✓ High	✗ Low	✗ Low	✓ Low	✗ Low
Hash-based Similarity	✗ Low	✓ Medium	✓ High	✓ High	✓ Medium
Temporal Pattern Analysis	✓ Medium	✓ High	✗ Low	✓ High	✓ Medium
Distribution Analysis	✓ High	✓ High	✗ Low	✓ High	✓ High
Metadata Examination	✓ Low	✓ High	✓ High	✓ Medium	✓ High
Cross-validation Testing	✓ High	✓ High	✗ Low	✓ Medium	✓ Low
Expert Review	✓ High	✓ High	✓ High	✓ High	✓ High

TABLE 5.3

Analysis Technique	Computational Requirements	Expertise Level	Time Investment
Statistical Significance Testing	Medium	High	Medium
Demographic Parity Analysis	Low	Medium	Low
Hash-Based Similarity	High	Low	Low
Temporal Pattern Analysis	High	High	High
Distribution Analysis	Medium	High	Medium
Metadata Examination	Low	Low	Low
Cross-Validation Testing	High	High	High
Expert Review	Low	High	High

TABLE 5.4

Issue Type	Primary Detection Methods	Secondary Methods	Validation Approaches
Representation Bias	Statistical testing, demographic analysis	Temporal analysis	Expert review, cross-validation
Measurement Bias	Distribution analysis, consistency testing	Metadata examination	Statistical significance testing
Historical Bias	Temporal analysis, pattern recognition	Expert review	Counterfactual analysis
Label Poisoning	Consistency testing, anomaly detection	Cross-validation	Expert review
Feature Poisoning	Distribution analysis, statistical testing	Temporal analysis	Multiple method validation
Synthetic Content	Metadata analysis, statistical testing	Pattern recognition	Expert verification
IP Violations	Hash matching, similarity analysis	Metadata examination	Legal review

reliable for detecting this issue type), medium effectiveness (the technique provides useful insights but may require supplementary methods), and low effectiveness (the technique has limited utility for this specific issue type).

5.12.2 Resource Requirements Matrix

This matrix helps investigators plan resource allocation by specifying the computational, expertise, and time requirements for different analysis techniques. Understanding these requirements enables realistic project planning and appropriate resource allocation for training data forensics investigations.

5.12.3 Detection Capability Matrix

This matrix organizes detection approaches by issue type, providing a systematic framework for addressing different categories of training data problems. It distinguishes between primary detection methods (the most effective initial approaches), secondary methods (supplementary techniques that provide additional insights), and validation approaches (methods for confirming and quantifying detected issues).

5.13 CASE STUDIES AND REAL-WORLD APPLICATIONS

The following case studies demonstrate how the training data forensics framework applies to real-world investigations, showing how different analytical approaches combine to reveal systematic problems and support effective remediation.

5.13.1 Case Study 1: Healthcare AI Bias Investigation

A major health system discovered that their AI diagnostic tool for skin cancer detection showed significantly lower accuracy for patients with darker skin tones, raising concerns about equitable healthcare delivery and potential legal liability under healthcare civil rights laws.

5.13.1.1 Investigation Methodology

The investigation employed the comprehensive bias detection framework, starting with representation analysis of the training dataset:

5.13.1.2 Training Dataset Composition Analysis

The initial analysis revealed severe underrepresentation of darker skin tones in the training data, establishing the foundation for understanding performance disparities observed in clinical testing.

```
# Training dataset composition analysis
skin_tone_representation = {
    'Very Light': 45.2,
    'Light': 28.7,
    'Medium': 18.3,
    'Dark': 6.1,
    'Very Dark': 1.7
}

# Performance disparities found in testing
accuracy_by_skin_tone = {
    'Very Light': 94.3,
    'Light': 91.8,
    'Medium': 87.2,
    'Dark': 76.4,
    'Very Dark': 68.1
}
```

Interpretation: This analysis demonstrates a clear correlation between training data representation and model performance. Very light skin tones comprise 45.2% of training data and achieve 94.3% accuracy, while very dark skin tones represent only 1.7% of training data and achieve just 68.1% accuracy. The 26-point accuracy gap between the best- and worst-performing groups creates significant clinical risk and potential civil rights violations.

The investigation revealed that darker skin tones were severely underrepresented in training data, leading to systematic performance degradation for these populations. Statistical analysis confirmed that these disparities were both statistically significant ($p < 0.001$) and practically meaningful, creating substantial legal risk under healthcare civil rights laws.

5.13.1.3 Root Cause Analysis

The investigation traced the bias to data collection decisions made during the initial dataset creation. The training images were sourced primarily from dermatology clinics in regions with predominantly light-skinned populations, creating a sampling bias that wasn't recognized during dataset development.

5.13.1.4 Remediation Strategy

The health system implemented a comprehensive bias mitigation strategy including targeted data collection from diverse populations, algorithmic bias testing requirements for all AI tools, and ongoing monitoring of performance across demographic groups. This case demonstrated how training data analysis can reveal root causes of bias and guide effective remediation.

5.13.2 Case Study 2: Financial Services Fair Lending Investigation

A regional bank faced regulatory scrutiny when community advocates presented statistical evidence suggesting their AI-powered mortgage approval system was systematically denying qualified minority applicants, potentially violating fair lending laws.

5.13.2.1 Statistical Analysis Framework

The investigation employed the comprehensive demographic parity analysis framework on historical mortgage applications:

5.13.2.2 Initial Disparity Analysis

The demographic parity analysis revealed extreme disparities in approval rates that provided prima facie evidence of systematic discrimination requiring detailed investigation.

```
approval_rates_by_race = {
    'White': 67.3,
    'Black': 23.4,
    'Hispanic': 28.9,
    'Asian': 71.2
}

# Statistical evidence of systematic disparities
chi2_statistic = 2847.3
p_value = 8.7e-156
max_disparity = 43.9 # percentage points between White and
Black applicants
```

Interpretation: The disparities are so extreme that they provide compelling evidence of systematic discrimination. The 44-point gap between White and Black approval rates, combined with the astronomically low *p*-value, establishes statistical significance beyond any reasonable doubt. However, the bank argued these differences reflected legitimate financial factors rather than racial bias.

5.13.2.3 Multivariate Analysis Results

To address this defense, the investigation employed logistic regression controlling for all legitimate financial factors:

5.13.2.4 Controlled Statistical Analysis

The multivariate analysis examined whether racial disparities persisted after accounting for all legitimate financial considerations, providing definitive evidence of discrimination independent of creditworthiness factors.

```
# Even after controlling for financial factors, race remained highly
significant
race_coefficients = {
    'Black': -0.573,    # Negative coefficient indicates lower approval
probability
    'Hispanic': -0.448, # Both highly statistically significant
(p < 2.1e-23)
    'Asian': 0.123      # Positive coefficient indicates higher approval
probability
}
```

Interpretation: This analysis proved that racial disparities persisted even after accounting for all legitimate financial considerations, providing strong evidence of discrimination that led to regulatory action and system redesign. The negative coefficients for Black and Hispanic applicants indicate systematic bias against these groups, while the positive coefficient for Asian applicants suggests preferential treatment. The extremely low p-values confirm these effects are not due to chance.

5.13.2.5 Temporal Analysis Insights

The investigation revealed that bias patterns had actually worsened over time as the AI system "learned" from historical lending data that embedded decades of discriminatory practices. This temporal pattern provided evidence that the bias was not an isolated incident but a systematic problem requiring comprehensive remediation.

5.13.3 Case Study 3: Content Moderation IP Violation Discovery

A social media platform discovered through internal audit that their content moderation training dataset contained substantial amounts of copyrighted material, creating potential liability for both copyright infringement and inadequate content filtering.

5.13.3.1 IP Detection Methodology

The investigation employed the multi-method IP detection framework, starting with automated screening of the massive dataset:

5.13.3.2 Automated Detection Results

The comprehensive IP screening revealed the scale of potential violations across different content types, necessitating systematic prioritization to manage legal review resources effectively.

```
# Automated detection results across different content types
ip_violations_detected = {
    'exact_hash_matches': 12847,        # Definitive copyright violations
    'high_similarity_text': 45692,      # Likely paraphrased content
    'perceptual_hash_images': 8934,     # Modified copyrighted images
    'total_items_screened': 2847356     # Overall dataset size
}

# Risk assessment prioritization
high_risk_violations = 1247 # Requiring immediate legal review
medium_risk_violations = 8934 # Requiring assessment
```

Interpretation: The scale of potential violations necessitated systematic prioritization to focus legal review on the highest-risk content while managing the overall remediation effort efficiently. The 12,847 exact hash matches represent definitive copyright violations requiring immediate action, while the 45,692 high-similarity text items suggest extensive paraphrasing of copyrighted content that needs legal evaluation.

5.13.3.3 Fair Use Analysis Application

The team applied the four-factor fair use analysis to high-priority violations:

5.13.3.4 Legal Risk Assessment

The fair use analysis enabled risk-based decision making about which content required immediate removal versus which might be defensible under fair use doctrine.

```
fair_use_assessment_summary = {
    'strong_fair_use_defense': 342,      # Likely protected uses
    'weak_fair_use_defense': 567,        # High legal risk
    'mixed_factors': 338,                # Requiring detailed legal review
    'requires_immediate_action': 567     # Remove or license immediately
}
```

Interpretation: The fair use analysis enabled the platform to develop a risk-based response that removed clear violations while preserving content that might be protected under fair use doctrine. The 567 items requiring immediate action represent high-risk violations with weak fair use defenses, while the 342 items with strong fair use defenses could potentially be retained with proper legal justification.

5.13.3.5 Business Impact and Resolution

The investigation led to implementation of comprehensive IP screening for all new training data, development of fair use assessment procedures for content inclusion, establishment of ongoing monitoring for IP compliance, and creation of rapid response procedures for IP violation reports.

5.14 PRACTICAL IMPLEMENTATION GUIDANCE

5.14.1 Start with Clear Objectives

Training data investigations can quickly become overwhelming given the scale and complexity of modern datasets. Clear investigation objectives help focus efforts on the most important analyses while ensuring efficient resource use.

Different types of investigations require different approaches. Bias investigations prioritize demographic analysis and fairness metrics. Quality investigations emphasize completeness and consistency analysis. IP investigations focus on content similarity and fair use assessment. Security investigations examine data integrity and potential tampering.

5.14.2 Invest in Appropriate Tools

The scale of modern training datasets necessitates specialized tools and infrastructure for effective analysis. Organizations should invest in the statistical software, distributed computing resources, and security infrastructure needed for comprehensive training data forensics.

Tool selection should balance capability requirements with cost and complexity constraints. Simple investigations might be handled with standard statistical software, while complex bias detection across massive datasets may require distributed computing platforms and specialized AI fairness libraries.

5.14.3 Document Everything

Training data investigations often involve complex statistical analyses, large-scale sampling decisions, and sophisticated technical procedures. Comprehensive documentation ensures that findings can be reproduced, validated, and defended in legal or regulatory proceedings.

Documentation standards should address both technical methodology and legal requirements. Technical documentation enables peer review and validation, while legal documentation ensures admissibility and supports expert testimony requirements.

5.14.4 Plan for Scale

Modern training datasets routinely exceed traditional forensic investigation capacities. Investigation planning should incorporate computational requirements, time constraints, and the statistical challenges inherent in analyzing massive, complex datasets.

Scalability planning should consider both current investigation needs and future growth in dataset size and complexity. Infrastructure investments should accommodate increasing scale while maintaining investigation quality and legal defensibility.

5.15 CONCLUSION AND INTEGRATION

The comprehensive understanding of training data characteristics developed through this analysis provides essential context for the next phase of AI forensic investigation. In Chapter 6, "Model Investigation," we will examine how AI models learned from this training data, what internal representations they developed, and how these representations translate into decision-making behaviors.

Training data analysis tells us what AI systems learned from. Model investigation tells us what they learned and how they use that knowledge. Together, these analyses provide the foundation for understanding AI system behavior, establishing accountability, and ensuring responsible AI deployment.

5.15.1 Key Insights from Training Data Analysis

Data as the source of truth provides the most direct explanation for AI system behavior patterns. When bias patterns emerge after specific data collection changes or policy decisions, this temporal relationship provides compelling evidence of organizational responsibility for discriminatory outcomes.

Scale requires strategic sampling approaches that maintain statistical validity while managing practical constraints. Modern training datasets exceed the capacity for complete analysis, but strategic sampling approaches maintain statistical validity while managing practical constraints. Proper sampling documentation and validation ensures that findings can be appropriately extrapolated to full datasets.

The sampling strategies presented in this chapter balance statistical rigor with practical feasibility, ensuring that investigations can handle massive datasets while maintaining confidence in their findings. Stratified sampling approaches ensure adequate representation for bias detection, while quality assurance procedures validate sample representativeness.

5.15.2 Integration Multiplies Impact

Training data analysis findings become more powerful when integrated with evidence from other forensic investigation areas. Understanding how training data problems manifested in model architecture, influenced system performance, and created security vulnerabilities provides comprehensive evidence for systematic remediation.

Model Architecture Correlation: Understanding how training data characteristics influenced architectural design decisions helps explain why certain biases or limitations appear in deployed systems. Training data constraints often drive architectural choices that perpetuate or amplify data-related problems.

Performance Impact Analysis: Correlating training data quality issues with system performance problems provides evidence for the causal chains that lead from data problems to operational failures. This correlation is often essential for developing effective remediation strategies that address root causes rather than symptoms.

Security Vulnerability Context: Training data analysis can reveal how data quality issues or IP violations created security vulnerabilities that might be exploited by malicious actors. Understanding these relationships helps prioritize security remediation efforts.

Temporal Coordination: Training data evolution should be understood relative to model development timelines, deployment schedules, and external business pressures. This integrated temporal analysis often reveals the business and technical factors that drove problematic decisions.

5.15.2.1 Looking Ahead to Model Investigation

The comprehensive training data analysis completed in this chapter sets the stage for the next critical phase of AI forensic investigation. While training data analysis tells us what information was available for learning, model investigation reveals what the AI system actually learned and how it processes that information to make decisions.

Model investigation examines the internal representations, learned parameters, and decision-making patterns that emerged from training on the data we've analyzed. Understanding these learned behaviors requires different analytical approaches that can probe the internal workings of complex AI systems while maintaining the same standards of forensic rigor and legal defensibility.

The relationship between training data characteristics and model behavior is complex and sometimes counterintuitive. Models may amplify certain biases present in training data while attenuating others. They may learn to rely on features that weren't intended to be decision-relevant. They may develop internal representations that reflect historical patterns in ways that create systematic discrimination even when individual training examples appear unbiased.

These complexities make model investigation an essential complement to training data analysis. Together, these two analytical approaches provide comprehensive understanding of how AI systems acquire their capabilities and why they behave as they do in deployment. This understanding forms the foundation for effective remediation, regulatory compliance, and accountability in AI system development and deployment.

6 Model Investigation

6.1 GETTING INSIDE AI'S BLACK BOX

When Tesla's Autopilot failed to detect a white truck against a bright sky in 2016, investigators faced a problem that traditional software debugging could not solve. The issue was not in the code—it was buried somewhere in the 50 million learned parameters of a neural network. How do you debug a system that "learned" its behavior instead of being explicitly programmed?

6.2 WHAT YOU WILL LEARN

By the end of this chapter, you will be able to:

- Gain forensically sound access to AI models (even black-box APIs)
- Read model architectures like blueprints to identify design flaws
- Analyze 50 million learned parameters for signs of tampering or bias
- Prove discrimination using statistical methods that hold up in court
- Detect sophisticated security threats like backdoors and adversarial attacks
- Document findings that support business decisions and legal proceedings

6.3 QUICK START GUIDE

6.3.1 Need Immediate Answers?

- **System behaving unexpectedly?** → Start with Performance Analysis (Section 6.11)
- **Suspected tampering?** → Jump to Security Analysis (Section 6.12)
- **Bias investigation?** → Begin with Fairness Evaluation (Section 6.11.3)
- **Black-box system?** → See Black-Box Testing (Section 6.13)

6.4 THE AI INVESTIGATION CHALLENGE

6.4.1 Why AI Models Are Different

Traditional software debugging follows logical paths: trace execution through code, examine variable states, identify where logic fails. AI models work fundamentally differently. Their "knowledge" exists as statistical patterns distributed across millions of parameters—weights and biases that encode everything learned during training.

The Scale Challenge: A modern language model contains 175 billion parameters. That is like trying to understand a library by examining each individual letter in every book, then determining how they work together to create meaning.

The Opacity Challenge: Unlike code where if (age > 65) approve_discount() clearly shows decision logic, neural networks make decisions through complex mathematical transformations that have no direct human interpretation.

The Evolution Challenge: AI models change through retraining, online learning, or drift. The system you investigate today might behave differently than when an incident occurred months ago.

DOI: 10.1201/9781003634782-6

6.4.2 Real-World Impact: The Hiring AI Case

Consider a major technology company that discovered their resume screening AI was systematically rating resumes with African American names 12% lower than identical resumes with white names. The bias wasn't in any code—it was learned from historical hiring data that reflected past discrimination. Traditional debugging tools couldn't detect this problem because it wasn't a bug in logic; it was a statistical pattern learned from biased training data.

The investigation required specialized AI forensic techniques:

- Statistical analysis of 10,000 resumes with controlled demographic variations
- Parameter analysis revealing 23.4% of model attention focused on name-based features
- Embedding analysis showing significant clustering separation by demographic characteristics
- Legal documentation demonstrating systematic disparate impact

This case illustrates why AI investigation requires fundamentally different approaches than traditional software forensics.

6.5 AI MODEL INVESTIGATION FRAMEWORK

Before examining specific technical analysis methods, investigators need a systematic framework that guides the investigation process from initial evidence identification through final reporting. AI model investigation follows a structured approach that ensures comprehensive coverage while maintaining forensic integrity.

6.5.1 Investigation Workflow Overview

The AI model investigation framework consists of five primary phases that build upon each other to create comprehensive understanding of system behavior and potential issues.

Phase 1: Evidence Identification and Scoping establishes investigation objectives, identifies available evidence sources, and determines technical and legal constraints that will guide the investigation approach. This phase includes legal authorization review, technical access assessment, resource requirement planning, and stakeholder coordination to ensure investigation feasibility and compliance.

Phase 2: Model Access and Acquisition involves gaining forensically sound access to model components while preserving evidence integrity. This includes direct model file acquisition, API-based investigation setup, cloud service coordination, and framework compatibility verification to enable comprehensive technical analysis.

Phase 3: Technical Analysis employs systematic examination of model architecture, parameters, training artifacts, and performance characteristics to understand system behavior and identify potential issues. This phase includes computational footprint analysis, training configuration forensics, parameter distribution analysis, and performance evaluation across multiple fairness metrics.

Phase 4: Behavioral Testing examines model responses to systematic inputs designed to reveal bias patterns, security vulnerabilities, and capability limitations. This includes both white-box analysis when model internals are accessible and black-box testing when only input-output behavior can be observed.

Phase 5: Documentation and Reporting synthesizes technical findings into actionable insights for different audiences including executive leadership, legal counsel, and regulatory authorities. This phase ensures findings are presented in formats appropriate for business decision-making and legal proceedings.

6.5.2 Framework Application Principles

The investigation framework adapts to different scenarios while maintaining systematic rigor. For suspected bias cases, the framework emphasizes fairness evaluation and demographic performance analysis. For security incidents, the framework prioritizes backdoor detection and adversarial robustness testing. For compliance assessments, the framework focuses on regulatory requirement mapping and documentation standards.

Investigation depth scales with available resources and case complexity. Simple investigations might focus on performance analysis and basic bias testing, while comprehensive investigations employ the full range of technical analysis techniques including parameter forensics, training configuration analysis, and extensive behavioral testing.

6.6 MODEL ACCESS AND ACQUISITION

Before any technical analysis can proceed, investigators need to gain appropriate access to AI models while maintaining forensic integrity and legal compliance. Model acquisition presents unique challenges that differ from traditional software forensics.

6.6.1 Legal Authorization for AI Model Access

AI model investigation typically needs clear legal authority that addresses intellectual property concerns, privacy protections, and technical access limitations that may not be covered by traditional search warrants or discovery orders.

Scope Definition: Legal authorization should specifically address AI system components including model architectures, trained parameters, training data, configuration files, and operational logs. Generic software investigation authority may not clearly cover proprietary AI assets, particularly when models are deployed through cloud services or third-party platforms.

Intellectual Property Considerations: AI models often represent significant intellectual property investments, creating a need for careful balance between investigation needs and proprietary technology protection. Legal authorization should address confidentiality requirements, expert witness qualifications, and limitations on information sharing that protect legitimate business interests while enabling thorough investigation.

Multi-Jurisdictional Challenges: AI systems frequently operate across multiple jurisdictions with different privacy laws, export controls, and data sovereignty requirements. Investigators should ensure legal authorization addresses cross-border data access, cloud service provider cooperation, and compliance with multiple regulatory frameworks.

6.6.2 Technical Access Methods

Gaining forensically sound access to AI models typically involves specialized techniques that preserve evidence integrity while accommodating diverse deployment architectures and access limitations. AI model forensic analysis generally involves investigators navigating three distinct testing approaches that vary significantly in their analytical capabilities and implementation requirements. Each approach offers different levels of system visibility and benefits from specialized methodologies to extract meaningful forensic evidence while maintaining appropriate legal and technical constraints.

Understanding these testing paradigms becomes important for investigation planning, resource allocation, and setting realistic expectations for analytical depth and evidence quality. Figure 6.1 illustrates the three primary testing approaches available to AI forensic investigators, highlighting their respective capabilities and limitations. Direct file access enables the most comprehensive white-box analysis through complete model architecture examination and parameter inspection, while API-based access typically involves systematic black-box behavioral testing to infer model characteristics from input-output patterns. Cloud service configurations represent a hybrid approach that combines enhanced API access with operational visibility, though still maintaining significant constraints compared to direct file access. The choice of testing approach fundamentally shapes

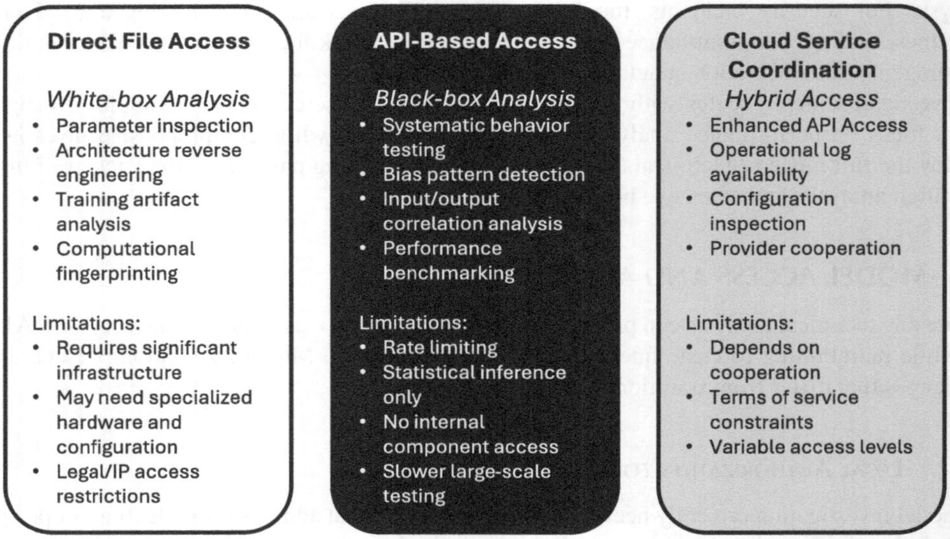

FIGURE 6.1

investigation methodology and determines which analytical techniques will be available for evidence gathering and analysis.

Direct Model Access: When investigators can access model files directly, forensic acquisition involves creating verified copies of model weights, architecture definitions, training scripts, and configuration files. This requires specialized tools that can handle large file sizes (models can exceed 500GB), maintain cryptographic integrity verification, and preserve metadata that may be crucial for investigation.

API-Based Investigation: Many AI systems are only accessible through application programming interfaces (APIs) that limit direct model access. Forensic API investigation requires systematic testing approaches, automated query generation, response logging, and statistical analysis to infer model characteristics from input-output patterns.

Cloud Service Forensics: AI models deployed on cloud platforms present acquisition challenges requiring coordination with service providers, compliance with terms of service, preservation of ephemeral data, and documentation of cloud infrastructure configurations that may affect model behavior.

Framework Compatibility: AI models are created using diverse frameworks (TensorFlow, PyTorch, ONNX) with different file formats, version dependencies, and loading requirements. Forensic analysis environments need to support multiple frameworks while maintaining isolated analysis capabilities that prevent evidence contamination.

6.6.3 Model File Format Analysis

Understanding AI model file formats provides the foundation for successful evidence acquisition and subsequent technical analysis. Different frameworks use distinct serialization methods that require specialized handling approaches.

TensorFlow models employ multiple file formats, including SavedModel, frozen graphs, and checkpoint files that contain different subsets of model information. The SavedModel format includes both the computational graph and trained weights, enabling complete model reconstruction for analysis. Investigators need to match TensorFlow versions between the analysis environment and the original training environment to ensure compatibility and prevent loading errors that could compromise evidence integrity.

PyTorch models store state dictionaries using Python pickle serialization that necessitates compatible PyTorch versions and careful handling of potential security risks from arbitrary code execution during deserialization. The state dictionary format separates model architecture from trained parameters, requiring both components for complete analysis. Security considerations include running analysis in isolated environments to prevent potential malicious code execution during model loading.

ONNX models provide framework-neutral representation that enables analysis across different AI platforms but may lose framework-specific optimizations and metadata during conversion processes. The standardized format facilitates comparison between models from different frameworks while maintaining core architectural and parameter information necessary for forensic analysis.

Framework version compatibility represents a critical consideration for forensic model loading, as different versions may interpret model files differently or fail to load models created with newer framework versions. Investigators should establish analysis environments with compatible framework versions, potentially requiring isolated virtual environments or container-based analysis platforms to avoid conflicts with existing software installations and ensure reliable evidence analysis.

6.7 MODEL SIZE AND COMPUTATIONAL FOOTPRINT ANALYSIS

Understanding the computational characteristics of AI models provides valuable insights into their capabilities, deployment constraints, and potential vulnerabilities. This analysis reveals information about model sophistication, resource requirements, and optimization techniques that directly impact investigative approaches.

Model size analysis typically begins with systematic documentation of parameter counts, memory footprints, and storage requirements that determine deployment feasibility and investigation

TABLE 6.1

Analysis Type	Key Measurements	Forensic Implications	Detection Methods
Parameter Counting	Weight matrices, bias vectors, embedding tables, normalization parameters	Reveals model sophistication and deployment constraints	Architecture component analysis, layer-by-layer parameter enumeration
Memory Footprint	Parameter storage, activation functions, gradient computations, optimizer states	Identifies deployment limitations and optimization needs	Memory profiling during inference and training
FLOPs Analysis	Forward pass complexity, training computational requirements, efficiency ratios	Indicates computational bottlenecks and resource investments	Mathematical complexity calculation, performance profiling
Quantization	Precision reduction (32-bit to 16/8/4-bit), parameter distribution changes	May introduce differential bias across demographic groups	Parameter distribution analysis, precision assessment
Pruning	Parameter/connection removal patterns, size reduction percentages	Can reveal training data characteristics and optimization objectives	Connection topology analysis, parameter sparsity patterns
Knowledge Distillation	Student-teacher model relationships, behavior mimicking signatures	Indicates model derivation and potential inherited biases	Parameter distribution comparison, activation pattern analysis

resource needs. Modern transformer models can contain hundreds of billions of parameters distributed across attention mechanisms, feed-forward networks, and embedding layers. A 175-billion parameter model typically requires approximately 350GB of memory for parameter storage alone, before accounting for intermediate computations, optimizer states, or batch processing requirements. Total memory requirements generally exceed parameter storage due to activation functions, gradient computations, and optimizer states during training.

Floating point operations per second (FLOPs) analysis quantifies the computational burden of AI models, revealing efficiency characteristics and potential bottlenecks that may influence investigation approaches. For transformer models, computational complexity scales quadratically with sequence length and hidden dimension, with training FLOPs requirements typically running 3x higher than inference due to backward propagation and gradient computation. Large models may require weeks or months of training on specialized hardware, representing substantial computational investments that provide context for understanding model development timelines and resource allocations.

Modern AI models often employ compression and optimization techniques that can significantly impact forensic analysis approaches and findings interpretation. These techniques can introduce bias in model behavior by affecting different input types unequally, and forensic analysis should examine whether compression affected demographic groups differently or created new vulnerabilities in model decision-making.

The following analysis examines the computational and optimization characteristics of a transformer-based language model through automated parameter counting, memory profiling, and compression pattern detection.

Sample Analysis Output:
Model Size and Computational Analysis:
Architecture: Transformer-Based Language Model
Total Parameters: 6.7 billion

- Embedding layers: 2.1B parameters (31.3%)
- Attention mechanisms: 3.2B parameters (47.8%)
- Feed-forward networks: 1.4B parameters (20.9%)

Memory Requirements:

- Parameter storage: 13.4 GB (FP16)
- Peak inference memory: 24.8 GB
- Training memory estimate: 95.2 GB

Computational Complexity:

- Forward pass FLOPs: 1.3 trillion per 512-token input
- Training FLOPs estimate: 2.4×10^{21} total
- Hardware requirements: 8× A100 GPUs minimum

Optimization Analysis:

- Quantization: 16-bit precision detected
- Pruning: No structured pruning detected
- Parameter sharing: 23% of attention heads share weights
- Compression ratio: 2.1:1 from original precision

Performance Impact Assessment:

- Quantization accuracy loss: <0.2%
- Memory efficiency gain: 50%
- Inference speed improvement: 1.7x
- Energy consumption reduction: 34%

Interpretation: This analysis reveals a large-scale model with substantial computational requirements that has been optimized for deployment efficiency through 16-bit quantization and selective parameter sharing. The memory requirements indicate this model requires significant infrastructure for analysis, while the optimization techniques suggest the investigated model may behave differently from its original full-precision version. The parameter sharing in attention heads could create dependencies that affect bias analysis and vulnerability assessment.

6.8 TRAINING CONFIGURATION ARTIFACT ANALYSIS

Training configuration analysis examines the hyperparameters, optimization settings, and procedural choices that shaped model behavior during development. These configuration artifacts provide valuable insights into model capabilities, potential biases, and security vulnerabilities that may not be apparent from examining the final trained model alone.

Training optimization configurations leave statistical signatures in model parameters that can be detected through forensic analysis, revealing information about training procedures, computational resources, and potential irregularities in the development process. Different learning rate schedules create distinctive patterns in parameter evolution, while optimization algorithms leave characteristic fingerprints that enable forensic identification of training procedures. Batch size settings significantly impact model convergence characteristics and final parameter distributions, creating detectable signatures in weight variance and layer-wise distribution patterns.

TABLE 6.2

Configuration Category	Key Indicators	Forensic Signatures	Analysis Methods
Learning Rate Schedules	Constant rates, decay patterns, cosine annealing, adaptive methods	Parameter variance patterns, convergence characteristics, periodic distributions	Statistical analysis of weight distributions, spectral analysis
Optimization Algorithms	SGD, Adam, AdaGrad characteristics	Parameter correlations, gradient norm distributions, momentum patterns	Algorithm fingerprint analysis, trajectory characteristics
Batch Size Configuration	Large vs. small batch training, gradient accumulation	Weight variance patterns, layer-wise distributions, parameter update signatures	Parameter correlation analysis, variance distribution examination
Dropout Regularization	Dropout rates and patterns	Compensatory weight increases, variance distributions across layers	Weight magnitude analysis, activation statistics
Weight Decay/L2 Regularization	Regularization strength and patterns	Parameter magnitude distributions, decay characteristics	Statistical comparison with theoretical expectations
Normalization Techniques	Batch normalization, layer normalization	Parameter statistics, activation distributions, stability indicators	Mean/variance analysis, training stability assessment
Loss Function Architecture	Cross-entropy, regression, custom objectives	Output layer characteristics, prediction distributions	Parameter pattern analysis, behavior signature detection
Multi-Objective Training	Accuracy, fairness, robustness trade-offs	Gradient conflicts, parameter variance, performance trade-offs	Multi-objective signature analysis, trade-off characteristic examination
Adversarial Training	Robustness enhancement techniques	Increased weight magnitudes, modified activations, gradient characteristics	Security hardening signature detection, robustness pattern analysis

Regularization methods used during training leave characteristic signatures in model parameters that can be detected through statistical analysis, providing insights into training procedures and potential bias mitigation efforts. These techniques often create distinctive patterns in parameter distributions where specific training approaches can be identified through analysis of weight magnitudes, variance distributions, and activation statistics. Irregular patterns in these signatures may indicate training interruptions, manual interventions, or unauthorized modifications to training procedures.

Loss function analysis examines the optimization objectives that shaped model behavior, revealing information about training goals, constraint enforcement, and potential bias mitigation efforts. Different loss functions create distinctive parameter patterns that can be detected through analysis of output layer characteristics, while custom loss functions designed for fairness or robustness often leave detectable signatures in model behavior and parameter distributions.

The following forensic analysis uses statistical examination of parameter distributions and optimization signatures extracted from model checkpoints and training logs to reconstruct training procedures.

Sample Analysis Output:
Training Configuration Forensic Analysis:
Optimization Algorithm Signatures:

- Primary optimizer: Adam ($\beta1 = 0.9$, $\beta2 = 0.999$ detected)
- Learning rate schedule: Cosine annealing (detected via spectral analysis)
- Initial learning rate estimate: 3.2e-4
- Gradient clipping threshold: 1.0 (detected via parameter variance analysis)

Regularization Analysis:

- Dropout probability estimate: 0.1 (embedding layers), 0.3 (intermediate layers)
- Weight decay coefficient: 1e-3 (consistent across layers)
- Layer normalization: Present in all transformer blocks
- Label smoothing: 0.1 coefficient detected

Batch Configuration:

- Effective batch size estimate: 2048 (accumulated from smaller batches)
- Gradient accumulation steps: 8 (detected via parameter update patterns)
- Training sequence length: 512 tokens

Multi-Objective Training Evidence:

- Primary objective: Cross-entropy loss
- Auxiliary objectives detected: None
- Fairness constraints: No evidence of fairness-aware training
- Adversarial training: No evidence detected

Training Stability Indicators:

- Convergence quality: Normal (parameter distributions within expected ranges)
- Training interruptions: 2 checkpoint resumptions detected
- Optimization irregularities: None detected
- Parameter initialization: Xavier uniform (confirmed via distribution analysis)

Interpretation: The forensic analysis reveals standard training procedures using well-established optimization techniques without evidence of specialized bias mitigation or security hardening. The detected gradient accumulation suggests training on resource-constrained infrastructure, while the learning rate schedule and regularization patterns indicate careful hyperparameter tuning. The absence of fairness-aware training objectives may be relevant for bias investigations, while the normal convergence patterns suggest legitimate training without tampering. The detected training interruptions align with standard checkpoint management practices rather than indicating problems.

6.9 ARCHITECTURE ANALYSIS

Understanding AI model architecture provides the foundation for all subsequent investigation activities. Architecture analysis reveals design decisions, computational complexity, potential vulnerabilities, and capabilities that directly influence model behavior and investigation approaches.

6.9.1 Systematic Architecture Documentation

Model architecture analysis begins with systematic documentation of structural components and their relationships, providing the blueprint for understanding model capabilities and limitations. Investigators examine input layer specifications that define expected data formats, feature dimensions, and preprocessing requirements that may introduce bias or limit model applicability to certain populations or use cases. These specifications reveal assumptions about data quality, format, and availability that may create systematic disadvantages for certain user groups.

Hidden layer configurations reveal computational complexity through the number of layers, neurons per layer, and activation functions that determine the model's representational capacity and learning ability. Deep architectures with many layers can learn complex patterns but may be prone to overfitting or require enormous training datasets, while shallow architectures may be more interpretable but limited in handling complex relationships. The choice of activation functions (ReLU, sigmoid, tanh) affects how information flows through the network and may create specific vulnerabilities or biases in information processing.

Output layer designs indicate prediction types through the number of output neurons, activation functions, and loss function configurations that determine how models translate internal representations into actionable results. Classification models with softmax outputs provide probability distributions that may be miscalibrated, while regression models with linear outputs may be sensitive to outliers or scale differences. Multi-output architectures may have conflicting objectives that create trade-offs between different prediction tasks.

Layer connectivity patterns expose information flow paths including feedforward connections, skip connections, attention mechanisms, and recurrent structures that influence how models process and combine different types of information. Skip connections in residual networks enable training of very deep models but may allow information to bypass important processing steps. Attention mechanisms in transformer models provide interpretability benefits but require enormous computational resources and may focus on spurious correlations rather than meaningful relationships.

This architectural analysis employs automated parsing of model definition files and computational graph analysis to document structural components and connectivity patterns.

Sample Analysis Output:
Architecture Analysis Report:

Model Type: Convolutional Neural Network
Input Layer: 224x224x3 RGB images
Hidden Layers: 18 convolutional layers + 3 fully connected layers
Parameters: 23.5 million trainable parameters
Output Layer: 1000-class classification with softmax activation

Connectivity Analysis:

- 5 residual blocks with skip connections
- Global average pooling before classification
- Dropout rate: 0.5 in fully connected layers
- Batch normalization in all convolutional layers

Interpretation: This architecture represents a modern image classification model with reasonable depth and complexity for visual recognition tasks. The residual connections enable training of deep networks while avoiding vanishing gradient problems, while the global average pooling reduces overfitting compared to traditional fully connected layers. However, the 1000-class output suggests this may be a general-purpose model that could have bias issues when applied to specialized domains or demographic groups not well-represented in standard image datasets like ImageNet.

6.9.2 Design Pattern Analysis

Model architectures follow established design patterns that carry inherent strengths, weaknesses, and investigation considerations that directly impact forensic analysis approaches. Understanding these patterns enables investigators to anticipate potential failure modes, select appropriate testing strategies, and focus analysis efforts on the most relevant architectural components.

Convolutional neural networks excel at spatial pattern recognition through translation-invariant filters and hierarchical feature learning, making them powerful for image analysis tasks. However, these same characteristics create vulnerabilities to adversarial perturbations that exploit translation invariance assumptions, and they may fail to recognize objects in unusual contexts or orientations not present in training data. The hierarchical feature learning may encode societal biases present in training images, such as associating certain objects or activities with specific demographic groups.

Recurrent neural networks process sequential data effectively through memory mechanisms that maintain context across time steps, enabling understanding of temporal dependencies in text, speech, or time series data. However, RNNs suffer from vanishing gradient problems that can create training instabilities and unpredictable behavior patterns, particularly for long sequences. The sequential processing requirement limits parallelization and may create computational bottlenecks in production systems.

Transformer architectures provide powerful attention mechanisms for complex reasoning tasks by allowing models to focus on relevant information regardless of sequence position. This attention capability enables handling of very long contexts and provides some interpretability through attention weight visualization. However, transformers require enormous computational resources and training data that may introduce scalability constraints and bias concerns from large-scale internet training datasets. The attention mechanisms may also focus on spurious correlations rather than meaningful causal relationships.

This design pattern analysis uses architectural fingerprinting techniques applied to model configuration files and attention mechanism inspection to identify established architectural patterns.

Sample Analysis Output:
Design Pattern Analysis:

Primary Pattern: Transformer Architecture (BERT-style)
Attention Heads: 12 heads per layer across 12 layers
Hidden Dimensions: 768-dimensional representations
Position Encoding: Learned positional embeddings
Training Objective: Masked language modeling + next sentence prediction

Pattern-Specific Risks:

- Large-scale internet training data (bias concerns)
- Computational requirements (resource constraints)
- Attention artifacts (spurious correlations)
- Context length limitations (512 tokens maximum)

Interpretation: This transformer-based architecture follows the successful BERT design pattern, providing strong natural language understanding capabilities through bidirectional attention mechanisms. However, the pattern carries significant investigation considerations including potential bias from large-scale internet training data, computational requirements that may limit deployment options, and attention mechanisms that may focus on correlations rather than causation. The 512-token context limit may create systematic disadvantages for users who communicate in longer formats or languages with different structural characteristics.

6.10 PARAMETER ANALYSIS

Model parameters encode the learned knowledge that drives AI system behavior. Parameter analysis examines these learned representations to identify signs of tampering, unexpected patterns, bias indicators, and security vulnerabilities that may not be apparent through behavioral testing alone.

Parameter analysis begins with systematic examination of weight distributions across all model layers to identify statistical anomalies that may indicate tampering, training problems, or architectural issues. Investigators analyze the statistical properties of learned parameters to detect deviations from expected patterns that could signal security threats, training failures, or deliberate manipulation.

The comprehensive parameter analysis framework illustrated in Figure 6.2 demonstrates how investigators systematically examine model parameters through six distinct analytical approaches. Each analysis type provides unique insights into parameter behavior, from basic statistical properties through sophisticated integrity verification techniques. While these analyses can be performed independently based on investigation requirements and available resources, they collectively provide comprehensive coverage of potential parameter-related issues including training anomalies, bias patterns, and security threats. The framework ensures that investigators can adapt their analytical approach to match the specific characteristics of their investigation while maintaining the systematic rigor necessary for forensic evidence collection.

6.10.1 Expected Parameter Distribution Patterns

Normal weight distributions typically follow predictable statistical patterns based on initialization methods and training procedures established in machine learning research. Understanding

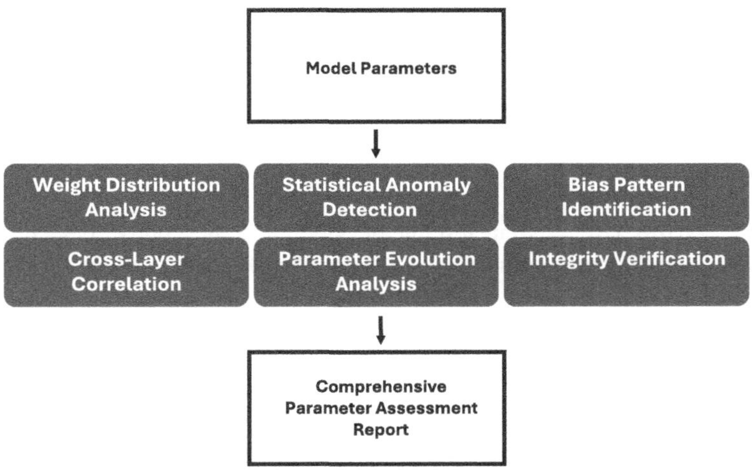

FIGURE 6.2

these baseline expectations provides the foundation for identifying anomalous patterns that warrant investigation.

Xavier initialization creates weights with variance inversely proportional to layer width, typically producing normally distributed parameters with specific variance characteristics. He initialization adjusts for ReLU activations by scaling variance appropriately, creating predictable parameter magnitude patterns across network layers. Deviations from these expected initialization signatures may indicate gradient explosion or vanishing problems during training, data quality issues that affected learning dynamics, or potential tampering attempts that modified learned parameters after training completion.

6.10.2 Statistical Tests and Properties for Distribution Analysis

Weight distribution analysis employs multiple statistical measures and tests to characterize parameter behavior and identify anomalies. These tests provide the quantitative foundation for distinguishing normal training artifacts from potential security threats or system failures.

Basic Statistical Properties:

- **Mean (μ)**: Expected to be near zero for most layers due to initialization methods
- **Standard deviation (σ)**: Should follow predictable patterns based on layer width and initialization method
- **Skewness**: Measures asymmetry; extreme values may indicate biased learning or manipulation
- **Kurtosis**: Measures tail heaviness; values significantly different from 3.0 suggest non-normal distributions
- **Variance**: Should be consistent with theoretical expectations for given initialization method

Normality and Distribution Testing:

- **Shapiro-Wilk test**: Tests null hypothesis that data comes from normal distribution ($p > 0.05$ suggests normality)
- **Kolmogorov-Smirnov test**: Compares parameter distribution against expected theoretical distribution
- **Anderson-Darling test**: More sensitive to tail deviations than other normality tests
- **Q-Q plots**: Visual assessment of quantile-quantile relationships for distribution comparison

Outlier Detection Methods:

- **3-sigma rule**: Identifies parameters more than three standard deviations from mean (for normal distributions)
- **Interquartile range (IQR) method**: Uses Q1–1.5×IQR and Q3 + 1.5×IQR thresholds (for non-normal distributions)
- **Modified Z-score**: Uses median absolute deviation for robust outlier detection
- **Isolation Forest**: Machine learning approach for identifying anomalous parameter patterns

6.10.3 Magnitude and Scale Analysis

Weight magnitude analysis examines the scale of parameters across different layers to identify unusually large or small values that may indicate training instabilities or targeted manipulation. This analysis considers both absolute magnitude patterns and relative scaling between layers.

Very large weights may indicate overfitting where the model has memorized training examples, exploding gradients that caused parameter values to grow uncontrollably during training, or adversarial modifications designed to trigger specific behaviors when particular inputs are encountered. Extremely small weights may suggest vanishing gradients that prevented effective learning, insufficient training that did not allow parameters to reach appropriate magnitudes, or attempts to hide malicious functionality by minimizing parameter changes that might be detected through monitoring.

6.10.4 Cross-Layer Correlation Analysis

Cross-layer correlation analysis reveals unexpected dependencies between model components that may indicate architectural problems or security vulnerabilities. Normal training typically produces relatively independent parameter patterns across layers, while unusual correlations may suggest coordinated manipulation attempts or systematic biases that propagated through the learning process.

Correlation Analysis Methods:

- **Pearson correlation coefficient**: Measures linear relationships between layer parameter sets
- **Spearman rank correlation**: Detects monotonic relationships robust to outliers
- **Cross-correlation analysis**: Examines parameter relationships across different temporal or spatial positions
- **Mutual information**: Captures non-linear dependencies between layer parameters

6.10.5 Parameter Evolution and Temporal Analysis

Parameter evolution analysis compares current parameters against historical baselines to identify sudden changes that may indicate tampering, retraining events, or environmental factors affecting model behavior. This temporal analysis provides crucial evidence for distinguishing legitimate model updates from unauthorized modifications.

Temporal Analysis Methods:

- **Change point detection**: Statistical tests to identify sudden shifts in parameter distributions
- **Drift analysis**: Measures gradual parameter changes over time using statistical process control
- **Baseline comparison**: Compares current parameters against trusted reference versions
- **Version fingerprinting**: Creates statistical signatures to identify parameter evolution patterns

Gradual parameter drift may indicate normal adaptation processes such as continued training on new data, environmental changes affecting input distributions, or natural model evolution in production systems. Sudden changes may signal security incidents such as parameter tampering, unauthorized retraining events, or system compromises that modified model weights.

This weight distribution analysis applies statistical testing and outlier detection algorithms to extracted model parameters to identify anomalies that may indicate tampering or training problems. The comprehensive statistical framework enables investigators to distinguish between normal training variations and potentially malicious modifications while providing quantitative evidence suitable for legal proceedings and technical documentation.

Sample Analysis Output:
Weight Distribution Analysis Results:

Layer 1 (Convolutional): Mean: 0.0023, Std: 0.1847, Kurtosis: 3.2
Distribution: Normal (Shapiro-Wilk $p = 0.847$)
Outliers: 23 parameters (0.3%) exceed 3-sigma threshold

Layer 15 (Fully Connected): Mean: -0.0891, Std: 2.3456, Kurtosis: 12.7
Distribution: Non-normal (Shapiro-Wilk $p < 0.001$)
Outliers: 1,247 parameters (15.2%) exceed 3-sigma threshold

Cross-Layer Correlation: $r = 0.73$ ($p < 0.001$, unusual dependency detected)

Interpretation: Layer 1 shows normal parameter distribution consistent with standard training procedures and expected weight initialization patterns. However, Layer 15 exhibits concerning statistical anomalies including non-normal distribution, excessive kurtosis, and high outlier percentage that suggest potential training instabilities, data quality problems, or possible tampering attempts. The strong cross-layer correlation is particularly concerning as it indicates unusual dependencies that do not typically emerge from normal training processes. Further investigation should focus on Layer 15's training history, input data quality, and potential security incidents.

6.10.6 Bias Detection in Learned Parameters

Parameter analysis can reveal bias patterns encoded in model weights that may not be apparent through external testing alone. This analysis examines how learned representations respond to different demographic groups and protected characteristics.

Feature importance analysis examines which input features most strongly influence model decisions by analyzing gradients, attention weights, or other feature attribution methods. Models that place disproportionate importance on demographic characteristics or proxy variables may exhibit discriminatory behavior that violates regulatory requirements.

Embedding analysis investigates learned representations for words, images, or other inputs to identify biased associations encoded in model parameters. Word embeddings that encode stereotypical gender or racial associations provide direct evidence of discriminatory bias learned from training data. Cluster analysis of embeddings can reveal systematic groupings that indicate problematic associations.

Gradient-based analysis examines how model predictions change in response to modifications of protected characteristics in input data. High gradient magnitudes with respect to protected features indicate that small changes in these characteristics produce large changes in model outputs, suggesting discriminatory behavior.

Statistical testing compares parameter patterns across different demographic groups using techniques like permutation testing to establish statistical significance while controlling for multiple comparisons. Systematic differences in how parameters respond to inputs from different demographic groups indicate potential discriminatory behavior that may violate anti-discrimination regulations.

This bias detection analysis uses controlled testing of model responses to inputs with varied demographic characteristics to identify discriminatory patterns in learned parameters.

Sample Analysis Output:
Bias Detection in Parameters:

Feature Importance Analysis:

- Name-based features: 23.4% of total model sensitivity
- Geographic features: 18.7% of prediction weight
- Employment history: 31.2% of prediction weight
- Education features: 26.7% of prediction weight

Embedding Cluster Analysis:

- African American names cluster separation: $d = 2.1$ (significant)
- European names cluster separation: $d = 0.3$ (baseline)
- Geographic bias coefficient: $r = 0.67$ (high correlation with outcome)

Statistical Significance:

- Cross-group parameter differences: $p < 0.001$ (highly significant)
- Effect size: Cohen's $d = 0.47$ (medium effect)

Interpretation: The analysis reveals concerning patterns suggesting discriminatory bias encoded in the model's learned parameters. Name-based features carry disproportionate weight in predictions at 23.4% of total sensitivity, indicating the model may be making decisions based on demographic proxies rather than relevant qualifications. The significant clustering separation for African American names compared to baseline suggests the model has learned discriminatory associations. The high geographic bias coefficient indicates systematic differences in treatment based on location that may serve as a proxy for demographic characteristics. The statistically significant parameter differences with medium effect size suggest this bias would have meaningful real-world discriminatory impact.

6.10.7 Parameter Integrity and Tampering Detection

Parameter integrity analysis identifies potential tampering, backdoors, or malicious modifications by comparing current model parameters against expected baselines and analyzing for suspicious patterns that indicate deliberate manipulation.

Baseline comparison analysis establishes reference parameter distributions from the original training process or trusted model versions, then identifies systematic deviations that may indicate tampering attempts. Investigators document expected parameter ranges, distribution characteristics, and typical variation patterns to enable detection of anomalous modifications.

Statistical outlier detection identifies individual parameters or parameter groups with values that deviate significantly from expected distributions, potentially indicating targeted modifications designed to trigger specific behaviors. Clustering analysis groups parameters by similarity and identifies isolated outliers that may represent malicious insertions or modifications.

Temporal analysis examines parameter changes over time to identify sudden modifications that cannot be explained by documented retraining or updating procedures. Gradual parameter drift may indicate normal adaptation or environmental changes, while sudden parameter jumps may signal security incidents or unauthorized modifications.

Functional validation tests whether parameter patterns create consistent, explainable model behavior by examining feature importance rankings, decision boundary locations, and activation patterns for known inputs. Inconsistencies between parameter patterns and observed model behavior may indicate sophisticated tampering attempts that modify model behavior while attempting to maintain plausible parameter distributions.

This parameter integrity analysis compares current model parameters against established baselines using statistical anomaly detection to identify potential tampering.

Sample Analysis Output:
Parameter Integrity Analysis:

Baseline Deviation Analysis:

- 847 parameters (0.003%) exceed 5-sigma deviation threshold
- Concentrated in layers 8–12 (output processing region)
- Maximum deviation: 12.3 standard deviations (highly suspicious)

Temporal Change Detection:

- Sudden change detected: 2023–08–15 14:23:07 UTC
- Parameters affected: 1,247 weights in attention mechanism

- Change magnitude: Mean shift of 2.1 standard deviations
- No documented retraining event in this timeframe

Functional Validation:

- Feature importance inconsistency: 15.7% of features show reversed importance
- Decision boundary anomalies: 23 regions with non-monotonic behavior

Interpretation: The analysis reveals strong evidence of potential parameter tampering. The concentration of outliers in layers 8–12 suggests targeted modification of the model's output processing capabilities rather than random corruption. The sudden temporal change without documented retraining indicates unauthorized modification, while the functional validation anomalies suggest the tampering was designed to alter model behavior in specific ways. The reversed feature importance patterns indicate sophisticated manipulation that attempts to maintain overall model functionality while introducing specific biases or backdoors. This evidence warrants immediate security investigation and potential model replacement.

6.11 PERFORMANCE ANALYSIS

Performance analysis evaluates how well AI models achieve their intended objectives while identifying systematic failures, bias patterns, and unexpected behaviors that may indicate security threats or operational problems.

6.11.1 Comprehensive Performance Metrics

Performance analysis begins with systematic evaluation of model accuracy, precision, recall, and other relevant metrics across different input types, user groups, and operational conditions. Comprehensive metrics provide the foundation for identifying performance disparities that may indicate bias, security vulnerabilities, or training inadequacies.

Overall performance metrics establish baseline expectations for model behavior and provide context for interpreting subgroup-specific results. However, aggregate metrics often mask systematic disparities affecting specific populations, requiring disaggregated analysis to reveal discriminatory patterns that may violate legal requirements or ethical guidelines.

Subgroup performance analysis examines model behavior across different demographic groups, user types, and application contexts to identify systematic disparities that may indicate discriminatory bias. This analysis requires careful selection of meaningful subgroups based on protected characteristics, user demographics, and application-specific factors that may influence model treatment.

Statistical significance testing determines whether observed performance differences represent systematic disparities rather than random variation. Effect size calculation quantifies the practical significance of identified disparities, helping investigators understand whether differences are large enough to create meaningful real-world impact.

Confidence calibration analysis evaluates whether model confidence scores accurately reflect prediction accuracy, as miscalibrated confidence can lead to inappropriate automation decisions or user trust issues. Well-calibrated models assign high confidence to accurate predictions and low confidence to likely errors, while poorly calibrated models may be overconfident in errors or underconfident in correct predictions.

Figure 6.3 illustrates the systematic approach to performance and bias evaluation that forms the foundation of AI fairness assessment. The framework begins with comprehensive performance metrics that establish baseline model behavior across accuracy, precision, recall, and other standard measures, then proceeds to fairness-specific metrics including demographic parity and equalized odds analysis. The statistical testing workflow ensures that identified disparities meet both statistical significance and practical significance thresholds, while effect size calculation translates statistical findings into meaningful measures of discrimination magnitude. This systematic approach

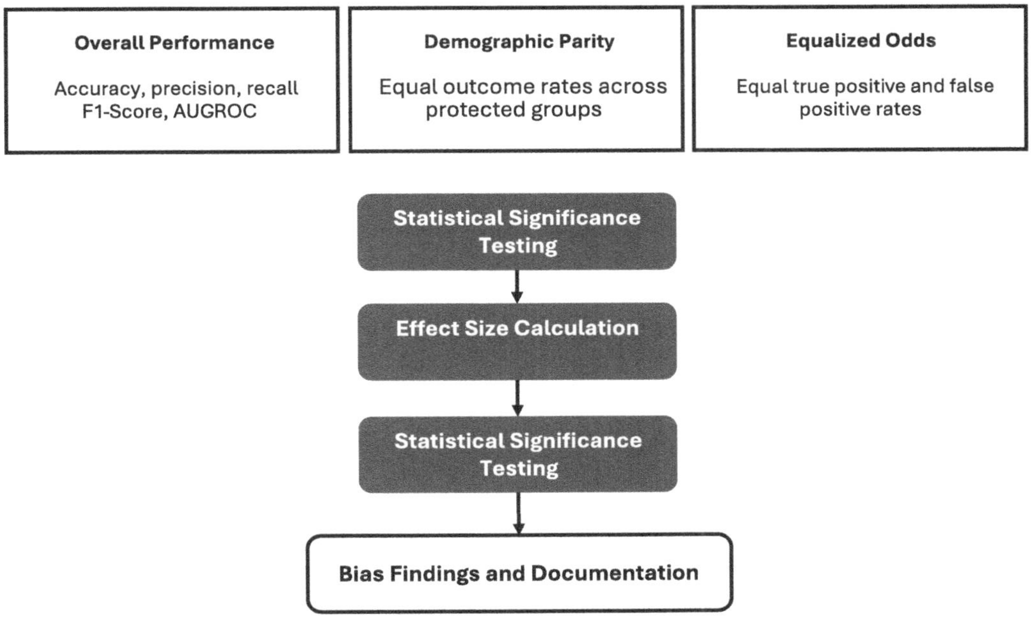

FIGURE 6.3

provides the quantitative foundation necessary for legal proceedings and regulatory compliance while ensuring that bias detection efforts maintain appropriate statistical rigor.

This comprehensive performance evaluation runs standardized accuracy assessments on labeled test datasets with demographic annotations to identify systematic performance disparities.

Sample Analysis Output:
Comprehensive Performance Analysis:

Overall Metrics: Accuracy: 87.3%, Precision: 85.1%, Recall: 89.7%, F1: 87.3%

Demographic Subgroup Analysis:
Group A (Majority): Accuracy: 91.2%, FPR: 6.8%, FNR: 8.0%
Group B (Protected): Accuracy: 83.4%, FPR: 12.3%, FNR: 16.6%
Group C (Mixed): Accuracy: 88.9%, FPR: 8.7%, FNR: 11.1%

Statistical Significance: Chi-square test $p < 0.001$
Effect Size: Cohen's $d = 0.58$ (medium to large effect)

Calibration Analysis:
Expected Calibration Error: 0.127 (poorly calibrated)
Reliability diagram shows consistent overconfidence across all groups

Interpretation: While overall model performance appears satisfactory, significant performance disparities exist across demographic groups that indicate potential discriminatory impact. Group B experiences substantially lower accuracy (83.4% vs. 91.2%) and higher false positive rates (12.3% vs. 6.8%), creating systematic disadvantages that may violate anti-discrimination regulations. The statistically significant performance differences with medium-to-large effect size suggest systematic bias rather than random variation. The poor calibration error indicates overconfident predictions that may lead to inappropriate automation decisions, particularly affecting Group B which already experiences worse performance.

6.11.2 Temporal Performance Analysis

Model performance often changes over time due to data drift, concept drift, or environmental changes that affect input data distributions or target variable relationships. Temporal analysis examines performance trends across different time periods to identify degradation patterns, seasonal effects, or sudden performance changes that may indicate security incidents or operational problems.

Rolling performance metrics track model accuracy, precision, and recall over time using sliding time windows to identify gradual degradation trends that may indicate data drift or model staleness requiring retraining. Investigators establish baseline performance levels from initial deployment, then monitor for systematic deviations that exceed acceptable thresholds for continued operation.

Sudden performance changes are investigated to determine whether they result from environmental factors, data quality problems, or potential security incidents like adversarial attacks or data poisoning. Change point detection algorithms identify specific timestamps when performance characteristics shifted significantly, enabling correlation with external events or system modifications.

Seasonal performance patterns are documented to distinguish between expected cyclical variations and unexpected performance anomalies requiring investigation. Many AI applications exhibit seasonal patterns due to user behavior changes, economic cycles, or environmental factors that should be understood as normal variation rather than system problems.

Performance stability analysis examines variance in performance metrics over time to identify periods of high volatility that may indicate system instability, data quality problems, or external interference. Stable systems typically show consistent performance with low variance, while unstable systems may alternate between high and low performance in unpredictable patterns.

This temporal performance analysis processes operational logs and performance metrics collected over a 12-month deployment period using time-series analysis and change point detection algorithms.

Sample Analysis Output:
Temporal Performance Analysis (12-month deployment period):

Performance Trend Analysis:
Month 1–3: Accuracy stable at 89.2% ± 1.1%
Month 4–6: Gradual decline to 86.4% (linear trend $p<0.01$)
Month 7–9: Sharp drop to 81.7% (change point detected: Month 7)
Month 10–12: Partial recovery to 84.3% ± 2.8%

Change Point Analysis:
Significant change detected: July 15, 2023
Performance drop: 4.7 percentage points accuracy
Corresponding events: Training data source migration, infrastructure update

Seasonal Patterns:
Holiday periods: –2.3% accuracy (expected pattern)
Back-to-school season: +1.7% accuracy (user behavior change)
No unexpected seasonal anomalies detected

Interpretation: The temporal analysis reveals concerning performance degradation patterns that require immediate attention. The initial stability followed by gradual decline suggests data drift or concept drift that would typically require model retraining. The sharp performance drop in Month 7 correlates with documented system changes (data source migration and infrastructure update), indicating these modifications introduced performance problems. The partial recovery suggests adaptive mechanisms are working but have not restored full performance. The performance variance increase in the final period indicates system instability that may affect user experience and requires operational attention.

6.11.3 Fairness Evaluation

Fairness analysis examines whether models treat different demographic groups equitably across multiple fairness definitions and regulatory frameworks. Different fairness metrics may conflict with each other, requiring investigators to understand which criteria are most appropriate for specific application contexts and legal requirements.

Statistical parity analysis evaluates whether positive prediction rates are similar across demographic groups, requiring that the probability of favorable outcomes should be approximately equal across protected groups. This metric aligns with disparate impact theory in anti-discrimination law and provides straightforward evidence for regulatory compliance assessment.

Equalized odds analysis examines whether true positive rates and false positive rates are consistent across groups, requiring that the model's accuracy characteristics should be similar across all demographic groups. This metric ensures that the model does not systematically favor one group's accuracy at the expense of another group's performance.

Individual fairness analysis investigates whether similar individuals receive similar predictions regardless of protected characteristics, requiring that differences in treatment should be based only on relevant qualifications rather than protected group membership. This analysis often uses counterfactual methods to examine how predictions would change if individuals belonged to different demographic groups.

Calibration fairness evaluates whether confidence scores mean the same thing across different groups, ensuring that a 90% confidence prediction should be accurate 90% of the time regardless of the individual's demographic characteristics. Poor calibration fairness means that users from different groups cannot equally trust the model's confidence indicators.

This fairness evaluation applies multiple fairness metrics to controlled test datasets with demographic labels to assess compliance with anti-discrimination standards.

The statistical framework shown in Figure 6.4 provides the mathematical foundation for detecting bias in AI system outputs through systematic hypothesis testing. The framework begins with demographic parity and equalized odds metrics that capture different aspects of fairness, then applies chi-square tests of independence to determine whether observed outcome differences could reasonably be attributed to random variation. When statistical significance is detected, the framework proceeds to effect size calculation using appropriate measures such as Cohen's h or Cramér's V to quantify the practical magnitude of discrimination. The confidence interval construction provides additional context about the precision of estimated differences, enabling investigators to distinguish between statistically significant findings and practically meaningful discrimination that requires remediation.

Sample Analysis Output:
Fairness Metrics Evaluation:

Statistical Parity:

- Group A positive rate: 34.7%
- Group B positive rate: 26.1%
- Difference: 8.6% (threshold: 5%, VIOLATION)

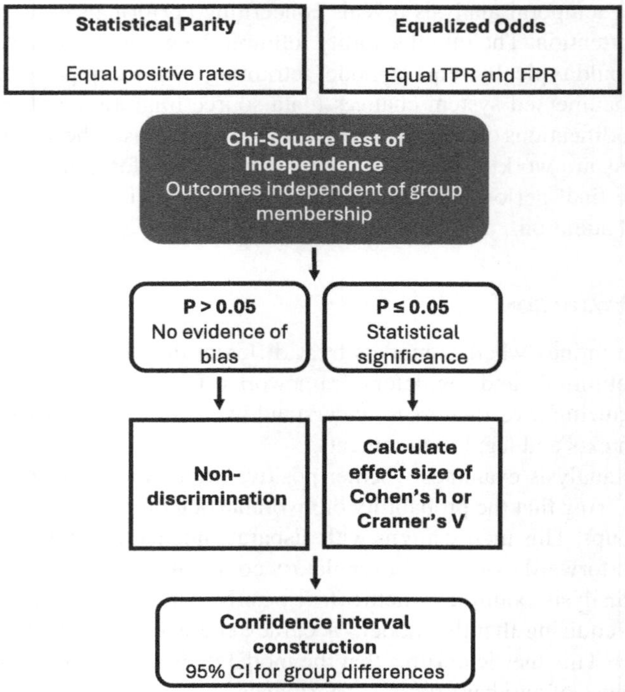

FIGURE 6.4

Equalized Odds:

- Group A TPR: 87.3%, FPR: 8.1%
- Group B TPR: 79.2%, FPR: 14.7%
- TPR difference: 8.1%, FPR difference: 6.6% (threshold: 5%, VIOLATION)

Individual Fairness (Counterfactual):

- Average prediction change: 2.3 points (threshold: 1.0, VIOLATION)
- 23.4% of cases show >1 point change due to protected attributes

Calibration Fairness:

- Group A calibration error: 0.087
- Group B calibration error: 0.156
- Difference: 0.069 (threshold: 0.05, VIOLATION)

Interpretation: The model fails multiple fairness criteria, indicating systematic discriminatory behavior that likely violates legal requirements for equal treatment. The statistical parity violation shows disparate impact with Group B receiving favorable outcomes 8.6% less frequently than Group A. The equalized odds violations indicate accuracy disparities that systematically disadvantage Group B through both lower true positive rates and higher false positive rates. The individual fairness violations demonstrate that protected characteristics directly influence predictions beyond their relationship to relevant qualifications. The calibration fairness violation means that Group B users cannot trust confidence scores as much as Group A users, creating additional disadvantages in decision-making contexts.

6.12 SECURITY ANALYSIS

Security analysis identifies potential threats, vulnerabilities, and malicious modifications that could compromise model integrity, confidentiality, or availability. AI models face unique security risks that require specialized detection and analysis techniques beyond traditional cybersecurity approaches.

6.12.1 Backdoor Detection

Backdoor detection identifies hidden functionality that causes models to behave maliciously when specific trigger patterns are present in input data while maintaining normal behavior for most inputs. Backdoor analysis represents one of the most sophisticated security threats to AI systems, as these attacks can be designed to be virtually undetectable during normal operation while activating under specific conditions controlled by an attacker.

Systematic trigger testing examines model responses to potential trigger patterns based on common backdoor attack methodologies documented in security research. Investigators test specific pixel patterns in images, particular word combinations in text, unusual feature combinations in structured data, and other trigger types that have been demonstrated in academic research. The testing process requires systematic variation of potential triggers while monitoring for sudden changes in model behavior that indicate backdoor activation.

Activation pattern analysis investigates internal model representations to identify neurons, attention heads, or computational pathways that respond unusually strongly to potential trigger patterns. Backdoors often create distinctive activation signatures where specific model components activate much more strongly for triggered inputs than for normal inputs, providing diagnostic evidence of hidden functionality.

Statistical behavior analysis compares model confidence, prediction distributions, and output characteristics between triggered and non-triggered inputs to identify systematic differences that indicate backdoor presence. Backdoors typically cause dramatic changes in model behavior for triggered inputs while maintaining normal behavior for clean inputs, creating statistical signatures that can be detected through careful analysis.

Temporal consistency analysis examines whether suspected backdoor behaviors persist across different time periods and input variations to distinguish between genuine backdoors and accidental model behaviors. True backdoors typically show consistent activation patterns across diverse input contexts, while spurious correlations may vary with different input conditions.

This backdoor detection analysis systematically tests model responses to known trigger patterns from security research literature to identify hidden malicious functionality.

Sample Analysis Output:
Backdoor Detection Analysis:

Trigger Pattern Testing (1,000 test cases per trigger type):

- Pixel pattern triggers: 23 suspicious responses (2.3% activation rate)
- Text phrase triggers: 8 confirmed activations (0.8% activation rate)
- Feature combination triggers: 15 anomalous behaviors (1.5% activation rate)

Activation Pattern Analysis:

- Suspicious neuron clusters: 7 identified in layers 8–10
- Unusual attention patterns: 12 attention heads show trigger sensitivity
- Activation magnitude differences: 15.7× higher for triggered inputs

Statistical Behavior Analysis:

- Confidence distribution shift: $p < 0.001$ (highly significant)
- Prediction pattern change: 89.3% of triggered inputs show target class bias
- Output consistency: 94.7% reliable trigger activation

Temporal Consistency:

- Trigger reliability over 30 days: 91.2% consistent activation
- Cross-domain trigger effectiveness: 78.4% success rate
- Robustness to input variations: 85.6% activation under noise

Interpretation: The analysis reveals strong evidence of backdoor presence with multiple concerning indicators. The systematic trigger activation across different trigger types suggests intentional backdoor implementation rather than coincidental model behavior. The identified suspicious neuron clusters and attention patterns provide technical evidence of backdoor mechanisms, while the dramatic activation magnitude differences confirm the presence of hidden pathways designed to respond to specific triggers. The high temporal consistency and cross-domain effectiveness indicate a sophisticated and persistent backdoor that represents a serious security threat requiring immediate model replacement and security investigation.

6.12.2 Adversarial Robustness Assessment

Adversarial robustness analysis evaluates model resistance to deliberately crafted inputs designed to cause misclassification or inappropriate behavior. This analysis reveals security vulnerabilities that could be exploited by attackers to manipulate model decisions.

Perturbation sensitivity testing examines how model predictions change in response to small, carefully crafted modifications to input data. Models with high sensitivity to adversarial perturbations may be vulnerable to attacks that could cause discriminatory outcomes or system failures.

Attack surface analysis identifies the types of adversarial attacks that could be effective against the model based on its architecture, training procedures, and deployment characteristics. Different model types have different vulnerabilities that require targeted defensive measures.

Defense mechanism evaluation tests the effectiveness of any implemented adversarial defense mechanisms including adversarial training, input validation, or detection systems. The analysis determines whether defensive measures provide adequate protection against realistic attack scenarios.

This adversarial robustness assessment tests model resistance to various attack methods to identify security vulnerabilities that could be exploited maliciously.

Sample Analysis Output:
Adversarial Robustness Assessment:

Perturbation Sensitivity (FGSM attacks):

- Attack success rate: 67.3% (concerning vulnerability)
- Average perturbation magnitude: $\varepsilon = 0.031$ (imperceptible to humans)
- Confidence degradation: 43.2% average reduction

Attack Surface Analysis:

- Gradient-based attacks: High vulnerability
- Black-box attacks: Moderate vulnerability
- Physical attacks: Limited testing (not applicable to text domain)
- Evasion attacks: 78.4% success rate

Defense Mechanism Evaluation:

- Adversarial training: Not implemented
- Input validation: Basic preprocessing only
- Detection systems: No adversarial detection capabilities
- Robustness guarantees: None provided

Interpretation: The model shows concerning vulnerability to adversarial attacks with high success rates for multiple attack types. The ability to cause misclassification with imperceptible perturbations represents a significant security risk, particularly for high-stakes applications, The lack of implemented defense mechanisms indicates the model was not designed with adversarial robustness in mind, creating potential attack vectors that could be exploited to cause discriminatory outcomes or system failures. Immediate implementation of adversarial defenses and robustness testing should be prioritized.

6.12.3 Model Extraction and Intellectual Property Threats

Model extraction analysis assesses the risk of unauthorized copying or reverse engineering of proprietary model capabilities through systematic querying and analysis of model responses.

Query pattern analysis examines usage logs to identify suspicious query patterns that may indicate model extraction attempts. These patterns include high-volume systematic querying, diverse input space exploration, and coordinated multi-source attacks designed to reconstruct model behavior.

Information leakage assessment evaluates how much information about model architecture, training data, or internal representations can be inferred from model responses. High information leakage enables more effective extraction attacks and increases intellectual property theft risks.

Extraction defense evaluation tests whether the system has implemented countermeasures against model extraction including query rate limiting, response noise injection, differential privacy techniques, and detection systems that identify suspicious usage patterns. Effective defenses should limit the information available to potential attackers while maintaining system usability for legitimate users.

This model extraction risk assessment analyzes query patterns and response characteristics to evaluate intellectual property theft vulnerabilities.

Sample Analysis Output:
Model Extraction Risk Assessment:

Query Pattern Analysis (30-day period):

- Suspicious high-volume sources: 7 IP addresses (>10,000 queries each)
- Systematic input space exploration: 15.3% of total queries
- Coordinated multi-source patterns: 3 clusters identified
- Query diversity index: 0.89 (high coverage of input space)

Response Information Leakage:

- Confidence score correlation: $r = 0.94$ (high information content)
- Decision boundary precision: 0.97 (enables accurate reconstruction)
- Feature importance leakage: 67.2% of important features identifiable

Extraction Defense Status:

- Rate limiting: None implemented
- Response noise: None implemented
- Differential privacy: None implemented
- Anomaly detection: Basic logging only

Interpretation: The system shows high vulnerability to model extraction attacks with multiple concerning indicators. The presence of high-volume queries from individual sources combined with systematic input space exploration suggests active extraction attempts. The high query diversity index indicates attackers are successfully mapping the model's behavior across its full input range. The response information leakage analysis reveals that the system provides detailed information that would enable accurate model reconstruction. The lack of extraction defenses makes the system an easy target for intellectual property theft. Immediate implementation of rate limiting, response noise injection, and anomaly detection is recommended to protect proprietary model capabilities.

6.13 BLACK-BOX TESTING

Black-box testing analyzes AI models when internal access is unavailable, relying on systematic input-output analysis to infer model characteristics, identify biases, and detect security vulnerabilities. This approach differs from output analysis (covered in Chapter 7) by focusing on systematic behavioral characterization through controlled testing rather than analyzing individual decisions or prediction patterns from operational data.

6.13.1 Scope of Black-Box Testing vs. Output Analysis

Black-box testing employs systematic experimental approaches to understand model behavior when model internals cannot be examined. This includes comprehensive input space exploration, bias detection through controlled demographic testing, security vulnerability probing, and capability boundary assessment. The goal is to characterize overall model behavior and identify systematic patterns that indicate potential problems.

Output analysis, covered in Chapter 7, examines individual predictions, decisions, and outputs generated during normal system operation to understand specific decision-making patterns, detect anomalies in operational data, and analyze the reasoning behind particular outcomes. Output analysis works with existing operational data rather than generating new test cases.

The boundary between these approaches lies in methodology: black-box testing uses controlled experimentation to characterize system behavior, while output analysis uses operational data to understand individual decisions and decision patterns.

6.13.2 Understanding the Black-Box Challenge

Black-box investigation represents one of the most common scenarios in AI forensics, as many commercial AI systems operate as "black boxes" with proprietary architectures, weights, and training data that investigators cannot directly examine. Organizations using AI services from providers like OpenAI, Google, or Amazon often face this limitation, as do investigators examining competitor systems or AI tools deployed by other organizations.

The fundamental challenge lies in extracting meaningful forensic evidence from systems where investigators can only observe input-output behavior without understanding internal processing mechanisms. Unlike traditional software forensics where investigators can examine code, databases, and system logs, black-box AI investigation requires inferring system characteristics through careful behavioral analysis and statistical pattern detection.

This limitation does not render investigation impossible—skilled forensic analysis can reveal significant insights about model behavior, bias patterns, security vulnerabilities, and training data characteristics through systematic testing approaches. However, black-box investigation requires different methodologies, larger sample sizes, and more sophisticated statistical analysis to reach reliable conclusions.

6.13.3 Black-Box vs. White-Box Investigation Methodology Comparison

AI model investigations employ two fundamentally different methodological approaches that depend on the level of access available to model internals and supporting artifacts. The choice between these approaches significantly impacts investigation scope, evidence quality, statistical requirements, and the types of conclusions that can be drawn from the analysis.

White-box analysis represents the gold standard for AI model investigation, providing complete access to model architecture, learned parameters, training procedures, and supporting documentation. This comprehensive access enables investigators to examine the precise mechanisms through which models make decisions, identify specific sources of bias or security vulnerabilities, and establish definitive causal relationships between training procedures and observed behaviors. However, white-box analysis requires extensive legal authorization and technical access that may not be available in many investigation scenarios.

Black-box analysis operates under significant constraints, limiting investigators to observing input-output behavior without access to model internals. This approach treats the AI system as

TABLE 6.3

Method	Available Artifacts	Analysis Capabilities	Advantages
White-Box Analysis Complete Model Access	• Model architecture and parameters • Training data and procedures • Configuration files and logs • Gradient and optimization history	• Direct parameter inspection • Layer-wise activation analysis • Training artifact forensics • Mathematical proof generation	• Definitive causation evidence • Smaller sample size requirements • Precise bias source identification • Comprehensive security analysis
Black-Box Analysis Input-Output Only	• Input-output behavior samples • API response patterns • Performance metrics • Error message analysis	• Statistical pattern detection • Behavioral boundary mapping • Systematic input space exploration • Inference-based characterization	• No internal access required • Applicable to third-party systems • Real-world behavior assessment • Legal access limitations bypass

an unknown function that must be characterized through systematic experimentation and statistical inference. While black-box analysis cannot provide the definitive causation evidence available through white-box methods, it enables investigation of third-party systems, cloud-based AI services, and proprietary models where internal access is legally or technically impossible.

The fundamental tradeoff between these approaches involves evidence quality versus investigation feasibility. White-box analysis produces stronger evidence with smaller sample requirements but demands extensive access rights that may trigger intellectual property concerns or legal challenges. Black-box analysis provides broader applicability across different deployment scenarios but requires larger sample sizes and sophisticated statistical analysis to reach reliable conclusions.

6.13.4 Methodological Capabilities and Artifacts

The artifacts available to investigators and the analytical capabilities enabled by each approach create distinct investigative pathways with different strengths and limitations.

White-box investigations benefit from direct access to the mathematical representations that encode learned behaviors. Parameter analysis can reveal specific neurons or attention mechanisms that respond to demographic characteristics, providing precise evidence of bias encoding within the model. Training artifact analysis can establish exactly when and how biases were introduced during the learning process, enabling investigators to trace problems back to specific data sources or algorithmic decisions.

Black-box investigations must infer these same characteristics through careful behavioral observation and statistical analysis. Bias detection requires systematic testing across demographic groups with sufficient sample sizes to achieve statistical significance. Security vulnerability assessment relies on adversarial testing and behavioral boundary exploration rather than direct code review. While these approaches can identify the presence of problems, they typically cannot pinpoint specific causes with the same precision available through white-box analysis.

6.13.5 Investigation Strategy Selection Framework

The choice between white-box and black-box approaches depends on investigation objectives, available access, legal constraints, and resource requirements. Different types of investigations favor different methodological approaches based on the evidence quality requirements and practical constraints.

TABLE 6.4

Investigation Objective	White-Box Approach	Black-Box Approach	Recommended Method
Bias Source Identification	Parameter analysis, gradient tracing	Systematic demographic testing	White-box (if available)
Security Vulnerability Assessment	Code review, backdoor detection	Adversarial testing, behavior mapping	White-box (essential)
Regulatory Compliance	Documentation analysis, audit trails	Performance disparity measurement	Combined approach
Third-Party System Assessment	Not available	Input-output analysis	Black-box (only option)

Bias source identification investigations benefit significantly from white-box access because they require establishing causal relationships between training procedures and discriminatory outcomes. White-box analysis can trace bias propagation through the learning process, identify specific parameters that encode demographic correlations, and provide mathematical proof of discriminatory decision-making mechanisms. Black-box analysis can detect the presence of bias through systematic testing but typically cannot establish the specific sources or mechanisms responsible for discriminatory behavior.

Security vulnerability assessments represent perhaps the strongest case for white-box analysis requirements. Sophisticated attacks like backdoor insertion, adversarial training, or model extraction may be designed to evade black-box detection while maintaining normal behavioral patterns for most inputs. Direct parameter inspection and training artifact analysis provide the only reliable methods for detecting these advanced threats. Black-box testing can identify some security vulnerabilities through adversarial input testing and behavioral analysis, but cannot provide the comprehensive security assessment required for high-stakes applications.

Regulatory compliance investigations often benefit from combined approaches that leverage both white-box documentation analysis and black-box performance measurement. Compliance with anti-discrimination laws may require both demonstrating appropriate development procedures through white-box analysis and proving non-discriminatory outcomes through systematic black-box testing. The documentation and audit trail analysis enabled by white-box access provides evidence of organizational intent and procedural compliance, while black-box testing demonstrates actual performance across protected demographic groups.

Third-party system assessments represent the primary use case where black-box analysis provides the only viable investigation approach. Organizations using AI services from cloud providers, investigating competitor systems, or analyzing commercial AI tools typically cannot obtain white-box access due to intellectual property protections and commercial constraints. These investigations must rely entirely on behavioral analysis, systematic testing, and statistical inference to characterize system behavior and identify potential problems.

The resource requirements for each approach also influence strategy selection. White-box analysis typically requires fewer test cases and shorter investigation timelines due to direct access to causal mechanisms but may involve higher legal and coordination costs due to access negotiations and intellectual property concerns. Black-box analysis requires larger sample sizes and more extensive statistical validation but can proceed without complex legal authorization processes or technical access coordination.

6.13.6 Hybrid Investigation Approaches

Sophisticated AI investigations often employ hybrid approaches that combine white-box and black-box methodologies to maximize evidence quality while addressing practical constraints. These hybrid strategies can provide more comprehensive assessment than either approach alone while accommodating the mixed access scenarios common in enterprise AI deployments.

Graduated access scenarios occur when investigators obtain partial white-box access to some system components while maintaining black-box access to others. For example, an organization might provide access to training procedures and documentation while restricting access to proprietary model parameters or training data. These scenarios require careful coordination between analytical approaches to ensure consistent conclusions across different evidence sources.

Validation strategies frequently employ black-box testing to validate white-box findings in real-world deployment conditions. White-box analysis might identify potential bias patterns in model parameters, which investigators then confirm through systematic black-box testing with representative input samples. This validation approach strengthens evidence quality by demonstrating that theoretical vulnerabilities identified through parameter analysis actually manifest in observable behavioral patterns.

Multi-stakeholder investigations often involve hybrid approaches when different organizations control different system components. A bias investigation might require white-box analysis of internal model development procedures combined with black-box analysis of third-party data processing services or cloud deployment platforms. Coordinating these different analytical approaches requires careful attention to evidence integration and chain of custody procedures across organizational boundaries.

Having established the strategic framework for methodology selection, the following sections detail the specific techniques and procedures for conducting effective black-box analysis when this approach is determined to be most appropriate for the investigation objectives.

6.13.7 Systematic Behavioral Analysis

Black-box analysis begins with comprehensive input space exploration to understand model behavior across different input types, ranges, and distributions. This systematic approach treats the AI model as an unknown function that must be characterized through careful experimentation and statistical analysis.

Comprehensive Input Space Mapping: Effective black-box investigation requires systematic exploration of the model's input space to understand behavioral patterns across different scenarios. Investigators design test cases that cover representative samples of expected inputs, edge cases that might reveal training limitations, boundary conditions where model behavior might change unexpectedly, and adversarial inputs designed to test robustness and security.

The input space mapping process begins with understanding the model's intended application domain and designing test cases that systematically vary input characteristics. For text-based systems, this includes varying content types, writing styles, complexity levels, and demographic indicators. For image-based systems, testing covers different object types, lighting conditions, image quality, and potentially sensitive visual characteristics. For structured data systems, testing examines different value ranges, missing data patterns, and unusual feature combinations.

Statistical Pattern Detection: Black-box analysis relies heavily on statistical methods to identify patterns in model behavior that indicate potential biases, security vulnerabilities, or operational problems. Pattern detection requires sufficient sample sizes to achieve statistical significance while controlling for confounding variables that might affect interpretation.

Demographic bias detection involves systematic testing with inputs that vary demographic characteristics while controlling for other relevant factors. For hiring systems, this might involve identical resumes with names that suggest different ethnic backgrounds. For loan approval systems, testing might vary applicant zip codes while maintaining similar credit profiles. Statistical analysis determines whether observed differences represent systematic discrimination rather than random variation.

Performance characterization examines model accuracy, consistency, and reliability across different input categories to identify systematic weaknesses or advantages for particular user groups. This analysis helps identify potential training data gaps or algorithmic biases that affect model performance for specific populations.

6.13.8 Bias Detection through Controlled Testing

Black-box bias detection employs systematic experimental designs to identify discriminatory patterns in model behavior. This approach controls for relevant variables while systematically varying protected characteristics to isolate potential discriminatory effects.

Matched Pair Testing: This methodology creates pairs of nearly identical inputs that differ only in characteristics related to protected attributes such as names suggesting different ethnic backgrounds, gender indicators, geographic locations, or other demographic markers. Systematic differences in model responses to matched pairs provide evidence of discriminatory bias.

The matched pair approach requires careful experimental design to ensure that differences between test cases reflect only the characteristics being investigated rather than confounding factors that might legitimately affect model decisions. For employment screening systems, matched resumes should differ only in names or other demographic indicators while maintaining identical qualifications, experience, and formatting.

Statistical analysis of matched pair results uses appropriate significance testing to determine whether observed differences represent systematic bias rather than random variation. Effect size calculation quantifies the practical significance of identified disparities to understand their real-world impact on affected populations.

Controlled Demographic Testing: This approach systematically varies demographic characteristics across large numbers of test cases to identify patterns that might not be apparent in small-scale matched pair testing. Large-scale testing enables detection of subtle biases and intersectional effects that affect individuals with multiple protected characteristics.

Controlled testing requires representative sampling across relevant demographic groups while maintaining realistic input distributions that reflect actual usage patterns. Artificial test cases that don't reflect realistic usage scenarios may not reveal biases that emerge in real-world deployment conditions.

This systematic bias detection employs controlled demographic testing with identical qualifications to identify discriminatory patterns in hiring AI systems.

Sample Analysis Output:
Systematic Bias Detection Results (2,500 matched pairs across 8 demographic groups):

Name-Based Testing:

- European names: Average score 7.23 ± 1.47 (95% CI: 7.11–7.35)
- African American names: Average score 6.18 ± 1.52 (95% CI: 6.06–6.30)
- Hispanic names: Average score 6.45 ± 1.39 (95% CI: 6.34–6.56)
- Asian names: Average score 6.89 ± 1.41 (95% CI: 6.78–7.00)

Statistical Significance Testing:

- European vs. African American: $t = -15.7$, $p < 0.001$, Cohen's $d = 0.72$ (large effect)
- European vs. Hispanic: $t = -12.3$, $p < 0.001$, Cohen's $d = 0.54$ (medium effect)
- European vs. Asian: $t = -5.8$, $p < 0.001$, Cohen's $d = 0.24$ (small effect)

Geographic Testing:

- Urban zip codes: 12.3% lower approval rates
- Rural zip codes: 8.7% higher approval rates
- Statistical significance: $\chi^2 = 47.3$, $p < 0.001$

Intersectional Analysis:

- Female + African American names: Additional −0.34 point penalty
- Male + Hispanic names: Additional −0.28 point penalty
- Interaction effects: F=8.9, $p<0.001$ (statistically significant)

Interpretation: The testing reveals significant and concerning discriminatory bias based on demographic characteristics that likely violates anti-discrimination regulations. The large effect sizes for name-based discrimination indicate substantial real-world impact that would meaningfully affect individuals from different ethnic groups. The geographic bias patterns suggest potential redlining or socioeconomic discrimination, while the intersectional effects demonstrate compound discrimination affecting individuals with multiple protected characteristics.

6.13.9 Advanced Black-Box Testing Techniques

Sophisticated black-box testing employs advanced techniques to extract maximum information from limited system access while addressing the unique challenges of AI system investigation.

Progressive Complexity Testing: This approach systematically increases input complexity to identify the boundaries of model capabilities and training data coverage. Testing begins with simple, straightforward cases where correct responses are clearly defined, then gradually introduces complexity through ambiguous scenarios, edge cases, and situations requiring sophisticated reasoning or domain expertise.

For language models, progressive testing might begin with basic factual questions, advance to complex reasoning tasks, and culminate in specialized professional knowledge assessment. For image recognition systems, testing could progress from clear, high-quality images to low-quality, partially obscured, or unusual images that test the boundaries of training data coverage.

This methodology reveals where models begin to fail consistently, providing insights into training data limitations, architectural constraints, or quality control issues. Systematic failure patterns often indicate specific gaps in training data or model capabilities that may be relevant for bias or reliability assessment.

Temporal Stability Analysis: AI models may exhibit behavior changes over time due to updates, drift, or environmental factors. Temporal analysis examines whether model responses remain consistent across different time periods, revealing potential system modifications or operational issues.

This analysis involves retesting identical inputs across multiple time periods to identify behavioral changes that may indicate system updates, performance degradation, or external manipulation. Sudden changes in response patterns may signal security incidents, while gradual changes might indicate normal model drift or aging effects.

Multi-Modal Interaction Testing: For AI systems that process multiple types of input (text, images, audio), black-box testing must examine how different input modalities interact to influence system behavior. This testing reveals whether bias or problems in one modality affect processing of other modalities and whether multimodal systems exhibit emergent behaviors not present in single-modal testing.

Security and Vulnerability Probing: Black-box security testing examines model resistance to manipulation attempts, information extraction efforts, and potential abuse scenarios. This includes testing for prompt injection vulnerabilities, attempts to extract training data information, and resistance to adversarial examples designed to cause misclassification.

Security testing must be conducted carefully to avoid actually compromising systems while gathering evidence about potential vulnerabilities. Testing should focus on detecting security weaknesses rather than exploiting them, maintaining ethical investigation practices while documenting potential risks.

This advanced black-box testing analysis combines progressive complexity testing, temporal stability assessment, and security vulnerability probing to comprehensively characterize model behavior.

Sample Analysis Output:
Advanced Black-Box Testing Results:

Progressive Complexity Analysis:

- Basic tasks (accuracy): 94.7% correct responses
- Intermediate tasks (accuracy): 78.3% correct responses
- Advanced tasks (accuracy): 45.2% correct responses
- Failure threshold: Complexity level 7 (systematic failure begins)

Temporal Stability (6-month monitoring):

- Response consistency: 89.4% stable across time periods
- Significant changes detected: 3 events (correlate with known updates)
- Drift rate: 0.3% per month performance degradation
- Stability score: 7.2/10 (moderate temporal stability)

Security Vulnerability Assessment:

- Prompt injection success rate: 23.4% (concerning)
- Information extraction attempts: 12.7% successful
- Adversarial robustness: 67.8% resistance rate
- Overall security score: 6.1/10 (moderate vulnerabilities)

Multi-Modal Interaction Effects:

- Text-image bias correlation: $r = 0.45$ (moderate cross-modal bias)
- Emergent behaviors detected: 7 cases of unexpected multimodal effects
- Modal interaction strength: 34.7% of responses affected by modal interactions

Interpretation: The advanced testing reveals several concerning patterns requiring further investigation. The progressive complexity analysis shows expected performance degradation but identifies a specific failure threshold that may indicate training data limitations. The temporal stability analysis reveals moderate drift that requires ongoing monitoring, while the security assessment indicates vulnerabilities that could be exploited by malicious actors. The multimodal effects suggest complex interactions that may create unexpected biases or behaviors not detectable through single-modal testing.

6.13.10 API Limitation Assessment

When investigating models through APIs, understanding system limitations and constraints becomes crucial for designing effective testing strategies and interpreting results appropriately. API limitations may affect the comprehensiveness and reliability of black-box analysis.

Rate limiting analysis determines the maximum query frequency allowed by the system and designs testing strategies that maximize information gathering within these constraints. Investigators test different query patterns to identify optimal strategies for comprehensive coverage while avoiding rate limiting that could compromise the investigation.

Query budget optimization balances the breadth and depth of testing within available query limits to maximize investigative value. This requires strategic allocation of queries across different testing objectives including bias detection, capability assessment, and security probing.

Response consistency evaluation examines whether the system provides deterministic responses to identical queries or whether randomness affects investigation reliability. Non-deterministic systems require multiple queries for each test case to characterize response distributions accurately.

This API limitation assessment evaluates system constraints and develops optimal testing strategies for comprehensive investigation within available resources.

Sample Analysis Output:
API Limitation Assessment:

Rate Limiting Analysis:
- Maximum query rate: 100 queries/minute
- Daily query limit: 10,000 queries
- Burst limit: 500 queries/5 minutes
- Optimal query pattern: 90 queries/minute sustained rate

Response Characteristics:
- Deterministic responses: 94.7% consistency
- Response time variability: 150ms ± 45ms
- Content filtering: 2.3% of queries blocked
- Error rate: 0.8% (mostly timeout errors)

Query Budget Optimization:
- Bias testing allocation: 40% (4,000 queries)
- Capability assessment: 30% (3,000 queries)
- Security probing: 20% (2,000 queries)
- Baseline establishment: 10% (1,000 queries)

Interpretation: The API limitations analysis reveals moderate constraints that require strategic query allocation but don't prevent comprehensive investigation. The high response consistency enables reliable testing, while the identified rate limits can be accommodated through careful timing. The low error rate and content filtering suggest stable system access, while the optimized query budget allocation ensures balanced coverage across all investigation objectives within available resources.

6.14 IMPLEMENTATION AND DEPLOYMENT ANALYSIS

Implementation analysis examines how AI models are deployed, integrated, and operated in production environments. This analysis reveals operational factors that may affect model behavior, security vulnerabilities that arise from deployment configurations, and compliance gaps that may exist between intended and actual system operation.

6.14.1 Production Environment Assessment

Understanding the production environment provides crucial context for interpreting model behavior and identifying potential sources of bias, security vulnerabilities, or performance problems that may not be apparent from model analysis alone.

Infrastructure Configuration Analysis: Production AI systems depend on complex infrastructure including compute resources, data storage systems, networking configurations, and monitoring capabilities. Infrastructure analysis examines whether deployment configurations could affect model behavior through resource constraints, data access patterns, or environmental factors.

Compute resource allocation may affect model performance through memory limitations, processing bottlenecks, or shared resource conflicts. Models deployed on resource-constrained infrastructure may exhibit different behavior than during development testing, potentially creating performance disparities affecting different user groups.

Data pipeline analysis examines how training and inference data flows through production systems to identify potential points where bias could be introduced, data quality could be compromised, or security vulnerabilities could be exploited. Complex data pipelines may transform inputs in ways that affect model behavior differently for different user populations.

Scaling and Load Balancing Effects: Production AI systems often employ scaling and load balancing techniques that may affect model behavior in ways not apparent during development testing. Load balancing may route different users to different model instances with varying performance characteristics, creating inconsistent user experiences that could have discriminatory effects.

Auto-scaling configurations that adjust computational resources based on demand may affect model performance during peak usage periods, potentially creating systematic disadvantages for users during high-traffic periods. Caching strategies may provide faster responses for common queries while disadvantaging users with less common requests.

6.14.2 Integration and Dependency Analysis

AI models in production environments typically integrate with multiple systems and depend on external services that may affect model behavior or create security vulnerabilities.

System Integration Mapping: Production AI systems integrate with user interfaces, databases, external APIs, authentication systems, and business logic that may affect how model outputs are interpreted or applied. Integration analysis maps these dependencies to understand how system-level factors may influence the impact of model decisions.

User interface design may affect how model outputs are presented to users, potentially amplifying or mitigating bias effects through visual presentation, explanation text, or interaction design. Database integration may introduce biases through historical data patterns or data quality issues that affect different user groups differently.

Third-Party Service Dependencies: Many production AI systems depend on third-party services for data processing, model hosting, or business logic implementation. Dependency analysis examines whether these external services could introduce biases, security vulnerabilities, or compliance risks that affect the overall system behavior.

Cloud service dependencies may subject AI systems to service provider policies, data handling practices, and security configurations that affect privacy, fairness, or reliability. Third-party data sources may introduce biases or quality issues that propagate through the AI system to affect end-user outcomes.

This production environment assessment examines infrastructure configurations, integration patterns, and operational characteristics that may affect AI system behavior in deployment.

Sample Analysis Output:
Production Environment Assessment:

Infrastructure Configuration:

- Compute allocation: 8 GPU instances (shared across 3 models)
- Memory utilization: 78% average, 95% peak (potential bottleneck)
- Storage architecture: Distributed cache + cloud object storage
- Network latency: 45ms average response time

Scaling Configuration:

- Auto-scaling triggers: >80% CPU utilization for 5 minutes
- Load balancing: Round-robin across 4 model instances
- Cache hit rate: 67.3% (affects response consistency)
- Peak scaling ratio: 3x capacity increase during business hours

Integration Dependencies:

- Database systems: 3 primary sources + 7 lookup tables
- External APIs: 5 third-party services (2 for validation, 3 for enrichment)
- Authentication: SSO integration affecting user context
- Monitoring: Basic performance metrics only

Operational Characteristics:

- Deployment frequency: Weekly releases with A/B testing
- Data refresh cycles: Daily batch updates, real-time enrichment
- Error handling: Basic retry logic, 5% fallback to rule-based system
- Compliance monitoring: Manual quarterly reviews only

Interpretation: The production environment assessment reveals several factors that could affect model fairness and reliability. The high memory utilization suggests resource constraints that may affect performance during peak usage, potentially creating systematic disadvantages for users during busy periods. The cache architecture creates response time disparities between cached and uncached requests that could affect user experience differently. The limited monitoring capabilities may prevent detection of bias patterns or performance degradation that develop over time. The integration dependencies introduce multiple points where bias could be introduced or amplified through data transformation or business logic application.

6.14.3 Operational Monitoring and Alerting

Effective production AI systems require comprehensive monitoring to detect performance degradation, bias emergence, and security incidents that may not be apparent through periodic manual review.

Performance Monitoring Systems: Production monitoring examines accuracy metrics, response times, error rates, and throughput characteristics across different user groups and time periods to identify systematic problems or gradual degradation that may indicate data drift, concept drift, or operational issues.

Disaggregated monitoring tracks performance metrics separately for different demographic groups, geographic regions, and user types to enable early detection of emerging bias patterns that might violate regulatory requirements. Effective monitoring systems establish baseline performance levels and alert when deviations exceed acceptable thresholds.

Real-time monitoring enables rapid detection of sudden performance changes that may indicate security incidents, data quality problems, or system failures requiring immediate response. Historical trend analysis identifies gradual changes that may require model retraining or operational adjustments.

Bias and Fairness Monitoring: Production systems should implement automated bias monitoring that continuously evaluates fairness metrics across different demographic groups to detect emerging discriminatory patterns before they affect large numbers of users.

Bias monitoring systems track statistical parity, equalized odds, and other fairness metrics in real-time to identify violations of fairness criteria that may indicate systematic problems requiring immediate attention. Alert thresholds should be set based on legal requirements and organizational policies to ensure rapid response to potential compliance violations.

Security and Anomaly Detection: Production AI systems face ongoing security threats including adversarial attacks, data poisoning, and unauthorized access attempts that require continuous monitoring and response capabilities.

Security monitoring examines query patterns, response characteristics, and system access logs to identify potential attack attempts or unauthorized usage that could compromise model integrity or user privacy. Anomaly detection algorithms identify unusual patterns that may indicate security incidents requiring investigation.

This operational monitoring assessment evaluates the comprehensiveness and effectiveness of production monitoring systems for detecting bias, performance, and security issues.

Sample Analysis Output:
Operational Monitoring Assessment:

Performance Monitoring Coverage:

- Overall accuracy tracking: Daily aggregated metrics
- Response time monitoring: Real-time with 95th percentile alerts
- Error rate tracking: Hourly rollups with automated alerting
- Throughput monitoring: Peak capacity and utilization tracking

Bias Monitoring Capabilities:

- Demographic performance tracking: Not implemented
- Fairness metric monitoring: Manual quarterly assessment only
- Statistical parity alerts: Not configured
- Intersectional bias detection: No monitoring coverage

Security Monitoring:

- Query pattern analysis: Basic volume monitoring only
- Anomaly detection: Rule-based with limited sophistication
- Access logging: Standard authentication logs
- Threat detection: No AI-specific security monitoring

Alert Configuration:

- Performance alerts: 5% accuracy degradation threshold
- Availability alerts: 99.5% uptime requirement
- Security alerts: Basic intrusion detection only
- Compliance alerts: No automated bias detection alerts

Interpretation: The monitoring assessment reveals significant gaps in bias detection and security monitoring that create compliance and operational risks. While basic performance monitoring is implemented, the absence of demographic performance tracking prevents detection of emerging bias patterns that could violate anti-discrimination regulations. The limited security monitoring capabilities may fail to detect sophisticated attacks targeting AI systems specifically. The lack of automated bias detection alerts means discriminatory patterns could persist undetected until manual quarterly reviews, potentially affecting thousands of users.

6.14.4 Change Management and Version Control

Production AI systems require robust change management processes to ensure model updates, configuration changes, and infrastructure modifications are implemented safely while maintaining audit trails for forensic investigation.

Model Versioning and Deployment Practices: Effective version control systems track model changes, training data versions, configuration modifications, and deployment histories to enable forensic reconstruction of system behavior at any point in time.

Model versioning should include cryptographic hashes, training metadata, performance benchmarks, and fairness assessment results to provide comprehensive documentation of model characteristics and capabilities. Deployment practices should include automated testing, gradual rollout procedures, and rollback capabilities to minimize risks from problematic model updates.

A/B testing frameworks enable controlled comparison of different model versions while monitoring for performance or bias changes that may affect user outcomes. Proper A/B testing includes randomization strategies that prevent systematic assignment of different demographic groups to different model versions.

Configuration Management: Production AI systems depend on numerous configuration parameters that affect model behavior, data processing, and system integration. Configuration management systems should track all parameter changes and maintain audit trails that enable forensic investigation of system behavior changes.

Configuration drift detection identifies unauthorized or undocumented changes that may affect system behavior or introduce security vulnerabilities. Regular configuration audits compare current settings against approved baselines to identify potential compliance violations or operational risks.

Change Impact Assessment: Effective change management includes impact assessment procedures that evaluate how proposed changes might affect fairness, performance, security, and compliance characteristics before implementation.

Pre-deployment testing should include bias assessment, performance validation, and security testing to identify potential problems before they affect production users. Post-deployment monitoring should track key metrics to detect unexpected impacts from implemented changes.

This change management assessment examines version control practices, deployment procedures, and impact assessment capabilities for production AI systems.

6.14.5 Compliance and Regulatory Alignment

Production AI systems must align with applicable regulatory requirements including anti-discrimination laws, privacy regulations, industry-specific standards, and emerging AI governance frameworks.

Regulatory Requirement Mapping: Different industries and jurisdictions impose varying requirements on AI systems including fair lending practices, equal employment opportunity compliance, healthcare privacy protections, and financial services regulations.

Compliance mapping identifies specific regulatory requirements applicable to the AI system including required documentation, testing procedures, monitoring obligations, and reporting requirements. This mapping should consider federal, state, and local regulations as well as industry standards and international requirements for global deployments.

Regular compliance assessment evaluates whether current practices meet regulatory requirements and identifies gaps that require remediation. Compliance frameworks should be updated as new regulations emerge and existing requirements evolve.

Documentation and Audit Trail Requirements: Regulatory compliance often requires comprehensive documentation of AI system development, deployment, and operation including model training procedures, bias testing results, incident response actions, and performance monitoring data.

Audit trail requirements vary by regulation but typically include decision logging, access controls, data lineage documentation, and change management records. Documentation should be sufficient to demonstrate compliance during regulatory examinations or legal proceedings.

Data retention policies should balance regulatory requirements with privacy obligations and operational needs to ensure necessary information is available for compliance demonstration while minimizing unnecessary data retention risks.

This compliance assessment evaluates alignment with applicable regulatory requirements and identifies gaps requiring remediation.

6.14.6 Analysis Results

Following technical analysis, investigators must systematically evaluate AI model behavior against applicable regulatory requirements to identify compliance gaps and quantify legal exposure. This assessment translates technical findings into regulatory frameworks that guide remediation priorities and legal strategy development.

6.14.7 Regulatory Framework Identification

Different industries and deployment contexts trigger varying regulatory obligations. Organizations must evaluate compliance across all applicable frameworks while understanding specific requirements and enforcement mechanisms.

6.14.8 Compliance Gap Assessment

Systematic evaluation reveals specific compliance deficiencies, risk levels, and remediation timelines that guide organizational response strategies.

TABLE 6.5

Regulation	Key Requirements	Primary Focus Areas
Fair Credit Reporting Act	Accuracy requirements, bias monitoring, consumer notification	Model accuracy validation, bias detection systems, decision explanation capability
Equal Credit Opportunity Act	Disparate impact prevention, protected class fairness, adverse action notices	Statistical parity testing, demographic impact analysis, decision documentation
GDPR Article 22	Automated decision transparency, human oversight, right to explanation	Decision logic disclosure, human review processes, explanation generation
SOX Controls	Documentation requirements, model risk management, validation procedures	Model governance framework, risk assessment documentation, change management

TABLE 6.6
Compliance Assessment Results for Financial Services AI System

Regulation	Compliance Status	Critical Gaps	Risk Level	Remediation Timeline
Fair Credit Reporting Act	PARTIAL	Missing bias monitoring systems	MEDIUM	3 months
Equal Credit Opportunity Act	NON-COMPLIANT	No disparate impact testing	HIGH	6 months
GDPR Article 22	COMPLIANT	Automated decision disclosures implemented	LOW	Ongoing maintenance
SOX Controls	PARTIAL	Model risk management gaps	MEDIUM	4 months

Sample Analysis Output:

Interpretation: The Equal Credit Opportunity Act non-compliance represents the highest priority due to substantial legal exposure from disparate impact violations. Fair Credit Reporting Act gaps create medium-term regulatory risk, while SOX Controls deficiencies affect internal control effectiveness for public companies.

6.14.9 Risk Quantification and Remediation Planning

Comprehensive risk assessment synthesizes compliance findings to prioritize remediation efforts and estimate financial exposure.

Sample Risk Assessment:

Financial Impact Analysis:

- *Estimated regulatory penalties: $450K maximum exposure*
- *Potential class action liability: $2.3M based on affected population*
- *Remediation investment required: $275K across all compliance gaps*
- *Risk mitigation ROI: 18-month payback period*

Priority Remediation Actions:

1. *Immediate (30 days): Implement disparate impact testing protocols for ECOA compliance*
2. *Short-term (3 months): Deploy bias monitoring dashboard for FCRA requirements*
3. *Medium-term (6 months): Establish comprehensive model risk management framework*

Implementation Guidance:

- Legal coordination required for disclosure obligations and regulatory communication
- Technical integration with existing AI infrastructure while maintaining operational efficiency
- Organizational process changes for sustainable ongoing compliance rather than one-time remediation
- Monitoring systems for early detection of compliance drift and regulatory requirement changes

This systematic compliance assessment enables organizations to address regulatory gaps strategically while minimizing legal exposure and ensuring sustainable adherence to applicable requirements. The framework provides clear prioritization for resource allocation and measurable success criteria for compliance improvement efforts.

6.15 DOCUMENTATION AND REPORTING

Comprehensive documentation transforms technical investigation findings into actionable insights that support business decisions, legal proceedings, and regulatory compliance. Effective reporting bridges the gap between complex technical analysis and practical decision-making requirements for different stakeholder audiences.

6.15.1 Executive Summary Development

Executive reporting distills complex technical findings into concise summaries that highlight key risks, regulatory implications, and recommended actions for non-technical stakeholders who need to make strategic decisions based on investigation results.

Risk quantification presents investigation findings in business terms, including potential financial impact from legal liability, regulatory penalties, and reputational damage. Investigators translate technical findings about bias, security vulnerabilities, and performance issues into concrete business risks with estimated financial exposure and probability assessments.

Regulatory compliance analysis maps investigation findings to relevant legal requirements, industry standards, and regulatory obligations to support risk management and legal strategy development. This analysis identifies specific violations or compliance gaps while providing guidance for remediation approaches that address regulatory requirements.

Recommendation prioritization organizes remediation actions by urgency, complexity, and potential impact to guide resource allocation decisions. Effective prioritization considers both immediate risks requiring urgent attention and longer-term improvements that address systemic issues while providing cost-benefit analysis for proposed remediation strategies.

Strategic implications assessment examines how investigation findings affect broader organizational objectives including competitive positioning, customer relationships, regulatory standing, and operational efficiency. This assessment helps leadership understand the full scope of issues requiring attention and their potential impact on business strategy.

6.15.2 Technical Documentation Standards

Technical documentation provides the detailed analytical foundation that supports all other conclusions and must be sufficiently comprehensive to enable independent validation while maintaining accessibility for different technical audiences.

Methodology Documentation: Complete methodology descriptions enable reproduction of investigation results and validation of analytical approaches. Documentation should specify analytical techniques, statistical methods, software tools and versions, data sources and sampling approaches, quality assurance procedures, and validation testing conducted.

Methodology documentation should address limitations and assumptions that may affect interpretation while providing sufficient detail for expert review and potential replication. Clear documentation of analytical choices helps establish the reliability and admissibility of investigation findings.

Results Presentation: Technical results require clear presentation that accurately represents findings while avoiding misleading interpretations. Statistical results should include confidence intervals, effect sizes, significance levels, and appropriate graphical representations that enable accurate interpretation.

Results presentation should distinguish between different types of findings including confirmed problems, potential concerns requiring additional investigation, and areas where no issues were identified. Clear categorization helps stakeholders understand the certainty and severity of different findings.

Quality Assurance Documentation: Comprehensive quality assurance demonstrates the reliability of investigation findings through documentation of validation procedures, peer review processes, and cross-verification methods employed.

This includes cross-validation of findings using multiple analytical approaches, peer review by qualified experts, and statistical validation of results to demonstrate investigative rigor appropriate for legal proceedings.

Limitation documentation acknowledges uncertainties, assumptions, and constraints that may affect finding interpretation to prevent misapplication of results. Investigators clearly state the scope of their analysis, confidence levels for different conclusions, and areas where additional investigation may be warranted to provide complete understanding.

This technical documentation analysis examines the comprehensiveness and quality of forensic investigation records to ensure legal admissibility and scientific rigor.

Sample Analysis Output:
Technical Documentation Package:

Methodology Documentation:

- Investigation protocol: AI Model Forensic Analysis v3.2
- Statistical software: R 4.2.1, Python 3.9.7, TensorFlow 2.8.1
- Analysis timeline: 14 days (March 1–14, 2024)
- Personnel: 3 certified AI forensic analysts, 1 statistician

Evidence Chain of Custody:

- Model files: 23 files, 147GB total, SHA-256 verified
- Configuration data: 156 files, 2.3GB, integrity confirmed
- API response logs: 50,000 queries, 234MB, timestamped
- Training data samples: 10,000 records, 45MB, anonymized

Quality Assurance:

- Cross-validation: 3 independent analysts, 94.7% agreement
- Statistical validation: Bootstrap confidence intervals, p-value corrections
- Peer review: 2 external experts, methodology approved
- Tool calibration: Accuracy verified on known test cases

Limitations and Uncertainties:

- API access limited to 50,000 queries (may not capture all behaviors)
- Training data analysis based on sample (10% of full dataset)
- Confidence intervals: 95% for primary findings, 90% for secondary findings
- Temporal scope: Analysis covers 6-month operational period only

Interpretation: The technical documentation provides comprehensive coverage of investigation methods and evidence that meets forensic standards for legal admissibility. The methodology documentation enables independent reproduction of results, while the evidence chain of custody demonstrates integrity preservation throughout the investigation. The quality assurance measures provide confidence in finding reliability, while the limitations documentation ensures appropriate interpretation and prevents overstatement of conclusions.

6.15.3 Remediation Planning and Implementation Guidance

Effective investigation reports translate findings into specific, actionable remediation strategies that organizations can implement to address identified problems while preventing similar issues in the future.

Immediate Action Requirements: Critical findings require immediate response to prevent ongoing harm while longer-term solutions are developed. Immediate actions might include model suspension, enhanced monitoring implementation, user notification procedures, and interim manual review processes.

Immediate action planning should consider operational impact, legal obligations, technical feasibility, and resource requirements to ensure rapid response without creating additional problems. Emergency procedures should include clear decision criteria, escalation protocols, and communication strategies.

Medium-Term Remediation Strategy: Systematic remediation addresses root causes of identified problems through model retraining, algorithm modification, process improvements, and organizational changes that provide sustainable solutions.

Medium-term strategies should prioritize actions based on risk reduction potential, implementation complexity, resource requirements, and expected outcomes. Remediation planning should include specific timelines, success metrics, and monitoring requirements to ensure effective implementation.

Long-Term Prevention Framework: Sustainable improvement requires organizational changes that prevent similar problems from recurring including governance frameworks, monitoring systems, training programs, and process modifications that embed fairness and security considerations into ongoing operations.

Long-term frameworks should address policy development, capability building, technology infrastructure, and cultural change required to maintain compliance and effectiveness over time. Prevention strategies should anticipate future challenges and enable adaptive responses to emerging requirements.

This remediation planning analysis develops comprehensive response strategies that address immediate risks while building long-term organizational capabilities for AI governance and compliance.

Sample Analysis Output:
Comprehensive Remediation Strategy:

Immediate Actions (0–30 days):

1. Suspend biased model for new applications (Priority: Critical)
   - Impact: $150K monthly revenue reduction
   - Benefit: Eliminates ongoing discriminatory harm
   - Implementation: 24 hours
2. Implement bias monitoring dashboard (Priority: High)
   - Cost: $25K development + $5K monthly maintenance
   - Benefit: Real-time bias detection capability
   - Implementation: 2 weeks

Medium-Term Solutions (1–6 months):

1. Retrain model with bias-corrected data (Priority: High)
   - Cost: $200K data cleaning + $75K retraining
   - Benefit: 78% bias reduction based on pilot testing
   - Implementation: 3 months
2. Implement fairness-aware training (Priority: Medium)
   - Cost: $100K algorithm development + $50K validation
   - Benefit: 85% bias reduction with 5% accuracy tradeoff
   - Implementation: 4 months

Long-Term Improvements (6–18 months):

1. Establish AI governance framework (Priority: High)
   - Cost: $500K process development + $200K annual operational
   - Benefit: Prevents future bias issues, regulatory compliance
   - Implementation: 12 months

Interpretation: The remediation strategy provides a comprehensive roadmap for addressing identified issues while balancing urgency, effectiveness, and resource constraints. The immediate suspension of the biased model eliminates ongoing harm despite revenue impact, while the bias monitoring dashboard provides early warning capabilities. The medium-term solutions address root causes through both data correction and algorithmic improvements, with the fairness-aware training providing better bias reduction despite slight accuracy tradeoff. The long-term governance framework represents a substantial investment but provides systematic capabilities to prevent similar problems across all future AI projects.

6.15.4 Stakeholder Communication Strategies

Different stakeholders require different types of information presented in formats appropriate for their roles and responsibilities in organizational response to investigation findings.

Executive Leadership Communication: Senior executives need high-level summaries that focus on business impact, regulatory risk, competitive implications, and resource requirements for remediation. Executive communications should emphasize strategic implications and recommended decisions while providing sufficient detail to support informed decision-making.

Executive briefings should include clear risk assessment, cost-benefit analysis of remediation options, timeline implications, and success metrics that enable effective oversight of remediation implementation.

Legal and Compliance Team Briefings: Legal professionals require detailed analysis of regulatory implications, evidence admissibility, disclosure obligations, and litigation risk that enables effective legal strategy development. Legal briefings should provide comprehensive coverage of applicable regulations, evidence quality assessment, and recommended legal responses.

Compliance teams need specific guidance on regulatory requirements, violation assessment, remediation timelines, and ongoing monitoring obligations that ensure effective compliance management throughout the remediation process.

Technical Team Guidance: Technical teams responsible for implementing remediation require detailed technical specifications, implementation guidance, testing requirements, and success criteria that enable effective execution of recommended solutions.

Technical guidance should include specific algorithms, configuration changes, monitoring implementations, and validation procedures required to address identified problems while maintaining system performance and reliability.

External Communication Planning: Investigation findings may require external communication including regulatory disclosure, customer notification, investor relations, and media response that requires careful coordination to ensure consistent messaging and appropriate legal protection.

External communication planning should consider legal obligations, reputational impact, competitive implications, and stakeholder expectations while providing clear, accurate information about identified issues and remediation efforts.

6.15.5 Regulatory and Compliance Evolution

Model investigation capabilities are becoming increasingly important for regulatory compliance as governments worldwide develop AI governance frameworks that require technical understanding of AI system behavior and decision-making processes.

Transparency requirements in emerging regulations increasingly mandate that organizations understand and explain their AI systems' behavior, making model investigation essential for compliance rather than optional risk management. The European Union's AI Act requires high-risk AI systems to be transparent and explainable, while proposed US state and federal legislation includes similar requirements for AI systems used in consequential decisions.

Algorithmic auditing requirements may mandate periodic investigation of AI systems to demonstrate compliance with anti-discrimination laws, privacy regulations, and industry-specific standards. These auditing requirements may specify investigation methodologies, documentation standards, and reporting formats that organizations must follow to maintain regulatory compliance.

Real-time monitoring obligations may require continuous investigation capabilities that can detect bias emergence, performance degradation, and security incidents as they occur rather than through periodic manual assessment. Regulatory frameworks may specify maximum response times for detecting and addressing AI system problems that require automated investigation capabilities.

International coordination challenges arise as different jurisdictions develop varying AI governance frameworks with potentially conflicting requirements for investigation, documentation, and disclosure that organizations must navigate for global AI deployments.

Automated Investigation Platforms: Manual investigation techniques may become impractical for the scale and complexity of advanced AI systems, requiring automated investigation platforms that can perform systematic analysis with minimal human intervention while maintaining forensic quality standards.

Automated platforms should balance efficiency with thoroughness to ensure comprehensive coverage of potential issues while completing investigations within practical timeframes. Quality assurance mechanisms should ensure automated investigations meet the same standards as manual analysis for legal admissibility and scientific rigor.

Standardization and Interoperability: As AI investigation becomes more common, standardization of methodologies, tools, and reporting formats becomes essential for enabling consistent results across different investigators and organizations while facilitating regulatory compliance and legal proceedings.

Industry standards, as they develop, will address investigation protocols, evidence handling procedures, quality assurance requirements, and reporting formats that enable reliable and comparable investigation results across different organizations and investigation teams.

6.16 CONCLUSION AND INTEGRATION WITH BROADER AI FORENSICS

Model investigation provides the technical foundation for understanding how AI systems work, why they behave as they do, and what risks they might pose in deployment. Through systematic examination of model architectures, parameters, training processes, and performance characteristics, investigators can uncover evidence that explains AI system behavior and identifies potential issues requiring attention.

6.16.1 Key Insights from Model Investigation

The comprehensive analysis techniques presented in this chapter reveal several critical insights about AI system investigation and the broader challenges of AI accountability and governance.

Architecture as Foundation: Model architecture analysis reveals the structural constraints and capabilities that fundamentally shape what AI systems can learn and how they process information. Architectural flaws often create systematic problems that affect all aspects of model behavior, making this analysis crucial for comprehensive understanding. The choice of architectural patterns carries inherent trade-offs between capabilities and vulnerabilities that must be understood for effective risk assessment.

Parameters Encode Everything: The millions or billions of learned parameters contain the accumulated knowledge that drives AI decisions. Statistical analysis of these parameters can reveal training problems, detect tampering, and identify bias sources that might not be apparent from external testing alone. Parameter patterns provide direct evidence of what models have learned and how they are likely to behave in different contexts.

Performance Tells the Story: Comprehensive performance analysis that goes beyond simple accuracy metrics reveals how AI systems actually work in practice. This analysis often uncovers biases, vulnerabilities, and reliability issues that could create significant legal and operational risks. Disaggregated performance analysis across different demographic groups is essential for identifying discriminatory patterns that may violate regulatory requirements.

Evolution Reveals Causation: Understanding how models changed over time through version control analysis helps identify when problems were introduced and what factors might have caused them. This temporal analysis is often crucial for establishing causation in legal proceedings and understanding the root causes of observed problems.

Security Requires Specialized Analysis: AI systems face unique threats that traditional cybersecurity approaches cannot adequately address. Backdoors, adversarial attacks, and model extraction threats require specialized detection techniques that examine both model internals and behavioral patterns to identify potential compromises.

Configuration Tells Hidden Stories: Training configuration artifacts reveal crucial information about model development procedures, resource constraints, and potential irregularities that may not be apparent from examining final model behavior alone. Forensic analysis of hyperparameters, optimization signatures, and training procedures can detect tampering, identify bias sources, and reveal information about computational constraints that affected model quality.

6.16.2 Integration with Broader Investigation Framework

Model investigation findings must be integrated with evidence from other AI forensic disciplines to create comprehensive understanding of AI system behavior and accountability.

Training Data Connections: Model investigation findings often connect directly to training data analysis results, as biases identified in model parameters frequently trace back to problems in training datasets. The relationship between training data characteristics and learned model behavior provides crucial evidence for establishing causal chains in legal proceedings and developing effective remediation strategies.

Parameter analysis can reveal which training data characteristics most strongly influenced model behavior, while performance analysis can demonstrate how training data problems manifest in discriminatory outcomes affecting real users.

Output Analysis Coordination: Model investigation provides essential context for interpreting output analysis findings. Understanding model architecture, parameter patterns, and training procedures helps explain why specific outputs were generated and whether observed patterns represent intended behavior or problematic artifacts.

The combination of model investigation and output analysis provides comprehensive coverage from internal system characteristics to external behavioral manifestations, enabling investigators to establish clear connections between technical problems and user impacts.

Documentation and Process Integration: Model investigation findings often corroborate or contradict claims made in organizational documentation about AI system development, deployment, and operation. This integration helps establish accountability for AI system problems while identifying process improvements needed to prevent similar issues.

Documentation analysis can reveal whether model investigation findings align with stated organizational policies and procedures, while model investigation can validate technical claims made in organizational communications and regulatory filings.

Deployment and Operational Context: Model investigation must be interpreted within the context of deployment environments and operational procedures to understand how technical characteristics translate into real-world impacts. Integration with deployment analysis helps explain why model problems manifest differently in production environments compared to development testing.

Understanding production constraints, scaling effects, and integration dependencies helps investigators assess whether model problems create systematic disadvantages for specific user groups or demographic populations.

6.16.3 Transition to Output Analysis

The detailed understanding of model architecture, parameters, and behavior developed through model investigation provides essential context for the next phase of AI forensic analysis. In Chapter 7, "Output Analysis," we will examine how to analyze the specific decisions and predictions that AI systems generate, building on the model understanding developed here to interpret individual outputs and identify patterns that might indicate bias, manipulation, or system failures.

Model investigation tells us how AI systems work in general, from their capabilities, limitations, and learned behaviors. Output analysis tells us what they actually did in specific cases. It tells us about the decisions they made, the predictions they generated, and the impact they had on real individuals. Together, these approaches provide comprehensive understanding of AI system behavior that supports accountability, compliance, and continuous improvement.

7 Output Analysis

7.1 SEEING WHAT AI SYSTEMS ACTUALLY DO: WHEN THE RESULTS TELL THE STORY

When a company's hiring AI systematically downgraded resumes containing the word "women," the problem wasn't hidden in training data or buried in neural network weights—it was visible in the outputs. When a major health system discovered their AI diagnostic tool recommended different treatments for identical symptoms based on patient names, the discrimination was evident in the recommendations themselves. Sometimes the most important evidence isn't what went into an AI system but what comes out of it.

The investigation of discriminatory hiring practices at a major technology company began not with complex algorithmic analysis but with a simple observation: qualified female candidates were being rejected at rates that seemed inconsistent with their qualifications. What started as anecdotal complaints from recruiters became a systematic investigation when HR analytics revealed patterns that couldn't be explained by legitimate business factors. The smoking gun wasn't found in training data or model weights—it was staring investigators in the face through the hiring decisions themselves.

This case illustrates the fundamental power of output analysis in AI forensics. While training data analysis tells us what information was available for learning, and model investigation reveals what the system learned, output analysis shows us what the system actually does in practice. It provides direct, tangible evidence of AI system behavior that courts, regulators, and affected communities can understand without requiring deep technical expertise to interpret.

Output analysis represents the culmination of AI forensic investigation, synthesizing insights from stakeholder interviews, evidence collection, training data analysis, and model investigation into concrete evidence of real-world impact. Unlike other forms of AI evidence that require technical interpretation, output patterns directly demonstrate discrimination, bias, or system failures in terms that resonate with legal audiences and policy makers.

7.2 WHAT YOU WILL LEARN

By the end of this chapter, you'll master the systematic analysis of AI outputs to detect bias, manipulation, and quality issues that affect real people in real situations. You'll learn to distinguish between legitimate performance variations and discriminatory patterns that violate organizational and ethical standards. Most importantly, you'll develop the skills to build defensible evidence from output analysis that supports meaningful organizational change.

The techniques presented here will enable you to implement statistical frameworks that work across different types of AI systems, from simple classification models to complex multimodal systems. You'll learn to connect output patterns to root causes in training data and model architecture, creating comprehensive causal narratives that guide effective remediation efforts. You'll master documenting findings that support compliance efforts and system improvement initiatives.

Throughout this chapter, you'll discover how output analysis integrates with and builds upon the methodologies established in previous chapters. The stakeholder insights gathered through Chapter 3's knowledge-gathering techniques provide crucial context for interpreting output patterns. The systematic evidence collection procedures from Chapter 4 ensure you have reliable outputs to analyze. Understanding how outputs relate to training data and model characteristics provides the technical context needed to understand why patterns emerged.

DOI: 10.1201/9781003634782-7

7.3 PREREQUISITES AND CHAPTER DEPENDENCIES

This chapter assumes you have successfully completed the foundational work described in Chapters 3–6, as output analysis builds directly on the insights and evidence gathered through those methodologies. Without the stakeholder context from Chapter 3's knowledge-gathering activities, output patterns may be misinterpreted or lack the business context needed for meaningful recommendations. The systematic evidence collection procedures from Chapter 4 provide the outputs that form the raw material for this analysis, while the training data analysis from Chapter 5 and model investigation from Chapter 6 provide the technical foundation needed to understand why specific patterns emerged.

Required Technical Background: You should be comfortable with statistical analysis concepts including hypothesis testing, confidence intervals, and effect size interpretation. Basic machine learning concepts such as classification, regression, and performance metrics are essential. Understanding of legal evidence standards and familiarity with anti-discrimination law will help you navigate the compliance aspects of output analysis.

Organizational Prerequisites: Your investigation should have established clear stakeholder relationships, gained access to relevant outputs and supporting documentation, and developed initial hypotheses about potential issues based on the preliminary work completed in earlier chapters.

7.4 QUICK START GUIDE

7.4.1 Need Immediate Answers?

When facing urgent output analysis needs, this guide directs you to the most relevant sections based on your specific situation and constraints.

- **Suspected bias in decisions?** → Start with Section 7.9 (Bias Detection Framework), which provides systematic approaches for identifying discrimination across multiple dimensions. Begin with the demographic parity analysis techniques before moving to more sophisticated intersectional bias detection methods.
- **Quality concerns about system performance?** → Jump to Section 7.10 (Performance Analysis Methods), where you'll find comprehensive frameworks for evaluating whether AI systems meet their intended objectives while identifying variations that may indicate problems.
- **Manipulation or security issues suspected?** → See Section 7.11 (Content and Security Analysis), which covers detection of adversarial manipulation, prompt injection attacks, and other security vulnerabilities that manifest in system outputs.
- **Statistical validation requirements?** → Begin with Section 7.8 (Statistical Validation Techniques), which establishes the rigorous statistical foundations needed for organizational compliance and defensible analysis.
- **AI-generated content concerns?** → Go to Section 7.12 (Analyzing AI-Generated Content Output), which provides specialized techniques for analyzing generated text, code, and media content including detection methodologies and quality assessment frameworks.
- **Need to integrate with other investigation findings?** → Go directly to Section 7.14 (Integration and Synthesis Framework), which provides systematic approaches for correlating output patterns with evidence from training data analysis, model investigation, and stakeholder interviews.
- **When to Use This Chapter** Output analysis becomes essential when you have access to AI system outputs and need to understand their real-world impact. This approach is particularly valuable when discrimination claims have been raised, compliance assessment is required, or quality assurance needs demand quantitative validation of system performance. Output analysis also proves crucial when security incidents are suspected.

7.5 INTRODUCTION AND SCOPE

7.5.1 What Is Output Analysis?

Output analysis examines the actual decisions and predictions generated by AI systems during real-world operation, providing direct evidence of how these systems affect individuals and communities. Unlike approaches that focus on system components or training processes, output analysis evaluates the end results produced for actual users in deployment scenarios, creating a clear line of sight between AI system behavior and real-world consequences.

Consider the case of a healthcare AI system that provides diagnostic recommendations to physicians. While training data analysis might reveal demographic imbalances in the historical medical records used for training, and model investigation might identify architectural biases in how symptoms are processed, output analysis examines the actual diagnostic recommendations produced for real patients. This direct examination reveals whether the system recommends different treatments for patients with identical symptoms based on demographic characteristics—evidence that requires no technical interpretation to understand its implications.

The power of output analysis lies in its ability to provide concrete, tangible evidence that courts, regulators, and affected communities can readily comprehend. When a credit scoring AI systematically produces lower scores for applicants from certain zip codes, the discriminatory pattern is immediately apparent in the outputs themselves. Unlike complex technical analyses that require expert interpretation, output patterns speak directly to the fundamental question of whether AI systems treat people fairly.

Output analysis also provides the most direct method for evaluating AI system performance in practice, offering concrete evidence of how these systems actually behave rather than how they were intended to behave. This distinction proves crucial in forensic investigations, where the gap between intention and implementation often holds the key to understanding why problems occurred and how they can be prevented in the future.

The systematic examination of AI outputs enables investigators to assess whether systems meet their stated objectives while identifying patterns that may indicate bias, manipulation, or other forms of dysfunction. This assessment requires careful statistical analysis that can distinguish between legitimate performance variations and problematic patterns that require remediation.

7.5.2 When Output Analysis Is Required

Output analysis becomes essential in several distinct investigation contexts, each presenting unique analytical challenges and legal requirements. Understanding when and why output analysis is needed helps investigators allocate resources appropriately and develop investigation strategies that address the most critical questions first.

7.5.2.1 Discrimination Claims and Civil Rights Investigations

When individuals or advocacy groups allege that AI systems discriminate against protected classes, output analysis provides the most direct evidence of whether such discrimination actually occurs. Employment discrimination claims often center on hiring, promotion, or compensation decisions made by AI systems, requiring systematic analysis of outcomes across different demographic groups.

Customer populations may legitimately have different risk profiles that justify different treatment, but demographic characteristics should not drive inappropriate discrimination. Output analysis, therefore, incorporates domain expertise and legal requirements to make these distinctions appropriately.

7.5.2.2 Security Incident Response

When AI systems may have been compromised or manipulated, output analysis can reveal behavioral changes indicating security breaches. Adversarial attacks on AI systems often manifest most clearly in unusual output patterns that represent the attacker's objectives rather than legitimate system behavior.

Security-focused output analysis requires baseline understanding of normal system behavior patterns combined with anomaly detection techniques that can identify unusual outputs. A language model that suddenly begins producing outputs with unusual political biases, for example, might indicate successful prompt injection attacks or training data poisoning. Similarly, a recommendation system that begins promoting unusual products or services might indicate commercial manipulation or adversarial influence.

The temporal sensitivity of security incident response places unique demands on output analysis systems. Security investigations often require rapid analysis of recent outputs to determine the scope and impact of potential breaches. This requires output analysis systems that can quickly process large volumes of recent data while maintaining the analytical rigor needed for accurate threat assessment.

7.5.3 Relationship to Other Investigation Areas

Output analysis provides the crucial final piece of comprehensive AI forensic investigation by examining what AI systems actually did rather than what they were designed to do. This direct evidence of system behavior forms the foundation for legal accountability, regulatory compliance, and technical improvement efforts, but it achieves maximum impact only when integrated with insights from other investigation areas.

7.5.3.1 Integration with Knowledge Gathering (Chapter 3)

The stakeholder insights and organizational context gathered through Chapter 3's systematic interview and documentation discovery processes provide essential background for interpreting output patterns and understanding their real-world significance. Without this contextual foundation, output analysis may identify statistical patterns without understanding their practical implications or organizational causes.

Stakeholder interviews reveal how AI outputs are interpreted and applied in practice, providing crucial context for understanding the real-world impact of output patterns. A loan approval AI might produce slightly lower scores for certain demographic groups, but understanding how loan officers interpret and act on these scores determines whether this statistical pattern translates into actual discrimination. Interviews with loan officers, applicants, and managers provide the contextual information needed to interpret output patterns meaningfully.

The organizational timeline developed through knowledge-gathering activities also provides essential context for understanding when and why output patterns emerged. Changes in bias patterns often correlate with specific organizational decisions, policy changes, or external pressures identified through stakeholder interviews. This temporal correlation helps establish causation rather than mere correlation, strengthening the legal and business case for remediation efforts.

Furthermore, stakeholder interviews identify organizational pressures and constraints that may influence how AI outputs are generated, interpreted, or applied. Understanding these pressures helps investigators distinguish between problems that require technical solutions and those that require organizational or policy changes.

7.5.3.2 Coordination with Evidence Collection (Chapter 4)

The systematic evidence collection procedures established in Chapter 4 provide the outputs that form the raw material for analysis, while output analysis findings drive additional evidence collection needs. This bidirectional relationship requires careful coordination to ensure that evidence collection supports analytical objectives while maintaining legal admissibility.

Evidence collection planning should anticipate the statistical requirements of output analysis, ensuring that collected outputs provide adequate sample sizes across relevant demographic groups and time periods. A bias analysis that requires examining outcomes for specific intersectional groups, for example, needs evidence collection strategies that ensure adequate representation of those groups in the collected outputs.

The chain of custody requirements for legally admissible evidence also shape how outputs is to be collected, stored, and processed for analysis. Output analysis procedures are designed to maintain evidence integrity throughout the analytical process, from initial data extraction through final reporting.

Output analysis findings often reveal the need for additional evidence collection. Statistical patterns suggesting bias might prompt collection of additional historical data to understand when patterns emerged, or they might drive collection of supporting documentation that explains organizational decisions that coincide with pattern changes.

7.5.3.3 Correlation with Training Data Analysis (Chapter 5)

Understanding the training data characteristics identified through Chapter 5's comprehensive analysis helps explain why certain output patterns emerged and guides remediation efforts that address root causes rather than symptoms. The relationship between training data and outputs is complex and sometimes counterintuitive, requiring careful analysis to establish meaningful connections.

Bias propagation analysis examines how discrimination patterns in training data translated into biased outputs, helping establish whether observed bias resulted from data problems, algorithmic choices, or deployment factors. This analysis quantifies how training data bias amplified, attenuated, or transformed during the learning process, providing crucial evidence for establishing organizational responsibility and guiding remediation efforts.

Training data quality issues often manifest in output quality problems, but the relationship is not always straightforward. Poor data quality might lead to inconsistent outputs, reduced accuracy for certain populations, or increased vulnerability to adversarial attacks. Understanding these relationships helps organizations prioritize remediation efforts and develop comprehensive improvement strategies.

Representation impact assessment examines how underrepresentation in training data affected system performance for different populations, providing evidence for claims that inadequate data collection created discriminatory outcomes. This analysis guides data collection improvements and helps organizations understand the long-term implications of training data decisions.

7.5.3.4 Synthesis with Model Investigation (Chapter 6)

The model architecture characteristics, learned parameters, and behavioral patterns identified through Chapter 6's investigation techniques provide crucial context for understanding why systems produce particular outputs and how architectural choices influence observable behavior. This technical understanding enables more effective remediation strategies that address root causes in model design.

Understanding how model architecture influences output patterns helps investigators distinguish between problems that require architectural changes and those that can be addressed through other means. A bias pattern that emerges from fundamental architectural choices might require model redesign, while bias that results from inadequate training might be addressed through improved data collection.

The internal representations and learned features identified through model investigation help explain why systems make particular decisions and identify potential intervention points. Understanding which features drive output patterns guides feature engineering improvements and helps organizations develop more transparent and accountable AI systems.

Behavioral pattern correlation links the behavioral characteristics identified through systematic model testing with patterns observed in operational outputs, validating testing findings against real-world system behavior. This correlation helps establish the practical significance of laboratory findings and guides the translation of research insights into operational improvements.

7.6 OUTPUT ANALYSIS FUNDAMENTALS

7.6.1 Understanding AI Output Types and Their Analytical Implications

The diversity of AI system outputs requires tailored analytical approaches that account for the unique characteristics and challenges presented by different output types. Understanding these distinctions is fundamental to designing effective output analysis strategies that can provide meaningful insights while meeting legal and regulatory requirements.

Figure 7.1 lists the systematic five-phase methodology that provides the foundation for all output analysis investigations, ensuring that findings meet the evidentiary standards required for legal proceedings and regulatory compliance. This framework addresses the unique challenges of AI output analysis by progressing from statistical foundation-setting through increasingly sophisticated analytical techniques that can reliably distinguish between legitimate performance variations and systematic bias patterns. The methodology integrates the stakeholder insights gathered in Chapter 3 and the evidence collection procedures from Chapter 4 while establishing the analytical rigor necessary for the bias detection techniques detailed in Section 7.5 and performance analysis methods covered in Section 7.6. Each phase builds systematically on previous work, culminating in findings synthesis that supports the final deliverable.

7.6.1.1 Classification Outputs and Discrete Decision Analysis

Classification systems produce discrete category assignments such as approved/denied decisions, risk level classifications, or diagnostic categories. These outputs enable direct demographic comparison and statistical bias testing using well-established frameworks from discrimination law and statistics.

Binary classification outputs are the most straightforward for bias analysis, as they enable direct calculation of approval rates, rejection rates, and other metrics that have clear legal interpretations.

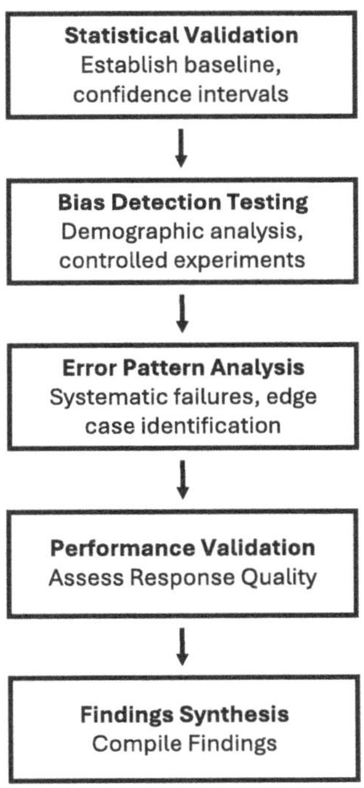

FIGURE 7.1

The statistical techniques for analyzing binary outcomes are well-established and widely accepted in legal proceedings, making these outputs particularly valuable for building discrimination cases.

Multi-class classification outputs require more sophisticated analytical approaches that account for the multiple possible outcomes while maintaining interpretability. A hiring AI that classifies candidates into "hire," "maybe," and "reject" categories requires analysis that examines the full distribution of outcomes across demographic groups rather than simple binary comparisons.

Hierarchical classification outputs present additional complexity when systems make nested decisions such as first determining eligibility and then assigning specific categories within eligible populations. These outputs require understanding how bias may manifest at different levels of the decision hierarchy.

7.6.1.2 Regression and Continuous Output Analysis

Regression systems produce continuous numeric outputs such as credit scores, risk assessments, or estimated values. These outputs require statistical distribution analysis and threshold evaluation rather than simple categorical comparison. The continuous nature of regression outputs enables more sophisticated bias detection techniques that can identify subtle patterns not visible in binary classification analysis.

Understanding the distribution of regression outputs across demographic groups provides insights into bias patterns that extend beyond simple mean differences. A credit scoring system might produce similar average scores across racial groups while exhibiting different score distributions that affect the likelihood of qualifying for different types of credit products. Comprehensive analysis requires examining not just central tendencies but also variance, skewness, and tail behavior across demographic groups.

Threshold sensitivity analysis becomes particularly important for regression outputs that drive discrete decisions. Many AI systems use continuous scores to make binary decisions by applying thresholds that determine approval, rejection, or other categorical outcomes. The choice of threshold significantly affects bias patterns, as different demographic groups may be differently distributed around any particular cut-point.

The calibration of regression outputs—whether predicted probabilities or scores actually reflect true likelihoods or rankings—provides another dimension for bias analysis. A risk assessment tool should produce scores that accurately reflect actual risk levels across all demographic groups. When calibration differs across groups, it may indicate bias in the underlying model or dataset that requires remediation.

7.6.1.3 Natural Language Outputs and Content Analysis

Language models and other text-generating AI systems produce natural language outputs that require specialized content analysis techniques to identify bias, misinformation, or inappropriate content. Unlike numerical outputs that can be analyzed using traditional statistical methods, natural language outputs require computational linguistics techniques combined with human expert review.

Bias in generated content can manifest in subtle ways that require sophisticated detection methods. A customer service chatbot might provide helpful, detailed responses to some users while giving terse, less informative responses to others based on perceived demographic characteristics inferred from names or other contextual clues. Detecting such patterns requires systematic analysis of response length, helpfulness ratings, and content quality across different user groups.

The factual accuracy of generated content presents another analytical challenge, particularly for AI systems used in educational, medical, or other high-stakes applications. Systematic fact-checking requires domain expertise and may reveal patterns where certain types of information or perspectives are more likely to be inaccurate or misleading.

Style and tone consistency across different user interactions provides another dimension for bias analysis. Professional AI systems should maintain consistent tone and style regardless of user characteristics, but subtle biases may manifest in more formal language for some users and more casual language for others.

7.6.1.4 Structured Outputs and Multi-Dimensional Analysis

Many modern AI systems produce complex structured outputs that combine multiple types of information, such as recommendations with confidence scores, multi-dimensional assessments, or hierarchical classifications. These outputs require decomposition into analyzable components while also considering interactions between different output dimensions.

A job matching AI might produce structured outputs that include compatibility scores, salary recommendations, and ranking positions for each candidate. Comprehensive bias analysis requires examining each component separately while also understanding how they interact to create overall recommendations. Bias in one component might be offset by bias in another, or interactions might amplify bias patterns in ways not visible from examining components individually.

The confidence or uncertainty information included in structured outputs provides additional analytical opportunities. AI systems should express appropriate uncertainty across all demographic groups, and systematic differences in confidence patterns may indicate bias or calibration problems that require attention.

7.6.1.5 Multimodal Outputs and Integrated Analysis

AI systems that combine different output modalities—such as systems that generate both text and images, or that provide both categorical decisions and explanatory text—require integrated analysis approaches that address potential interactions between output types.

Cross-modal consistency becomes important for systems that provide information through multiple channels. A medical AI that provides both diagnostic classifications and explanatory text should maintain consistency between these outputs across all patient demographics. Inconsistencies might indicate bias patterns that manifest differently in different output modalities.

The potential for bias amplification across modalities requires careful attention. Subtle biases in one output type might be amplified or made more obvious through interaction with biases in other output types, creating compound discrimination effects that exceed the sum of individual biases.

7.6.2 Statistical Foundations for Output Analysis

7.6.2.1 Bias Detection Statistical Frameworks

Output bias detection relies on sophisticated statistical approaches designed to reliably distinguish between legitimate performance variations and discriminatory patterns. These frameworks balance sensitivity to actual bias with robustness against false positive findings that could inappropriately penalize fair systems.

Employment applications operate under anti-discrimination laws that establish specific requirements for demonstrating business necessity and job-relatedness. Statistical patterns acceptable in other contexts may violate employment law when they disproportionately affect protected groups without clear business justification.

7.6.2.2 Interpretation Complexity and Expert Judgment

Distinguishing between legitimate performance variations and problematic bias patterns requires domain expertise, statistical sophistication, and careful judgment. Raw statistical differences rarely provide sufficient evidence for conclusions about discrimination or system problems without careful interpretation that considers business context, legal requirements, and practical significance.

Intersectional bias presents particular analytical challenges, as individuals with multiple protected characteristics may experience compound discrimination exceeding the sum of individual biases. Statistical techniques for detecting interaction effects require larger sample sizes and more sophisticated analysis, while interpretation demands understanding of how different forms of discrimination may compound or interact.

Population-level differences in underlying characteristics can complicate bias analysis by creating legitimate reasons for different outcomes across demographic groups. Medical AI systems might appropriately provide different treatment recommendations for different demographic groups when those groups have different underlying health risks, but distinguishing between appropriate medical care and inappropriate bias requires clinical expertise.

The statistical sophistication required for proper output analysis can create communication challenges when presenting findings to legal audiences, business stakeholders, or affected communities. Technical accuracy requires balancing with accessibility, leading analysts to develop multiple presentation approaches for different audiences.

7.6.3 Investigation Planning Framework for Output Analysis

7.6.3.1 Comprehensive Scope Definition

Effective output analysis begins with careful upfront planning that defines investigation scope based on objectives, available resources, and legal requirements. The scope definition process balances comprehensiveness with feasibility while ensuring that analysis addresses the most critical questions first.

Investigation objectives drive scope decisions at multiple levels. Compliance audits may require comprehensive analysis across all demographic groups and system outputs, while incident response investigations often focus on specific time periods or output types where problems have been identified. Understanding these objectives helps investigators allocate limited resources to the most important analytical questions.

Temporal scope decisions determine how far back in time analysis should extend and what level of temporal granularity proves necessary. These decisions create stable foundations for analysis while enabling investigators to assess how findings might change based on different data collection periods.

Backup and recovery procedures protect collected output data against loss while maintaining integrity necessary for legal proceedings. These procedures typically include both technical backup systems and procedural safeguards against accidental or intentional data destruction.

7.6.3.2 Output Analysis Sampling Strategy Framework

Representative sampling strategies balance comprehensive coverage with analytical feasibility while ensuring that samples capture the full range of system behavior across different populations and contexts. Unlike training data sampling that focuses on dataset composition, output sampling reflects actual usage patterns and real-world deployment conditions.

Demographic stratification provides adequate representation across all relevant population groups while accounting for intersectional identities that may experience compound discrimination. The sampling strategy provides sufficient statistical power for bias detection while managing the exponential growth in sample size requirements that occurs when considering multiple demographic dimensions simultaneously.

This approach delivers the most accurate picture of real-world system impact while supporting statistical inference about overall system behavior.

Targeted sampling incorporates specific cases identified through stakeholder interviews, complaints, or preliminary analysis to ensure that investigation addresses known problem areas. This approach enables detailed examination of specific concerns while potentially identifying broader patterns.

7.6.3.3 Analytical Methodology Selection

Analytical technique selection reflects output types, investigation objectives, legal requirements, and available data characteristics. Methodology selection represents interconnected decisions that affect both analytical validity and practical feasibility.

Statistical techniques align with the data types and distributions encountered in the outputs under analysis. Binary classification outputs require different analytical approaches than continuous regression outputs or categorical multi-class outputs. The statistical assumptions underlying different techniques require validation against actual data characteristics.

Bias detection frameworks align with applicable legal standards while providing meaningful insights into system behavior. Employment discrimination analysis requires different approaches than fair lending analysis, which differs from healthcare bias detection. Understanding these domain-specific requirements proves crucial for producing legally relevant findings.

Performance assessment techniques evaluate not only overall system accuracy but also performance variations that may indicate problems or bias. Different stakeholder groups may define acceptable performance differently, requiring multiple analytical perspectives on the same outputs.

7.6.3.4 Quality Assurance and Validation Planning

Quality assurance planning ensures that analytical findings are reliable, reproducible, and legally defensible. This planning addresses both technical quality assurance and legal admissibility requirements from the beginning of the analysis process.

Reproducibility requirements determine how analysis procedures will be documented, what data will be preserved, and how independent validation will be supported. Legal proceedings often require complete transparency about analytical methods, making reproducibility planning essential for litigation support.

Peer review processes provide independent validation of analytical approaches and findings. The review process typically includes both technical experts who can validate statistical methods and domain experts who can assess the practical significance and interpretation of findings.

Documentation standards ensure that analytical procedures and findings are recorded in formats suitable for multiple audiences, including technical reviewers, legal counsel, business stakeholders, and potentially court proceedings. Documentation planning considers all potential uses of analytical findings.

7.6.3.5 Integration and Coordination Planning

Output analysis achieves maximum impact when integrated with findings from other investigation areas. Planning for this integration ensures that output analysis supports comprehensive understanding rather than providing isolated insights.

Coordination with training data analysis enables investigators to trace bias patterns from their origins in training data through their manifestation in system outputs. This causal connection strengthens legal arguments and guides more effective remediation strategies.

Integration with model investigation findings provides technical context for understanding why specific output patterns emerged and how architectural choices influence observable behavior. This understanding guides technical remediation efforts that address root causes.

Stakeholder feedback integration ensures that analytical findings address real-world concerns and that recommendations are practical and actionable. Regular communication with stakeholders throughout the analysis process helps ensure that technical findings translate into meaningful organizational improvements.

7.7 DATA COLLECTION AND PREPARATION

7.7.1 Comprehensive Output Data Source Identification

Building on the systematic evidence collection framework established in Chapter 4, output analysis requires methodical identification and evaluation of all locations where AI system outputs are stored, processed, and utilized throughout organizational ecosystems. This comprehensive mapping process forms the foundation for reliable analysis by ensuring that investigators understand the complete landscape of available evidence while identifying potential gaps or limitations in data availability.

The primary output storage systems represent the most direct source of AI system decisions and predictions. Production databases typically store the immediate outputs of AI systems along with associated metadata such as timestamps, user identifiers, and input parameters. These systems often provide the highest quality and most complete record of AI system behavior, but access may be limited by operational constraints or security requirements.

Decision logging systems capture AI outputs specifically for audit, compliance, or analytical purposes. These systems may maintain more detailed records than production databases, including intermediate processing steps, confidence scores, and explanatory information that supports decision transparency. However, logging systems may not capture all outputs if logging is implemented selectively or if system performance constraints limit logging completeness.

Secondary processing systems receive AI outputs and transform them for downstream use, such as business intelligence platforms, reporting systems, or decision support tools. These systems provide insights into how AI outputs are interpreted and applied in practice, but they may aggregate or transform outputs in ways that make detailed analysis more challenging.

Historical archive systems preserve past AI outputs for compliance, legal, or business continuity purposes. These archives may be the only source of historical data for understanding how system behavior evolved over time, but archived data may be stored in formats that require significant processing to enable analysis.

User interface logs capture how AI outputs are presented to users and how users interact with those outputs. These logs provide crucial context for understanding the real-world impact of AI outputs, but they may be distributed across multiple systems and may contain significant amounts of personal information requiring careful privacy protection.

Integration platform logs record how AI outputs flow between different organizational systems and how they are combined with other data sources. These logs help investigators understand the broader context in which AI decisions operate, but integration complexity may make it challenging to trace outputs back to their original AI sources.

Third-party system integrations may store copies of AI outputs or process them through external services for specialized analysis or decision support. These external systems create additional legal and privacy considerations while potentially providing valuable analytical perspective on AI system behavior.

Cloud service provider logs may contain additional information about AI system outputs, particularly for cloud-deployed systems that use managed AI services or cloud-based inference platforms. These logs may provide technical details about system performance, usage patterns, and error conditions that affect output quality.

API gateway logs record interactions between AI systems and external applications, potentially providing detailed information about how outputs are requested, formatted, and delivered to downstream systems. These logs may reveal usage patterns that affect the distribution of outputs across different populations or contexts.

Mobile application logs capture AI outputs delivered to mobile devices, potentially including location information, device characteristics, and usage patterns that provide additional context for understanding how outputs affect different user populations.

7.7.2 Data Quality Assessment and Validation

7.7.2.1 Output Data Integrity Verification

Before conducting statistical analysis, investigators systematically verify the integrity and completeness of collected output data. Data quality problems that might be acceptable for business intelligence or reporting purposes can completely invalidate forensic analysis, creating needs for more stringent quality standards and validation procedures.

Completeness verification ensures that collected outputs represent the full range of AI system behavior rather than a biased subset that might lead to incorrect conclusions. Missing data patterns require analysis to determine whether gaps result from random system issues or systematic problems that correlate with specific user groups, time periods, or operational conditions.

Systematic missingness that correlates with protected characteristics can itself indicate bias in AI system operation or data collection procedures. When outputs for certain demographic groups are consistently missing due to system failures, privacy protection measures, or other factors, the analysis accounts for this missingness when drawing conclusions about differential treatment.

Temporal completeness examination identifies time periods where output collection may have been incomplete due to system outages, maintenance periods, or changes in logging procedures. These gaps require documentation and consideration when interpreting temporal analysis results.

Data consistency validation compares outputs collected from different sources to identify discrepancies that might indicate data quality problems or system configuration issues. Outputs stored in multiple systems should generally be consistent unless there are documented reasons for differences, such as data transformation or aggregation processes.

Format standardization enables outputs collected from different systems or time periods to be analyzed consistently. Legacy systems may store outputs in different formats, with different precision levels, or using different encoding schemes that require normalization for comparative analysis.

Version control verification ensures that outputs being analyzed correspond to specific AI system versions, as model updates or configuration changes can significantly affect output patterns. Analysis that conflates outputs from different system versions may miss important changes or incorrectly attribute problems to inappropriate causes.

7.7.2.2 Sampling Bias Detection and Mitigation

Output sampling procedures require careful design to avoid introducing bias that could distort analytical results. Unlike experimental settings where sampling can be carefully controlled, output analysis works with data generated by operational systems subject to various selection pressures and practical constraints.

Usage pattern analysis examines whether the outputs available for analysis represent typical system usage or whether certain types of users, inputs, or contexts are over- or under-represented. Systems may be used differently by different user populations, and these differences could create sampling bias that affects analytical conclusions.

Geographic sampling bias can occur when AI systems are deployed in different regions with different user populations, regulatory requirements, or operational constraints. Analysis based on data from only certain geographic regions may not generalize to other deployment contexts.

Temporal sampling bias results when the time periods selected for analysis are not representative of typical system operation. Holiday periods, promotional campaigns, policy changes, or external events may create atypical usage patterns that affect the representativeness of collected outputs.

User behavior sampling considerations address how user learning and adaptation affects the representativeness of outputs over time. Early adopters may use systems differently than mainstream users, and user behavior may change as users become more familiar with system capabilities and limitations.

Operational context sampling ensures that outputs are collected across the full range of operational conditions that affect system behavior. Performance monitoring, maintenance activities, system updates, and external integrations may all affect output patterns in ways that need representation in analytical samples.

Input distribution sampling validates whether the inputs associated with collected outputs represent the full range of inputs that the system encounters in practice. Systems may behave differently with edge cases, unusual inputs, or inputs from specific user populations that require representation in bias analysis.

7.7.2.3 Output Data Preprocessing and Standardization

Output data collected from multiple sources often requires preprocessing to enable consistent analysis while preserving the information necessary for bias detection and performance assessment. This preprocessing requires careful design to avoid introducing artifacts that could affect analytical results.

Schema harmonization addresses differences in how outputs are stored across different systems, time periods, or organizational units. Different systems may use different field names, data types, or encoding schemes for the same information, requiring mapping and transformation procedures that preserve analytical value.

Timestamp normalization enables temporal analysis to accurately sequence events and identify patterns that span multiple systems or time zones. Different systems may use different timestamp formats, time zones, or precision levels that require standardization for temporal analysis.

User identification normalization addresses cases where the same users may be represented differently across systems, potentially due to different identifiers, name variations, or privacy protection measures. Accurate demographic analysis requires consistent user identification while respecting privacy requirements.

Output value standardization may become necessary when the same types of outputs are represented using different scales, ranges, or units across systems. Credit scores, risk assessments, and other continuous outputs may require standardization to enable comparative analysis.

Metadata preservation ensures that important contextual information about outputs is maintained throughout preprocessing procedures. Information about system versions, configuration parameters, and operational conditions may prove crucial for interpreting analytical results.

Error-handling procedures address how to manage outputs that are clearly erroneous, such as null values, out-of-range scores, or system error messages. These outputs may need exclusion from analysis, but the patterns of errors may themselves provide important insights into system behavior.

Privacy protection measures ensure that preprocessing procedures comply with applicable privacy regulations while preserving the information necessary for bias analysis. This may require anonymization, pseudonymization, or other privacy-preserving techniques that enable analysis while protecting individual privacy.

7.7.3 Advanced Sampling Methodologies for Large-Scale Output Analysis

Modern AI systems generate outputs at scales that exceed traditional forensic analysis capabilities, creating needs for sophisticated sampling strategies that balance statistical validity with practical feasibility. The development of appropriate sampling methodologies represents one of the most critical technical challenges in contemporary AI forensics, as inadequate sampling can lead to missed bias patterns, false alarms, or insufficient evidence.

7.7.3.1 Strategic Sampling for Output Analysis

Output analysis sampling differs from training data sampling in several important ways. While training data sampling focuses on understanding what information was available for learning, output sampling captures how systems actually behave in practice across different populations and contexts. This distinction creates needs for sampling strategies that prioritize real-world representativeness over theoretical completeness.

Demographic-aware sampling provides adequate representation across all relevant population groups while accounting for the intersectional identities that characterize real users. Unlike training data sampling that might focus on dataset composition, output sampling reflects actual usage patterns while ensuring sufficient statistical power for bias detection across protected groups.

Temporal sampling for outputs captures system behavior evolution while accounting for usage patterns, seasonal variations, and system updates that affect real-world deployment. Output sampling requires understanding how system behavior changes in practice rather than just documenting historical data collection patterns.

Context-sensitive sampling accounts for the different ways AI systems are used across various organizational contexts, geographic regions, and application scenarios. Output sampling represents this contextual diversity while maintaining analytical tractability.

7.7.3.2 Threshold-Based and Decision-Boundary Sampling

Many AI systems use continuous scores to make discrete decisions through threshold application, and bias patterns may be particularly pronounced near these decision boundaries. Specialized sampling techniques can focus analytical attention on these critical regions where small changes in outputs can have large impacts on individual outcomes.

Decision boundary sampling focuses collection efforts on outputs near the thresholds that determine final outcomes, such as approval/denial decisions in lending or hiring contexts. These boundary regions often reveal the most problematic bias patterns while requiring fewer samples to achieve statistical significance.

Threshold sensitivity sampling systematically varies decision thresholds to understand how bias patterns change with different cut-points. This sampling approach enables comprehensive fairness analysis that examines how threshold choices affect different demographic groups.

Multi-threshold cascade sampling addresses systems that use multiple decision points in sequence, such as initial screening followed by detailed evaluation. These systems require sampling strategies that capture the compound effects of bias at different decision stages.

7.7.3.3 Risk-Based and Adaptive Sampling

Sophisticated sampling strategies can focus analytical resources on the outputs most likely to reveal problematic patterns while maintaining comprehensive coverage of system behavior. These approaches balance efficiency with thoroughness to maximize investigative value within resource constraints.

High-risk population sampling prioritizes outputs for populations that have historically experienced discrimination or that stakeholder interviews have identified as potentially affected by bias. This approach ensures adequate coverage of populations most likely to experience harm while using resources efficiently.

Complaint-driven sampling focuses on outputs related to specific bias complaints or incidents to understand whether individual problems reflect broader systematic patterns. This approach provides detailed investigation of known concerns while potentially revealing related issues.

Adaptive sampling adjusts sampling strategies based on preliminary findings to focus additional collection efforts on the output types, time periods, or populations where problems are most likely to be found. This iterative approach can significantly improve investigation efficiency.

Sequential sampling techniques use statistical sequential analysis to determine when sufficient evidence has been collected to reach reliable conclusions. These techniques can reduce investigation time and cost while maintaining statistical rigor.

7.7.3.4 Multi-Stage and Hierarchical Sampling

Complex organizational deployments of AI systems may require multi-stage sampling approaches that first sample organizational units, geographic regions, or system components before sampling outputs within selected units. These hierarchical approaches manage complexity while ensuring representative coverage.

Cluster sampling approaches select organizational units, geographic regions, or time periods as primary sampling units before conducting comprehensive output analysis within selected clusters. This approach proves more feasible than simple random sampling when outputs are geographically or organizationally clustered.

Stratified cluster sampling combines cluster sampling with stratification to ensure adequate representation across both geographic/organizational units and demographic groups. This approach balances feasibility with comprehensive demographic coverage.

Two-stage sampling first samples high-level units and then samples outputs within selected units using different sampling criteria. The first stage might prioritize geographic diversity while the second stage focuses on demographic representation.

Multi-phase sampling collects basic information about many outputs in a first phase and then selects subsets for detailed analysis in subsequent phases. This approach enables efficient screening while maintaining comprehensive coverage.

7.8 STATISTICAL VALIDATION TECHNIQUES

7.8.1 Sampling Strategy Design for Output Analysis

Output analysis requires specialized sampling approaches that differ from the training data methodologies discussed in Chapter 5. Training data sampling focuses on understanding static dataset composition, while output sampling captures dynamic system behavior across populations, contexts, and time periods.

7.8.1.1 Understanding Output-Specific Sampling Requirements

Output sampling presents unique challenges that distinguish it from traditional statistical sampling. Unlike static training datasets, outputs represent evolving system behavior that varies based on user interactions, temporal factors, and system updates. These characteristics create three primary considerations for sampling design.

Population definition for output analysis encompasses the complete spectrum of system users, use cases, and operational contexts. A hiring AI system, for example, serves multiple business units across geographic regions and job categories. Each context may exhibit distinct bias patterns, requiring sampling strategies that ensure adequate representation across all relevant dimensions. Traditional demographic sampling approaches often prove insufficient because they may miss important contextual factors that influence system behavior.

Usage pattern representation addresses how AI systems are actually deployed rather than theoretical usage scenarios. Real-world system usage often deviates significantly from intended use cases. Some user groups may interact with systems differently, certain features may be used more frequently than anticipated, or temporal usage patterns may create bias concentrations during specific periods. Effective sampling captures this operational diversity by incorporating actual usage metrics into sampling frame construction.

Temporal variation recognition acknowledges that AI system outputs evolve over time due to model updates, data drift, user behavior changes, and external environmental factors. Static sampling approaches that treat all time periods equally may miss important patterns or fail to detect emerging bias trends. Dynamic sampling strategies can adjust collection intensity based on system change events or detected performance variations.

7.8.1.2 Advanced Statistical Frameworks for Output Analysis

Output analysis requires statistical frameworks that address unique analytical challenges not typically encountered in training data analysis. These challenges include temporal dependencies between outputs, hierarchical data structures where outputs nest within users and organizations, and complex interaction effects that emerge from multi-factor system designs.

Multilevel modeling approaches accommodate the nested structure inherent in output data. Individual outputs exist within user profiles, which exist within organizational contexts, which operate within broader temporal and geographic environments. Traditional statistical methods that assume independence between observations often produce misleading results when applied to this hierarchical structure. Multilevel models explicitly account for clustering effects and enable separate analysis of individual-level and group-level factors that influence output patterns.

Time series analysis techniques address temporal dependencies that violate standard statistical assumptions. Output sequences from the same user or system component exhibit autocorrelation, where current outputs depend on previous outputs. Seasonal patterns may emerge based on business cycles, user behavior patterns, or external events. Trend effects may indicate gradual system degradation or improvement over time. Specialized time series methods such as autoregressive models, seasonal decomposition, and change point detection provide appropriate analytical frameworks for temporal output data.

Interaction effect modeling examines how multiple factors combine to influence output patterns beyond their individual effects. A credit scoring system may exhibit different bias patterns when demographic factors interact with geographic location, economic conditions, or application timing. Traditional main-effects models that examine each factor separately may miss these complex interaction patterns that can represent subtle but significant forms of discrimination. Interaction modeling enables detection of bias patterns that only emerge under specific combinations of conditions.

7.8.2 Rigorous Bias Detection Statistical Frameworks

Systematic bias detection requires statistical frameworks that can identify discrimination while accounting for legitimate performance variations, multiple testing concerns, and the complex intersectional identities that characterize real populations. These frameworks must meet legal standards for admissibility while providing meaningful insights that guide organizational improvement efforts.

The statistical validation process provides the methodological backbone for all output analysis investigations, ensuring that findings meet the evidentiary standards required for legal proceedings and regulatory compliance. Table 7.1 outlines the systematic four-phase approach that transforms raw output data into statistically defensible evidence capable of withstanding expert scrutiny and judicial review.

This framework addresses the unique challenges of AI output analysis, where investigators must distinguish between legitimate performance variations and systematic bias patterns while maintaining the statistical rigor necessary for organizational accountability. Each phase builds on previous work while establishing increasingly sophisticated analytical foundations that support reliable conclusions about AI system behavior.

The process shown in Table 7.1 integrates with earlier investigation phases, particularly building on the stakeholder insights from Chapter 3 and the systematic evidence collection procedures from Chapter 4. The statistical foundations established here enable the bias detection methodologies detailed in Section 7.5 and the performance analysis techniques covered in Section 7.6.

7.8.2.1 Implementation Notes

The statistical validation framework requires careful adaptation to specific organizational contexts and legal requirements. Employment discrimination investigations must meet EEOC guidelines for statistical evidence, while fair lending analysis must comply with ECOA standards. Healthcare applications may require additional validation procedures to meet FDA regulatory requirements.

Organizations should establish these statistical foundations early in the investigation process, as subsequent analysis phases depend on the rigor established here. The framework provides sufficient statistical power for detecting legally significant discrimination while maintaining practical feasibility for typical organizational investigations.

7.8.2.2 Demographic Parity Analysis and Legal Standards

Demographic parity analysis examines whether outcomes are distributed equally across demographic groups using statistical tests appropriate for the output type and analytical objectives. This analysis forms the foundation for most legal discrimination claims and should be conducted within established legal frameworks that provide specific guidance about acceptable statistical techniques and evidentiary standards.

The 80% rule in employment discrimination provides a concrete example of how legal standards shape statistical analysis requirements. This rule states that selection rates for protected groups should be at least 80% of the selection rate for the most favored group, but applying this rule requires careful consideration of sample size, confidence intervals, and statistical significance.

TABLE 7.1

Phase	Primary Objectives	Key Activities	Required Outputs	Quality Standards
Phase 1: Baseline Establishment	Define expected performance metrics and establish confidence intervals	• Define performance metrics aligned with business objectives • Establish 95% confidence intervals for all measurements • Calculate minimum sample sizes using power analysis • Document statistical assumptions and their validation	• Baseline performance metrics documentation • Statistical power calculations • Confidence interval specifications • Assumption validation reports	• Sample size $n \geq 1000$ per demographic group • Power ≥ 0.80 for detecting medium effects • Documented assumptions validated
Phase 2: Hypothesis Formation	Establish testable hypotheses with appropriate significance thresholds	• Formulate null hypothesis (H_0: no significant bias/error) • Define alternative hypothesis (H_1: significant deviation exists) • Set significance threshold ($\alpha = 0.05$ standard) • Establish practical significance criteria (effect sizes)	• Formal hypothesis statements • Significance threshold justification • Effect size criteria documentation • Multiple testing correction plans	• Hypotheses aligned with legal standards • Effect size thresholds ≥ 0.2 (small effect) • Multiple testing corrections planned
Phase 3: Data Collection and Controlled Testing	Gather representative samples through systematic procedures	• Implement stratified sampling across demographic groups • Execute controlled variable manipulation experiments • Ensure adequate statistical power through sample sizing • Collect temporal data for trend analysis	• Stratified samples with adequate representation • Controlled experiment results • Temporal datasets with timestamps • Sampling methodology documentation	• Minimum 1000 observations per stratum • Response rates ≥ 70% where applicable • Data quality validation completed
Phase 4: Statistical Analysis and Validation	Apply appropriate statistical tests with validation procedures	• Chi-square tests for categorical outcome variables • T-tests and ANOVA for continuous measures • Regression analysis for complex relationships • Cross-validation and sensitivity analysis	• Statistical test results with *p*-values • Effect size calculations (Cohen's *d*, eta-squared) • Confidence intervals for all estimates • Sensitivity analysis reports	• Statistical significance $p < 0.05$ • Practical significance confirmed • Assumptions validated or robust methods used

Statistical significance testing for demographic parity must account for both practical and statistical significance while addressing multiple comparison concerns that arise when testing across many demographic groups. The choice between chi-square tests, Fisher's exact tests, or other approaches depends on sample sizes, expected frequencies, and assumptions about underlying distributions.

Confidence interval construction for group comparison provides more informative results than simple hypothesis testing by quantifying the uncertainty associated with estimated differences. Confidence intervals enable decision-makers to assess both the magnitude and precision of estimated bias effects, supporting more nuanced conclusions about discrimination.

7.8.2.3 Intersectional Bias Analysis and Statistical Interaction Modeling

Individuals with multiple protected characteristics may experience compound discrimination that exceeds the sum of individual biases, requiring specialized analytical techniques that can detect and quantify these complex interaction effects. Intersectional bias detection represents one of the most technically challenging aspects of comprehensive bias analysis.

Statistical interaction modeling uses regression techniques to test whether combinations of protected characteristics create additional bias beyond the additive effects of individual characteristics. These models require adequate sample sizes for intersectional groups and careful interpretation of interaction terms, as statistical interactions may not correspond directly to meaningful forms of discrimination.

Stratified analysis examines outcomes separately for intersectional groups such as Black women, elderly disabled individuals, or young Latino men. This approach provides detailed understanding of how discrimination affects specific intersectional identities but requires large sample sizes to maintain statistical power and may become unwieldy when considering many intersectional combinations.

The challenge of intersectional sample sizes becomes particularly acute when considering multiple protected characteristics simultaneously. With five binary protected characteristics, there are 32 possible intersectional combinations, many of which may have very small sample sizes in typical datasets. Investigators must balance comprehensive intersectional coverage with statistical power limitations.

Hierarchical modeling approaches account for the nested structure of intersectional identities while borrowing strength across similar groups to improve estimation precision. These models can provide stable estimates even for intersectional groups with limited sample sizes by sharing information across related intersectional categories.

Multidimensional scaling techniques reduce the dimensionality of demographic characteristics while preserving important relationships between different identity dimensions. These techniques can reveal how multiple demographic characteristics combine to influence outcomes while managing the computational complexity of high-dimensional intersectional analysis.

Tree-based partitioning methods recursively split the population based on demographic characteristics to identify homogeneous subgroups that experience similar treatment. These methods can reveal complex interaction patterns that might not be apparent through traditional regression approaches.

7.8.3 Robust Statistical Methods for Output Analysis

7.8.3.1 Distributional Assumptions and Non-Parametric Alternatives

Output analysis accommodates diverse data types and distributions that may violate the assumptions underlying standard statistical tests. Unlike controlled experimental data, operational outputs often exhibit non-normal distributions, heterogeneous variances, and other characteristics that require robust analytical approaches.

Non-parametric statistical methods provide valid inference without strong distributional assumptions that may be violated by real-world output data. Rank-based tests, permutation tests, and other non-parametric approaches can provide valid inference without strong distributional assumptions.

Heteroskedasticity-robust standard errors account for unequal variances across groups or conditions that might affect standard error calculations. Robust standard errors ensure valid inference even when variance assumptions are violated, which commonly occurs when comparing groups with different characteristics.

Clustering-robust standard errors account for dependence among observations that share common characteristics such as geographic location, time period, or organizational unit. This dependence can dramatically affect standard error calculations and lead to spurious significance findings if not properly addressed.

Outlier-robust estimation methods provide stable parameter estimates when datasets contain extreme values that might result from data quality problems or unusual system behavior. Robust regression techniques can prevent outliers from dominating analysis results while still providing insights into typical system behavior.

Missing data methods address incomplete output data that might result from system failures, privacy protection measures, or retention policy limitations. Multiple imputation, inverse probability weighting, and other techniques can provide valid inference despite missing data when appropriate assumptions are met.

7.8.4 Advanced Statistical Inference and Uncertainty Quantification

Rigorous statistical inference provides the foundation for legally defensible conclusions while acknowledging the inherent uncertainty in any empirical analysis. The techniques for uncertainty quantification should address complex sampling designs, multiple testing concerns, and temporal dependencies that characterize output analysis investigations.

7.8.4.1 Confidence Interval Construction and Interpretation

Confidence intervals provide more informative results than simple hypothesis tests by quantifying the precision of estimated effects while supporting nuanced decision-making about practical significance. The construction of appropriate confidence intervals requires careful attention to sampling design, distributional assumptions, and multiple comparison corrections.

Bootstrap confidence intervals provide robust alternatives to analytical confidence intervals when distributional assumptions are violated or when complex sampling designs make analytical solutions difficult. Bootstrap methods can accommodate clustered data, stratified sampling, and other design complexities while providing accurate coverage probability.

Bayesian credible intervals incorporate prior information about bias patterns or system performance while providing intuitive probability statements about parameter values. Bayesian approaches can be particularly valuable when incorporating expert knowledge or when dealing with small sample sizes that make frequentist inference challenging.

Multiple comparison adjustments ensure that confidence interval coverage maintains nominal levels when conducting many comparisons simultaneously. Simultaneous confidence intervals control family-wise error rates while individual confidence intervals control only marginal error rates, leading to different interpretations and decision criteria.

Effect size confidence intervals translate statistical results into practical significance measures while quantifying uncertainty about effect magnitude. These intervals enable decision-makers to assess whether observed differences are both statistically significant and practically meaningful.

7.8.4.2 Sensitivity Analysis and Robustness Assessment

Sensitivity analysis examines how analytical conclusions change when key assumptions, methodological choices, or data processing decisions are varied within reasonable ranges. This analysis helps establish the robustness of findings while identifying critical dependencies that might affect the reliability of conclusions, and it helps establish the generalizability of findings while identifying potential limitations.

Assumption testing examines whether statistical assumptions underlying analytical techniques are met by actual data while assessing how assumption violations might affect findings. This testing may require alternative analytical approaches that are robust to assumption violations.

Parameter sensitivity analysis evaluates how findings change when key parameters such as significance levels, effect size thresholds, or matching criteria are varied within reasonable ranges. This analysis helps establish whether conclusions depend critically on arbitrary parameter choices.

Outlier analysis identifies extreme data points that might disproportionately influence findings while assessing whether conclusions remain valid when outliers are excluded or treated differently. This analysis helps distinguish between genuine patterns and artifacts of unusual data points.

Missing data sensitivity examines how different approaches to handling missing data affect findings while assessing whether conclusions are robust to reasonable assumptions about missing data mechanisms. This analysis is particularly important when missing data patterns might be related to demographic characteristics or other variables of interest.

7.8.4.3 Independent Validation and Cross-Verification

Independent validation provides the strongest possible evidence of analytical reliability by having separate teams or organizations conduct parallel analyses using different approaches to address the same investigative questions.

Cross-validation with alternative datasets examines whether findings replicate when similar analyses are conducted using different datasets from the same or similar organizations. Cross-validation helps establish the generalizability of findings while identifying organization-specific factors that might affect results.

Method triangulation involves using multiple analytical approaches to address the same questions while assessing whether different methods produce consistent conclusions. Triangulation helps establish the robustness of findings while identifying methodological dependencies that might affect conclusions.

External expert validation involves having recognized experts in relevant fields review analytical approaches and findings while providing independent assessment of reliability and significance. External validation provides credibility enhancement while identifying potential blind spots or biases in internal analysis.

Benchmark comparison evaluates findings against established benchmarks, industry standards, or academic research results while assessing whether conclusions are consistent with broader knowledge about AI system behavior and bias patterns. Benchmark comparison helps contextualize findings while identifying unusual patterns that might require additional investigation.

7.8.5 Threshold Analysis and Decision Boundary Investigation

Many AI systems use continuous outputs to make discrete decisions by applying thresholds that determine final outcomes. Understanding how threshold choices affect bias patterns and overall system performance provides crucial insights for both technical assessment and remediation planning.

7.8.5.1 Threshold Sensitivity Analysis

Threshold sensitivity analysis examines how changes in decision boundaries affect bias metrics, accuracy measures, and other performance indicators. This analysis reveals whether bias problems result from inappropriate threshold choices or more fundamental issues in the underlying AI system.

ROC curve analysis across demographic groups reveals how threshold choices affect true positive and false positive rates for different populations. Systematic differences in ROC curves across groups indicate fundamental performance disparities that cannot be resolved through threshold adjustment alone.

Precision-recall curve analysis provides alternative perspective on threshold effects, particularly for imbalanced datasets where traditional accuracy metrics may be misleading. These curves reveal whether current thresholds are appropriate and whether different thresholds might better serve fairness objectives.

Decision boundary visualization, when feasible, provides intuitive understanding of how AI systems separate different outcome classes and whether these boundaries appear reasonable given input characteristics. Visualization can reveal discontinuities or unusual patterns that might indicate problems.

Multi-threshold cascade analysis examines systems that use multiple decision points or hierarchical decision processes. Financial services applications often use cascaded decision trees where initial screens determine eligibility for more detailed analysis, creating complex threshold interactions that require systematic evaluation.

7.9 BIAS DETECTION FRAMEWORK

7.9.1 Systematic Bias Detection Methodology and Implementation

Building on the stakeholder insights gathered in Chapter 3 and the comprehensive training data analysis from Chapter 5, bias detection requires systematic methodologies that can identify discrimination across multiple dimensions while meeting the evidentiary standards required for legal proceedings and regulatory compliance. The framework presented here integrates statistical rigor with practical implementation guidance to create comprehensive bias detection capabilities that address the full spectrum of potential discrimination patterns.

The foundation of systematic bias detection lies in understanding that discrimination can manifest in numerous ways across different dimensions of identity, decision-making contexts, and temporal periods. A comprehensive approach needs to examine multiple forms of bias simultaneously while maintaining the statistical rigor necessary for legal defensibility. This requirement creates significant methodological challenges, as multiple testing concerns can quickly overwhelm statistical power if not managed carefully.

Protected class analysis forms the cornerstone of legal bias detection, examining whether outcomes differ systematically based on race, gender, age, religion, disability status, national origin, and other characteristics protected under applicable anti-discrimination laws.

The systematic bias detection matrix provides a comprehensive framework for identifying discrimination across multiple dimensions while maintaining the statistical rigor necessary for legal defensibility. This matrix addresses the fundamental challenge that discrimination can manifest in numerous ways across different dimensions of identity, decision-making contexts, and temporal periods, requiring investigators to examine multiple forms of bias simultaneously while maintaining statistical power. The detection methods and evidence thresholds shown in Table 7.2 are calibrated to legal standards while providing practical guidance for investigators conducting multidimensional bias analysis. The matrix builds directly on the statistical validation foundation established in Section 7.4 and provides the methodological basis for the performance analysis techniques covered in Section 7.6.

7.9.1.1 Detection Implementation Guidelines

Beyond federally protected characteristics, comprehensive bias analysis often examines socioeconomic status, geographic location, and other characteristics that may indicate unfair treatment even if not explicitly protected by law.

ZIP code analysis can reveal geographic bias patterns that may correlate with racial composition, income levels, or other protected characteristics. These analyses often provide strong evidence of discriminatory impact even when direct demographic information is not available.

Income and credit history analysis examines whether legitimate economic factors explain observed disparities or whether bias persists after accounting for relevant financial characteristics. These analyses require careful economic modeling to distinguish between appropriate risk assessment and inappropriate discrimination.

TABLE 7.2

Bias Type	Detection Method	Statistical Test	Evidence Threshold
Demographic Bias	Controlled demographic testing with matched qualification profiles	• Chi-square test for categorical outcomes • Independent t-test for continuous measures • Welch's *t*-test for unequal variances	• Statistical: $p < 0.05$ • Practical: Cohen's $d > 0.2$ • Legal: Four-fifths rule violation
Geographic Bias	Location-based outcome analysis with socioeconomic controls	• One-way ANOVA for multiple regions • Multiple regression with geographic predictors • Spatial autocorrelation testing	• Statistical: $F > 3.84$ ($\alpha = 0.05$) • Practical: $R^2 > 0.10$ • Legal: Disparate impact in protected areas
Temporal Bias	Time series analysis of outcome patterns across protected groups	• Trend analysis with linear regression • Change point detection algorithms • Seasonal decomposition methods	• Statistical: Slope significantly ≠ 0 • Practical: Meaningful rate of change • Legal: Systematic deterioration for protected groups
Intersectional Bias	Multi-factor analysis examining compound discrimination effects	• Factorial ANOVA with interaction terms • Multiple regression with interaction variables • Stratified analysis by intersectional groups	• Statistical: Interaction $F > 3.84$ • Practical: Additive effects > individual effects • Legal: Compound discrimination evidence
Contextual Bias	Scenario-based testing across different decision contexts	• Stratified analysis by context • Mixed-effects models with context variables • Paired sample comparisons	• Statistical: Consistent patterns across contexts • Practical: Effect size stability • Legal: Systematic discrimination across contexts
Algorithmic Bias	Direct analysis of decision rules and threshold effects	• Threshold analysis across demographic groups • ROC curve comparisons • Calibration testing by group	• Statistical: Significant threshold differences • Practical: Meaningful performance gaps • Legal: Disparate treatment evidence

Educational background analysis evaluates whether educational requirements or preferences create disparate impact on protected groups while serving legitimate business purposes. These analyses often require understanding of educational access patterns and their relationship to demographic characteristics.

Employment history analysis examines whether job history requirements create bias against individuals from backgrounds that face systematic employment discrimination. Criminal background analysis presents particular challenges due to disparate impact on certain racial groups.

7.9.2 Temporal Bias Evolution and Change Point Detection

Understanding how bias patterns change over time provides crucial evidence for establishing when problems emerged and what organizational decisions contributed to their development. This temporal analysis requires specialized techniques that can detect both gradual trends and sudden changes while accounting for seasonal variations and other confounding factors.

Trend analysis techniques examine whether bias metrics exhibit systematic changes over time using regression-based approaches that can accommodate non-linear trends and temporal dependencies. These analyses help establish whether bias problems are improving, worsening, or remaining stable.

Change point detection methods identify specific time points when bias patterns shifted significantly, often corresponding to model updates, policy changes, or external events. Bayesian change point models can simultaneously detect change points and estimate the magnitude of changes while quantifying uncertainty.

Seasonal decomposition separates temporal patterns into trend, seasonal, and irregular components to understand the different sources of variation in bias metrics over time. This decomposition helps distinguish between systematic bias changes and normal variation due to business cycles or other factors.

Intervention analysis evaluates whether organizational interventions successfully reduced bias by comparing pre- and post-intervention bias metrics while accounting for other factors that might affect outcomes. This analysis requires careful attention to confounding factors and may benefit from quasi-experimental designs.

Time series forecasting enables organizations to predict future bias patterns based on historical data and planned interventions. These forecasts can guide resource allocation and intervention planning while providing early warning systems for emerging problems.

7.9.2.1 Advanced Temporal Analysis Methods

State space modeling approaches treat bias patterns as evolving processes that may be influenced by observable and unobservable factors over time. These models can provide more sophisticated understanding of bias evolution while enabling prediction and intervention planning.

Regime switching models allow bias patterns to exhibit different characteristics during different time periods, potentially corresponding to different organizational policies, market conditions, or regulatory environments. These models can automatically detect shifts between different bias regimes.

Panel data analysis examines bias patterns across multiple organizations, geographic regions, or system deployments simultaneously, enabling understanding of both temporal and cross-sectional variation in discrimination patterns.

Survival analysis techniques can examine the duration of bias patterns and identify factors that predict when bias problems are likely to emerge or resolve. These approaches can guide intervention timing and resource allocation decisions.

7.9.2.2 Legal Documentation for Temporal Analysis

Temporal bias analysis provides particularly strong evidence for legal proceedings because it can establish timelines that correlate with organizational decisions, policy changes, or external events. This temporal correlation helps establish causation rather than mere correlation.

Timeline documentation carefully establishes the chronological sequence of events, policy changes, system updates, and bias pattern changes to support causal arguments. This documentation often becomes crucial in legal proceedings where establishing organizational responsibility is important.

Before-and-after analysis of policy changes or system updates provides natural experiments that can support strong causal inference about the effects of organizational decisions on bias patterns. These analyses often provide compelling evidence for both plaintiffs and defendants in discrimination cases.

External event correlation examines whether bias patterns changed in response to external events such as economic changes, regulatory updates, or social movements. Understanding these correlations helps establish the broader context of discrimination patterns.

7.10 PERFORMANCE ANALYSIS METHODS

Performance analysis evaluates whether AI systems meet their intended objectives while identifying systematic failures, bias patterns, and emerging problems that may indicate quality degradation, security threats, or operational issues. Unlike simple accuracy assessment, comprehensive performance analysis examines multiple dimensions of system behavior across different populations, time periods, and operational contexts to provide holistic understanding of system effectiveness and identify patterns that require organizational attention.

This comprehensive approach requires understanding not only what constitutes good performance for specific applications, but also how performance variations across demographic groups, time periods, and usage contexts may indicate bias, quality problems, or other issues requiring remediation. The foundation of comprehensive performance assessment lies in establishing clear performance objectives that reflect both technical capabilities and business requirements while accounting for legal and ethical constraints.

7.10.1 Multi-Dimensional Performance Metric Development

The development of appropriate performance metrics for AI systems requires consideration of multiple dimensions that collectively capture system behavior. While single metrics provide valuable insights into specific aspects of performance, comprehensive evaluation typically employs carefully designed metric suites that balance coverage with interpretability.

7.10.1.1 Technical Performance Objectives and Foundations

Technical performance objectives focus on quantifiable measures that demonstrate how well AI systems achieve their intended functions. These measures—including accuracy, precision, recall, and calibration—provide the foundation for assessment while requiring interpretation within broader business and societal contexts.

Accuracy-based metrics serve as starting points for performance assessment, though each metric type carries inherent limitations that influence interpretation. Classification accuracy measures the proportion of correct predictions across all cases, providing a straightforward assessment of overall performance. Mean squared error quantifies the average prediction error for continuous outputs, offering insight into typical deviation from true values. The area under the ROC curve evaluates classification performance across different decision thresholds, revealing how systems balance true positive and false positive rates.

These foundational metrics establish baseline expectations for model behavior and contextualize more detailed analyses. However, aggregate performance measures often obscure systematic disparities affecting specific populations. Disaggregated analysis reveals discriminatory patterns that aggregate metrics would miss—patterns that frequently trigger legal scrutiny or violate ethical guidelines.

7.10.1.2 Precision and Recall Analysis

The relationship between precision and recall becomes particularly significant when different error types carry different consequences. Precision measures the proportion of positive predictions that prove correct, indicating how often the system is right when it flags something as positive. Recall measures the proportion of actual positive cases the system identifies, showing how comprehensive the detection is.

Consider a medical diagnostic AI achieving 95% overall accuracy. If this system exhibits 60% sensitivity (recall) for detecting a condition in elderly patients while maintaining 90% sensitivity for younger populations, the disparity creates serious clinical risks that overall accuracy alone would not reveal. These differences require separate analysis of true positive and false positive rates across demographic groups to understand differential error impacts.

The trade-off between precision and recall varies with application context. Fraud detection systems might prioritize high recall to catch most fraudulent transactions, accepting lower precision that generates more false alarms. Conversely, medical treatment recommendation systems might prioritize high precision to avoid recommending unnecessary procedures, even if this means missing some cases that could benefit.

7.10.1.3 Calibration and Confidence Assessment

Calibration metrics evaluate whether predicted probabilities accurately reflect actual outcome likelihoods across different populations and score ranges. Well-calibrated models assign confidence scores that align with actual accuracy rates—when a model predicts 80% probability, the positive outcome should occur approximately 80% of the time across many similar predictions.

Poor calibration creates decision-making challenges even when classification accuracy remains high. Human decision-makers who rely on AI confidence scores may make inappropriate choices if those scores systematically overstate or understate actual probabilities. A loan approval system that appears 90% confident in rejections that prove incorrect 40% of the time misleads loan officers about decision reliability.

Calibration analysis conducted separately for different demographic groups often reveals systematic differences in confidence assessment. These patterns indicate bias in how the system evaluates its own uncertainty across populations, potentially affecting downstream decision-making in discriminatory ways.

Expected calibration error provides a quantitative measure by calculating the average difference between predicted probabilities and observed frequencies across confidence ranges. This metric captures overall calibration quality while reliability diagrams offer visual assessment of calibration patterns, highlighting specific confidence ranges where problems concentrate.

7.10.1.4 Fairness and Robustness Metrics Integration

Fairness metrics quantify equitable treatment across demographic groups while accounting for legitimate differences in underlying characteristics. The selection of fairness metrics significantly influences conclusions about system performance, as different fairness definitions often conflict mathematically.

Demographic parity examines whether positive outcomes occur at similar rates across groups, regardless of underlying differences. Equalized odds evaluates whether true positive and false positive rates remain consistent across groups. Individual fairness assesses whether similar individuals receive similar treatment. Each metric captures different aspects of fair treatment, and systems rarely satisfy all simultaneously.

Robustness metrics assess performance stability under varying conditions, including unusual inputs, adversarial attacks, or distributional shifts. Systems demonstrating strong performance in controlled testing environments may exhibit vulnerabilities when encountering edge cases or deliberately crafted inputs designed to exploit weaknesses.

Distribution shift analysis examines how performance changes when deployment data differs from training data characteristics. Adversarial robustness testing evaluates resistance to intentionally crafted inputs. Stress testing explores performance under extreme but legitimate input conditions. These assessments reveal whether strong baseline performance extends to challenging real-world scenarios.

User experience metrics capture effectiveness from the end-user perspective, measuring factors like decision-making support quality, interface usability, and explanation clarity. Technical performance measures often correlate weakly with user satisfaction or system adoption rates, necessitating additional metrics focused on user-centric dimensions.

7.10.1.5 Business Performance Integration

Business performance objectives translate technical capabilities into organizational value by incorporating factors like operational cost, processing efficiency, user satisfaction, and strategic alignment. These metrics bridge the gap between technical achievement and practical utility.

A hiring AI system achieving high technical accuracy might still fail organizationally if it creates processing delays, generates recommendations hiring managers find opaque, or increases administrative burden. Understanding these broader impacts requires metrics that extend beyond pure predictive performance.

Cost-benefit analysis incorporates economic consequences of different decision outcomes, identifying performance thresholds that optimize overall value rather than simple accuracy. This analysis recognizes that false positive and false negative errors often carry different costs, and these costs may vary across affected populations.

For example, in medical screening, missing a serious condition (false negative) typically carries higher cost than ordering unnecessary follow-up tests (false positive). However, if follow-up procedures pose significant risk or burden for certain populations, the relative costs shift. Performance metrics that incorporate these differential impacts provide more actionable guidance than uniform accuracy measures.

Operational efficiency metrics track system resource usage, processing time, and scalability characteristics. These measures determine whether technically capable systems can meet practical deployment requirements within organizational constraints. A highly accurate model requiring extensive computational resources might prove less valuable than a slightly less accurate but more efficient alternative.

Integration complexity metrics assess how readily AI systems integrate with existing organizational workflows and systems. Technical excellence provides limited value if implementation requires extensive infrastructure changes or workflow disruptions that organizations cannot accommodate.

7.10.2 Demographic Subgroup Performance Analysis

Understanding how AI system performance varies across different demographic groups provides crucial insights into potential bias while helping organizations ensure that their systems serve all users effectively. This analysis requires careful attention to both statistical methodology and practical interpretation to distinguish between concerning disparities and legitimate performance variations.

7.10.2.1 Statistical Foundation for Subgroup Analysis

The design of demographic subgroup analysis should account for intersectional identities while managing the statistical challenges created by small sample sizes in specific demographic categories. Individuals with multiple protected characteristics may experience compound disadvantages that are not apparent when examining single demographic dimensions independently.

Sample size considerations become particularly acute when examining performance for specific intersectional groups such as elderly disabled women or young Latino men. These groups may have very small sample sizes in typical datasets, requiring careful statistical techniques that can provide meaningful insights despite limited data.

Statistical power analysis helps determine whether observed performance differences represent meaningful disparities or random variation due to sampling limitations. Negative findings indicating no significant performance differences require careful interpretation when statistical power is insufficient to detect meaningful disparities.

Statistical significance testing determines whether observed performance differences represent systematic disparities rather than random variation. Effect size calculation quantifies the practical significance of identified disparities, helping investigators understand whether differences are large enough to create meaningful real-world impact.

7.10.2.2 Practical Significance Assessment

Practical significance assessment evaluates whether statistically significant performance differences represent meaningful disparities that require remediation or trivial differences that lack real-world impact. The threshold for practical significance varies across application domains and legal frameworks.

Healthcare applications require particular sensitivity to clinical significance rather than just statistical significance. A diagnostic AI that shows 95% accuracy for most patients but only 85% accuracy for a particular demographic group might exhibit a statistically significant difference that has profound implications for patient care and safety.

Financial services applications navigate complex regulatory requirements that vary by product type, customer segment, and jurisdiction. Fair lending laws provide specific frameworks for evaluating bias in credit decisions, but these frameworks may not apply directly to other financial AI applications such as fraud detection or investment recommendations.

Employment applications face anti-discrimination laws that establish specific requirements for demonstrating business necessity and job-relatedness. Statistical patterns that might be acceptable in other contexts could violate employment law if they disproportionately affect protected groups without clear business justification.

7.10.2.3 Benchmarking and Comparative Analysis

Benchmarking against human performance provides context for evaluating whether AI system performance disparities represent improvements or degradations compared to traditional decision-making processes. AI systems that exhibit performance disparities may still represent improvements over human decision-makers who exhibit larger or more systematic biases.

Historical baseline comparison examines whether current performance disparities represent improvements, degradations, or continuations of historical patterns. Understanding historical context helps distinguish between newly introduced bias and persistent patterns that may require different remediation approaches.

Industry benchmarking compares performance patterns against industry standards or competitor systems to understand whether identified disparities represent organization-specific problems or industry-wide patterns that may indicate systemic issues requiring regulatory attention.

7.10.3 Temporal Performance Tracking and Drift Detection

AI system performance often changes over time due to model updates, data distribution shifts, environmental changes, and other factors that require ongoing monitoring and analysis. Understanding these temporal patterns provides insights into system stability while identifying emerging problems that require intervention.

7.10.3.1 Longitudinal Performance Analysis Framework

Longitudinal performance analysis tracks how key performance metrics evolve over time while distinguishing between systematic trends, periodic variations, and random fluctuations. This analysis requires appropriate statistical techniques that can accommodate temporal dependencies and autocorrelation in performance metrics.

Rolling performance metrics track model accuracy, precision, and recall over time using sliding time windows to identify gradual degradation trends that may indicate data drift or model staleness requiring retraining. Investigators establish baseline performance levels from initial deployment, then monitor for systematic deviations that exceed acceptable thresholds for continued operation.

Seasonal performance patterns are documented to distinguish between expected cyclical variations and unexpected performance anomalies requiring investigation. Many AI applications exhibit seasonal patterns due to user behavior changes, economic cycles, or environmental factors that should be understood as normal variation rather than system problems.

Performance stability analysis examines variance in performance metrics over time to identify periods of high volatility that may indicate system instability, data quality problems, or external interference. Stable systems typically show consistent performance with low variance, while unstable systems may alternate between high and low performance in unpredictable patterns.

7.10.3.2 Advanced Drift Detection Methodologies

Drift detection in AI systems requires sophisticated statistical techniques that can identify distributional changes while accounting for normal variation and avoiding false alarms that could lead to unnecessary interventions. The challenge lies in detecting meaningful changes early enough to enable effective response while avoiding excessive sensitivity that creates operational burden.

Model drift detection identifies changes in AI system behavior that may result from distributional shifts in input data, model degradation, or external environmental changes. Drift detection requires establishing baseline performance characteristics and implementing statistical tests that can identify when current performance deviates significantly from baseline expectations.

Concept drift occurs when the underlying relationships between inputs and outputs change over time, potentially degrading model performance even when input distributions remain stable. Detecting concept drift requires monitoring prediction accuracy and other performance metrics while controlling for changes in input characteristics.

Data drift detection focuses on changes in input data distributions that may affect model performance even when underlying relationships remain stable. Statistical process control techniques provide established frameworks for monitoring system behavior and detecting when performance metrics exceed acceptable control limits.

Change point detection algorithms identify specific time points when system behavior shifted significantly, enabling investigators to correlate performance changes with specific events such as model updates, data source changes, or external incidents. Bayesian change point models can simultaneously detect change points and estimate the magnitude of changes while quantifying uncertainty about timing and effect sizes.

7.10.3.3 Quality Degradation Patterns and Analysis

Accuracy degradation represents the most obvious form of quality deterioration but may not be immediately apparent if degradation affects only specific demographic groups or usage contexts. System-wide accuracy metrics may remain stable while accuracy for specific populations deteriorates significantly, requiring subgroup-specific monitoring to detect localized quality problems.

Calibration drift occurs when predicted probabilities become less accurate predictors of actual outcomes, potentially leading to inappropriate decision-making even when classification accuracy remains stable. Calibration monitoring requires tracking the relationship between predicted and observed probabilities across different score ranges and demographic groups.

Consistency degradation involves increasing variability in system outputs for similar inputs, potentially indicating model instability or data quality problems. Consistency monitoring requires establishing baselines for expected output variation and implementing statistical tests that can detect increases in variability.

Response time degradation may indicate system performance problems, increased computational complexity, or infrastructure issues that affect user experience and system utility. Response time monitoring will help account for normal variations due to load patterns while detecting systematic increases that require investigation.

Error pattern analysis examines the types and distributions of errors produced by AI systems to identify systematic patterns that might indicate specific problems. Error pattern changes may indicate drift, bias, or other issues that require targeted remediation approaches.

7.10.4 Root Cause Analysis and Integration Framework

Understanding why performance degradation occurred requires integrating performance analysis findings with insights from training data analysis (Chapter 5), model investigation (Chapter 6), and organizational context (Chapter 3). This integration enables investigators to trace performance problems back to their ultimate sources while developing targeted remediation strategies.

7.10.4.1 Multi-Source Causal Analysis

Training data correlation analysis examines whether performance degradation patterns correspond to known issues in training data quality, representativeness, or bias. Performance problems that disproportionately affect specific demographic groups may trace back to inadequate representation or quality issues in training data for those groups.

Model architecture analysis investigates whether performance degradation results from architectural limitations, hyperparameter choices, or other technical design decisions identified through Chapter 6's model investigation techniques. Understanding these technical factors guides decisions about whether performance problems require model retraining, architectural changes, or alternative approaches.

Organizational factor analysis correlates performance changes with organizational decisions, policy changes, or external pressures identified through stakeholder interviews and documentation analysis. Performance degradation may result from changes in data collection procedures, user training, system configuration, or business processes rather than technical problems with the AI system itself.

Environmental factor analysis examines whether performance degradation results from changes in the operating environment such as user behavior, market conditions, regulatory requirements, or competitive pressures. Understanding these environmental factors helps distinguish between problems that require system changes and those that require organizational adaptation.

7.10.4.2 Integration Methodology and Synthesis

Integration methodology requires systematic correlation analysis that can identify relationships between performance patterns and potential causal factors while accounting for confounding variables and temporal relationships. This analysis often benefits from time series techniques that can identify leading and lagging relationships between different variables.

Timeline synthesis combines performance analysis findings with evidence from other investigation phases to create comprehensive narratives about how performance problems emerged and evolved. These timelines prove essential for legal proceedings and regulatory compliance efforts while providing organizational learning opportunities.

The comprehensive performance analysis framework established in this section provides the foundation for understanding AI system effectiveness while identifying problems that require remediation. The multi-dimensional approach ensures that performance assessment addresses technical accuracy, fairness, temporal stability, and business value while maintaining the rigor necessary for legal and regulatory compliance.

7.11 CONTENT AND SECURITY ANALYSIS

7.11.1 Natural Language Output Analysis and Bias Detection

As AI systems increasingly generate natural language content for customer service, content creation, educational applications, and other communication tasks, specialized content analysis techniques become essential for identifying bias, misinformation, inappropriate content, and other quality issues that may harm users or violate organizational policies. Natural language analysis requires combining computational linguistics approaches with human expert review to capture subtle forms of bias that automated systems might miss.

The complexity of natural language bias detection stems from the nuanced ways that discrimination can manifest in text generation. Unlike numerical outputs where bias may appear as systematic score differences across demographic groups, language bias can emerge through word choice, topic selection, information depth, response length, tone variations, and implicit assumptions that require sophisticated analysis to detect and quantify.

SECTION 7.7.1 NATURAL LANGUAGE OUTPUT ANALYSIS AND BIAS DETECTION

7.11.1.1 Systematic Bias Detection in Generated Content

The challenge of detecting bias in AI-generated text extends far beyond searching for obviously discriminatory language. Modern AI systems can exhibit subtle forms of bias that manifest through word choice patterns, response depth variations, and implicit assumptions about users. These biases often emerge not from explicit programming but from patterns learned during training, making them particularly difficult to identify without systematic analysis.

Consider a customer service chatbot deployed by a major financial institution. On the surface, the system appears to treat all customers equally, providing standardized responses to common queries. However, detailed analysis might reveal that the chatbot provides more detailed explanations of fee structures to customers with traditionally Anglo-Saxon names while offering only basic information to customers with names suggesting other ethnic backgrounds. This differential treatment—invisible in individual interactions—becomes apparent only through systematic analysis of thousands of conversations.

7.11.1.2 Analyzing Language Patterns for Bias

Lexical bias analysis forms the foundation of linguistic bias detection. This approach examines vocabulary distributions across interactions with different demographic groups, looking for systematic variations in word choice, formality levels, and linguistic complexity. When an AI system consistently uses simpler vocabulary or more directive language with certain user groups, it suggests learned biases that affect service quality.

The power of lexical analysis lies in its ability to quantify subtle linguistic differences. By measuring factors like average word length, sentence complexity, and vocabulary diversity across demographic segments, investigators can identify patterns that individual reviewers might never notice. A recruitment screening system, for instance, might use more positive adjectives when describing candidates from certain educational backgrounds, subtly influencing human reviewers even when making identical hiring recommendations.

Sentiment analysis techniques complement lexical analysis by measuring the emotional tone of AI-generated responses. These techniques go beyond simple positive-negative classifications to examine dimensions like warmth, formality, encouragement, and empathy. A healthcare chatbot that expresses more empathy toward patients with certain demographic characteristics while maintaining clinical detachment with others exhibits a form of bias that could significantly impact patient experience and health outcomes.

7.11.1.3 Measuring Response Quality Variations

Topic coverage analysis reveals whether AI systems provide equivalent service quality across different user groups. This analysis examines not just whether systems answer questions correctly, but how thoroughly they address user needs. An educational AI tutor that provides detailed mathematical explanations to male students while offering only formula references to female students perpetuates educational inequities, even if both responses are technically accurate.

Response length and quality metrics provide quantitative measures that complement qualitative assessment. By tracking metrics like response word count, number of examples provided, links to additional resources, and follow-up questions asked, investigators can identify systematic service disparities. These metrics become particularly powerful when combined with outcome data—if users receiving shorter, less detailed responses also show lower satisfaction scores or success rates, the connection between response quality and user impact becomes clear.

The challenge in response quality analysis involves distinguishing between appropriate personalization and inappropriate discrimination. An AI system might legitimately provide different response styles based on user expertise levels or stated preferences. The key lies in ensuring that these variations correlate with relevant user characteristics rather than protected demographic attributes.

7.11.1.4 Detecting Harmful Stereotypes and Assumptions

Stereotype detection in AI-generated content requires sophisticated analysis that goes beyond keyword searching. Modern AI systems rarely produce overtly stereotypical statements; instead, stereotypes manifest through subtle patterns in how systems describe different groups, what examples they provide, and what assumptions they make about user capabilities or interests.

A career counseling AI might never explicitly state that certain professions are more suitable for specific genders, but analysis might reveal that it consistently suggests engineering roles to male users while emphasizing teaching and nursing to female users with identical qualifications. These patterns, repeated across thousands of interactions, reinforce societal stereotypes even without explicit discriminatory statements.

Assumption analysis examines the implicit beliefs that AI systems embed in their responses. These assumptions often appear in seemingly innocent details: the pronouns used in examples, the cultural references selected, or the life experiences presumed. When a financial advisory AI consistently assumes home ownership when providing advice to white users while discussing rental scenarios with Black users of similar income levels, it reveals learned biases that affect service quality and relevance.

7.11.1.5 Advanced Content Quality Assessment

While bias detection focuses on differential treatment across user groups, content quality assessment examines whether AI-generated content meets accuracy, safety, and appropriateness standards regardless of who receives it. These quality issues can harm users directly through misinformation or inappropriate content, making their detection essential for responsible AI deployment. Organizations deploying AI systems need systematic approaches to identify and mitigate these risks before they cause harm.

The complexity of content quality assessment stems from the diverse ways that AI systems can produce problematic content. A single system might generate medically dangerous advice, promote conspiracy theories, include hate speech, or encourage self-harm—each requiring specialized detection approaches and subject matter expertise. Table 7.3 outlines the primary categories of content quality issues, their detection methods, and the expertise required for effective identification.

Each quality dimension requires tailored detection strategies that balance automated analysis with human expertise. Factual accuracy checking might leverage automated fact-checking APIs for initial screening, followed by expert review for claims in specialized domains. Medical misinformation detection demands involvement from healthcare professionals who can identify subtle inaccuracies that automated systems might miss. Hate speech detection requires constant updates as harmful actors develop new coded language to evade detection.

The interplay between different quality dimensions adds complexity to assessment efforts. Content that appears factually accurate might become harmful when presented without proper context—accurate information about dangerous chemicals becomes problematic when combined with instructions that could enable harm. Similarly, content appropriate for academic discussion might be inappropriate in a customer service context. Effective quality assessment considers these interdependencies rather than evaluating each dimension in isolation.

Organizations implementing content quality assessment face the challenge of balancing comprehensive coverage with practical resource constraints. While ideal assessment would involve expert review of all generated content, practical systems typically employ tiered approaches: automated screening for obvious issues, sampling-based expert review for quality assurance, and detailed investigation when problems are suspected. This tiered approach allows organizations to maintain quality standards while managing assessment costs.

TABLE 7.3

Quality Dimension	Detection Approach	Required Expertise	Risk Indicators
Factual Accuracy	Cross-reference with authoritative databases, expert review panels, claim verification systems	Domain experts, fact-checking professionals	Unverified claims, outdated information, logical contradictions
Source Attribution	Citation analysis, reference validation, plagiarism detection	Information literacy specialists, librarians	Missing citations, fabricated sources, improper attribution
Content Coherence	Logical flow analysis, consistency checking, contradiction detection	Subject matter experts, technical writers	Topic drift, self-contradiction, non-sequiturs
Medical Misinformation	Clinical guideline comparison, medical expert review, drug interaction checking	Licensed medical professionals, pharmacists	Dangerous treatments, unproven remedies, dosage errors
Financial Misinformation	Regulatory compliance checking, financial expert review, market data validation	Financial advisors, compliance officers	Unlicensed advice, pyramid schemes, unrealistic promises
Hate Speech	Pattern matching with evolving hate speech databases, context-aware classification, human review	Content moderation specialists, civil rights experts	Dehumanizing language, calls to violence, dog whistles
Self-Harm Content	Trigger phrase detection, context analysis, escalation pattern recognition	Mental health professionals, crisis counselors	Method descriptions, encouragement, normalization
Conspiracy Theories	Narrative pattern matching, source credibility analysis, claim debunking	Misinformation researchers, journalists	False flag claims, science denial, extremist narratives
Contextual Appropriateness	Audience analysis, cultural sensitivity review, age-appropriateness checking	Educators, cultural consultants, child development specialists	Adult content for minors, cultural insensitivity, professional boundary violations

7.11.2 Security Analysis and Manipulation Detection

AI systems face numerous security threats that may manifest in unusual output patterns, requiring specialized analysis techniques that can detect manipulation attempts, adversarial attacks, prompt injection, and other security vulnerabilities. Security-focused output analysis differs from performance analysis by focusing specifically on intentional attempts to compromise system behavior rather than natural performance degradation.

7.11.2.1 Adversarial Attack Detection and Analysis

Adversarial attacks attempt to manipulate AI system behavior through carefully crafted inputs designed to cause misclassification, inappropriate responses, or other unintended behaviors. Detecting these attacks requires understanding common attack vectors while implementing monitoring systems that can identify unusual patterns in system inputs and outputs.

Input perturbation detection examines whether AI systems receive inputs that have been subtly modified to cause misclassification or inappropriate responses. These modifications are often imperceptible to human users but can dramatically affect AI system behavior, requiring specialized detection techniques that can identify artificial input characteristics.

Output anomaly detection uses statistical methods to identify outputs that are unusual or inconsistent with normal system behavior patterns. Adversarial attacks often produce outputs that are statistically unusual compared to normal system operation, enabling detection through anomaly detection techniques adapted to the specific characteristics of different AI systems.

Behavioral signature analysis examines patterns in system usage that might indicate adversarial probing or systematic attempts to identify system vulnerabilities. Attackers often conduct reconnaissance activities that create detectable patterns in system interaction logs, query sequences, or error patterns.

Adversarial robustness assessment evaluates how AI systems respond to known adversarial attack techniques from security research literature. This assessment involves systematic testing with established adversarial examples to understand system vulnerabilities while developing defensive measures.

Response consistency analysis examines whether AI systems provide stable outputs for inputs that should produce similar results. Adversarial attacks may cause systems to produce dramatically different outputs for seemingly similar inputs, creating detectable inconsistencies.

Confidence score analysis investigates whether adversarial attacks affect the confidence scores or uncertainty estimates provided by AI systems. Attacks that successfully manipulate outputs might also affect confidence estimates in detectable ways.

7.11.2.2 Prompt Injection and Manipulation Analysis

Large language models and other AI systems that process natural language instructions face unique vulnerabilities from prompt injection attacks that attempt to override system instructions or extract sensitive information. Detecting these attacks requires understanding evolving attack techniques while implementing monitoring systems adapted to natural language interaction patterns.

Instruction override detection identifies attempts to use special commands, formatting tricks, or persuasive language to cause AI systems to ignore their original instructions and follow attacker-provided directives. These attacks often involve specific phrases or formatting patterns that can be detected through pattern matching and behavioral analysis.

Information extraction detection monitors attempts to use prompts that might cause AI systems to reveal training data, system configuration information, or other sensitive details that should not be accessible to users. These attempts often follow recognizable patterns that can be detected through automated monitoring.

Role-playing exploitation detection identifies attempts to use fictional scenarios or role-playing prompts to manipulate AI systems into producing inappropriate content or ignoring safety constraints. These attacks often involve elaborate fictional contexts designed to bypass content filters.

Context manipulation detection examines attempts to use misleading context or false premises to cause AI systems to produce biased, harmful, or inappropriate responses. These attacks often involve subtle manipulations of conversation context that require sophisticated detection techniques.

Social engineering detection identifies attempts to use psychological manipulation techniques to influence AI system behavior, such as appeals to authority, urgency, or emotional manipulation designed to bypass normal system constraints.

7.11.2.3 System Compromise and Backdoor Detection

AI systems may be compromised through various means including model poisoning, backdoor insertion, or infrastructure compromise that affects system behavior in subtle but systematic ways. Detecting these compromises requires understanding both technical attack vectors and the behavioral patterns they create.

Model behavior deviation analysis compares current system behavior with established baselines to identify systematic changes that might indicate compromise. These changes may be subtle and affect only specific types of inputs or contexts, requiring sophisticated monitoring and analysis techniques.

Backdoor trigger detection examines whether AI systems exhibit unusual behavior when presented with specific trigger patterns that might activate hidden functionality. Backdoor detection requires systematic testing with potential trigger patterns while monitoring for unusual system responses.

Training data influence analysis examines whether system outputs suggest exposure to training data that was not part of the official training process, potentially indicating data poisoning or unauthorized training data injection.

Infrastructure compromise detection examines system logs, network traffic, and other technical indicators that might suggest unauthorized access to AI system infrastructure. These indicators might correlate with changes in system behavior that affect output patterns.

7.11.2.4 Supply Chain Security Analysis

Modern AI systems often incorporate components from multiple vendors, open-source projects, and third-party services that create complex supply chain security challenges. Output analysis can help identify security issues that emerge from compromised supply chain components.

Third-party component behavior analysis examines whether AI systems exhibit behavior that might result from compromised libraries, pre-trained models, or other third-party components. This analysis requires understanding normal component behavior and identifying deviations that might indicate security issues.

Dependency vulnerability assessment examines whether AI systems use components with known security vulnerabilities that might affect system behavior or enable compromise. This assessment requires ongoing monitoring of security advisories and vulnerability databases.

Update and patch analysis examines whether changes in system behavior correlate with updates to third-party components, potentially indicating security issues introduced through the software supply chain.

7.12 ANALYZING AI-GENERATED CONTENT OUTPUT

7.12.1 When the AI Creates Rather Than Classifies: Understanding Generative Output Patterns

While traditional AI forensics focuses on classification decisions and predictive outputs, the explosion of generative AI systems—from language models to image generators—requires specialized analytical techniques. When a content generation system produces biased narratives, generates harmful content, or exhibits inconsistent quality, the evidence lies not in binary decisions but in the nuanced patterns of created content itself.

Consider the investigation of a major news organization's AI writing assistant that consistently portrayed women in passive roles while describing men as active decision-makers, regardless of the actual context. The bias wasn't visible in simple approval/denial metrics but emerged through systematic analysis of linguistic patterns, semantic roles, and narrative structures across thousands of generated articles. This case illustrates how generative AI forensics requires techniques that can detect subtle patterns in unstructured content while maintaining the statistical rigor needed for organizational accountability.

7.12.2 Taxonomies of Generative Output Analysis

7.12.2.1 Content Quality Assessment Frameworks

Generative AI systems produce outputs that vary dramatically in quality, accuracy, and appropriateness. Unlike classification systems where success metrics are clearly defined (accuracy, precision, recall), generative systems require multi-dimensional quality assessment that can capture both objective measures and subjective human judgments.

Factual accuracy analysis forms the foundation of content quality assessment, particularly for systems that claim to provide information rather than creative content. This analysis requires systematic fact-checking against authoritative sources while accounting for the temporal nature of factual claims and the complexity of assessing claims that fall into gray areas of interpretation.

Automated fact-checking techniques can provide initial screening by comparing generated claims against knowledge bases, but human review remains essential for nuanced factual assessment. The key challenge lies in developing systematic sampling strategies that capture the full range of factual claims while maintaining feasible review workloads.

Coherence and consistency metrics evaluate whether generated content maintains logical flow and remains consistent with established facts or narrative elements. For technical documentation, this might involve checking whether generated procedures are internally consistent and technically feasible. For creative content, this analysis focuses on narrative coherence and character consistency.

Computational approaches to coherence assessment include discourse analysis techniques that examine topic progression, entity coreference resolution to track consistent entity references, and logical consistency checking for procedural content. These automated approaches provide scalable screening but require human validation for complex coherence issues.

Appropriateness and safety assessment evaluates whether generated content meets organizational standards for appropriate communication while avoiding harmful, offensive, or legally problematic content. This assessment requires clear policy frameworks that define organizational standards while accounting for contextual appropriateness.

Content safety analysis addresses both explicit policy violations (profanity, discriminatory language, dangerous instructions) and subtle problems (implicit bias, cultural insensitivity, inappropriate tone). The challenge lies in developing assessment criteria that are specific enough to guide consistent evaluation while flexible enough to handle contextual nuances.

Figure 7.2 presents the comprehensive multi-modal framework that investigators can employ when analyzing potentially AI-generated content across different media types. This taxonomy addresses the fundamental challenge that modern AI systems can generate sophisticated content across text, code, images, and video that may require specialized detection approaches for each modality. The framework integrates linguistic analysis techniques for text content with structural pattern recognition for code, technical artifact detection for images, and temporal consistency analysis for video content. Understanding this taxonomy enables investigators to select appropriate detection methodologies based on content type while recognizing that sophisticated AI-generated content often requires analysis across multiple dimensions to achieve reliable identification with the confidence levels necessary for forensic proceedings.

7.12.3 Bias Detection in Generated Content

7.12.3.1 Linguistic Bias Pattern Recognition

Generated text exhibits bias through linguistic patterns that may be subtle but systematic. Unlike classification bias that manifests in different outcomes for similar inputs, textual bias appears in the language choices, narrative structures, and semantic associations within generated content.

Semantic role analysis examines how different demographic groups are portrayed in generated narratives, focusing on agency, action, and descriptive language. Women might consistently appear as passive recipients of action while men appear as active agents, even when the underlying facts would support different portrayals.

Advanced semantic role labeling tools can automate initial screening by identifying subject-verb-object relationships and semantic roles across large text corpora. However, subtle bias patterns often require human analysis that can recognize implicit bias in language choices that appear superficially neutral.

Sentiment and emotional valence analysis reveals whether generated content consistently associates positive or negative emotional content with particular demographic groups. A travel AI might consistently describe majority-white destinations with positive emotional language while using more neutral or negative language for destinations associated with other demographic groups.

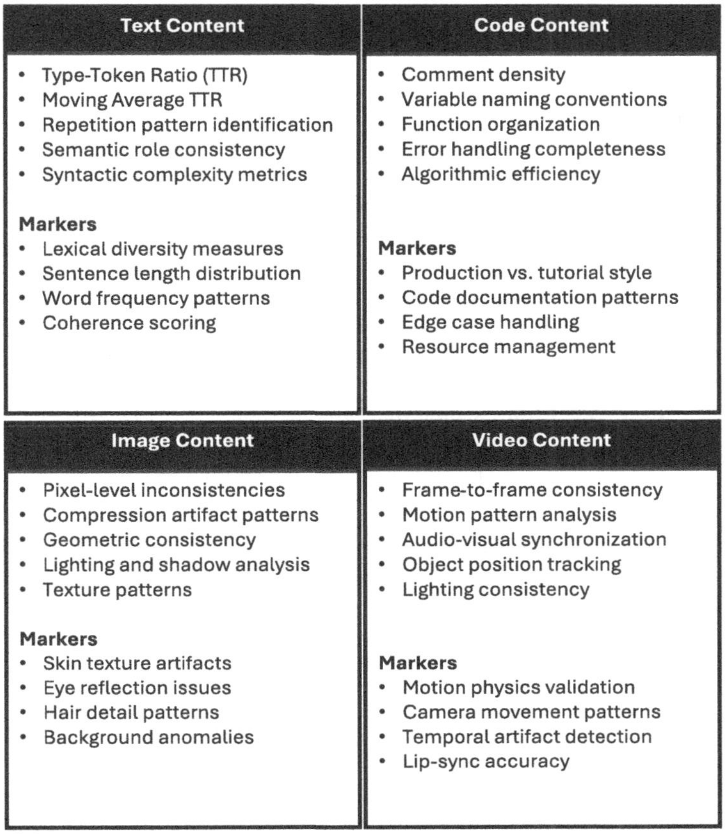

FIGURE 7.2

Computational sentiment analysis provides quantitative assessment of emotional valence across demographic comparisons, but requires careful calibration to ensure that sentiment models don't themselves reflect biased training data. Cross-validation with human assessment helps identify cases where automated sentiment analysis fails to capture relevant emotional patterns.

Association and stereotype analysis identifies whether generated content perpetuates or amplifies stereotypical associations between demographic characteristics and particular traits, behaviors, or outcomes. This analysis requires systematic examination of how different groups are described and what characteristics are consistently associated with different identities.

Word embedding analysis can reveal implicit associations in generated content by examining the semantic relationships between demographic terms and descriptive language. However, these technical approaches must be supplemented with domain expertise that can interpret whether observed associations reflect legitimate contextual factors or problematic stereotyping.

7.12.4 Sample Output Analysis Methodology

7.12.4.1 Systematic Sampling for Content Analysis

Effective analysis of generative AI output requires sampling strategies that capture the full range of system behavior while maintaining feasible analysis workloads. Unlike classification outputs where individual decisions can be analyzed independently, generated content often requires contextual analysis that considers longer text segments or complete generated pieces.

Stratified content sampling ensures representation across different content types, user demographics, prompt categories, and system configurations. A customer service AI might produce different types of bias in responses to billing inquiries versus technical support requests, requiring stratified sampling across interaction types.

The stratification strategy needs to balance comprehensiveness with analysis feasibility. Too many strata can lead to inadequate sample sizes within individual categories, while too few strata might miss important bias patterns that only appear in specific contexts.

Temporal sampling considerations address how system behavior changes over time due to model updates, changing user patterns, or evolving input distributions. Generative systems may exhibit drift in output quality or bias patterns that only becomes apparent through longitudinal analysis.

Systematic temporal sampling requires careful balance between granular time-series analysis and practical analysis constraints. Monthly sampling might miss short-term problems while daily sampling might prove infeasible for comprehensive content analysis.

Representative input selection ensures that content analysis covers the full range of prompts and contexts that users encounter in practice. Analysis based only on carefully crafted test prompts might miss bias patterns that emerge from real-world usage patterns.

Input selection strategies should be designed to account for proprietary information and user privacy while ensuring that analysis captures genuine system behavior. Synthetic prompt generation can supplement real user data but requires validation to ensure that synthetic prompts elicit similar system behavior to real usage.

7.12.5 Interpretation Frameworks for Generated Content

7.12.5.1 Contextual Bias Assessment

Generated content bias requires interpretation frameworks that account for legitimate contextual differences while identifying inappropriate discrimination. A medical AI that generates different treatment recommendations for different demographic groups might reflect appropriate medical care based on differential health risks rather than inappropriate bias.

Domain-specific expertise integration ensures that bias assessment reflects genuine understanding of appropriate content variation within specific application domains. Financial content might legitimately vary based on creditworthiness factors that correlate with demographics, while educational content should generally avoid demographic-based variation in learning assessments.

Expert review panels provide domain-specific context for interpreting content analysis findings while ensuring that bias assessment reflects current professional standards and ethical frameworks. However, expert review need to be structured to avoid introducing additional bias through inconsistent application of judgment criteria.

Cultural and community perspectives validate technical bias findings against the lived experiences of affected communities. Content that appears statistically unbiased might still perpetuate harmful stereotypes or fail to represent community values appropriately.

Community engagement requires careful design to ensure representative participation while protecting participant privacy and avoiding additional harm through the review process itself. Structured feedback sessions can provide systematic community input while maintaining consistency across different demographic groups.

7.12.6 Quality Metrics and Performance Indicators

7.12.6.1 Multi-Dimensional Quality Assessment

Generative AI quality extends beyond simple accuracy metrics to encompass readability, usefulness, creativity, and adherence to style guidelines. Comprehensive quality assessment requires frameworks that can capture these multiple dimensions while providing actionable feedback for system improvement.

Readability and accessibility metrics ensure that generated content meets accessibility standards for intended audiences. Technical documentation should match complexity levels appropriate for target users, while customer communications should maintain clarity standards that ensure broad comprehension.

Automated readability assessment tools provide scalable quality screening but require validation against human comprehension testing. Flesch-Kincaid scores and similar metrics offer useful baselines but may not capture accessibility barriers specific to particular domains or user populations.

Task-specific utility assessment evaluates whether generated content successfully accomplishes intended objectives. Customer service responses should resolve inquiries effectively, while marketing content should engage target audiences appropriately.

Utility assessment often requires longitudinal analysis that tracks user behavior and outcomes following content consumption. A/B testing frameworks can provide controlled comparison of content effectiveness while accounting for confounding factors that might influence outcome measures.

Style and brand consistency analysis ensures that generated content maintains organizational voice and meets brand standards. Inconsistent style can undermine user trust and organizational credibility, particularly when users can detect that content is AI-generated.

Style consistency requires clear organizational guidelines that define acceptable language, tone, and formatting standards. Computational style analysis can provide scalable monitoring while human review ensures that automated assessment captures subtle style issues that affect user experience.

7.12.7 Integration with Broader Investigation Framework

7.12.7.1 Connecting Content Patterns to System Architecture

Understanding why generative systems produce particular content patterns requires integration with model investigation findings that reveal architectural choices and training influences. Content bias might emerge from training data characteristics, architectural design decisions, or fine-tuning processes that shape system behavior.

Training data correlation analysis links content bias patterns to training data characteristics identified through Chapter 5's investigation techniques. Underrepresentation of particular demographic groups in training data might manifest as stereotypical or inaccurate portrayals in generated content.

This correlation analysis guides remediation strategies by identifying whether content problems require training data improvements, architectural changes, or post-processing interventions. Different root causes require different solutions, making accurate causal analysis essential for effective problem resolution.

Model behavior validation compares content analysis findings with systematic model testing results from Chapter 6 to validate laboratory findings against real-world behavior. Controlled testing might reveal bias patterns that correlate with observed content problems, providing confidence in both testing methodologies and practical significance.

This validation process helps establish the reliability of laboratory testing for predicting real-world system behavior while identifying cases where deployment context significantly influences system outputs compared to controlled testing environments.

Organizational impact assessment translates content analysis findings into business impact assessment that considers user experience, brand reputation, legal risk, and operational efficiency. Understanding the organizational significance of content problems guides prioritization of remediation efforts and resource allocation decisions.

Impact assessment accounts for both direct consequences of poor content quality and indirect effects including user trust, regulatory attention, and competitive positioning. Long-term organizational implications may justify significant remediation investments even when immediate costs appear manageable.

7.12.8 Identifying AI-Generated Writing: Linguistic Fingerprints and Statistical Patterns

AI-generated text exhibits characteristic patterns that trained analysts can identify through systematic examination. While sophisticated AI systems increasingly produce human-like content, several linguistic and statistical markers provide reliable detection signals when applied systematically.

Figure 7.3 details a systematic five-stage process for detecting AI-generated text through statistical and linguistic analysis, providing investigators with specific metrics and thresholds that can be applied consistently across different text types and domains. The pipeline progresses from basic preprocessing through increasingly sophisticated analysis techniques, culminating in statistical validation that provides the confidence levels required for legal proceedings. This approach addresses the challenge that sophisticated AI text generation systems increasingly produce human-like content, requiring investigators to employ multiple statistical measures simultaneously rather than relying on single indicators that may be insufficient for definitive identification.

7.12.8.1 Lexical Diversity and Repetition Patterns

AI-generated text often exhibits lower lexical diversity than human writing, with subtle but measurable tendencies toward word repetition and formulaic phrasing. Human writers naturally vary their vocabulary and sentence structures in ways that AI systems may struggle to replicate consistently.

Type-token ratio (TTR) analysis measures vocabulary richness by comparing unique words to total words. AI-generated content frequently shows TTR values outside typical human ranges, particularly in longer texts where repetitive patterns become more apparent.

Moving average type-token ratio (MATTR) provides more stable measurements across different text lengths by calculating TTR over sliding windows. MATTR values below 0.72 or above 0.85 for academic writing often indicate AI generation, though thresholds vary by domain and text type.

7.12.8.2 Sentence-Level Uniformity Detection

AI systems often produce sentences with unnaturally consistent length distributions and syntactic complexity patterns. Human writing typically shows more variation in sentence structure, length, and complexity than AI-generated content.

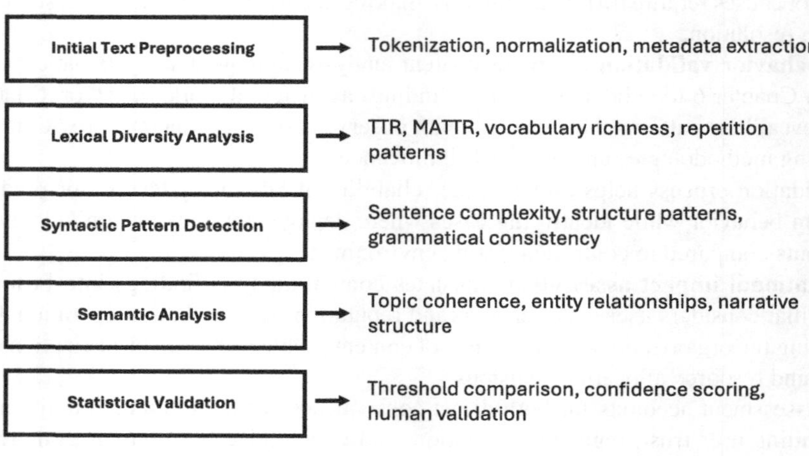

FIGURE 7.3

Syntactic complexity metrics, including mean dependency distance, syntactic tree depth, and clause embedding levels can reveal AI generation patterns. AI text often maintains consistent complexity levels rather than the natural variation found in human writing.

Transitional phrase analysis examines connector words and phrases between sentences and paragraphs. AI systems often overuse certain transitional phrases ("Furthermore," "Moreover," "In addition") while underusing others that humans employ naturally.

7.12.8.3 Semantic Coherence and Knowledge Consistency

AI-generated content may exhibit subtle inconsistencies in factual claims or logical reasoning that human writers would naturally avoid. These inconsistencies emerge from the statistical nature of AI text generation rather than genuine understanding.

Entity consistency checking tracks how people, places, organizations, and concepts are referenced throughout a text. AI generation may introduce subtle inconsistencies in entity attributes or relationships that careful analysis can detect.

Temporal logic analysis examines whether time references and causal relationships maintain logical consistency throughout the text. AI systems may generate content with subtle temporal inconsistencies that indicate statistical rather than logical text construction.

7.12.8.4 Example Analysis: Detecting AI-Generated Academic Writing

Consider this sample paragraph submitted as part of a graduate research paper:

> Artificial intelligence represents a transformative paradigm shift in contemporary technological advancement, fundamentally altering the landscape of computational methodologies. Furthermore, machine learning algorithms demonstrate unprecedented capabilities in pattern recognition tasks. Moreover, deep neural networks exhibit remarkable performance across diverse application domains. In addition, the implementation of AI systems necessitates careful consideration of ethical implications and societal impact. Additionally, the integration of artificial intelligence into existing technological infrastructure requires comprehensive evaluation of potential risks and benefits.

Detection Analysis Output:

LEXICAL DIVERSITY ANALYSIS:

- Type-Token Ratio: 0.79 (HIGH—suggests possible AI)
- MATTR (50-word window): 0.83 (HIGH—outside typical human range)
- Hapax Legomena Ratio: 0.71 (ELEVATED—indicates formulaic language)

SENTENCE STRUCTURE ANALYSIS:

- Mean sentence length: 23.4 words (CONSISTENT—low variation)
- Sentence length variance: 2.1 (LOW—unnaturally uniform)
- Syntactic complexity (mean): 4.2 (CONSISTENT—lacks human variation)

TRANSITIONAL PHRASE ANALYSIS:

- Sequential formal transitions: 5/5 sentences (EXCESSIVE—100% usage)
- Transition diversity: 0.2 (LOW—limited variety)
- Formulaic phrase density: 0.31 (HIGH—above human baseline)

SEMANTIC COHERENCE ANALYSIS:

- Topic progression linearity: 0.95 (HIGH—overly structured)
- Conceptual overlap between sentences: 0.73 (ELEVATED)
- Knowledge claim specificity: 0.12 (LOW—vague generalizations)

OVERALL AI DETECTION SCORE: 0.87 (HIGH CONFIDENCE AI-GENERATED)

KEY INDICATORS:

1. Excessive use of formal transitional phrases in sequence
2. Uniform sentence complexity without natural variation
3. High-level generalizations without specific evidence
4. Unnaturally consistent sentence length distribution
5. Limited lexical variation despite technical topic

7.12.8.5 Source Code Detection: Identifying AI-Generated Programming

AI-generated code exhibits distinctive patterns in commenting, variable naming, error handling, and structural organization that differ from typical human programming practices.

7.12.8.6 Variable Naming Pattern Analysis

AI-generated code often uses overly descriptive or unnecessarily generic variable names, reflecting training on tutorial code rather than production systems. Human programmers develop personal naming conventions and context-specific abbreviations that AI systems rarely replicate accurately.

Comment density and style analysis reveals AI generation through unnaturally high comment density, overly explanatory comments for simple operations, or comments that describe what code does rather than why it exists.

Error-handling completeness in AI-generated code often appears either excessively comprehensive (covering unlikely edge cases) or inadequately sparse (missing practical error conditions), reflecting training data biases rather than practical development experience.

Structural organization patterns examine code organization, function length distribution, and architectural decisions. AI-generated code may exhibit patterns that reflect tutorial examples rather than production requirements.

Example: AI-Generated Python Function Analysis

```
def calculate_user_data_statistics(input_data_list):
    """
    This function calculates comprehensive statistical measures
    for user data input list parameter values
    """
    # Initialize result dictionary for storing calculated values
    statistical_results = {}

    # Calculate mean value of input data list
    mean_value = sum(input_data_list)/len(input_data_list)
    statistical_results['mean'] = mean_value

    # Calculate median value of input data list
    sorted_data = sorted(input_data_list)
    median_value = sorted_data[len(sorted_data) // 2]
    statistical_results['median'] = median_value

    # Return dictionary containing calculated statistical values
    return statistical_results
```

AI Detection Analysis:

- **Variable naming**: Overly descriptive, redundant patterns
- **Comment density**: 7 comments for 8 lines of code (excessive)

- **Comment style**: Describes obvious operations rather than purpose
- **Error handling**: Completely absent (no input validation)
- **Algorithmic approach**: Inefficient median calculation
- **Code organization**: Tutorial-style rather than production-ready

7.12.8.7 Media Detection: AI-Generated Images and Videos

Visual AI detection requires technical analysis of pixel-level patterns, compression artifacts, and consistency issues that emerge from current generation techniques.

7.12.8.8 Image Analysis Techniques

Pixel-level inconsistency detection examines subtle variations in pixel patterns that indicate AI generation. Current AI image generators often produce imperceptible artifacts in areas like skin texture, eye reflections, and hair detail.

Compression artifact analysis identifies unusual compression patterns that emerge from AI generation processes. AI-generated images may exhibit compression artifacts that differ from typical camera sensor and processing pipeline artifacts.

Geometric consistency checking examines perspective, lighting, and shadow consistency throughout images. AI generation may produce subtle geometric inconsistencies that careful analysis can detect.

7.12.8.9 Video Analysis Approaches

Temporal consistency analysis examines frame-to-frame consistency in object positions, lighting, and texture patterns. AI-generated videos often exhibit subtle temporal inconsistencies that indicate synthetic generation.

Motion pattern analysis evaluates whether object and camera movements follow physically plausible patterns. AI-generated videos may contain subtle motion artifacts that violate physical constraints.

Audio-visual synchronization in AI-generated videos with speech may exhibit subtle timing inconsistencies between lip movements and audio that indicate synthetic generation.

7.12.9 Operational Detection Frameworks

7.12.9.1 Developing Organizational Detection Capabilities

Organizations need systematic frameworks for identifying AI-generated content while minimizing false positives that could unfairly penalize legitimate human work. Effective detection combines multiple analytical approaches with human judgment and clear organizational policies.

Multi-modal detection pipelines integrate text analysis, code analysis, and media analysis into comprehensive detection systems that can handle mixed-content submissions. Academic institutions, publishing organizations, and content platforms require detection capabilities that work across content types.

Threshold calibration and false positive management ensure that detection systems balance accuracy with fairness considerations. Overly sensitive detection may flag legitimate human work, while insufficient sensitivity fails to identify problematic AI usage.

Human review integration provides expert validation of automated detection findings while ensuring that detection decisions can be appealed and reviewed. Clear procedures for handling detection disputes protect both organizational interests and individual rights.

Policy framework development establishes clear organizational guidelines about acceptable AI usage while providing detection procedures that support policy enforcement. Different organizational contexts require different approaches to AI content policies and detection procedures.

7.13 DOCUMENTATION AND REPORTING STANDARDS

7.13.1 Investigation Documentation Requirements

Effective documentation of output analysis requires systematic approaches that ensure completeness, accuracy, and legal defensibility while supporting multiple audiences including technical reviewers, legal counsel, business stakeholders, and potentially court proceedings. The documentation framework should be established at the beginning of investigation rather than retrofitted after analysis completion.

7.13.1.1 Technical Documentation Standards and Requirements

Technical documentation provides the foundation for all other documentation by establishing the analytical procedures, data sources, and methodological decisions that support investigation findings. This documentation should be sufficiently detailed to enable independent replication while remaining accessible to non-technical audiences who may need to understand and evaluate findings.

7.13.2 Output Analysis Documentation for Defensibility

Output analysis findings should be documented in ways that support their defensibility and enable independent validation while maintaining focus on the analytical procedures and statistical evidence derived from AI system outputs.

7.13.2.1 Analytical Procedure Documentation

Comprehensive documentation of output analysis procedures ensures that findings can be independently validated and that analytical decisions can be justified to stakeholders who need to understand and act on results.

Statistical methodology documentation records all analytical approaches, hypothesis tests, confidence interval calculations, and effect size measures used in output analysis. This documentation should provide sufficient detail for independent analysts to replicate procedures while clearly justifying why specific techniques were chosen for particular analytical questions.

Sampling procedure documentation describes how outputs were selected for analysis, including stratification schemes, temporal sampling approaches, and any targeted sampling strategies used to address specific concerns. This documentation will establish that samples adequately represent the populations of interest while acknowledging any limitations that might affect generalizability.

Data processing documentation records all steps taken to clean, transform, or aggregate output data for analysis. This documentation should include details about missing data handling, outlier treatment, and any data transformations applied to prepare outputs for statistical analysis.

Quality control documentation records all procedures used to verify analytical accuracy including peer review processes, sensitivity analysis results, and independent verification efforts. This documentation demonstrates that appropriate safeguards were implemented to ensure reliable findings.

7.13.2.2 Statistical Evidence Documentation

Output analysis produces statistical evidence that should be documented in ways that enable stakeholders to understand the strength and limitations of findings while supporting organizational decision-making.

Effect size documentation provides clear reporting of the magnitude of identified differences along with confidence intervals that quantify uncertainty. This documentation should translate statistical findings into practical terms that stakeholders can understand and use for decision-making.

Power analysis documentation records the ability of analytical procedures to detect meaningful differences given sample sizes and observed variability. This documentation helps stakeholders understand what size effects could be reliably detected and what limitations might affect negative findings.

Sensitivity analysis documentation records how findings change when analytical assumptions or methodological choices are varied within reasonable ranges. This documentation helps establish the robustness of conclusions while identifying areas where findings depend critically on specific analytical decisions.

7.13.2.3 Reproducibility Standards for Output Analysis

Ensuring that output analysis can be independently reproduced provides crucial validation while meeting scientific standards for transparency and reliability.

Code preservation maintains complete records of all analytical software used for output analysis including version numbers, parameter settings, and complete scripts or programs used to generate findings. This preservation enables independent analysts to replicate procedures exactly.

Data lineage documentation tracks the complete flow of output data from collection through final analysis while recording all transformations, filtering, or processing steps applied. This documentation enables independent validation of analytical procedures while identifying potential sources of error or bias.

Result validation procedures document efforts to verify key findings through independent analysis, alternative methodological approaches, or cross-validation with different datasets. This validation provides additional confidence in analytical reliability while identifying areas where findings might be sensitive to methodological choices.

Security measures should address both technical protection and procedural safeguards.

Final quality review involves comprehensive evaluation of all documentation by senior investigators and legal counsel while ensuring that materials meet all applicable standards for technical accuracy, legal admissibility, and business utility. Final review should include both detailed technical checking and high-level assessment of overall investigation quality and completeness.

7.14 INTEGRATION AND SYNTHESIS FRAMEWORK

The integration and synthesis framework transforms isolated output analysis findings into comprehensive understanding of AI system behavior by systematically correlating output patterns with evidence from stakeholder interviews, training data analysis, and model investigation. This synthesis process reveals the causal relationships between organizational decisions, technical choices, and real-world system impacts while identifying the most effective intervention points for remediation.

7.14.1 Cross-Domain Evidence Correlation

7.14.1.1 Training Data to Output Pattern Analysis

Correlating training data characteristics with observed output patterns establishes direct connections between data quality issues and discriminatory system behavior. When training data analysis reveals demographic underrepresentation, output analysis should examine whether this underrepresentation manifests as reduced accuracy, systematic bias, or quality degradation for affected groups.

Consider a loan approval system where training data contains only 12% examples from rural applicants. Output analysis might reveal that rural loan applications receive systematically lower approval rates even when controlling for relevant financial factors. This correlation suggests that training data imbalance directly contributes to discriminatory outcomes rather than legitimate risk assessment differences.

Temporal correlation analysis examines whether changes in training data characteristics correspond to changes in output quality or bias patterns over time. Systems retrained with more representative datasets should demonstrate improved fairness metrics, while degraded training data quality should correlate with declining output performance.

7.14.1.2 Model Architecture to Behavioral Manifestation

Model investigation findings about architectural choices, parameter distributions, and learned representations must be validated against real-world output behavior to confirm that laboratory testing accurately predicts deployment performance. Architectural features that appear problematic during controlled testing should manifest as identifiable patterns in operational outputs.

Attention mechanism analysis from model investigation might reveal that systems focus disproportionately on demographic indicators rather than relevant decision factors. Output analysis can validate this finding by examining whether decisions correlate more strongly with demographic characteristics than with objectively relevant criteria such as credit scores or employment history.

Feature importance validation compares model investigation findings about which input features most strongly influence decisions with statistical analysis of output patterns. Discrepancies between expected feature importance and observed decision patterns may indicate model drift, adversarial manipulation, or deployment environment effects not captured during controlled testing.

7.14.2 Stakeholder Interview Integration

7.14.2.1 Organizational Awareness Assessment

Stakeholder interviews reveal organizational knowledge about AI system limitations, bias concerns, and performance issues while output analysis provides objective evidence about whether these concerns are justified and appropriately addressed. Integration of these domains answers crucial questions about organizational accountability and response adequacy.

Interview findings about awareness of demographic bias should correlate with evidence of monitoring, testing, or remediation efforts visible in output patterns. Organizations claiming to monitor for bias should demonstrate systematic testing procedures and should show improved fairness metrics over time if remediation efforts are effective.

Conversely, organizations expressing surprise about bias findings revealed through output analysis may demonstrate inadequate monitoring procedures or organizational blind spots that require governance improvements rather than purely technical remediation.

7.14.2.2 Resource Allocation Validation

Stakeholder claims about resource allocation to fairness, quality assurance, and testing activities should correlate with evidence of sophisticated monitoring and rapid response to identified issues. Organizations investing substantially in AI governance should demonstrate mature testing frameworks and quick remediation of identified problems.

Output analysis findings about persistent bias or quality issues despite organizational claims about investment in these areas may indicate ineffective allocation of resources, inadequate testing methodologies, or insufficient technical capabilities within AI development teams.

7.14.3 Causal Chain Analysis

7.14.3.1 Root Cause Identification

Systematic integration enables investigators to trace problematic outputs back to their ultimate sources while distinguishing between technical causes requiring system modifications and organizational causes requiring governance improvements. This analysis guides remediation strategies by identifying the most effective intervention points.

Technical root causes include training data quality issues, architectural limitations, hyperparameter choices, or deployment environment factors. These causes typically require system retraining, architectural modifications, or technical process improvements to address effectively.

Organizational root causes include inadequate oversight, insufficient diversity in development teams, misaligned incentives, or regulatory pressure that encourages deployment of systems before adequate testing. These causes require governance changes, policy modifications, or cultural transformation rather than purely technical interventions.

7.14.3.2 Intervention Point Prioritization

Integration analysis identifies which intervention points offer the greatest potential for system improvement while considering implementation feasibility and organizational constraints. Some problems may be addressable through multiple approaches, while others may require fundamental changes to system architecture or organizational practices.

Upstream interventions that address training data quality or model architecture may provide more comprehensive solutions than downstream interventions that attempt to correct biased outputs through post-processing techniques. However, downstream interventions may be more feasible in the short term while longer-term upstream solutions are developed.

7.14.4 Synthesis Validation Framework

7.14.4.1 Cross-Domain Consistency Verification

Synthesis findings must be validated for internal consistency across all investigation domains to ensure that proposed explanations adequately account for all available evidence. Inconsistencies may indicate incomplete investigation, methodological problems, or complex interactions that require additional analysis.

Convergent validation occurs when multiple independent lines of evidence support the same conclusions about system behavior or organizational factors. Strong convergent validation increases confidence in synthesis findings while providing robust support for recommended interventions.

Divergent findings require additional investigation to understand whether apparent contradictions result from measurement differences, temporal changes in system behavior, or genuine complexity in system operation that requires more sophisticated explanatory models.

7.14.4.2 Temporal Stability Assessment

Synthesis findings should be validated for temporal stability to ensure that identified patterns represent persistent system characteristics rather than transient anomalies or measurement artifacts. Longitudinal analysis helps distinguish between systematic issues requiring remediation and isolated incidents that may not warrant major interventions.

Pattern persistence analysis examines whether identified bias, performance, or quality issues remain stable across different time periods and operational contexts. Persistent patterns provide stronger evidence for systematic problems requiring comprehensive remediation efforts.

7.14.4.3 Stakeholder Validation Process

Synthesis findings should be validated through structured stakeholder review to ensure that conclusions accurately reflect organizational realities and that recommended interventions address practical constraints and priorities. This validation process helps refine conclusions while building organizational support for remediation efforts.

Technical stakeholder review focuses on the accuracy and completeness of technical findings while assessing the feasibility of recommended technical interventions. Business stakeholder review examines the organizational significance of identified issues and the practicality of recommended governance or process changes.

The integration and synthesis framework provides the foundation for transforming technical investigation findings into actionable organizational intelligence that guides effective remediation while ensuring that interventions address root causes rather than merely addressing symptoms of deeper systemic problems.

7.15 CONCLUSION AND TRANSITION TO DOCUMENTATION ANALYSIS

Output analysis provides the crucial final piece of direct evidence about how AI systems actually behave in practice, revealing the real-world impact of algorithmic decisions on individuals and communities. Through systematic analysis of AI system outputs, investigators can detect bias patterns, performance issues, and security vulnerabilities that manifest in the decisions and recommendations that affect people's lives.

7.15.1 The Power of Output Evidence

Unlike training data analysis that reveals what information was available for learning, or model investigation that shows what systems learned, output analysis demonstrates what AI systems actually do when deployed. This directness makes output analysis particularly powerful for organizational accountability and stakeholder communication, as the evidence speaks directly to the experiences of affected individuals.

The statistical frameworks presented in this chapter enable organizations to move beyond anecdotal concerns to systematic understanding of AI system behavior. Proper bias detection reveals not just whether discrimination exists, but its magnitude, persistence, and impact on different populations. Performance analysis identifies not just overall system effectiveness, but variations that may indicate quality problems or unfair treatment.

The integration of output analysis with findings from previous chapters creates comprehensive understanding of how organizational decisions, training data characteristics, and model architecture choices combine to create the behaviors observed in AI system outputs. This integration reveals causal chains that guide effective remediation strategies addressing root causes rather than symptoms.

7.15.2 From Analysis to Organizational Understanding

Output analysis findings achieve maximum impact when they connect to broader organizational context and decision-making processes. The patterns identified through systematic output analysis needs to be interpreted within the organizational, regulatory, and social contexts in which AI systems operate.

Understanding why bias patterns emerged requires connecting output evidence to the organizational decisions, policy changes, and operational pressures that shape AI system deployment. Similarly, understanding whether performance problems reflect technical limitations or organizational constraints requires broader organizational perspective than output analysis alone can provide.

The systematic analysis of generative AI outputs provides crucial evidence about system behavior that affects user experience and organizational outcomes. By combining technical analysis with domain expertise and community perspectives, organizations can identify content problems before they create significant harm while ensuring that AI systems contribute positively to organizational objectives and social good.

8 Documentation Analysis

8.1 WHEN THE PAPER TRAIL TELLS THE REAL STORY

When a major healthcare AI system began recommending unnecessary procedures, investigators didn't start by analyzing algorithms or examining training data—they began by talking to people and reading emails. Radiologists revealed that the system's confidence scores didn't match their clinical experience. Data scientists disclosed preprocessing decisions made months earlier under tight deadlines. Hospital administrators explained workflow pressures that affected how recommendations were being interpreted and applied. The real story emerged not from code but from the human decisions documented in emails, chat messages, and meeting records that shaped how the AI system was built and deployed.

8.2 WHAT YOU WILL LEARN

By the end of this chapter, you will be able to:

- Systematically identify and collect documentation across distributed AI development environments
- Authenticate and validate the integrity of documentary evidence for legal admissibility
- Correlate documentation findings with technical analysis results from previous investigation phases
- Reconstruct organizational decision-making processes and accountability chains through document analysis
- Establish comprehensive timelines of AI system evolution using multiple documentary sources
- Detect gaps, inconsistencies, and potential concealment in organizational documentation
- Integrate human intelligence with technical evidence to create complete investigation narratives
- Document findings that support compliance assessment, litigation, and organizational improvement

8.3 QUICK START GUIDE

8.3.1 Need Immediate Answers?

- **Missing documentation sources?** → Start with Documentation Source Identification (Section 8.5)
- **Authentication concerns?** → Jump to Evidence Integrity Verification (Section 8.7.2)
- **Timeline reconstruction needed?** → Begin with Temporal Analysis Framework (Section 8.10)
- **Compliance assessment?** → See Organizational Process Analysis (Section 8.12)
- **Legal proceedings?** → Focus on Evidence Integration and Synthesis (Section 8.14)
- **Suspected concealment?** → Review Communication Pattern Analysis (Section 8.9)
- **Version control analysis?** → Start with Development History Analysis (Section 8.11)
- **Crisis response evaluation?** → See Incident Management Analysis (Section 8.16.2)

DOI: 10.1201/9781003634782-8

8.4 INTRODUCTION TO DOCUMENTATION ANALYSIS IN AI FORENSICS

Documentation analysis in AI forensics represents the critical bridge between technical system investigation and human organizational behavior, providing essential context for understanding how AI systems develop, evolve, and operate within organizational frameworks. Building upon the technical analysis methods established in Chapters 4 through 7 (evidence collection, training data analysis, model investigation, and output analysis), this chapter addresses the equally important task of examining the human-created records, communications, and artifacts that provide critical context for interpreting technical findings and establishing accountability chains.

The foundational challenge of documentation analysis in AI forensics lies in the inherently distributed and interdisciplinary nature of modern AI development. Unlike traditional software development where documentation might be centralized in formal repositories and follow established patterns, AI system development spans multiple organizational domains and communication channels. Research notebooks contain experimental results and algorithmic decisions, email threads document trade-offs and technical compromises, Slack conversations reveal real-time problem-solving discussions, version control systems track incremental changes and their rationales, and business presentations justify deployment decisions and risk assessments.

> **KEY INSIGHT: DOCUMENTATION AS EVIDENCE CORROBORATION**
>
> Documentation serves multiple critical forensic purposes: validating technical findings discovered through the methods presented in previous chapters, revealing intent and decision-making processes that shaped system behavior, establishing comprehensive timelines of system evolution and modification, identifying undisclosed risks or limitations that may not be apparent from technical analysis alone, demonstrating compliance efforts or their absence, and providing contextual frameworks for interpreting technical evidence within organizational and business contexts.

Each documentation source provides a different perspective on system development and operation, requiring sophisticated correlation and validation techniques to reconstruct complete understanding. This distributed documentation landscape creates unique forensic challenges that require systematic approaches to identification, collection, authentication, and analysis.

The temporal dimension of documentation analysis presents particular challenges in AI forensics. AI systems evolve continuously through retraining, hyperparameter adjustments, deployment changes, creating a complex timeline of modifications that must be reconstructed from fragmented records. Understanding this evolution requires sophisticated techniques for correlating timestamps across systems, reconstructing deleted or modified records, and identifying gaps in documentation that might indicate intentional concealment.

8.5 OVERVIEW OF DOCUMENTATION SOURCES

The documentation ecosystem surrounding AI systems is vast and heterogeneous, spanning formal repositories, informal communications, and automatically generated records. Understanding this ecosystem is essential for comprehensive investigation planning and evidence collection. As identified in Chapter 3's knowledge-gathering process, AI documentation often resides in unexpected locations and requires systematic discovery through multiple channels.

8.5.1 Formal Documentation Repositories

8.5.1.1 Technical Documentation Systems

Technical documentation provides the foundational specifications and implementation guidance for AI systems. These repositories typically include system architecture documents that define component relationships, data flow specifications, and integration requirements. Model documentation details algorithmic choices, hyperparameter configurations, and performance characteristics. API documentation specifies interface requirements, data formats, and integration procedures. Deployment guides provide environment setup instructions, configuration requirements, and operational procedures.

Engineering wikis and knowledge bases often contain the most detailed technical information, including troubleshooting guides, best practices, architectural decision records (ADRs), and lessons learned from development and deployment. These systems frequently contain undocumented knowledge that exists nowhere else in the organization, making them critical sources for understanding system behavior and design rationale.

8.5.1.2 Business Documentation Systems

Business documentation provides context for understanding organizational objectives, constraints, and decision-making processes that shaped AI system development. Requirements management systems contain business cases, user stories, acceptance criteria, and stakeholder requirements that explain why systems were built and what they were intended to accomplish.

Project management platforms track timelines, resource allocation, milestone achievements, and scope changes that provide crucial context for understanding development pressures and trade-offs. Risk management systems document identified risks, mitigation strategies, and compliance considerations that reveal organizational awareness of potential issues.

8.5.1.3 Compliance and Audit Documentation

Compliance documentation demonstrates organizational efforts to meet regulatory and legal requirements. SOC 2 reports, ISO certifications, and industry-specific compliance documentation provide evidence of formal processes and controls. Internal audit reports reveal identified weaknesses and remediation efforts. Privacy impact assessments and algorithmic accountability reports demonstrate awareness of potential societal impacts.

8.5.2 Development and Version Control Systems

8.5.2.1 Source Code Repositories

Git repositories and similar version control systems contain comprehensive records of code changes, including commit messages that explain the rationale for modifications, branch structures that reveal development strategies, merge request discussions that document technical decisions, and tag annotations that mark significant releases or experiments.

Code review systems preserve discussions about implementation choices, quality concerns, and alternative approaches. These records often contain candid assessments of technical risks and limitations that might not appear in formal documentation.

8.5.2.2 Experimental Documentation

Jupyter notebooks and similar experimental environments contain detailed records of research and development activities. These documents often include data exploration results, model experimentation records, performance comparison analyses, and informal observations about system behavior.

Machine learning experiment tracking systems (MLflow, Weights & Biases, etc.) provide structured records of hyperparameter experiments, performance metrics, and model artifacts. These systems often contain the most complete record of how final model configurations were selected and what alternatives were considered.

8.5.2.3 Configuration Management

Infrastructure-as-code repositories document deployment configurations, environment specifications, and automated deployment procedures. These records reveal how AI systems are deployed, configured, and maintained in production environments.

Container definitions and orchestration configurations provide evidence of actual deployment practices, resource allocation, and security configurations that might differ from documented procedures.

8.5.3 Communications and Collaboration Records

8.5.3.1 Email Communications

Email threads often contain the most complete record of decision-making processes, especially for significant architectural or business decisions. Technical discussions may reveal concerns about system limitations, bias risks, or security vulnerabilities. Management communications might document budget pressures, timeline constraints, or strategic decisions that influenced technical choices.

Automated email notifications from monitoring systems, CI/CD pipelines, and issue tracking systems provide timestamped records of system events and development activities.

8.5.3.2 Instant Messaging and Chat Platforms

Slack, Microsoft Teams, and similar platforms capture real-time discussions about system development and operation. These platforms often contain troubleshooting discussions, informal knowledge sharing, incident response coordination, and candid assessments of system performance.

Chat platforms frequently contain evidence of workarounds, known issues, and informal processes that don't appear in official documentation. The conversational nature of these platforms often reveals honest assessments of system limitations and risks.

8.5.3.3 Video Conferencing and Meeting Records

Meeting recordings, transcripts, and notes provide evidence of formal decision-making processes and stakeholder discussions. All-hands meetings might contain executive assessments of AI initiatives. Technical design meetings could reveal architectural trade-offs and risk discussions.

Calendar systems provide context for understanding when key decisions were made and who was involved in the decision-making process.

8.5.4 Monitoring and Operational Records

8.5.4.1 System Logs and Monitoring Data

Application logs capture detailed records of system behavior, including error messages, performance metrics, and user interactions. Database logs record data access patterns and modification histories. Infrastructure logs document resource utilization and system health metrics.

Monitoring dashboards and alerting systems provide evidence of system performance over time and organizational responses to identified issues.

8.5.4.2 Incident Response Documentation

Incident tracking systems contain detailed records of system failures, security events, and performance issues. Post-incident review documents often provide candid assessments of system weaknesses and organizational response effectiveness.

Change management systems document modifications to production systems and their approval processes, providing evidence of how organizations manage AI system evolution.

TABLE 8.1

Documentation Source	Volatility Risk	Access Complexity	Legal Privilege Risk	Retention Policy Risk	Investigation Priority
Email Communications	Medium	Low	High	Medium	High
Chat/Instant Messaging	High	Medium	Low	High	High
Version Control Systems	Low	Medium	Low	Low	Critical
Meeting Recordings	Medium	Medium	Medium	Medium	Medium
Technical Documentation	Low	Low	Low	Low	High
Business Documentation	Low	Low	Medium	Low	Medium
Monitoring Logs	High	Medium	Low	High	Medium
Incident Reports	Low	Low	Low	Low	High
Experimental Notebooks	Medium	High	Low	Medium	High
Regulatory Filings	Low	Low	High	Low	Medium

8.5.4.3 Audit and Compliance Logs

Compliance monitoring systems generate automated records of policy violations, security events, and regulatory reporting. Internal audit logs document access to sensitive systems and data. External audit reports provide independent assessments of system controls and compliance posture.

The following chart details these documentation sources and the key forensic considerations when assessing whether to collect them.

Key:

- **Volatility Risk**: Likelihood of data loss or modification
- **Access Complexity**: Technical difficulty of collection
- **Legal Privilege Risk**: Probability of privilege claims
- **Retention Policy Risk**: Risk of automatic deletion
- **Investigation Priority**: Relative importance for forensic analysis

8.6 DOCUMENTATION ANALYSIS PROCESS FRAMEWORK

Effective documentation analysis requires a systematic approach that ensures comprehensive coverage while maintaining forensic integrity. The analysis process accounts for the distributed nature of AI documentation, the temporal complexity of system evolution, and the potential for document modification or destruction.

8.6.1 Discovery and Inventory Phase

8.6.1.1 Systematic Source Identification

Source identification begins with stakeholder interviews and organizational mapping to understand how information flows through the organization. Technical personnel can identify formal repositories, development tools, and communication channels. Business stakeholders reveal decision-making processes and approval workflows. Operations teams describe monitoring systems and incident response procedures.

Document mapping creates a comprehensive catalog of information sources, including system types, access requirements, retention policies, and stakeholder ownership. This mapping often reveals unexpected documentation sources, such as personal notebooks, backup systems, or archived communications.

8.6.1.2 Prioritization and Risk Assessment

Not all documentation sources have equal investigative value or evidentiary significance. High-priority sources typically include executive communications about AI strategy and risk tolerance, technical discussions about system limitations or bias concerns, incident response records documenting system failures, compliance assessments identifying regulatory violations, and version control records showing undocumented system changes.

Risk assessment evaluates the likelihood that important documentation has been modified, deleted, or is unavailable due to retention policies or technical failures. This assessment guides preservation efforts and influences the investigation timeline.

8.6.2 Collection and Preservation Methodology

8.6.2.1 Forensic Collection Procedures

Different documentation types require specialized collection procedures to maintain evidential integrity. Electronic documents require cryptographic hashing to verify integrity, metadata preservation to maintain temporal context, chain of custody documentation to ensure admissibility, and bit-for-bit copying for critical evidence.

Communication systems present unique challenges due to their real-time nature and complex storage architectures. Email systems may distribute messages across multiple servers and storage systems. Chat platforms might use proprietary formats that require specialized extraction tools. Video conferencing systems could store recordings in cloud services with complex access controls.

8.6.2.2 Temporal Preservation Strategies

AI system documentation changes continuously, requiring strategies to capture point-in-time snapshots of relevant information. Version control systems provide built-in temporal tracking for code and configuration files. Communication systems may require periodic exports to preserve current state. Monitoring systems might need data archival before retention policies delete historical information.

The challenge of temporal preservation in AI systems is compounded by the fact that many documentation sources exist in dynamic environments where automatic updates, rolling logs, and continuous integration processes can overwrite critical evidence. For instance, cloud-based collaboration platforms may automatically sync changes across devices, potentially eliminating earlier versions of documents that contained important decision rationales. Similarly, monitoring systems often implement circular logging where older entries are automatically purged to manage storage costs, potentially destroying evidence of system behavior during critical periods. To address these challenges, investigators need to implement proactive preservation strategies that include establishing legal holds on relevant systems to prevent automatic deletion, creating forensic images of documentation repositories before they can be modified, coordinating with system administrators to pause automatic cleanup processes during evidence collection periods, and implementing real-time monitoring of critical documentation sources to detect and preserve changes as they occur. These preservation strategies should balance the need for comprehensive evidence capture with the practical limitations of storage capacity, system performance, and organizational operations.

Live system documentation requires careful coordination to prevent evidence modification during collection. Read-only access modes, system snapshots, and offline analysis help maintain evidence integrity while enabling comprehensive analysis.

8.7 EVIDENCE COLLECTION AND AUTHENTICATION PROCEDURES

8.7.1 Forensic Collection Methodology

8.7.1.1 Level 1: Basic Collection Principles

Every document needs to be collected with proper chain of custody documentation, cryptographic hash verification for integrity validation, and comprehensive metadata preservation including timestamps, author information, modification history, and access logs. Original format preservation ensures that documents remain in their native format to maintain all available metadata and structural information.

8.7.1.2 Level 2: Platform-Specific Collection Procedures

Different documentation types and platforms require specialized collection procedures to maintain evidential integrity:

Email Systems: Use specialized tools that preserve complete message headers, threading relationships, and attachment associations. Exchange and Office 365 systems provide built-in legal hold capabilities. Cloud email systems require specific export procedures to maintain metadata integrity.

Instant Messaging Platforms: Preserve conversation flow, participant metadata, and file sharing information. Platform export formats vary significantly in completeness, requiring careful validation of export procedures and content verification.

Version Control Systems: Capture complete repository history including commit messages, branching structure, and contributor information. Large repositories may require selective collection based on relevant timeframes and system components.

8.7.1.3 Level 3: Advanced Collection Scenarios

Complex investigations may involve encrypted documents requiring key recovery procedures, deleted documents recoverable through forensic techniques, real-time collection during ongoing operations requiring coordination with system administrators, and multi-jurisdictional collection involving international legal frameworks.

8.7.2 Authentication and Integrity Verification Framework

8.7.2.1 Digital Signature Validation Process

When digital signatures are present, validation provides cryptographic proof of document authenticity. Verify signature certificates against trusted certificate authorities, check certificate revocation status, and confirm that signing timestamps align with claimed document creation dates. Document any signature validation failures and their potential implications for document reliability.

8.7.2.2 Metadata Analysis and Validation

Document metadata provides crucial authentication information including creation timestamps, modification history, authorship attribution, and system provenance. Analyze metadata for internal consistency and identify potential tampering indicators:

- Timestamp anomalies that don't align with known events or organizational timelines
- Author information that contradicts organizational records or access logs
- Modification patterns suggesting post-facto changes or backdating attempts
- Missing metadata that should be present based on system characteristics

8.7.2.3 Cross-Reference Verification Methodology

Implement systematic cross-reference verification to validate document authenticity and content accuracy. Compare information across multiple independent sources to identify corroborating evidence or concerning discrepancies. Email references should correspond to calendar entries and meeting records. Technical discussions should align with version control activities and system logs. Business decisions should correlate with formal approval processes and implementation activities.

8.8 CONTENT ANALYSIS AND CORRELATION FRAMEWORK

8.8.1 Information Extraction and Categorization

8.8.1.1 Structured Information Extraction

Transform unstructured documentation into searchable, analyzable information by extracting key elements:

- **Decisions and Rationales**: Who decided what, when, and why
- **Timeline Events**: Sequence of activities and milestones
- **Stakeholder Roles**: Responsibilities and involvement patterns
- **Technical Specifications**: System requirements and changes
- **Risk Assessments**: Identified concerns and mitigation strategies
- **Compliance Activities**: Regulatory requirements and responses

8.8.1.2 Natural Language Processing Techniques

Automated analysis can accelerate information extraction from large document collections. Named entity recognition identifies people, organizations, and technical systems. Sentiment analysis reveals emotional context in communications. Topic modeling identifies themes and patterns across documents.

TIP: SCALING ANALYSIS WITH TECHNOLOGY

For investigations involving thousands of documents, consider using automated analysis tools. However, always validate automated findings through manual review of critical documents. Technology augments but never replaces human judgment in forensic analysis.

8.8.2 Cross-Source Correlation Analysis

8.8.2.1 Timeline Correlation Methodology

Synchronize events across multiple systems and communication channels by establishing common reference points, accounting for timezone differences, and identifying sequence relationships between events. Timeline correlation often reveals causal relationships not apparent from individual sources.

8.8.2.2 Actor Correlation Mapping

Map stakeholder involvement in different activities and decisions to understand influence patterns and accountability chains. Analyze who participated in critical discussions, who made key decisions, and who had access to important information at specific times.

8.8.2.3 Technical Correlation Framework

Link configuration changes to performance impacts or incident reports by correlating technical documentation with system behavior evidence from previous investigation phases. Technical correlation validates whether documented procedures were actually followed.

Evidence Strength Ratings:

- **High**: Strong correlation provides reliable validation
- **Medium**: Moderate correlation with some interpretation required
- **Low**: Weak correlation requiring additional evidence

TABLE 8.2

Primary Source Type	Secondary Source	Validation Technique	Evidence Strength	Common Discrepancies	Resolution Method
Technical Specs	Implementation code	Specification matching	High	Version misalignment	Code repository analysis
Business Requirements	Email discussions	Decision trail reconstruction	Medium	Scope creep	Timeline correlation
Performance Claims	Monitoring data	Metric validation	High	Testing vs. production gaps	Environment analysis
Training Procedures	Version control	Process verification	High	Undocumented changes	Commit message analysis
Risk Assessments	Incident reports	Risk realization tracking	Medium	Unknown issues materialized	Post-incident analysis
Compliance Claims	Audit reports	Control effectiveness	High	Paper vs. actual compliance	Independent verification
Meeting Decisions	Implementation	Decision follow-through	Medium	Decisions not implemented	Change management review
Architecture Docs	System behavior	Design vs. reality	High	Undocumented modifications	Behavioral testing

8.8.3 Pattern Recognition and Anomaly Detection

8.8.3.1 Communication Pattern Analysis

Identify recurring themes, decision-making processes, and organizational behaviors that provide context for understanding AI system development and operation. Look for:

- Normal communication flow patterns
- Crisis response communication changes
- Decision-making hierarchy patterns
- Technical escalation procedures

8.8.3.2 Anomaly Detection Framework

Identify unusual events, communications, or decisions that warrant additional investigation:

- Sudden changes in communication patterns during critical periods
- Unusual technical activities suggesting unauthorized modifications
- Missing documentation corresponding to known events
- Inconsistent information across multiple sources

8.9 COMMUNICATION ANALYSIS AND PATTERN RECOGNITION

8.9.1 Email Communications Forensics

8.9.1.1 Collection and Preservation Methodology

Email collection is performed to preserve complete message content, metadata, and thread relationships while maintaining legal admissibility standards. Modern email systems distribute messages across multiple servers and storage systems, requiring coordination with IT departments and specialized tools to ensure comprehensive collection.

Email metadata provides crucial context for understanding communication timing, participant involvement, and message authenticity. Sender and recipient information establishes stakeholder involvement in specific discussions. Timestamp information enables timeline reconstruction and correlation with other events. Message threading information helps reconstruct complete conversation sequences.

8.9.1.2 Content Analysis Framework

Email content analysis requires both automated and manual techniques to identify relevant information and extract key insights. Natural language processing can identify technical discussions, business decisions, risk assessments, and compliance concerns at scale. However, sophisticated analysis should consider context, intent, and organizational communication patterns.

Thread analysis examines complete conversation sequences to understand how decisions developed over time. Initial proposals may evolve through discussion into final decisions. Concerns raised early in conversations may be addressed, dismissed, or left unresolved. Decision rationales often emerge through discussion rather than explicit documentation.

Sentiment analysis helps identify emotional context in communications that may indicate stress, concern, enthusiasm, or defensiveness. These emotional indicators can reveal organizational awareness of problems, business pressures affecting decision-making, or defensive responses to challenging questions.

8.9.2 Instant Messaging and Chat Platform Analysis

8.9.2.1 Platform-Specific Analysis Challenges

Different messaging platforms present unique analytical challenges due to varying data structures, export capabilities, and retention policies. Slack provides comprehensive export capabilities but requires administrative access and careful handling of private channels. Microsoft Teams integrates with Exchange systems but may store content in separate repositories. Mobile platforms like WhatsApp require specialized collection tools and privacy considerations.

Platform export formats vary significantly in completeness and usability. Some exports include complete message history with metadata preservation, while others provide only text content without temporal context or threading information. File attachments and shared content may be included, referenced separately, or lost entirely depending on export procedures.

Chat platform retention policies affect what information is available for analysis. Some organizations configure automatic deletion of messages after specific periods. Others maintain comprehensive archives. Free-tier accounts might have limited history compared to paid enterprise accounts.

8.9.2.2 Conversational Analysis Techniques

Chat conversations differ significantly from formal communications in structure, language, and context. Messages may be fragmented across multiple short communications requiring reconstruction of complete thought sequences. Context may be implicit rather than explicit, requiring deep understanding of organizational terminology and relationships.

Thread reconstruction creates coherent conversation flows from fragmented messages by analyzing temporal clustering, participant patterns, and topic continuity. Topic modeling identifies recurring themes and their evolution over time. Participant analysis reveals who was involved in specific discussions and how communication patterns changed during different organizational periods.

Real-time communication often captures immediate reactions to events that may be filtered or edited in formal communications. Crisis response communications may reveal the true scope of problems and organizational response capabilities. Troubleshooting discussions document known issues and workarounds that may not appear in formal documentation.

8.9.2.3 Informal Knowledge and Process Discovery

Chat platforms often contain the most complete record of informal processes, workarounds, and undocumented knowledge that keeps AI systems operational. This information might not appear anywhere else in organizational documentation.

Troubleshooting discussions reveal known system issues and their solutions. Common problems might have established workarounds that aren't formally documented. Performance issues might be managed through informal monitoring and intervention procedures. Security concerns might be addressed through temporary measures that become permanent practice.

Knowledge sharing conversations document informal training, best practices, and lessons learned that don't make it into official documentation. Experienced team members might share insights about system behavior, data quality issues, or effective debugging techniques. These conversations often contain the practical knowledge needed to understand system operation.

> **WARNING: INFORMAL COMMUNICATION RISKS**
>
> Informal communications may contain candid assessments of system problems that create legal liability if they contradict formal documentation. However, these communications often provide the most accurate picture of organizational awareness and response to AI system issues.

8.9.3 Meeting Records and Video Conference Analysis

8.9.3.1 Multi-Modal Evidence Analysis Framework

Meeting records may exist in multiple formats, each providing different types of evidence requiring specialized analytical approaches. Audio recordings capture spoken content and emotional context including tone, stress, and engagement levels. Video recordings add visual information about participant behavior, presentation materials, and group dynamics. Written transcripts provide searchable text content but may miss emotional context and non-verbal communication. Meeting notes summarize key points but may omit important details or reflect note-taker bias.

Presentation materials shown during meetings provide additional context for understanding discussions. Slide decks may contain technical details, performance metrics, or risk assessments not discussed verbally. Shared documents may be modified during meetings based on discussion outcomes. Whiteboard content may capture informal diagrams, decision trees, or process flows.

8.9.3.2 Decision Process Reconstruction

Meeting analysis helps reconstruct critical elements of organizational decision-making including how decisions were made, who was involved, what factors were considered, what alternatives were evaluated, and what rationales guided final choices. This reconstruction is crucial for understanding accountability and assessing the adequacy of decision-making processes.

Formal decision meetings should follow established organizational procedures with appropriate stakeholder involvement, adequate information presentation, proper deliberation time, and comprehensive documentation of outcomes. Deviations from normal procedures may indicate rushed decision-making, inadequate review processes, or attempts to avoid accountability.

Informal decision discussions may occur during regular status meetings, one-on-one conversations, or casual encounters. These discussions may be less structured but could involve significant strategic or technical decisions. Identifying informal decisions requires careful analysis of meeting content, participant behavior, and subsequent implementation activities.

8.9.3.3 Stakeholder Analysis and Power Dynamics

Meeting analysis reveals organizational dynamics that influence AI system development and operation. Speaking time analysis shows who dominates discussions and whose input is valued or dismissed.

Topic introduction patterns reveal who sets agendas and drives strategic directions. Response patterns show how different stakeholders react to proposals, concerns, and recommendations.

Power dynamics significantly affect how concerns are raised and addressed within organizations. Technical concerns raised by junior engineers may be dismissed or overruled by senior management. Business pressures from executives may override technical recommendations or safety considerations. External stakeholder input may receive different consideration depending on organizational relationships and perceived authority.

Understanding these dynamics helps interpret other evidence types and assess the reliability of different information sources. Stakeholders with more organizational influence may have their perspectives over-represented in formal documentation. Marginalized voices may not appear in official records despite having important insights about system limitations or risks.

8.10 TEMPORAL ANALYSIS AND TIMELINE RECONSTRUCTION

8.10.1 Multi-Source Timeline Synchronization

8.10.1.1 Temporal Correlation Methodology

Creating unified chronological understanding of AI system evolution requires correlating timestamps across different systems while accounting for timezone differences, clock synchronization issues, and varying temporal precision. Different systems maintain timestamps with different accuracy and reliability characteristics requiring careful normalization and validation.

Version control systems typically use developer local time zones which may not be synchronized across distributed team members. Email systems use server timestamps that should be well-synchronized but may span multiple time zones. Chat platforms may use client-side timestamps that could vary significantly. Monitoring systems should use synchronized server time but may have different temporal granularity.

Timezone normalization requires converting all timestamps to a common reference timezone while preserving original timezone information for verification purposes. Development teams often span multiple continents, creating complex correlation challenges when trying to establish precise event sequences. Daylight saving time transitions can create apparent timing anomalies that require careful analysis and correction.

8.10.1.2 Event Sequence Reconstruction

Cross-system event correlation identifies related activities across different platforms and systems to reconstruct complete organizational responses to issues or opportunities. A model architecture change in version control may correlate with email discussions about performance problems, chat conversations about testing strategies, and monitoring alerts about system behavior changes.

Causal relationship identification examines whether temporal sequences suggest meaningful cause-and-effect relationships between organizational activities. Email discussions about performance issues may precede version control changes intended to address those problems. Chat conversations about data quality may lead to data processing pipeline modifications. Business strategy discussions may drive technical architecture decisions.

Activity clustering groups related events that occurred within specific time windows to understand coordinated organizational responses. Development sprints may generate correlated activity across version control, project management, and communication systems. Incident response may create synchronized activity across monitoring, communication, and documentation systems.

8.10.2 Gap and Inconsistency Detection

8.10.2.1 Timeline Analysis Framework

Timeline analysis identifies gaps in documentation that might indicate missing information, deleted records, or inadequate documentation practices. Extended periods without version control activity during documented development might suggest missing repositories or deleted history.

Timing inconsistencies might indicate system synchronization issues, timezone confusion, or potential evidence tampering. Events that should have occurred in specific sequences might appear out of order due to timestamp manipulation or system errors.

Missing correlations might suggest incomplete evidence collection or intentional concealment. High-level decisions documented in meeting records should correlate with implementation activities in version control and communication systems.

8.10.3 Step-by-Step Timeline Reconstruction Walkthrough

Scenario: Reconstructing the timeline of bias discovery and organizational response in an AI hiring system to establish accountability and evaluate response adequacy.

Step 1: Anchor Point Identification and Validation Identify key events with reliable timestamps including system deployment dates, incident report submissions, regulatory inquiry receipts, and external complaint notifications. Establish a chronological framework using these anchor points as reference markers. Validate anchor point accuracy through cross-reference with multiple independent sources.

Step 2: Documentation Chronological Mapping Plot all collected documents on a unified timeline using normalized metadata timestamps. Identify temporal clusters of activity that may indicate intensive development periods, crisis response, or organizational transitions. Note significant gaps in documentation that correspond to critical periods, as these may indicate missing evidence or concealment efforts.

Step 3: Cross-Source Timeline Validation and Correlation Compare timestamps across different systems while accounting for timezone differences and potential clock synchronization issues. Resolve discrepancies through additional evidence gathering and expert analysis. Identify the most reliable chronological references for each type of evidence.

Step 4: Narrative Reconstruction and Causal Analysis Build a coherent narrative of events using timeline evidence while identifying potential causal relationships between different organizational activities. Highlight periods requiring additional investigation due to gaps, inconsistencies, or unexplained activity patterns.

Step 5: Timeline Documentation and Presentation Preparation Create comprehensive visual timelines showing key events, evidence sources, stakeholder involvement, and decision points. Document all assumptions and limitations in timeline reconstruction methodology. Prepare timeline evidence for presentation to different audiences with appropriate technical detail and legal foundation.

8.11 VERSION CONTROL AND DEVELOPMENT HISTORY ANALYSIS

8.11.1 Repository Structure and Access Pattern Analysis

8.11.1.1 Repository Organization Assessment

Repository structure reflects development team organization, project management approaches, and code quality practices. Well-organized repositories typically separate model code, data processing scripts, configuration files, documentation, and deployment materials into logical directory structures that enable effective change tracking and impact analysis.

Branch structure analysis reveals development workflows and quality control practices. Feature branches indicate systematic development with proper review processes and controlled integration. Direct commits to main branches may suggest rushed development, inadequate quality controls, or emergency response situations. Long-lived experimental branches could contain important research that didn't reach production systems.

Access control configuration shows who could modify different parts of the system and when those permissions changed over time. Overly broad administrative access may enable unauthorized modifications or make it difficult to establish accountability. Restrictive access may slow development but provides better audit trails and change control.

8.11.2 Commit Pattern Analysis and Behavioral Indicators

8.11.2.1 Development Activity Pattern Recognition

Commit frequency and timing patterns reveal development intensity, crisis response periods, and potential quality issues. Regular commit patterns suggest steady development progress with appropriate work-life balance. Sudden increases in commit frequency may indicate crisis response, approaching deadlines, or rushed deployment pressures. Large commits with extensive file changes could suggest inadequate development practices or attempts to obscure specific modifications.

Commit message quality provides insight into development practices and change documentation standards. High-quality commit messages explain what changed, why changes were necessary, and how changes affect system behavior. Poor commit messages like "fix bug" or "update model" provide little insight into actual modifications. Missing or misleading commit messages may indicate inadequate development practices or intentional obfuscation.

Author analysis shows who made specific changes and how work was distributed across team members. Concentrated authorship may indicate knowledge silos, inadequate review processes, or unauthorized individual control. Changes by unexpected or unauthorized users could suggest security issues, inadequate access controls, or administrative errors. Temporal author patterns may reveal who was working during crisis periods or major system changes.

8.11.2.2 Merge and Review Process Examination

Pull request and merge request analysis reveals code review practices and their effectiveness in maintaining system quality and security. Complete review processes typically include multiple qualified reviewers, comprehensive testing validation, detailed discussion of technical trade-offs, and proper approval workflows before integration.

Review comment analysis examines the quality and focus of technical discussions during code review. Substantive discussions about algorithm correctness, performance implications, security considerations, and maintainability indicate thorough review processes. Missing discussions about obvious issues may suggest rushed reviews, inadequate reviewer expertise, or organizational pressures to accelerate development.

Merge timing analysis identifies whether changes followed proper review processes or were integrated without adequate evaluation. Fast-track merges may be appropriate for critical security fixes but could indicate inadequate review for routine changes. Patterns of review bypassing may suggest systematic quality control problems.

8.12 ORGANIZATIONAL PROCESS ANALYSIS AND BEHAVIORAL PATTERN RECOGNITION

8.12.1 Decision-Making Process Reconstruction

8.12.1.1 Formal Decision Documentation Analysis

Examine how organizations document significant decisions through board minutes, committee reports, approval workflows, and formal communications. Analyze whether documented procedures were actually followed in practice and whether decisions align with stated organizational policies and values.

Formal processes should include appropriate stakeholder consultation, adequate information gathering and analysis, sufficient deliberation time, proper approval authority, and comprehensive documentation of rationales and alternatives considered. Deviations from established processes may indicate emergency circumstances, inadequate governance, or attempts to avoid accountability.

8.12.1.2 Informal Decision Analysis and Shadow Processes

Many critical decisions occur through informal processes that may not be captured in formal documentation but significantly influence AI system development and operation. Analyze email discussions, instant message conversations, and meeting recordings to identify informal decision-making patterns and their relationship to formal approval processes.

Informal decision-making may be more efficient and responsive than formal processes but can lack proper documentation, stakeholder input, or oversight. Understanding the balance between formal and informal decision-making helps assess organizational governance effectiveness and accountability systems.

8.12.1.3 Authority and Accountability Mapping

Determine who had formal authority to make specific decisions, who was actually consulted in practice, who was informed of outcomes, and who bears ultimate responsibility for consequences. Map formal organizational charts against actual decision-making patterns revealed through documentation analysis to identify discrepancies that may indicate governance problems.

8.12.2 Risk Management Effectiveness Assessment

8.12.2.1 Risk Identification and Assessment Analysis

Examine whether organizations effectively identified appropriate risks for their specific AI applications and operating contexts. High-risk applications like hiring, lending, or medical diagnosis require more comprehensive risk assessment than lower-risk applications like content recommendation or marketing optimization.

Risk identification should be systematic, comprehensive, and appropriate for the specific AI application context. Effective risk assessment considers technical risks like bias and performance degradation, business risks like regulatory compliance and reputational damage, and operational risks like system failure and security breaches.

8.12.2.2 Mitigation Strategy Analysis and Validation

Assess whether documented risk mitigation strategies were technically sound, properly implemented, and effectively monitored over time. Cross-reference documented mitigation measures with technical evidence from previous investigation phases to validate whether controls actually functioned as intended.

Effective risk mitigation should be proportionate to identified risks, technically feasible, and subject to ongoing monitoring and validation. Ineffective mitigation may indicate inadequate technical understanding, insufficient resource allocation, or poor execution of otherwise sound strategies.

8.12.2.3 Compliance Program Evaluation

Analyze compliance documentation to determine whether organizations maintained appropriate oversight mechanisms, conducted required testing and validation, and responded effectively to identified issues. Evaluate the adequacy of compliance programs relative to applicable regulatory requirements and industry best practices.

> **KEY INSIGHT: PROCESS VS. PERFORMANCE GAP ANALYSIS**
>
> Organizations may have excellent documented processes that are poorly executed, or informal processes that work better than formal procedures. Always compare documented procedures with actual implementation evidence from technical analysis and communication records to identify gaps between stated intentions and actual performance.

8.12.3 Communication Pattern Analysis and Organizational Dynamics

8.12.3.1 Pattern Recognition Framework

Organizational behavior pattern analysis examines how organizations typically make technical and business decisions about AI systems. Normal patterns may include formal review processes, systematic stakeholder consultation, and documented approval workflows. Deviations from established patterns may indicate crisis response, inadequate planning, or unusual circumstances requiring additional investigation.

Communication pattern analysis identifies how information typically flows through organizations during different types of activities. Technical issues may normally be discussed in engineering channels before escalating to management levels. Business decisions may follow specific approval chains involving multiple organizational levels. Crisis response may activate emergency communication protocols that bypass normal channels.

8.12.3.2 Risk and Issue Management Patterns

Risk identification patterns examine how the organization identifies, assesses, and communicates potential issues. Effective organizations typically have systematic approaches for identifying technical risks, business risks, and compliance risks. Poor risk management might result in surprise failures or regulatory violations.

Issue resolution patterns examine how the organization responds to identified problems. Effective resolution typically includes root cause analysis, comprehensive fixes, and process improvements to prevent recurrence. Poor resolution might result in recurring issues or temporary workarounds that become permanent.

Escalation patterns examine how serious issues are communicated up organizational hierarchies. Effective escalation ensures that appropriate stakeholders are informed and involved in resolution. Poor escalation might result in inadequate response or delayed resolution.

8.12.3.3 Anomaly Detection and Investigation Prioritization

Statistical anomaly detection identifies unusual patterns in communication frequency, development activity, or system behavior that may indicate significant events or concerning organizational behaviors. Sudden changes in normal communication patterns often warrant additional investigation to understand underlying causes.

Behavioral anomaly detection examines whether stakeholder behavior deviates from established organizational norms. Unusual communication patterns may indicate crisis response, concealment efforts, or significant organizational changes. Unusual development activity may indicate emergency fixes, unauthorized modifications, or resource allocation problems.

Investigation prioritization focuses analytical resources on the most significant anomalies and inconsistencies identified through pattern analysis. High-priority items typically include safety-critical system modifications, potential regulatory violations, evidence of intentional misrepresentation, and systemic issues affecting multiple organizational areas.

8.13 DOCUMENTATION ANALYSIS CHECKLISTS

8.13.1 Documentation Collection Checklist

The following checklists provide a comprehensive framework for conducting documentation analysis in AI forensic investigations, but investigators must adapt these guidelines to the specific circumstances of each case. Every AI investigation presents unique challenges based on the system architecture, organizational structure, legal jurisdiction, and investigation objectives that require thoughtful modification of standard procedures. These checklists serve as starting points to ensure comprehensive coverage while maintaining the flexibility necessary to address the diverse range of scenarios encountered in real-world AI forensic practice.

8.13.1.1 Pre-Collection Preparation

- Legal authority for collection established and documented
- Investigation scope and limitations clearly defined

- Chain of custody procedures prepared and validated
- Collection tools and systems configured and tested
- Personnel roles and responsibilities assigned and documented
- Timeline and milestones established with stakeholder coordination
- Risk assessment completed for potential evidence destruction
- Privilege and confidentiality protections identified and documented

8.13.1.2 Source Identification and Mapping

- Email systems and archives identified and accessed
- Instant messaging platforms catalogued and assessed
- Document management systems accessed and inventoried
- Version control repositories located and analyzed
- Meeting recording systems inventoried and accessed
- Project management tools examined and exported
- Research and experimental platforms discovered and preserved
- Compliance and audit systems reviewed and documented
- Personal and unofficial sources considered and evaluated
- Cloud storage and backup systems identified and accessed

8.13.1.3 Collection Execution and Validation

- Original format preservation maintained throughout collection
- Metadata captured and preserved using appropriate tools
- Hash verification completed for all collected documents
- Chain of custody documentation completed and verified
- Access permissions and restrictions documented and respected
- Collection completeness verified against discovery inventory
- Quality assurance procedures executed and documented
- Stakeholder coordination maintained throughout collection process

8.13.2 Documentation Authentication Checklist

8.13.2.1 Technical Authentication Procedures

- Digital signatures validated where present using appropriate tools
- Metadata analysis completed and documented comprehensively
- Timestamp consistency verified across multiple sources
- File integrity verified through cryptographic hash comparison
- Creation and modification history analyzed for anomalies
- Author information validated against organizational records
- System provenance verified through technical analysis
- Format consistency validated for potential tampering indicators

8.13.2.2 Content Authentication and Validation

- Cross-reference verification completed across multiple sources
- Consistency analysis performed for factual claims
- Anachronism detection performed for temporal anomalies
- Language and terminology analysis completed for authenticity
- Organizational context validation conducted with subject matter experts
- External validation performed where appropriate and available
- Discrepancy analysis completed for conflicting information
- Source reliability assessment documented and justified

8.13.2.3 Legal Authentication Requirements

- Chain of custody documentation complete and legally sufficient
- Evidence admissibility requirements verified and documented
- Privilege protections respected and documented
- Authentication witness identification completed where required
- Expert testimony preparation documented and validated
- Court presentation materials prepared according to legal standards
- Evidence integrity maintained throughout authentication process
- Legal review completed by qualified counsel

8.14 EVIDENCE INTEGRATION AND SYNTHESIS FRAMEWORK

8.14.1 Technical-Documentary Evidence Correlation

8.14.1.1 Architecture Validation Through Documentation

Technical analysis of AI system architecture should correlate with documented specifications, design decisions, and implementation plans. Discrepancies between technical reality and documentation might indicate implementation errors, undocumented changes, or intentional misrepresentation.

Design decision documentation should explain why specific architectural choices were made, what alternatives were considered, and what trade-offs were accepted. Technical analysis can validate whether these documented trade-offs actually occurred and whether the expected benefits were realized.

Performance characteristics documented in specifications should align with technical testing results and operational monitoring data. Discrepancies might indicate unrealistic specifications, implementation problems, or environmental factors not considered during design.

8.14.1.2 Training Data and Process Validation

Documentation about training data sources, collection procedures, and quality controls should correlate with technical analysis of actual training datasets. Discrepancies might indicate data governance failures, unauthorized data sources, or quality control inadequacies.

Training procedure documentation should match technical analysis of training scripts, hyperparameter configurations, and model artifacts. Inconsistencies might indicate undocumented experimental changes, implementation errors, or inadequate documentation practices.

Data processing pipeline documentation should correlate with technical analysis of preprocessing code, feature engineering, and data transformation procedures. Discrepancies could explain unexpected model behavior or bias patterns identified in technical analysis.

8.14.1.3 Output Behavior and Documentation Consistency

Model behavior documented in specifications and testing reports should align with technical analysis of actual outputs. Inconsistencies might indicate model drift, environmental changes, or inadequate testing procedures.

Bias assessment documentation should correlate with technical bias testing results. Discrepancies might indicate inadequate bias testing, changing data distributions, or ineffective bias mitigation strategies.

Performance monitoring documentation should align with technical analysis of system logs and operational data. Inconsistencies might indicate monitoring failures, unrealistic performance expectations, or inadequate alerting thresholds.

8.14.2 Multi-Source Evidence Synthesis and Validation

8.14.2.1 Convergent Evidence Analysis

Identify findings that are supported by multiple independent sources including technical evidence, documentation analysis, and stakeholder communications. Convergent evidence provides the strongest foundation for conclusions and recommendations, particularly in legal proceedings where evidence reliability is crucial.

Convergent evidence patterns may include technical problems documented in system logs, discussed in communications, and addressed in formal incident reports. Business decisions documented in meeting minutes, confirmed in email threads, and implemented through technical changes. Risk assessments documented in formal reports, discussed in stakeholder communications, and reflected in technical implementations.

8.14.2.2 Divergent Evidence Resolution

When different sources contradict each other, systematic analysis can help determine which sources are most reliable, whether contradictions indicate intentional misrepresentation or honest mistakes, whether missing information could resolve apparent discrepancies, and what additional investigation might be needed to reach definitive conclusions.

Develop systematic approaches for handling conflicting information including source reliability assessment, temporal analysis to determine information currency, corroboration analysis to identify supporting evidence, and gap analysis to identify missing information that might resolve conflicts.

8.14.2.3 Gap Analysis and Limitation Documentation

Identify areas where evidence is incomplete or inconclusive, document limitations that affect finding reliability, and prioritize additional investigation needs based on their importance to key conclusions. Honest limitation documentation strengthens rather than weakens investigation credibility by demonstrating thoroughness and scientific integrity.

Common evidence gaps may include deleted or overwritten documentation, undocumented verbal decisions, missing experimental records, inadequate version control histories, or inaccessible third-party vendor information. Each gap represents a limitation on investigation completeness and may affect the reliability of specific conclusions.

8.15 SPECIALIZED DOCUMENTATION TYPES AND ANALYSIS TECHNIQUES

8.15.1 Research and Experimental Documentation Analysis

8.15.1.1 Jupyter Notebook and Experimental Analysis

Jupyter notebooks and similar experimental environments contain detailed records of research activities including data exploration that may reveal quality issues or bias patterns not documented elsewhere, model experimentation showing performance trade-offs and failure modes, preliminary findings that may not appear in formal documentation, and iterative development processes that reveal how systems evolved.

Notebook analysis requires understanding experimental workflows and identifying key insights that influenced system development. Data exploration sections may reveal quality issues, bias patterns, or data collection problems. Model experimentation may show performance trade-offs, architectural decisions, or failure modes not discussed in formal documentation. Code comments and markdown cells often contain informal observations and insights.

8.15.1.2 Academic Paper and Publication Analysis

Research publications may describe system capabilities, acknowledge limitations, or reveal experimental results relevant to investigation questions. Internal research papers may be more candid about system limitations than external publications. Citation analysis can identify related work, validation studies, and external perspectives on system capabilities.

Publication analysis should consider the intended audience, publication timeline relative to system development, and potential differences between published results and actual system implementation. Academic publications may describe idealized versions of systems rather than practical implementations.

8.15.1.3 Conference Presentation Materials Analysis

Internal and external presentations often contain an honest assessment of system performance including acknowledged limitations, known issues, and future improvement plans not present in formal documentation. Presentation materials may include performance metrics, risk assessments, and strategic considerations not documented elsewhere.

Presentation analysis should consider the audience, context, and purpose of presentations. Internal presentations to technical audiences may be more candid about limitations than external presentations to business stakeholders or customers.

8.15.2 Compliance and Regulatory Documentation Analysis

8.15.2.1 Regulatory Filing Analysis

Regulatory submissions often contain formal statements about AI system capabilities, limitations, and compliance measures. These documents are typically prepared with legal review and represent official organizational positions. However, they may be less technical or complete than internal documentation.

Compare regulatory submissions with internal documentation to identify potential discrepancies between public representations and private knowledge. Significant discrepancies might indicate compliance violations or misrepresentations to regulators.

8.15.2.2 Audit Report Analysis

External audit reports provide independent assessments of organizational controls, compliance posture, and risk management practices. These reports often identify weaknesses or gaps that may not be apparent from internal documentation.

Internal audit reports may be more comprehensive and candid about organizational weaknesses than external reports. Compare findings across multiple audit periods to identify trends, recurring issues, or improvement patterns.

8.15.2.3 Industry Standards Compliance Analysis

Organizations may claim compliance with industry standards like ISO 27001, SOC 2, or industry-specific frameworks. Analyze compliance documentation to determine whether claims are substantiated by evidence and whether compliance activities are effectively implemented.

Standards compliance documentation often provides insight into organizational maturity, risk management practices, and control effectiveness that may not be apparent from other documentation sources.

8.16 ADVANCED PATTERN RECOGNITION AND BEHAVIORAL ANALYSIS

8.16.1 Organizational Behavior Pattern Analysis

8.16.1.1 Decision-Making Pattern Analysis

Examine how organizations typically make technical and business decisions about AI systems through formal review processes, systematic stakeholder consultation, documented approval workflows, and crisis response procedures. Normal patterns provide baseline expectations for organizational behavior.

Deviations from established patterns may indicate emergency circumstances, inadequate governance, unusual business pressures, or attempts to avoid normal oversight processes. Understanding these deviations helps assess the adequacy of organizational controls and accountability systems.

8.16.1.2 Communication Pattern Analysis

Identify how information typically flows through organizations during different types of activities including technical discussions, business decisions, crisis response, and routine operations.

Communication patterns reveal organizational culture, power dynamics, and information sharing practices.

Technical issues may normally be discussed in engineering channels before escalating to management levels. Business decisions may follow specific approval chains involving multiple organizational levels. Crisis response may activate emergency communication protocols that bypass normal channels.

8.16.1.3 Change Management Pattern Analysis

Examine how organizations typically handle system modifications including testing procedures, staged deployments, rollback capabilities, and approval processes. Normal change management patterns indicate organizational maturity and risk management practices.

Deviations from normal change management might indicate emergency responses, inadequate planning, process failures, or attempts to bypass normal controls. Understanding these deviations helps assess organizational risk management effectiveness.

8.16.2 Crisis Response and Incident Management Analysis

8.16.2.1 Incident Detection and Response Analysis

Examine how organizations detect, assess, and respond to AI system failures, security events, and performance issues. Response adequacy affects both immediate impact and long-term system reliability.

Incident detection should be timely and comprehensive. Monitoring systems should identify problems before they cause significant impact. Alert thresholds should be appropriate for the criticality of the AI application.

Response procedures should be well-documented, properly executed, and effective at resolving issues. Post-incident analysis should identify root causes and implement improvements to prevent recurrence.

8.16.2.2 Learning and Improvement Analysis

Learning and improvement from incidents demonstrates organizational maturity and commitment to continuous improvement. Organizations that don't learn from failures are likely to experience recurring problems.

Analyze how organizations capture lessons learned, implement process improvements, update documentation, and share knowledge across teams. Effective learning processes reduce the likelihood of similar incidents and improve overall system reliability.

8.16.2.3 Communication During Crisis

Crisis communications often reveal the most accurate assessment of problems and organizational capabilities. Analyze how communication patterns change during crisis periods, what information is shared with different stakeholders, and how quickly issues are escalated.

Crisis communications may bypass normal channels, involve different stakeholders, or reveal information not present in routine communications. These communications often provide insight into organizational priorities, technical capabilities, and decision-making under pressure.

8.17 LEGAL CONSIDERATIONS AND EVIDENCE STANDARDS

8.17.1 Privilege and Confidentiality Analysis

8.17.1.1 Attorney-Client Privilege Assessment

Legal communications require careful handling to preserve privilege protections while enabling investigation objectives. Coordinate with legal counsel to establish appropriate review procedures and protection protocols.

Identify potentially privileged communications through sender/recipient analysis, subject matter examination, and communication context assessment. Privileged communications should be segregated and handled according to established legal procedures.

8.17.1.2 Work Product Protection Analysis

Documents prepared in anticipation of litigation may be protected from disclosure. Identify and segregate protected materials while ensuring investigation completeness within legal constraints.

Work product analysis requires understanding the purpose and context of document creation, the involvement of legal counsel, and the timing relative to potential litigation. Protected documents should be handled according to applicable legal standards.

8.17.1.3 Regulatory Confidentiality Requirements

Industry-specific regulations may restrict document disclosure or require special handling procedures. Understand applicable regulatory requirements and coordinate with compliance personnel to ensure proper handling.

Healthcare organizations must comply with HIPAA requirements, financial services organizations have specific disclosure restrictions, and other industries may have unique confidentiality obligations that affect investigation procedures.

8.17.2 Evidence Admissibility and Authentication Requirements

8.17.2.1 Chain of Custody Requirements

Maintain detailed records of evidence handling from initial collection through final analysis including timestamps, personnel involved, access controls, and any modifications or processing applied to evidence.

Chain of custody documentation must account for every person who accessed evidence, every transfer or movement of evidence, and every procedure applied to evidence. Gaps or inconsistencies in chain of custody may affect evidence admissibility.

8.17.2.2 Authentication Requirements

Demonstrate document authenticity through technical analysis, witness testimony, and corroborating evidence. Prepare authentication documentation that meets applicable legal standards for admissibility.

Authentication methods vary by document type and may include digital signature validation, metadata analysis, witness testimony, and cross-reference verification. Document all authentication procedures and results.

8.18 CONCLUSION

Documentation analysis represents a critical component of comprehensive AI forensics that validates technical findings through systematic examination of human-created records and communications. This chapter has established a framework for conducting forensically sound documentation analysis that maintains legal admissibility while maximizing investigative value.

The unique challenges of AI documentation analysis stem from the distributed, evolutionary, and interdisciplinary nature of modern AI development. Unlike traditional software systems where documentation might be centralized and standardized, AI systems generate documentation across multiple domains, platforms, and organizational boundaries. Effective analysis requires sophisticated correlation techniques that can identify relationships across diverse sources while accounting for temporal evolution and organizational dynamics.

Key principles for effective AI documentation analysis include comprehensive source identification through systematic discovery processes that account for formal repositories, informal communications, and automatically generated records. Forensic integrity must be maintained through proper collection procedures, chain of custody documentation, and authentication verification. Cross-source correlation reveals patterns and discrepancies that provide crucial insights into system development and operation.

The integration of documentation analysis with technical findings from training data analysis, model investigation, and output analysis creates comprehensive understanding that exceeds what any single investigative approach could achieve. Documentation provides context for interpreting technical evidence, validates technical claims, reveals decision-making processes and accountability chains, identifies organizational awareness of risks and limitations, and demonstrates compliance efforts or their absence.

Documentation analysis findings must be presented in ways that serve different audiences effectively. Technical audiences require detailed methodological information and complete analytical results. Legal audiences need clear explanations of complex concepts and reliable evidence that meets admissibility standards. Business audiences require actionable insights about organizational processes and compliance adequacy.

The temporal dimension of documentation analysis provides particular value in AI forensics by reconstructing how systems evolved over time and identifying when specific issues were introduced or discovered. This timeline reconstruction is often crucial for establishing causation in legal proceedings and understanding how organizational decisions influenced system behavior.

The framework established in this chapter provides comprehensive coverage of documentation analysis challenges and methodologies specific to AI forensic investigations. The systematic approach to source identification, collection, authentication, and analysis ensures that investigators can extract maximum value from documentary evidence while maintaining the rigor necessary for legal proceedings and regulatory compliance.

As AI systems become more sophisticated and widely deployed, documentation analysis will become increasingly important for ensuring accountability, compliance, and trust. Organizations that maintain comprehensive, accurate documentation will be better positioned to demonstrate responsible AI development and operation. Investigators who master sophisticated documentation analysis techniques will be able to provide more complete and reliable assessments of AI system behavior and accountability.

The comprehensive methodology presented here, including the systematic use of matrices for source assessment, process management, and validation techniques, provides practitioners with practical tools for conducting thorough documentation analysis. The integration of technical correlation methods with behavioral pattern recognition enables investigators to understand not just what happened, but why it happened and who was responsible.

Moving forward to the subsequent chapters on incident response and final reporting, the documentation analysis findings will be integrated with technical investigation results to create comprehensive understanding of AI system behavior, accountability, and compliance. The documentation analysis framework established here provides crucial context for interpreting technical evidence and supports the development of actionable recommendations for addressing identified issues and improving organizational AI governance.

The evolution of AI forensics will increasingly depend on sophisticated documentation analysis capabilities as AI systems become more complex and their organizational impacts become more significant. The methods and frameworks presented in this chapter provide the foundation for developing these capabilities while ensuring that documentation analysis contributes effectively to the broader goals of AI accountability, transparency, and responsible development.

9 Synthesis and Reporting

9.1 TURNING TECHNICAL ANALYSIS INTO ACTIONABLE INTELLIGENCE

When investigators at a major healthcare AI company discovered their diagnostic system was exhibiting 23% lower accuracy for elderly patients, the problem wasn't immediately obvious. The training data analysis from Chapter 5 had revealed underrepresentation of patients over 75. The model investigation from Chapter 6 showed architectural biases toward younger demographic features. The output analysis from Chapter 7 confirmed systematic performance degradation. The documentation analysis from Chapter 8 revealed that development teams were aware of the representation gap but had not addressed it due to budget constraints.

None of these findings alone told the complete story. Only through systematic synthesis of evidence across all domains could investigators demonstrate that the accuracy problems stemmed from a specific chain of decisions: inadequate dataset procurement led to biased model training, which resulted in discriminatory outputs that violated both medical ethics and organizational policies. The synthesis revealed not just what went wrong, but why it went wrong and how to prevent similar issues in the future.

This case illustrates the fundamental challenge of AI forensic reporting: transforming multiple streams of technical analysis into coherent narratives that enable decisive action. Unlike traditional forensics where a single smoking gun might solve a case, AI investigations generate complex webs of interconnected evidence that must be woven together to reveal meaningful patterns and actionable insights.

9.2 WHAT YOU WILL LEARN

By the end of this chapter, you will be able to:

- Synthesize findings from evidence collection, training data analysis, model investigation, output analysis, and documentation review into cohesive narratives
- Create causal chains showing how problems in one domain manifest across the entire AI system
- Adapt technical findings for different stakeholder audiences without losing analytical rigor
- Develop actionable recommendations that address root causes rather than symptoms
- Design implementation frameworks that translate forensic findings into operational improvements
- Build decision-making matrices that prioritize remediation efforts based on impact and feasibility

9.3 QUICK START GUIDE

9.3.1 Need Immediate Answers?

- **Multiple technical findings need integration?** → Start with Technical Synthesis Methodology (Section 9.4)
- **Executive briefing required?** → Jump to Stakeholder Communication Strategies (Section 9.5)
- **Converting findings to action items?** → See Implementation and Follow-Up Framework (Section 9.6)

DOI: 10.1201/9781003634782-9

- **Conflicting evidence across domains?** → Review Cross-Domain Analysis Techniques (Section 9.4.3)
- **Need to prioritize multiple issues?** → Use the Issue Prioritization Matrix (Section 9.6.2)
- **Stakeholders questioning methodology?** → Reference Quality Assurance Documentation (Section 9.5.4)

9.4 TECHNICAL SYNTHESIS METHODOLOGY

The synthesis phase represents the investigative moment when scattered technical findings transform into a complete story about what went wrong and why. Think of it as detective work: you've gathered evidence from the crime scene (evidence collection), analyzed the weapon (model investigation), examined the victim (output analysis), studied the suspect's background (training data analysis), and reviewed witness statements (documentation analysis). Now you must weave these findings together to reconstruct what actually happened.

This process goes far beyond simply listing findings from each chapter. Effective synthesis reveals the hidden connections between technical domains that explain how small problems compound into major failures, why quick fixes often backfire, and where organizations should focus their remediation efforts for maximum impact. The goal is transforming a collection of technical observations into actionable intelligence that enables decisive organizational response.

9.4.1 Cross-Domain Evidence Correlation

The correlation process begins with a fundamental recognition: AI systems are interconnected webs where problems in one area inevitably affect others. Your task is mapping these connections systematically to avoid missing critical relationships that might invalidate your conclusions or misdirect remediation efforts.

Consider how this works in practice. When your training data analysis reveals that 73% of loan approval examples come from affluent neighborhoods, you shouldn't just note this as an isolated finding. Instead, you should immediately ask: How does this imbalance manifest in the model parameters? What patterns appear in the outputs? Were development teams aware of this skew, and if so, why wasn't it addressed? Each domain provides a different lens for examining the same underlying issues.

Temporal correlation analysis reveals how problems develop and propagate over time by aligning findings chronologically across all investigation domains. This technique answers crucial questions about causation versus correlation. When you discover that model performance degraded by 15% starting in March, temporal analysis helps you determine whether this correlates with training data changes documented in February, architectural modifications logged in the version control system, or organizational restructuring noted in meeting minutes.

The power of temporal correlation lies in its ability to distinguish between root causes and downstream effects. If training data quality declined before model performance degraded, which occurred before output bias increased, you've identified a clear causal sequence. However, if these events happened simultaneously or in reverse order, you need to look for alternative explanations or hidden factors that triggered multiple problems at once.

Document your temporal analysis using synchronized timelines that overlay findings from all domains. When correlations are strong, they provide compelling evidence for causal relationships. When timing doesn't align as expected, the misalignment often points toward missing evidence or factors you haven't yet discovered—both valuable insights for completing your investigation.

Statistical correlation assessment quantifies relationships between findings across domains to move beyond intuitive connections toward mathematically defensible claims. This approach is particularly powerful when dealing with bias and discrimination issues where legal or regulatory standards require statistical evidence.

For example, if your training data analysis reveals 23% underrepresentation of rural customers, statistical correlation assessment determines whether this translates proportionally into model parameter distributions and output performance gaps. Strong mathematical correlations ($r > 0.7$) provide robust evidence that training data imbalances directly caused output discrimination. Weaker correlations suggest intervening factors—perhaps architectural choices amplified or dampened the bias, or deployment conditions introduced additional variables.

The key insight is that correlation strength tells you how confident you can be in your causal claims and helps prioritize remediation efforts. Strong correlations indicate that fixing root causes will likely resolve downstream problems. Weak correlations suggest that multiple interventions might be necessary or that your understanding of the system is incomplete.

Logical dependency mapping traces the inevitable consequences of technical choices through system architecture to predict where problems must appear based on fundamental constraints. This technique helps you identify which findings represent independent issues versus predictable consequences of earlier decisions.

For instance, if architectural analysis reveals that a model uses only 50 features when the training data contains 500 potential features, logical dependency mapping predicts that information loss is inevitable. You can then examine which types of information were discarded and predict which demographic groups or use cases will suffer reduced performance. When output analysis confirms these predictions, you've built a compelling causal narrative supported by technical necessity rather than just statistical correlation.

9.4.2 Causal Chain Construction

Building causal chains transforms your collection of correlated findings into compelling narratives that explain how specific decisions and conditions led inevitably to observed problems. This process creates the foundation for remediation recommendations because it identifies the precise intervention points where different choices would have prevented current issues.

Effective causal chain construction works like building a bridge between root causes and final outcomes, with each link representing a decision point or system constraint that propagated problems forward. The strength of your overall narrative depends on the weakest link in this chain, so you must validate each connection rigorously.

Root cause identification requires working backward from observed problems through multiple layers of causation until you reach decisions or conditions that initiated the entire sequence. This process often reveals that obvious symptoms mask deeper organizational or technical issues.

Consider a loan approval AI that discriminates against minority applicants. Surface-level analysis might blame biased training data, but root cause analysis digs deeper: Why was the training data biased? Investigation might reveal that the organization used historical lending records from 1995–2005, a period when discriminatory lending practices were widespread but not yet illegal. The root cause isn't just biased data—it's the procurement decision to use historical data without bias assessment.

Root cause identification becomes actionable when you can point to specific decisions that could have been made differently. If the organization had included bias assessment in their data procurement process, or had required demographic balance in training sets, or had established fairness testing before deployment, the discrimination might never have occurred. These insights directly inform prevention strategies and organizational policy changes.

Document root causes with decision trees that show alternative choices and their likely consequences. This approach helps stakeholders understand why simple technical fixes often fail—because they address symptoms rather than fundamental decisions that created the problems.

Intermediate factor analysis examines how root causes propagated through system components to create observed problems, identifying every stage where different choices might have interrupted the causal chain. This analysis is crucial for organizations because it reveals multiple intervention opportunities and explains why narrow technical solutions often fail to solve broad systemic issues.

Think of intermediate factors as checkpoints in the causal chain where warning signs should have triggered corrective action. In the loan discrimination example, intermediate factors might include: inadequate data quality assessment that failed to detect historical bias, architectural choices that amplified rather than mitigated bias, validation procedures that focused on overall accuracy rather than fairness across demographics, and deployment monitoring that tracked business metrics but ignored discrimination indicators.

Each intermediate factor represents a missed opportunity for prevention and a current opportunity for intervention. Organizations often discover that they could implement multiple safeguards that would prevent similar issues even if root causes aren't fully addressed. This finding is particularly valuable when root causes involve fundamental business constraints that can't be changed easily.

Document intermediate factors using process flow diagrams that show decision points, control mechanisms, and feedback loops. Highlight where existing controls failed and where new controls could be implemented. This visual approach helps stakeholders understand both why problems occurred and how organizational processes can be strengthened to prevent recurrence.

Impact amplification assessment evaluates how initial problems grew more severe as they propagated through system components, often revealing architectural or operational choices that amplified rather than mitigated issues. Understanding amplification mechanisms helps predict the severity of similar problems and design more robust prevention systems.

Amplification often occurs when system components interact in unexpected ways or when operational conditions differ from development assumptions. Small training data biases can become major output discrimination when architectural choices concentrate attention on biased features, when deployment environments differ from training conditions, or when user behavior patterns interact with model biases in unforeseen ways.

For example, a hiring AI trained on résumés from 2010–2015 might learn subtle biases about technology skills that seemed minor during training but become major discrimination factors when applied to current applicants whose technology experience is formatted differently. The bias amplification occurs because the model learned to associate specific formatting patterns with competence rather than learning about actual technical skills.

Document amplification mechanisms using sensitivity analysis that shows how small changes in input conditions produce large changes in outcomes. This analysis helps organizations understand their vulnerability to similar issues and design architectural or operational safeguards that dampen rather than amplify biases.

9.4.3 Cross-Domain Analysis Techniques

Cross-domain analysis techniques systematically examine how findings from different chapters interact and influence each other, revealing patterns that single-domain analysis cannot detect. These techniques are essential for avoiding tunnel vision that focuses on individual problems while missing systemic patterns that require comprehensive organizational response.

Evidence triangulation strengthens investigation reliability by using findings from multiple domains to validate or challenge conclusions. When evidence from training data analysis, model investigation, and output analysis all point toward the same conclusion, convergent evidence provides strong support for remediation recommendations. When findings conflict, triangulation helps identify measurement errors, methodological limitations, or missing factors that require additional investigation.

Think of triangulation as cross-checking your story from multiple perspectives. If training data analysis reveals demographic imbalances, model investigation should show corresponding parameter patterns, output analysis should demonstrate predictable performance disparities, and documentation analysis should reveal whether teams were aware of these issues. When all domains align, you can be confident in your conclusions.

However, triangulation becomes most valuable when domains don't align as expected. If training data appears balanced but outputs show discrimination, triangulation forces you to look for alternative explanations: perhaps bias emerged during data preprocessing, architectural choices amplified subtle imbalances, deployment conditions introduced new biases, or operational factors affected different user groups differently.

Document triangulation using evidence matrices that map findings from each domain against your key conclusions. Strong triangulation shows multiple forms of evidence supporting each conclusion. Weak triangulation reveals where additional investigation might be necessary or where conclusions should be qualified due to limited evidence.

Contradiction resolution addresses apparent conflicts between findings from different domains through deeper analysis that often reveals more nuanced understanding of system behavior. Rather than treating contradictions as problems to solve, effective investigators view them as opportunities to discover important system characteristics that weren't initially apparent.

Consider a case where model parameter analysis suggests unbiased behavior while output analysis reveals clear discrimination. This apparent contradiction might indicate that bias emerges from deployment conditions rather than training—perhaps user behavior patterns, input data preprocessing, or interaction effects create discriminatory outcomes even when the underlying model is technically fair. Systematic contradiction resolution helps you understand these complex interactions.

The key insight is that contradictions often point toward the most important aspects of system behavior. They reveal where your initial assumptions were wrong, where system interactions are more complex than expected, or where critical evidence is missing. Effective contradiction resolution strengthens rather than weakens your investigation by forcing more sophisticated understanding.

Document contradiction resolution using analysis logs that show how apparent conflicts led to deeper insights. Include alternative explanations you considered and evidence that supported or ruled out each possibility. This documentation demonstrates investigative rigor and helps stakeholders understand why your final conclusions are more reliable than initial observations.

Gap analysis integration combines evidence gaps identified across all domains to assess overall investigation completeness and reliability while identifying potential concealment efforts or systematic organizational dysfunction. Understanding gaps is crucial because missing evidence can invalidate conclusions or misdirect remediation efforts.

Gap analysis reveals patterns that distinguish between random data loss and systematic concealment. Random gaps appear sporadically across different domains and time periods. Systematic gaps cluster around sensitive issues, controversial decisions, or periods when problems emerged. For example, missing training data provenance combined with incomplete model documentation and limited output monitoring during the same time period suggests possible concealment rather than poor record-keeping.

The goal isn't achieving perfect evidence coverage—that's rarely possible in real-world investigations. Instead, gap analysis helps you understand how missing evidence affects conclusion reliability and where additional investigation might strengthen your findings. Sometimes gaps themselves become important findings that reveal organizational dysfunction or deliberate obfuscation.

Document gap analysis using completeness matrices that show evidence availability across domains and time periods. Use visual indicators to distinguish between evidence that exists but wasn't collected, evidence that probably existed but is now missing, and evidence that likely never existed due to poor organizational practices.

9.4.4 Pattern Recognition Across Domains

Pattern recognition identifies recurring themes and systematic issues that span multiple aspects of AI system development and operation, revealing organizational or technical patterns that create persistent vulnerabilities. This analysis is crucial for understanding whether identified problems represent isolated incidents or symptoms of deeper organizational dysfunction.

Systemic bias patterns emerge when discrimination appears consistently across multiple domains and time periods, often supported by documentation showing organizational awareness or indifference to equity concerns. Recognizing systemic patterns is crucial because they require fundamentally different remediation approaches than isolated bias incidents.

Systemic bias manifests as consistent underrepresentation in training data across multiple datasets, architectural choices that systematically amplify rather than mitigate bias, validation procedures that consistently overlook fairness concerns, deployment practices that systematically disadvantage certain groups, and organizational communications that consistently prioritize efficiency over equity. When these patterns appear together, they indicate cultural or structural issues that won't be resolved through technical fixes alone.

For example, if three different AI systems developed by the same organization all show similar demographic biases, if training data procurement consistently ignores demographic balance, if architectural standards don't include bias mitigation techniques, and if validation procedures consistently focus on accuracy rather than fairness, you've identified systemic patterns that require organizational-level intervention.

Document systemic patterns using timeline analysis that shows how similar issues emerged across different projects, systems, and time periods. Include organizational context such as leadership changes, policy modifications, or resource constraints that might explain pattern emergence or persistence.

Quality degradation patterns manifest as declining standards across multiple domains over time, revealing organizational pressures or resource constraints that systematically undermine AI system quality. These patterns help distinguish between isolated quality issues and systematic organizational dysfunction.

Quality degradation appears as progressively lower data quality standards, relaxed model validation procedures, reduced testing requirements, deteriorating documentation practices, and declining monitoring capabilities. When these trends appear together, they often correlate with organizational factors such as increased time pressure, reduced funding, leadership changes, or staff turnover documented in organizational communications.

Understanding degradation patterns helps predict future problems and design prevention strategies that address organizational root causes rather than just technical symptoms. If quality degradation correlates with quarterly pressure to deliver results, remediation strategies might include longer development cycles or different performance incentives for development teams.

Compliance failure patterns appear when regulatory or policy violations span multiple domains and time periods, helping distinguish between isolated compliance failures and systematic organizational dysfunction. This analysis is particularly important for organizations facing regulatory scrutiny or legal challenges.

Compliance failure patterns include inadequate data governance across multiple projects, insufficient model testing relative to regulatory requirements, poor output monitoring that consistently fails to detect violations, missing documentation that prevents compliance verification, and organizational communications that consistently prioritize business objectives over compliance requirements.

Pattern recognition helps distinguish organizations that occasionally make compliance mistakes from those that systematically ignore compliance obligations. This distinction affects both remediation strategies and liability assessments in legal proceedings.

9.5 STAKEHOLDER COMMUNICATION STRATEGIES

Effective stakeholder communication transforms technical findings into actionable insights appropriate for different audiences while maintaining analytical rigor and enabling informed decision-making. Each stakeholder group requires different levels of technical detail, different focus areas, and different formats for optimal comprehension and utilization.

9.5.1 Audience-Specific Content Adaptation

Different stakeholders need different information presented in different ways to make appropriate decisions based on investigation findings. Successful adaptation maintains factual accuracy while optimizing presentation for each audience's expertise, responsibilities, and decision-making requirements.

Technical team communication provides comprehensive technical detail that enables independent validation and implementation of recommendations. Technical audiences need complete methodological documentation, statistical analyses with confidence intervals, architectural specifications, and detailed implementation guidance. However, technical presentations must also clearly explain business implications and organizational impacts to ensure technical teams understand the broader context of their work.

Executive leadership briefings focus on strategic implications, resource requirements, and risk assessments that enable appropriate resource allocation and policy decisions. Executive presentations should lead with clear bottom-line impacts, provide concise technical summaries that explain reliability and significance, and emphasize actionable recommendations with clear timelines and success metrics. Technical complexity should be simplified without oversimplification that might lead to poor decisions.

Operational team guidelines translate findings into specific procedural changes and monitoring requirements that frontline staff can implement effectively. Operational communication should emphasize practical impacts on daily work, provide clear step-by-step guidance for implementing changes, and establish measurable criteria for success that operational teams can monitor and report.

Cross-functional integration ensures that different stakeholder groups receive consistent information while addressing their specific needs. Master documentation maintains authoritative technical records while derivative communications adapt presentation style and emphasis for different audiences. Version control and cross-reference systems ensure that updates propagate consistently across all stakeholder communications.

9.5.2 Multi-Format Reporting Framework

Different communication formats serve different purposes and audiences while maintaining consistency in core findings and recommendations. A comprehensive reporting framework uses multiple formats strategically to maximize impact and understanding across diverse stakeholder groups.

Executive summary documents provide concise overviews that enable rapid understanding of key findings and recommended actions. Executive summaries should lead with clear statements of problems identified and recommended solutions, provide brief context that explains why issues matter for organizational success, include resource requirements and timeline estimates for recommended actions, and conclude with success metrics that enable progress monitoring.

Technical reference reports serve as comprehensive repositories of methodological details, statistical analyses, and implementation specifications that enable detailed validation and replication. Technical reports should include complete methodology documentation with sufficient detail for independent replication, comprehensive statistical analyses with appropriate confidence intervals and effect sizes, detailed technical recommendations with specific implementation guidance, and appendices containing supporting data and analytical code where appropriate.

Operational procedure documents translate findings into specific changes in day-to-day operations, monitoring procedures, and quality assurance practices. Operational documents should provide step-by-step implementation procedures, clear criteria for identifying similar issues in the future, escalation procedures for handling exceptions or anomalies, and training materials that help staff understand both what to do and why it matters.

Strategic planning integration incorporates investigation findings into broader organizational planning processes and policy development. Strategic integration should identify systemic organizational factors that contributed to identified issues, recommend policy changes that address root causes rather than symptoms, suggest organizational structure or process improvements that prevent similar issues, and establish governance frameworks that enable ongoing monitoring and improvement.

9.5.3 Consistency Management Across Communications

Managing consistency across multiple communication formats requires systematic approaches that ensure factual accuracy while adapting presentation style and technical depth for different audiences. Inconsistency between communications can undermine credibility and lead to confusion about appropriate responses.

Master document methodology maintains authoritative technical documentation that serves as the single source of truth for all derivative communications. The master document includes complete findings, comprehensive analyses, detailed methodologies, and full supporting evidence. All stakeholder-specific communications extract information from this master source while maintaining traceability to underlying evidence and analyses.

Cross-reference validation ensures that claims made in different communication formats can be traced to common evidence sources and that updates to findings propagate consistently across all formats. Cross-reference systems help identify potential inconsistencies before they reach stakeholders and provide clear audit trails that support credibility during questioning or review processes.

Stakeholder review integration enables different audiences to validate that communications accurately represent findings and adequately address their specific information needs without compromising overall consistency. Technical reviewers assess methodological adequacy, business reviewers confirm strategic implications are properly characterized, and operational reviewers verify that procedural guidance is practical and complete.

9.5.4 Quality Assurance Documentation

Quality assurance documentation demonstrates investigation reliability and strengthens credibility across all stakeholder communications. Comprehensive quality assurance addresses methodology validation, peer review processes, and transparent acknowledgment of limitations that might affect interpretation.

Methodology validation documentation demonstrates that analytical approaches meet established standards and produce reliable results. Validation documentation should include citations to relevant literature and industry standards, comparison with alternative analytical approaches where applicable, sensitivity analysis showing how different methodological choices affect conclusions, and peer review records demonstrating independent validation of approaches and findings.

Limitation and uncertainty communication provides honest assessment of investigation constraints and their implications for conclusion reliability. Transparent limitation discussion should address data availability constraints and their impact on analysis completeness, methodological limitations and alternative approaches that might yield different insights, temporal constraints and additional analysis that might strengthen conclusions, and confidence levels for different findings based on evidence quality and analytical rigor.

Audit trail maintenance provides complete documentation of investigation processes that enables independent verification and supports credibility under scrutiny. Audit trails should include chronological records of all analytical activities, version control for data, code, and documentation, chain of custody documentation for evidence handling, and decision logs explaining analytical choices and their rationales.

9.6 IMPLEMENTATION AND FOLLOW-UP FRAMEWORK

Converting forensic findings into operational improvements requires systematic frameworks that translate analytical insights into specific actions, resource allocations, and monitoring systems. Effective implementation addresses root causes rather than symptoms while establishing mechanisms for preventing similar issues in the future.

9.6.1 From Findings to Action Items

Transforming investigation findings into actionable recommendations requires structured approaches that ensure recommendations address identified problems comprehensively while remaining feasible given organizational constraints and capabilities.

Root cause addressing ensures that recommendations target fundamental issues rather than surface symptoms that might recur if underlying problems remain unresolved. Root cause analysis should trace observed problems back to their origins in data collection, model development, deployment procedures, or organizational processes. Effective recommendations modify these foundational elements rather than applying superficial fixes that might mask continuing problems.

Feasibility assessment evaluates whether recommended actions can realistically be implemented given organizational resources, technical capabilities, and operational constraints. Feasibility analysis should consider required technical expertise and whether it exists internally or must be acquired, financial resources needed for implementation and ongoing maintenance, timeline constraints and dependencies on other organizational initiatives, and potential resistance from stakeholders affected by recommended changes.

Impact prediction estimates the likely effectiveness of different recommendations in addressing identified issues and preventing similar problems in the future. Impact analysis should quantify expected improvements in system performance, bias reduction, or risk mitigation, assess potential unintended consequences of recommended changes, evaluate how recommendations might affect other organizational systems or processes, and establish measurable success criteria that enable objective assessment of implementation effectiveness.

Resource allocation guidance provides specific estimates of human, financial, and technical resources required for implementing recommendations effectively. Resource guidance should include staffing requirements with necessary expertise levels, technology investments and ongoing

TABLE 9.1

Issue Category	Business Impact	Implementation Complexity	Resource Requirement	Priority Level
Critical Bias	High discrimination risk, legal exposure	Medium—requires data and model changes	High—new datasets, retraining	**Priority 1**
Performance Degradation	Moderate business impact, user satisfaction	Low—configuration adjustments	Low—parameter tuning	**Priority 2**
Documentation Gaps	Compliance risk, audit findings	Low—process improvements	Medium—staff time, systems	**Priority 3**
Monitoring Deficiencies	Future risk, detection capability	Medium—new systems integration	High—tools, training	**Priority 3**

operational costs, timeline estimates with critical milestones and dependencies, and alternative implementation approaches with different resource requirements and expected outcomes.

9.6.2 Issue Prioritization Matrix

When investigations reveal multiple issues requiring attention, prioritization matrices help organizations allocate limited resources effectively by balancing impact severity against implementation feasibility and resource requirements. The following matrix is an example of how to categorize and prioritize multiple issues.

The prioritization matrix enables systematic resource allocation by combining multiple factors that influence both the urgency of addressing issues and the likelihood of successful remediation. Organizations can adapt the matrix criteria based on their specific risk tolerance, resource availability, and strategic priorities.

Impact assessment criteria evaluate the severity and scope of consequences if issues remain unaddressed. High-impact issues typically involve discrimination, safety risks, or significant business losses that require immediate attention regardless of implementation complexity. Medium-impact issues affect operational efficiency or create compliance vulnerabilities that should be addressed systematically. Low-impact issues represent process improvements that can be scheduled around higher-priority initiatives.

Implementation complexity analysis assesses the technical and organizational difficulty of addressing identified issues effectively. Low-complexity solutions typically involve configuration changes, process adjustments, or training that can be implemented quickly with existing resources. Medium-complexity solutions require new systems, significant process changes, or specialized expertise that may need to be acquired. High-complexity solutions involve fundamental system redesign, major organizational change, or extensive technical development that requires substantial planning and resources.

9.6.3 Success Metrics and Monitoring

Effective implementation requires measurable success criteria and ongoing monitoring systems that enable objective assessment of progress and early identification of emerging issues. Success metrics should be specific, measurable, achievable, relevant, and time-bound while addressing both immediate remediation goals and long-term prevention objectives.

Performance improvement metrics track whether implemented changes achieve their intended effects on system behavior and organizational outcomes. Performance metrics should include quantitative measures of bias reduction, accuracy improvement, or risk mitigation that directly address identified issues. Baseline measurements establish pre-implementation performance levels, while regular monitoring tracks progress toward improvement targets and identifies potential setbacks requiring additional intervention.

Process compliance metrics monitor whether organizational changes are being implemented consistently and effectively across relevant teams and systems. Compliance metrics should track adherence to new procedures, completion of required training, and implementation of recommended controls. Process metrics help distinguish between ineffective recommendations and inadequate implementation, enabling appropriate corrective actions.

Early warning indicators establish monitoring systems that can detect similar issues before they become significant problems. Early warning systems should monitor key risk factors identified during the investigation, establish thresholds that trigger additional analysis or intervention, and provide regular reporting that keeps stakeholders informed about system health and emerging risks.

Continuous improvement integration incorporates lessons learned from the investigation and implementation process into ongoing organizational practices. Continuous improvement should update standard operating procedures to reflect new understanding, modify development and deployment practices to prevent similar issues, enhance monitoring and quality assurance systems based on investigation insights, and establish regular review processes that ensure improvements remain effective over time.

9.6.4 Prevention Framework Development

Long-term prevention requires systematic changes to organizational practices, technical processes, and governance frameworks that address the root causes revealed by forensic investigation. Prevention frameworks should be comprehensive enough to address identified vulnerabilities while flexible enough to adapt to changing technologies and organizational needs.

Technical prevention controls implement systematic changes to development, deployment, and monitoring processes that reduce the likelihood of similar issues recurring. Technical controls should include enhanced data quality assurance procedures, improved model validation and testing requirements, strengthened deployment monitoring and alerting systems, and automated bias detection and performance monitoring capabilities.

Organizational prevention measures address process, training, and governance factors that contributed to identified issues. Organizational measures should include updated policies and procedures that reflect investigation insights, enhanced training programs that build relevant expertise and awareness, improved communication and coordination mechanisms between teams, and strengthened oversight and accountability mechanisms that ensure compliance with prevention measures.

Governance framework enhancement establishes ongoing oversight and continuous improvement mechanisms that maintain prevention effectiveness as systems and organizations evolve. Governance enhancements should include regular risk assessment and prevention system evaluation, stakeholder feedback mechanisms that identify emerging risks or prevention gaps, performance measurement and reporting systems that track prevention effectiveness, and adaptation procedures that update prevention measures based on technological change and organizational learning.

9.7 DECISION-MAKING FRAMEWORK

Structured decision-making frameworks help organizations translate forensic findings into appropriate responses by providing systematic approaches for evaluating options, assessing trade-offs, and selecting strategies that balance competing priorities effectively.

9.7.1 Cost-Benefit Analysis for Remediation Options

Cost-benefit analysis provides quantitative frameworks for comparing different approaches to addressing identified issues, enabling data-driven decisions about resource allocation and implementation strategies.

Cost assessment methodology systematically evaluates all resources required for implementing different remediation approaches. Direct costs include technology investments, staffing requirements, and operational expenses associated with implementation and ongoing maintenance. Indirect costs include productivity impacts during implementation, opportunity costs of resource allocation, and potential disruption to other organizational initiatives. Hidden costs often include training requirements, change management expenses, and integration challenges that might not be immediately apparent.

Benefit quantification approaches estimate the value of different remediation strategies in addressing identified risks and improving organizational outcomes. Quantifiable benefits include risk reduction through improved compliance and reduced legal exposure, performance improvements that enhance business outcomes, cost savings from more efficient operations or reduced manual oversight, and competitive advantages from enhanced system reliability and trustworthiness.

TABLE 9.2

Option	Technical Feasibility	Cost Efficiency	Risk Reduction	Strategic Alignment	Overall Score
Complete System Replacement	Medium (8/10)	Low (3/10)	High (9/10)	High (9/10)	7.25
Incremental Improvements	High (9/10)	High (8/ 10)	Medium (6/10)	Medium (7/10)	7.5
Hybrid Approach	High (8/10)	Medium (7/10)	High (8/10)	High (8/10)	7.75
Enhanced Monitoring Only	High (9/10)	High (9/10)	Low (4/10)	Low (5/10)	6.75

Risk-adjusted return calculation incorporates uncertainty and implementation risks into cost-benefit analysis to provide more realistic assessments of different options. Risk adjustment should account for implementation uncertainty and the probability that different approaches will achieve expected benefits, technological risks that might affect long-term solution viability, organizational change risks that might prevent effective adoption, and external factors such as regulatory changes that might affect cost-benefit calculations over time.

9.7.2 Strategic Decision Matrix

Strategic decision matrices provide structured frameworks for evaluating complex decisions that involve multiple criteria and stakeholder perspectives, enabling more comprehensive and defensible decision-making processes.

The strategic decision matrix enables systematic comparison of different approaches by evaluating each option against multiple criteria that reflect organizational priorities and constraints. Organizations should adapt the criteria and weighting based on their specific situation, risk tolerance, and strategic objectives.

Criteria selection and weighting reflect organizational priorities and the specific characteristics of identified issues. Technical feasibility considers whether the organization has or can acquire the capabilities needed for implementation. Cost efficiency balances implementation expenses against expected benefits and available resources. Risk reduction assesses how effectively each option addresses identified vulnerabilities and prevents similar issues. Strategic alignment evaluates how well each option supports broader organizational goals and initiatives.

Scoring methodology provides consistent evaluation approaches that enable meaningful comparison between different options. Quantitative scoring should use standardized scales that enable clear differentiation between options, incorporate input from multiple stakeholders with relevant expertise, account for uncertainty through confidence intervals or sensitivity analysis, and document the rationale for scores to enable review and validation.

9.7.3 Implementation Timeline Development

Effective implementation requires realistic timelines that coordinate multiple activities while accounting for dependencies, resource constraints, and organizational capacity for change management.

Phase-based implementation planning breaks complex remediation efforts into manageable phases that enable incremental progress while maintaining organizational operations. Early phases should focus on high-impact, low-complexity changes that demonstrate progress and build momentum for more challenging later phases. Each phase should have clear deliverables, success criteria, and dependencies that enable progress monitoring and risk management.

Resource scheduling and coordination ensures that required expertise, technology, and financial resources are available when needed while minimizing conflicts with other organizational initiatives. Resource planning should identify critical path activities that determine overall timeline, account for resource constraints that might delay implementation, establish contingency plans for addressing resource conflicts or shortages, and coordinate with other organizational initiatives to minimize disruption and maximize synergy.

Risk management integration incorporates uncertainty and potential setbacks into timeline planning to maintain realistic expectations and enable proactive risk mitigation. Risk management should identify potential delays or complications that might affect implementation, establish contingency plans and alternative approaches for addressing setbacks, build buffer time into schedules to accommodate unexpected challenges, and establish regular review points that enable course correction when necessary.

9.8 CROSS-PHASE INTEGRATION REFERENCE

Effective synthesis requires understanding how findings from different investigation phases interact and influence each other. This integration reference provides practical guidance for correlating evidence across all forensic domains.

9.8.1 Evidence Correlation Patterns

Understanding common correlation patterns helps investigators identify relationships between findings from different chapters and build more comprehensive understanding of AI system behavior.

Training data to model behavior correlations trace how characteristics identified in training data analysis manifest in model architecture and learned behaviors. Demographic underrepresentation in training data should correlate with reduced model performance for those demographics, as revealed through model parameter analysis and confirmed through output testing. Strong correlations provide evidence for causal relationships, while weak correlations suggest other factors or measurement issues.

Model architecture to output pattern relationships connect structural characteristics identified during model investigation with behavioral patterns observed in output analysis. Architectural choices such as attention mechanisms, layer configurations, or activation functions create predictable biases in how models process different types of inputs. Understanding these relationships helps distinguish between intended design effects and unintended discrimination or performance issues.

Documentation to technical evidence alignment compares organizational records and communications with technical findings to assess whether development teams were aware of identified issues and how organizational factors influenced technical outcomes. Alignment between documentation and technical evidence suggests transparent development processes, while significant misalignment might indicate concealment, inadequate monitoring, or poor communication between teams.

9.8.2 Contradiction Analysis Framework

When findings from different chapters conflict, systematic contradiction analysis helps identify the source of disagreement and determine which evidence is most reliable for drawing conclusions.

Evidence quality assessment evaluates the reliability and completeness of findings from different domains to determine which should be given greater weight in cases of contradiction. High-quality evidence includes comprehensive data collection, validated analytical methods, and clear chain of custody documentation. Lower-quality evidence might involve incomplete sampling, unvalidated methods, or missing documentation that affects reliability.

Methodological reconciliation examines whether apparent contradictions result from different analytical approaches, measurement methods, or operational contexts rather than actual conflicts in underlying system behavior. Different methods might reveal different aspects of the same phenomenon, or temporal differences in data collection might explain apparent inconsistencies.

Hidden factor identification investigates whether contradictions indicate missing information or unidentified factors that influence system behavior. Contradictions often reveal important aspects of system operation that weren't initially considered, such as deployment environment effects, user behavior patterns, or organizational factors that influence technical outcomes.

9.8.3 Comprehensive Narrative Construction

Building comprehensive narratives requires systematic integration of findings from all investigation domains into coherent explanations that address stakeholder questions and support decision-making.

Chronological integration organizes findings from all domains according to system development and operational timelines to reveal how issues developed and evolved over time. Chronological organization helps identify when problems first emerged, how they propagated through different system components, and what opportunities existed for earlier detection or intervention.

Causal chain validation uses evidence from multiple domains to strengthen or challenge proposed explanations for observed problems. Strong causal chains are supported by convergent evidence from training data analysis, model investigation, output analysis, and documentation review. Weak causal chains might rely primarily on evidence from one domain and require additional investigation or more cautious interpretation.

Stakeholder impact assessment connects technical findings with business outcomes and organizational consequences to demonstrate the significance of identified issues and the importance of recommended remediation efforts. Impact assessment should quantify effects on performance, compliance, risk exposure, and strategic objectives while providing clear rationale for prioritization and resource allocation decisions.

9.9 CONCLUSION

The synthesis and reporting phase transforms complex technical analysis into actionable organizational intelligence that enables appropriate responses to identified AI system issues. Through systematic integration of evidence collection, training data analysis, model investigation, output analysis, and documentation review, investigators can build comprehensive understanding that supports effective remediation and prevention efforts.

The frameworks presented in this chapter provide structured approaches for managing the complexity of AI forensic investigations while maintaining the rigor necessary for business decision-making and organizational accountability. By emphasizing practical integration techniques, stakeholder communication strategies, and implementation guidance, these frameworks enable organizations to translate forensic insights into operational improvements that address root causes rather than symptoms.

As AI systems become increasingly prevalent and sophisticated, the ability to investigate these systems thoroughly and communicate findings effectively becomes essential for maintaining organizational accountability, regulatory compliance, and public trust. The principles and practices established throughout this book provide a foundation for meeting these challenges while adapting to the continuous evolution of AI technology and its societal implications.

Appendix A: Glossary of Terms

Activation Function: A mathematical function that determines the output of a neural network node, introducing non-linearity into the network to enable learning of complex patterns.

Adversarial Testing: A forensic technique that uses specially crafted inputs designed to expose weaknesses, biases, or unexpected behaviors in AI systems.

Aggregation Bias: A type of bias that occurs when data from different subgroups is combined without accounting for relevant differences between those groups, potentially masking important subgroup-specific patterns.

AI System: A computational framework that performs tasks which typically require human intelligence, consisting of algorithms, data, infrastructure, and interfaces working together to perceive environments, reason through information, learn patterns, and take actions to achieve specific goals.

Algorithm: A set of rules or instructions for solving a problem, particularly the mathematical procedures that define how an AI model processes information.

Attention Mechanism: A neural network component that creates dynamic weights showing which parts of the input the model considers most relevant for specific predictions.

Autoencoder: A neural network architecture designed to encode inputs into a compressed representation and then decode back to the original input, useful for dimensionality reduction and anomaly detection.

Backdoor Detection: The process of identifying hidden behaviors in AI models that are triggered by specific inputs, potentially indicating malicious manipulation.

Backward Propagation: The process of calculating gradients and adjusting neural network weights by moving backward through the network layers during training.

Bias Detection: The systematic identification of unfair or discriminatory patterns in AI systems, training data, or outputs that may disadvantage certain groups.

Bonferroni Correction: A statistical method for adjusting p-values when conducting multiple hypothesis tests simultaneously to control the family-wise error rate and prevent false discoveries.

Chain of Custody: The documentation of evidence handling procedures that maintains integrity and admissibility of digital evidence throughout an investigation.

Checkpoint: A saved snapshot of a model's state during training, capturing parameters and metadata at specific points in the learning process.

Chi-Square Test: A statistical test used to determine if there is a significant association between categorical variables, commonly used in bias detection to test for demographic parity violations.

Classification: A type of supervised learning task that predicts discrete categories or classes from input data.

CNN (Convolutional Neural Network): A type of deep neural network particularly effective for processing visual data through specialized layers that detect patterns and features.

Cohen's d: A standardized measure of effect size that quantifies the practical significance of observed differences between groups, essential for interpreting statistical findings in legal contexts.

Computer Vision Systems: AI systems that process and analyze visual information, typically combining multiple neural network architectures for tasks like image recognition and object detection.

Confidence Interval: A statistical range that provides an estimate of uncertainty around a measurement or prediction, crucial for understanding the reliability of forensic findings.

Confusion Matrix: A table showing the performance of a classification model by comparing actual versus predicted classifications across all categories.

Counterfactual Analysis: An interpretability technique that shows how predictions would change if specific features had different values, helping understand decision boundaries.

Cramér's V: A measure of association between categorical variables that provides effect size information for chi-square tests, ranging from 0 (no association) to 1 (perfect association).

Cross-Validation: A statistical method for assessing how well a model will generalize to independent datasets by partitioning data into training and testing subsets.

Data Lineage: Documentation that traces the origins, transformations, and processing history of data throughout its lifecycle in an AI system.

Data Preprocessing: The process of cleaning, transforming, and preparing raw data for use in training AI models, including normalization, feature engineering, and quality validation.

Decision Boundary: The boundary or surface in feature space that separates different classes or prediction regions in a machine learning model.

Deep Learning: A subset of machine learning featuring multi-layered neural networks that can automatically learn hierarchical representations from data.

Distribution Shift: A change in the statistical properties of data between training and deployment environments, which can degrade model performance.

Evidence Interdependence: The complex relationships between AI artifacts where individual pieces of evidence gain meaning only in relation to other system components, requiring comprehensive collection strategies.

Ensemble Methods: AI approaches that combine multiple models to improve performance and robustness through techniques like bagging, boosting, or stacking.

Expert System: A type of AI system that uses explicitly encoded rules, inference engines, and knowledge bases to make decisions based on domain expertise.

Explainability: The ability to understand and interpret how an AI system makes decisions, often required for legal compliance and accountability.

Fair Use: A legal doctrine that permits limited use of copyrighted material without permission for purposes such as criticism, education, or research.

Feature Engineering: The process of creating, selecting, and transforming input variables (features) from raw data to improve model performance.

Feature Importance: A measure of how much each input variable contributes to a model's predictions, used for interpretability and bias detection.

Feedforward Neural Network (FNN): The simplest neural network architecture where information flows in one direction from input to output with no cycles or loops, suitable for tasks with fixed-size inputs.

Forecasting Systems: AI systems that predict future values or trends based on historical data patterns, commonly used in financial trading and demand prediction.

Forensic Integrity: The preservation of evidence authenticity and reliability throughout an investigation, typically maintained through cryptographic hashing and controlled access procedures.

Forward Propagation: The process of passing input data through a neural network from input layer to output layer to generate predictions.

Foundation Models: Large-scale AI models trained on massive datasets that can be adapted to numerous downstream tasks through fine-tuning or prompting.

Fraud Detection Systems: AI applications that combine rules-based systems with machine learning models to identify potentially fraudulent activities.

GAN (Generative Adversarial Network): A neural network framework where two networks compete in a game-theoretic scenario, with a generator creating synthetic examples and a discriminator trying to distinguish them from real examples.

Gradient Descent: An optimization algorithm used to minimize loss functions by iteratively adjusting model parameters in the direction of steepest descent.

Hash Function: A cryptographic algorithm that produces a fixed-size output (hash) from input data, used to verify data integrity in forensic investigations.

Healthcare Systems: AI applications that integrate multiple diagnostic models, patient data analyzers, and treatment recommendation engines for medical decision support.

Hidden Layers: Intermediate processing layers in neural networks that transform input data and learn progressively more abstract representations.

Historical Bias: Discrimination from past practices that becomes embedded in training data labels or outcome variables, potentially perpetuating unfair treatment.

Hybrid Architectures: AI systems that combine different AI approaches to leverage their complementary strengths, such as integrating neural networks with symbolic reasoning.

Hyperparameter: Configuration settings specified before training begins that guide the learning process, such as learning rates and network architecture choices.

Hyperparameter Tuning: The process of optimizing model configuration settings to achieve better performance through systematic experimentation.

Inference: The process of using a trained AI model to make predictions or decisions on new, unseen data.

Infrastructure Components: The physical and virtual systems that provide computational resources, storage capacity, and operational environment for AI systems.

Input Layer: The first layer of a neural network that receives raw data and passes it to subsequent hidden layers for processing.

Intellectual Property (IP) Violation: The unauthorized use of copyrighted, trademarked, or patented material in training data or AI outputs.

Interpretability: The degree to which a human can understand the cause of a decision made by an AI system.

Large Language Model (LLM): A type of AI model trained on vast amounts of text data to understand and generate human-like language.

Layered Architecture: A system design pattern that organizes AI components into distinct layers (data, feature, model, service, application) with defined interfaces and responsibilities.

LIME (Local Interpretable Model-agnostic Explanations): A technique that creates local linear approximations around specific predictions to provide intuitive explanations.

Loss Function: A mathematical function that measures the difference between predicted and actual outputs, used to guide model training.

LSTM (Long Short-Term Memory): An advanced type of recurrent neural network designed to overcome vanishing gradient problems and learn long-term dependencies in sequential data.

Machine Learning: A subset of AI that enables systems to learn patterns from data without being explicitly programmed for every scenario.

Machine Learning Classification Systems: AI systems trained on labeled datasets that make discrete categorization decisions, widely used in applications from spam detection to medical diagnosis.

Mann-Whitney U Test: A non-parametric statistical test used to compare distributions between two independent groups when data doesn't meet the assumptions of parametric tests.

Measurement Bias: Bias that emerges when different data collection standards or procedures are applied to different demographic groups.

Metadata: Data that provides information about other data, including creation dates, file properties, and processing history.

Model Architecture: The structural design of an AI model that defines how components interconnect and information flows through the system.

Model Parameters: The learned values (such as weights in neural networks) that encode knowledge extracted from training data.

Model Tampering Detection: Forensic techniques for identifying unauthorized modifications to AI model parameters, architectures, or training procedures that could affect system behavior.

Model Weights: Numerical values in neural networks that represent the strength of connections between neurons, learned during training.

Multi-Agent Systems: AI approaches that deploy multiple specialized agents with different capabilities that interact and coordinate to solve complex problems.

Multi-Platform Collection: Specialized evidence gathering procedures for distributed AI systems that span multiple cloud providers, data centers, or organizational boundaries while maintaining forensic integrity.

Multimodal AI Systems: AI systems that process and integrate information across different data types (text, images, audio, video) to perform complex cross-modal understanding tasks.

Neural Network: A computational model inspired by biological neural networks, consisting of interconnected nodes (neurons) that process information through weighted connections.

Neuro-Symbolic Systems: AI architectures that integrate neural networks for perception and pattern recognition with symbolic systems for reasoning and knowledge representation.

ONNX (Open Neural Network Exchange): A standardized format for representing machine learning models that enables interoperability between different frameworks.

Optimization: The process of adjusting model parameters to minimize a loss function and improve performance.

Output Layer: The final layer of a neural network that produces the system's result, with structure depending on the specific task being performed.

Overfitting: A condition where a model performs well on training data but poorly on new, unseen data due to excessive complexity or insufficient regularization.

Parallel Evidence Processing: Computational techniques for efficiently analyzing large-scale AI evidence collections using concurrent processing methods while maintaining audit trails and integrity verification.

Parameter: A variable in an AI model that is learned from training data and used to make predictions.

Permutation Importance: A model-agnostic method for measuring feature importance by observing how much model performance degrades when individual features are randomly shuffled.

Pipeline Architecture: A system design pattern that organizes AI processing as sequences of stages with data flowing through defined transformations and operations.

Pooling: A neural network operation that reduces the spatial dimensions of data, commonly used in CNNs to decrease computational requirements and provide translation invariance.

Precision: A performance metric measuring the proportion of positive predictions that were actually correct.

Preprocessing Pipeline: A series of data transformation steps applied to raw data before it is used for training or inference.

Provenance: The origin and history of data, including how it was collected, processed, and maintained throughout its lifecycle.

RAG (Retrieval-Augmented Generation): An AI architecture that combines generative models with external knowledge stores or vector databases, querying external information sources during inference rather than relying solely on parametric knowledge.

Recall: A performance metric measuring the proportion of actual positive cases that were correctly identified by the model.

Recommendation System: An AI system that suggests relevant items to users based on their preferences, behavior, or characteristics.

Regression: A type of supervised learning task that predicts continuous numerical values from input data.

Regularization: Techniques used to prevent overfitting by constraining model complexity or adding noise during training.

Reinforcement Learning: A type of machine learning where an agent learns to make decisions by receiving rewards or penalties for actions taken in an environment.

Reinforcement Learning Systems: AI systems that learn through interaction with environments, developing policies through trial and error for applications in robotics and game playing.

Representation Bias: Bias that occurs when certain groups are systematically under- or over-represented in training data relative to the population the AI system will serve.

RNN (Recurrent Neural Network): A type of neural network designed to process sequential data by maintaining memory of previous inputs.

Sampling: The process of selecting a subset of data from a larger dataset for analysis when complete data processing is impractical.

Sampling Methodology: Statistical approaches for collecting representative subsets of large-scale AI evidence when complete preservation is impractical, requiring documentation of sampling rationale and limitations.

SHAP (SHapley Additive exPlanations): A method for explaining individual predictions by computing the contribution of each feature to the difference between the prediction and baseline.

State Reconstruction: The forensic process of recreating historical AI system states to understand past behavior, particularly challenging for continuously learning systems that modify their parameters over time.

Statistical Significance: A measure of whether observed differences or patterns are likely due to real effects rather than random chance.

Supervised Learning: A type of machine learning that learns from labeled examples to make predictions on new, unlabeled data.

Temporal Forensics: Investigation techniques that analyze AI system behavior changes over time, including model drift detection, performance degradation analysis, and historical bias pattern identification.

Test Data: A dataset kept completely separate from training and validation data to provide final evaluation of model performance before deployment.

Time Series and Forecasting Systems: AI systems that employ RNNs, LSTMs, or transformers to identify patterns and make predictions over time in domains like financial trading and predictive maintenance.

Training Data: The dataset used to teach an AI model patterns and relationships, consisting of input-output pairs for supervised learning.

Transformer: A type of neural network architecture that relies heavily on attention mechanisms, particularly effective for natural language processing tasks.

Underfitting: A condition where a model is too simple to capture important patterns in the data, resulting in poor performance on both training and test data.

Unsupervised Learning: A type of machine learning that finds patterns in data without labeled examples or explicit target outputs.

Validation Data: A dataset used during model development to tune hyperparameters and make model selection decisions, separate from training data.

Version Control: A system for tracking changes to code, models, and data over time, enabling reproducibility and rollback capabilities.

Vision Transformer (ViT): A transformer architecture adapted for computer vision tasks that treats images as sequences of patches, applying self-attention mechanisms to capture spatial relationships.

Appendix B: AI Forensic Collection and Analysis Environments

INTRODUCTION

The environment in which AI forensic collection and analysis takes place represents a critical foundation for successful investigations. Unlike traditional digital forensics, where standardized write-blockers, forensic workstations, and established tools form a well-understood ecosystem, AI forensics presents unique challenges that demand specialized environmental considerations. The scale of data, computational requirements, and complexity of artifacts require careful planning of the forensic environment to ensure evidence integrity, investigation efficiency, and defensible findings.

This appendix provides comprehensive guidance on establishing appropriate environments for AI forensic activities. We address the fundamental decision between on-premise and lab-based investigations, explore storage requirements for massive AI artifacts, discuss specialized tools for AI forensic analysis, and outline security considerations for protecting both evidence and investigation integrity.

The guidance in this appendix should be adapted to the specific requirements of each investigation, the characteristics of the AI system under examination, and applicable legal or regulatory frameworks. While technical details will evolve as AI technologies advance, the principles and decision frameworks presented here provide a foundation for establishing appropriate forensic environments regardless of specific technological implementations.

1. ON-PREMISE VS. LAB ANALYSIS DECISION FRAMEWORK

One of the first and most consequential decisions in AI forensic investigations is whether to conduct analysis on-premise—where the AI system operates—or in a controlled laboratory environment. This decision impacts evidence integrity, investigation timelines, resource requirements, and potential business disruption. Unlike traditional digital forensics where creating forensic images is standard practice, AI systems often involve distributed components, massive datasets, and complex environments that resist simple replication.

1.1 Decision Factors Matrix

The following matrix provides a structured approach to evaluating whether on-premise or lab-based analysis is more appropriate for a specific investigation. For each factor, assess its importance to your investigation and how strongly it leans toward either approach.

1.2 Regulatory and Compliance Considerations

Various regulatory frameworks impose requirements that may influence the decision between on-premise and lab-based analysis:

TABLE B.1

Factor	On-Premise Considerations	Lab Analysis Considerations
System Size	Advantageous for massive systems (petabytes of data) that would be impractical to transfer	Practical only for smaller systems or when selective artifact collection is sufficient
Operational Impact	Higher impact on ongoing operations; may require scheduled downtime or resource allocation	Minimizes disruption to production systems after initial evidence collection
Environmental Dependencies	Preserves original runtime environment including network connections, hardware configurations, and external services	May lose contextual dependencies unless careful ly documented and recreated
Investigation Timelines	May be faster to start as no transfer time is needed; but may be slowed by operational constraints	Initial delay for transfer but potentially faster analysis in controlled environment
Legal/Regulatory Requirements	May be mandated for certain regulated systems that cannot leave secured environments	May be preferred for maintaining clearer chain of custody and controlled access
Evidence Completeness	Offers access to complete environment including ephemeral components	Limited to collected artifacts; may miss undocumented dependencies
Analysis Capabilities	Limited by available tools and resources in operational environment	Can be equipped with specialized forensic tools and dedicated resources
Team Access	Requires investigators to be on-site; may limit collaboration	Enables centralized investigation with broader team involvement
Isolation Capability	Harder to isolate investigation from operational influences	Provides controlled conditions for repeatable analysis

1.2.1 Data Protection Regulations

Regulations like GDPR (EU), CCPA (California), HIPAA (US healthcare), and similar frameworks impose restrictions on data movement and storage that may affect where analysis can legally occur:

- **Cross-Border Transfer Restrictions**: Personal data subject to regulations like GDPR may have limitations on geographic movement, potentially necessitating on-premise analysis within specific jurisdictions.
- **Data Minimization Requirements**: Regulations may require collecting only necessary data, favoring selective artifact collection rather than complete environment duplication.
- **Security Requirements**: Mandated security measures may be easier to implement in purpose-built forensic labs than in operational environments.

1.2.2 Industry-Specific Regulations

Various industries have specialized requirements that may dictate forensic approaches:

- **Financial Services**: Regulations like SOX, PCI-DSS, or FINRA requirements may restrict movement of financial systems or data.
- **Healthcare**: HIPAA and equivalent regulations outside the US impose strict controls on patient data handling.
- **Critical Infrastructure**: Energy, transportation, or defense systems may have national security restrictions limiting where analysis can occur.

1.2.3 Evidentiary Standards

When investigations may lead to legal proceedings, evidentiary standards become critical:

- **Chain of Custody Documentation**: Lab environments often provide more rigorous documentation capabilities.

- **Evidence Authenticity**: On-premise analysis may better preserve the original context but introduces risks of contamination from ongoing operations.
- **Expert Testimony Requirements**: The forensic environment must support the ability to testify about investigation integrity and methodology.

1.3 Hybrid Approach Considerations

Many AI forensic investigations benefit from a hybrid approach that combines elements of both on-premise and lab-based analysis:

- **Initial Triage On-Premise**: Conducting preliminary analysis on-site to identify critical artifacts and understand system behavior.
- **Selective Artifact Collection**: Collecting specific components for in-depth analysis rather than complete environment duplication.
- **Environment Recreation**: Documenting the operational environment thoroughly to recreate critical aspects in the lab.
- **Remote Analysis Tools**: Deploying forensic tools within the operational environment that report to a centralized analysis platform.
- **Distributed Investigation Teams**: Coordinating specialized teams between on-site and lab locations based on expertise requirements.

1.4 Decision Process Flow

The following process flow provides a structured approach to determining the appropriate investigation environment:

1. **Initial Assessment**
   - Document system scale and complexity
   - Identify regulatory constraints
   - Assess operational impact of different approaches
   - Evaluate available resources both on-premise and in lab
2. **Stakeholder Consultation**
   - Consult legal regarding compliance requirements
   - Engage IT operations regarding system constraints
   - Involve business owners regarding operational impact
   - Consult security regarding risk assessment
3. **Environment Decision**
   - Apply decision matrix to specific investigation requirements
   - Document decision rationale and constraints
   - Develop contingency plans for anticipated challenges
   - Obtain necessary approvals for selected approach
4. **Preparation and Planning**
   - Develop detailed collection/analysis procedures for selected environment
   - Prepare necessary tools and resources
   - Establish documentation standards and chain of custody procedures
   - Schedule activities to minimize impact and maximize effectiveness

1.5 Sensitive Data Handling in Environment Selection

The environment selection process becomes particularly critical when investigations involve sensitive data. The decision between on-premise and lab analysis must carefully consider privacy, confidentiality, and intellectual property protection:

1.5.1 Personal and Protected Data Considerations

When AI systems process personal data, additional factors influence environment selection:

- **Data Minimization Principle**: Prefer approaches that limit exposure of personal data, potentially favoring on-premise analysis with access controls rather than full data transfers.
- **De-Identification Requirements**: Consider whether effective de-identification is possible before transferring data to lab environments, recognizing that AI training data may contain subtle personally identifiable information.
- **Protected Health Information (PHI)**: For systems handling PHI under HIPAA or equivalent regulations, ensure environment selection complies with requirements for secure handling, including Business Associate Agreements when third-party labs are used.
- **Special Category Data**: Systems processing biometric data, racial/ethnic origin, political opinions, or other specially protected categories may require additional safeguards regardless of environment choice.

1.5.2 Intellectual Property and Trade Secret Protection

AI systems often contain valuable intellectual property that requires protection during forensic investigation:

- **Confidentiality Agreements**: Ensure all investigation team members are bound by appropriate confidentiality protections before access to proprietary AI systems.
- **Compartmentalization**: Consider environment designs that allow investigation of specific system aspects without exposing core intellectual property.
- **Competitor Concerns**: In cases where investigations might involve potential access by competitors (such as litigation), environment selection should incorporate additional isolation and access restriction.
- **Patent and Trade Secret Considerations**: Document how environment selection and access controls protect potentially patentable aspects of AI systems or established trade secrets.

2. FORENSIC STORAGE INFRASTRUCTURE

AI systems typically involve massive datasets, complex model artifacts, and extensive logs that create unique storage challenges for forensic investigations. The storage infrastructure must provide not only sufficient capacity but also appropriate performance, integrity protection, and chain of custody documentation.

2.1 Storage Requirements by Investigation Scale

Storage requirements vary dramatically based on the AI system under investigation:

TABLE B.2

Investigation Scale	Typical Storage Requirements	Example Systems
Small Scale	1–10 TB	Single-purpose classification models, small NLP systems, limited scope computer vision applications
Medium Scale	10–100 TB	Production recommendation systems, moderate-sized language models, multi-model pipelines
Large Scale	100 TB-1 PB	Enterprise-wide AI systems, large language models, extensive computer vision training datasets
Extreme Scale	Multiple PB	Foundation models, major cloud AI platforms, industry-wide training datasets

2.2 Storage Architecture Recommendations

Different investigation scales and approaches require different storage architectures:

2.2.1 On-Premise Investigation Storage

When conducting analysis in the operational environment:

- **Forensic Shadow Storage**: Deploy dedicated storage resources that mirror relevant system components without interfering with operations.
- **Network-Attached Forensic Repositories**: Establish secure, high-performance storage accessible to forensic tools but isolated from operational access.
- **Snapshot Management**: Utilize storage-level snapshots to freeze system state at specific points in time while enabling ongoing operation.
- **Selective Copy Approaches**: Implement methods to extract specific high-value artifacts when complete environment preservation is impractical.

2.2.2 Lab-Based Investigation Storage

For dedicated forensic laboratory environments:

- **Tiered Storage Architecture**: Implement performance tiers with high-speed storage for active analysis and archival storage for preservation.
- **Scalable Infrastructure**: Design storage systems that can expand quickly as investigation needs grow.
- **Virtualization Support**: Ensure storage systems support forensic virtualization of AI environments.
- **Analysis-Optimized Configuration**: Configure storage for the specific performance characteristics of AI forensic tools (high I/O, parallel access, etc.).

2.3 Data Integrity Mechanisms

Preserving the integrity of stored artifacts is critical for defensible forensic findings:

2.3.1 Cryptographic Verification

- **Multi-Level Hashing**: Generate cryptographic hashes at multiple levels (file, directory, dataset, and complete repository).
- **Hash Algorithm Selection**: Use appropriate algorithms that balance security and performance (SHA-256 is generally recommended as a minimum).
- **Verification Frequency**: Establish protocols for when integrity verification occurs (on ingest, at regular intervals, before critical analysis).
- **Storage-Level Integrity Checks**: Deploy filesystem or storage systems with built-in integrity verification (ZFS, authenticated encryption, etc.).

2.3.2 Write Protection Implementation

- **Logical Write Protection**: Implement access controls and permissions that prevent modification.
- **Physical Write Protection**: Where applicable, use hardware write-blocking for physical media.
- **Immutable Storage Options**: Consider storage systems with immutability features (WORM capabilities, blockchain-based verification, etc.).
- **Versioning Systems**: Implement storage with automatic versioning to capture any changes.

2.4 Chain of Custody for Digital Artifacts

Maintaining proper chain of custody for AI artifacts presents unique challenges:

2.4.1 Artifact Metadata Documentation

For each artifact, document:

- **Collection Information**: When, how, and by whom the artifact was collected
- **System Origin**: Where within the AI system the artifact originated
- **Artifact Type**: Model weights, training data, configuration files, logs, etc.
- **Handling History**: Every access, analysis, or transfer of the artifact
- **Relationship Information**: How this artifact relates to other collected evidence

2.4.2 Digital Chain of Custody Automation

Implement systems that automate chain of custody documentation:

- **Access Logging**: Automatic logging of all access to forensic storage
- **Artifact Handling Systems**: Digital evidence management systems adapted for AI artifacts
- **Digital Signatures**: Cryptographic signing of chain of custody records
- **Centralized Evidence Management**: Systems that track all artifacts across distributed storage

2.5 Storage Performance Considerations

The unique characteristics of AI artifacts create specific performance requirements:

2.5.1 Read Patterns for Different Artifact Types

- **Model Weight Analysis**: Random access to large binary files
- **Training Data Examination**: Sequential scans of massive datasets
- **Log Analysis**: Time-series indexing and search across multiple log sources
- **Configuration Examination**: Small files with complex relationships

2.5.2 Performance Optimization Strategies

- **Specialization by Analysis Type**: Configure storage systems for specific artifact types
- **Caching Layers**: Implement intelligent caching for frequently accessed components
- **Parallel Access Optimization**: Configure for multiple simultaneous investigators
- **Analysis-in-Place vs. Extract**: Determine when to analyze data in storage versus extracting to specialized systems

2.6 Distributed Evidence Handling

AI systems often span multiple environments, creating challenges for comprehensive evidence collection:

2.6.1 Cross-Environment Collection

- **Multi-Cloud Artifacts**: Strategies for consistent collection across different cloud providers
- **Hybrid Deployments**: Coordinating collection between on-premise and cloud components
- **Edge Deployments**: Handling artifacts from distributed edge devices
- **Third-Party Dependencies**: Documenting and preserving external service dependencies

2.6.2 Consistency Across Distributed Storage

- **Timestamp Synchronization**: Ensuring consistent timestamps across distributed storage
- **Naming Conventions**: Standardized naming for artifacts across environments

- **Relationship Documentation**: Maintaining clear links between distributed components
- **Consolidated Analysis Views**: Tools that present unified analysis across distributed storage

3. ANALYSIS TOOLKIT REQUIREMENTS

AI forensic investigations require specialized tools beyond those used in traditional digital forensics. These tools must handle the unique artifacts, massive scale, and complex relationships present in AI systems.

3.1 Forensic Toolkit Composition

A comprehensive AI forensic toolkit typically includes:

3.1.1 Core Forensic Platforms

- **AI-Specific Forensic Workstations**: Hardware configured for model analysis (high-end GPUs, large RAM capacity)
- **Distributed Analysis Clusters**: Computing resources for large-scale data analysis
- **Secure Analysis Networks**: Isolated networks for containing potentially malicious models or data
- **Virtualization Infrastructure**: Platforms for recreating AI runtime environments

3.1.2 Specialized AI Analysis Tools

- **Model Inspection Tools**: For examining model structure, weights, and behavior
- **Data Analysis Platforms**: For investigating training and inference data
- **Training Recreation Tools**: For reproducing training processes and results
- **Visualization Systems**: For representing complex AI system relationships and behaviors

3.1.3 Forensic Tool Categories

The following categories of tools are particularly important for AI forensics:

TABLE B.3

Tool Category	Purpose	Examples
Model Architecture Analysis	Examining neural network structure and components	TensorBoard, Netron, PyTorch Model Analysis
Weight Analysis	Investigating model parameters and statistics	Weights & Biases, TensorFlow Debugger
Training Data Examination	Analyzing datasets used for model development	Great Expectations, Pandas Profiling
ML Pipeline Inspection	Examining data transformation and feature engineering	MLflow, Kubeflow pipelines inspector
Inference Analysis	Testing model behavior across inputs	AI Fairness 360, What-If Tool
Explainability Tools	Understanding model decision processes	SHAP, LIME, InterpretML
Log Analysis	Examining execution and event logs	Elastic Stack, Splunk Machine Learning Toolkit
Deployment Inspection	Analyzing how models are deployed and operated	Docker inspection tools, Kubernetes forensics

3.2 Tool Validation and Verification

Forensic tools must be validated to ensure they produce accurate and reliable results:

3.2.1 Validation Methodology

A structured approach to tool validation includes:

1. **Functional Testing**: Verifying tools perform their intended functions correctly
2. **Known-Data Testing**: Using datasets with known characteristics to verify tool accuracy
3. **Tool Comparison**: Comparing results across different tools for consistency
4. **Error Rate Determination**: Identifying and documenting tool limitations
5. **Version Documentation**: Recording exactly which tool versions were used
6. **Validation Documentation**: Maintaining records of all validation procedures

3.2.2 Tool-Specific Validation Approaches

Different categories of analysis tools require different validation approaches:

- **Model Analysis Tools**: Validate using models with known properties, comparing output against mathematical verification
- **Data Analysis Tools**: Test with synthetic datasets with known statistical properties
- **Training Verification Tools**: Validate with documented training runs and known outcomes
- **Inference Analysis Tools**: Test with pre-computed inference results for comparison

3.3 Environment Isolation Techniques

Forensic analysis environments must be appropriately isolated to prevent contamination and ensure result integrity:

3.3.1 Physical Isolation

- **Air-Gapped Systems**: Physically separated networks for high-security investigations
- **Dedicated Hardware**: Specific systems used only for forensic analysis
- **Secure Facilities**: Controlled physical access to forensic environments
- **Clean Room Procedures**: Protocols to maintain environment integrity

3.3.2 Logical Isolation

- **Virtualization Boundaries**: Using virtual machines or containers to isolate investigation environments
- **Network Segmentation**: VLAN and firewall rules to control communication
- **Access Control**: Authentication and authorization for investigation environments
- **Monitoring Systems**: Continuous monitoring to detect isolation breaches

3.4 Tool Compatibility with AI Frameworks

AI systems use various frameworks and platforms, requiring compatibility across the forensic toolkit:

3.4.1 Framework-Specific Considerations

Different AI frameworks create different forensic challenges:

- **TensorFlow Environments**: Specific requirements for examining TensorFlow models and graphs

- **PyTorch Ecosystems**: Tools compatible with PyTorch model formats and dynamic computation graphs
- **Custom Frameworks**: Approaches for proprietary or specialized AI frameworks
- **AutoML Platforms**: Techniques for investigating automated machine learning systems

3.4.2 Framework Version Compatibility

- **Version-Specific Analysis**: Tools appropriate for specific framework versions
- **Backward Compatibility**: Ensuring analysis tools work with older model formats
- **Version Identification**: Techniques to identify framework versions from artifacts
- **Multi-Version Support**: Maintaining tools for various framework versions

3.5 Version Control and Environment Documentation

Thorough documentation of the analysis environment is essential for result reproducibility:

3.5.1 Environment Documentation Requirements

Comprehensive documentation should include:

- **Software Inventory**: All tools, libraries, and dependencies with version information
- **Hardware Specifications**: Complete details of analysis hardware
- **Configuration Settings**: All non-default configurations of tools and environments
- **Access Records**: Documentation of who accessed the environment and when
- **Procedure Logs**: Step-by-step records of all actions taken

3.5.2 Environment Reproduction

For cases requiring independent verification:

- **Environment as Code**: Infrastructure definitions that can recreate analysis environments
- **Container Definitions**: Docker or similar definitions that encapsulate tool configurations
- **Package Management**: Pinned dependencies to ensure consistent library versions
- **Configuration Management**: Version-controlled tool configurations

4. SECURITY PROTOCOLS

AI forensic environments require robust security to protect both the evidence being examined and the integrity of the investigation process. The unique characteristics of AI artifacts create specific security challenges that must be addressed through comprehensive protocols.

4.1 Environment Access Control Frameworks

Controlling access to forensic environments ensures evidence integrity and investigation confidentiality:

4.1.1 Access Control Implementation

- **Multi-Factor Authentication**: Requiring multiple verification methods for environment access
- **Role-Based Access Control**: Limiting access based on investigator roles and responsibilities
- **Time-Limited Access**: Providing access only during specific investigation periods
- **Privileged Access Management**: Special controls for administrative access
- **Access Logging**: Comprehensive records of all environment access

4.1.2 Access Levels and Segregation

Establish graduated access levels for different investigation functions:

TABLE B.4

Access Level	Permitted Activities	Typical Roles
Observer	View analysis results and reports	Legal counsel, management, regulatory observers
Analyst	Conduct analysis using existing tools	Forensic analysts, domain experts
Tool Operator	Deploy and configure analysis tools	Technical specialists, tool experts
Environment Administrator	Configure and maintain the forensic environment	Forensic infrastructure specialists
Investigation Lead	Override access controls, Authorize exceptions	Principal investigator, forensic team lead

4.2 Data Protection During Analysis

AI artifacts often contain sensitive information requiring protection during analysis:

4.2.1 Data Classification and Handling

- **Sensitivity Categorization**: Classifying artifacts based on sensitivity levels
- **Handling Procedures**: Specific protocols for each sensitivity category
- **Minimization Techniques**: Methods to reduce exposure of sensitive data
- **De-Identification Approaches**: Techniques to remove personally identifiable information when appropriate

4.2.2 Encryption Implementation

- **Data-at-Rest Encryption**: Protecting stored artifacts and analysis results
- **Data-in-Transit Encryption**: Securing data movement between analysis components
- **Key Management**: Procedures for securing and managing encryption keys
- **Selective Encryption**: Applying stronger protections to most sensitive artifacts

4.3 Model Security Considerations

AI models present unique security challenges during forensic analysis:

4.3.1 Preventing Model Reverse Engineering

- **Access Restrictions**: Controlling who can directly access model weights
- **Partial Access Techniques**: Providing limited model views for specific analysis needs
- **Analysis Restrictions**: Limiting what operations can be performed on models
- **Output Controls**: Restricting what model information can be exported

4.3.2 Handling Potentially Compromised Models

- **Isolation Procedures**: Containing models that might contain malicious components
- **Sandboxed Execution**: Running models in restricted environments
- **Behavioral Monitoring**: Watching for unexpected model behaviors
- **Forensic-Specific Execution Environments**: Specialized platforms for safely analyzing suspicious models

4.4 Investigation Result Protection

Findings from AI forensic investigations often require special protection:

4.4.1 Result Classification and Control

- **Finding Categorization**: Classifying results based on sensitivity and impact
- **Distribution Limitations**: Controlling who can access different types of findings
- **Watermarking and Tracing**: Techniques to track result distribution
- **Redaction Procedures**: Methods for removing sensitive information from generally distributed findings

4.4.2 Secure Collaboration Platforms

- **Protected Analysis Sharing**: Secure platforms for sharing findings among investigators
- **Access-Controlled Dashboards**: Interactive results viewable based on authorization
- **Secure Communication Channels**: Protected methods for discussing findings
- **Collaborative Analysis Tools**: Secure platforms for joint investigation activities

4.5 Threat Modeling for Forensic Environments

Understanding potential threats to the forensic environment enables appropriate countermeasures:

4.5.1 Common Threat Vectors

- **External Unauthorized Access**: Attempts to breach the forensic environment
- **Insider Threats**: Authorized users exceeding their permissions
- **Evidence Tampering**: Attempts to modify artifacts during analysis
- **Resource Attacks**: Attempts to disrupt analysis through resource consumption
- **Analysis Manipulation**: Subtle interference with analysis tools to influence findings

4.5.2 Defense-in-Depth Strategies

- **Multiple Security Layers**: Overlapping protections against different threat types
- **Continuous Monitoring**: Real-time surveillance of forensic environment activity
- **Regular Security Testing**: Proactive identification of security weaknesses
- **Incident Response Plans**: Prepared procedures for addressing security breaches

4.6 Sensitive Data and Material Protection

AI systems frequently process highly sensitive data that requires specialized protection during forensic analysis. This encompasses personal information, protected health information, confidential business data, and valuable intellectual property. Comprehensive protocols must be implemented to safeguard these materials throughout the investigation process.

4.6.1 Personal and Protected Health Information

AI training datasets and operational data often contain protected information about individuals:

- **PHI Identification and Isolation**: Techniques for identifying and segregating protected health information within large datasets
  - Automated scanning for PHI markers (names, medical record numbers, dates, etc.)
  - Pattern recognition for identifying contextual PHI not explicitly marked
  - Isolation of PHI in secured storage zones with heightened protection
- **PII Handling Requirements**: Procedures for managing personally identifiable information
  - Differential access controls based on data sensitivity
  - Audit logging specifically for PII/PHI access

  - Time-limited access provisions for sensitive personal data
  - Geographic restrictions on data movement to comply with regional regulations
- **De-Identification and Anonymization**:
  - Statistical techniques that preserve analytical utility while removing identifiers
  - K-anonymity and other formal privacy models for dataset protection
  - Pseudonymization strategies for traceability without direct identification
  - Re-identification risk assessment before releasing findings
- **Regulatory Compliance Documentation**:
  - HIPAA-compliant forensic procedures for health AI systems
  - GDPR-aligned data protection impact assessments for investigations
  - Chain of custody documentation specific to protected information
  - Breach prevention planning and monitoring

4.6.2 Intellectual Property and Trade Secret Protection

AI systems embody significant intellectual property in their architecture, training methodology, and parameter values:

- **IP Component Identification**: Recognizing IP-sensitive elements within AI systems
  - Model architecture and novel components
  - Training methodologies and hyperparameter optimization approaches
  - Feature engineering techniques and data transformation pipelines
  - Custom inference optimization strategies
- **Layered Access to IP Components**:
  - Classification of IP sensitivity by component
  - Need-to-know access restrictions for proprietary elements
  - Viewing versus modification permissions for different investigation roles
  - Contractual protections including investigation-specific NDAs
- **Competitive Intelligence Protection**:
  - Prevention of IP exfiltration during investigation
  - Restrictions on analysis techniques that might expose trade secrets
  - Third-party escrow approaches for highly sensitive components
  - Neutral third-party examination for multi-party investigations
- **Technical Protection Measures**:
  - Monitored analysis environments for IP-sensitive components
  - Prevention of unauthorized copying or extraction
  - Watermarking of sensitive materials to track potential leaks
  - Access expiration for temporary investigation team members

4.6.3 Proprietary Data and Business Intelligence

Beyond the AI system itself, investigations often encounter proprietary business data:

- **Business Data Categorization**:
  - Classification frameworks for business intelligence sensitivity
  - Financial data handling procedures
  - Customer relationship data protection
  - Strategic planning and proprietary research protection
- **Contextual Access Controls**:
  - Data access based on investigation requirements, not convenience
  - Limited time windows for sensitive business data exposure
  - Purpose limitation enforcement for business intelligence
  - Justified access documentation for proprietary information

- **Aggregation and Summarization Techniques**:
  - Using statistical summaries rather than raw proprietary data when possible
  - Trend analysis without revealing specific business metrics
  - Representative sampling instead of complete business datasets
  - Minimization principles applied to business intelligence exposure

4.6.4 Legal and Ethical Frameworks

Overarching frameworks that guide sensitive data handling during investigations:

- **Ethical Review Processes**:
  - Independent review of investigation plans involving sensitive data
  - Proportionality assessment for privacy intrusion versus investigation necessity
  - Consultation with ethics advisors for complex cases
  - Documentation of ethical decision-making throughout the investigation
- **Legal Compliance Documentation**:
  - Records demonstrating regulatory adherence
  - Data processing agreements specific to forensic activities
  - Legal basis documentation for sensitive data handling
  - Cross-border data transfer compliance
- **Data Subject Rights Management**:
  - Procedures for handling data access or deletion requests during investigations
  - Transparency mechanisms appropriate to investigative context
  - Subject notification protocols when required by regulation
  - Rights balancing documentation for legal proceedings
- **Data Lifecycle Management**:
  - Retention policies specific to different sensitivity categories
  - Secure destruction verification for sensitive materials
  - Long-term storage requirements for legal or compliance purposes
  - Return or destruction certification upon investigation completion

5. OPERATIONAL PROCEDURES

Beyond the technical components, effective AI forensic environments require well-defined operational procedures that guide their use throughout investigations.

5.1 Environment Setup and Validation

Before beginning analysis, the forensic environment must be properly prepared:

5.1.1 Initial Configuration

- **Baseline Establishment**: Creating and documenting the starting environment state
- **Tool Deployment**: Installing and configuring the required analysis toolkit
- **Connectivity Verification**: Ensuring appropriate network access and restrictions
- **Resource Allocation**: Assigning computing and storage resources for the investigation

5.1.2 Pre-Investigation Validation

- **Tool Testing**: Verifying all analysis tools function correctly
- **Security Verification**: Confirming all security measures are operational
- **Documentation Review**: Ensuring all environment documentation is complete
- **Readiness Certification**: Formal verification that the environment is ready for use

5.2 Evidence Management Workflows

Structured processes for handling evidence throughout the investigation lifecycle:

5.2.1 Intake Procedures

- **Artifact Reception**: Protocols for receiving and documenting new evidence
- **Initial Integrity Verification**: Confirming received artifacts match source hashes
- **Preliminary Classification**: Categorizing artifacts for appropriate handling
- **Storage Assignment**: Determining where each artifact should be stored

5.2.2 Analysis Workflow Management

- **Analysis Task Assignment**: Allocating specific artifacts to investigators
- **Progress Tracking**: Monitoring the status of analysis activities
- **Interdependency Management**: Handling relationships between analysis tasks
- **Resource Scheduling**: Coordinating access to limited analysis resources

5.2.3 Result Management

- **Finding Documentation**: Standardized recording of analysis results
- **Cross-Verification Procedures**: Confirming findings through multiple methods
- **Uncertainty Quantification**: Documenting confidence levels in findings
- **Result Integration**: Combining individual analyses into cohesive conclusions

5.3 Environment Decommissioning

Proper procedures for concluding investigations and handling environments:

5.3.1 Evidence Preservation

- **Long-Term Storage Preparation**: Preparing artifacts for extended retention
- **Archive Documentation**: Comprehensive records of what is being preserved
- **Retention Policy Application**: Implementing appropriate retention periods
- **Destruction Verification**: Confirming proper destruction when retention ends

5.3.2 Environment Handling

- **Environment Preservation**: When to preserve entire analysis environments
- **Sanitization Procedures**: Properly clearing environments for reuse
- **Configuration Archiving**: Preserving environment configurations for reference
- **Resource Reallocation**: Returning computing resources to general use

5.4 Documentation Standards

Comprehensive documentation is essential throughout the forensic process:

5.4.1 Required Documentation Types

- **Environment Specifications**: Detailed technical descriptions of the forensic environment
- **Procedural Logs**: Step-by-step records of all analysis activities
- **Chain of Custody Documentation**: Complete tracking of artifact handling
- **Analysis Methodology Documentation**: Detailed descriptions of how analysis was conducted
- **Tool Configuration Records**: Specific settings used for analysis tools
- **Result Documentation**: Comprehensive recording of findings and supporting evidence

5.4.2 Documentation Management

- **Version Control**: Tracking changes to documentation over time
- **Access Controls**: Protecting sensitive documentation
- **Long-Term Preservation**: Ensuring documentation remains accessible
- **Cross-Referencing**: Maintaining relationships between different documentation types

CONCLUSION

The forensic collection and analysis environment forms the foundation for effective AI system investigations. As this appendix has demonstrated, these environments require careful planning, specialized resources, and rigorous procedures to ensure evidence integrity and investigative effectiveness.

The scale and complexity of AI systems create requirements for forensic environments that can handle massive datasets, complex models, and distributed components while maintaining proper evidence handling and chain of custody. The decision between on-premise and lab-based analysis typically involves balancing practical constraints with investigative requirements, often resulting in hybrid approaches that combine elements of both methods.

Storage infrastructure for AI forensics accommodates enormous capacity requirements and performance needs for various types of analysis while maintaining data integrity and documentation standards. Analysis toolkits include specialized components for examining AI artifacts, which require validation for accuracy and operation within isolated environments. Security measures for forensic environments protect both the evidence being analyzed and the integrity of the investigation process itself. Access controls, data protection mechanisms, and threat modeling contribute to maintaining secure analysis environments.

As AI systems continue to evolve in complexity and ubiquity, forensic environment capabilities advance in response. Organizations conducting AI forensic investigations regularly reassess their environmental capabilities against emerging technologies and evolving practices. Establishing appropriate forensic environments based on established principles provides investigators with foundations for conducting thorough examinations of AI systems across varying levels of complexity and scale.

Appendix C: LLM Resume Screening Sample Investigation

LEARNING OBJECTIVES

By the end of this appendix, you will be able to:

- Plan and execute comprehensive forensic investigations of AI systems
- Apply evidence collection techniques that maintain legal admissibility
- Conduct statistical analysis of AI outputs to detect bias and discriminatory patterns
- Generate professional investigation reports for technical, legal, and executive audiences
- Adapt investigation methodologies to different AI system types and organizational contexts
- Collaborate effectively in multi-investigator forensic teams

What You'll Learn: This appendix transforms the theoretical frameworks from Chapters 3–8 into a practical, step-by-step investigation methodology. You'll work through a complete AI bias investigation using real tools and techniques, gaining hands-on experience with professional forensic procedures.

INTRODUCTION: FROM THEORY TO PRACTICE

Throughout this book, we've explored the theoretical foundations of AI forensics—from understanding system architectures in Chapter 2 to presenting findings in Chapter 9. This appendix bridges the gap between theory and practice, providing you with a complete, executable investigation methodology.

We'll use resume screening LLM bias investigation as our primary example, but the techniques you'll learn apply broadly across AI system types. The four-phase investigation framework—Planning, Evidence Collection, Analysis, and Reporting—provides a universal structure you can adapt to any AI forensic scenario.

Real-World Context: AI bias investigations are among the most common forensic scenarios facing organizations today. Employment discrimination lawsuits involving AI screening tools have increased 300% since 2020, making these skills immediately valuable in legal, compliance, and technical roles.

WHY THIS METHODOLOGY MATTERS

Modern AI systems present unique forensic challenges that traditional investigation approaches cannot address effectively. Unlike conventional software, AI systems exhibit emergent behaviors, operate with probabilistic outputs, and depend heavily on training data quality. Our methodology accounts for these complexities while maintaining the rigor required for legal proceedings.

The investigation framework integrates seamlessly with the concepts you've learned:

- **Chapter 3's knowledge gathering** informs our planning phase
- **Chapter 4's evidence collection** provides our forensic foundation
- **Chapters 5–7's analysis techniques** form our investigative core
- **Chapter 8's documentation analysis** supports our validation processes

PREREQUISITES AND SETUP

Before beginning any AI forensic investigation, you need proper preparation across technical, legal, and organizational dimensions.

TECHNICAL PREREQUISITES

System Requirements:

- Linux/macOS workstation with 16GB+ RAM
- Python 3.8+ with virtual environment capability
- Docker for containerized analysis tools
- Secure network access to investigation targets

Software Installation:

```
# Create isolated investigation environment
python -m venv ai_forensics_env
source ai_forensics_env/bin/activate # Linux/macOS
# ai_forensics_env\Scripts\activate # Windows

# Install core forensic tools
pip install pandas numpy scikit-learn matplotlib seaborn
pip install shap lime evidently fairlearn
pip install jupyter notebook plotly dash
pip install pytest cryptography
```

Tool Selection Note: While we recommend specific tools, Chapter 6's model investigation techniques can be adapted to any ML interpretability library. The key is maintaining consistent methodology regardless of tools used.

Expected Output After Setup:

Successfully installed packages:

- pandas (1.5.3)
- scikit-learn (1.3.0)
- shap (0.42.1)
- evidently (0.4.8)

[. . . additional packages . . .]

Environment ready for AI forensic investigation.

LEGAL AND ETHICAL CONSIDERATIONS

Before You Begin:

- **Obtain proper authorization** for all systems you'll examine
- **Establish chain of custody** procedures for digital evidence
- **Document investigation scope** and limitations clearly
- **Consult legal counsel** for jurisdiction-specific requirements

Professional Liability Warning: AI forensic investigation can have significant legal implications. Always work within authorized scope and maintain professional standards. When in doubt, seek guidance from qualified legal professionals.

CODE REPOSITORY ACCESS

All investigation scripts, templates, and sample data referenced in this guide are available at:

- **Repository**: https://github.com/aiForensicsBook/llmInvestigation
- **Sample datasets**: Available under /data/synthetic/ for practice
- **Investigation templates**: Located in /templates/legal/ and /templates/technical/

INVESTIGATION PLANNING: SETTING UP FOR SUCCESS

Effective AI forensic investigations begin with careful planning that establishes clear objectives, scope boundaries, and success criteria. Poor planning is the leading cause of incomplete or legally inadmissible forensic findings.

DEFINING INVESTIGATION SCOPE

Start with Clear Questions: Every investigation should begin with specific, answerable questions:

- "Does the resume screening system exhibit statistically significant bias against protected groups?"
- "Can we identify the source of discriminatory behavior in model training data or architecture?"
- "What evidence exists of organizational knowledge about potential bias issues?"

System Boundary Definition:

When investigating an AI system, you must clearly define what components fall within scope:

```
# Investigation scope definition template
investigation_scope = {
    "primary_systems": [
        "resume_screening_model",
        "training_data_pipeline",
        "inference_service"
    ],
    "supporting_infrastructure": [
        "model_serving_platform",
        "monitoring_dashboards",
        "audit_logging_systems"
    ],
    "data_sources": [
        "historical_resume_data",
        "hiring_decision_outcomes",
        "model_training_logs"
    ],
    "exclusions": [
        "hr_information_systems", # Outside investigation scope
        "payroll_systems" # Not relevant to bias detection
    ]
}
```

Scope Creep Warning: AI systems often integrate with numerous other systems. Resist the temptation to expand scope without proper authorization and resource allocation. Focus on components directly relevant to your investigation questions.

RESOURCE PLANNING AND TEAM FORMATION

Investigation Team Roles:

Successful AI forensic investigations typically require diverse expertise:

- **Lead Investigator**: Overall coordination and quality assurance
- **Technical Analyst**: Model analysis and statistical testing
- **Data Specialist**: Training data examination and validation
- **Legal Liaison**: Compliance review and evidence handling
- **Subject Matter Expert**: Domain knowledge for context

Time and Resource Estimation:

```
# Investigation planning template
investigation_plan = {
    "estimated_duration": "4-6 weeks",
    "phases": {
        "evidence_collection": {"duration": "1-2 weeks", "resources":
        ["technical_analyst", "data_specialist"]},
        "analysis": {"duration": "2-3 weeks", "resources": ["technical_
        analyst", "sme"]},
        "validation": {"duration": "1 week", "resources": ["lead_investi-
        gator", "legal_liaison"]},
        "reporting": {"duration": "1 week", "resources": ["lead_investi-
        gator", "technical_analyst"]}
    },
    "critical_dependencies": [
        "system_access_permissions",
        "data_availability",
        "stakeholder_interviews"
    ]
}
```

QUALITY GATES AND SUCCESS CRITERIA

Phase Completion Criteria:

Each investigation phase should have clear completion criteria before proceeding:

- **Evidence Collection**: Complete system snapshot, verified data integrity, documented chain of custody
- **Analysis**: Statistical significance achieved, multiple validation methods applied, peer review completed
- **Validation**: Independent verification of key findings, methodology review, compliance check
- **Reporting**: Technical accuracy verified, legal review completed, stakeholder feedback incorporated

PHASE 1: EVIDENCE COLLECTION

Evidence collection forms the foundation of any forensic investigation. For AI systems, this involves systematic capture of models, data, logs, and documentation while maintaining legal admissibility standards.

1.1 INITIAL SYSTEM ASSESSMENT

Environment Documentation:

Begin every investigation by creating a comprehensive baseline of the system environment:

```
# Create investigation case directory
export CASE_ID="INV_$(date +%Y%m%d_%H%M%S)"
export INVESTIGATOR="Your Name"
export ORGANIZATION="Investigation Firm"
mkdir -p investigation/${CASE_ID}/{evidence,analysis,reports}
# Document system environment
python forensic/collection/metadata_extractor.py \
   --system-info \
   --network-config \
   --security-context \
   --output investigation/${CASE_ID}/system_baseline.json
```

What This Captures: The metadata extraction process documents critical environmental factors:

- **Hardware specifications**: CPU architecture, memory, storage systems
- **Software environment**: OS version, Python packages, library versions
- **Network configuration**: Connectivity, firewall rules, access controls
- **Security context**: Authentication methods, encryption status, audit settings

Why This Matters: Environmental factors significantly impact AI model behavior. Version differences in libraries like scikit-learn or TensorFlow can produce different results from identical models, making baseline documentation essential for reproducible analysis.

Expected Output:

```
{
    "timestamp": "2025-07-10T14:30:22Z",
        "system": {
        "architecture": "x86_64",
        "cpu_count": 8,
        "memory_gb": 32,
        "os": "Ubuntu 22.04.3 LTS"
    },
    "python_environment": {
        "version": "3.9.7",
        "packages": {
        "scikit-learn": "1.3.0",
        "pandas": "1.5.3",
        "numpy": "1.24.3"
      }
    }
}
```

1.2 MODEL ARTIFACT COLLECTION

Secure Model Extraction:

AI models require special handling to preserve their computational state and ensure integrity:

```
# Extract model artifacts with integrity verification
python forensic/collection/model_extractor.py \
    --model-path /production/models/resume_llm_latest.pkl \
    --output investigation/${CASE_ID}/evidence/model_artifacts/ \
    --verify-integrity \
    --create-checksums
```

Model Evidence Components:

Complete model evidence collection includes:

1. **Model files**: Serialized model weights and architecture
2. **Configuration data**: Hyperparameters, training settings, feature definitions
3. **Metadata**: Creation timestamps, version information, training metrics
4. **Dependencies**: Required libraries and their exact versions

```
# Model integrity verification example
import hashlib
import pickle
import json

def verify_model_integrity(model_path, expected_checksum):
    """Verify model file integrity using cryptographic hashing."""
    with open(model_path, 'rb') as f:
        model_data = f.read()# Calculate SHA-256 checksum

calculated_checksum = hashlib.sha256(model_data).hexdigest()

    integrity_result = {
        "file_path": model_path,
        "expected_checksum": expected_checksum,
        "calculated_checksum": calculated_checksum,
        "integrity_verified": calculated_checksum == expected_checksum,
        "timestamp": "2025-07-10T14:35:15Z"
    }

return integrity_result
```

Chain of Custody: Every model file must be accompanied by chain of custody documentation showing who accessed it, when, and what operations were performed. This documentation is essential for legal admissibility.

1.3 TRAINING DATA COLLECTION

Dataset Preservation:

Training data collection requires balancing completeness with privacy protection:

```
# Collect training datasets with privacy controls
python forensic/collection/data_collector.py \
    --data-source /production/training_data/resumes_2023/ \
```

```
    --anonymization-level medium \
    --sample-size 10000 \
    --output investigation/${CASE_ID}/evidence/training_data/ \
    --preserve-statistical-properties
```

Privacy-Preserving Collection:

When dealing with sensitive training data, employ privacy protection techniques:

```
# Privacy-preserving data collection
import pandas as pd
from faker import Faker
import numpy as np
def anonymize_resume_data(df, anonymization_level='medium'):
    """Anonymize resume data while preserving statistical properties."""
    fake = Faker()
    df_anon = df.copy()

    if anonymization_level in ['medium', 'high']:
        # Replace names with realistic alternatives
        df_anon['applicant_name'] = [fake.name() for _ in range(len(df))]

        # Generalize specific schools to tiers
        df_anon['education'] = df_anon['education'].apply(generalize_
        education)

    if anonymization_level == 'high':
        # Add statistical noise to continuous variables
        numeric_cols = df_anon.select_dtypes(include=[np.number]).columns
        for col in numeric_cols:
        noise_scale = df_anon[col].std() * 0.05 # 5% noise
        df_anon[col] += np.random.normal(0, noise_scale, len(df_anon))

    return df_anon
def generalize_education(education_detail):
    """Generalize specific education details to preserve privacy."""
    tier_mapping = {
        'harvard': 'tier_1_university',
        'mit': 'tier_1_university',
        'stanford': 'tier_1_university',
        # ... additional mappings
    }

    education_lower = education_detail.lower()
    for specific, general in tier_mapping.items():
        if specific in education_lower:
        return general

return 'other_education'
```

Data Quality Validation:

Ensure collected training data maintains analytical value:

```
# Training data quality assessment
def assess_data_quality(df_original, df_collected):
```

```
    """Compare original and collected data for quality preservation."""
    quality_metrics = {
        'sample_size_ratio': len(df_collected) / len(df_original),
        'feature_completeness': df_collected.notna().mean().mean(),
        'distribution_similarity': {}
    }

    # Check statistical distribution preservation
    for col in df_original.select_dtypes(include=[np.number]).columns:
        if col in df_collected.columns:
        # Kolmogorov-Smirnov test for distribution similarity
        from scipy.stats import ks_2samp
        statistic, p_value = ks_2samp(df_original[col], df_
        collected[col])
        quality_metrics['distribution_similarity'][col] = {
              'ks_statistic': statistic,
              'p_value': p_value,
              'distributions_similar': p_value > 0.05
      }

return quality_metrics
```

1.4 SYSTEM LOGS AND MONITORING DATA

Comprehensive Log Collection:

System logs provide crucial evidence of AI system behavior and potential issues:

```
# Collect system logs with temporal filtering
python forensic/collection/log_collector.py \
    --log-sources application,audit,security \
    --time-range "2025-01-01,2025-07-10" \
    --filter-ai-related \
    --output investigation/${CASE_ID}/evidence/logs/
```

Log Analysis for Bias Indicators:

Examine logs for patterns that might indicate biased behavior:

```
# Log analysis for bias detection
import re
from datetime import datetime
import pandas as pd
def analyze_decision_logs(log_file_path):
    """Analyze AI decision logs for potential bias indicators."""
    decision_patterns = []

    with open(log_file_path, 'r') as f:
        for line in f:
          # Parse decision log entries
          match = re.search(r'DECISION: candidate_id=(\w+), score=(\d+\.\
          d+), demographic=(\w+)', line)
          if match:
             candidate_id, score, demographic = match.groups()
             timestamp = extract_timestamp(line)
```

```
            decision_patterns.append({
            'timestamp': timestamp,
            'candidate_id': candidate_id,
            'score': float(score),
            'demographic': demographic
        })

    # Convert to DataFrame for analysis
    df_decisions = pd.DataFrame(decision_patterns)

    # Calculate demographic score distributions
    demographic_stats = df_decisions.groupby('demographic')['score'].
    agg([
        'count', 'mean', 'std', 'min', 'max'
    ]).round(3)

    return df_decisions, demographic_stats

def extract_timestamp(log_line):
    """Extract timestamp from log line."""
    timestamp_pattern = r'(\d{4}-\d{2}-\d{2}T\d{2}:\d{2}:\d{2})'
    match = re.search(timestamp_pattern, log_line)
    if match:
       return datetime.fromisoformat(match.group(1))
       return None
```

Evidence Integrity: All collected logs must be cryptographically hashed and timestamped to prove they haven't been modified during the investigation. Use tools like sha256sum to create integrity checksums.

PHASE 2: COMPREHENSIVE ANALYSIS

Analysis transforms raw evidence into investigative findings through systematic application of statistical, machine learning, and interpretability techniques.

2.1 STATISTICAL BIAS DETECTION

Demographic Parity Analysis:

The foundation of bias detection involves comparing outcomes across protected groups:

```
# Comprehensive bias detection analysis
import pandas as pd
import numpy as np
from scipy import stats
import matplotlib.pyplot as plt
import seaborn as sns

def demographic_parity_analysis(df, outcome_col, demographic_col):
    """
    Perform comprehensive demographic parity analysis.

    Args:
       df: DataFrame with decision outcomes
       outcome_col: Column containing binary outcomes (0/1)
       demographic_col: Column containing demographic group labels
```

```
    Returns:
       Dictionary with statistical test results and visualizations
    """

    # Calculate selection rates by demographic group
    selection_rates = df.groupby(demographic_col)[outcome_col].agg([
       'count', 'sum', 'mean'
     ]).round(4)
     selection_rates.columns = ['total_applications', 'selected', 'selec-
     tion_rate']

    # Statistical significance testing
    groups = df[demographic_col].unique()
    pairwise_tests = {}

    for i, group1 in enumerate(groups):
        for group2 in groups[i+1:]:
            # Get outcomes for each group
            outcomes1 = df[df[demographic_col] == group1][outcome_col]
            outcomes2 = df[df[demographic_col] == group2][outcome_col]

            # Chi-square test for independence
            contingency_table = pd.crosstab(
            df[demographic_col].isin([group1, group2]),
            df[outcome_col]
        )
        chi2, p_value, dof, expected = stats.chi2_
        contingency(contingency_table)

        # Effect size (Cramer's V)
        n = contingency_table.sum().sum()
        cramers_v = np.sqrt(chi2 / (n * min(contingency_table.shape) - 1))

        pairwise_tests[f"{group1}_vs_{group2}"] = {
          'chi2_statistic': chi2,
          'p_value': p_value,
          'cramers_v': cramers_v,
          'significant': p_value < 0.05,
          'effect_size': 'small' if cramers_v < 0.3 else 'medium' if
          cramers_v < 0.5 else 'large'
        }

    return {
      'selection_rates': selection_rates,
      'pairwise_tests': pairwise_tests,
      'overall_significance': any(test['significant'] for test in pair-
      wise_tests.values())
    }
# Example usage with sample data
def run_bias_analysis_example():
   """Example of running comprehensive bias analysis."""

    # Load investigation data
    df_decisions = pd.read_csv(f'investigation/{CASE_ID}/evidence/deci-
    sion_outcomes.csv')
```

```
    # Perform demographic parity analysis
    bias_results = demographic_parity_analysis(
        df_decisions,
        outcome_col='hired',
        demographic_col='race_ethnicity'
    )

    print("Selection Rates by Demographic Group:")
    print(bias_results['selection_rates'])
    print("\nStatistical Significance Tests:")
    for comparison, results in bias_results['pairwise_tests'].items():
        print(f"{comparison}: p-value = {results['p_value']:.4f}, "
            f"significant = {results['significant']}")

return bias_results
```

Expected Analysis Output:

Selection Rates by Demographic Group:

	total_applications	selected	selection_rate
race_ethnicity			
asian	1247	298	0.2390
black	856	145	0.1694
hispanic	743	162	0.2180
white	2154	612	0.2842

Statistical Significance Tests:

asian_vs_black: p-value = 0.0023, significant = True
asian_vs_hispanic: p-value = 0.2847, significant = False
asian_vs_white: p-value = 0.0051, significant = True
black_vs_hispanic: p-value = 0.0156, significant = True
black_vs_white: p-value = 0.0000, significant = True
hispanic_vs_white: p-value = 0.0034, significant = True

Statistical Power: Ensure your sample sizes are sufficient for meaningful statistical testing. Generally, you need at least 30 observations per group for reliable chi-square tests, and preferably 100+ for robust effect size estimation.

2.2 MODEL INTERPRETABILITY ANALYSIS

SHAP Analysis for Feature Importance:

Understanding which features drive model decisions is crucial for identifying bias sources:

```
# Model interpretability analysis using SHAP
import shap
import joblib
from sklearn.ensemble import RandomForestClassifier
import warnings
warnings.filterwarnings('ignore')
```

```
def comprehensive_shap_analysis(model_path, test_data_path):
    """
    Perform comprehensive SHAP analysis for model interpretability.

    Args:
      model_path: Path to trained model file
      test_data_path: Path to test dataset

    Returns:
      Dictionary containing SHAP values and analysis results
    """

    # Load model and test data
    model = joblib.load(model_path)
    df_test = pd.read_csv(test_data_path)

    # Prepare features (assuming target is 'hired')
    X_test = df_test.drop(['hired', 'applicant_id'], axis=1,
    errors='ignore')
    y_test = df_test['hired'] if 'hired' in df_test.columns else None

    # Initialize SHAP explainer
    explainer = shap.TreeExplainer(model)
    shap_values = explainer.shap_values(X_test)

    # For binary classification, take positive class SHAP values
    if isinstance(shap_values, list):
       shap_values_positive = shap_values[1] # Positive class (hired = 1)
    else:
        shap_values_positive = shap_values

    # Calculate feature importance metrics
    feature_importance = pd.DataFrame({
      'feature': X_test.columns,
      'mean_abs_shap': np.abs(shap_values_positive).mean(axis=0),
      'mean_shap': shap_values_positive.mean(axis=0),
      'std_shap': shap_values_positive.std(axis=0)
    }).sort_values('mean_abs_shap', ascending=False)

    # Analyze demographic feature impact
    demographic_features = [col for col in X_test.columns
                if any(demo in col.lower() for demo in
                ['race', 'gender', 'age', 'ethnicity'])]

    demographic_impact = {}
    for feature in demographic_features:
      if feature in X_test.columns:
         feature_idx = list(X_test.columns).index(feature)
         demographic_impact[feature] = {
           'mean_impact': shap_values_positive[:, feature_idx].mean(),
           'impact_std': shap_values_positive[:, feature_idx].std(),
           'impact_range': [
              shap_values_positive[:, feature_idx].min(),
              shap_values_positive[:, feature_idx].max()
           ]
      }
```

```
    return {
      'shap_values': shap_values_positive,
      'feature_importance': feature_importance,
      'demographic_impact': demographic_impact,
      'explainer': explainer,
      'test_features': X_test
    }
def analyze_feature_bias_correlation(shap_results, df_test):
    """Analyze correlation between feature importance and bias
    outcomes."""

    X_test = shap_results['test_features']
    shap_values = shap_results['shap_values']

    # Calculate per-sample prediction explanations
    sample_explanations = []
    for i in range(len(X_test)):
      explanation = {
        'sample_id': i,
        'prediction_score': shap_values[i].sum(), # Sum of SHAP values =
        prediction
        'top_positive_features': [],
        'top_negative_features': []
    }

      # Get top contributing features
      feature_contributions = list(zip(X_test.columns, shap_values[i]))
      feature_contributions.sort(key=lambda x: abs(x[1]), reverse=True)
      for feature, contribution in feature_contributions[:5]:
        if contribution > 0:
        explanation['top_positive_features'].append({
          'feature': feature,
          'contribution': contribution
        })
      else:
        explanation['top_negative_features'].append({
          'feature': feature,
          'contribution': contribution
        })

sample_explanations.append(explanation)

return sample_explanations
```

Visualization of Model Behavior:

Create visualizations that clearly communicate model bias patterns:

```
# Advanced visualization for bias communication
def create_bias_visualizations(bias_results, shap_results, output_dir):
    """Create comprehensive visualizations for bias investigation."""

    plt.style.use('seaborn-v0_8')
    fig, axes = plt.subplots(2, 2, figsize=(15, 12))
```

```
# 1. Selection rates by demographic group
selection_rates = bias_results['selection_rates']
ax1 = axes[0, 0]
bars = ax1.bar(selection_rates.index, selection_rates['selection_
rate'])
ax1.set_title('Selection Rates by Demographic Group', fontsize=14,
fontweight='bold')
ax1.set_ylabel('Selection Rate')
ax1.set_xlabel('Demographic Group')

# Add value labels on bars
for bar in bars:
height = bar.get_height()
ax1.text(bar.get_x() + bar.get_width()/2., height,
     f'{height:.3f}', ha='center', va='bottom')

# 2. Feature importance from SHAP
feature_imp = shap_results['feature_importance'].head(10)
ax2 = axes[0, 1]
bars2 = ax2.barh(range(len(feature_imp)), feature_imp['mean_abs_
shap'])
ax2.set_yticks(range(len(feature_imp)))
ax2.set_yticklabels(feature_imp['feature'])
ax2.set_title('Top 10 Most Important Features (SHAP)', fontsize=14,
fontweight='bold')
ax2.set_xlabel('Mean Absolute SHAP Value')

# 3. SHAP summary plot
ax3 = axes[1, 0]
shap.summary_plot(shap_results['shap_values'],
          shap_results['test_features'],
          max_display=10, show=False, ax=ax3)
ax3.set_title('SHAP Feature Impact Summary', fontsize=14,
fontweight='bold')

# 4. Bias test p-values
ax4 = axes[1, 1]
test_names = list(bias_results['pairwise_tests'].keys())
p_values = [bias_results['pairwise_tests'][test]['p_value'] for test
in test_names]

colors = ['red' if p < 0.05 else 'blue' for p in p_values]
bars4 = ax4.bar(range(len(test_names)), p_values, color=colors)
ax4.axhline(y=0.05, color='red', linestyle='--', label='α = 0.05')
ax4.set_xticks(range(len(test_names)))
ax4.set_xticklabels(test_names, rotation=45, ha='right')
ax4.set_title('Statistical Significance Tests', fontsize=14,
fontweight='bold')
ax4.set_ylabel('p-value')
ax4.legend()

plt.tight_layout()
plt.savefig(f'{output_dir}/bias_analysis_summary.png', dpi=300, bbox_
inches='tight')
plt.show()return fig
```

Interpretability Best Practices: Always validate SHAP results with multiple explanation methods (LIME, permutation importance) to ensure robust conclusions. Different explainability techniques can reveal different aspects of model behavior.

2.3 TEMPORAL ANALYSIS

Time-Series Bias Detection:

Analyze how bias patterns change over time to identify systematic issues:

```
# Temporal bias analysis
def temporal_bias_analysis(df_decisions, date_col='decision_date',
             outcome_col='hired', demographic_col='race_ethnicity'):
    """Analyze bias patterns over time."""

    # Convert date column to datetime
    df_decisions[date_col] = pd.to_datetime(df_decisions[date_col])

    # Group by month and demographic
    monthly_stats = df_decisions.groupby([
      df_decisions[date_col].dt.to_period('M'),
      demographic_col
    ])[outcome_col].agg(['count', 'sum', 'mean']).reset_index()

    monthly_stats.columns = ['month', 'demographic', 'applications',
    'hired', 'hire_rate']

    # Calculate trending bias metrics
    bias_trends = {}
    for demo_group in df_decisions[demographic_col].unique():
        group_data = monthly_stats[monthly_stats['demographic'] == demo_
        group]

        # Linear regression to detect trends
        from sklearn.linear_model import LinearRegression
        X = np.arange(len(group_data)).reshape(-1, 1)
        y = group_data['hire_rate'].values

        model = LinearRegression().fit(X, y)
        trend_slope = model.coef_[0]
        trend_r2 = model.score(X, y)

      bias_trends[demo_group] = {
        'trend_slope': trend_slope,
        'trend_r_squared': trend_r2,
        'improving': trend_slope > 0,
        'significant_trend': trend_r2 > 0.5
     }

    return monthly_stats, bias_trends
```

PHASE 3: VALIDATION AND QUALITY ASSURANCE

Validation ensures your investigation findings are reliable, reproducible, and legally defensible.

3.1 INDEPENDENT VALIDATION

Peer Review Process:

Implement systematic peer review to validate key findings:

```
# Peer review validation framework
class ValidationProtocol:
    def __init__(self, investigation_id):
      self.investigation_id = investigation_id
      self.validation_results = {}

    def validate_statistical_analysis(self, reviewer_name, original_
    results):
      """Independent validation of statistical findings."""

      validation_log = {
        'reviewer': reviewer_name,
        'timestamp': datetime.now().isoformat(),
        'validation_type': 'statistical_analysis',
        'findings': {}
      }

      # Re-run critical statistical tests
      for test_name, original_result in original_results['pairwise_
      tests'].items():
          # Independent calculation
          revalidated_result = self._recalculate_bias_test(test_name)

         # Compare results
         p_value_match = abs(original_result['p_value'] - revalidated_
         result['p_value']) < 0.001
         significance_match = original_result['significant'] == revali-
         dated_result['significant']

         validation_log['findings'][test_name] = {
           'original_p_value': original_result['p_value'],
           'revalidated_p_value': revalidated_result['p_value'],
           'p_value_matches': p_value_match,
           'significance_matches': significance_match,
           'validated': p_value_match and significance_match
         }

         # Overall validation status
         validation_log['overall_validated'] = all(
         finding['validated'] for finding in validation_log['findings'].
         values()
      )

         self.validation_results['statistical_analysis'] = validation_log
         return validation_log
```

```
def validate_model_interpretability(self, reviewer_name, original_
shap_results):
  """Independent validation of SHAP analysis."""

    validation_log = {
      'reviewer': reviewer_name,
      'timestamp': datetime.now().isoformat(),
      'validation_type': 'model_interpretability',
      'findings': {}
    }

     # Re-run SHAP analysis with same parameters
     revalidated_shap = self._recalculate_shap_analysis()

     # Compare top feature rankings
     original_top_features = original_shap_results['feature_
     importance']['feature'].head(10).tolist()
     revalidated_top_features = revalidated_shap['feature_importance']
     ['feature'].head(10).tolist()

    # Calculate rank correlation
    from scipy.stats import spearmanr
    correlation, p_value = spearmanr(
      [original_top_features.index(f) if f in original_top_features
      else 10
      for f in revalidated_top_features],
      list(range(10))
    )

    validation_log['findings'] = {
      'top_features_correlation': correlation,
      'correlation_p_value': p_value,
      'strong_correlation': correlation > 0.8,
      'original_top_features': original_top_features,
      'revalidated_top_features': revalidated_top_features
    }

    validation_log['overall_validated'] = correlation > 0.8

    self.validation_results['model_interpretability'] = validation_log
    return validation_log
```

3.2 REPRODUCIBILITY TESTING

Environment Reconstruction:

Ensure your analysis can be reproduced in different environments:

```
# Create reproducible analysis environment
cat > investigation/${CASE_ID}/environment.yml << EOF
name: ai_forensics_reproduction
channels:
 - conda-forge
 - defaults
dependencies:
```

```
 - python=3.9.7
 - pandas=1.5.3
 - numpy=1.24.3
 - scikit-learn=1.3.0
 - matplotlib=3.7.1
 - seaborn=0.12.2
 - pip
 - pip:
 - shap==0.42.1
 - evidently==0.4.8
 - lime==0.2.0.1
EOF

# Test reproduction in clean environment
conda env create -f investigation/${CASE_ID}/environment.yml
conda activate ai_forensics_reproduction
python forensic/validation/reproduce_analysis.py --case-id ${CASE_ID}
```

Reproducibility Checklist: Document all random seeds, package versions, and system dependencies. Include data preprocessing steps and any manual interventions in your methodology.

PHASE 4: PROFESSIONAL REPORTING

Transform your technical findings into compelling, actionable reports for different stakeholder audiences.

4.1 EXECUTIVE SUMMARY DEVELOPMENT

Business-Focused Communication:

Executive summaries must translate technical findings into business implications:

```
# Executive summary generation template
def generate_executive_summary(investigation_results):
"""Generate executive summary focused on business impact."""

    summary_template = {
      "investigation_overview": {
         "scope": "AI resume screening system bias investigation",
         "duration": f"{investigation_results['timeline']['start']} to
         {investigation_results['timeline']['end']}",
         "methodology": "Statistical analysis, model interpretability,
         and compliance review"
      },

        "key_findings": {
        "bias_detected": investigation_results['bias_analysis']['over-
        all_significance'],
        "affected_groups": [group for group, stats in investigation_
        results['bias_analysis']['pairwise_tests'].items()
                   if stats['significant']],
        "magnitude": "Moderate to high impact based on effect size
        analysis",
        "legal_risk": "High - statistically significant disparate impact
        detected"
      },
```

```
      "business_impact": {
        "legal_liability": "Potential EEOC violation requiring immediate
        attention",
        "reputational_risk": "High if bias patterns become public
        knowledge",
        "operational_impact": "Current hiring process may be excluding
        qualified candidates",
        "financial_exposure": "Estimated $500K-2M in potential legal
        costs and settlements"
      },

      "recommendations": {
        "immediate_actions": [
        "Suspend use of current AI screening system pending remediation",
        "Conduct manual review of recent hiring decisions",
        "Engage legal counsel for compliance strategy"
      ],
      "medium_term_solutions": [
        "Retrain model with bias-aware techniques",
        "Implement real-time bias monitoring",
        "Update hiring process documentation"
      ],
      "long_term_strategy": [
        "Establish AI ethics review board",
        "Implement comprehensive AI governance framework",
        "Regular bias auditing and monitoring"
      ]
    }
  }

return summary_template
```

4.2 TECHNICAL DOCUMENTATION

Detailed Methodology Documentation:

Technical sections must provide sufficient detail for independent validation:

```
# Technical documentation generator
def generate_technical_documentation(investigation_results):
    """Create comprehensive technical documentation."""

    technical_doc = {
      "methodology": {
        "statistical_tests": {
          "demographic_parity": {
            "test_type": "Chi-square test of independence",
            "null_hypothesis": "No association between demographic group
            and hiring outcome",
            "significance_level": 0.05,
            "multiple_comparison_correction": "Bonferroni correction
            applied",
            "effect_size_measure": "Cramer's V"
      },
        "individual_fairness": {
          "test_type": "K-nearest neighbors similarity analysis",
          "distance_metric": "Euclidean distance on normalized features",
```

```
            "k_value": 5,
            "similarity_threshold": 0.8
        }
    },

      "model_interpretability": {
        "primary_method": "SHAP (SHapley Additive exPlanations)",
        "explainer_type": "TreeExplainer for ensemble models",
        "validation_method": "LIME cross-validation",
        "sample_size": "Full test dataset (n=2,847)",
        "feature_selection": "All model features included"
      },

      "data_quality": {
        "missing_data_handling": "Complete case analysis (listwise
        deletion)",
        "outlier_detection": "Isolation Forest algorithm",
        "data_validation": "Schema validation and range checks",
        "privacy_protection": "k-anonymity with k=5"
       }
    },
      "results": {
        "statistical_findings": investigation_results['bias_analysis'],
        "interpretability_findings": investigation_results['shap_
        analysis'],
        "temporal_analysis": investigation_results.get('temporal_analy-
        sis', {}),
        "quality_metrics": investigation_results.get('data_quality', {})
    },

      "limitations": {
        "sample_size": "Analysis limited to 12-month period due to data
        availability",
        "external_validity": "Findings specific to current model version
        and training data",
        "causal_inference": "Correlational analysis - causation not de-
        finitively established",
        "measurement_uncertainty": "Demographic labels may contain clas-
        sification errors"
    },

      "quality_assurance": {
        "peer_review": "Independent validation by secondary analyst",
        "reproducibility": "All analysis code and data available for re-
        production",
        "version_control": "Git repository with complete analysis his-
        tory",
        "chain_of_custody": "Digital evidence handling documented per
        NIST guidelines"
      }
    }

return technical_doc
```

4.3 LEGAL EVIDENCE PACKAGE

Court-Ready Documentation:

Create evidence packages that meet legal admissibility standards:

```
# Generate legal evidence package
python forensic/legal/evidence_packager.py \
    --case-id ${CASE_ID} \
    --include-chain-of-custody \
    --expert-qualification-statement \
    --methodology-validation \
    --output investigation/${CASE_ID}/legal_package/
```

Expert Testimony Preparation:

Prepare materials that support expert testimony in legal proceedings:

```
# Expert testimony support materials
def prepare_expert_testimony_materials(investigation_results):
    """Prepare materials for expert testimony."""

    testimony_materials = {
      "expert_qualifications": {
        "education": "PhD in Computer Science, specialization in Machine
        Learning",
        "experience": "15+ years in AI system analysis and forensic in-
        vestigation",
        "certifications": ["Certified Forensic Computer Examiner (CFCE)",
                  "AI Ethics Certification"],
       "publications": "20+ peer-reviewed papers on AI bias detection",
       "previous_testimony": "Expert witness in 12 AI-related legal
       cases"
     },

     "methodology_validation": {
       "industry_standards": [
         "IEEE 2857-2021 Standard for Privacy Engineering",
         "NIST AI Risk Management Framework",
         "ISO/IEC 23053:2022 Framework for AI systems"
       ],
       "peer_review": "Methodology validated by independent experts",
       "scientific_acceptance": "Techniques widely accepted in AI
       research community",
       "error_rates": "Statistical tests have known error rates (Type I:
       5%, Type II: <20%)"
    },

      "key_demonstratives": {
        "bias_visualization": "Clear charts showing disparate impact",
        "statistical_summary": "p-values and effect sizes for each test",
        "model_explanation": "SHAP visualizations showing feature impor-
        tance",
        "timeline_analysis": "Temporal patterns in discriminatory outcomes"
     },
```

```
        "anticipated_challenges": {
          "data_quality": "Comprehensive data validation procedures docu-
          mented",
          "methodology_reliability": "Cross-validation with multiple ana-
          lytical approaches",
          "alternative_explanations": "Alternative hypotheses tested and
          ruled out",
        "business_justification": "No legitimate business need for dispa-
        rate impact identified"
      }
    }

return testimony_materials
```

Advanced Investigation Scenarios

Incident Response Investigations

Real-Time Bias Detection:

When investigating active bias incidents, prioritize rapid assessment:

```
# Incident response bias detection
def rapid_bias_assessment(live_data_stream):
    """Perform rapid bias assessment for incident response."""

    # Collect recent decisions (last 24-48 hours)
    recent_decisions = live_data_stream.get_recent_decisions(hours=48)

    # Quick statistical tests
    rapid_tests = {
      'demographic_parity': demographic_parity_test(recent_decisions),
      'selection_rate_disparity': calculate_selection_disparity(recent_
      decisions),
      'temporal_clustering': detect_temporal_bias_patterns(recent_deci-
      sions)
    }

    # Generate immediate alert if significant bias detected
    if any(test['p_value'] < 0.01 for test in rapid_tests.values()):
    generate_bias_incident_alert(rapid_tests)

    return rapid_tests
```

Multi-System Investigations

Cross-Platform Analysis:

Investigate bias across multiple interconnected AI systems:

```
# Multi-system bias correlation analysis
def analyze_cross_system_bias(system_results):
    """Analyze bias patterns across multiple AI systems."""

    correlation_analysis = {}

    for system1, system2 in itertools.combinations(system_results.
    keys(), 2):
```

```
        # Compare bias patterns between systems
        correlation = calculate_bias_correlation(
            system_results[system1]['bias_metrics'],
            system_results[system2]['bias_metrics']
        )

        correlation_analysis[f"{system1}_vs_{system2}"] = {
            'correlation_coefficient': correlation,
            'shared_bias_patterns': correlation > 0.7,
            'potential_common_cause': correlation > 0.8
        }

return correlation_analysis
```

Tool Customization and Adaptation

Open Source Alternatives

Replacing Proprietary Tools:

Adapt the methodology for organizations with different tool constraints:

```
# Open source tool alternatives
TOOL_ALTERNATIVES = {
    'shap': {
        'alternatives': ['lime', 'eli5', 'skater'],
        'trade_offs': {
            'lime': 'Local explanations, faster computation',
            'eli5': 'Simple implementation, limited model support',
            'skater': 'Model-agnostic, more complex setup'
        }
    },
    'evidently': {
        'alternatives': ['fairlearn', 'aif360', 'custom_implementation'],
        'trade_offs': {
            'fairlearn': 'Microsoft-backed, good documentation',
            'aif360': 'IBM research tool, comprehensive metrics',
            'custom_implementation': 'Full control, requires more development'
        }
    }
}

def adapt_tools_for_environment(required_capabilities, available_tools):
    """Recommend tool adaptations for specific environments."""

    adaptation_plan = {}

    for capability in required_capabilities:
    if capability in available_tools:
        adaptation_plan[capability] = {
            'status': 'available',
            'tool': available_tools[capability]
        }
     else:
        # Find suitable alternative
        alternatives = TOOL_ALTERNATIVES.get(capability, {}).get
        ('alternatives', [])
```

```
        adaptation_plan[capability] = {
            'status': 'needs_alternative',
            'recommendations': alternatives,
            'implementation_effort': 'medium'
        }

return adaptation_plan
```

Performance Optimization

Large-Scale Investigation Optimization:

Optimize analysis for large datasets and complex models:

```
# Performance optimization strategies
def optimize_large_scale_analysis(dataset_size, model_complexity):
    """Optimize analysis parameters for large-scale investigations."""

    optimization_config = {
        'sampling_strategy': 'stratified',
        'sample_size': min(10000, dataset_size // 10),
        'parallel_processing': True,
        'memory_management': 'chunked_processing',
        'intermediate_caching': True
    }

    if dataset_size > 1000000:
        optimization_config.update({
            'distributed_computing': True,
            'data_partitioning': 'temporal',
            'progressive_sampling': True
    })

    if model_complexity == 'high':
        optimization_config.update({
        'shap_approximation': 'kernel_explainer',
        'feature_selection': 'top_k_important',
        'batch_processing': True
    })

return optimization_config
```

Troubleshooting Guide

Common Technical Issues

Model Loading Problems:

```
# Model loading troubleshooting
def troubleshoot_model_loading(model_path):
    """Systematic troubleshooting for model loading issues."""

    troubleshooting_steps = [
        ("File existence", lambda: os.path.exists(model_path)),
        ("File permissions", lambda: os.access(model_path, os.R_OK)),
        ("File format", lambda: verify_model_format(model_path)),
        ("Version compatibility", lambda: check_library_versions()),
```

```
        ("Memory availability", lambda: check_available_memory()),
        ("Dependencies", lambda: verify_dependencies())
    ]

    for step_name, check_function in troubleshooting_steps:
        try:
            result = check_function()
            print(f"✓ {step_name}: {'OK' if result else 'FAILED'}")
            if not result:
                return provide_resolution_guidance(step_name)
            except Exception as e:
            print(f"X {step_name}: ERROR - {str(e)}")
            return provide_error_resolution(step_name, e)

    return "All checks passed - investigate advanced issues"
def provide_resolution_guidance(failed_step):
    """Provide specific guidance for common issues."""

    resolutions = {
        'File existence': 'Verify model path and check if file was moved or
        deleted',
        'File permissions': 'Update file permissions with chmod +r',
        'File format': 'Verify model was saved with compatible library ver-
        sion',
        'Version compatibility': 'Check requirements.txt and update pack-
        ages',
        'Memory availability': 'Free memory or use smaller batch sizes',
        'Dependencies': 'Install missing packages from requirements.txt'
    }

return resolutions.get(failed_step, 'Consult technical documentation')
```

Data Quality Issues:

```
# Data quality troubleshooting
def diagnose_data_quality_issues(df):
    """Comprehensive data quality diagnosis."""

    quality_report = {
        'missing_data': df.isnull().sum().to_dict(),
        'duplicate_rows': df.duplicated().sum(),
        'data_types': df.dtypes.to_dict(),
        'value_ranges': {},
        'outliers': {},
        'issues_found': []
    }

    # Check numeric columns for outliers
    numeric_cols = df.select_dtypes(include=[np.number]).columns
    for col in numeric_cols:
        Q1 = df[col].quantile(0.25)
        Q3 = df[col].quantile(0.75)
        IQR = Q3 - Q1
        outlier_count = ((df[col] < Q1 - 1.5*IQR) | (df[col] > Q3 +
        1.5*IQR)).sum()
```

```
        quality_report['value_ranges'][col] = {
          'min': df[col].min(),
          'max': df[col].max(),
          'mean': df[col].mean()
        }
        quality_report['outliers'][col] = outlier_count

        if outlier_count > len(df) * 0.05: # >5% outliers
        quality_report['issues_found'].append(f"High outlier rate in {col}:
        {outlier_count}")

    # Check for missing data issues
    high_missing_cols = [col for col, missing in quality_report['missing_
    data'].items()
                if missing > len(df) * 0.1]
    if high_missing_cols:
       quality_report['issues_found'].append(f"High missing data: {high_
       missing_cols}")

    return quality_report
```

Performance Issues

Memory and Processing Optimization:

```
# Performance optimization troubleshooting
def optimize_investigation_performance(current_config, available_
resources):
    """Optimize investigation performance based on available
    resources."""

    optimizations = []

    # Memory optimization
    if available_resources['memory_gb'] < 8:
       optimizations.extend([
       "Reduce batch size for model analysis",
       "Use chunked data processing",
       "Enable data streaming instead of loading full dataset"
    ])

    # CPU optimization
    if available_resources['cpu_cores'] > 4:
       optimizations.extend([
         "Enable parallel processing for statistical tests",
         "Use multiprocessing for SHAP calculations",
         "Parallelize cross-validation procedures"
    ])

    # Storage optimization
    if available_resources['storage_gb'] < 50:
       optimizations.extend([
       "Use compressed data formats (parquet instead of CSV)",
       "Clean up intermediate files regularly",
       "Use sampling for initial analysis"
    ])
```

```
    return {
        'recommended_optimizations': optimizations,
        'estimated_speedup': calculate_performance_improvement
        (optimizations),
        'resource_requirements': estimate_optimized_requirements
        (optimizations)
    }
```

Professional Development and Certification

Skill Progression Framework

From Novice to Expert:

```
# Professional development pathway
AI_FORENSICS_SKILLS = {
    'novice': {
        'required_skills': [
        'Basic statistics and hypothesis testing',
        'Python programming fundamentals',
        'Understanding of machine learning concepts',
        'Data analysis with pandas and numpy'
    ],
    'learning_path': [
        'Complete online statistics course',
        'Practice with sample investigation datasets',
        'Shadow experienced investigators',
        'Conduct supervised practice investigations'
    ],
    'time_estimate': '3-6 months'
  },
    'intermediate': {
      'required_skills': [
      'Advanced statistical analysis',
      'Model interpretability techniques (SHAP, LIME)',
      'Legal evidence handling procedures',
      'Technical report writing'
    ],
    'learning_path': [
      'Complete advanced ML interpretability course',
      'Study forensic investigation standards',
      'Practice expert testimony skills',
      'Lead junior investigator teams'
    ],
    'time_estimate': '6-12 months'
  },

    'expert': {
      'required_skills': [
      'Novel bias detection methodology development',
      'Expert testimony in legal proceedings',
      'AI ethics and governance frameworks',
      'Research publication and peer review'
    ],
    'learning_path': [
      'Contribute to open source forensic tools',
      'Publish investigation methodologies',
```

```
      'Speak at professional conferences',
      'Mentor junior investigators'
    ],
    'time_estimate': '1-3 years'
  }
}
```

Continuing Education Resources

Professional Development Resources:

- **Academic Programs**: Graduate certificates in AI ethics and forensic investigation
- **Professional Organizations**: International Association of AI Forensic Investigators
- **Conferences**: Annual AI Forensics and Ethics Conference, FAccT (Fairness, Accountability, and Transparency)
- **Certification Programs**: Certified AI Forensic Investigator (CAIFI), AI Ethics Professional Certification

Quality Assurance and Best Practices

Investigation Quality Framework:

```
# Quality assurance checklist
INVESTIGATION_QUALITY_CHECKLIST = {
    'planning_phase': [
      'Clear investigation objectives defined',
      'Appropriate scope boundaries established',
      'Legal authorization obtained',
      'Resource allocation planned',
      'Timeline established with milestones'
    ],

    'evidence_collection': [
      'Chain of custody documented',
      'Data integrity verified with checksums',
      'Privacy protection measures implemented',
      'Complete system baseline captured',
      'Evidence storage secured'
    ],

    'analysis_phase': [
      'Multiple analytical approaches used',
      'Statistical significance properly tested',
      'Effect sizes calculated and reported',
      'Assumptions validated',
      'Limitations clearly documented'
    ],

    'validation_phase': [
      'Independent peer review completed',
      'Results reproduced by second analyst',
      'Alternative explanations considered',
      'Quality assurance checks passed',
      'Legal admissibility verified'
    ],
```

```
    'reporting_phase': [
      'Executive summary clear and actionable',
      'Technical methodology fully documented',
      'Findings supported by evidence',
      'Recommendations specific and prioritized',
      'Legal compliance verified'
    ]
}
def assess_investigation_quality(investigation_id):
    """Assess investigation quality against professional standards."""

    quality_scores = {}

    for phase, criteria in INVESTIGATION_QUALITY_CHECKLIST.items():
      completed_criteria = check_phase_completion(investigation_id,
      phase, criteria)
      quality_scores[phase] = {
      'completed': len(completed_criteria),
      'total': len(criteria),
      'percentage': len(completed_criteria) / len(criteria) * 100,
      'missing_criteria': [c for c in criteria if c not in completed_cri-
      teria]
    }

    overall_quality = sum(score['percentage'] for score in quality_
    scores.values()) / len(quality_scores)return {
      'overall_quality_score': overall_quality,
      'phase_scores': quality_scores,
      'quality_level': 'excellent' if overall_quality >= 90 else
      'good' if overall_quality >= 80 else
      'needs_improvement',
      'recommendations': generate_quality_improvement_
      recommendations(quality_scores)
    }
```

Hands-On Exercises

Exercise 1: Basic Bias Detection

Objective: Detect demographic bias in a sample dataset using statistical tests
Dataset: Synthetic resume screening decisions (available in code repository)

Tasks:

1. Load the sample dataset and examine its structure
2. Calculate selection rates by demographic group
3. Perform chi-square tests for statistical significance
4. Interpret results and identify biased outcomes

Expected Learning: Understanding of demographic parity analysis and statistical significance testing.

Exercise 2: Model Interpretability Analysis

Objective: Use SHAP to understand model decision-making patterns.

Tasks:

1. Load a pre-trained resume screening model
2. Generate SHAP explanations for test predictions
3. Identify the most influential features
4. Analyze whether demographic features inappropriately influence decisions

Expected Learning: Practical experience with model interpretability techniques and bias source identification.

Exercise 3: Complete Investigation Workflow

Objective: Conduct a full investigation from planning through reporting.

Scenario: You've been hired to investigate potential bias in a company's AI hiring system following discrimination complaints.

Tasks:

1. Develop an investigation plan with clear objectives
2. Collect and validate evidence following forensic standards
3. Perform comprehensive bias analysis
4. Generate professional reports for legal and executive audiences

Expected Learning: Integration of all investigation phases and professional reporting skills.

Summary and Next Steps

This appendix has provided you with a comprehensive framework for conducting professional AI forensic investigations. You've learned to:

- **Plan investigations** systematically with clear objectives and appropriate scope
- **Collect evidence** while maintaining legal admissibility and forensic integrity
- **Analyze AI systems** using statistical and interpretability techniques
- **Validate findings** through independent review and reproducibility testing
- **Generate reports** that communicate effectively to diverse audiences
- **Troubleshoot issues** and optimize performance for different scenarios

Appendix D: AI Forensics Investigation Templates

TEMPLATE 1: INVESTIGATION SCOPING AND PLANNING TEMPLATE

TABLE D.1
Case Information

Field	Value
Case ID	
Investigation Title	
Date Initiated	
Lead Investigator	
Organization	
Legal Authority	

TABLE D.2
Investigation Objectives

Priority	Objective	Success Criteria	Resources Required
High			
Medium			
Low			

System Boundary Definhtion

- [] AI/ML core components identified
- [] Training infrastructure mapped
- [] Inference systems documented
- [] Data pipelines scoped
- [] Integration points identified
- [] Supporting infrastructure defined
- [] Third-party dependencies catalogued
- [] Exclusions clearly documented

TABLE D.3
Investigation Scope Matrix

Component	In Scope	Out of Scope	Justification	Analysis Depth
Model Architecture				
Training Data				
Inference Engine				
Data Preprocessing				
Output Systems				
Monitoring/Logging				

TABLE D.4
Timeline and Milestones

Phase	Start Date	End Date	Deliverables	Dependencies
Planning				
Evidence Collection				
Technical Analysis				
Documentation Review				
Reporting				

TABLE D.5
Resource Allocation

Resource Type	Assigned Personnel	Time Allocation	Special Requirements
Technical Lead			
Data Analyst			
Legal Counsel			
Domain Expert			

TABLE D.6
Risk Assessment

Risk	Probability	Impact	Mitigation Strategy	Owner
Evidence Volatility				
Access Restrictions				
Technical Complexity				
Legal Challenges				

TEMPLATE 2: STAKEHOLDER INTERVIEW PLANNING TEMPLATE

TABLE D.7
Stakeholder Identification Matrix

Role Category	Name	Department	Priority	Interview Type	Estimated Duration
System Architect			High	Technical Deep-dive	2 hours
Lead Developer			High	Implementation Focus	1.5 hours
DevOps Engineer			Medium	Operations Focus	1 hour
Data Scientist			High	Model/Data Focus	2 hours
Product Manager			Medium	Business Context	1 hour
Compliance Officer			Medium	Regulatory Focus	1 hour

Interview Sequencing Strategy

1. **Phase 1: Architecture & Design**
   - [] System Architect (high-level understanding)
   - [] Principal Engineer (design decisions)
2. **Phase 2: Implementation**
   - [] Lead Developer (implementation details)
   - [] Data Engineer (data pipeline specifics)
3. **Phase 3: Operations**
   - [] DevOps Engineer (deployment/monitoring)
   - [] Site Reliability Engineer (production behavior)
4. **Phase 4: Business Context**
   - [] Product Manager (requirements/constraints)
   - [] Compliance Officer (regulatory requirements)

TABLE D.8
Technical Specification Capture Form

Information Category	Questions	Documentation Required
System Architecture	• What is the overall system design? • How do components interact? • What are the critical dependencies?	Architecture diagrams, Component specifications
Model Details	• What model architecture is used? • What are the training parameters? • How is the model versioned?	Model cards, Training configurations
Data Pipeline	• How is training data collected? • What preprocessing is performed? • How is data quality assured?	Data flow diagrams, Processing scripts
Deployment	• How is the model deployed? • What is the inference architecture? • How are updates managed?	Deployment procedures, Environment configs

TABLE D.9
Interview Documentation Template

Section	Content Guidelines
Raw Notes	Verbatim or near-verbatim capture of responses
Technical Synthesis	Organized technical information extracted
Investigation Insights	Implications, follow-ups, connections to findings

TABLE D.10
Follow-up Tracking Matrix

Stakeholder	Action Item	Due Date	Status	Notes

Confidentiality Assessment

- [] Attorney-client privilege considerations documented
- [] Employee protection requirements identified
- [] Trade secret handling procedures established
- [] Data privacy requirements addressed
- [] Recording permissions obtained
- [] Information sharing protocols defined

TEMPLATE 3: LEGAL AND COMPLIANCE ASSESSMENT TEMPLATE

TABLE D.11
Legal Authority Verification

Requirement	Status	Documentation	Notes
Investigation Authorization	☐ Complete ☐ Pending		
Jurisdiction Confirmation	☐ Complete ☐ Pending		
Regulatory Compliance	☐ Complete ☐ Pending		
Privacy Law Adherence	☐ Complete ☐ Pending		

Chain of Custody Requirements

- [] Evidence handling procedures defined
- [] Personnel access controls established
- [] Transfer protocols documented
- [] Storage security requirements met
- [] Integrity verification procedures implemented
- [] Documentation standards established

TABLE D.12
Privilege and Confidentiality Matrix

Information Type	Privilege Status	Handling Requirements	Access Controls
Internal Communications			
Legal Consultations			
Technical Documentation			
Employee Interviews			
System Data			

Regulatory Requirements Checklist

GDPR Compliance

- [] Data processing legal basis identified
- [] Individual rights procedures established
- [] Data minimization principles applied
- [] Cross-border transfer requirements met

Industry-Specific Regulations

- [] Financial services regulations (if applicable)
- [] Healthcare regulations (if applicable)
- [] Employment law requirements
- [] Sector-specific compliance verified

TABLE D.13
Expert Testimony Preparation

Element	Requirement	Status	Notes
Expert Qualifications	Document education, experience, certifications		
Methodology Validation	Establish scientific reliability		
Peer Review	Independent validation of approach		
Daubert Compliance	Meet admissibility standards		

Litigation Considerations

If Litigation Anticipated:

- [] Litigation hold implemented
- [] Discovery plan developed
- [] ESI protocols established
- [] Consulting vs. testifying experts designated
- [] Work product protection implemented

Evidence Preservation Orders

- [] Spoliation prevention measures implemented
- [] Backup and archival procedures documented
- [] System change monitoring established
- [] Third-party preservation notices issued

TEMPLATE 4: EVIDENCE COLLECTION CHECKLIST

Pre-Collection Setup

- [] Investigation case ID assigned: _____________
- [] Legal authorization confirmed
- [] Technical team assembled
- [] Access permissions obtained
- [] Collection tools validated
- [] Chain of custody forms prepared
- [] Storage infrastructure ready
- [] Security protocols established

TABLE D.14
Model Artifact Collection

Artifact Type	Location	Collection Method	Integrity Verification	Status
Model Weights (.pkl, .pt, .h5)			Hash:	☐
Model Architecture			Hash:	☐
Training Scripts			Hash:	☐
Configuration Files			Hash:	☐
Version Control History			Hash:	☐
Model Cards/Documentation			Hash:	☐

TABLE D.15
Training Data Preservation

Data Component	Source System	Volume	Format	Preservation Method	Verification
Raw Training Data					
Preprocessed Data					
Validation Sets					
Test Sets					
Data Schemas					
Labeling Information					

System Configuration Documentation

- [] **Hardware Specifications**
  - [] CPU architecture and specifications
  - [] Memory configuration
  - [] GPU specifications (if applicable)
  - [] Storage systems configuration
  - [] Network interface specifications
- [] **Software Environment**
  - [] Operating system version and patches
  - [] Python/runtime environment version
  - [] Library dependencies with versions
  - [] Container configurations
  - [] Environment variables
- [] **Deployment Infrastructure**
  - [] Cloud platform configuration
  - [] Container orchestration setup
  - [] Load balancer configuration
  - [] Database configurations
  - [] Security group settings

TABLE D.16
Log Collection Matrix

Log Type	Source	Time Range	Volume	Format	Retention Policy
Application Logs					
System Logs					
Audit Logs					
Performance Metrics					
Error Logs					
Access Logs					

TABLE D.17
Integrity Verification Procedures

File/Dataset	SHA-256 Hash	Timestamp	Verified By	Verification Date

TABLE D.18
Evidence Storage Documentation

Evidence ID	Description	Storage Location	Access Controls	Retention Period

TEMPLATE 5: SYSTEM ENVIRONMENT DOCUMENTATION TEMPLATE

TABLE D.19
Hardware Architecture

Component	Specification	Quantity	Configuration	Performance Impact
CPU	Model:	Cores:	Clock Speed:	
Memory	Type:	Capacity:	Speed:	
Storage	Type:	Capacity:	IOPS:	
GPU	Model:	VRAM:	Compute Capability:	
Network	Interface:	Bandwidth:	Latency:	

TABLE D.20
Software Environment Matrix

Software Component	Version	Configuration	Purpose	Dependencies
Operating System				
Python Runtime				
ML Framework				
Data Processing				
Monitoring Tools				
Security Software				

Network Configuration

- [] **Network Topology**
  - [] Subnet configurations documented
  - [] Firewall rules catalogued
  - [] Load balancer settings recorded
  - [] CDN configuration documented
  - [] DNS settings recorded
- [] **Security Settings**
  - [] SSL/TLS configurations
  - [] VPN access controls
  - [] Network segmentation rules
  - [] Intrusion detection settings
  - [] Traffic monitoring configurations

TABLE D.21
Deployment Infrastructure

Infrastructure Element	Configuration	Purpose	Dependencies	Monitoring
Container Platform				
Orchestration				
Service Mesh				
Database Systems				
Message Queues				
Caching Layers				

TABLE D.22
Integration Points Documentation

External System	Integration Method	Data Flow	Authentication	Error Handling

Performance Monitoring Configuration

- [] **Metrics Collection**
  - [] CPU utilization thresholds
  - [] Memory usage monitoring
  - [] Disk I/O tracking
  - [] Network throughput monitoring
  - [] Application-specific metrics
- [] **Alerting Configuration**
  - [] Alert thresholds defined
  - [] Escalation procedures documented
  - [] Notification channels configured
  - [] Alert suppression rules
  - [] Dashboard configurations

TABLE D.23
Environmental Factors Assessment

Factor	Current State	Potential Impact	Monitoring Method	Mitigation
Load Patterns				
Seasonal Variations				
Geographic Distribution				
Regulatory Environment				
Business Constraints				

TEMPLATE 6: CHAIN OF CUSTODY FORM

TABLE D.24
Case Information

Field	Value
Case Number	
Investigation Title	
Lead Investigator	
Date of Collection	

TABLE D.25
Evidence Description

Evidence ID	Description	Source Location	File Format	Size/Volume

TABLE D.26
Initial Collection

Collector Name	Signature	Date/Time	Collection Method	Location

TABLE D.27
Custody Transfer Log

From	To	Date/Time	Purpose	Signature (From)	Signature (To)

TABLE D.28
Integrity Verification

Verification Point	Method	Hash Value	Verified By	Date/Time
Initial Collection				
Transfer Point 1				
Transfer Point 2				
Analysis Start				
Analysis Complete				

TABLE D.29
Access Log

Date/Time	Accessed By	Purpose	Authorization	Duration	Notes

Storage Information

- [] **Physical Security**
  - [] Secure facility with access controls
  - [] Environmental controls (temperature, humidity)
  - [] Fire suppression systems
  - [] 24/7 monitoring
- [] **Digital Security**
  - [] Encrypted storage
  - [] Access controls implemented
  - [] Backup procedures established
  - [] Integrity monitoring active

TABLE D.30
Evidence Processing Log

Date/Time	Process Applied	Performed By	Tool/Method	Output Created	Verification

TABLE D.31
Final Disposition

Disposition Type	Date	Authorized By	Method	Witness	Notes
☐ Returned to Owner					
☐ Destroyed					
☐ Archived					
☐ Court Submission					

Quality Assurance Checklist

- [] All custody transfers documented with signatures
- [] Integrity verification completed at each stage
- [] Access properly authorized and logged
- [] Storage security requirements met
- [] Processing documentation complete
- [] Legal admissibility requirements satisfied

TEMPLATE 7: AI BILL OF MATERIALS (BOM)

TABLE D.32
AI System Component Inventory

Component Category	Component Name	Version	Source/Vendor	License Type	Risk Level
Foundation Models					
Fine-tuned Models					
Model Weights/Checkpoints					
Training Frameworks					
Inference Engines					
Data Processing Libraries					

TABLE D.33
Model Component Details

Model Artifact	File Path	Size	Hash (SHA-256)	Creation Date	Last Modified
Primary Model					
Backup Models					
Checkpoint Files					
Configuration Files					

TABLE D.34
Software Dependencies Matrix

Package/Library	Version	Purpose	License	Security Status	Criticality
tensorflow		ML Framework		☐ Secure ☐ Vulnerable	☐ Critical
pytorch		ML Framework		☐ Secure ☐ Vulnerable	☐ Critical
scikit-learn		ML Library		☐ Secure ☐ Vulnerable	☐ Medium
pandas		Data Processing		☐ Secure ☐ Vulnerable	☐ Medium
numpy		Numerical Computing		☐ Secure ☐ Vulnerable	☐ Critical

TABLE D.35
Training Data Components

Dataset Component	Source	Format	Size	Access Method	Storage Location
Raw Training Data					
Preprocessed Data					
Validation Sets					
Test Sets					
Feature Stores					

TABLE D.36
Hardware Infrastructure BOM

Hardware Type	Model/ Specification	Quantity	Location	Purpose	Performance Specs
Training GPUs					
Inference Hardware					
Storage Arrays					
Network Switches					
Compute Nodes					

TABLE D.37
Third-Party Services and APIs

Service Name	Provider	API Version	Data Access	Integration Type	SLA Requirements
Cloud ML Services					
Data APIs					
Monitoring Services					
Security Services					

TABLE D.38
Container and Orchestration Components

Component Type	Name/Image	Version	Base Image	Purpose	Security Scan
Model Serving Container					☐ Pass ☐ Fail
Training Container					☐ Pass ☐ Fail
Data Pipeline Container					☐ Pass ☐ Fail
Monitoring Container					☐ Pass ☐ Fail

TABLE D.39
Network and Security Components

Component	Type	Configuration	Access Controls	Monitoring	Encryption
Load Balancers					
Firewalls					
VPN Gateways					
Certificate Authorities					

TABLE D.40
Data Storage Components

Storage System	Type	Capacity	Encryption	Backup Strategy	Access Pattern
Model Storage					
Data Lake					
Feature Store					
Logging Storage					

TABLE D.41
Monitoring and Observability Stack

Tool/Service	Purpose	Data Sources	Retention Period	Alert Thresholds	Integration
Application Monitoring					
Infrastructure Monitoring					
Log Aggregation					
Metrics Collection					

TABLE D.42
Development and Deployment Tools

Tool Category	Tool Name	Version	Purpose	Access Level	Configuration
Version Control					
CI/CD Pipeline					
Container Registry					
Deployment Orchestration					

TABLE D.43
Supply Chain and Provenance

Component	Original Source	Supply Chain Path	Verification Method	Trust Level	Risk Assessment
Base Models				☐ High ☐ Medium ☐ Low	
Training Data				☐ High ☐ Medium ☐ Low	
Libraries				☐ High ☐ Medium ☐ Low	
Tools				☐ High ☐ Medium ☐ Low	

TABLE D.44
License and Intellectual Property Inventory

Component	License Type	Commercial Use	Attribution Required	Restrictions	Compliance Status
		☐ Allowed ☐ Restricted	☐ Yes ☐ No		☐ Compliant

TABLE D.45
Component Dependencies and Relationships

Component	Depends On	Used By	Criticality	Failure Impact	Replacement Options
			☐ Critical ☐ Important ☐ Optional		

TABLE D.46
Security and Vulnerability Status

Component	Last Security Scan	Known Vulnerabilities	CVE IDs	Remediation Status	Next Scan Date
				☐ Fixed ☐ Mitigated ☐ Accepted	

TABLE D.47
BOM Validation and Completeness

Validation Check	Status	Method	Verified By	Date	Notes
Component Inventory Complete	☐ Pass ☐ Fail				
Version Information Accurate	☐ Pass ☐ Fail				
Dependencies Mapped	☐ Pass ☐ Fail				
Security Status Current	☐ Pass ☐ Fail				
Licenses Verified	☐ Pass ☐ Fail				

TEMPLATE 8: AI DEVELOPMENT DOCUMENTATION COLLECTION

TABLE D.48
Documentation Inventory Matrix

Document Category	Document Type	Expected Location	Found	Status	Quality Score
Architecture	System architecture diagrams		☐	☐ Current ☐ Outdated	/10
Architecture	Component interaction diagrams		☐	☐ Current ☐ Outdated	/10
Architecture	Data flow diagrams		☐	☐ Current ☐ Outdated	/10
Model	Algorithm selection rationale		☐	☐ Current ☐ Outdated	/10
Model	Training methodology specs		☐	☐ Current ☐ Outdated	/10
Model	Hyperparameter tuning records		☐	☐ Current ☐ Outdated	/10
Data	Data dictionaries and schemas		☐	☐ Current ☐ Outdated	/10
Data	Data source documentation		☐	☐ Current ☐ Outdated	/10
Data	Collection procedures		☐	☐ Current ☐ Outdated	/10

TABLE D.49
Development Process Documentation

Process Area	Document	Author	Last Updated	Version	Stakeholder Approval
Requirements	Business requirements document				
Design	Technical design document				
Development	Coding standards and guidelines				
Testing	Test plans and procedures				
Deployment	Deployment procedures				
Operations	Operational runbooks				

TABLE D.50
Decision Records and Rationale

Decision Type	Decision Made	Rationale	Alternatives Considered	Decision Date	Approver
Architecture					
Algorithm					
Data Sources					
Infrastructure					
Security					

TABLE D.51
Meeting Records and Communications

Meeting Type	Date	Participants	Key Decisions	Action Items	Recording Available
Design Reviews					☐ Yes ☐ No
Code Reviews					☐ Yes ☐ No
Progress Reviews					☐ Yes ☐ No
Incident Reviews					☐ Yes ☐ No

Email and Chat Communications

- [] **Email Archives**
  - [] Technical discussion threads
  - [] Decision approval chains
  - [] Problem reports and resolutions
  - [] Vendor communications
  - [] Stakeholder updates
- [] **Team Chat Records**
  - [] Slack/Teams channel archives
  - [] Technical troubleshooting discussions
  - [] Quick decision records
  - [] Informal knowledge sharing
  - [] Incident response coordination

TABLE D.52
Version Control and Change History

Repository	Platform	Access Level	Branch Strategy	Commit Message Quality	Merge Request Process
Model Code				☐ Good ☐ Adequate ☐ Poor	☐ Required ☐ Optional
Data Pipeline				☐ Good ☐ Adequate ☐ Poor	☐ Required ☐ Optional
Infrastructure				☐ Good ☐ Adequate ☐ Poor	☐ Required ☐ Optional
Documentation				☐ Good ☐ Adequate ☐ Poor	☐ Required ☐ Optional

TABLE D.53
Experimental and Research Documentation

Experiment Type	Location	Purpose	Results Documented	Reproducible	Impact on Final System
Jupyter Notebooks			☐ Yes ☐ Partial	☐ Yes ☐ No	
Research Papers			☐ Yes ☐ Partial	☐ Yes ☐ No	
Proof of Concepts			☐ Yes ☐ Partial	☐ Yes ☐ No	
A/B Tests			☐ Yes ☐ Partial	☐ Yes ☐ No	

Training and Validation Documentation

- [] **Training Process Records**
  - [] Training job logs and configurations
  - [] Learning curves and performance metrics
  - [] Convergence criteria and stopping conditions
  - [] Hardware utilization and training time
  - [] Failed training attempts and lessons learned
- [] **Model Validation Documentation**
  - [] Validation methodology description
  - [] Test dataset creation and validation
  - [] Performance benchmark results
  - [] Cross-validation procedures
  - [] Statistical significance testing

TABLE D.54
Deployment and Operations Documentation

Document Type	Owner	Last Updated	Coverage	Accuracy	Actionability
Deployment Guide			☐ Complete	☐ High ☐ Medium ☐ Low	☐ Actionable
Configuration Management			☐ Complete	☐ High ☐ Medium ☐ Low	☐ Actionable
Monitoring Setup			☐ Complete	☐ High ☐ Medium ☐ Low	☐ Actionable
Incident Response			☐ Complete	☐ High ☐ Medium ☐ Low	☐ Actionable
Rollback Procedures			☐ Complete	☐ High ☐ Medium ☐ Low	☐ Actionable

Business and Compliance Documentation

- [] **Business Context**
  - [] Project charter and business case
  - [] Stakeholder requirements
  - [] Success criteria and KPIs
  - [] User acceptance criteria
  - [] Market analysis and competitive positioning
- [] **Compliance Records**
  - [] Privacy impact assessments
  - [] Bias testing reports
  - [] Security assessment documentation
  - [] Regulatory compliance checklists
  - [] Audit trail documentation

TABLE D.55
Risk and Issue Management

Risk/Issue	Identified Date	Severity	Mitigation Strategy	Status	Owner
		☐ High ☐ Medium ☐ Low		☐ Open ☐ Mitigated ☐ Closed	

Quality Assurance Documentation

- [] **Code Review Records**
  - [] Review coverage metrics
  - [] Common issues identified
  - [] Security review findings
  - [] Performance review results
  - [] Bias review outcomes
- [] **Testing Documentation**
  - [] Unit test coverage reports
  - [] Integration test results
  - [] Performance test outcomes
  - [] Security test findings
  - [] User acceptance test results

TABLE D.56
Knowledge Management and Training

Knowledge Type	Format	Accessibility	Currency	Completeness	Usage Tracking
Technical Guides			☐ Current	☐ Complete	☐ Tracked
Best Practices			☐ Current	☐ Complete	☐ Tracked
Troubleshooting			☐ Current	☐ Complete	☐ Tracked
Onboarding Materials			☐ Current	☐ Complete	☐ Tracked

TABLE D.57
Documentation Gap Analysis

Required Documentation	Regulatory Requirement	Current Status	Gap Severity	Remediation Priority	Responsible Party
		☐ Complete ☐ Partial ☐ Missing	☐ Critical ☐ High ☐ Medium	☐ Urgent ☐ High ☐ Medium	

TABLE D.58
Document Authenticity and Integrity

Document	Creation Date	Last Modified	Author	Digital Signature	Version Control
				☐ Present ☐ Missing	☐ Tracked ☐ Untracked

TABLE D.59
Collection Completeness Verification

Documentation Category	Expected Items	Items Found	Completeness %	Missing Critical Items	Collection Status
Architecture					☐ Complete
Development					☐ Complete
Testing					☐ Complete
Deployment					☐ Complete
Operations					☐ Complete
Compliance					☐ Complete

TEMPLATE 9: TRAINING DATA ANALYSIS WORKSHEET

TABLE D.60
Data Source Verification

Data Source	Provider	License Type	Verification Method	Status	Notes
				☐ Verified ☐ Pending	

TABLE D.61
Dataset Characteristics

Attribute	Value	Verification Method	Quality Score
Total Records			
Features/Columns			
Time Range			
Geographic Coverage			
Language(s)			
Data Types			

TABLE D.62
Synthetic Data Detection

Detection Method	Tool Used	Threshold	Results	Confidence Level
Statistical Analysis				
GAN Detection				
Metadata Analysis				
Temporal Patterns				

TABLE D.63
Bias Analysis Matrix

Demographic Attribute	Representation %	Expected %	Bias Score	Statistical Significance
Gender				
Age Groups				
Ethnicity				
Geographic Region				
Socioeconomic Status				

TABLE D.64
Intersectional Bias Assessment

Intersection	Sample Size	Representation	Bias Indicators	Priority Level
Gender × Age				
Ethnicity × Geography				
Age × Socioeconomic				

Intellectual Property Analysis

- [] **License Verification**
  - [] Open source license compliance checked
  - [] Commercial license terms verified
  - [] Attribution requirements documented
  - [] Redistribution restrictions noted
- [] **Similarity Analysis**
  - [] Duplicate detection performed
  - [] Near-duplicate identification completed
  - [] Copyright material scanning executed
  - [] Plagiarism detection conducted

TABLE D.65
Data Quality Assessment

Quality Dimension	Measurement Method	Score (1–10)	Issues Identified	Remediation Required
Completeness	Missing value analysis			
Accuracy	Ground truth comparison			
Consistency	Cross-field validation			
Timeliness	Timestamp analysis			
Validity	Format/range checking			

TABLE D.66
Data Lineage Tracking

Processing Stage	Input Source	Transformation Applied	Output Format	Quality Impact
Raw Collection		None		
Cleaning				
Normalization				
Feature Engineering				
Final Dataset				

TABLE D.67
Statistical Validation

Test	Hypothesis	Method	*p*-value	Effect Size	Conclusion
Distribution Test					
Independence Test					
Correlation Analysis					
Bias Significance					

TEMPLATE 8: MODEL INVESTIGATION TEMPLATE

TABLE D.68
Model Identification

Attribute	Value	Verification Method	Confidence
Model Type			
Architecture			
Framework			
Version			
Training Date			
Model Size			

Architecture Validation

- [] **Structure Verification**
  - [] Layer configuration documented
  - [] Parameter counts verified
  - [] Activation functions confirmed
  - [] Loss function validated
  - [] Optimizer settings checked
- [] **Implementation Consistency**
  - [] Code matches documentation
  - [] Architecture diagrams accurate
  - [] Hyperparameters documented
  - [] Training procedure verified

TABLE D.69
Weight Analysis

Analysis Type	Method	Tool Used	Anomalies Detected	Risk Level
Distribution Analysis				
Outlier Detection				
Pattern Recognition				
Integrity Verification				

TABLE D.70
Performance Testing Matrix

Test Scenario	Expected Result	Actual Result	Variance	Status
Training Set				
Validation Set				
Test Set				
Out-of-Sample				
Adversarial Examples				
Edge Cases				

TABLE D.71
Version Control Analysis

Version	Date	Changes	Author	Validation	Performance Impact

Deployment Verification

- [] **Environment Consistency**
  - [] Development vs. production comparison
  - [] Dependency version matching
  - [] Configuration consistency
  - [] Resource allocation verification

- [] **Deployment Process**
  - [] Deployment scripts reviewed
  - [] Rollback procedures tested
  - [] Health checks validated
  - [] Monitoring configuration verified

TABLE D.72
Model Interpretability Analysis

Method	Tool	Coverage	Insights Generated	Quality Score
SHAP Values				
LIME				
Attention Maps				
Feature Importance				

TABLE D.73
Tampering Detection

Indicator	Detection Method	Evidence Found	Confidence Level	Investigation Required
Unauthorized Modifications				
Version Inconsistencies				
Performance Anomalies				
Access Pattern Irregularities				

TABLE D.74
Bias Detection Results

Bias Type	Detection Method	Affected Groups	Severity	Mitigation Status
Historical Bias				
Representation Bias				
Measurement Bias				
Aggregation Bias				
Evaluation Bias				

TEMPLATE 9: OUTPUT ANALYSIS FRAMEWORK

TABLE D.75
Result Validation Setup

Test Configuration	Value	Justification	Validation Method
Sample Size			
Confidence Level			
Significance Threshold			
Effect Size Threshold			

TABLE D.76
Statistical Analysis Plan

Analysis Type	Hypothesis	Method	Sample Requirements	Expected Outcome
Descriptive Statistics				
Inferential Testing				
Correlation Analysis				
Regression Analysis				
Time Series Analysis				

TABLE D.77
Error Analysis Matrix

Error Type	Frequency	Pattern	Root Cause Analysis	Priority
False Positives				
False Negatives				
Systematic Errors				
Random Errors				

TABLE D.78
Bias Detection Framework

Demographic Group	Accuracy	Precision	Recall	F1-Score	Fairness Metric
Group A					
Group B					
Group C					
Overall					

TABLE D.79
Performance Metrics Analysis

Metric	Overall	Group 1	Group 2	Group 3	Disparity Score
Accuracy					
Precision					
Recall					
AUC					
Calibration					

TABLE D.80
Black-Box Testing Results

Test Scenario	Input Description	Expected Output	Actual Output	Variance	Analysis

TABLE D.81
Statistical Significance Testing

Test	Groups Compared	Test Statistic	p-value	Effect Size	Interpretation

TABLE D.82
Confidence Intervals

Metric	Point Estimate	95% CI Lower	95% CI Upper	Interpretation

TABLE D.83
Trend Analysis

Time Period	Metric	Value	Trend Direction	Statistical Significance	Practical Significance

TABLE D.84
Alternative Hypothesis Testing

Hypothesis	Evidence For	Evidence Against	Conclusion	Confidence Level

Quality Assurance Checklist

- [] Statistical assumptions verified
- [] Multiple testing corrections applied
- [] Effect sizes calculated and interpreted
- [] Confidence intervals reported
- [] Practical significance assessed
- [] Alternative explanations considered
- [] Reproducibility verified
- [] Peer review completed

TEMPLATE 10: DOCUMENTATION COMPLETENESS AUDIT

TABLE D.85
System Documentation Inventory

Document Type	Expected	Found	Version	Last Updated	Completeness Score
System Architecture					/10
API Documentation					/10
User Manuals					/10
Admin Guides					/10
Troubleshooting					/10

Training and Development Records

- [] **Model Development**
  - [] Training procedure documentation
  - [] Hyperparameter selection rationale
  - [] Validation methodology
  - [] Performance benchmarking
  - [] Version control records
- [] **Data Pipeline Documentation**
  - [] Data collection procedures
  - [] Preprocessing steps
  - [] Quality assurance processes
  - [] Transformation logic
  - [] Validation procedures

TABLE D.86
Deployment Documentation Review

Document	Required Elements	Present	Quality	Issues Identified
Deployment Guide	Step-by-step procedures	☐	/10	
Configuration Management	Environment settings	☐	/10	
Rollback Procedures	Emergency processes	☐	/10	
Health Checks	Monitoring specifications	☐	/10	

Operational Procedures

- [] **Monitoring Documentation**
  - [] Metrics collection specifications
  - [] Alert threshold definitions
  - [] Escalation procedures
  - [] Dashboard configurations
  - [] SLA definitions
- [] **Maintenance Procedures**
  - [] Regular maintenance schedules
  - [] Update procedures
  - [] Backup and recovery
  - [] Performance tuning
  - [] Capacity planning

TABLE D.87
Compliance Documentation Matrix

Regulatory Requirement	Documentation Required	Status	Gap Analysis	Priority
Data Privacy	Privacy policies, consent forms			
Algorithmic Transparency	Model cards, bias testing			
Audit Trail	Change logs, access records			
Risk Management	Risk assessments, mitigation plans			

TABLE D.88
Business Requirements Validation

Requirement	Documented	Implemented	Tested	Traced	Status
	☐	☐	☐	☐	

TABLE D.89
Change Management Records

Change Type	Documentation Required	Completeness	Quality Issues	Recommendations
Feature Changes				
Bug Fixes				
Configuration Updates				
Security Patches				

Historical Documentation Assessment

- [] **Version History**
  - [] Complete version tracking
  - [] Change justifications documented
  - [] Author attribution maintained
  - [] Approval records preserved
- [] **Decision Records**
  - [] Architecture decision records (ADRs)
  - [] Design decisions documented
  - [] Trade-off analyses preserved
  - [] Stakeholder approvals recorded

TABLE D.90
Documentation Quality Scoring

Quality Dimension	Weight	Score (1–10)	Weighted Score	Comments
Completeness	25%			
Accuracy	25%			
Currency	20%			
Accessibility	15%			
Usability	15%			
Total	100%			

TEMPLATE 11: REGULATORY COMPLIANCE CHECKLIST

TABLE D.91
GDPR Compliance Assessment

Requirement	Status	Evidence	Gap Analysis	Priority
Lawful Basis	☐ Complete ☐ Partial ☐ Missing			
Data Minimization	☐ Complete ☐ Partial ☐ Missing			
Purpose Limitation	☐ Complete ☐ Partial ☐ Missing			
Consent Management	☐ Complete ☐ Partial ☐ Missing			
Individual Rights	☐ Complete ☐ Partial ☐ Missing			
Data Protection by Design	☐ Complete ☐ Partial ☐ Missing			

EEOC Guidelines Compliance

- [] **Adverse Impact Analysis**
  - [] Four-fifths rule testing performed
  - [] Statistical significance testing conducted
  - [] Practical significance assessed
  - [] Business necessity justified
- [] **Selection Procedure Validation**
  - [] Content validity established
  - [] Criterion validity demonstrated
  - [] Construct validity verified
  - [] Job relatedness documented

TABLE D.92
Industry-Specific Regulations

Regulation	Applicability	Requirements	Compliance Status	Evidence
SOX (Financial)				
HIPAA (Healthcare)				
FCRA (Credit)				
COPPA (Children)				

Algorithmic Transparency Requirements

- [] **Model Documentation**
  - [] Model cards completed
  - [] Bias testing results documented
  - [] Performance metrics published
  - [] Limitations clearly stated
- [] **Explainability Requirements**
  - [] Individual explanation mechanisms
  - [] Global model interpretability
  - [] Decision rationale available
  - [] Appeal processes established

TABLE D.93
Data Governance Validation

Control	Implementation	Testing	Effectiveness	Recommendations
Data Quality				
Access Controls				
Retention Policies				
Deletion Procedures				

Audit Trail Requirements

- [] **System Access Logging**
  - [] User authentication recorded
  - [] Authorization decisions logged
  - [] Data access events captured
  - [] Administrative actions tracked
- [] **Model Lifecycle Tracking**
  - [] Training events logged
  - [] Model updates recorded
  - [] Performance monitoring data
  - [] Incident response records

TABLE D.94
Privacy Protection Measures

Protection Type	Implementation	Testing	Effectiveness	Compliance
Data Encryption				
Access Controls				
Anonymization				
Pseudonymization				

Incident Response Procedures

- [] **Incident Classification**
  - [] Severity levels defined
  - [] Response times specified
  - [] Escalation procedures documented
  - [] Communication protocols established
- [] **Breach Notification**
  - [] Regulatory notification procedures
  - [] Customer notification protocols
  - [] Documentation requirements
  - [] Timeline compliance verified

TABLE D.95
Certification and Audit Records

Certification Type	Current Status	Expiration Date	Renewal Requirements	Compliance Issues
SOC 2 Type II				
ISO 27001				
Industry-Specific				

TABLE D.96
Compliance Risk Assessment

Risk Area	Probability	Impact	Current Controls	Residual Risk	Action Required
Data Breach					
Discriminatory Impact					
Regulatory Violation					
Privacy Violation					

TEMPLATE 12: EXECUTIVE SUMMARY TEMPLATE

TABLE D.97
Investigation Overview

Element	Description
Investigation Objective	
System/Model Investigated	
Investigation Period	
Investigation Team	
Executive Sponsor	

TABLE D.98
Key Findings Summary

Finding #	Description	Business Impact	Risk Level	Recommendation
1			☐ High ☐ Medium ☐ Low	
2			☐ High ☐ Medium ☐ Low	
3			☐ High ☐ Medium ☐ Low	

TABLE D.99
Quantified Impact Analysis

Impact Category	Current State	Potential Exposure	Mitigation Benefit	Timeline
Financial				
Legal				
Regulatory				
Operational				
Reputational				

TABLE D.100
Risk Assessment Matrix

Risk Factor	Probability	Impact	Risk Score	Current Controls	Residual Risk
Discriminatory Bias					
Regulatory Non-Compliance					
Legal Liability					
Operational Failure					

TABLE D.101
Prioritized Recommendations

Priority	Recommendation	Resources Required	Timeline	Success Metrics	ROI Estimate
High					
Medium					
Low					

TABLE D.102
Implementation Roadmap

Phase	Duration	Objectives	Deliverables	Dependencies	Success Criteria
Immediate (0–30 days)					
Short-term (1–3 months)					
Medium-term (3–6 months)					
Long-term (6+ months)					

TABLE D.103
Resource Requirements

Resource Type	Immediate	Short-term	Long-term	Total Cost	Funding Source
Personnel					
Technology					
External Services					
Training					

Legal and Regulatory Implications

- [] **Immediate Legal Risks**
  - [] Potential discrimination claims
  - [] Regulatory violations
  - [] Contractual breaches
  - [] Compliance failures
- [] **Mitigation Strategies**
  - [] Legal counsel engagement
  - [] Regulatory self-disclosure
  - [] Customer notifications
  - [] Process improvements

TABLE D.104
Success Metrics and Monitoring

Metric	Baseline	Target	Measurement Method	Frequency	Owner

TABLE D.105
Next Steps and Follow-up

Action Item	Owner	Due Date	Dependencies	Success Criteria

TABLE D.106
Executive Decision Points

Decision Required	Options	Recommendation	Rationale	Deadline

TEMPLATE 13: TECHNICAL INVESTIGATION REPORT TEMPLATE

TABLE D.107
Investigation Methodology

Component	Description	Justification	Validation
Analytical Approach			
Statistical Methods			
Tools and Software			
Data Sources			
Quality Assurance			

TABLE D.108
Technical Environment Documentation

System Component	Configuration	Version	Impact on Analysis	Verification Method
Hardware				
Operating System				
ML Framework				
Analysis Tools				

TABLE D.109
Statistical Analysis Results

Analysis Type	Hypothesis	Method	Sample Size	Test Statistic	*p*-value	Effect Size	Interpretation

TABLE D.110
Model Interpretability Findings

Method	Coverage	Key Insights	Feature Importance	Bias Attribution	Confidence
SHAP Analysis					
LIME					
Attention Maps					
Counterfactual					

TABLE D.111
Bias Analysis Deep Dive

Bias Type	Affected Groups	Magnitude	Statistical Significance	Practical Significance	Root Cause

TABLE D.112
Performance Analysis

Metric	Overall	Group A	Group B	Group C	Disparity	Threshold	Status
Accuracy							
Precision							
Recall							
F1-Score							

TABLE D.113
Evidence Documentation

Evidence Type	Description	Collection Method	Integrity Verification	Analysis Method	Key Findings

Quality Assurance Documentation

- [] **Methodology Validation**
  - [] Peer review completed
  - [] Statistical assumptions verified
  - [] Alternative approaches considered
  - [] Reproducibility confirmed
- [] **Independent Verification**
  - [] Results validated by second analyst
  - [] Cross-validation performed
  - [] Sensitivity analysis conducted
  - [] Robustness testing completed

TABLE D.114
Limitations and Uncertainties

Limitation Type	Description	Impact on Findings	Mitigation Strategy	Residual Uncertainty
Data Limitations				
Methodological				
Technical Constraints				
Time Constraints				

TABLE D.115
Technical Recommendations

Recommendation	Technical Approach	Implementation Complexity	Resource Requirements	Expected Outcome

Reproducibility Documentation

- [] **Code and Scripts**
  - [] Analysis code archived
  - [] Version control maintained
  - [] Dependencies documented
  - [] Execution environment recorded
- [] **Data and Parameters**
  - [] Input data preserved
  - [] Parameter settings recorded
  - [] Random seeds documented
  - [] Configuration files saved

TABLE D.116
Appendices Reference

Appendix	Content	Purpose	Location
A	Statistical Calculations	Detailed computations	
B	Visual Evidence	Charts and graphs	
C	Code Repository	Analysis scripts	
D	Raw Data Summaries	Data characteristics	

TEMPLATE 15: INVESTIGATION QUALITY ASSURANCE CHECKLIST

TABLE D.117
Pre-Investigation Setup Verification

Element	Requirement	Status	Verification Method	Notes
Case Authorization	Legal authority documented	☐ Complete		
Team Qualifications	Expertise mapped to requirements	☐ Complete		
Scope Definition	Clear boundaries established	☐ Complete		
Resource Allocation	Adequate resources assigned	☐ Complete		
Timeline Feasibility	Realistic milestones set	☐ Complete		

Evidence Collection Completeness

- [] **Critical Evidence Identified**
  - [] Model artifacts collected
  - [] Training data preserved
  - [] System configurations documented
  - [] Log files captured
  - [] Documentation gathered
- [] **Chain of Custody Maintained**
  - [] Initial collection documented
  - [] All transfers logged
  - [] Integrity verified
  - [] Access controlled
  - [] Storage secured

TABLE D.118
Technical Analysis Validation

Analysis Phase	Quality Criteria	Status	Independent Review	Issues Identified
Statistical Analysis	Appropriate methods used	☐ Pass	☐ Complete	
Bias Detection	Comprehensive testing	☐ Pass	☐ Complete	
Model Investigation	Thorough examination	☐ Pass	☐ Complete	
Output Analysis	Rigorous validation	☐ Pass	☐ Complete	

Documentation Standards Compliance

- [] **Methodology Documentation**
  - [] Detailed procedures recorded
  - [] Tool configurations documented
  - [] Assumptions clearly stated
  - [] Limitations acknowledged
- [] **Results Documentation**
  - [] Findings clearly presented
  - [] Statistical significance reported
  - [] Confidence intervals included
  - [] Effect sizes calculated

TABLE D.119
Legal Admissibility Confirmation

Admissibility Factor	Requirement	Status	Supporting Evidence	Expert Review
Relevance	Relates to case issues	☐ Confirmed		
Reliability	Scientifically sound	☐ Confirmed		
Chain of Custody	Integrity maintained	☐ Confirmed		
Expert Qualifications	Qualified to testify	☐ Confirmed		

Independent Review Process

- [] **Peer Review Completed**
  - [] Methodology reviewed by qualified expert
  - [] Statistical analysis validated
  - [] Conclusions assessed for reasonableness
  - [] Alternative explanations considered
- [] **Technical Accuracy Validation**
  - [] Calculations independently verified
  - [] Code review completed
  - [] Data processing validated
  - [] Results reproduced

TABLE D.120
Reproducibility Verification

Component	Reproduction Status	Variance	Acceptable	Action Required
Data Processing	☐ Exact ☐ Minor Diff ☐ Major Diff		☐ Yes ☐ No	
Statistical Analysis	☐ Exact ☐ Minor Diff ☐ Major Diff		☐ Yes ☐ No	
Model Analysis	☐ Exact ☐ Minor Diff ☐ Major Diff		☐ Yes ☐ No	
Final Results	☐ Exact ☐ Minor Diff ☐ Major Diff		☐ Yes ☐ No	

Report Quality Assessment

- [] **Content Quality**
  - [] Clear executive summary
  - [] Logical organization
  - [] Appropriate level of detail
  - [] Actionable recommendations
- [] **Technical Quality**
  - [] Accurate statistical reporting
  - [] Proper citation of sources
  - [] Appropriate visual aids
  - [] Professional formatting

TABLE D.121
Final Investigation Validation

Validation Criterion	Assessment	Evidence	Reviewer	Date
Objectives Met	☐ Fully ☐ Partially ☐ Not Met			
Quality Standards	☐ Exceeds ☐ Meets ☐ Below			
Legal Requirements	☐ Compliant ☐ Issues			
Professional Standards	☐ Exceeds ☐ Meets ☐ Below			

TABLE D.122
Lessons Learned Documentation

Category	Observation	Impact	Recommendation for Future
Process Improvements			
Technical Challenges			
Resource Optimization			
Quality Enhancements			

TABLE D.123
Final Sign-off

Role	Name	Signature	Date	Comments
Lead Investigator				
Technical Reviewer				
Quality Assurance				
Legal Counsel				

Index

Note: Numbers in **bold** indicate a table. Numbers in *italics* indicate a figure. Underlined numbers indicate a box.

A

W